SELECTIONS FROM THE PRISON NOTEBOOKS OF ANTONIO GRAMSCI

SELECTIONS FROM THE

PRISON NOTEBOOKS

OF

ANTONIO GRAMSCI

edited and translated by

QUINTIN HOARE

and

GEOFFREY NOWELL SMITH

INTERNATIONAL PUBLISHERS

New York

Published simultaneously by Lawrence & Wishart, London, and
International Publishers, New York

First edition, 1971
Third Printing, 1975

ISBN 0–7178–0270–1 (Cloth); ISBN 0–7178–0397–X (Paperback)
Library of Congress Catalog Card Number 73–77646

Printed in the United States of America

CONTENTS

ACKNOWLEDGEMENTS

The editors would like to express their thanks to the Istituto Gramsci in Rome, holders of the copyright on Gramsci's Prison Notebooks, for permission to publish the present selection and for allowing them to consult and to copy from the photostat of Gramsci's manuscript in the possession of the Institute. Particular thanks for their assistance are due to Dr Elsa Fubini and Prof. Valentino Gerratana of the staff of the Institute, and to the director, Franco Ferri. The initiative for the publication of this volume came from Roger Simon and Steve Bodington, who have supervised its progress throughout, making many invaluable suggestions, and without whose stimulus the work would have taken even longer to complete.

We would like to acknowledge our indebtedness to certain books without which the General Introduction could not have been written. The most important of these sources is the series of books on Turin working-class history and the early history of the Italian Communist Party by Paolo Spriano. Also indispensable were Giuseppe Fiori's biography, the Tasca archive material published in the Annali Feltrinelli in 1960 and 1966, and the Marx Memorial Library's collection of Comintern congress reports, etc.

Geoffrey Nowell Smith would like to thank all those who helped or took part in the preparation of his sections of this edition, in particular Rosalind Delmar, a constant collaborator on the volume from its inception; John Merrington, Ian Steedman, Norman Geras and Michael Evans; and Shirley Hill, who produced a flawless typescript of his part of the translation.

PREFACE

EXISTING EDITIONS

The present edition comprises a selection of texts from the Notebooks (*Quaderni del carcere*) written by Gramsci in prison between 1929 and 1935. There is still no critical edition of the *Quaderni* in Italian, though one is in course of preparation at the Istituto Gramsci in Rome. A preliminary edition containing the bulk of Gramsci's original material, excepting translations and rejected drafts, was brought out by the Turin publisher Einaudi in six volumes between 1948 and 1951, under the editorship of Felice Platone. The same edition contains a volume of Prison Letters (*Lettere dal carcere*, 1947), now superseded by a more complete edition, and a series of volumes of the pre-1926 writings, from the period prior to Gramsci's imprisonment. Our selection is based on this Einaudi edition of the *Quaderni*, with the addition of one or two previously unpublished texts and with a slight rearrangement of the order in certain places. References to the Einaudi or to other selections or translations of Gramsci's works are given in these pages as follows:

Quaderni

MS.	*Il materialismo storico e la filosofia di Benedetto Croce*, 1948.
Int.	*Gli intellettuali e l'organizzazione della cultura*, 1949.
Ris.	*Il Risorgimento*, 1949.
NM.	*Note sul Machiavelli, sulla politica e sullo Stato moderno*, 1949.
LVN.	*Letteratura e vita nazionale*, 1950.
PP.	*Passato e presente*, 1951.

Letters

LC.	*Lettere dal carcere*, edited by S. Caprioglio and E. Fubini Nuovo Universale Einaudi, Turin 1965.

Other editions referred to

GF.	*2000 pagine di Gramsci*, edited by N. Gallo and G. Ferrata, Vol. I, "Nel tempo della lotta, 1914–1926", Il Saggiatore, Milan 1964. On pp. 797–819 of this volume is published Gramsci's important essay on the Southern Question (written immediately prior to his arrest): *Alcuni temi della quistione meridionale*, hereafter referred to as "*Alcuni temi*".
	(Vol. II consists of letters. Two further volumes are in preparation.)

OC. *Oeuvres choisies de Antonio Gramsci*, Editions Sociales, Paris, 1959.

A previous English translation of some of the works of Gramsci contained in this volume, together with one or two of the earlier writings, translated and edited by Louis Marks, was published by Lawrence and Wishart in 1957, under the title *The Modern Prince and other Essays*. There also exist a number of Italian anthologies and of translations of Gramsci's works into other languages. For a selective bibliography of works of and about Gramsci we refer the reader to the note at the end of the English translation of Giuseppe Fiori's biography of Gramsci (*Antonio Gramsci, Life of a Revolutionary*, translated by Tom Nairn, New Left Books, London 1970).

GRAMSCI'S PRISON NOTEBOOKS

The problem of making a selection from Gramsci's *Quaderni* or Prison Notebooks is complicated by two factors: the fragmentary character of the writings themselves, and the uncertain status of the Notebooks in Gramsci's intentions. From references in the Notebooks and in Gramsci's letters from prison it is possible to obtain some indication of how Gramsci intended his work to be understood. Soon after his arrest he wrote to his sister-in-law Tatiana (19 March 1927: LC. pp. 57–60) about a project of writing something "für ewig" (for ever), something which would also serve to absorb him and "give a focus to [his] inner life". He mentions a plan for a history of the Italian intellectuals, together with studies on linguistics, on the theatre of Pirandello and on serial novels and popular literary taste. However, in another letter to Tatiana (15 December 1930: LC. pp. 389–92) he writes: "thinking 'disinterestedly' or study for its own sake are difficult for me . . . I do not like throwing stones in the dark; I like to have a concrete interlocutor or adversary", and he speaks of the "polemical nature" of his entire intellectual formation. Early in 1932, in a note in one of his *Quaderni* (Q.XXVIII), he describes a programme of "principal essays" wider in scope than the previous one, with more political and philosophical content, fairly close in its general outlines to what has actually come down to us in the *Quaderni*. It is this programme which forms the basis of the ordering of the material of the Notebooks carried out by the Einaudi editors after the war. Even so, many difficulties remain. Ill health and the unavailability of books in the prison forced him to leave unfinished, to abandon or to modify certain plans. With his transfer to the prison clinic in 1933 and consequent partial recovery, he began to recopy, reorder and rework much of the material from the earlier notebooks. But he did so with an extra caution, eliminating any surviving words or phrases, like the name of Marx or the word "class", which might attract the attention of the censor and so cause his work to be brought to an end. Most significantly of all, in a note in one of the *Quaderni* entitled "Questions of Method" (see below pp. 382–86) he offers a warning, ostensibly about Marx but equally if not more applicable to himself, against confusing unfinished or unpublished work with works published and approved by an author during his lifetime. In the same note he also refers to the importance and to the inherent difficulties of reconstructing the "intellectual biography" of an author. To perform such a task, in relation to the Prison Notebooks, would be an immensely valuable but also intricate labour. In default of this, however, and given the circumstances in which the texts were written, any unequivocal assertions about the aim and status of Gramsci's theoretical project as contained or sketched out in the Notebooks are necessarily speculative and must be recognised as such.

THIS EDITION: SELECTION AND TRANSLATION

While the above observations can be construed most simply as a warning against taking as definitive or as having an unambiguous intention texts whose form is often provisional and whose intention is in some way veiled or uncertain, the problem of the fragmentary character of Gramsci's original manuscript poses more immediate problems. Gramsci's prison *Quaderni* number thirty-three in all, several of them containing notes on a number of different subjects or written over a period of a couple of years. Many of the notes are isolated jottings. Others are so placed in the *Quaderno* as to make their insertion into the main structure of Gramsci's arguments at best hypothetical. Longer texts, about whose coherence and general order there can be no doubt, are often partially revised in such a way that it is necessary, in editing the text, to intersperse the revised or rewritten sections with passages of which only an earlier draft exists. Both in the classification of the notes according to subject and in the ordering of particular items, we have, broadly speaking, followed the lines laid down in the Einaudi edition, which also provides the basis of the text used for the translation. At the same time we have not hesitated, in the interests of clarity of presentation, to depart from the Einaudi order wherever this seemed to us justified on philological grounds, by reference to the original *Quaderni*. We have also, where relevant (e.g. in the political sections), appended in square brackets the date of the *Quaderno* from which a text is taken. The texts that we have used are as follows.

The essays on the Intellectuals and on Education belong together in Gramsci's original manuscript (*Quaderno* XXIX, ff. 1–12). We have translated the texts as they appear in the Einaudi volume *Gli intellettuali* on pp. 3–19, 97–103 and 106–14.

The sections on Italian History and on Politics have necessitated the most reordering, both in relation to the Einaudi edition and to the original *Quaderni*. The "Notes on Italian History" in this edition come mainly from the Einaudi volume *Il Risorgimento*. One passage, "Material for a Critical Essay on Croce's Two Histories", is previously unpublished, and we have also integrated into the text one passage from each of the Einaudi volumes *Il materialismo storico*, *Note sul Machiavelli* and *Passato e presente*.

The "Notes on Politics" were all included, with the exception of one previously unpublished text—"Self-criticism and the Hypocrisy of Self-criticism"—in the Einaudi volumes *Note sul Machiavelli* and *Passato e presente*. Within the political sections however our ordering, in terms of a rough division into two parts, on the Party and on the State, is original. The Einaudi order here is not satisfactory, but it is equally impossible to follow the *Quaderni*. The principal source for the notes is a late *Quaderno* (XXX, datable to 1933–34) in which a number of earlier texts are rewritten in a more polished form but in an order which has no particular internal coherence. Drafts of some of the same texts, together with notes on related topics, are to be found in a number of other *Quaderni*, written between 1929 and 1933. Short of a literal reproduction of all these texts, or a massive critical apparatus, out of place in an edition of this size and scope, there is clearly no alternative to a reordering of some kind, aimed at presenting to the reader a selection of texts which is as reasonably comprehensive and coherent as possible, while making it clear, through the dates appended at the end of each passage, roughly where each stands in terms of Gramsci's original project.

The essay "Americanism and Fordism" derives from a single *Quaderno*, number V, and is translated here as it appears, slightly reordered, in the *Note sul Machiavelli*.

The philosophical texts have been translated, with one or two minor changes, as they appear in the Einaudi volume *Il materialismo storico*. The essays "Some Preliminary Points of Reference" and "Critical Notes on an Attempt at Popular Sociology" are fairly complete in the original *Quaderni*. Those entitled "Problems of Philosophy and History" and "Some Problems in the Study of the Philosophy of Praxis" are the result of some reordering by the Einaudi editors.

In translating our aim has been to combine the demands of a readable English style with a respect not only for the precise content but also for the flavour of an original which, in its fragmentary and elliptical character and its frequent recourse to tricks to deceive the prison censor, bears distinct traces of the difficult circumstances under which it was written. Names of well-known Marxists and Communists are almost always given in the *Quaderni* in the form of a substitute or a circumlocution. Thus Marx is referred to as "the founder of the philosophy of praxis", Lenin as "Ilich" or "Vilich" [V. Ilich], Trotsky as "Leon Davidovitch" or "Bronstein" and so on. Similarly certain identifiable concepts of Marxism Leninism such as the class struggle or the dictatorship of the proletariat are usually masked under innocuous sounding titles. All such names or phrases have been left in the original form used by Gramsci, but explained either by square brackets in the text or by a footnote. In the case of concepts this has been done not merely in order to preserve the feel of the original text but also to avoid imposing too simplistic an interpretation on phrases which often have a conceptual value of their own. Thus "philosophy of praxis" is both a euphemism for Marxism and an autonomous term used by Gramsci to define what he saw to be a central characteristic of the philosophy of Marxism, the inseparable link it establishes between theory and practice, thought and action.

TERMINOLOGY

Questions of censorship apart, Gramsci's terminology presents a number of difficulties to the translator. Wherever possible we have tried to render each term of Gramsci's with a single equivalent, as close as possible to the original. In one particular set of cases this has proved impossible, and that is with the group of words centred around the verb *dirigere* (*dirigente*, *direttivo*, *direzione*, etc.). Here we have in part followed the normal English usage dictated by the context (e.g. *direzione* = leadership; *classe dirigente* = ruling class) but in certain cases we have translated *dirigente* and *direttivo* as "directive" in order to preserve what for Gramsci is a crucial conceptual distinction, between power based on "domination" and the exercise of "direction" or "hegemony". In this context it is also worth noting that the term "hegemony" in Gramsci itself has two faces. On the one hand it is contrasted with "domination" (and as such bound up with the opposition State/Civil Society) and on the other hand "hegemonic" is sometimes used as an opposite of "corporate" or "economic-corporate" to designate an historical phase in which a given group moves beyond a position of corporate existence and defence of its economic position and aspires to a position of leadership in the political and social arena. Non-hegemonic groups or classes are also called by Gramsci "subordinate", "subaltern" or sometimes "instrumental". Here again we have preserved Gramsci's original terminology despite the strangeness that some of these words have in English and despite the fact that it is difficult to discern any systematic difference in Gramsci's usage between, for instance, subaltern and subordinate. The Hegelian sense of the word "momento", meaning an aspect of a situation in its concrete (not necessarily temporal) manifestations, has generally been rendered as "moment" but sometimes as "aspect". Despite Marx's strictures (in *The German Ideology*) on the abuse of this word, it occurs frequently in Gramsci in both its senses, and confusion is made worse by the fact that Italian, unlike German, does not distinguish the two senses of the word according to gender. In particular cases where there seemed to us any difficulty with a word or concept we have referred the reader to a footnote, as also with any passage where the translation is at all uncertain. In general we have preferred to footnote too much rather than too little, on the assumption that readers familiar with, say, the history of the Third International might nevertheless find useful some explanation, however elementary, of the specialised vocabulary of Kantian philosophy, while philosophers who know their Hegel and Marx might be less at home in the history of the Italian Risorgimento.

The translation and notes for the essays on Education and for the writings on the Risorgimento and on politics are by Quintin Hoare; those for the essay on the Intellectuals, for "Americanism and Fordism" and for the philosophical sections are by Geoffrey Nowell Smith. With the exception of the section on Gramsci's intellectual background, the General Introduction is by Quintin Hoare.

NOTES

Explanatory notes by the English editors and translators have been indicated on each page by superior numerals, Gramsci's own notes, as contained in the originals, by asterisks.

We have preferred, for ease of reference, to place all the notes on the pages to which they refer rather than place editors' notes at the end of each section or at the end of the book—although this means that occasionally an editorial note has had to be added below one of the author's notes.

GENERAL INTRODUCTION

By the autumn of 1926, the world's first fascist régime had been in power for four years in Italy. Its character was still very much a matter of dispute, not least within the Italian Communist Party and the Third International. Was it a specific, national phenomenon or the precursor of an international trend? Was it a novel socio-political formation or one that was basically just the Italian equivalent of other, more traditional forms of reaction—such as the Russian Black Hundreds after 1905 or the anti-labour repression which ravaged American socialism in the early years of this century or the *Freikorps* which underpinned the social-democratic government of Noske and Scheidemann in Germany after 1918? Did its essence lie in its social base in the urban petty bourgeoisie and the rural bourgeoisie, or in its role as the new, more brutal instrument of big capital's dominion?

These uncertainties about how fascism should be defined were accompanied by equal uncertainty about its stability and historical prospects. It was still widely believed by communist leaders that the ruling class might decide that the fascist option was too costly, and switch to a social-democratic alternative. The notion that social-democracy was the "left wing of the bourgeoisie" had been generally accepted, for example, by Italian communists since Zinoviev first put it forward in 1922 (by 1924 this had become "the left wing of fascism"). Moreover, it was true that the fascists had not entirely suppressed bourgeois political institutions; indeed, even communist members still sat in the fascist-dominated parliament. And during the crisis which had followed the fascist assassination of the social-democrat deputy Matteotti in June 1924, the régime had genuinely appeared to totter and its backers to hesitate. But in fact fascist power already had immensely strong foundations. It had inaugurated a system of repression incomparably more thoroughgoing and efficient than any previous form of reaction. By the end of 1925 it was quite clear that any idea of the régime splitting in the foreseeable future under the force of its own internal contradictions was an illusion. Throughout 1926 Mussolini had been effectively playing at cat and mouse with the opposition parties—at least at the legal level.

Finally, in the autumn of 1926, on the pretext of an alleged attempt on his life, Mussolini decided to make an end of even the semblance of bourgeois democracy that still survived. All remaining opposition organisations and their publications were banned, and a new, massive series of arrests was launched throughout the country. Among those arrested was Antonio Gramsci. Gramsci was a member of parliament—but the régime was no longer interested in niceties about parliamentary immunity. He had also, since August 1924, been the general secretary of the Communist Party—though of course under such political conditions the identity of party officials was kept secret. He was 35 years old. At his trial in 1928, the official prosecutor ended his peroration with the famous demand to the judge: "We must stop this brain working for twenty years!" But, although Gramsci was to be dead long before those twenty years were up, released, his health broken, only in time to die under guard in a clinic rather than in prison, yet for as long as his physique held out his jailers did not succeed in stopping his brain from working. The product of those years of slow death in prison were the 2,848 pages of handwritten notes which he left to be smuggled out of the clinic and out of Italy after his death, and of which this volume is a selection.

Our introduction will make no attempt to offer a general *interpretation* of Gramsci's Prison Notebooks, but will concentrate rather on giving a brief outline of the political and intellectual experience which formed, inevitably, the background to and the point of departure for Gramsci's writing during his imprisonment.

Early Life

Antonio Gramsci was born in 1891, in the small town of Ales in Sardinia. His father came originally from Naples and had been intended to be a lawyer. But the death of his own father, a colonel in the *Carabinieri*, meant that he had to abandon his studies; he found a job as registrar in the small Sardinian town of Ghilarza. There he met Gramsci's mother, who was the daughter of a local inspector of taxes and had the rare attainment, in an area of 90 per cent illiteracy, of being able to read and write. Any ambitions the couple might have had for their children were rudely dashed, however, in 1897 when the father was suspended from his job, without pay, on suspicion of peculation. The following year he was put under arrest and in 1900 he was sentenced to nearly six years imprisonment. To what extent he was guilty of the charges, which were undoubtedly motivated by his opposition to the political party in power locally, is not very important; corruption is anyway endemic in that type of society. The essential fact is that from 1898 to 1904, when her husband was released from prison and found a new—albeit inferior—job, Gramsci's mother was forced to bring up her seven children, alone, with no source of income other than her meagre earnings as a seamstress and the proceeds from the sale of a small plot of land, in conditions of dire poverty.

Antonio's health was an added problem. He had a malformation of the spine, which the doctors attempted to cure by having him suspended for long periods from a beam on the ceiling, and when he grew up he became hunch-backed and was barely five feet tall. He also suffered from internal disorders which brought him close to death as a small child, and which were to recur throughout his adult life, accompanied by severe nervous complications, and to culminate in his death at the age of 46.

In 1898 Antonio started school at Ghilarza, but his education was interrupted for a couple of years at the end of his elementary schooling since none of his brothers was earning and he had to go out to work. His father's release enabled him to return to school, in the neighbouring town of Santulussurgiu. It was an appallingly bad school, but nevertheless, by dint of application and the help afforded by his literate home background, he managed in 1908 to pass the examination to enter the senior *liceo* in Cagliari.

When in Cagliari he lodged with his elder brother Gennaro, now a white-collar worker and recently returned from military service in Turin. Gennaro, whose experience on the mainland had turned him into a socialist militant, helped to introduce Antonio to politics, and from 1906 used to send socialist pamphlets back to his younger brother at home. An equally formative influence was provided by the wave of social protest that swept Sardinia in the same year, and was brutally repressed by troops from the mainland. The form taken by the repression, both military and legal, gave a great impetus to the cause of Sardinian nationalism, and it was to this cause that Gramsci first adhered. Experience of the working-class movement in Turin was to lead Gramsci to abandon his attachment to nationalism as such, but he never lost the concern, imparted to him in these early years, with peasant problems and the complex dialectic of class and regional factors. A unique surviving essay from his schooldays at Cagliari shows him, too, already progressing from a Sardinian to an internationalist and anti-colonialist viewpoint, as vehement in his opposition to European imperialism in China as in his repetition of what (he recalled in 1924) was the favourite slogan of his schooldays: "Throw the mainlanders into the sea!"

In 1906 mainland troops were called in to repress the Sardinian peasantry. Later on, however, Gramsci was to discover the opposite side of the coin—Sardinian troops being used to hold down the workers of Turin. In general, the conflicts between industrial "North" and rural "South" tended to obscure more basic class questions. Since 1887, the growing industry of the North had been favoured by protectionist policies which kept out foreign capital, and secured its dominance of the domestic market. This protectionism provided the basis of an effective community of interests between big industrial capital and the reformist working-class organisations—a community of interests which was fostered by the policies of Giovanni Giolitti, the dominant bourgeois politician of the years preceding the First World War. But its impact on agricultural Italy was, with the exception of the cereal-producers in the Centre and North, calamitous: the peasants were no longer able to export their produce, and at the same time were forced to buy the products of Italian industry rather than the far cheaper goods made in the more advanced industrial countries. This was the main basis of what became the "Southern Question". One of its consequences was that the socialism which spread in the South and the islands was not that of the P.S.I. (Socialist Party of Italy) or the trade unions, but a kind of mélange of socialist and liberal theories which can be traced back to the ideas and activity of Carlo Pisacane during the Risorgimento, and which was propagated most notably by Gaetano Salvemini in the period preceding the First World War. This "Southernism" was almost certainly Gramsci's political position, broadly speaking, at the time of his arrival in Turin in 1911. Salvemini in particular, an early socialist who resigned from the party because of its reformism and indifference to rural and Southern concerns, was to be a major intellectual influence in Gramsci's political formation.

In 1911 Gramsci, having managed to recoup the losses caused by his indifferent and interrupted early schooling, won a scholarship for poor students from Sardinia to the University of Turin, sitting the examination at the same time as a future student friend and fellow communist, Palmiro Togliatti. The scholarship grant was miserably inadequate, and cold and malnutrition played havoc with Gramsci's already precarious health. During 1913–15 he was desperately ill most of the time, and eventually he was forced to abandon his studies, despite his talent, especially for philology and linguistics generally, and despite the encouragement of several of his teachers. However, there was a more important reason even than his impossible personal situation which finally decided him to leave the university. This was the fact of his growing political commitment.

Intellectual Formation

It was during his years at Turin University that Gramsci first came into serious contact with the intellectual world of his time. The deficiencies of liberal Italy had created a certain vogue for socialist ideas even in bourgeois circles, and many of the professors at the University had links with the socialist movement. Foremost among these were Umberto Cosmo, a literary historian and Dante scholar, with whom Gramsci became friends and whom he subsequently was to criticise for his bourgeois style of attachment to the workers' movement, and Annibale Pastore, whose lectures on Marxism Gramsci attended. Here he was introduced to the particular brand of Hegelianised "philosophy of praxis" to which he remained in an ambiguous critical relationship right to the end of his working life.

The term "philosophy of praxis", best known today in connection with Gramsci's Prison Notebooks, in which it is used partly for its own sake and partly as a euphemism to deceive the censor, was introduced into Italy by Antonio Labriola, the only Italian theoretical Marxist of any consequence before the first world war. Labriola, who died in 1904, was a philosopher and historian who had come round to Marxism and to participation in the socialist movement fairly late in life, bringing with him distinct traces of a Hegelian intellectual formation. He saw the essence of Marxism in the unique nexus it established between theoretical and practical activity, and maintained the unity of philosophy and history; he distinguished himself from the Hegelian school mainly by his insistence on the primacy of concrete relations over consciousness. Labriola's ideas, particularly on the interpretation of history, were extremely influential, but mainly in intellectual circles and often in a distorted form which accentuated their latent idealism at the expense of their materialist base. The phrase "philosophy of praxis" in particular entered into the parlance of a specifically anti-materialist tendency of which the major exponents were Rodolfo Mondolfo and, in a marginal way, Giovanni Gentile.

Gentile's role in the development of Italian Marxism was limited to one thing: his translation, the first into Italian, of Marx's *Theses on Feuerbach*, which he interpreted idealistically as referring to the process of cognition rather than to the real world and man's relation to it. Gentile's flirtation with Marxism was brief and superficial. His theory of praxis soon degenerated into a philosophy of the "pure act", of voluntarist and proto-fascist inspiration. He later became a major ideologue of fascism and was executed by the partisans during the resistance.

Mondolfo was a far more serious figure, and after Labriola's death the leading philosopher of Italian socialism. His main contribution to Marxism lay in his attempt to drive a wedge between the "philosophical" Marx and the more empirical Engels. Mondolfo and his school were also responsible to a large extent for the idealistic interpretation of Labriola. The use, common to Labriola, Mondolfo and Gramsci of the same phrase "philosophy of praxis" has led some commentators to posit a common idealist matrix for the three thinkers. This is a view that must be treated with caution. In one feature Gramsci's mature thought is in accord with Mondolfo's ideas and that is in its constant underplaying of the materialist element in Marx's work, which, in Gramsci at least, is replaced with a stress on "immanentism" and the elimination of metaphysics. On the whole, however, Gramsci shows himself critical of Mondolfo and concerned to reassert the substantial Marxism of Labriola against both those Marxists who had criticised him for idealism and the idealists who had tried to claim him for their own. That Mondolfo's approach to Marxism entered into his own culture at this early period is certain, but as Gramsci himself was to point out, in relation to Marx, there is a distinction to be made between the personal philosophical culture of an author—what he has read and absorbed and maybe rejected at various periods of his life—and his own original philosophy.

A far more important philosophical and cultural influence imparted to Gramsci in his early years was that of Benedetto Croce. Croce had been a pupil of Labriola and for a short period, between 1895 and 1900, professed himself a Marxist. He soon defected, declaring Marxism to be useful only as a "simple canon of historical enquiry and research" and pronouncing, with characteristic arrogance, "the death of theoretical Marxism in Italy" coincidental with his own defection. Croce's influence on the whole of Italian culture right up to the present time cannot be overestimated. Despite his abandonment of Marxism many of his ideas continued to strike an echoing chord among young intellectuals of the left in the pre-fascist period: notably his secularism and his opposition to the previously dominant ideology of positivism.

Politically his role was always ambiguous. His calls for ethical renewal had dangerous overtones, as his support for Mussolini in the early twenties was to show. But his continued association with the French theorist of syndicalism, Georges Sorel, helped to sustain the illusion that his could be a philosophy for the Left.

Looking back on his student days, Gramsci was to describe himself self-critically as having been, in his youth, "tendentially Crocean", and many of his early articles have a distinct Crocean ring about them. This personal, though culturally imparted, Crocean influence on Gramsci himself must be carefully distinguished from the attitude which emerges from the *Quaderni*, where Croce is considered more objectively as a philosopher and as a dominant figure in contemporary culture. Much of Gramsci's philosophical notebooks is devoted to a rigorous critique of Crocean philosophy in its relation to Marxism. In his prison writings he refers constantly to the need to combat Croceanism, both as a diffuse ideology and as a specific philosophical system, sometimes casting Croce in the role of a Dühring, to be polemically destroyed, but more often seeing him as comparable to Hegel as a thinker whose work could be profited from in the struggle to renew Marxist thought and liberate it from positivistic accretions.

The substance of Gramsci's mature critique of Croce's philosophy relates to the latter's reduction of historical movement from a struggle of opposites to a merely conceptual dialectic, the "dialectic of distincts". While, Gramsci contended, such a schema might have its place in the philosophy of a society in which real conflicts had been eliminated and where the unity of knowledge and being, impossible in a class society, had finally been achieved, it was unable to offer an account of the actual concrete character of a history fundamentally determined by the class struggle. This abstraction of real history into an ethereal realm of distinct concepts went hand in hand, in Crocean philosophy, with a radical denial of politics. The distinct "categories" of the Crocean system allow for the existence of four sciences, Aesthetics, Economics, Logic and Ethics, relating to the pursuit respectively of the Beautiful, the Useful, the True and the Good. Politics, in this conception, can only be a composite entity, a mere "passion", of no philosophical value. In Gramsci's thought, by contrast, politics figures, philosophically, as the central human activity, the means by which the single consciousness is brought into contact with the social and natural world in all its forms.

The critique to which Gramsci subjects Crocean idealism in the prison *Quaderni* is motivated, however, less by an abstract concern to expose its intellectual inadequacies than by an awareness of the need to destroy the influence which Croceanism, and Croce himself, had on all aspects of Italian cultural and even political life. Whereas in the period leading up to the first world war much of what Croce said and did could be held to have a positive value—his leftish sympathies, his revaluation of a "romantic" tradition in Italian culture from Vico through De Sanctis up to the present, his opposition to contemporary positivism—the rise of fascism and Croce's ambiguous attitude to it had turned his role into a pernicious and reactionary one. Unlike Gentile, Croce did not play a direct and active part in the elaboration of fascist cultural policy and even managed to draw intellectual credit from the fact of his abstention from public life after 1926. But the fact remains that he did support the régime at the outset and that the theoretical character of his later opposition was of a singularly insipid and depoliticising kind, whose effect on the intellectual strata subject to Crocean influence was at best to inspire a certain withdrawal from fascist vulgarity, but which more often promoted a habit of "justificationism" with regard to the régime far more extensive than any provoked by Hegel's supposed glorification of the Prussian monarchy.

The war and fascism provided a brutal litmus test for many progressive and *avant-garde* intellectuals and artists beside Croce. Among those who supported or were at least complicit with the régime were D'Annunzio, Pirandello, Marinetti the futurist poet, together with most of his acolytes, the meridionalist Prezzolini, former editor of *La Voce*, Mario Missiroli and countless others. Many of these had been important figures in Gramsci's cultural formation, at a time when they had held advanced positions in the world of Italian culture and before Gramsci's own Marxism had matured and taken its definitive form. Not only Gramsci but the whole *Ordine Nuovo* group of Communists in Turin had been influenced by the cultural ferment of the prewar years and it is a sign of the complexity and confusion of the Italian situation that a group such as the Futurists, for example, whose Russian equivalents, led by Mayakovsky, had played a leading role in the formation of the Soviet *avant-garde*, should in Italy have degenerated into the barrel-organs of fascism. Be that as it may the whole question of the Italian intellectuals, their provincialism, their cosmopolitanism, their role in the power structure of Church and State, particularly in the South, was to become a major subject of Gramsci's reflection in prison. His critique is never sectarian. It starts from a realistic assessment of the objective weakness of the Italian intelligentsia with a view to recuperating those ideas and those forces which could contribute to the formation of a "national-popular" consciousness in association with the rising power of the proletariat. Even Crocean idealism, despite its evident anti-popular bias, is not totally dismissed, and those features of it which had positively impressed Gramsci in his youth are brought out and used, even, as an aid to the criticism of orthodox Marxism itself.

Socialist Politics in Turin

When Gramsci arrived in Turin, the city was the red capital of Italy—Gramsci was to call it Italy's Petrograd—home of its most advanced industry and above all of FIAT. By the end of the war, FIAT was to be the biggest producer of tractors in Europe; its workers were to increase from 4,000 in 1913 to 20,000 in 1918; by 1915, it was exporting armoured cars and aeroplanes to the Entente countries in great quantities. Turin's population rose from some 400,000 in 1911 (20 per cent of them industrial workers) to over 500,000 in 1918 (30 per cent of them industrial workers)—and this despite the fact that between 5 and 10 per cent of the population was in the army and therefore not included in the 1918 total. Of the Turin working class, some 40 per cent was made up of women, and these were in the vanguard of all the major proletarian upheavals which shook the city between 1912 and 1920.

One consequence of the specific character of Turin's capitalism was that, unlike the other major industrial cities of the country, it was relatively satisfied by the boom which it experienced in 1914–15, and hence favoured the policy of neutrality advocated by Giolitti. It was above all heavy industry—iron, steel, coal, shipping—which stood to gain from war. But the cotton and wool factories which still represented by far the greater part of Turin's industry, and the vehicle industry which was soon destined to outstrip these, were both so overwhelmed by orders from the belligerent Entente countries that they saw no need for direct intervention in the war. They had absorbed whatever unemployed labour they could find among the recent immigrants and especially among the women of the population, they were short of skilled labour and were intent above all on introducing new methods of raising productivity—the Taylorism which was to interest both Lenin and Gramsci so much—and in maintaining industrial peace as far as was possible.

The latter task was a formidable one. The proletariat of Turin was the most advanced and combative in Italy. As early as 1904–6, it had demonstrated a high degree of solidarity and a readiness to take to the streets. Although it suffered a series of massive defeats in 1907, which were followed by years which saw the apogee of Giolittian "industrial peace" and the rapid growth of a collaborationist trade-union movement, nevertheless in 1912 the metal-workers (those not organised in unions!) embarked upon a strike "to the end". This was defeated, after 75 days of struggle; but the metalworkers came out again—this time led by the union, the FIOM—in the spring of 1913, and after a 93-day strike won a considerable victory (partly as a result of government intervention against the employers' dangerous intransigence). These struggles were the background to Gramsci's first years in Turin. They won him from his youthful Southernism, demonstrating that the workers were the real enemy of the Northern industrialists, despite the collaborationism of their reformist leaders, and that they were thus the potential ally and leader of the peasant masses of the South. As war approached, and after its outbreak, the struggles of the Turin proletariat became yet more massive, and at the same time more political. The key stages in this trajectory were the general strike of June 1914, following the bloody repression of an anti-war demonstration at Ancona; the huge anti-war demonstrations and general strike of May 1915; and above all the insurrection of August 1917.

When Gramsci arrived in Turin, the two dominant influences on the younger generation of socialists were Salvemini, and Mussolini who was the acknowledged leader of the party's left wing and the editor of *Avanti!*, the party newspaper. Salvemini's impassioned crusading against the indifference of the reformist working-class leaders to the plight of the Southern peasantry has already been discussed. He had violently opposed the imperialist expansion into Libya in 1912, and had been beaten up by government thugs. His newspaper was entitled *Unità*, with the implication that genuine unity between North and South on a basis of equality remained to be fought for; years later in 1923 Gramsci proposed the same name for the new organ of the P.C.I. (Communist Party of Italy) "because . . . we must give special importance to the Southern question". The influence of Mussolini was as great. An equally harsh critic of the Libyan expedition, and of the passivity of the reformist party officials, Mussolini wrote in the accents of Sorel, exalting the combativity of the masses and the potentialities of the general strike as a weapon in the class war. In this period he was also a passionate opponent of all forms of militarism. His youth and voluntarist temperament won him the admiration and loyalty of the younger generation, which he was only to forfeit in 1914 when he became an advocate of Italian intervention during the war.

To understand the complex internal life of Italian socialism in these years, it is essential to stress that the party itself was only one of the forces in play: the socialist trade union federation (C.G.L.), the socialist deputies in parliament, the socialist local councillors, and the powerful cooperative institutions were none of them subject in any effective sense to party discipline. The primary concern of the party leadership throughout the war years was to play a unitary role in relation to these various forces; such a role could of its nature not be a revolutionary one, even though some at least of the party leaders were subjectively genuine revolutionaries. At the same time, the leadership was edged steadily to the left (in words at any rate) in response to the growing unpopularity of the war, the increasing militancy of the industrial workers, and later to the immense impact of the Russian revolutions. These twin, conflicting pressures combined to create the "maximalism" (Italian equivalent of the "centrism" which was an international phenomenon after the war, and whose most important expression was the German U.S.P.D.) which was to dominate the Italian Left until it was crushed by fascism, and of which Serrati, the editor of *Avanti!* after Mussolini's defection, was the most important and most honourable expression.

In the course of the war years, a reformist Right, based primarily on the parliamentary deputies and the trade unions and led by Turati, Treves and d'Aragona, emerged as a coherent entity. Its main characterising feature, especially after the catastrophic defeat of the Italian army at Caporetto in 1917, was its readiness to accept patriotic slogans. The official party position was defined by the party secretary Lazzari as "Neither support nor sabotage", and the principal source of dissent within the movement was the argument over whether or not support could be given to the various committees (for aid to war victims, industrial mobilisation, etc.) formed to assist the war effort. The Right was favourable to participation in these, but the party leadership remained true to its "abstentionist" principles. Though positive as far as it went, this had some extremely negative consequences for the future. For the leadership had a "left" enough position to prevent the emergence of any effective organised Left until well after the war, while it was in no genuine sense revolutionary in its practice; at the same time, it profoundly alienated the petit-bourgeois strata—susceptible to patriotic slogans —who were to provide the social basis for fascism. Although there was a diffuse "Left" within the party, and this even constituted itself briefly as an "intransigent-revolutionary" faction in mid-1917, it overlapped to a great extent with the party leadership. It differed from official policy mainly on issues of "principle"—in its insistence that violence is inevitable as the midwife of revolution; that the reformists collaborating with the committees should be expelled; that the bourgeois notion of the "nation" should be repudiated, etc. The faction did also advocate a more active encouragement of mass resistance to the war, but it never elaborated any really distinct strategy. Although the "intransigent" faction of 1917 was in a sense the forerunner of the communist fraction of 1919–20, it was short-lived and acted as the conscience of the party rather than as an alternative, left leadership. Many of its most prominent members, were to become centrists rather than communists after Livorno (see below).

At the outbreak of war, the Turin branch of the P.S.I. had some 1,000 members, of whom perhaps four-fifths were workers. This total was quickly reduced by conscription to not more than 500, and in the course of the war—despite the huge upsurge of revolutionary consciousness among the masses—almost certainly was further reduced by police repression, until in the last year of war the section almost ceased to have any public existence. The section, during the course of the war, became one of the bastions of the intransigent wing of the party, and this was especially true of the younger members, such as Gramsci.

Gramsci's first political associate and mentor after his arrival in Turin was Angelo Tasca, who subsequently became the leader of the right wing of the P.C.I. until his expulsion after the left turn in 1929. Tasca, the son of a railway worker, born in the same year as Gramsci, had been active in the socialist party since 1909. In May 1912 he gave Gramsci a copy of *War and Peace* with the inscription "To my fellow student of today, and my fellow militant—I hope—of tomorrow". In November 1912 Gramsci moved to Tasca's street, and a year later to the same building, at more or less the same time as he joined the Socialist Party. Tasca had risen to national prominence within the party at its 1912 youth conference, when he had clashed with the man who was to dominate the P.C.I. in its first years, and subsequently to lead its left faction until his expulsion in 1930: Amadeo Bordiga. Bordiga, the son of an agricultural economist, grew up in an intellectual socialist milieu in Naples, and through his immense energy—Gramsci was to describe him as capable of as much work as three others put together—soon imposed himself as the leader of the intransigent opposition to the reformist socialism which dominated the local party organisation. Whereas the young Turin socialists, in their reaction against the class collaborationism and passivity of the old socialist leaders, were influenced above all by Crocean idealism and Sorelian voluntarism, by Salvemini's Southernism, and by the experience of the mass proletarian struggles of Italy's most advanced industrial city, Bordiga's reaction took a different course. He fought for a return to Marxist orthodoxy, principled, intransigent, but also already showing the inflexibility and indeed dogmatism which were to characterise his political career. He also fought, however, for a national perspective for revolutionary strategy, at a time when Gramsci was still thinking in local terms; it was this factor above all, together with his early understanding of the role of the revolutionary party, which ensured his dominance in the P.C.I. at its foundation.

At the 1912 youth congress mentioned above, Tasca had demanded that *Avanguardia*, the youth organ of the Party, should become the bearer of a new culture and set out to renovate the intellectual patrimony of Italian socialism. Bordiga heaped derision on this "culturalism": "The need for study is what a congress of schoolteachers proclaims—not a congress of socialists", etc. Gramsci, years later in his Prison Notebooks, was to write of this clash: "It is often claimed that [Bordiga's] 'economistic' extremism was justified by [Tasca's] cultural opportunism . . . but might it not be replied, vice versa, that the cultural opportunism was justified by the economistic extremism? In reality, neither one nor the other was 'justifiable' nor should they ever be justified. They should be 'explained' realistically as twin aspects of the same immaturity and the same primitivism" (PP pp. 73–4). Gramsci's achievement within the P.C.I. was to win it away from Bordiga without delivering it to Tasca.

During these early years in Turin, Gramsci also made the acquaintance of other future leaders of the P.C.I.—notably Togliatti and Terracini. Since the two latter, together with Gramsci and Tasca, formed the nucleus of collaborators responsible for the creation of *L'Ordine Nuovo* in 1919, there has been a tendency to read back their association as a group into the war years, which was not the case. Togliatti was essentially a student friend, whose political activity really dated from the end of the war; when war broke out he volunteered to serve in the medical corps. Tasca was called up immediately in May 1915. Terracini, who had joined the Socialist youth organisation at the age of sixteen in 1911, was arrested in September 1916 for distributing anti-war propaganda, and after a month in gaol was also conscripted. Gramsci alone spent the war years in Turin.

Gramsci's first political initiative was a blunder, and one that was to cost him dear. In October 1914, when Mussolini began to shift away from the official party position of neutrality in the war, Gramsci wrote an article in the party press defending him. The mistake was hardly surprising, given Gramsci's political inexperience; Mussolini was the unchallenged leader of the P.S.I.'s left wing, and nobody, of course, could foresee his future trajectory. The internationalism of Lenin was utterly unknown in Italy at the time. Gramsci was motivated above all by scorn for the passivity of the official party position "Neither support, nor sabotage", for what was in effect nothing but a policy of "clean hands". He wrote: "Revolutionaries see history as a creation of their own spirit, as being made up of a continuous series of violent tugs at the other forces of society—both active and passive, and they prepare the maximum of favourable conditions for the definitive tug (revolution); they must not be content with the provisional slogan 'absolute neutrality', but must transform it into that of 'active, operative neutrality'." It quickly became clear, of course, that Mussolini's perspective was a very different one, and Gramsci did not venture into print again for over a year. Despite his irreproachable record of opposition to the imperialist war in the ensuing years, the accusation of "interventionism" was still to be hurled at him years later by political opponents, on the basis of this one article.

However, in 1915 Gramsci joined the staff of the Socialist Party weekly *Il Grido del Popolo*, and became a full-time journalist. During the war years, he developed into a formidable political commentator. He wrote on every aspect of Turin's social and political life; on the strikes and demonstrations of the Turin working class; on international events such as the Zimmerwald Conference or the Armenian massacres. As the theatre critic of *Avanti!*, the party daily, from 1916 on, he was one of the first to recognise the importance of Pirandello. His influence extended far outside the ranks of the party itself. In 1916, Gramsci spoke in public for the first time, addressing meetings on Romain Rolland, on the

French Revolution, on the Paris Commune, and (taking as his cue Ibsen's play *The Doll's House*) on the emancipation of women. However, before 1917 Gramsci did not play any very prominent part in the life of the Turin party organisation. 1917 was the turning-point in his political formation: it was the year of the Russian revolutions and of the great proletarian insurrection in Turin.

When the news of the February Revolution in Russia filtered through, Gramsci was in no two minds about its significance, despite the sketchiness of the censored press reports. As early as 29 April 1917, he wrote in *Il Grido del Popolo*, the party weekly: "The bourgeois press . . . has told us how the autocracy's power has been replaced by another power which is not yet clearly defined and which they hope is bourgeois power. They have been quick to establish a parallel between the Russian Revolution and the French Revolution, and have found that the events are similar. . . . We, however, are convinced that the Russian Revolution is not simply an event but a proletarian act, and that it must naturally debouch into a socialist régime." Yet Gramsci's understanding of the true achievement of the Bolsheviks, or even knowledge of who precisely the Bolsheviks were (see, e.g. his article "Kerensky-Chernov" of 29/9/17), was inevitably still quite limited. Above all, he did not yet at all realise the importance of Lenin's theory and practice of the revolutionary, vanguard party. He responded above all to the affirmation of proletarian will which he discerned in the Bolshevik Revolution; after October, he wrote a famous article, of great interest despite its all-too-evident idealist misconceptions, entitled "The Revolution against *Das Kapital*". In this article he counterposed Lenin's achievement as an affirmation of revolutionary will against the determinism which dominated the Second International—a determinism justified with the help of a positivist interpretation of Marx's *Capital*. In his view "the Bolsheviks . . . are not 'Marxists' . . . they have not compiled on the basis of the Master's works an external doctrine, made up of dogmatic assertions. . . . They live the thought of Marx, that which can never die, which is the continuation of Italian and German idealist thought, and which in Marx was contaminated by positivistic and naturalistic incrustations". The parallel with Marx's own assertion that he was not a "Marxist" is obvious; Gramsci was already more of a Marxist than he knew, but what he did, decisively, reject was the "Marxism" which held that there was "a fatal necessity for a bourgeoisie to be formed in Russia, for a capitalist era to open, before the proletariat might even think of rising up, of their own class demands, of their revolution". In other words the "Marxism" of the Mensheviks or of the Second International.

The impact of the Russian revolutions of 1917 was perhaps more rapid in Turin than anywhere else in Europe. Hostility to the war had been general in the city from the start, and had grown in intensity as the conflict continued. The first months of 1917 were punctuated by numerous industrial struggles launched to counter the effects of food shortages and rising prices; in the vanguard were the women workers, above all in the textile factories. As soon as the news of the February Revolution began to filter through, the idea of "doing the same as in Russia" spread like wildfire. By May the prefect of the city was asking the Government to proclaim the province of Turin a "war zone". Socialist speakers urged workers to "come to meetings in future . . . with revolvers . . ." to use against the police, and stressed that "it is imperative not to waste time, but to work actively for a general insurrection, get hold of bombs . . .", etc. These fiery words were not in fact accompanied by any serious concrete preparation for any such course of action on the part of the socialist leaders, but they seized the imagination of the mass of workers in Turin, and of many workers in the other Italian cities. A typical attitude in this period was that of Serrati: on 8 May he was arguing at a national meeting of the socialist leadership that they should assume responsibility for co-ordinating the current struggles with a view to channelling them towards a general insurrection; after his resolution was defeated, he subsequently urged moderation on the intransigents of Turin—in line with the priority which he was long to continue to give to party unity.

In August 1917, on the occasion of yet another failure of bread supplies, the Turin proletariat rose in a spontaneous insurrection. Barricades went up in the working-class quarters, and the centre of the city was besieged. In so far as there was any organisation on the insurgent side, it was provided by the anarchists. The intransigent socialist leaders were as impotent as the reformist deputies or trade union officials. This impotence of the socialist leaders was to be demonstrated repeatedly during the next three years. The insurrection lasted for four days, and machine-guns and tanks had to be brought into the fray before the last barricades fell. Some fifty workers were killed in the fighting, and almost one thousand were subsequently either imprisoned or sent to the front by order of the courts. The August events showed with dramatic clarity both the immense revolutionary spirit of the Turin proletariat, and the wretched inadequacy of its political organisations.

Before the August events, Gramsci had held no important post within the Turin party section, but when, in their wake, virtually all the socialist leaders were arrested, he was elected to the "Provisional Committee" which directed the semi-clandestine activities to which the party was reduced in the city until the war ended. He also became editor of *Il Grido del Popolo*, which was a key position when the press was almost the only aspect of the party's activity which was able to continue a legal existence. His political position was evolving in the direction of a break not merely with the "centrist" party leadership, but also with the "purism" of the intransigent Left. In October 1917, a meeting was held between the principal leaders of the intransigent faction mentioned earlier and representatives of the party leadership, including Serrati and Lazzari. This was followed in November by a secret conference held in Florence, with the aim of working out a common platform before the party's next national congress. By this time the only major point which separated the "intransigents" and the party centre—although it was to prove a crucial one—was their respective views on what should be done about the reformists: the centre was not prepared to expel them. Gramsci attended the conference as one of the two delegates from Turin, although he was not a member of the intransigent faction (which dominated the Turin party organisation). The net result of the conference was a declaration of support for the Zimmerwald and Kienthal congresses of anti-war socialists, and a formal condemnation of the reformists, Turati and the rest, who had compromised with social-patriotism. In this, it was a perfect example of the "purism" of Italian maximalist socialism, concerned above all with the preservation of principles, and offering no concrete strategy for political action. However, Bordiga, whose opposition to the war had from 1914 gone beyond the "Neither support, nor sabotage" of the leadership, and who was of all Italian socialists during this period the nearest to Leninist positions, made a speech which ended with the words: "It is essential to act. The proletariat in the factories is tired. But it is armed. We must act." Gramsci spoke in his support. The two future leaders of the P.C.I. had met for the first time. Bordiga already enjoyed national stature as one of the most uncompromising of the leaders of the party's left wing for the past five years; Gramsci was attending his first national party function. In the three years which were to intervene between this meeting and the founding of the Communist Party at Livorno, Gramsci was to emerge as the main theorist of the factory council movement which focused the struggles of the most advanced section of the Italian proletariat in Turin, and as such he was to become a national figure. But in terms of party activity Bordiga was to be the unchallenged leader of that Left which was to become first the communist fraction within the P.S.I., and later the P.C.I.; it was not until 1923 that Gramsci began to question that supremacy. At all events the combination of intransigence with an emphasis on action in Bordiga's speech to the Florence conference must have struck a chord in Gramsci. His political position was very different, in reality, from Bordiga's, but they shared a total impatience with the passivity of the party leaders. (It was incidentally at this meeting that Gramsci was first to be accused by a maximalist speaker of "voluntarism" and "Bergsonianism"—an accusation which was often to be repeated by opponents in the years to come.)

In 1918, after the war had ended, the idea that the revolution was on the agenda was common to both sides in the class struggle, in Italy as in most of continental Europe. But beyond the first, tremendous revelation of October, that the socialist revolution *could be made*, even in a country where the objective conditions were apparently "not ripe", the impact was a dual one, the lessons drawn of two kinds. Firstly, the supreme lesson for party militants everywhere was the role played by a highly organised, disciplined revolutionary party. In Italy, the quickest to appreciate this lesson was Amadeo Bordiga, and it is this more than anything else that explains his absolute dominance of the P.C.I. at its formation. But October had a second meaning, which for the proletarian masses was primary, and this was as the installation of *Soviet* power. The idea of these new institutions of proletarian power, which could both play a role in the revolutionary process and provide the institutional basis for the proletarian State, swept round the world. Germany in 1918, of course, provides the most familiar and striking example of this inspiration, with the largely spontaneous springing up of workers' and soldiers' councils throughout the country. But in Italy, too, and above all in proletarian Turin, the impact of the Soviet model was immense. And during the next three years, Gramsci became the theorist and propagandist of an attempt to emulate that model in Turin. One result of this option was to delay his understanding of the central importance of the revolutionary party, so that he was not to play a determining role in the formation of the P.C.I. But at the same time it meant that Gramsci was at the centre of the main struggle of the Italian working class in the post-war period—a struggle which was to furnish the new P.C.I. with the essential of its working-class base. Moreover, Gramsci's writings of this period retain their theoretical interest and indeed relevance to this day.

Ordine Nuovo, the "Red Years" and the Founding of the P.C.I.

The War ended in November 1918, and the two years that followed were marked by a constant, and growing, conviction on the part of most of the ruling class in Italy as among the mass of workers and socialists that the revolution was inevitable, and was only a matter of time. Yet by the time that the P.C.I. was founded in January 1921, the revolutionary wave was on the ebb; the workers had been defeated and had lost their confidence in the possibility of revolution. Big capital, shocked by what it saw as unnecessary concessions made by Giolitti to the working class and the socialists, was looking for a blunter instrument. And fascist squads had started their punitive expeditions in the autumn of 1920. The debate about whether a revolution was really on the cards in 1919–20 can of course never be conclusively resolved one way or the other; but what is certain is that even if the ruling class could not go on in the old way, and the oppressed classes were not prepared to go on in the old way, the revolutionary vanguard party which was needed to lead the assault on the bourgeois State did not exist until after the revolutionary crisis was over.

Furthermore, the notion that the ruling class could not go on in the old way requires careful examination. It is true that there were no ruling-class parties to confront the mushrooming P.S.I.; the country was governed by makeshift coalitions of parliamentary cliques and personal followings. It is true that the war was followed by a catastrophic economic crisis—the *lira* lost 80 per cent of its value between 1914 and 1920; the budgetary deficit rose from 214 millions in 1914–15 to 23,345 millions in 1918–19, with the main tax burden falling on the petite bourgeoisie; wheat production fell from 52 million quintals in 1911–13 to 38 million in 1920, and 40 per cent of the balance of payments deficit was accounted for by food imports; production dropped after the war by 40 per cent in the engineering industries, 20 per cent in chemicals, 15 per cent in mining, etc.; coal prices were over 16 times higher in 1920 than they had been in 1913; etc., etc.—to which the various governments seemed to have no solution. It is true that there was a general feeling of impotence in the bourgeois press and among bourgeois politicians, in the face of the growth of industrial militancy and the advances of the P.S.I. Yet there is another side to this picture. Italian capitalism had been given an enormous shot in the arm by the war, and the process of concentration of capital was proceeding at a vertiginous pace. Between 1915 and 1917, the average rate of profit in industry went up from 4·26% to 7·75%; in advanced sectors the progress was dramatic—e.g. steel 6·3%–16·55%, vehicle manufacture 8·2%–30·5%. Production of iron and steel multiplied five times in the course of the war, and firms like FIAT increased their capital tenfold. These advances did indeed have a calamitous effect on the agricultural sector of the economy, and, by eliminating large numbers of small firms, helped to proletarianise important petit-bourgeois strata. Nevertheless industrial capital was in a particularly aggressive and confident mood in the immediate post-war period. Moreover, at least one bourgeois politician, Giolitti, had a coherent political strategy—of restraining the more intransigent employers and backing the reformist trade-union leaders—and, in the event, this strategy proved extremely successful, above all in the critical month of the factory occupations of September 1920. It would be utterly mistaken to portray fascism as a desperate last resort of a threatened ruling class. On the contrary, it was only *after* the defeat of the working class in 1920 that the big industrialists (and Giolitti) decided that the moment had come to replace the velvet glove by the iron fist, and gave financial support and tacit approval respectively to the fascist squads.

In order to understand the "Great Fear" of the Italian bourgeoisie in this period, it is essential to grasp the character of the "maximalism" which dominated the P.S.I. After the event, commentators of every political persuasion were united in the view that the party had never at any moment seriously considered the problem of how to make the revolution, nor made any serious preparations for it. However, at the time, the verbal statements of its leaders and the party's adhesion to the Third International created a very different impression. The process whereby, from 1917 on, the party leaders shifted their positions to the left, to converge with the "intransigents", has already been mentioned. When the Third International was founded, in March 1919, the P.S.I., although its delegates could not get to Moscow in time for the First Congress, immediately declared its adhesion—a decision that was ratified at the P.S.I.'s congress in October by an overwhelming majority. At this congress, a 65 per cent majority voted for a resolution calling for the installation of Soviets in place of the institutions of bourgeois democracy, and for a transitional régime of dictatorship of the proletariat. In the November 1919 general elections, the P.S.I. received almost two million votes, and returned 156 deputies to parliament, out of a total of 508 seats. Party membership rose from 20,000 at the end of the war to 87,000 in 1919, 180,000 in 1920; membership of the C.G.L. rose in the same period from 250,000 to two million. But despite its revolutionary language, the P.S.I. neither organised itself for insurrection, nor sought allies for the industrial proletariat (four million strong at this time) among the peasants or agricultural labourers (each of whom represented a further four millions, approximately). Although the peasants were occupying feudal estates in the South throughout the revolutionary years, the party made no attempt to co-ordinate their struggles. It allowed the catholic Popular Party to organise the mass of small peasants in North and Central Italy. And it neither carried out any serious work in the army, nor organised the proletariat militarily. Finally, it alienated the urban petite bourgeoisie and the demobilised officers and failed to channel their resentments (caused by their critical economic and social position) against the ruling class.

In April 1919, Gramsci, Tasca, Togliatti and Terracini took the decision to found a weekly "review of socialist culture". Gramsci, a year later, when the *Ordine Nuovo* had become something very different, wrote critically of their original intentions: "When, in April 1919, three, or four, or five of us decided to begin publishing this review *Ordine Nuovo*, none of us (perhaps) had any thought of changing the face of the world or of opening a new historical era. None of us (perhaps: some had fantasies of 6,000 subscribers in a few months) had any rosy illusions about the possible success of the project. Who were we? What did we represent? What slogan did we have to offer? Alas! The only sentiment which united us, in our meetings of that period, was based on a vague enthusiasm for a vague proletarian culture; we wanted to act, to act, to act, we felt trapped, without perspective, amid the feverish life of those months following the armistice, when the cataclysm of Italian society seemed imminent." These words were written in polemical vein, against Angelo Tasca; for from June 1919 on, Gramsci, supported by Togliatti and Terracini, had found the "slogan" which was to characterise *Ordine Nuovo*, i.e. the idea of the Factory Councils as the Italian equivalent of the Soviets, and had met a growing dissent from Tasca. Nevertheless, it is certainly true that neither Gramsci nor the others could have had any idea in April 1919 either of the course that the proletarian struggles would take in Turin or of the influence that their modest journal would come to wield among the workers of the city.

At all events, less than a month after the appearance of the first number Gramsci was already writing: "The history of the class struggle has entered a decisive phase after the concrete experience of Russia: the international revolution has acquired form and body since the Russian proletariat invented (in the Bergsonian sense) the State of the Councils, digging into its experience as an exploited class, extending to the entire collectivity a system and order which synthesises the proletarian form of economic life organised in the factories around the shop committees, and the form of its political life organised in the neighbourhood associations, in the town and village sections, in the provincial and regional federations in which the Socialist Party is articulated." And by June the idea that the shop committees (*commissioni interne*) were the potential nucleus for factory councils, which would be the first stage in the creation of Italian "soviets", was expressed by Gramsci in an *Ordine Nuovo* editorial "Democrazia Operaia" in unambiguous terms. This thematic became the hallmark of *Ordine Nuovo* and of the group which coalesced around it. During the succeeding eighteen months the journal became the ideological motor of a proletarian struggle in Turin which was not merely the most advanced of those revolutionary years in Italy, but which persuaded the leaders of the Third International that a proletarian revolution was imminent. Although its circulation was only about 3,000 copies in 1919, and averaged at most 5,000 in 1920, it nevertheless was a genuine "organiser" in the Leninist sense, and both played an essential part in the organisation of factory councils in all the factories of any size in Turin and also provided the P.C.I. with the major part of its working-class base.

This is not the place for an analysis of the theoretical position worked out in the pages of the weekly *Ordine Nuovo* in the twenty months of its existence. Its main features, however, and also its main weaknesses must be indicated briefly, for an appreciation of its relation to Gramsci's mature thought. The idea of "Soviets" was common currency on the Italian Left in this period, from the reformists at one extreme to Bordiga, whose journal in Naples was entitled *Il Soviet*, at the other. But *Ordine Nuovo* distinguished itself from the rest of the Left in four important ways. First, and most important, it related its theories directly to the practice of the Turin working class; it had a *programme* for the realisation of a soviet system, and fought for that programme. By the summer of

1920, there were councils in all the main factories of the city. Secondly, the new institutions were to be completely independent of the traditional working-class organisations; they were to be institutions of *the whole proletariat*, including non-organised workers, anarchists, etc. This conception was bitterly attacked by all sectors of the Italian Left, and was the real cause of Tasca's dissent. For Gramsci's conception saw the councils as the institutions whereby the dictatorship of the proletariat would be exercised, institutions which stood towards the "voluntary", "private" associations such as the party and the trade union in a relation of "State" to "government". This apparent subordination of the traditional working-class organisations was a source of scandal to the Left as a whole, for whom Serrati certainly spoke when he asserted that "the dictatorship of the proletariat is the conscious dictatorship of the Socialist Party".

In the third place, *Ordine Nuovo* saw the factory councils and the territorial Soviets which would subsequently be based on them as the embryos of the future socialist state. And fourthly it claimed that: "The real development of the revolutionary process occurs below the surface, in the obscurity of the factory and in the obscurity of the consciousness of the numberless masses whom capitalism subjects to its laws"; "the revolution is proletarian and communist only in so far as it is a liberation of productive and proletarian forces"; "we, as Marxists, must strive to grasp the terms of the problem of power in the productive organism".

These ideas were attacked particularly sharply by Bordiga, as a form of gradualism. "This, call it reformism or syndicalism, is defined by the erroneous view that the proletariat can emancipate itself by winning ground in economic relations, while capitalism still holds political power through its control of the State." Bordiga was not wrong to point out syndicalist tendencies in Gramsci's thought at this time. The ideas developed in the pages of *Ordine Nuovo* were deeply influenced both by Daniel de Leon, the theorist of the Wobblies, and by the British shop stewards' movement. Moreover, Gramsci certainly underestimated the role of the State, and hence had not grasped the role of the revolutionary party in organising the seizure of power. But at the same time, it is something of a paradox that Bordiga, who so early appreciated the implications of the Bolshevik revolution, and who was aware two years before Gramsci of the need to break organisationally with the socialism of the Second International, should have so little understood the need to break with that Second International socialism ideologically as well, and should have continued to share its rigidly mechanical conception of the relationship between party and masses.

For the *Ordine Nuovo* group's immense merit was its grasp of the role of the masses, and their spontaneous action, in the revolutionary process. Oddly, in view of the accusation of "voluntarism" which was so often to be hurled at them in these years, they were the only Italian Marxists to attempt to pose the problem of revolution in non-voluntarist terms. Gramsci, in November 1919, wrote: "Even if a revolutionary minority succeeded in seizing power violently, that minority would be overthrown the next day by the backlash of capitalism's mercenary forces . . . the communist revolution is a necessity in Italy more for international reasons than for reasons inherent to the process of development of the national productive apparatus . . . The revolution finds the great popular masses of Italy still amorphous, still fragmented. . . ." In Gramsci's view, it was only through the creation of organisms capable of uniting the masses and channelling their spontaneity, that the revolution could command majority assent and hence overcome definitively the power of the capitalist State.

However, it was not until the spring of 1920, on the eve of the great Turin metalworkers' strike, that Gramsci began to pose correctly the relation between mass institutions and the revolutionary party. He then wrote an article—destined, to the horror of the P.S.I. delegates, to be described by Lenin as "fully in keeping with the fundamental principles of the Third International"—entitled "For a Renewal of the Socialist Party", in which he said, notably: "The existence of a cohesive and strongly disciplined Communist Party which, through its factory, trade-union and co-operative nuclei, co-ordinates and centralises within its own executive committee all of the proletariat's revolutionary activity, is the fundamental and indispensable condition for attempting any Soviet experiment." But by this time, as Gramsci was to recognise with bitter self-criticism in subsequent years, the task of national co-ordination of the proletariat's revolutionary activity had been left too late. The April metalworkers' strike was in fact the high point of revolutionary mass struggle in the postwar years; and it was only after its defeat that the *Ordine Nuovo* group attempted to sink its theoretical differences with Bordiga, in order to participate in the process of creating an Italian Communist Party. It was only after the defeat of the factory occupations in September, i.e. after the effective end of the period of postwar revolutionary upsurge, that the Party was in fact formed—on Bordiga's terms.

The April strike was provoked by the employers. Their objective was explicitly the ending of "dual power" in the factories, i.e. the destruction or emasculation of the *commissioni interne.* That they succeeded, despite a month's strike by the metalworkers, ten days of general strike throughout Turin and the province of Piedmont, and the organisation of an urban Soviet defended by armed workers, was due not to the huge armed force which was concentrated in the city—"an army of police . . . cannon and machine-guns at all strategic points" as Gramsci described it—but to the failure of the Turin comrades to secure the support of the party or trade unions nationally, and to draw in workers outside Piedmont. Their failure to organise earlier on a national scale now caught up with them, and Turin stood alone. *Avanti!* refused to print the manifesto put out by the Turin section of the party, calling for the solidarity of workers in the rest of the country. The party executive moved its National Council meeting from Turin to Milan during the strike. *Ordine Nuovo*'s appeals for an urgent tabling of the question of insurrection were ignored. And although the result of the strike—a compromise limiting the power of the *commissioni interne*—was not seen immediately in Turin as a decisive turning-point, it was nonetheless the moment at which the proletarian advance of the postwar period was checked.

The summer of 1920 was a critical period for the *Ordine Nuovo* group. In May Bordiga, who had begun to organise a national communist fraction in the previous autumn, called a meeting in Florence of the various left groups within the Socialist Party. His own fraction called itself the "abstentionist" fraction, and had already made electoral abstentionism the basic differentiating feature of its positions. The Third International, which had been counselling restraint, since it hoped that the communists would carry a majority in the P.S.I., sent a representative; Gramsci attended as an observer. Gramsci proposed, on behalf of the Turin comrades not already members of Bordiga's abstentionist fraction, that a national communist fraction should be formed on a non-abstentionist platform, in line with Comintern recommendations. This was rejected, and Gramsci returned to Turin isolated. The unity of the *Ordine Nuovo* group was lost in these months. Tasca's dissent from the entire factory council thematic as developed by Gramsci came into the open, and he urged a turn back towards the traditional working-class organisations. Terracini and Togliatti drew nearer to the maximalists who dominated the Turin section of the P.S.I., and the former was co-opted into the party leadership; they did not follow Gramsci in his moves towards Bordiga, but formed their own "electionist" faction as a rival to the "abstentionists". Gramsci spent the following months promoting communist education groups in the factories; he later described Togliatti and Terracini as having "rejoined Tasca" in this period. *Ordine Nuovo* was no more able to organise nationally after the April moment of truth than it had been before.

In July 1920, the Comintern held its Second Congress. The Italian delegates ranged from Bordiga to the reformist trade-union leader d'Aragona; all were received warmly, especially Serrati, who had known Lenin since the Zimmerwald Congress. However, despite the illusions undoubtedly harboured on the revolutionary character of the P.S.I.—illusions which were to persist for at least another three years, and which were to be an important cause of the P.C.I.'s long resistance to the United Front policy—nevertheless, criticisms of Serrati's reluctance to expel the reformists were already beginning to be voiced. The Italian delegates learnt with surprise and dismay of Lenin's approval of the *Ordine Nuovo* positions. The two main programmatic bases of the Congress were the 21 points—which were to prove unacceptable to Serrati—and Lenin's *Left-wing Communism, an Infantile Disorder*—which was directed against Bordiga, among others. But it would be quite incorrect to present the "right" and "left" deviations on the same plane. The Congress was held at a moment of huge confidence in the revolutionary prospects. The International's support was growing at immense speed. The Red Army was advancing towards Warsaw. It was the immediacy of the task of making the revolution which made it so essential to expel the reformists and to forge communist parties adequate to that task. Right-wing opportunism was the enemy—left-wing communism merely an infantile disorder to be outgrown. Bordiga abandoned abstentionism after the Congress vote; Serrati, however, was adamant in his refusal either to change the name of the P.S.I. or to expel the reformists. Bordiga came away from the Congress determined not only to create the P.C.I. as soon as possible, but to exclude from it all "centrists". The real gulf between him and the International was not on the comparatively unimportant issue (given the revolutionary perspectives of the period) of abstentionism, but on the far more essential question of whether it was necessary to win the majority of the working class. Bordiga's position was then, and always remained, an utterly rigid one; the party should be pure and hard, and if it followed the correct policies then the mass of the working class would of course follow its lead. The idea of trying to win the majority of the P.S.I. was of no interest to him, since he was already convinced of their irrevocable "centrism". On the other hand, he was equally opposed to mass movements, such as the Turin factory councils, which were not strictly controlled by the party. Ultimately his line resulted in an almost complete immobilism.

However, Bordiga's supremacy among the communists in the P.S.I. was total. He had been the most intransigent of the left leaders, and by a long way the first to organise on a national level. His implacable anti-centrism was shared by all the Left, especially the youth organisation, who were so impatient to have done with the P.S.I. that they could not be restrained from setting up an autonomous communist youth section on their own in August 1920. It was precisely because Gramsci's anti-centrism was as implacable as Bordiga's own that he took so long to face up to the consequences of his dissent from other aspects of Bordiga's leadership. Indeed, he never clearly distanced himself from Bordiga's position on the United Front strategy at all, at least until after his arrest, and then only in part. Yet differences with Bordiga there certainly were, from the very beginning. For Gramsci was to say (in 1923) of the way in which the P.C.I. was formed, i.e. of the failure to win the majority of the socialist workers to the new party, that this was "without a doubt reaction's greatest triumph": not an opinion shared by Bordiga. At all events, this summer of 1920 was the moment when *Ordine Nuovo* lost its unity and momentarily its sense of direction, and when Bordiga's supremacy among Italian communists was decisively consolidated.

In September 1920, as the Italian delegates were returning from the Comintern Congress, the occupation of the factories broke out in Milan, and quickly spread throughout the country. As Gramsci was to stress subsequently, this confrontation was one chosen by the employers, however impressive the proletarian response may have been. Upon the threat of a lockout, workers at the Romeo plant occupied the factory. The unions encouraged the spread of this tactic to other factories, as a defensive move in the industrial struggle. But the movement soon assumed a scale and character which far exceeded anybody's expectations, the unions' most of all. It was now that the real impact of *Ordine Nuovo*'s ideas and agitation made itself felt. Factory councils sprang up everywhere, not merely in Turin, and not merely in the engineering industry. In many places, and notably at Turin, production continued. Where possible, the workers armed the factories, expecting a counter-blow from the State. But although the movement was by far the greatest in scale of all the working-class struggles of this revolutionary period in Italy, the balance was heavily weighted against the workers. The trade unions were from the start looking for a compromise solution. When, for tactical reasons, the reformist trade-union leaders challenged the P.S.I. leadership to make good their revolutionary words, offering their resignations if the P.S.I. wished to assume leadership of the unions directly and to organise an insurrection, the P.S.I. leaders at once refused. They, too, were anxious to find a way out of the situation, which was outside their control. They asked the Turin representatives (who included Terracini, as well as maximalists who would join the P.C.I. at its founding congress at Livorno like Gennari) whether the Turin proletariat was prepared to take the lead in an insurrectionary bid for power. But the Turin representatives, quite apart from their suspicions—only too justified in view of the events of April—that they were being cast in the role of sacrificial lambs, knew very well that the arms and military preparation even of the workers of Italy's "Petrograd" were totally inadequate for such an enterprise. The *Ordine Nuovo* might have implanted an *idea* that had caught the imagination of the masses; the intransigents and Bordiga's abstentionist fraction might have defined an *attitude* which rejected all compromises; but not even these forces—and how much less the mass organisations, the Party and the trade unions—had made any serious attempt to organise the proletariat, on a national scale, for a revolutionary assault on the capitalist State. All Giolitti, who had become Prime Minister again in June, had to do was to restrain the more hot-headed employers who would have liked the troops sent in—an action which might have provoked precisely the immense mass reaction which alone could have escalated the confrontation to a struggle for state power—and to wait until the workers had fully realised that their leaders' revolutionary words were empty rhetoric. Then, there was no difficulty in reaching a compromise, by means of an offer of industrial co-partnership which was to be echoed with equal success by another threatened bourgeois politician forty-eight years later in France. Even the term "participation" used so skilfully by De Gaulle in 1968 was used before him by Giolitti, although the latter also spoke of "trade-union control". At all events, the bait was sufficient for the reformist leadership of the C.G.L., which was only waiting to be hooked and brought to land; a compromise was reached, and the factory occupations were called off. The *Ordine Nuovo* group, whose thematic had been translated into revolutionary practice by the working class of all Italy, were entirely impotent at the national-organisational level; matters were decided between Giolitti and the C.G.L., and the revolutionary phase of postwar Italy was effectively brought to a close.

For despite Giolitti's success, the employers were in no mood to be satisfied with the compromise he had achieved. Many of them saw the notional "control" which he was prepared to grant the unions as a mortal threat to their positions of power. It was in the autumn of 1920 that fascist squads began to carry out raids on behalf of the landowners of North and Central Italy against both the socialist and Catholic peasant associations, and against socialist-controlled municipalities such as that of Bologna or socialist papers such as the Trieste daily *Il Lavoratore*. And it was also during this period that a number of industrialists began to pour funds into Mussolini's organisation. In all probability Giolitti too was a source of finance for the fascists in this period. At all events Bonomi, Giolitti's ex-socialist Minister of War, in October 1920 sent out a circular giving effective encouragement to demobilised officers to join the *Fasci*. And the entire early development of fascism from the marginal phenomenon of 1919 to the mass phenomenon of 1920 was assisted by massive State connivance.

During this same period, the communist fraction within the P.S.I. assumed public form and prepared for the party's January 1921 National Conference at Livorno. Communist sections were formed throughout the country. The failure of the occupation of the factories had demonstrated what the communists had been saying for months, that the centrist leaders of the P.S.I. could not make the revolution; it gave a real urgency to the recommendations contained in the International's 21 points. The International appears to have believed during this period that the communists would carry the majority of the P.S.I.; Gramsci may have shared this illusion. But Gramsci did not share the International's limited view of the objectives to be pursued *vis-à-vis* the centrist leaders. For while the International was merely concerned to secure an acceptance of its discipline and the twenty-one points, Gramsci, like Bordiga, sought an emphatic rejection of the entire past of Italian socialism—seen as responsible for the defeats of the last two years. Togliatti was to describe the intensity of this rejection: "The Livorno split was essentially, and predominantly, an act of struggle against centrism. . . . We fought root and branch against Turati and Modigliani [the reformists], but as for Serrati, we hated him . . . The main obstacle was not the reformists but maximalist centrism." It was an attitude which was at the root of the Italian party's long resistance to Comintern directives.

In the manifesto of the communist fraction which was published on 15 October 1920 in Milan, over the signatures of Bordiga, Gramsci, Terracini and others, Bordiga's supremacy was obvious. The entire *Ordine Nuovo* thematic was absent, as was any reference to the relation between party and masses, to soviet democracy, to organisation in the factories, etc. The emphasis was on discipline and centralism, and on purity of principles. There were undoubted differences of perspective between the various components of the future P.C.I. Quite apart from the ideas developed in *Ordine Nuovo*, which Gramsci had certainly not abandoned wholesale as subsequent events were to show, there was a clear difference of perspective with respect to the overall political prospects. Whereas Bordiga dismissed the significance of fascism, believing that a social-democratic "solution" was the most likely for the ruling class to adopt, Gramsci had as early as April 1920 written that the two possibilities were black reaction or proletarian revolution (though he too was to waver in this view in the coming years, and to speak on frequent occasions of the probability of a social-democratic solution). But both shared a conviction that revolution was still very much on the immediate agenda; and Gramsci was at this time convinced, too, that the only possible way in which the communist party could be formed was on Bordiga's terms.

At all events, the communist delegates went to Livorno with 58,783 votes, compared so the Centre's 98,028 and the reformists' 14,695. The first communist to speak, Secondino Tranquilli (subsequently known as Ignazio Silone) the editor of the youth paper, asked the communist delegates to "burn the effigy of unity". They left the conference singing the *Internationale*, and held their own founding congress in a neighbouring hall. The Central Committee elected had six abstentionist members, two *Ordine Nuovo* (Gramsci and Terracini), and seven ex-maximalists; but Bordiga was in fact more entirely dominant than these numbers would suggest, since he quickly won over the entire C.C. to his views, with the sole partial exception of Gramsci, who was thus totally isolated. It was to be three years before he would find the political confidence, and establish the autonomous political positions, which would permit him to challenge Bordiga's leadership of the new party.

The P.C.I. under Bordiga 1921–1923

At the time of the Livorno Congress and the foundation of the

P.C.I., Gramsci was not yet thirty. He had less than four years of serious political activity behind him. The three years that followed—years which saw the consolidation of fascist power in Italy, the reflux of the revolution internationally, the beginnings of the struggle for power within the Russian party, and a growing rift between the Italian party and the Third International—represent a period of uncertainty and indeed at times anguish in Gramsci's political career. Until all his work for the years between 1922 and 1926 has been published, and until more is known about his life and activity in Moscow (May 1922–November 1923) and in Vienna (December 1923–May 1924), it will not be possible to reconstruct fully his political biography for these crucial years. Hopefully, by the time that the introduction to an English selection of Gramsci's early writings comes to be written, many of the existing gaps will have been filled. At all events, we have limited our objectives here to giving an extremely schematic indication of the complex historical context within which Gramsci's political activity was inserted—in terms of three main, interrelated determinants: international developments and the united front; Italian developments and fascism; the struggle against Bordiga and Tasca inside the party.

For most historians writing with the hindsight of today, the period of possible revolution in the West in the wake of the First World War and the October Revolution was a brief one, over effectively by 1921 at the latest. This is no place to discuss the correctness of this estimate. What must, however, be stressed is that this was by no means the view of communists throughout the early twenties, despite all the setbacks and defeats. The notion that the proletarian revolution was no longer on the immediate agenda was the hallmark of the social-democrats, and was fiercely rejected by all currents within the Third International.

The response of the Comintern to what were, at that time, seen as *temporary* ebbings of the revolutionary tide was, fundamentally, the united front policy. This characterised Comintern strategy, despite fluctuations in interpretation, at least until 1925–6. Its basic idea was that the communists, now that they had expelled, or split from, the reformists, should seek to engage the latter in forms of common action; only thus could they win a majority in the working class—which has a fundamental interest in unity, whether in defensive or in offensive action. As Lenin put it: "The purpose and sense of the tactics of the united front consist in drawing more and more masses of the workers into the struggle against capital, even if it means making repeated offers to the leaders of the II and II½ Internationals to wage this struggle together. When the majority of the workers have already established their class, i.e. their Soviet, and not 'general national' (i.e. in common with the bourgeoisie) representation, and have overthrown the political domination of the bourgeoisie, then the tactics of the united front, of course, cannot require co-operation with parties such as that of the Mensheviks and the S.R.s, for these have turned out to be opponents of Soviet power"; and again: "If there are still people at the enlarged meeting of the Executive who have not grasped the fact that the tactic of the united front will help us to overthrow the leaders of the II and II½ Internationals, these people should have an extra number of popular lectures and talks read to them" (*Collected Works*, Vol. 42, pp. 411 and 401). The slogan "To the masses" which was launched at the Third World Congress in 1921 was a recognition that in most cases (there were exceptions like Bulgaria) the communist parties were not yet followed by the majority of workers, and that only when they were would revolution be attainable.

This eminently dialectical tactic required an unremitting struggle against left and right deviations in the interpretation of it, and ultimately broke down in the "right" and "left" zigzags of 1927–8 and 1929–34. On the one hand, a number of parties, among them the P.C.I., had the greatest reluctance in accepting the hated centrists as in any sense potential allies—even if the object was partly to discredit them. They rejected the idea that it was necessary to win the majority of the working class. The entire history of the P.C.I. between 1921 and 1924 was characterised by a series of disagreements with the Comintern which all turned on this point. The most that the Italian communists—and here Gramsci or Togliatti did not differ from Bordiga—were prepared to accept was what they termed the united front "from below"; but clearly this was tantamount to a rejection of the tactic, since the only reason for it at all was the impossibility as yet of establishing direct contact with the majority of the working class or of by-passing their reformist or centrist leaders.

On the other hand, in those years of revolutionary reflux, there was immensely strong pressure to accept, even without necessarily being conscious of so doing, the reformists' abandonment of all revolutionary perspective. This "liquidationist" danger was an ever-present reality in the minds of communists like Bordiga or Gramsci, who saw the Comintern continually placing what they regarded as false hopes in the P.S.I. and negotiating with its leaders directly, and who were only too aware that the main supporter of the united front inside the Italian party was precisely Tasca, whom they suspected of not sharing their implacable spirit of rupture with the entire tradition of Italian socialism. Togliatti expressed such fears, for example, when at a 1923 Central Committee meeting he spoke of the Comintern's directive to pursue a policy of fusion with the P.S.I. after the latter's expulsion of the reformists. He said: "The greatest risk was and still is that, under the cover of the fusion policy, there will be a growth of tendencies which cannot be called anything else but 'liquidatory' of the communist party and movement; that what I termed above our first and most important achievement in the consciousness of the Italian masses will be forgotten"; the achievement in question was "the demonstration of the necessity for every future political development of the Italian proletariat to take place on bases radically different from those that have been traditional in the socialist movement".

The roots of the schism between the new P.C.I. and the Comintern go back, of course, well before the united front policy was proclaimed in December 1921. Lenin had sharply condemned Bordiga's abstentionism in 1920. In the summer of 1921, the International had been highly critical of the P.C.I.'s attitude to the *arditi del popolo* (see note 25 on p. 230 below). At the Third World Congress in June, the Italian party had aligned itself with the new leadership of the German party in support of the "theory of the offensive" (formulated notably by Bela Kun); that theory was the object of harsh criticism from Trotsky in his keynote report to the Congress, and when Terracini, the P.C.I. spokesman, defended it he found himself at the receiving end of one of Lenin's most devastating polemical broadsides. Terracini had invoked the positions of the previous World Congress in support of the P.C.I.'s views, but the year which separated the two Congresses had seen the proclamation of N.E.P., a swift growth of Italian fascism, and the failure of the "March Action" in Germany; Zinoviev, at the end of March and under pressure from Lenin, had written an article speaking of the slow-down of the revolutionary tempo. Despite the arguments of the important German and Italian parties for the theory of the offensive, the Congress was marked by a new determination to win the majority of the working class and launched the slogan "to the masses"—in an adumbration of the united front. Moreover, it was at this time that a major disagreement about policy inside Italy came to the fore—a disagreement that was to last until the popular front period in the thirties. This concerned the attitude to be taken up towards the P.S.I. Already in this summer of 1921, the P.C.I. leaders were deeply suspicious of the hopes placed by the International in the P.S.I.; the latter had not yet expelled the reformists, but the International generally believed that they would and that the P.C.I. should then fuse with them, while the P.C.I. leaders were utterly opposed to any such perspective, even if the reformists were to be expelled.

In December 1921, the united front policy was formally launched by the Comintern Executive; it meant common action between the rival Internationals, between rival left parties, and in the trade-union field. The Italian party was resolutely opposed to it, and was at the most prepared to accept a limited application of it in the trade-union field. Togliatti, in the same Central Committee meeting of 1923 quoted above, went on to say: ". . . it was obvious that, so shortly after our formation as an autonomous party, we were resistant to any tactical shift which might . . . cause the mass of the party and of the proletariat to forget what for us was the first, solidly won position . . . Hence our reservations about an immediate application by us of the united front in the political field . . .". In the Enlarged Executive meeting of February/March 1922, Terracini again attacked the entire new policy, and was rebuked by Lunacharsky, Radek, Trotsky and Zinoviev in turn.

The disagreement continued throughout 1922. In March, the P.C.I. held its second Congress at Rome. The Congress theses (see note 103 on p. 200 below), whose main section on tactics was drafted by Bordiga and Terracini, were attacked by Trotsky and Radek on behalf of the Comintern Executive, and again by Kolarov the Comintern representative at the Congress itself. Kolarov was answered not only by Bordiga and Terracini, but also by Gramsci—who argued that the P.S.I. with whom the Comintern wished the communists to fuse was fundamentally a peasant rather than a proletarian party! Kolarov's intervention was of critical importance for future developments in the party, since it stimulated the emergence of a right-wing opposition group headed by Tasca, who stood for a full application of the united front policy. However, for the moment the Bordigan executive was reconfirmed by the congress as a united bloc; the right minority was not represented in the party's leading bodies; and Gramsci was sent to Moscow as the P.C.I. representative to the Comintern Executive.

In the remainder of the year the rift between the Italian party and the Comintern widened yet further. Zinoviev attacked the Italians violently for not participating in the *Alleanza del Lavoro*—a front of trade unions, formed on the initiative of the anarcho-syndicalist railwaymen's union and to which the C.G.L. gave its support. On the other hand, the P.C.I. was bitterly critical of Zinoviev's negotiations with the P.S.I., which in October expelled the reformists and affirmed its adhesion to the Third International. At the Fourth World Congress in November, substantial differences were evident on the nature of fascism, on the slogan of "workers' governments", and above all on the issue of fusion with the P.S.I.

With respect to fascism, Zinoviev in his opening address tended to dismiss it as a transitory phenomenon. He concentrated his fire on the social-democrats—whom he now defined as the "left wing of the bourgeoisie". Radek's report on the capitalist offensive, however, was in marked contrast—and may very well have been influenced by Gramsci. It stressed the petit-bourgeois components of fascism, the sectarianism shown by the proletarian organisations towards the ex-combatants, and the aid of the big bourgeoisie in fascism's rise to power—while reiterating that the fundamental class contradiction remained that between bourgeoisie and proletariat. This complex analysis was in sharp contrast to that of Bordiga, who in the main report to the Congress on fascism refused any distinction between the general capitalist counter-offensive and fascism, and spoke of the latter's convergence with social-democracy, describing fascism as a great unity movement of the dominant class. He stated that "fascism has introduced no novel elements into traditional bourgeois politics or ideology". The Congress as a whole tended to accept Radek's view of the danger of Italian fascism, almost certainly inspired by Gramsci; but ironically enough Gramsci himself—who had foreseen the possibility of fascist victory in Italy so early and had developed the essential elements of an adequate analysis of the new phenomenon—was to oscillate over the ensuring years in his analysis. Bordiga characteristically remained unswervingly loyal to his univocal view, but Gramsci like the rest of the P.C.I. leaders was to show continuing uncertainty, stressing now the petit-bourgeois origins of fascism, now its internal contradictions, now its agrarian component, now the predominance of finance capital, and now its function as an expression of the entire ruling class. To some extent it was Tasca who was most consistently to develop Gramsci's early intuitions in the next years, and who was to be most consistent in his emphasis on the specificity of fascism, while Gramsci was still not free of Bordiga's influence.

The Italians also differed sharply from the majority of the Fourth Congress on the issue of "workers' governments"—a slogan conceived by Zinoviev, and attacked violently by Bordiga. The slogan was indeed more than a little ambiguous, and was to be interpreted in widely divergent ways in the coming years, not least by Zinoviev himself. But the real bone of contention was the issue of fusion with the P.S.I., which was the subject of prolonged discussion. Gramsci, Bordiga and the other delegates belonging to the majority were obdurate in their resistance to the Comintern pressure. Tasca, on the other hand, was strongly in favour of the fusion proposals. In the course of the discussion, Trotsky seems to have made an attempt to persuade Gramsci to differentiate himself from Bordiga, asking whether each individual Italian delegate was free to vote as he wished; when this produced no result, Trotsky launched a bitter attack on the Italian positions: "This is the *ne plus ultra* of disagreement between the P.C.I. and the communist international—anything further would mean open rupture . . . Gramsci is demanding a privilege of intransigence for Italy. On the question of the united front you made a bloc with France and Spain. The others have now recognised that they were wrong, but you refuse to do so . . . You continue to repeat the same error on every issue . . . We propose that you should accept the collective adhesion [of the P.S.I.] first, and then you can make an individual selection afterwards . . . If you do not have the sympathy of the broad masses, you will not be able to maintain a legal existence. If you are bent on limiting your base you will end up without a base at all and will be regarded as a sect." Finally, on 24 November, an ultimatum over the signatures of Lenin, Trotsky, Zinoviev, Radek and Bukharin was delivered to the Italian party. And it was then, for the first time, that a rift appeared—if only briefly—in the Bordigan majority. For whereas Bordiga was for a purely formal acceptance of discipline, but an effective policy of non-application of the Comintern's directives, Gramsci disagreed. He feared that continued resistance would bring the right-wing minority and Tasca to power in the party, and the majority of the Italian delegates shared his desire for a more active policy than that favoured by Bordiga. The upshot was that Gramsci and Scoccimarro, together with Tasca, participated in the fusion committee nominated by the Congress, while Bordiga boycotted it. However, this difference of opinion between Bordiga and Gramsci was still essentially tactical—although Gramsci was later to claim that he had not dared to press it further in the absence of support among the other P.C.I. leaders in Italy, and for fear of handing power in the party to Tasca. At all events, the consequences were minimal, since the fusion issue was resolved once and for all a couple of months later by the predominance within the P.S.I.—despite the expulsion of the reformists, and against all the Comintern's expectations—of an anti-fusionist majority headed by Nenni.

It was at about this time that the Comintern began to make serious probings with respect to the possibility of changing the P.C.I. leadership—although as early as the autumn of 1921 overtures had been made to Gramsci to join the party executive in order to act as a counter-balancing influence *vis-à-vis* Bordiga. Now Rakosi (Rakosi, Kuusinen and Humbert-Droz were the three Secretaries to the Executive Committee of the Communist International in this period) offered Gramsci the leadership directly, with what Gramsci described sarcastically as "the diplomatic delicacy which was characteristic of him"; Gramsci's response was to reject in embarrassment the notion that the problems of the P.C.I. could be solved by such manipulative means. Indeed, it cannot be stressed too strongly that it is quite impossible to understand the transition from the Bordiga leadership of 1921–3 to the Gramsci leadership of 1924–6 simply by reference to Comintern influence. It is necessary also to consider the actual history of the party's political experience in Italy, and the context within which it had to operate.

The P.C.I. was formed in the first period of widespread fascist terror. Although at Livorno it commanded delegate votes equivalent to two thirds of those of the maximalist centre, its real strength after the split proved to be far smaller. In the April 1921 general elections, the communists won 290,000 votes, while the socialists won over a million and a half. Party membership was around 40,000 in 1921, of whom 98 per cent were workers and less than ½ per cent (245 in all) intellectuals. In that summer, while fascist violence continued, Mussolini simultaneously engaged in complex parliamentary manoeuvres. In August, the P.S.I.—who were so opposed to any armed resistance to fascism that they had actually published in *Avanti!* an extract from Papini's *Story of Christ* under the banner headline: "Do Not Resist!"—signed a pacification pact with the fascists. The situation in 1921–2 was dominated by a grave economic crisis, and the weakness of successive bourgeois governments. Wages declined by some 30 per cent; there were half a million unemployed by the beginning of 1922; C.G.L. membership dropped from two million to 800,000, and P.S.I. membership from over 200,000 at Livorno to 100,000 in October 1921, 70,000 in October 1922 before the party congress, and 25,000 after the expulsion of the reformists at the congress. Throughout the early months of

1922, there was a continual *dialogue des sourds* between the P.C.I., hostile to any alliance with the other left organisations but pressing for a general strike and direct action against fascism; the reformist-led C.G.L., whose aim was to detach itself from the maximalist-dominated P.S.I. and form a Labour Party which could participate in a government coalition; and the P.S.I., which was locked in a sterile combination of verbal intransigence with total passivity in practice. In the summer of 1922, fascist violence broke out anew, and a general strike was finally called for 31 July; this was, however, effectively sabotaged by the C.G.L. leaders, and crushed by fascist counter-blows. This action was the last massive expression of popular resistance to fascism, and its defeat had a decisive negative impact on the morale of the proletariat. When Mussolini "marched" on Rome in October 1922, the P.C.I.'s call for a general strike found no response. During 1922, P.C.I. membership, although resisting far better than that of the other left parties, nevertheless fell to about 25,000 in September.

The fascist seizure of power in October 1922 was predictably enough followed by a vast wave of repression. In late 1922 and above all early 1923, it crushed most of the oppositional party organisations and press. Terracini wrote in February 1923: "The fascist government has unleashed the long announced anti-communist round-up. In a week the police has arrested more than 5,000 comrades, including all our area secretaries, all communist trade-union organisers, all our local councillors. Moreover, it has succeeded in seizing all our party funds, and thus in delivering what is perhaps a mortal blow to our press . . . a real man-hunt by the police hand-in-glove with the fascist squads . . . Our party is not submitting, or yielding; a quarter of our members under arrest, our organisation shattered, our press silenced, our branches dissolved, deprived of our leader comrade Bordiga who is under personal danger of death or torture, the Italian Communist Party has already reassumed its function and its activity." And indeed, although the party's illegal organisation proved to have serious weaknesses in this first test of its effectiveness, nevertheless some important successes were registered; notably the printing and distribution of a clandestine edition of *Ordine Nuovo* (now a party daily), and the holding of a number of public meetings in spite of the atmosphere of terror. However, the magnitude of the blow which had been struck at the young party needs no emphasising, and is an index of the total failure to appreciate the dangers of fascism under Bordiga's leadership. It would be unjust to claim that the P.C.I. leadership was responsible for the fascist seizure of power—as both Tasca and Radek were at different times to suggest—but it certainly gravely underestimated its significance, and continued to do so until 1926. Even Gramsci did not prior to his arrest arrive at a consistent and adequate appreciation of the specificity of the new type of régime, and as for Bordiga, his declaration in 1924 that "the bourgois counter-revolution for us is the proof of the inevitability of the revolution" eloquently sums up his determined rejection of the idea that the fascist seizure of power was anything to worry about at all.

The Interregnum in the Italian Party 1923–24

The arrest of Bordiga and the massive blow which had been struck at the entire party organisation meant that the time when the Comintern, as mentioned earlier, began seriously to prospect the possibility of making changes in the P.C.I. leadership in order to bring the party into line coincided with a moment in which external circumstances compelled provisional changes in any case. It was to be well over a year before a new, coherent leadership emerged, with positions as sharply distinguished from those of Bordiga as they were from those of Tasca. It was to be another year after that before the new leadership gained unshakeable control. But the events of early 1923, when fascist repression reduced active membership of the P.C.I. to little more than 5,000, and when the original leadership was shattered by arrest and exile, so that a replacement leadership on the ground had perforce to be installed, was decisive in breaking Bordiga's grip on the party.

Yet it must be emphasised that the significance of what had happened was by no means appreciated at the time by the Italian communist leaders involved. Throughout 1923, Gramsci, Terracini, Togliatti, Scoccimarro and the other members of the future "centre" of 1924 continued to support Bordiga—and with the partial exception of Gramsci they did so by conviction. They all, including Gramsci, continued to see Tasca and the Right as the principal threat. During the early months of 1923, the International tended to lay the blame both for the failure to fuse with the socialists and for the successes of fascism at the P.C.I.'s door. This was Tasca's view, and his reports to the Comintern during this period tended increasingly to assume the character of a bid for the leadership. The result, throughout 1923, was a closing of ranks in the majority behind Bordiga. The correspondence exchanged in late 1923 and early 1924 between the future members of the "centre" leadership of 1924–6 shows them all apprehensive of the danger of Tasca winning power in the party with Comintern backing, and hence all unwilling to contemplate a break of any kind with Bordiga. Moreover, all of them, including Gramsci, continued throughout 1923 to share the greater part of Bordiga's perspectives, even though they were becoming increasingly anxious about the rift with the Comintern which these entailed. Although according to Gramsci himself, and judging by the correspondence referred to above, a "centre" group of a kind began to take form from the time of the Fourth World Congress, it did so only in an absolutely unorganised and barely conscious fashion. It was not until the end of 1923, after his move to Vienna in November, that Gramsci took the initiative in a series of letters to Togliatti, Terracini, Scoccimarro, Leonetti and others towards constituting a new leading group without Bordiga or his followers.

The P.C.I. executive in the first years of its existence consisted of five men, all solid supporters of Bordiga, despite their differing political pasts prior to Livorno; Bordiga himself, Grieco, Terracini, Repossi and Fortichiari. Now Bordiga and Grieco had been arrested, and Fortichiari—who was responsible for the party's illegal organisation—went to Moscow to discuss how best to organise resistance to the fascist régime. Terracini was left as the *de facto* leader of the party within Italy, and, at the Comintern's suggestion, he now co-opted Togliatti and Scoccimarro onto a new provisional executive, and Tasca onto the Central Committee; the latter was then sent to Paris to organise the Italian émigré community there (there were 45,000 Italian émigré workers in France in 1921; 200,000 in 1924; over 450,000 by 1926). In April, Terracini himself was called to Moscow, and Scoccimarro sent to Berlin. Togliatti was left in effective leadership of the party within Italy.

On 12 June 1923, there took place a meeting of the Enlarged Executive of the Comintern largely devoted to the Italian question. The polarisation of forces within the P.C.I. leadership had reached a new high point. Bordiga, in prison, represented an increasingly coherent position at one end of the spectrum: the Comintern policy for Italy would lead to the liquidation of the P.C.I.; the Comintern itself was showing signs of degeneration; the Italian party was a left vanguard struggling against this degeneration. At the other extreme, Tasca was urging full acceptance of the Comintern line. Moreover, he was involved in complex three-way negotiations with the Comintern and with the new "third-internationalist" minority faction inside the P.S.I. (headed by Serrati). Gramsci, Terracini, Togliatti and the other future members of the post-1924 centre group saw this line-up as a particularly grave "liquidationist" threat, and continued to solidarise with Bordiga.

The Comintern decided to instal a temporary "mixed" leadership, in the form of a provisional executive composed of Fortichiari, Scoccimarro and Togliatti from the old "majority", and Tasca and Vota from the minority. Bordiga was opposed to this solution, and advocated a typically abstentionist policy of "all power to the minority"; he subsequently persuaded Fortichiari to withdraw from the appointed executive (he was replaced by Gennari). Scoccimarro and Togliatti at first hesitated, but were persuaded to accept their posts by Gramsci. The position was now one of the most extreme complexity. The Comintern had for the first time nominated a new party leadership against the wishes of a majority of its own nominees. Bordiga, Fortichiari, Grieco and Repossi of the original P.C.I. executive all favoured an intransigent policy of non-collaboration in any such imposed executive; Togliatti, Terracini and Scoccimarro were equally unhappy about the imposed solution, but were persuaded by Gramsci that the dangers of accepting were less than those of allowing a right-wing leadership. Togliatti finally wrote to the others that he was prepared to accept the post given him by the Comintern Executive only on condition that the old leading group should constitute itself as a fraction and begin "an open polemic with the International and with the minority in the party, by means of a series of declarations of principle and polemics which must be not only communicated to the International but disseminated among the masses". As in the case of the tactical disagreement between Bordiga and Gramsci at the Fourth World Congress eight months earlier, the Bordigan majority was still not divided on substantial issues; but in this case, the practical consequences of a disagreement on tactics were to be incomparably greater. It was at this juncture that Gramsci began to search for a way out of the sterile impasse in which the Italian party found itself—although it was to be another six months before he was to begin concretely to prospect the possibility of creating a new centre majority without Bordiga.

By the summer of 1923, Gramsci had been in Moscow for a year. Remarkably little is known about this period in his life. One of the most surprising features of his published writings is the absence of any reflections on, or even descriptions of, Russia as he knew it in the eighteen months he spent there at what was a crucial period in the history of the revolution. What can be gleaned from his writing and outside sources is merely a few bare elements. He was very ill in the first months of his stay, and spent them in and out of a clinic. He attended the Fourth World Congress, in which his part has already been discussed above. He met Julia Schucht and fell in love; their few months together, in Moscow and when she came to Italy in 1925/6, were an isolated interlude of personal happiness in Gramsci's life. He was constantly expecting to be sent back to Italy, but the issue of a warrant for his arrest made this impossible. He sent Trotsky some information about Italian futurism, at the latter's request, to be included as an appendix to the original edition of *Literature and Revolution*. His Comintern activities are likely to have brought him into contact with Radek and with Zinoviev, and when he left Moscow and took his leave of the latter he told him of his intention to propose a new slogan of a "federal Soviet republic" for Italy. Lastly, as we shall see, his letters written from Vienna to Togliatti, Terracini and others in early 1924 show that his political sympathies at this time were with the Left in the Bolshevik Party.

It is very hard to judge, on the basis of material published to date, what Gramsci's overall attitude to Bordiga was during the first years of the P.C.I.'s existence. On the one hand, there are numerous documents testifying to a substantial identity of positions on all the most important issues. On the other, there is Gramsci's own testimony that his motives for accepting the Bordiga policies for so long were mainly tactical, and that he was later to blame himself bitterly for not differentiating himself from Bordiga earlier. At all events, it seems clear that such differences as there were concerned not so much questions of overall analysis, or of strategy even, as the relation between theory and practice. While broadly sharing Bordiga's views on the united front and the nature of social-democracy, and while not as yet having drawn any very consistent conclusions from what *was* a very different analysis of fascism, he did clearly disagree with Bordiga's lack of any positive strategy within Italy, with his entire conception of the party and its relation to the masses, and with his inflexibility—especially *vis-à-vis* the International.

There exist two documents which give a good idea of Gramsci's positions in this summer of 1923, and which show him after the Enlarged Executive meeting of June (when Zinoviev had criticised him for equivocating on the issue of fusion with the third internationalists) beginning to elaborate a new approach to the leadership problem, although still firmly opposed to the Comintern's policy on fusion. Firstly, in a memorandum on "Relations between the P.C.I. and the Comintern" now in the P.C.I. archives, he wrote: "The present majority of the C.P. intends to defend to the last its position and historical role in Italy, where the unified C.P. must be constituted with an ideological centre which is neither the traditional socialist one nor a compromise with that. We are defending the future of the Italian Revolution . . . We may have made mistakes and we are willing to amend them, but we are not willing to allow the centre of attraction and of assimilation of new elements entering the Italian section of the Comintern to be shifted on to a new basis—represented by individuals who want to make a compromise with the socialists on the fundamental issue. The attitude of the Comintern and the activity of its representatives is bringing disintegration and corruption into the communist ranks. We are determined to struggle against the elements who would liquidate our Party, and against the corrupt elements. The situation of illegality and exile makes this obligatory. We do not want what happened in Hungary and in Yugoslavia to be repeated in Italy. If the Comintern too receives a few blows as we strike back, we should not be blamed for that: it is a mistake to ally oneself with untrustworthy elements." The second document consists of a letter sent in late July to a number of comrades, including Togliatti, Terracini, Fortichiari and Leonetti, in which Gramsci wrote: "I am absolutely convinced that at present no useful results can come of any discussion that is limited by us to the organisational and juridical aspects of the Italian question; such a discussion could only make things worse and render our task more difficult and dangerous. What we need to do is to work concretely to prove, by Party activity and political work that is wholly adapted to the Italian situation, that we are what we claim to be; and to abandon the attitude of 'unappreciated geniuses' that we have maintained up to now." The final passage is a clear enough expression of Gramsci's criticisms of Bordiga at this moment.

Although, as we have already pointed out, it is still not possible to trace fully the itinerary of Gramsci's political development in these years, the documents quoted are unambiguous evidence of the basic elements of his position in the summer of 1923. They show the fatuity of the view that Gramsci was simply the "Comintern's man", parachuted into the leadership in place of the refractory Bordiga. If anybody was the Comintern's man at this time it was Tasca, and Gramsci did not differ from Bordiga in his condemnation of Comintern policy. On the other hand, the documents show

Gramsci beginning to arrive at an estimate of Bordiga's policy which was not so dissimilar from his earlier hostile judgement on the "intransigent" immobility of the P.S.I. leaders at the end of the war. From the time of his first, ill-starred entry into print on the subject of neutrality in 1914, one of the constants of Gramsci's position was his view that revolutionary politics must necessarily be an active intervention in history, and could not consist simply in adopting "correct" positions and waiting to be proved right, waiting for the historical process to provide the circumstances in which the ruling class would topple, the true revolutionaries would be acknowledged by the masses and socialism could be ushered in. In this summer of 1923, the contrast between Bordiga and Gramsci was already a sharp one, despite the considerable overlap between their views. Sharing a common estimate of the crucial importance of defending the party against the "liquidation" which—in their view—was threatened by the Comintern's tractations with the very centrists against whom the P.C.I. had been formed, Bordiga concluded that the International was degenerating and that it was necessary to organise an international opposition to fight that degeneration; whereas Gramsci concluded in effect that the party should assume fully the task of making the revolution in Italy—if need be despite the International. In a letter written a few months later from Vienna he was to write: "Amadeo approaches things from the viewpoint of an international minority, but we must approach things from the viewpoint of a national majority." This difference of perspective was to play a decisive part subsequently in determining Gramsci's attitude to the inner-party struggle in Russia.

Throughout 1923, the P.C.I. existed in a state of semi-legality. It was not banned as such, but its leaders, militants and press were subject to constant repression and harassment. April was the low point as far as membership was concerned—with little more than 5,000 in the party. The summer saw a slow build-up to some eight and a half thousand in November. However, in September Togliatti, Tasca, Vota and Gennari—i.e. four of the five members of the new provisional executive—were arrested. In October, the first trial of communists took place; it was a great personal triumph for Bordiga, and culminated in his release. In December Togliatti, Tasca and the others were also released. But in late December and in January 1924 new repressive measures once again reduced the communist press to total silence.

After his release, Bordiga had returned to Naples, and refused any position in the leadership. Instead, he drafted an open letter to all party militants aimed at reaffirming the views of the old majority of the P.C.I. *vis-à-vis* both the Comintern and the right-wing minority. Terracini, Togliatti, Scoccimarro and the others were all at first prepared to sign, but Gramsci refused point-blank, and in a series of letters won over the three mentioned above, Leonetti, Gennari, Tresso and Camilla Ravera: the centre group for the first time had a concrete existence. In November, Gramsci had moved from Moscow to Vienna, to take charge of a newly-founded Comintern bureau for anti-fascist action. This was the moment at which he seems finally to have decided to initiate the creation of a new centre majority without Bordiga, and to work to heal the rift with the Comintern. Although he was by no means won over to the Comintern's views on the united front policy, he was not prepared to follow Bordiga on his path of creating an international opposition, and was increasingly hostile to the immobility of his policies within Italy.

What Gramsci proposed as a way out of the impasse in which the P.C.I. found itself was a new strategy for the party in Italy, a strategy with close affinities with the old *Ordine Nuovo* thematic of 1919–20, and also a thorough-going renovation of the party itself, inspired by a quite different conception from that of Bordiga. As early as September 1923, in a letter to the P.C.I. executive written from Moscow on the subject of a proposal to found a new working-class daily newspaper in collaboration with the "third-internationalist" current which was in the process of being expelled from the P.S.I., Gramsci began to evoke some of the themes which were to inspire both his political practice between 1924 and 1926 and also his prison writings. He suggested *Unità* as the name of the new paper (see p. xxvi above), and proposed the slogan of a "federal republic of workers and peasants" as an intermediate "ideological preparation" for a soviet régime; this concern with the "Southern Question" and with the concrete form which the alliance of workers and peasants might take in Italy represented something quite new in the Italian party at that time. He also revived one of the main themes of *Ordine Nuovo* in a proposal to build on the *commissioni interne* as a counter to the reformist leadership of the C.G.L.—increasingly tending to compromise with fascism.

In the months which followed, in a series of letters to the other members of the new "centre" group of P.C.I. leaders, Gramsci outlined the main elements of the new strategy which he proposed they should fight for. The main objective should be to win for the P.C.I. a genuine mass base. To this end Gramsci proposed, on 1 March, four main areas of initiative: 1. intensive propaganda around the slogan of a worker and peasant government; 2. a struggle against the labour aristocracy, i.e. against reformism, aimed at cementing an alliance between the mass of workers in the North and the peasant masses in the South; the creation of a special organising committee for the South, and a study of the possibilities for organising an armed insurrection in the South; 3. an intensive programme of political education within the party—with the object of superseding the existing internal divisions—and the enlargement of the leadership; 4. the stepping up of communist activity among the émigré population, above all in France. In later letters, Gramsci propounded the idea of a "federal" perspective for the South; stressed the importance of attempting to stimulate the formation of nuclei of future factory councils (this was to be one of the fundamental elements of P.C.I. strategy in the ensuing two years, up to the moment of Gramsci's arrest); discussed the possible transitional stages which might intervene between the defeat of fascism and a proletarian revolution; and spoke of the importance of winning the Milan working class to communist positions as a precondition for the revolution in Italy.

But perhaps more important even than the new strategic aims which Gramsci outlined in these letters was the new conception of the party which he put forward. In the key letter of the entire correspondence, written on 9 February 1924, he wrote: "The error of the party has been to have accorded priority in an abstract fashion to the problem of organisation, which in practice has simply meant creating an apparatus of functionaries who could be depended on for their orthodoxy towards the official view . . . The communist party has even been against the formation of factory cells. Any participation of the masses in the activity and internal life of the party, other than on big occasions and following a formal decree from the centre, has been seen as a danger to unity and centralism. The party has not been seen as the result of a dialectical process in which the spontaneous movement of the revolutionary masses and the organising and directing will of the centre converge; it has been seen merely as something suspended in the air, something with its own autonomous and self-generated development, something which the masses will join when the situation is right and the crest of the revolutionary wave is at its highest point, or when the party centre decides to initiate an offensive and stoops to the level of the masses in order to arouse them and lead them into action. Naturally, since things do not work out in this way, areas of opportunistic infection have formed without the centre knowing anything about them. These have had their reflection in the parliamentary group, and subsequently, in a more organic form, in the minority." The continuity of this critique of the P.C.I. under Bordiga with Gramsci's earlier analysis of maximalism is evident, and it was to be expanded and more fully theorised in some of the key passages of the Prison Notebooks. For the moment, Gramsci began to develop these themes in the pages of *Ordine Nuovo*, which was resuscitated as a theoretical organ in March; he wrote the first numbers almost single-handed in Vienna, and clearly saw the new review as a key element in the intensive campaign of political education which was essential if the party was to be won to a new political strategy.

In the spring of 1924, the P.C.I. prepared to fight a general election—under a new weighted electoral code and in a climate of terror and electoral fraud. Fascism had succeeded in absorbing broad strata of the bourgeoisie and petite bourgeoisie behind its electoral list, and by now had won the support of the Vatican (provoking a split in the Popular Party—see note 14 on p. 62); it was backed by the decisive centres of financial and industrial capital. Most of the opposition parties favoured boycotting the election, but when the P.C.I. announced that it would participate the other anti-fascist parties followed suit. The P.C.I. proposed an electoral bloc, but this was refused; it therefore formed its own list, together with the "third-internationalists" who had been expelled from the P.S.I. and were to join the P.C.I. formally after the Fifth World Congress in June. The Comintern representative in Italy during this period—J. Humbert Droz—was particularly active in pressing the P.C.I. leaders to adopt a "flexible" policy towards the other anti-fascist forces; he worked very closely with Tasca and Vota, the minority members of the executive.

At the time of the electoral campaign, the P.C.I. had some 12,000 members (if the 2,000 "third-internationalists" are included). The youth organisation had a further 5,000. The communist trade-union committee controlled about a sixth of the 120,000 members who remained in the C.G.L. When the new party daily *Unità* appeared in February, it gained a circulation of about 25,000; the new *Ordine Nuovo* came out in March in 6,000 copies. The party was moderately successful in the elections, with 19 members elected to parliament, and it maintained its vote compared to the 1921 election far better than the two socialist parties. Among those elected was Gramsci, who returned to Italy in May.

During the electoral campaign, the Bordiga question had once more exploded, when the latter refused to lead or indeed to figure at all on the party's electoral list. He was now in a position of intransigent opposition nationally as well as internationally. An idea of the attitude of his followers at this time (although Gramsci was to stress that Bordiga himself did not hold such views) can be gained from a conversation which took place between Humbert Droz and Grieco (at that time an unquestioning follower of Bordiga), and which Droz reported to Zinoviev on 15 February 1924. Grieco had said: "The International and the party have an anti-communist line and it is the duty of certain leaders, when they perceive a serious deviation, to refuse to follow discipline . . . Certain comrades are so to speak predestined to be leaders. Bordiga, like Lenin, is one of these. Discipline cannot be applied to such men as it can to other members of the party; their historical mission is to apply discipline to others, not to respect it."

In May, a few days after Gramsci's return to Italy, the P.C.I. held a consultative conference near Como. Three separate sets of theses were presented by the Left (over the signatures of Bordiga, Grieco, Fortichiari and Repossi), the Centre (over the signatures of Gennari, Leonetti, Ravera, Scoccimarro and Togliatti), and the Right (over the signatures notably of Tasca, Vota and Berti). Although it had only consultative status, the voting on these theses was a good index of the balance of strength in the P.C.I. at that moment. It showed that the Centre had a slender majority in the Central Committee over the Right, but that the Left—which had of course refused to participate in the leading bodies of the party—was overwhelmingly stronger than the other two factions combined in the party apparatus as a whole.

The theses of the Right criticised the entire line of the P.C.I. since Livorno, and while welcoming the formation of the new Centre nevertheless held it co-responsible with the Left for that line. They stood on the positions of the Fourth World Congress—although as we shall see these were by this time in the process of revision, and the Right showed its awareness of this by warning against too wide an interpretation of the slogan of "workers' governments". The Centre theses, drafted by Togliatti while Gramsci was still in Vienna but supported by him on his return, took the position that the old leadership had been right to struggle against the minority, but wrong to oppose the line of the Fourth

Congress. They rejected the Rome Theses, and accepted a limited interpretation of the united front. As Zinoviev was shortly to do at the Fifth World Congress, they defined social-democracy as the "left wing of fascism". They saw "workers' governments" as a mobilising slogan useful for convincing the more backward sections of the masses that the conquest of power was on the agenda, but warned against the illusion that there must be intermediate phases before the installation of the proletarian dictatorship—indeed they stated that "the existence of a régime of permanent armed dictatorship opens up for Italy a period of 'permanent revolution' "; they defined fascism as "the armed dictatorship of a fraction of the capitalist bourgeoisie and the big landowners". The Left presented a much shorter set of theses simply reaffirming the correctness of the Rome Theses and of the entire line followed by the party since Livorno, accusing the Comintern of placing false hopes in the P.S.I. and stressing the dangers of the united front and workers' government slogans.

The entire situation in the party was referred to the Fifth World Congress which took place in the following month. It was still not certain what leadership solution the Comintern would decide on. However, a great deal had changed in the party in the preceding months. Bordiga's attitude by now was that only a change in the line of the Comintern as a whole would make it possible for the Left to participate once more in the party leadership; he regarded the new Centre as having succumbed to Tasca, and felt that the Right was the logical leadership in view of current Comintern strategy. The Right, on the other hand, no longer had a monopoly in urging the acceptance of Comintern policy in full; moreover, as we shall see, in the wake of the German events the tide was running against it in the International. In addition, Tasca himself to some extent drew nearer to the Centre from mid-March 1924 onwards, in the course of his collaboration with Togliatti at the head of the party; furthermore, for a number of reasons (including personal ones) he was anxious to withdraw for a time from leadership responsibilities, and in fact resigned from the Executive in April.

Thus the Centre was in fact in a much stronger position than it looked at Como; over the next years it absorbed Tasca and most of the Right, and defeated the Left within the party organisation as a whole, winning over not only its rank and file but also many of its leaders—such as Grieco in 1925. The new conception of the party itself and the distinctive strategy within Italy which Gramsci had begun to formulate in his exchange of letters with Togliatti,

Terracini and the others in early 1924 were in sharp contrast to what had gone before. But the decisive factor in the change of leadership between 1923 and 1924 was undoubtedly international—both in the particular sense of attitudes to, and the role played by, the Comintern, and, more importantly, in the wider sense of the way in which the relation between the national and international dimensions of revolution was conceived. In the crucial letter of 9 February already referred to, Gramsci wrote: "Amadeo . . . thinks that the tactic of the International reflects the Russian situation, i.e. was born on the terrain of a backward and primitive capitalist civilisation. For him, this tactic is extremely voluntaristic and theatrical, because only with an extreme effort of will was it possible to obtain from the Russian masses a revolutionary activity which was not determined by the historical situation. He thinks that for the more developed countries of central and western Europe this tactic is inadequate or even useless. In these countries the historical mechanism functions according to all the approved schemas of Marxism: there exists the historical determinism which was lacking in Russia, and therefore the over-riding task must be the organisation of the party as an end in itself. I think that the situation is quite different. Firstly, because the political conception of the Russian communists was formed on an international and not on a national terrain; secondly, because in central and western Europe the development of capitalism has determined not only the formation of broad proletarian strata, but also and as a consequence has created the higher stratum, the labour aristocracy with its appendages of trade-union bureaucracy and the social-democratic groups. The determination, which in Russia was direct and drove the masses into the streets for a revolutionary uprising, in central and western Europe is complicated by all these political superstructures, created by the greater development of capitalism; this makes the action of the masses slower and more prudent, and therefore requires of the revolutionary party a strategy and tactics altogether more complex and long-term than those which were necessary for the Bolsheviks in the period between March and November 1917. But the fact that Amadeo has this conception, and that he seeks to achieve its victory not merely on a national scale but also internationally, is one thing: he is a convinced man, and struggles with great skill and great elasticity to obtain his objective, to avoid compromising his theses, to postpone any Comintern sanctions which might prevent him from continuing until the historical period in which the revolution in western and central Europe deprives Russia of the hegemonic position it holds today. But that we, who are not convinced of the historical truth of this conception, should continue to ally ourselves with it politically and thereby give it the international status which it at present enjoys is quite another thing. Amadeo approaches things from the viewpoint of an international minority, but we must approach things from the viewpoint of a national majority."

The P.C.I. under Gramsci 1924–26

The two years in which Gramsci led the P.C.I. can be seen as closing an epoch: the epoch opened by the October Revolution in which individual communist parties elaborated their theoretical analyses and their strategies in terms of one basic premise—the actuality of the revolution. This is not, of course, to suggest that many communists did not thereafter, notably during the "third period", believe that revolution was on the immediate agenda. What it does mean is that from early in 1924 Comintern policies and Comintern politics had become increasingly bound up with the struggle in the Russian party, and by 1927 Russian developments became the determining factor.

Thus 1924–26 was a transitional phase, and it is extremely important to stress the room for manoeuvre still remaining in this period to an individual party such as the P.C.I. The coincidence between Comintern strategy and that of the Italian party after the Fifth World Congress in June 1924 was not simply a question of cause and effect; it was rather a question of a somewhat tactical "left" turn by the Comintern meshing in with the pre-existing "leftism" of the P.C.I. This is made quite clear by subsequent events. For in the spring of 1925 the Comintern was to reverse its "left" turn—after the fall of Macdonald in Britain and Herriot in France, the rise to power of Hindenburg in Germany and the repression of the K.P.D., the new consolidation of Mussolini's régime in Italy, and the reactionary turn of events in Poland and in Estonia—and speak of the temporary stabilisation of capitalism. Yet there was no corresponding rightward turn in the line of the Italian party, which was to undergo no significant modifications until after Gramsci's arrest. Perhaps part of the reason for the freedom of manoeuvre which this reveals—despite the bolshevisation of the communist parties in this same period—was the extremely complex power relations in the Comintern at this time. Zinoviev was President of the International throughout this period; in 1924 he was allied to Stalin and attacking Trotsky for his "anti-peasant" policies; by 1926 he was allied to Trotsky and attacking Stalin and Bukharin for their "pro-peasant" policies. From early in 1925 a Bukharinist Right began to emerge within the Comintern, and it was particularly significant for the Italian party that Humbert-Droz—already mentioned as the Comintern representative in Italy during 1924, and as a close associate of Tasca during that period—returned to Moscow in 1925 to take charge of the Latin section of the International; Droz was to establish excellent relations with Bukharin, and fall with him in 1929. The upshot of this complex situation seems to have been that Zinoviev on the one hand and the Bukharinist Right on the other effectively cancelled each other out for this period, with the result that it was possible for "leftist" policies in countries like Germany and Italy to coexist with "rightist" policies in countries like China, the United States, Britain or Yugoslavia. In each case, the determining factors were national rather than international.

This periodicity is of crucial importance in understanding the basic political coordinates of Gramsci's writings in prison. These have an organic continuity with the political universe within which Gramsci had operated prior to his arrest; they manifest a radical disjuncture from the political universe which existed by the time that they were written. This is perhaps a major reason for the opacity and oblique character of some of the central political reflections in the Prison Notebooks, on the revolution in the West, on the party, on the State, etc. And it is certainly the major reason for the inappropriateness of many of the attempts that have been made to interpret Gramsci in terms of criteria which had no meaning in his political universe: popular frontism, Stalinism, etc. Any theorisation of Gramsci's work must seek to set it firmly in its true historical context, and must seek to explain all, and not merely some, of its sometimes contradictory elements.

As has already been mentioned, after the Como conference it had been decided to refer the leadership situation in the Italian party to the forthcoming Fifth World Congress, due to begin in Moscow in late June 1924. The Italian delegates included Bordiga, Togliatti, Terracini, Tasca, Serrati, Grieco, Leonetti and Berti, all of whom arrived in Moscow early in the month. (Gramsci and Scoccimarro, however, had not yet left Italy when the Matteotti crisis broke out on June 12, and consequently cancelled their departure.) The strategies defined at the first four World Congresses can be interpreted as responses to the actual course of historical events—at least in Europe. The "left" turn which followed the German October of 1923, on the other hand, and which was reflected at the Fifth World Congress, can only be understood in terms of the inner-party struggle which had already broken out in the Soviet Union, and in terms of Zinoviev's manoeuvring to shift the blame for the German disaster.

In the last months of 1923 Zinoviev and Stalin had launched the campaign against "Trotskyism", the Forty Six had published their platform, and Trotsky had published his *New Course* articles. In October, the German party led by Brandler had been involved in an abortive attempt at an insurrectionary uprising. The rising was planned in Moscow by Zinoviev, and liaison between Moscow and the K.P.D. was entrusted personally to Radek. After the defeat, Zinoviev made Brandler the scapegoat for the entire affair, and Trotsky—who had believed in the possibility of a revolution in Germany—joined forces with Radek—who had not—to defend Brandler from carrying sole responsibility. Zinoviev backed the Left inside the German party—led by Fischer and Maslov—and they replaced Brandler. The latter was accused of rightism, and Zinoviev took the lead in swinging the Comintern decisively to the left. These manoeuvres were designed principally to prevent the German disaster being used by the Russian opposition to discredit Zinoviev himself.

Battle lines had been drawn publicly, and at the Fifth Congress the Russian majority leaders were above all preoccupied with preventing the opposition from winning international allies. The obvious candidate to lead an international fraction in support of the Russian opposition was Bordiga—in spite of the fact that Trotsky had led the attack on the latter's rejection of the united front at the Fourth Congress and on his espousal of the "theory of the offensive" at the Third. For there was an obvious convergence between Bordiga's views on the degeneration of the Comintern and Trotsky's on the degeneration inside the Bolshevik party. Zinoviev sought to prevent such an alliance by incorporating Bordiga into the Comintern leadership with the post of vice-president. He saw a bloc between the Centre and the Left as the best solution to the P.C.I.'s internal divisions, and as a consequence of the tactical shift to the left which he had made after the German defeat no longer viewed Tasca and the Right with the same favour.

However, these plans shipwrecked on the rocks of Bordiga's intransigence. He was prepared to accept a post on the Comintern Executive, since he needed to maintain international contacts in view of his perspective of organising an international Left minority faction; but he refused any leadership position within the P.C.I. Paradoxically, the Fifth Congress at one and the same time shifted the line of the International substantially onto the positions which Bordiga had been defending—united front from below, struggle on two fronts against fascism and against social-democracy, etc. (the line which the Gramsci leadership was to follow for the next two years), and at the same time it saw Bordiga's definitive isolation in organisational terms. Bordiga gave the main Congress report on fascism, and there was little argument with the equal stress which he laid on the struggle against fascism and that against social-democracy; Togliatti too spoke of social-democracy as the left wing of fascism, and differed from Bordiga more on questions of emphasis than on those of substance—stressing the need to make the P.C.I. a mass party, the need for more work among the peasantry, etc. Zinoviev, summing up the work of the Congress, spoke of two possible alternatives for capitalism in the era of its "irremediable crisis": "The Social-Democrats from the right wing of the labour movement are in a process of transition and more and more becoming converted into the left wing of the bourgeoisie, and in places, into a wing of fascism. This is the reason that it is historically incorrect to speak of the 'victory of fascism over social democracy'. Fascism and social democracy (so far as their leaders are concerned) are the right and left hands of modern capitalism, which has been somewhat weakened by the first imperialist war, and in the first battles of the workers against capitalism. Whatever Mussolini and Poincaré do on the one hand, or Macdonald and Herriot on the other, favour proletarian revolution. Whether they take the road of 'democracy' or that of fascism is of little consequence. They are all of them merely carrying water to the mill of the proletarian revolution." (See note 70 on p. 169.) This expressed very exactly Bordiga's view. However, he still preferred to remain in opposition within the P.C.I. Therefore, when a new Central Committee and Executive were nominated by a special commission at the close of the Congress, the Centre was given a majority on both bodies, with minority representation for the Right and for the "third-internationalists" who now became formally members of the party. The new executive was made up of Gramsci, Togliatti and Scoccimarro from the Centre, Mersù from the Right (Tasca did not want the post but was in the new C.C.), and the ex-third-internationalist socialist Maffi. Two months later Gramsci was elected to the new post of secretary-general of the party.

The Fifth World Congress on the surface represented a shift to the left, and since the analyses which it formulated corresponded broadly to those of both Centre and Left in the P.C.I. it definitively healed the rift between the Italian party and the International. But what was Gramsci's real estimate of its significance, and what explains the substantial shift in his international positions, notably on Russia itself, between the spring of 1924 and the spring of 1925? Some answer, even if a necessarily incomplete one, is essential to understanding certain of the key passages in the *Prison Notebooks*.

In February 1924, Gramsci had written: "Just as I did not believe a year ago that the International was moving to the right . . . I do not believe today that it is moving to the left." He rejected the simple explanation for the German débacle offered by Zinoviev, i.e. that Brandler was a rightist; Gramsci described Brandler's strategy in 1923 as if anything putschist, and dismissed the question of which of the two contending factions in the German party—the Brandler/Thalheimer pre-October leadership, or Zinoviev's protégés Fischer and Maslov who replaced them after the defeat—was "right" and which "left" as "a rather Byzantine question". Moreover, he was at this time broadly sympathetic to the outlook of the Left in the Russian party. He wrote: "It is well known that in November 1917, while Lenin and the majority of the party had gone over to Trotsky's view and intended to take over not merely political power but also economic power, Zinoviev and Kamenev remained in the traditional party view and wanted a revolutionary coalition government with the Mensheviks and Social-Revolutionaries . . . In the recent polemic which has broken out in Russia, it is clear that Trotsky and the opposition in general, in view of the prolonged absence of Lenin from the leadership of the party, have been greatly preoccupied about the danger of a return to the old mentality, which would be damaging to the revolution. Demanding a greater intervention of proletarian elements in the life of the party and a diminution of the powers of the bureaucracy, they want basically to ensure the socialist and proletarian character of the revolution and to prevent a gradual transition to that democratic dictatorship—carapace for a developing capitalism—which was still the programme of Zinoviev and Co. in November 1917. This seems to me to be the situation in the Russian party . . . the only novelty is the passage of Bukharin to the Zinoviev, Kamenev, Stalin group."

However, from the spring of 1924 onwards there was increasing pressure on communist parties to align themselves with the majority in the Russian party. From the passages quoted it is clear that Gramsci did not personally accept the version of the Russian inner-party struggle which was disseminated in Comintern circles at this time. But four main, inter-related factors combined to determine a substantial alignment with the successive dominant groups within the Russian party from this period onwards—an alignment which by 1926 at least was not merely tactical but based on conviction. In the first place, the terms of the struggle in Russia were filtered through to foreign communists via a Comintern apparatus which was henceforward increasingly itself an instrument of that struggle. Secondly, Gramsci made the healing of the breach with the Comintern and a full acceptance of international discipline the very foundation of the new Centre leadership and its basic difference with Bordiga. Thirdly, the issues of the Russian oppositions and the Left in the Italian party became inextricably mixed in the mid-twenties. The stances adopted by Trotsky and by Bordiga both raised analogous questions with regard to party discipline and the formation of fractions. Moreover, for a period—from 1925 to 1930—Bordiga aligned himself with Trotsky internationally; it became impossible for the Italian party to discuss Russian questions without reference to its own internal situation. Lastly, Gramsci's strategy in Italy was increasingly directed towards the Southern peasantry, and concerned with the forging of a worker-peasant alliance. In 1926, he saw the positions of the Joint Opposition in Russia as a threat to the latter. These four factors combined, in an often contradictory way as we shall see, to determine Gramsci's change of position; the contradictions are reflected in the *Prison Notebooks*.

Gramsci's return to Italy from Vienna in May 1924 preceded by less than a month the outbreak of the Matteotti crisis on 12 June. When the social-democratic leader was assassinated by fascist thugs, the régime seemed suddenly vulnerable and internally divided; its backers appeared to waver; and the opposition gained confidence. The first months of Gramsci's leadership saw a new room for manoeuvre for the party, and a considerable growth in its strength. Yet the crisis did not go so deep as the communist leaders thought, and the remaining two years of the P.C.I.'s open existence in Italy were to be a long defensive action against quite overwhelming odds.

As early as 1921–2, Gramsci had opposed the prevalent view in the Italian party that a fascist or military dictatorship was impossible. According to his own account, he had prevented such a view being incorporated in the Rome Theses. However, as we have already indicated, even he did not achieve in the years which followed a consistent or adequate appreciation of the fascist phenomenon—indeed it would have been impossible at that time to foresee the full potentialities of fascism as a new and *sui generis* form of bourgeois reactionary rule. Even before the Matteotti crisis broke out, in the spring of 1924 he was already writing of the possibility of a social-democratic "alternative" replacing fascism. He was critical of Bordiga for underestimating the internal contradictions of Italian capitalism and for believing that the specific forms of bourgeois rule were irrelevant and that the only perspective was one of a crisis of the capitalist system and the revolutionary upsurge and mass swing to communism which this crisis would necessarily entail. When Matteotti was murdered, and the régime appeared unconfident and divided, Gramsci became more than ever convinced that a social-democratic alternative was imminent, and that this would put proletarian revolution once more on the immediate agenda.

It is easy to see the similiarities as well as the differences between Gramsci's and Bordiga's perspectives. Both were based on a belief in the general crisis of the bourgeois order and in the actuality of the revolution. Both accepted only the united front "from below", and stressed the need to struggle not only against the régime itself but equally—or even primarily—against the social-democrats, the "left wing of the bourgeoisie". But whereas Bordiga saw fascism and social-democracy simply as two inter-changeable forms of bourgeois rule, rejected the notion that whether one form or the other happened to be adopted by Italian capitalism could be of any consequence to the P.C.I., and foresaw a direct replacement of the existing régime by the dictatorship of the proletariat, Gramsci's conception was a less reductionist one. He had always analysed fascism in terms of its social base, and he saw its disintegration in terms of the detachment of sections of this base—above all the urban petite bourgeoisie. He thought that a social-democratic "alternative" would be a short-lived and inherently unstable transitional phase—analogous to the Kerensky régime in the Soviet Union—and that it would quickly lead to a period of civil war, for which the proletariat must be prepared; but he also thought that initially the fall of fascism might see an increase of support for the social-democratic organisations.

After Matteotti's murder, the opposition parties left parliament and met in an alternative assembly on the Aventine. Although the P.C.I. at first participated in this, its attitude to the other anti-fascist parties remained unchanged. At a Central Committee meeting in mid-July, Scoccimarro argued that there were two possible outcomes to the crisis; either the most intransigent wing of fascism would take over and instal a yet more dictatorial régime, or there would be an agreement between the fascists and the opposition parties. Gramsci agreed with this assessment, and stressed that fascism could not possibly be overthrown except by mass struggle. In another Central Committee meeting the following month, Gramsci recognised that the democratic opposition parties remained the axis of popular anti-fascism, but emphasised that they must be combated for that very reason. He described the Aventine opposition as "semi-fascist". Underlying these positions was the belief that fascism was disintegrating, and that the real forces of the bourgeois State would pass over to the opposition—which was therefore the main danger. In Gramsci's view, the P.C.I.'s strategy in this situation must be an all-out attempt to capture the majority of the proletariat, and he picked out the creation of factory committees as the key immediate objective.

To resume Gramsci's perspective in this period, he did reject both the ultra-left view that there could be no transition whatever between fascism and the dictatorship of the proletariat (a view which was to characterise the third period), and the rightist view that communist aims should be limited for the moment to the struggle against fascism and the restoration of bourgeois democracy and that the fight against the social-democrats should therefore be suspended—implying that there would be a stable period of transition between fascism and the proletarian revolution (a view which was to characterise the period from 1927 to 1928). But within these two extremes, there was still considerable room for error, and it seems undeniable that Gramsci and the other P.C.I. leaders did seriously underestimate the strength and possibilities for internal development of the fascist régime.

The whole history of the P.C.I. in its remaining two years of semi-legal existence was marked by this failure of appreciation (which was in Gramsci's own case almost certainly one of the main factors in his decision to remain in Italy until he was arrested). The return of the P.C.I. deputies to parliament in November 1924 was inspired by a concern to expose the Aventine opposition in the event of the collapse of fascism which the party expected. Any idea of a united front other than "from below" was still rejected. When the fascists finally struck back in January 1925, and Mussolini's speech assuming responsibility for the Matteotti murder was followed by a new wave of repression, this was seen by the party as a mere episode. A compromise between fascism and the opposition was still confidently expected. (It should be stressed that the other opposition parties had an equally mistaken assessment of the true situation; the Aventine parties issued a statement at this time which declared "The moral battle has already been won"!).

P.C.I. membership at the end of 1924 had risen to about 25,000, and a legal apparatus of sections and federations was re-created side by side with the clandestine cells during the months following Matteotti's death. It was still an overwhelmingly working-class party, still firmly believing in the inevitability of the world defeat of capitalism in the wake of the October Revolution. Every strengthening of repression was taken as a sign of ruling-class weakness. It must be emphasised that the Left still dominated the party organisation as a whole. In the elections for new federation committees which took place between September and December 1924, Bordiga still controlled the majority of federations, and the most important ones: Turin, Milan, Rome, Naples to name only the largest. But the leadership too broadly shared the view that had been so succinctly expressed by Bordiga earlier in the year: "the bourgeois counter-revolution for us is the proof of the inevitability of the revolution".

Up to this time, the inner-party struggle in the Soviet Union had hardly impinged at all on the internal situation in the P.C.I. In the theses prepared for the Como conference—which had taken place in the aftermath of the first open phase of the conflict which opposed Zinoviev, Kamenev and Stalin to Trotsky and to the Forty Six—Bordiga and the Left had remained silent on the Russian question; Togliatti and the Centre had expressed general support for the majority in the Bolshevik party while stressing the need for detailed knowledge of the issues involved; only Tasca and the Right had raised the question in a substantive fashion, and had attacked Trotsky for endangering the unity of the Bolshevik leadership—in line with Zinoviev's presentation of the issue. It is true that during the conference itself, Gramsci was to draw the first analogy between the attitudes of Trotsky and Bordiga respectively to party discipline. But this analogy was not to be repeated again until the following year.

At the Fifth World Congress, the Russian inner-party struggle had been temporarily at a halt, at least on the surface; but it had been reopened when Trotsky published his *Lessons of October* in the autumn of 1924. It was after this that Bordiga began to align himself internationally with Trotsky—an alignment which was to last intermittently up to 1930, and which was to lead Gramsci and the other P.C.I. leaders to view the Russian party struggle to a very great extent in terms of their own conflict with Bordiga. The P.C.I. in fact first discussed the Russian question in a Central Committee meeting of February 1925, after Trotsky had made a declaration of discipline; in the following years, of course, events in Russia were to have a growing importance for the P.C.I.

The type of contradictions to which the assimilation of Bordiga and Trotsky was to lead was revealed dramatically in the course of this first discussion in February 1925. Bordiga had taken up some theses put forward by Trotsky in a speech on "Perspectives of World Development" the previous July, on the subject of the growing strength of American capitalism and its increasing hegemony over Europe. Gramsci attacked these in the following terms: "We reject these predictions which, by deferring the revolution indefinitely, would shift the entire tactics of the Communist International—which would have to go back to propagandistic and agitational activity among the masses. Moreover, they would shift the tactics of the Russian State since, if the European revolution is deferred for an entire historical period, if in other words the Russian working class for a long period of time is to be unable to count on the support of the proletariat of other countries, it is evident that the Russian revolution must be modified." The issues presented by Gramsci were real ones—Stalin had formulated his theory of "Socialism in One Country" for the first time only a few weeks earlier—but clearly the protagonists of the debate were reversed in Gramsci's presentation! (Incidentally, this discussion was probably the origin of Gramsci's subsequent interest in the specific character of American capitalism, developed notably in the notes on "Americanism and Fordism"—see pp. 277–318.)

But even at this Central Committee meeting, the main focus of the discussion was not any such theoretical issue, but the problem of fractions within the party; it was in terms of this that the analogy between Bordiga and Trotsky was most frequently drawn in the following years. This was the period of bolshevisation of the communist parties, and their closer alignment with the Russian party. In May at a Central Committee meeting Gramsci spoke of bolshevisation as a Leninist stabilisation of the communist parties, and defined Bordigism as a provincial tendency to refuse incorporation in a world organisation. (Bordiga, for his part, had long characterised Gramsci's strategy as a provincial tendency to view the problem of revolution in exclusively national terms.) Earlier, in March/April, at the important Fifth Enlarged Executive meeting of the Comintern at which the Fifth Congress strategy was redefined in a decisively "right-wing" sense, Stalin had put direct pressure on Scoccimarro to include an attack on Trotsky in his prepared speech on bolshevisation and the struggle against Bordiga. Bordiga himself had in February submitted an article in defence of Trotsky for publication in *Unità*. The question of fractionism in general, of the struggle against Bordiga in particular, and the question of Trotsky were now inextricably intertwined.

During the rest of 1925, events in Russia had less direct repercussions in Italy. Bordiga's article and Scoccimarro's Moscow speech on Trotsky were published by *Unità* in July, but without any accompanying discussion. In any case, during this period Trotsky had withdrawn from the inner-party struggle in the Soviet Union, and it was the dissensions between Stalin and Bukharin on the one hand and Zinoviev and Kamenev on the other which were now fast emerging. Gramsci always resisted the tendency current by that time in the Comintern to reduce substantive disagreements to simple factional disputes. In this period, the Comintern was generally following the lead given by Zinoviev at the Fifth Enlarged Executive meeting already referred to, in assimilating left and right oppositions as "right opportunist". Gramsci never accepted this type of crude amalgam, and continued to speak of right and left tendencies as two separate entities. When a date was announced for the forthcoming Third Congress of the party, he suggested that the pre-congress discussion could be a valuable opportunity for general reflection—not only on the internal state of the party, but on more fundamental problems of the worker-peasant alliance, etc.

But the situation was not one which allowed such calm, non-factional discussion. The process of bolshevisation was inexorably eroding the strength of the Left in the party. A number of factors contributed to this process: the Left's conflict with the Comintern and rejection of the latter's discipline; its leader's self-imposed isolation and refusal to accept posts of responsibility in the party; Gramsci's inner-party activity, especially among the youth; the new intake of militants who had joined the party in the period following Matteotti's murder; the influence inevitably exerted by the group at the centre which ran the party organisationally. It was hardly a surprise when in June the Left reacted to this loss of its support by openly organising as a fraction, and forming the *Comitato d'Intesa*—quickly condemned by both the party executive and the Comintern, and dissolved after an ultimatum from the latter. The fact that the formation of this committee happened to coincide with a new wave of fascist repression damaged the Left yet further. By the time the Third Congress of the party finally took place at Lyons in January 1926, the Centre controlled 90 per cent of the party. A total reversal of the respective strengths of the Left and the Centre had taken place in the eighteen months since Como. It was not surprising that the Lyons Congress thus took place in an atmosphere envenomed by bitter accusations of fractionism on the one hand, of undemocratic practices in the name of "bolshevization" on the other.

Throughout 1925, the fascist régime intensified the dictatorial character of its rule. The P.C.I.'s traditional view equating fascism and social-democracy was not abandoned, but it now began to be accompanied by a new awareness of fascism as a unifier of the ruling class and expression of its interests. "Fascism has given back to the bourgeoisie a class consciousness and class organisation", wrote Gramsci in February; at about the same time he wrote to Julia in Moscow that it was no longer possible to expect "any very imminent end to fascism as a régime . . .". But if anything the P.C.I. moved farther to the left under the impact of the new repression. Gramsci continued to speak of the need to liquidate the P.S.I. and its hold over the masses, and it was with this aim that the party campaigned around the slogan of "Worker and peasant committees". But now, in addition, Gramsci spoke of the need to "put on the agenda . . . the preparation for an insurrection. Recent political events mark the beginning of a phase in which insurrection has become the sole means for the masses to express their political will".

In April 1925, Togliatti was arrested; however, he was amnestied in June of the same year. In August, while preparations were being made for the party to go underground again completely, the party secretariat was discovered and Terracini arrested. The main focus of P.C.I. activity by now was the struggle for trade-union autonomy. In October, the employers' federation signed a pact with the fascist "corporations" (fake trade unions), in which the latter were given sole bargaining rights, and the *commissioni interne* were suppressed. The C.G.L. was by now reduced to a shadow of what it had once been, and its reformist leaders were already preparing to dissolve it entirely—although this did not prevent them from fighting a bitter factional struggle against the communists inside the unions. The strategy of the P.C.I. was a two-pronged one: to build up autonomous factory committees, and to defend C.G.L. independence so that "the trade-union movement will be reborn under our control", as Gramsci put it. It was at this point that a new disagreement with Tasca arose in the Central Committee, on an issue which was to become very important the following year. For Tasca criticised the whole attempt to stimulate the formation of autonomous factory committees, outside the established trade-union structure (it was substantially the same disagreement which had arisen in 1919–20), and called for an initiative towards the P.S.I. and an attempt to reach agreement with the reformist C.G.L. leaders for common action to defend the remnants of trade-union independence.

In November 1925, the opposition press was finally crushed and brought under fascist control, with the partial exception of the socialist and communist organs, *Avanti!* and *Unità*, which were permitted a continued semi-legal existence. Although by the end of 1925 the communist leaders did cease speaking of the possibility of compromise between fascism and the constitutional opposition, they neither made any distinction between anti-fascist struggle and the socialist revolution, nor did they revise their judgement on the P.S.I. as the last bastion of bourgeois reaction; they were to continue throughout 1926 to resist efforts which the Comintern now began to make to persuade them to pursue a serious united front policy. During the autumn of 1925, arrests of communists continued steadily, and the party was compelled to reorganise itself almost completely during this period in which it was preparing for its Third Congress—which had been postponed after Terracini's arrest, but was now scheduled to take place at Lyons in January 1926. It was something of an achievement that during 1925 the P.C.I. maintained its membership under extremely difficult conditions; by the end of the year it had some 27,000 members, largely organised in cells. However, to a considerable extent it had lost working-class members as a result of the repression, and had compensated for this by increased recruitment among the peasantry.

By the end of 1925, the party leaders were coming to recognise that the situation was indeed a qualitatively new one, and Gramsci began now to formulate a new strategic conception which he was to develop in the Congress Theses and in his 1926 essay on the Southern Question. The basic elements of this new conception were as follows: fascism had successfully united the Italian ruling class; but economic contradictions could not be resolved, and would progressively tend to detach the middle strata—especially in the South—

from the fascist bloc; this perspective meant that the alliance between northern proletariat and southern peasantry must be seen in new terms. At a Central Committee meeting in November 1925, Gramsci said: "In Italy the situation is revolutionary when the proletariat in the North is strong; if the proletariat in the North is weak, the peasants fall in behind the petite bourgeoisie. Conversely, the peasants of southern Italy represent an element of strength and revolutionary stimulus for the workers in the North. The northern workers and the southern peasants are thus the two immediate revolutionary forces (the southern peasants are 80 per cent controlled by the priests) to which we must devote all our attention. . . If we succeed in organising the southern peasants, we will have won the revolution; at the moment of the decisive action a transfer of the armed forces of the bourgeoisie from North to South to confront the insurrection of the southern peasantry allied to the northern proletariat will afford the workers greater possibilities for action. Our general task is therefore clear: organise the workers of the North and the southern peasants and forge their revolutionary alliance." And indeed, the two focuses of communist action in the last period of its semi-legal existence in Italy were the creation of base organisations in the factories and greatly intensified work among the peasantry.

The Lyons Congress saw the last major challenge by the Left inside the P.C.I. The main issues of the pre-congress discussion were bolshevisation and relations with the International. The platform of the Left turned on opposition to bolshevisation, especially to reorganisation on the basis of factory cells which it saw as creating a basis for a new corporativism, and on a condemnation of what it claimed was the "tacticism" of the Centre leadership; it laid the responsibility for the emergence of fractionism at the door of the leadership and of the Comintern. Gramsci and the Centre, on the other hand, violently attack the Left's "fractionism", and argued that bolshevisation should be seen as the construction of a real world communist party and that opposition to it was the result of provincial residues. The Centre's Congress Theses, published in October and drafted by Gramsci with the collaboration of Togliatti, give the most complete résumé of the leadership's analysis and strategy in this last period of semi-legal existence. The theses repudiated the entire socialist tradition in Italy prior to Livorno, and stressed the qualitative novelty introduced by the October Revolution and Leninism. (This was in marked contrast to the Bordigan view, expressed in the Rome Theses of 1922, that the P.C.I. was the continuer of the intransigent left tradition within the P.S.I., and that Lenin had resuscitated the true Marxism rather than adding anything new.) The theses went on to reaffirm that no revolution was possible in Italy other than a proletarian revolution to overthrow capitalism; to characterise the ruling-class bloc of northern industrialists and southern landowners; to analyse the role of the proletariat—which was compared with that of pre-revolutionary Russia, numerically small but advanced and highly concentrated, and whose strength was emphasised in view of the heterogenous and backward nature of the Italian social structure; to describe how fascism, whose original base had been in the urban petite bourgeoisie and the rural bourgeoisie, had become the tool of the capitalist class. The period was defined as one of preparation for revolution; stress was laid on the internal contradictions of fascism, which might lead to its imminent collapse, and also on inter-imperialist contradictions, notably between the United States and Britain, which made war not unlikely. The theses went on to formulate the concept of an alliance between the northern proletariat and the southern peasantry, and to define the anti-fascist opposition forces as so many links in a chain of reaction stretching from fascism to the P.S.I. The idea that any post-fascist democratic phase was possible was rejected; any transitional phase would be brief and unstable, and lead quickly to the outbreak of civil war. Lastly, the united front was given the most narrow possible definition, as merely a means for unmasking the reformists.

The Lyons Congress itself lasted for a week, and an extremely hard-hitting discussion ranged over the entire experience of the five years of the party's existence. Gramsci's main report lasted four hours, Bordiga's reply lasted seven! The congress was dominated by the ideological conflict between the Centre leadership and the Left, which invested every aspect of analysis, tactics and strategy. Yet significantly enough, when the disagreements with Tasca also came up in the discussion of trade-union strategy and the factory committees (and it must be remembered that the Right had not existed as a tendency since the Fifth World Congress, but had been effectively absorbed by the new leadership), the response of the Centre—Gramsci and Scoccimarro in particular—revealed a hostility as great as that shown towards the Left. Gramsci spoke of "a rightist conception, connected to the desire not to clash too seriously with the reformist trade-union bureaucracy which strenuously opposes any organisation of the masses". We have already sufficiently stressed the elements of continuity between the Left and

Centre leaderships not to need to emphasise that the differences between Gramsci and Tasca were just as fundamental as those between Gramsci and Bordiga. Moreover, in view of the depth of these differences, it says much for the type of leadership exercised by Gramsci that he made every effort to ensure that the tendencies within the party should all be represented in the party's leading bodies. And this time he succeeded in persuading Bordiga to join the Central Committee, together with another representative of the Left. Tasca too remained on the C.C., and a new executive—shortly to be renamed the Political Committee—consisting of Gramsci, Terracini (freed from prison shortly after the Congress), Togliatti, Scoccimarro, Camilla Ravera, Ravazzoli and Grieco was appointed. Togliatti, a month after the Congress, was sent to Moscow as P.C.I. representative to the Comintern.

There had been no discussion of the Russian question at the Lyons Congress. This was the moment when the conflict between Stalin and Bukharin on the one hand and Zinoviev, Kamenev and Krupskaya on the other hand had just exploded at the Fourteenth Congress to the Bolshevik Party in December 1925; Trotsky had been silent for almost a year, and it was only in April 1926 that he was to join forces with Zinoviev and Kamenev. But almost immediately after Lyons, the Sixth Enlarged Executive Committee meeting took place in Moscow, and inevitably the new inner-party struggle in Russia formed its background. Zinoviev was of course still President of the Comintern, and it had become essential for Stalin and Bukharin to prevent him from using the international organisation as a power base. The Central Committee of the Russian party therefore requested the other national sections of the Cominturn not to carry the discussion of the Russian question into the ranks of the International. However, they had not reckoned with Bordiga.

The Italian delegation was headed by Togliatti, and included Grieco, Gennari, Berti, Bordiga and several others. When the delegation met before the Congress to discuss the draft theses presented by Zinoviev, Bordiga declared that Russia was faced with two possible perspectives: advance towards socialism, or failure to continue this advance. He stated that the International had the duty to analyse these possibilities, and that the individual national sections could and should intervene. This meant of course direct defiance of the Russian Central Committee's request, and the Italian delegates—after Bordiga had left the meeting—decided to ask the Russian party for information on the Russian situation.

The next day a new meeting of the Italian delegates was arranged with Stalin. According to Berti, Bordiga had meanwhile had a long meeting with Trotsky. At all events, a prolonged and violent confrontation took place—to the considerable embarrassment of the other Italian delegates—between Stalin and Bordiga, in which the latter's questions ranged from the attitude taken up by Stalin towards the provisional government in 1917 prior to Lenin's return to the current policies being followed in the Soviet Union towards the middle peasantry. The next day, at the plenary session of the Congress, Bordiga made the sole oppositional speech. Lasting four hours, it was the most extended expression of his analysis of the relation between the Russian revolution, the International and the revolution in the West. "We were told: we only have one party which has achieved a victorious revolution, and that is the Russian Bolshevik Party. Therefore we must follow the path which led the Russian party to victory. That is quite true, but it is not sufficient. The Russian party fought in special conditions, that is to say in a country in which the feudal aristocracy had not yet been defeated by the capitalist bourgeoisie. It is necessary for us to know how to attack a modern democratic bourgeois State which, on the one hand, has its own means of corrupting and misleading the proletariat, and, on the other hand, can defend itself on the terrain of armed struggle more effectively than the Tsarist autocracy was able to do. This problem does not figure in the history of the Russian Communist Party . . . We are told that the correct solution is ensured by the leading role of the Russian party. But there are reservations to be made on that score. What is the leading factor within the Russian party itself? Is it the Leninist old guard? But after the recent events it is clear that this old guard can be divided. . . . The correct solution lies elsewhere. It is necessary to base ourselves on the whole International, on the whole world proletarian vanguard. Our organisation is like a pyramid and must be so, because everything must flow from the individual sectors towards a common summit. But this pyramid is balanced on its summit, and is too unstable. It must be turned the other way up . . . Given that the world revolution has not yet developed in other countries, it is necessary for Russian policy to be worked out in the closest relation to the general revolutionary policy of the proletariat . . . The basis for this struggle is certainly, and primarily, the Russian working class and its communist party, but it is essential also to base ourselves on the proletariat in the capitalist countries and on its class awareness—which is the result of its living relationship with the class enemy. The problem of Russian politics will not be resolved within the closed field of the Russian movement; the direct contribution of the entire communist proletarian International is necessary". We quote the speech at some length both because it gives some idea of the stature of Bordiga (he was almost the principal protagonist of the Congress; hardly a speech did not take up one or other of his arguments), and also because of the parallel between its thesis on the difference between the revolution in Russia and that in the West and some of Gramsci's most important prison reflections. The episode also presaged a new phase in the Italian inner-party struggle. For whereas Bordiga declared during the discussion that "The history of Lenin is the history of fractions", Togliatti was now explicit that in his view "The most serious danger is the danger of the extreme Left".

During the summer of 1926 the Joint Opposition, formed in April, suffered its first major defeat in July, over the Anglo-Soviet Trade-union Committee, and Zinoviev was excluded from the Politburo. Togliatti, working closely with Humbert Droz during this period in Moscow, was subjected to constant pressure by Droz and Bukharin to work for a shift in the P.C.I.'s "left" line, especially in the trade-union field. He was won over to their positions in April—and this fact was to assume its full significance after Gramsci's arrest, when Togliatti became effective leader of the party. (In the same month, Togliatti put forward the somewhat Machiavellian proposal in the Latin secretariat of the Comintern that Trotsky should be invited to write a polemical article against Bordiga, and Tasca another against the Right in the French party, as contributions to the struggle against left and right deviations.) But in Italy, the party leadership did not modify its attitude towards the trade unions—whose reformist leaders were in fact to accede to the fascist request to dissolve the C.G.L. formally only a few months later—throughout the year.

After the Enlarged Executive meeting, the P.C.I. respected the request of the Russian party not to intervene in, or comment upon, its internal struggle. When the July measures were taken against the Joint Opposition, *Unità* merely published a brief note—perhaps by Gramsci—supporting the disciplinary measures taken, but limiting its comment to the issue of fractionism and not entering into the substance of the discussion. However, in September Togliatti indicated from Moscow that the ban on discussion of the Russian question should be considered as no longer valid, and Gramsci published a series of polemical articles (directed against fascist newspaper accounts) which, although not intervening directly in the Russian debates, did represent a full expression of support for the majority in the Russian party. In particular, he wrote: "It is inevitable that in the mass of the peasantry there should appear differences, and that rich and middle peasants should arise; but the very fact that the former will always be a small minority means that their interests will clash with those of the mass of poor peasants and wage-earners. Their political influence will not therefore become dangerous, since the alliance between the poor peasants and the workers will be reinforced by these very developments." There is no question that Gramsci accepted the view of the majority in the Russian party that the line defended by the Joint Opposition would endanger the alliance of workers and peasants, and indeed he said as much in the famous letters which he wrote in early October, just before his arrest, on behalf of the P.C.I. Executive to the Russian Central Committee.

In the first of these two letters, Gramsci expressed the party leadership's official support for the Stalin/Bukharin majority in the Russian party, and accepted the majority's view that the Joint Opposition was endangering the alliance of workers and peasants and that it had been guilty of fractional activity. At the same time, however, Gramsci expressed the Italian party's fears about the course which the Russian inner-party struggle was taking, and stressed that "unity and discipline cannot be mechanical and coercive; they must be loyal and the result of conviction, and not those of an enemy unit imprisoned or besieged—thinking all the time of how to escape or make an unexpected counter-attack." In the second letter, Gramsci replied with very considerable acerbity to the reasons put forward by Togliatti in Moscow for not transmitting the P.C.I.'s first letter to the Russian Central Committee to whom it was addressed, dismissing these reasons as "vitiated by bureaucratism", etc. He wrote with very great eloquence of the importance of "the Leninist line" which "consists in struggling for the unity of the party, and not merely for external unity but for the rather more profound kind which involves there not being inside the party two political lines which diverge on every question". He expressed his pessimism about the chances of the Bolshevik Party in fact being able to maintain the unity which he saw as being so important an element of its strength. Once again, he stressed that the P.C.I.'s original letter had been "a whole indictment of the opposition".

In 1926, the last margin of semi-legality remaining to the P.C.I.

was progressively reduced, until in early November the fascist jaws finally closed on the remnants of opposition which had been allowed to exist until then. The year was a crucial one in the evolution of fascism, and it was now, under the impact of growing economic contradictions, that the basis of the corporate State and of the interventionist economic policies which were to characterise the régime in the thirties was first laid. The P.C.I., and notably Gramsci, were gradually coming to formulate a more coherent and sophisticated analysis of the régime and the contradictory social forces which supported it than they had previously held. But even so, the fundamental line did not alter. In October, the party executive could still issue a directive which said: "the problem of the P.S.I. for us is part of the more general problem of reorganising the industrial proletariat which our party has set itself. The maximalist party is a factor of disorganisation and disorientation of the masses: it represents a negative element of the situation which will have to be superseded and eliminated." Moreover, in August Tasca still felt it necessary to write to Gramsci that "The present economic crisis does not find at the helm of State a politically oscillating petit-bourgeois stratum, an easy prey to panic when faced with a situation of such seriousness; it finds a well-defined capitalist group, homogeneous, endowed with a political experience . . . The typical feature of the present period . . . remains . . . the direct taking over of the State apparatus by big capital, and the latter's decisive and commanding role in government policy". Tasca, characteristically, drew pessimistic conclusions of the type which caused Gramsci to consider him a "liquidator"; but, in the summer of 1926, his pessimism can hardly be regarded as unjustified.

On 31 October 1926, an alleged attempt was made on Mussolini's life by a 15-year-old boy; it was taken as the pretext for a new wave of repression. The Council of Ministers met on 5 November and drafted a series of emergency laws, to be debated in parliament on the 9th, which were designed to eliminate the remaining vestiges of bourgeois democracy in Italy. The party laid plans for Gramsci's escape to Switzerland, but he was unwilling to leave. Newspaper reports had led him to believe that only the Aventine deputies were in danger of losing their parliamentary immunity, and he decided, as a communist deputy, to participate in the debate on the new laws. He still almost certainly believed that the internal contradictions of the Italian ruling class were such as to make unlikely the total elimination of such residual obstacles to the régime as still remained. Moreover, it should be remembered that nobody in the party could have predicted either the twenty-year sentences that the communist leaders were now to receive, nor more importantly that the fascist régime had anything approaching such an extended future ahead of it. But the principal reason for Gramsci's refusal to leave Rome when his arrest must have seemed almost certain was reported by Camilla Ravera to Togliatti: "Antonio . . . observed that such a step should only be taken when the workers could see for themselves that it was absolutely justified and necessary; that leaders ought to remain in Italy until it became quite impossible for them to do so". In an "autobiographical note" written in prison, Gramsci confirms this: "The rule has been made that a captain must be the last to abandon his vessel in a shipwreck; that he must leave only when everybody else on board is safe. Some have even gone so far as to claim that in such cases the captain 'must' go down with his ship. Such assertions are less irrational than it might seem. Certainly, there may be certain cases in which there is no reason why the captain should not save himself first. But if such cases were made the basis for a rule, what guarantee would there be that a captain had done everything: (1) to prevent the shipwreck from occurring; (2) once it had occurred, to reduce human and material losses (material losses which represent future human losses) to a minimum? Only the 'absolute' rule that, in case of shipwreck, the captain is the last to leave his ship, and indeed may die with her, can provide this guarantee. Without it, collective life would become impossible; for nobody would be prepared to accept responsibility or continue activity which involved putting their lives in the hands of others."

Prison

Since Gramsci's arrest effectively isolated him from events in the outside world, we shall only give the briefest sketch of developments in the P.C.I. and the Comintern thereafter. In 1927 and 1928, the party was reduced to a tiny core of dedicated militants working underground—perhaps 6,000 in 1927 and fewer still in successive years until the lowest point was reached in 1934, when membership was probably (according to Comintern estimates) about 2,500. The leadership was now in exile, and in 1927 and 1928—the years of Bukharin's dominance in the Comintern—its nucleus consisted of Togliatti, Grieco and Tasca. A left opposition emerged in these years, centred on the youth organisation and its leaders Longo and Secchia, on positions which adumbrated those of the "third period". In 1929 came the left turn in Russia and the

International, and the crushing of Bukharin and the Right. Tasca, the P.C.I. representative in Moscow, opposed it and was expelled from the P.C.I. in the autumn; Togliatti and Grieco were won over to the positions of Longo and the youth (causing Bordiga reportedly to exclaim: "the party is coming back to me"). In place of the slogans of 1927–8—"popular revolution" against fascism; the "transitional phase" which would follow the popular revolution; the "republican assembly" which should be the intermediate objective—the leadership now spoke of the rising tide of revolution in Italy, the imminent fall of fascism, the disappearance of the social base for reformism, the impossibility of any transition between fascism and the dictatorship of the proletariat; in accordance with these theses, they proposed in March 1930 to move the party centre back to Italy.

In late 1929 an opposition emerged inside the Political Committee. Three of its eight members—Leonetti, Tresso and Ravazzoli—claimed that the change of line from the "right" line symbolised by Tasca to the "left" line as propounded by Longo was opportunistic, and that a serious self-criticism was required. However, the position of the "three" was not a very strong one tactically, since it involved simultaneously demanding self-criticism for the previous right line and opposing the change to the new left line. The situation came to a head in connection with the proposal to move the party centre back to Italy. The "three"—who were in fact responsible respectively for the underground party organisation, for the clandestine press, and for communist trade-union work (the C.G.L. had been dissolved by its reformist leaders, and reconstituted under communist leadership as a clandestine organisation)—opposed this as suicidal, and counter-proposed a plan to build up the underground organisation of a less voluntarist kind. The "three" were narrowly defeated, and soon after established contact with Trotsky (by now on Prinkipo)—for which they were expelled. The whole experience of the left turn was a disastrous one for the Italian party. The leadership was shattered; of the eight members of the 1928 Political Committee, five were expelled by 1931 (Tasca, the "three", and Silone—who was a moral and political casualty of the period). Bordiga too, still formally a member of the Central Committee although in prison, was expelled in 1930. In addition, the militants sent back to Italy as part of the new policy were arrested almost to a man or woman, and membership inside the country as we have mentioned was reduced to miniscule proportions by 1934, at the end of the "left" period.

After Gramsci's arrest, he was taken to the island of Ustica off the north coast of Sicily. The six weeks he spent in detention there were the last in which he enjoyed a relative freedom of movement and of extended contact with other militants. Among his fellow-prisoners was Bordiga, and the two collaborated in organising education courses for the political detainees. Gramsci taught history and geography and studied German: Bordiga was in charge of the scientific side. But on 20 January 1927, Gramsci was transferred to Milan. The journey lasted nineteen days, with the prisoners being transported—most of the time in chains—from prison to prison the length of the peninsula. After over a year in Milan, where he was kept in almost permanent isolation, punctuated only by the appearance of specially planted *agents provocateurs* to share his cell, and with no facilities for reading or writing other than of a limited number of personal letters, he was brought back to Rome to stand trial.

The trial, which began on 28 May 1928, was planned as a political showpiece. A special tribunal had been created to judge Gramsci, Terracini, Scoccimarro and twenty other defendants. The prisoners were accused of organising an armed insurrection. Legal arguments or evidence were largely irrelevant—the régime had decided that a conviction was necessary, to be followed by exemplary punishment. "For twenty years we must stop this brain from functioning", declared the Public Prosecutor, pointing to Gramsci. Sentence was passed on 4 June: twenty-two years for Terracini, who had been the main spokesman for the prisoners; twenty each for Gramsci, Scoccimarro and Roveda, and similarly severe sentences for the other defendants.

On 19 July, after another nightmare journey, Gramsci arrived at the prison of Turi, in the heel of Italy about twenty miles from Bari, in a state of near collapse from illness and exhaustion. This was to be his home for the next five and a half years, until his worsening health compelled a transfer to a prison clinic at Formia. It was here in Turi, from February 1929 onwards, that he set to work on his *Prison Notebooks*. Conditions in Turi were slightly better then they had been in Milan, if only because he was allowed to write and to receive books (if not as many as, or all those which, he would have wished), and because he had a limited contact with his fellow-prisoners. On the other hand, his health was worse and he must already have been preoccupied with the thought, however he might try to conceal it from himself, that he might not survive to the end of his prison term. To exacerbate his other sufferings, there were the unexplained silences of Julia, who spent much of these years in Moscow clinics with a series of nervous illnesses. However, Julia's elder sister Tatiana had settled in Italy, and was able to offer him some of the support which she knew that Julia was unable to give, and to send him regular news of Julia herself and their two children.

When Gramsci's strength permitted, he read voraciously, anything he was allowed to receive. Access to Marxist texts was restricted by prison censorship, and he was forced to supplement his reading of the originals by reference to commentaries and critiques. Many of the passages from Marx which occur in the philosophical and economic sections of the *Quaderni* coincide with those quoted by Benedetto Croce in his *Materialismo storico ed economia marxistica*. When he could not read books he read magazines and periodicals, thus keeping in touch with cultural developments while at the same time using his reading as material for a critique of bourgeois idiocy and of the confusion and backwardness of Italian intellectual life under fascism. He wrote copiously, filling his notebooks systematically in a small, crabbed and curiously precise hand, transcribing quotations and practising translations as well as developing his own thoughts.

He also wrote letters, to immediate friends and relations—to Tatiana, to Julia, to his children (the younger of whom was born after his arrest and whom he was never to see) and to his mother and sisters in Sardinia. These letters are an extraordinary document of human tenacity, and are justifiably reckoned one of the classics of modern Italian literature. Occasionally querulous, more often resigned, they rarely lapse into self-pity but instead are buoyed up constantly by an urgent desire to communicate information, ideas, projects or simply affection. Most striking of all is the sense they give of continuing perseverance in the face of deprivation and appalling physical suffering. Temperamentally introverted and inclined towards stoicism, Gramsci had little to rely on except force of will and the knowledge of belonging, even during this period of impotence and isolation, to a revolutionary movement. It was for this latter reason above all that, when in prison, he obstinately refused any privilege or special treatment that could possibly imply recognition of dependence on favours granted by the régime, but instead fought tooth and nail for his exact legal rights as a political prisoner.

The one moment in those prison years when we know that Gramsci both had some knowledge of political developments outside the prison (other than what he could obtain from the fascist press) and some possibility of political discussion was in the second half of 1930. In July, his brother Gennaro had visited him, and on Togliatti's instructions had informed him of the opposition of the "three" and their expulsion the month before. Gennaro reported to Togliatti that Gramsci had been in full agreement with the measures taken against the "three"; but years later in the sixties he told Fiori, Gramsci's biographer, that he had lied to save his brother from any possible condemnation by the party for "opportunism", and that in fact Gramsci had considered the opposition of the "three" to the left turn fully justified. This account tallies with the report sent to the party centre in 1933 by a communist who had been a fellow-prisoner of Gramsci's—Athos Lisa. According to Athos Lisa, violent discussions had arisen between the political prisoners in Turi—during their daily hour of exercise—after Gramsci had criticised the "left" turn, the policy of "frontal attack", and the elements of maximalism and underestimation of the strength of the fascist régime which it involved. The discussions had gone on for some time, with a majority of prisoners agreeing with Gramsci, and a minority, of whom Lisa was one, supporting the official line of the time. Among the themes outlined by Gramsci in the course of the discussion, according to Lisa, were the following: 1. the conception of the party as the organic intellectuals of the proletariat, indispensable if the latter is to win power; 2. the need for a military organisation capable of taking on the power of the bourgeois State—but a military organisation conceived of not in narrowly technical terms, but in essentially political ones; 3. the importance of the intermediate slogan of a "constituent assembly", as first a *means* of winning allies for the proletariat in its struggle against the ruling class, and subsequently as a *terrain* on which to struggle against "all projects of peaceful reform, demonstrating to the Italian working class how the only possible solution in Italy resides in the proletarian revolution"; 4. the need to replace the old Fifth World Congress slogan of the "worker and peasant government" by that of a "republic of worker and peasant soviets in Italy"; 5. the definition of fascism as a specific form of bourgeois reaction, characterised by the increasing predominance within it of finance capital, but whose origins are to be sought in certain specific features of Italian historical development—the absence of a genuine bourgeois revolution (implying not that a bourgeois revolution remained to be completed in Italy, but that fascism itself was the distorted Italian form of bourgeois revolution); the lack of class unity of the bourgeoisie; the weight of the Catholic Church—and whose immediate background was the "parallelism of forces" following the First World War, with both the fundamental classes, the bourgeoisie and the proletariat, too divided to defeat the other; 6. the existence of all the objective conditions for a conquest of power by the proletariat, but the imperative urgency—as a pre-condition for such a conquest of power—of realising the proletariat's hegemony over the peasantry.

It is therefore not surprising that Gramsci's letters from prison reveal a sense of isolation that was more than simply a physical one—but compounded terribly both by political preoccupations and by anxiety about Julia. Increasingly, Gramsci was forced back into himself. Much of the time, particularly towards the end of his stay in Turi, he was too ill even to read or write. Hunchbacked, sickly, having suffered at least three major breakdowns of his health even when he was free and able to enjoy medical attention and maintain a special diet, his years in prison were literally an eleven-year death-agony. His teeth fell out, his digestive system collapsed so that he could not eat solid food, his chronic insomnia became permanent so that he could go weeks without more than an hour or two of sleep at night; he had convulsions when he vomited blood, and suffered from headaches so violent that he beat his head against the walls of his cell. It is against this background that the achievement of the *Prison Notebooks* should be seen. When first arrested he had written to Tatiana: "I am obsessed by the idea that I ought to do something *für ewig* . . . I want, following a fixed plan, to devote myself intensively and systematically to some subject that will absorb me and give a focus to my inner life." His first concern was to resist, to find a means of reacting against the transformation of his existence that imprisonment entailed—the switch from participation in a collective enterprise to isolation and the danger of self-abandonment, from day-to-day struggle to a perspective that must needs be a long-term one, from the optimism of the will that is essential to any political activity to what must often during Gramsci's imprisonment have come very near to despair. The greatest danger for any political prisoner is that under the impact of his new situation the very reasons for his past struggle and his present plight will come to lose their validity for him. Gramsci once wrote—commenting on some lines of poetry by a certain Bini which said: "Prison is so finely-wrought a file, that, tempering one's thought, it makes of it a style"—"Was Bini really in prison? Perhaps not for long. Prison is so finely-wrought a file that it destroys thought utterly. It operates like the master craftsman who was given a fine trunk of seasoned olive wood with which to carve a statue of Saint Peter; he carved away, a piece here, a piece there, shaped the wood roughly, modified it, corrected it—and ended up with a handle for a cobbler's awl." Clearly, from the beginning of his imprisonment, Gramsci decided that his struggle was not ended. His most eloquent, and stark, vision of the new nature of that struggle is a note which he entitled "A Dialogue". "Something has changed, fundamentally. This is evident. What is it? Before, they all wanted to be the ploughmen of history, to play the active parts, each one of them to play an active part. Nobody wished to be the 'manure' of history. But is it possible to plough without first manuring the land? So ploughmen and 'manure' are both necessary. In the abstract, they all admitted it. But in practice? Manure for manure, as well draw back, return to the shadows, into obscurity. Now something has changed, since there are those who adapt themselves 'philosophically' to being 'manure', who know this is what they must be and adapt themselves. It is like the problem of the proverbial dying man. But there is a great difference, because at the point of death what is involved is a decisive action, of an instant's duration. Whereas in the case of the manure, the problem is a long-term one, and poses itself afresh at every moment. You only live once, as the saying goes; your own personality is irreplaceable. You are not faced abruptly with an instant's choice on which to gamble, a choice in which you have to evaluate the alternatives in a flash and cannot postpone your decision. Here postponement is continual, and your decision has continually to be renewed. This is why you can say that something has changed. There is not even the choice between living for a day as a lion, or a hundred years as a sheep. You don't live as a lion even for a minute, far from it: you live like something far lower than a sheep for years and years and know that you have to live like that. Image of Prometheus who, instead of being attacked by the eagle, is devoured by parasites. The Hebrews produced the image of Job. Only the Greeks could have imagined Prometheus, but the Hebrews were more realistic, more pitiless, and their hero more true to life."

As news of Gramsci's condition filtered through to the outside world, an international campaign was mounted in anti-fascist circles to demand his release. The campaign, organised notably by Piero Sraffa, a long-standing friend of Gramsci's now living in England, was at least partially successful. At the end of 1933, Gramsci was transferred from Turi to a clinic at Formia, a small town midway between Rome and Naples. The transfer was an urgent medical necessity. In the last year at Turi illnesses had taken grip of his entire organism, and he was slowly but inexorably being killed by lack of medical attention. At Formia he began gradually to recover somewhat, and was able to resume work on the notebooks. Despite his perilous condition, however, and in contravention of the fascist penal code itself, he was still held as a prisoner; his room had been specially converted as a prison cell, and he was harassed by brutal supervision.

The transfer to Formia had, in any case, come too late to save him. Renewed international pressure ensured that he was at least granted provisional liberty, in accordance with his constitutional rights, although in point of fact this meant no more than that the bars were removed from his window and that he was allowed to go for walks. Eventually, in August 1935, he was moved to a proper clinic, the "Quisisana" in Rome. He was now suffering from arterio-sclerosis, from a tubercular infection of the back known as Potts disease and from pulmonary tuberculosis, and was subject to high blood-pressure, angina, gout and acute gastric disorders. His prison sentence, less remissions, was due to expire on 21 April 1937, after which, if his health permitted, he hoped to retire to Sardinia for convalescence. But when the time came he was too ill to move from the clinic, and on 27 April he died. Tatiana, while making the funeral arrangements, managed to smuggle the thirty-three notebooks out of Gramsci's room and via the diplomatic bag to Moscow. They had been "the focus to my inner life", and the continuation in Gramsci's prison cell of his life as a revolutionary.

* * *

Some apology is perhaps needed for the unbalanced and schematic character of this introduction, and for its inevitable lacunae. We decided from the outset that there should be no attempt to offer any general interpretation of Gramsci's *Prison Notebooks* themselves, or any attempt to discuss the significance of his thought within Marxism as a whole. Gramsci has perhaps suffered more than any Marxist writer since Lenin from partial and partisan interpretation, both by supporters and opponents; the *Prison Notebooks* themselves, read seriously and in all their complexity, are the best antidote to this. We also felt that, given limited space, we should avoid duplicating what already exists in English—notably the biographies of Fiori and Cammett. Other gaps—particularly a fuller account of the economic, political and social conflicts in Italy in the early twenties, and of the part played in them by anti-fascist forces other than the P.C.I.—will be filled when a selection of Gramsci's early writings is published. We felt that it was indispensable to give priority to the central political experience of Gramsci's life as a revolutionary—to the class struggle in Turin, to the formation of the Italian Communist Party, to the rise and consolidation of fascism, to the strategic debates which took place in the P.C.I. and in the Comintern in those years. It is this central political experience, of course, that Gramsci was least able to write openly about in prison, with the result that those passages of the Notebooks where he discusses fascism, or communist strategy, are necessarily opaque and allusive. In order to have a basis from which to interpret these passages, it is essential to understand the political experience upon which the *Prison Notebooks* are a comment and of which they are the fruit. In a more general sense, too, the entire intellectual enterprise represented by the Notebooks can only be evaluated in relation to Gramsci's prior political experience; and only a grasp of that experience makes it possible to distinguish between the development and the critical reappraisal of earlier views.

We have tried to convey something of the calibre of the leaders of the P.C.I. in its first years, a calibre perhaps unmatched in any other of the Third International parties at the time. We have tried to show that none of them had a monopoly of correct positions; indeed, how could they have, when the party was formed *after* the defeat of the revolutionary upsurge which followed the October Revolution and the World War, and when its foundation was followed within two years by the fascist seizure of power—so that its experience was in fact one of long and bitterly fought defensive action, against overwhelming odds? We have tried to show that Tasca had a more realistic appreciation than either the Left or the Centre of the full significance of fascism, and that Bordiga had a fuller and earlier awareness than either the Centre or the Right of the implications for individual communist parties of events in Russia and in the International generally. We have also tried to show how Gramsci, in the brief period in which he led the P.C.I., successfully combated the maximalism, sectarianism and economism of Bordiga and the pessimism, "liquidationism" and culturalism of Tasca, while seeking to develop a genuinely Leninist political practice —both in terms of intra-party norms and of responsiveness to the spontaneous activity of the masses. Both Bordiga and Tasca failed to understand the dialectical relation between vanguard party and mass spontaneity: Bordiga saw the party as an élite which must above all guard itself against any contamination of its "pure" principles. Tasca, on the other hand, never understood the qualitative difference between the Leninist party and the parties of the Second International. Moreover, both were united in their suspicion of the factory councils in 1919–20. Gramsci's strategy, in contrast, turned entirely on the creation of autonomous class organisations of the proletariat and peasantry—in continuity with the conceptions of *Ordine Nuovo*, but now in dialectical relation with a vanguard party which alone could organise the taking of power and fight for revolution within the class organisms. This is the background against which the *Prison Notebooks* must be read.

I

PROBLEMS OF HISTORY AND CULTURE

I
THE INTELLECTUALS

INTRODUCTION

The central argument of Gramsci's essay on the formation of the intellectuals is simple. The notion of "the intellectuals" as a distinct social category independent of class is a myth. All men are potentially intellectuals in the sense of having an intellect and using it, but not all are intellectuals by social function. Intellectuals in the functional sense fall into two groups. In the first place there are the "traditional" professional intellectuals, literary, scientific and so on, whose position in the interstices of society has a certain inter-class aura about it but derives ultimately from past and present class relations and conceals an attachment to various historical class formations. Secondly, there are the "organic" intellectuals, the thinking and organising element of a particular fundamental social class. These organic intellectuals are distinguished less by their profession, which may be any job characteristic of their class, than by their function in directing the ideas and aspirations of the class to which they organically belong.

The implications of this highly original schema bear on all aspects of Gramsci's thought. Philosophically they connect with the proposition (p. 323) that "all men are philosophers" and with Gramsci's whole discussion of the dissemination of philosophical ideas and of ideology within a given culture. They relate to Gramsci's ideas on Education (pp. 26–43) in their stress on the democratic character of the intellectual function, but also on the class character of the formation of intellectuals through school. They also underlie his study of history and particularly of the *Risorgimento*, in that the intellectuals, in the wide sense of the word, are seen by Gramsci as performing an essential mediating function in the struggle of class forces.

Most important of all, perhaps, are the implications for the political struggle. Social Democracy, following Kautsky, has tended to see the relationship between workers and intellectuals in the Socialist movement in formal and mechanistic terms, with the intellectuals—refugees from the bourgeois class—providing theory and ideology (and often leadership) for a mass base of non-intellectuals, i.e. workers. This division of labour within the movement was vigorously contested by Lenin, who declares, in *What is to be Done*, that in the revolutionary party "all distinctions as between workers and intellectuals . . . must be obliterated". Lenin's attitude to the problem of the intellectuals is closely connected with his theory of the vanguard party, and when he writes about the need for socialist consciousness to be brought to the working class from outside, the agency he foresees for carrying this out is not the traditional intelligentsia but the revolutionary party itself, in which former workers and former professional intellectuals of bourgeois origin have been fused into a single cohesive unit. Gramsci develops this Leninist schema in a new way, relating it to the problems of the working class as a whole. The working class, like the bourgeoisie before it, is capable of developing from within its ranks its own organic intellectuals, and the function of the political party, whether mass or vanguard, is that of channelling the activity of these organic intellectuals and providing a link between the class and certain sections of the traditional intelligentsia. The organic intellectuals of the working class are defined on the one hand by their role in production and in the organisation of work and on the other by their "directive" political role, focused on the Party. It is through this assumption of conscious responsibility, aided by absorption of ideas and personnel from the more advanced bourgeois intellectual strata, that the proletariat can escape from defensive corporatism and economism and advance towards hegemony.

THE INTELLECTUALS

THE FORMATION OF THE INTELLECTUALS

Are intellectuals an autonomous and independent social group, or does every social group have its own particular specialised category of intellectuals? The problem is a complex one, because of the variety of forms assumed to date by the real historical process of formation of the different categories of intellectuals.

The most important of these forms are two:

1. Every social group, coming into existence on the original terrain of an essential function in the world of economic production, creates together with itself, organically, one or more strata[1] of intellectuals which give it homogeneity and an awareness of its own function not only in the economic but also in the social and political fields. The capitalist entrepreneur creates alongside himself the industrial technician, the specialist in political economy, the organisers of a new culture, of a new legal system, etc. It should be noted that the entrepreneur himself represents a higher level of social elaboration, already characterised by a certain directive [*dirigente*][2] and technical (i.e. intellectual) capacity: he must have a certain technical capacity, not only in the limited sphere of his activity and initiative but in other spheres as well, at least in those which are closest to economic production. He must be an organiser of masses of men; he must be an organiser of the "confidence" of investors in his business, of the customers for his product, etc.

If not all entrepreneurs, at least an *élite* amongst them must have the capacity to be an organiser of society in general, including all its complex organism of services, right up to the state organism, because of the need to create the conditions most favourable to the

---

[1] The Italian word here is "*ceti*" which does not carry quite the same connotations as "strata", but which we have been forced to translate in that way for lack of alternatives. It should be noted that Gramsci tends, for reasons of censorship, to avoid using the word class in contexts where its Marxist overtones would be apparent, preferring (as for example in this sentence) the more neutral "social group". The word "group", however, is not always a euphemism for "class", and to avoid ambiguity Gramsci uses the phrase "fundamental social group" when he wishes to emphasise the fact that he is referring to one or other of the major social classes (bourgeoisie, proletariat) defined in strict Marxist terms by its position in the fundamental relations of production. Class groupings which do not have this fundamental role are often described as "castes" (aristocracy, etc.). The word "category", on the other hand, which also occurs on this page, Gramsci tends to use in the standard Italian sense of members of a trade or profession, though also more generally. Throughout this edition we have rendered Gramsci's usage as literally as possible (see note on Gramsci's Terminology, p. xiii).

[2] See note on Gramsci's Terminology.

expansion of their own class; or at the least they must possess the capacity to choose the deputies (specialised employees) to whom to entrust this activity of organising the general system of relationships external to the business itself. It can be observed that the "organic" intellectuals which every new class creates alongside itself and elaborates in the course of its development, are for the most part "specialisations" of partial aspects of the primitive activity of the new social type which the new class has brought into prominence.*

Even feudal lords were possessors of a particular technical capacity, military capacity, and it is precisely from the moment at which the aristocracy loses its monopoly of technico-military capacity that the crisis of feudalism begins. But the formation of intellectuals in the feudal world and in the preceding classical world is a question to be examined separately: this formation and elaboration follows ways and means which must be studied concretely. Thus it is to be noted that the mass of the peasantry, although it performs an essential function in the world of production, does not elaborate its own "organic" intellectuals, nor does it "assimilate" any stratum of "traditional" intellectuals, although it is from the peasantry that other social groups draw many of their intellectuals and a high proportion of traditional intellectuals are of peasant origin.[4]

2. However, every "essential" social group which emerges into history out of the preceding economic structure, and as an expression

---

* Mosca's *Elementi di Scienza Politica* (new expanded edition, 1923) are worth looking at in this connection. Mosca's so-called "political class"[3] is nothing other than the intellectual category of the dominant social group. Mosca's concept of "political class" can be connected with Pareto's concept of the *élite*, which is another attempt to interpret the historical phenomenon of the intellectuals and their function in the life of the state and of society. Mosca's book is an enormous hotch-potch, of a sociological and positivistic character, plus the tendentiousness of immediate politics which makes it less indigestible and livelier from a literary point of view.

[3] Usually translated in English as "ruling class", which is also the title of the English version of Mosca's *Elementi* (G. Mosca, *The Ruling Class*, New York 1939). Gaetano Mosca (1858–1941) was, together with Pareto and Michels, one of the major early Italian exponents of the theory of political *élites*. Although sympathetic to fascism, Mosca was basically a conservative, who saw the *élite* in rather more static terms than did some of his fellows.

[4] Notably in Southern Italy. See below, "The Different Position of Urban and Rural-type Intellectuals", pp. 14–23. Gramsci's general argument, here as elsewhere in the *Quaderni*, is that the person of peasant origin who becomes an "intellectual" (priest, lawyer, etc.) generally thereby ceases to be organically linked to his class of origin. One of the essential differences between, say, the Catholic Church and the revolutionary party of the working class lies in the fact that, ideally, the proletariat should be able to generate its own "organic" intellectuals within the class and who remain intellectuals *of* their class.

of a development of this structure, has found (at least in all of history up to the present) categories of intellectuals already in existence and which seemed indeed to represent an historical continuity uninterrupted even by the most complicated and radical changes in political and social forms.

The most typical of these categories of intellectuals is that of the ecclesiastics, who for a long time (for a whole phase of history, which is partly characterised by this very monopoly) held a monopoly of a number of important services: religious ideology, that is the philosophy and science of the age, together with schools, education, morality, justice, charity, good works, etc. The category of ecclesiastics can be considered the category of intellectuals organically bound to the landed aristocracy. It had equal status juridically with the aristocracy, with which it shared the exercise of feudal ownership of land, and the use of state privileges connected with property.* But the monopoly held by the ecclesiastics in the superstructural field** was not exercised without a struggle or without limitations, and hence there took place the birth, in various forms (to be gone into and studied concretely), of other categories, favoured and enabled to expand by the growing strength of the central power of the monarch, right up to absolutism. Thus we find the formation of the *noblesse de robe*, with its own privileges, a stratum of administrators, etc., scholars and scientists, theorists, non-ecclesiastical philosophers, etc.

Since these various categories of traditional intellectuals experience through an "*esprit de corps*" their uninterrupted historical continuity and their special qualification, they thus put themselves forward as autonomous and independent of the dominant social group. This self-assessment is not without consequences in the ideological and political field, consequences of wide-ranging import. The whole of

---

* For one category of these intellectuals, possibly the most important after the ecclesiastical for its prestige and the social function it performed in primitive societies, the category of *medical men* in the wide sense, that is all those who "struggle" or seem to struggle against death and disease, compare the *Storia della medicina* of Arturo Castiglioni. Note that there has been a connection between religion and medicine, and in certain areas there still is: hospitals in the hands of religious orders for certain organisational functions, apart from the fact that wherever the doctor appears, so does the priest (exorcism, various forms of assistance, etc.). Many great religious figures were and are conceived of as great "healers": the idea of miracles, up to the resurrection of the dead. Even in the case of kings the belief long survived that they could heal with the laying on of hands, etc.

** From this has come the general sense of "intellectual" or "specialist" of the word "*chierico*" (clerk, cleric) in many languages of romance origin or heavily influenced, through church Latin, by the romance languages, together with its correlative "*laico*" (lay, layman) in the sense of profane, non-specialist.

idealist philosophy can easily be connected with this position assumed by the social complex of intellectuals and can be defined as the expression of that social utopia by which the intellectuals think of themselves as "independent", autonomous, endowed with a character of their own, etc.

One should note however that if the Pope and the leading hierarchy of the Church consider themselves more linked to Christ and to the apostles than they are to senators Agnelli and Benni,[5] the same does not hold for Gentile and Croce, for example: Croce in particular feels himself closely linked to Aristotle and Plato, but he does not conceal, on the other hand, his links with senators Agnelli and Benni, and it is precisely here that one can discern the most significant character of Croce's philosophy.

What are the "maximum" limits of acceptance of the term "intellectual"? Can one find a unitary criterion to characterise equally all the diverse and disparate activities of intellectuals and to distinguish these at the same time and in an essential way from the activities of other social groupings? The most widespread error of method seems to me that of having looked for this criterion of distinction in the intrinsic nature of intellectual activities, rather than in the ensemble of the system of relations in which these activities (and therefore the intellectual groups who personify them) have their place within the general complex of social relations. Indeed the worker or proletarian, for example, is not specifically characterised by his manual or instrumental work, but by performing this work in specific conditions and in specific social relations (apart from the consideration that purely physical labour does not exist and that even Taylor's phrase of "trained gorilla"[6] is a metaphor to indicate a limit in a certain direction: in any physical work, even the most degraded and mechanical, there exists a minimum of technical qualification, that is, a minimum of creative intellectual activity.) And we have already observed that the entrepreneur, by virtue of his very function, must have to some degree a certain number of qualifications of an intellectual nature although his part in society is determined not by these, but by the general social relations which specifically characterise the position of the entrepreneur within industry.

---

[5] Heads of FIAT and Montecatini (Chemicals) respectively. For Agnelli, of whom Gramsci had direct experience during the *Ordine Nuovo* period, see note 11 on p. 286.

[6] For Frederick Taylor and his notion of the manual worker as a "trained gorilla", see Gramsci's essay *Americanism and Fordism*, pp. 277–318 of this volume.

All men are intellectuals, one could therefore say: but not all men have in society the function of intellectuals.*

When one distinguishes between intellectuals and non-intellectuals, one is referring in reality only to the immediate social function of the professional category of the intellectuals, that is, one has in mind the direction in which their specific professional activity is weighted, whether towards intellectual elaboration or towards muscular-nervous effort. This means that, although one can speak of intellectuals, one cannot speak of non-intellectuals, because non-intellectuals do not exist. But even the relationship between efforts of intellectual-cerebral elaboration and muscular-nervous effort is not always the same, so that there are varying degrees of specific intellectual activity. There is no human activity from which every form of intellectual participation can be excluded: *homo faber* cannot be separated from *homo sapiens*.[7] Each man, finally, outside his professional activity, carries on some form of intellectual activity, that is, he is a "philosopher", an artist, a man of taste, he participates in a particular conception of the world, has a conscious line of moral conduct, and therefore contributes to sustain a conception of the world or to modify it, that is, to bring into being new modes of thought.

The problem of creating a new stratum of intellectuals consists therefore in the critical elaboration of the intellectual activity that exists in everyone at a certain degree of development, modifying its relationship with the muscular-nervous effort towards a new equilibrium, and ensuring that the muscular-nervous effort itself, in so far as it is an element of a general practical activity, which is perpetually innovating the physical and social world, becomes the foundation of a new and integral conception of the world. The traditional and vulgarised type of the intellectual is given by the man of letters, the philosopher, the artist. Therefore journalists, who claim to be men of letters, philosophers, artists, also regard themselves as the "true" intellectuals. In the modern world, technical education, closely bound to industrial labour even at the most primitive and unqualified level, must form the basis of the new type of intellectual.

On this basis the weekly *Ordine Nuovo*[8] worked to develop certain

---

* Thus, because it can happen that everyone at some time fries a couple of eggs or sews up a tear in a jacket, we do not necessarily say that everyone is a cook or a tailor.

[7] i.e. Man the maker (or tool-bearer) and Man the thinker.

[8] The *Ordine Nuovo,* the magazine edited by Gramsci during his days as a

forms of new intellectualism and to determine its new concepts, and this was not the least of the reasons for its success, since such a conception corresponded to latent aspirations and conformed to the development of the real forms of life. The mode of being of the new intellectual can no longer consist in eloquence, which is an exterior and momentary mover of feelings and passions, but in active participation in practical life, as constructor, organiser, "permanent persuader" and not just a simple orator (but superior at the same time to the abstract mathematical spirit); from technique-as-work one proceeds to technique-as-science and to the humanistic conception of history, without which one remains "specialised" and does not become "directive"[9] (specialised and political).

Thus there are historically formed specialised categories for the exercise of the intellectual function. They are formed in connection with all social groups, but especially in connection with the more important, and they undergo more extensive and complex elaboration in connection with the dominant social group. One of the most important characteristics of any group that is developing towards dominance is its struggle to assimilate and to conquer "ideologically" the traditional intellectuals, but this assimilation and conquest is made quicker and more efficacious the more the group in question succeeds in simultaneously elaborating its own organic intellectuals.

The enormous development of activity and organisation of education in the broad sense in the societies that emerged from the medieval world is an index of the importance assumed in the modern world by intellectual functions and categories. Parallel with the attempt to deepen and to broaden the "intellectuality" of each individual, there has also been an attempt to multiply and narrow the various specialisations. This can be seen from educational institutions at all levels, up to and including the organisms that exist to promote so-called "high culture" in all fields of science and technology.

School is the instrument through which intellectuals of various levels are elaborated. The complexity of the intellectual function in different states can be measured objectively by the number and

---

militant in Turin, ran as a "weekly review of Socialist culture" in 1919 and 1920. See Introduction, pp. xxxv ff.

[9] "*Dirigente.*" This extremely condensed and elliptical sentence contains a number of key Gramscian ideas: on the possibility of proletarian cultural hegemony through domination of the work process, on the distinction between organic intellectuals of the working class and traditional intellectuals from outside, on the unity of theory and practice as a basic Marxist postulate, etc.

gradation of specialised schools: the more extensive the "area" covered by education and the more numerous the "vertical" "levels" of schooling, the more complex is the cultural world, the civilisation, of a particular state. A point of comparison can be found in the sphere of industrial technology: the industrialisation of a country can be measured by how well equipped it is in the production of machines with which to produce machines, and in the manufacture of ever more accurate instruments for making both machines and further instruments for making machines, etc. The country which is best equipped in the construction of instruments for experimental scientific laboratories and in the construction of instruments with which to test the first instruments, can be regarded as the most complex in the technical-industrial field, with the highest level of civilisation, etc. The same applies to the preparation of intellectuals and to the schools dedicated to this preparation; schools and institutes of high culture can be assimilated to each other. In this field also, quantity cannot be separated from quality. To the most refined technical-cultural specialisation there cannot but correspond the maximum possible diffusion of primary education and the maximum care taken to expand the middle grades numerically as much as possible. Naturally this need to provide the widest base possible for the selection and elaboration of the top intellectual qualifications—i.e. to give a democratic structure to high culture and top-level technology—is not without its disadvantages: it creates the possibility of vast crises of unemployment for the middle intellectual strata, and in all modern societies this actually takes place.

It is worth noting that the elaboration of intellectual strata in concrete reality does not take place on the terrain of abstract democracy but in accordance with very concrete traditional historical processes. Strata have grown up which traditionally "produce" intellectuals and these strata coincide with those which have specialised in "saving", i.e. the petty and middle landed bourgeoisie and certain strata of the petty and middle urban bourgeoisie. The varying distribution of different types of school (classical and professional)[10] over the "economic" territory and the varying aspirations of different categories within these strata determine, or give form to, the production of various branches of

---

[10] The Italian school system above compulsory level is based on a division between academic ("classical" and "scientific") education and vocational training for professional purposes. Technical and, at the academic level, "scientific" colleges tend to be concentrated in the Northern industrial areas.

intellectual specialisation. Thus in Italy the rural bourgeoisie produces in particular state functionaries and professional people, whereas the urban bourgeoisie produces technicians for industry. Consequently it is largely northern Italy which produces technicians and the South which produces functionaries and professional men.

The relationship between the intellectuals and the world of production is not as direct as it is with the fundamental social groups but is, in varying degrees, "mediated" by the whole fabric of society and by the complex of superstructures, of which the intellectuals are, precisely, the "functionaries". It should be possible both to measure the "organic quality" [*organicità*] of the various intellectual strata and their degree of connection with a fundamental social group, and to establish a gradation of their functions and of the superstructures from the bottom to the top (from the structural base upwards). What we can do, for the moment, is to fix two major superstructural "levels": the one that can be called "civil society", that is the ensemble of organisms commonly called "private", and that of "political society" or "the State". These two levels correspond on the one hand to the function of "hegemony" which the dominant group exercises throughout society and on the other hand to that of "direct domination" or command exercised through the State and "juridical" government. The functions in question are precisely organisational and connective. The intellectuals are the dominant group's "deputies" exercising the subaltern functions of social hegemony and political government. These comprise:

1. The "spontaneous" consent given by the great masses of the population to the general direction imposed on social life by the dominant fundamental group; this consent is "historically" caused by the prestige (and consequent confidence) which the dominant group enjoys because of its position and function in the world of production.

2. The apparatus of state coercive power which "legally" enforces discipline on those groups who do not "consent" either actively or passively. This apparatus is, however, constituted for the whole of society in anticipation of moments of crisis of command and direction when spontaneous consent has failed.

This way of posing the problem has as a result a considerable extension of the concept of intellectual, but it is the only way which enables one to reach a concrete approximation of reality. It also clashes with preconceptions of caste. The function of organising social hegemony and state domination certainly gives rise to a particular division of labour and therefore to a whole hierarchy of qualifications in some of which there is no apparent attribution of directive or organisational functions. For example, in the apparatus of social and state direction there exist a whole series of jobs of a manual and instrumental character (non-executive work, agents rather than officials or functionaries).[11] It is obvious that such a distinction has to be made just as it is obvious that other distinctions have to be made as well. Indeed, intellectual activity must also be distinguished in terms of its intrinsic characteristics, according to levels which in moments of extreme opposition represent a real qualitative difference—at the highest level would be the creators of the various sciences, philosophy, art, etc., at the lowest the most humble "administrators" and divulgators of pre-existing, traditional, accumulated intellectual wealth.*

In the modern world the category of intellectuals, understood in this sense, has undergone an unprecedented expansion. The democratic-bureaucratic system has given rise to a great mass of functions which are not all justified by the social necessities of production, though they are justified by the political necessities of the dominant fundamental group. Hence Loria's[13] conception of the unproductive "worker" (but unproductive in relation to whom and to what mode of production?), a conception which could in part be justified if one takes account of the fact that these masses exploit their position to take for themselves a large cut out of the national income. Mass formation has standardised individuals both psychologically and in terms of individual qualification and has produced the same phenomena as with other standardised masses: competition which makes necessary organisations for the defence of

---

[11] "*funzionari*": in Italian usage the word is applied to the middle and higher echelons of the bureaucracy. Conversely "administrators" ("*amministratori*") is used here (end of paragraph) to mean people who merely "administer" the decisions of others. The phrase "non-executive work" is a translation of "[*impiego*] *di ordine e non di concetto*" which refers to distinctions within clerical work.

* Here again military organisation offers a model of complex gradations between subaltern officers, senior officers and general staff, not to mention the NCO's, whose importance is greater than is generally admitted. It is worth observing that all these parts feel a solidarity and indeed that it is the lower strata that display the most blatant *esprit de corps*, from which they derive a certain "conceit"[12] which is apt to lay them open to jokes and witticisms.

[12] "*boria*". This is a reference to an idea of Vico (see note 41 on p. 151).

[13] For Loria see note 108 on p. 458. The notion of the "unproductive labourer" is not in fact an invention of Loria's but has its origins in Marx's definitions of productive and unproductive labour in *Capital*, which Loria, in his characteristic way, both vulgarised and claimed as his own discovery.

professions, unemployment, over-production in the schools, emigration, etc.

THE DIFFERENT POSITION OF URBAN AND RURAL-TYPE INTELLECTUALS

Intellectuals of the urban type have grown up along with industry and are linked to its fortunes. Their function can be compared to that of subaltern officers in the army. They have no autonomous initiative in elaborating plans for construction. Their job is to articulate the relationship between the entrepreneur and the instrumental mass and to carry out the immediate execution of the production plan decided by the industrial general staff, controlling the elementary stages of work. On the whole the average urban intellectuals are very standardised, while the top urban intellectuals are more and more identified with the industrial general staff itself.

Intellectuals of the rural type are for the most part "traditional", that is they are linked to the social mass of country people and the town (particularly small-town) petite bourgeoisie, not as yet elaborated and set in motion by the capitalist system. This type of intellectual brings into contact the peasant masses with the local and state administration (lawyers, notaries, etc.). Because of this activity they have an important politico-social function, since professional mediation is difficult to separate from political. Furthermore: in the countryside the intellectual (priest, lawyer, notary, teacher, doctor, etc.), has on the whole a higher or at least a different living standard from that of the average peasant and consequently represents a social model for the peasant to look to in his aspiration to escape from or improve his condition. The peasant always thinks that at least one of his sons could become an intellectual (especially a priest), thus becoming a gentleman and raising the social level of the family by facilitating its economic life through the connections which he is bound to acquire with the rest of the gentry. The peasant's attitude towards the intellectual is double and appears contradictory. He respects the social position of the intellectuals and in general that of state employees, but sometimes affects contempt for it, which means that his admiration is mingled with instinctive elements of envy and impassioned anger. One can understand nothing of the collective life of the peasantry and of the germs and ferments of development which exist within it, if one does not take into consideration and examine concretely and in depth this effective subordination to the intellectuals. Every organic development of the peasant masses, up to a certain point, is linked to and depends on movements among the intellectuals.

With the urban intellectuals it is another matter. Factory technicians do not exercise any political function over the instrumental masses, or at least this is a phase that has been superseded. Sometimes, rather, the contrary takes place, and the instrumental masses, at least in the person of their own organic intellectuals, exercise a political influence on the technicians.

The central point of the question remains the distinction between intellectuals as an organic category of every fundamental social group and intellectuals as a traditional category. From this distinction there flow a whole series of problems and possible questions for historical research.

The most interesting problem is that which, when studied from this point of view, relates to the modern political party, its real origins, its developments and the forms which it takes. What is the character of the political party in relation to the problem of the intellectuals? Some distinctions must be made:

1. The political party for some social groups is nothing other than their specific way of elaborating their own category of organic intellectuals directly in the political and philosophical field and not just in the field of productive technique. These intellectuals are formed in this way and cannot indeed be formed in any other way, given the general character and the conditions of formation, life and development of the social group.*

2. The political party, for all groups, is precisely the mechanism which carries out in civil society the same function as the State carries out, more synthetically and over a larger scale, in political society. In other words it is responsible for welding together the organic intellectuals of a given group—the dominant one—and the traditional intellectuals.[14] The party carries out this function in strict dependence on its basic function, which is that of elaborating its own component parts—those elements of a social group which

---

* Within productive technique those strata are formed which can be said to correspond to NCO's in the army, that is to say, for the town, skilled and specialised workers and, for the country (in a more complex fashion) share-cropping and tenant farmers—since in general terms these types of farmer correspond more or less to the type of the artisan, who is the skilled worker of a mediaeval economy.

[14] Although this passage is ostensibly concerned with the sociology of political parties in general, Gramsci is clearly particularly interested here in the theory of the revolutionary party and the role within it of the intellectuals. See Introduction to this Section.

has been born and developed as an "economic" group—and of turning them into qualified political intellectuals, leaders [*dirigenti*] and organisers of all the activities and functions inherent in the organic development of an integral society, both civil and political. Indeed it can be said that within its field the political party accomplishes its function more completely and organically than the State does within its admittedly far larger field. An intellectual who joins the political party of a particular social group is merged with the organic intellectuals of the group itself, and is linked tightly with the group. This takes place through participation in the life of the State only to a limited degree and often not at all. Indeed it happens that many intellectuals think that they *are* the State, a belief which, given the magnitude of the category, occasionally has important consequences and leads to unpleasant complications for the fundamental economic group which *really* is the State.

That all members of a political party should be regarded as intellectuals is an affirmation that can easily lend itself to mockery and caricature. But if one thinks about it nothing could be more exact. There are of course distinctions of level to be made. A party might have a greater or lesser proportion of members in the higher grades or in the lower, but this is not the point. What matters is the function, which is directive and organisational, i.e. educative, i.e. intellectual. A tradesman does not join a political party in order to do business, nor an industrialist in order to produce more at lower cost, nor a peasant to learn new methods of cultivation, even if some aspects of these demands of the tradesman, the industrialist or the peasant can find satisfaction in the party.*

For these purposes, within limits, there exists the professional association, in which the economic-corporate activity of the tradesman, industrialist or peasant is most suitably promoted. In the political party the elements of an economic social group get beyond that moment of their historical development and become agents of more general activities of a national and international character. This function of a political party should emerge even more clearly from a concrete historical analysis of how both organic and traditional categories of intellectuals have developed in the context of different national histories and in that of the development of the various major social groups within each nation, particularly those groups whose economic activity has been largely instrumental.

* Common opinion tends to oppose this, maintaining that the tradesman, industrialist or peasant who engages in "politicking" loses rather than gains, and is the worst type of all—which is debatable.

The formation of traditional intellectuals is the most interesting problem historically. It is undoubtedly connected with slavery in the classical world and with the position of freed men of Greek or Oriental origin in the social organisation of the Roman Empire.

Note. The change in the condition of the social position of the intellectuals in Rome between Republican and Imperial times (a change from an aristocratic-corporate to a democratic-bureaucratic régime) is due to Caesar, who granted citizenship to doctors and to masters of liberal arts so that they would be more willing to live in Rome and so that others should be persuaded to come there. ("*Omnesque medicinam Romae professos et liberalium artium doctores, quo libentius et ispi urbem incolerent et coeteri appeterent civitate donavit.*" Suetonius, *Life of Caesar*, XLII.) Caesar therefore proposed: 1. to establish in Rome those intellectuals who were already there, thus creating a permanent category of intellectuals, since without their permanent residence there no cultural organisation could be created; and 2. to attract to Rome the best intellectuals from all over the Roman Empire, thus promoting centralisation on a massive scale. In this way there came into being the category of "imperial" intellectuals in Rome which was to be continued by the Catholic clergy and to leave so many traces in the history of Italian intellectuals, such as their characteristic "cosmopolitanism", up to the eighteenth century.

This not only social but national and racial separation between large masses of intellectuals and the dominant class of the Roman Empire is repeated after the fall of the Empire in the division between Germanic warriors and intellectuals of romanised origin, successors of the category of freedmen. Interweaved with this phenomenon are the birth and development of Catholicism and of the ecclesiastical organisation which for many centuries absorbs the major part of intellectual activities and exercises a monopoly of cultural direction with penal sanctions against anyone who attempted to oppose or even evade the monopoly. In Italy we can observe the phenomenon, whose intensity varies from period to period, of the cosmopolitan function of the intellectuals of the peninsula. I shall now turn to the differences which are instantly apparent in the development of the intellectuals in a number of the more important countries, with the proviso that these observations require to be controlled and examined in more depth.

As far as Italy is concerned the central fact is precisely the international or cosmopolitan function of its intellectuals, which is both cause and effect of the state of disintegration in which the peninsula remained from the fall of the Roman Empire up to 1870.

France offers the example of an accomplished form of harmonious development of the energies of the nation and of the intellectual categories in particular. When in 1789 a new social grouping makes its political appearance on the historical stage, it is already completely equipped for all its social functions and can therefore struggle for total dominion of the nation. It does not have to make any essential compromises with the old classes but instead can subordinate them to its own ends. The first intellectual cells of the new type are born along with their first economic counterparts. Even ecclesiastical organisation is influenced (gallicanism, precocious struggles between Church and State). This massive intellectual construction explains the function of culture in France in the eighteenth and nineteenth centuries. It was a function of international and cosmopolitan outward radiation and of imperialistic and hegemonic expansion in an organic fashion, very different therefore from the Italian experience, which was founded on scattered personal migration and did not react on the national base to potentiate it but on the contrary contributed to rendering the constitution of a solid national base impossible.

In England the development is very different from France. The new social grouping that grew up on the basis of modern industrialism shows a remarkable economic-corporate development but advances only gropingly in the intellectual-political field. There is a very extensive category of organic intellectuals—those, that is, who come into existence on the same industrial terrain as the economic group—but in the higher sphere we find that the old land-owning class preserves its position of virtual monopoly. It loses its economic supremacy but maintains for a long time a politico-intellectual supremacy and is assimilated as "traditional intellectuals" and as directive [*dirigente*] group by the new group in power. The old land-owning aristocracy is joined to the industrialists by a kind of suture which is precisely that which in other countries unites the traditional intellectuals with the new dominant classes.

The English phenomenon appears also in Germany, but complicated by other historical and traditional elements. Germany, like Italy, was the seat of an universalistic and supranational institution and ideology, the Holy Roman Empire of the German Nation, and provided a certain number of personnel for the mediaeval cosmopolis, impoverishing its own internal energies and arousing struggles which distracted from problems of national organisation and perpetuated the territorial disintegration of the Middle Ages. Industrial development took place within a semi-feudal integument that persisted up to November 1918, and the *Junkers* preserved a politico-intellectual supremacy considerably greater even than that of the corresponding group in England. They were the traditional intellectuals of the German industrialists, but retained special privileges and a strong consciousness of being an independent social group, based on the fact that they held considerable economic power over the land, which was more "productive"[15] than in England. The Prussian *Junkers* resemble a priestly-military caste, with a virtual monopoly of directive-organisational functions in political society, but possessing at the same time an economic base of its own and so not exclusively dependent on the liberality of the dominant economic group. Furthermore, unlike the English landowning aristocracy, the *Junkers* constituted the officer class of a large standing army, which gave them solid organisational cadres favouring the preservation of an *esprit de corps* and of their political monopoly.*

In Russia various features: the political and economico-commercial organisation was created by the Norman (Varangians), and religious organisation by the Byzantine Greeks. In a later period the Germans and the French brought to Russia the European experience and gave a first consistent skeleton to the protoplasm of Russian history. National forces were inert, passive and receptive, but perhaps precisely for this reason they assimilated completely the foreign influences and the foreigners themselves, Russifying them. In the more recent historical period we find the opposite phenomenon. An *élite* consisting of some of the most active, energetic, enterprising and disciplined members of the society emigrates abroad and assimilates the culture and historical experiences of the most advanced

---

[15] Gramsci is probably using the word "productive" here in the specifically Marxian sense of productive of surplus value or at any rate of surplus.

* In Max Weber's book, *Parliament and Government in the New Order in Germany*[16] can be found a number of elements to show how the political monopoly of the nobility impeded the elaboration of an extensive and experienced bourgeois political personnel and how it is at the root of the continual parliamentary crises and of the fragmentation of the liberal and democratic parties. Hence the importance of the Catholic centre and of Social democracy, which succeeded during the period of the Empire[17] in building up to a considerable extent their own parliamentary and directive strata, etc.

[16] Max Weber, *Parlament und Regierung im neugeordnetem Deutschland*. English translation in *From Max Weber: Essays in Sociology*, ed. H. H. Gerth and C. Wright Mills.

[17] i.e. up to the formation of the Weimar Republic in 1919.

countries of the West, without however losing the most essential characteristics of its own nationality, that is to say without breaking its sentimental and historical links with its own people. Having thus performed its intellectual apprenticeship it returns to its own country and compels the people to an enforced awakening, skipping historical stages in the process. The difference between this *élite* and that imported from Germany (by Peter the Great, for example) lies in its essentially national-popular character. It could not be assimilated by the inert passivity of the Russian people, because it was itself an energetic reaction of Russia to her own historical inertia.

On another terrain, and in very different conditions of time and place, the Russian phenomenon can be compared to the birth of the American nation (in the United States). The Anglo-Saxon immigrants are themselves an intellectual, but more especially a moral, *élite*. I am talking, naturally, of the first immigrants, the pioneers, protagonists of the political and religious struggles in England, defeated but not humiliated or laid low in their country of origin. They import into America, together with themselves, apart from moral energy and energy of the will, a certain level of civilisation, a certain stage of European historical evolution, which, when transplanted by such men into the virgin soil of America, continues to develop the forces implicit in its nature but with an incomparably more rapid rhythm than in Old Europe, where there exists a whole series of checks (moral, intellectual, political, economic, incorporated in specific sections of the population, relics of past régimes which refuse to die out) which generate opposition to speedy progress and give to every initiative the equilibrium of mediocrity, diluting it in time and in space.

One can note, in the case of the United States, the absence to a considerable degree of traditional intellectuals, and consequently a different equilibrium among the intellectuals in general. There has been a massive development, on top of an industrial base, of the whole range of modern superstructures. The necessity of an equilibrium is determined, not by the need to fuse together the organic intellectuals with the traditional, but by the need to fuse together in a single national crucible with a unitary culture the different forms of culture imported by immigrants of differing national origins. The lack of a vast sedimentation of traditional intellectuals such as one finds in countries of ancient civilisation explains, at least in part, both the existence of only two major political parties, which could in fact easily be reduced to one only (contrast this with the case of France, and not only in the post-war period when the multiplication of parties became a general phenomenon), and at the opposite extreme the enormous proliferation of religious sects.*

One further phenomenon in the United States is worth studying, and that is the formation of a surprising number of negro intellectuals who absorb American culture and technology. It is worth bearing in mind the indirect influence that these negro intellectuals could exercise on the backward masses in Africa, and indeed direct influence if one or other of these hypotheses were ever to be verified: 1. that American expansionism should use American negroes as its agents in the conquest of the African market and the extension of American civilisation (something of the kind has already happened, but I don't know to what extent); 2. that the struggle for the unification of the American people should intensify in such a way as to provoke a negro exodus and the return to Africa of the most independent and energetic intellectual elements, the ones, in other words, who would be least inclined to submit to some possible future legislation that was even more humiliating than are the present widespread social customs. This development would give rise to two fundamental questions: 1. linguistic: whether English could become the educated language of Africa, bringing unity in the place of the existing swarm of dialects? 2. whether this intellectual stratum could have sufficient assimilating and organising capacity to give a "national" character to the present primitive sentiment of being a despised race, thus giving the African continent a mythic function as the common fatherland of all the negro peoples? It seems to me that, for the moment, American negroes have a national and racial spirit which is negative rather than positive, one which is a product of the struggle carried on by the whites in order to isolate and depress them. But was not this the case with the Jews up to and throughout the eighteenth century? Liberia, already Americanised and with English as its official language, could become the Zion of American negroes, with a tendency to set itself up as an African Piedmont.[18]

In considering the question of the intellectuals in Central and South America, one should, I think, bear in mind certain funda-

---

* More than two hundred of these have, I think, been counted. Again one should compare the case of France and the fierce struggles that went on to maintain the religious and moral unity of the French people.

[18] The reference here is to the role of leadership among the Italian States assumed by Piedmont during the Risorgimento. For Gramsci's analysis of this phenomenon, see "The Function of Piedmont", pp. 104–106.

mental conditions. No vast category of traditional intellectuals exists in Central or South America either, but the question does not present itself in the same terms as with the United States. What in fact we find at the root of development of these countries are the patterns of Spanish and Portuguese civilisation of the sixteenth and seventeenth century, characterised by the effects of the Counter Reformation and by military parasitism. The change-resistant crystallisations which survive to this day in these countries are the clergy and a military caste, two categories of traditional intellectuals fossilised in a form inherited from the European mother country. The industrial base is very restricted, and has not developed complicated superstructures. The majority of intellectuals are of the rural type, and, since the latifundium is dominant, with a lot of property in the hands of the Church, these intellectuals are linked with the clergy and the big landowners. National composition is very unbalanced even among the white population and is further complicated by the great masses of Indians who in some countries form the majority of the inhabitants. It can be said that in these regions of the American continent there still exists a situation of the *Kulturkampf* and of the Dreyfus trial,[19] that is to say a situation in which the secular and bourgeois element has not yet reached the stage of being able to subordinate clerical and militaristic influence and interests to the secular politics of the modern State. It thus comes about that Free Masonry and forms of cultural organisation like the "positivist Church" are very influential in the opposition to Jesuitism. Most recent events (November 1930), from the *Kulturkampf* of Calles in Mexico[20] to the military-popular insurrections in Argentina, Brazil, Peru, Chile and Bolivia, demonstrate the accuracy of these observations.

Further types of formation of the categories of intellectuals and of their relationship with national forces can be found in India, China and Japan. In Japan we have a formation of the English

---

[19] "*Kulturkampf*" was the name given to the struggle waged by Bismarck, in the 1870s, with Liberal support, against Catholic opposition to Prussian hegemony. The Dreyfus case in France, which lasted from Dreyfus' first condemnation in 1894 to his final acquittal in 1906, coincided with a major battle fully to laicise the French educational system and had the effect of polarising French society into a militaristic, pro-Catholic, anti-Semitic Right, and an anti-Catholic Liberal and Socialist Left. Both *Kulturkampf* and Dreyfus case can also be seen as aspects of the bourgeois-democratic struggle against the residues of reactionary social forces.

[20] Plutarco Elias Calles was President of Mexico from 1924–28. It was under his Presidency that the religious and educational provisions of the new constitution were carried through, against violent Catholic opposition.

and German type, that is an industrial civilisation that develops within a feudal-bureaucratic integument with unmistakable features of its own.

In China there is the phenomenon of the script, an expression of the complete separation between the intellectuals and the people. In both India and China the enormous gap separating intellectuals and pcople is manifested also in the religious field. The problem of different beliefs and of different ways of conceiving and practising the same religion among the various strata of society, but particularly as between clergy, intellectuals and people, needs to be studied in general, since it occurs everywhere to a certain degree; but it is in the countries of East Asia that it reaches its most extreme form. In Protestant countries the difference is relatively slight (the proliferation of sects is connected with the need for a perfect suture between intellectuals and people, with the result that all the crudity of the effective conceptions of the popular masses is reproduced in the higher organisational sphere). It is more noteworthy in Catholic countries, but its extent varies. It is less in the Catholic parts of Germany and in France; rather greater in Italy, particularly in the South and in the islands; and very great indeed in the Iberian peninsula and in the countries of Latin America. The phenomenon increases in scale in the Orthodox countries where it becomes necessary to speak of three degrees of the same religion: that of the higher clergy and the monks, that of the secular clergy and that of the people. It reaches a level of absurdity in East Asia, where the religion of the people often has nothing whatever to do with that of books, although the two are called by the same name.

2
ON EDUCATION

INTRODUCTION

In 1923 the Mussolini government put through the first major reform of Italian education since the unification of the country sixty years earlier and the adoption of the Piedmontese educational system, as laid down by the Casati Act of 1859. The reform was drafted by, and named after, the idealist philosopher Giovanni Gentile, who was Mussolini's Minister of Education; but its main lines had in fact been worked out by Croce, who had held the same post in the Giolitti government of 1921. In the first decades of this century, Gentile and Croce had developed a wide-ranging critique of the existing school system, stigmatising it as "instruction" not "education", and as narrow, formal and sterile. They particularly attacked the learning by heart of Latin grammar and of philosophy and literature manuals. The watchwords of the Gentile reform were "educativity" and "active education", and Gramsci's object in his writing on education was in part to expose the rhetorical character of these slogans, and to show the practice which lay behind them.

Gramsci's preoccupations in his writing on education are still at the centre of educational debate today: the relations between education and class; vocationalism; the ideology of education; the "comprehensive" school. Moreover, the positions which emerge from his criticisms of the Gentile reform should be seen in the light of his personal situation. The apparently "conservative" eulogy of the old curriculum in fact often represents a device which allowed Gramsci to circumvent the prison censor, by disguising the future (ideal system) as the past in order to criticise the present. In a different way, Gramsci's insistence on the values of discipline and work in education must also be seen in terms of his own history. He was far from being hostile to the Rousseauesque tradition in education, though he was critical of it. His attitude is best suggested in his comment: "The active school is still in its romantic phase, in which the elements of struggle against the mechanical and Jesuitical school have become unhealthily exaggerated—through a desire to distinguish themselves sharply from the latter and for polemical reasons. It is necessary to enter the 'classical', rational phase, and to find in the ends to be attained the natural source for developing the appropriate methods and forms." But born into a backward peasant environment and deprived of either an adequate or a continuous education, Gramsci's success in school and university despite constant ill-health, under-nourishment and over-work was a triumph of intellectual purpose. Something of his individual experience is thus carried over into his repeated emphasis on learning as work. (Just as his childhood experience led him to value so highly an education which combated "folklore" and "magic".)

The relation between autobiography and sociological reflection in Gramsci's thought is, however, more intimate and complex even than this would suggest. For, as the last sentence of the second of these notes shows, it is with the creation of intellectuals from the working class that he is ultimately concerned, and his life was precisely the history of the formation of such an intellectual. In perhaps the key passage of his analysis, he wrote: "It was right to struggle against the old school, but reforming it was not so simple as it seemed. The problem was not one of model curricula but of men, and not just of the men who are actually teachers themselves but of the entire social complex which they express." This judgement sums up the whole dialectical character of education which it was the object of the preceding notes to suggest. The reference to the future, creating intellectuals from the working class, is fundamental to Gramsci's thought. It is the revolutionary perspective which structures his whole analysis. In the last resort, the work involved in education which Gramsci emphasises so much is at one and the same time the work by means of which he personally transcended his environment and the work required in the forging of a revolutionary party of the working class—the latter's "organic intellectuals".

ON EDUCATION

THE ORGANISATION OF EDUCATION AND OF CULTURE

It may be observed in general that in modern civilisation all practical activities have become so complex, and the sciences[1] so interwoven with everyday life, that each practical activity tends to create a new type of school for its own executives and specialists and hence to create a body of specialist intellectuals at a higher level to teach in these schools. Thus, side by side with the type of school which may be called "humanistic"—the oldest form of traditional school, designed to develop in each individual human being an as yet undifferentiated general culture, the fundamental power to think and ability to find one's way in life—a whole system of specialised schools, at varying levels, has been being created to serve entire professional sectors, or professions which are already specialised and defined within precise boundaries. It may be said, indeed, that the educational crisis raging today is precisely linked to the fact that this process of differentiation and particularisation is taking place chaotically, without clear and precise principles, without a well-studied and consciously established plan. The crisis of the curriculum and organisation of the schools, i.e. of the overall framework of a policy for forming modern intellectual cadres, is to a great extent an aspect and a ramification of the more comprehensive and general organic crisis.

The fundamental division into classical and vocational (professional) schools was a rational formula: the vocational school for the instrumental classes,[2] the classical school for the dominant classes and the intellectuals. The development of an industrial base both in the cities and in the countryside meant a growing need for the new type of urban intellectual. Side by side with the classical school there developed the technical school (vocational, but not manual), and this placed a question-mark over the very principle of a concrete programme of general culture, a humanistic programme of general culture based on the Græco-Roman tradition. This programme, once questioned, can be said to be doomed,

[1] "Sciences" in the sense of branches of human knowledge, rather than in the more restricted meaning which the word has taken on since the industrial revolution.

[2] *Classi strumentali* is a term used by Gramsci interchangeably with the terms *classi subalterne* or *classi subordinate*, and there seems no alternative to a literal translation of each which leaves the reader free to decide whether there is any different nuance of stress between them. See too the final paragraph of "History of the Subaltern Classes" on pp. 52–5 below.

since its formative capacity was to a great extent based on the general and traditionally unquestioned prestige of a particular form of civilisation.

The tendency today is to abolish every type of schooling that is "disinterested" (not serving immediate interests) or "formative"—keeping at most only a small-scale version to serve a tiny élite of ladies and gentlemen who do not have to worry about assuring themselves of a future career. Instead, there is a steady growth of specialised vocational schools, in which the pupil's destiny and future activity are determined in advance. A rational solution to the crisis ought to adopt the following lines. First, a common basic education, imparting a general, humanistic, formative culture; this would strike the right balance between development of the capacity for working manually (technically, industrially) and development of the capacities required for intellectual work. From this type of common schooling, via repeated experiments in vocational orientation, pupils would pass on to one of the specialised schools or to productive work.

One must bear in mind the developing tendency for every practical activity to create for itself its own specialised school, just as every intellectual activity tends to create for itself cultural associations of its own; the latter take on the function of post-scholastic institutions, specialised in organising the conditions in which it is possible to keep abreast of whatever progress is being made in the given scientific field.

It may also be observed that deliberative bodies tend to an ever-increasing extent to distinguish their activity into two "organic" aspects: into the deliberative activity which is their essence, and into technical-cultural activity in which the questions upon which they have to take decisions are first examined by experts and analysed scientifically. This latter activity has already created a whole bureaucratic body, with a new structure; for apart from the specialised departments of experts who prepare the technical material for the deliberative bodies, a second body of functionaries is created—more or less disinterested "volunteers", selected variously from industry, from the banks, from finance houses. This is one of the mechanisms by means of which the career bureaucracy eventually came to control the democratic regimes and parliaments; now the mechanism is being organically extended, and is absorbing into its sphere the great specialists of private enterprise, which thus comes to control both régimes and bureaucracies. What is involved is a necessary, organic development which tends to integrate the personnel specialised in the technique of politics with personnel specialised in the concrete problems of administering the essential practical activities of the great and complex national societies of today. Hence every attempt to exorcise these tendencies from the outside produces no result other than moralistic sermons and rhetorical lamentations.

The question is thus raised of modifying the training of technical-political personnel, completing their culture in accordance with the new necessities, and of creating specialised functionaries of a new kind, who as a body will complement deliberative activity. The traditional type of political "leader", prepared only for formal-juridical activities, is becoming anachronistic and represents a danger for the life of the State: the leader must have that minimum of general technical culture which will permit him, if not to "create" autonomously the correct solution, at least to know how to adjudicate between the solutions put forward by the experts, and hence to choose the correct one from the "synthetic" viewpoint of political technique.

A type of deliberative body which seeks to incorporate the technical expertise necessary for it to operate realistically has been described elsewhere,[3] in an account of what happens on the editorial committees of some reviews, when these function at the same time both as editorial committees and as cultural groups. The group criticises as a body, and thus helps to define the tasks of the individual editors, whose activity is organised according to a plan and a division of labour which are rationally arranged in advance. By means of collective discussion and criticism (made up of suggestions, advice, comments on method, and criticism which is constructive and aimed at mutual education) in which each individual functions as a specialist in his own field and helps to complete the expertise of the collectivity, the average level of the individual editors is in fact successfully raised so that it reaches the altitude or capacity of the most highly-skilled—thus not merely ensuring an ever more select and organic collaboration for the review, but also creating the conditions for the emergence of a homogeneous group of intellectuals, trained to produce a regular and methodical "writing" activity (not only in terms of occasional publications or short articles, but also of organic, synthetic studies).

Undoubtedly, in this kind of collective activity, each task produces new capacities and possibilities of work, since it creates ever

---

[3] Int., pp. 137 ff.

more organic conditions of work: files, bibliographical digests, a library of basic specialised works, etc. Such activity requires an unyielding struggle against habits of dilettantism, of improvisation, of "rhetorical" solutions or those proposed for effect. The work has to be done particularly in written form, just as it is in written form that criticisms have to be made—in the form of terse, succinct notes: this can be achieved if the material is distributed in time, etc.; the writing down of notes and criticisms is a didactic principle rendered necessary by the need to combat the habits formed in public speaking—prolixity, demagogy and paralogism. This type of intellectual work is necessary in order to impart to autodidacts the discipline in study which an orthodox scholastic career provides, in order to Taylorise[4] intellectual work. Hence the usefulness of the principle of the "old men of Santa Zita" of whom De Sanctis speaks in his memoirs of the Neapolitan school of Basilio Puoti:[5] i.e. the usefulness of a certain "stratification" of capabilities and attitudes, and of the formation of work-groups under the guidance of the most highly-skilled and highly-developed, who can accelerate the training of the most backward and untrained.

When one comes to study the practical organisation of the common school, one problem of importance is that of the various phases of the educational process, phases which correspond to the age and intellectual-moral development of the pupils and to the aims which the school sets itself. The common school, or school of humanistic formation (taking the term "humanism" in a broad sense rather than simply in the traditional one) or general culture, should aim to insert young men and women into social activity after bringing them to a certain level of maturity, of capacity for intellectual and practical creativity, and of autonomy of orientation and initiative. The fixing of an age for compulsory school attendance depends on the general economic conditions, since the latter may make it necessary to demand of young men and women, or even of children, a certain immediate productive contribution. The common school necessitates the State's being able to take on the expenditure which

---

[4] For Gramsci's analysis of Taylorism, see "Americanism and Fordism", below pp. 302 ff.

[5] De Sanctis in his memoirs recounts how as a child in Naples he was taken to be taught literary Italian at a school for the aristocracy of the city run in his home by the Marchese Puoti. Puoti used to refer to the elder boys, whose "judgement carried great weight, and when one of them spoke everyone fell silent, the marquis soonest of all, and was filled with admiration", as *gli anziani di Santa Zita*, in reference to Dante, *Inferno* XXI, 38. The "*anziani*" were the magistrates of the city of Lucca, whose patron saint was Zita.

at present falls on the family for the maintenance of children at school; in other words, it transforms the budget of the national department from top to bottom, expanding it to an unheard of extent and making it more complex. The entire function of educating and forming the new generations ceases to be private and becomes public; for only thus can it involve them in their entirety, without divisions of group or caste. But this transformation of scholastic activity requires an unprecedented expansion of the practical organisation of the school, i.e. of buildings, scientific material, of the teaching body, etc. The teaching body in particular would have to be increased, since the smaller the ratio between teachers and pupils the greater will be the efficiency of the school—and this presents other problems neither easy nor quick to solve. The question of school buildings is not simple either, since this type of school should be a college, with dormitories, refectories, specialised libraries, rooms designed for seminar work, etc. Hence initially the new type of school will have to be, cannot help being, only for restricted groups, made up of young people selected through competition or recommended by similar institutions.

The common school ought to correspond to the period represented today by the primary and secondary schools, reorganised not only as regards the content and the method of teaching, but also as regards the arrangement of the various phases of the educational process. The first, primary grade should not last longer than three or four years, and in addition to imparting the first "instrumental" notions of schooling—reading, writing, sums, geography, history—ought in particular to deal with an aspect of education that is now neglected—i.e. with "rights and duties", with the first notions of the State and society as primordial elements of a new conception of the world which challenges the conceptions that are imparted by the various traditional social environments, i.e. those conceptions which can be termed folkloristic. The didactic problem is one of mitigating and rendering more fertile the dogmatic approach which must inevitably characterise these first years. The rest of the course should not last more than six years, so that by the age of fifteen or sixteen it should be possible to complete all the grades of the common school.

One may object that such a course is too exhausting because too rapid, if the aim is to attain in effect the results which the present organisation of the classical school aims at but does not attain. Yet the new organisation as a whole will have to contain within itself the general elements which in fact make the course too slow today, at least for a part of the pupils. Which are these elements? In a whole series of families, especially in the intellectual strata, the children find in their family life a preparation, a prolongation and a completion of school life; they "breathe in", as the expression goes, a whole quantity of notions and attitudes which facilitate the educational process properly speaking. They already know and develop their knowledge of the literary language, i.e. the means of expression and of knowledge, which is technically superior to the means possessed by the average member of the school population between the ages of six and twelve. Thus city children, by the very fact of living in a city, have already absorbed by the age of six a quantity of notions and attitudes which make their school careers easier, more profitable, and more rapid. In the basic organisation of the common school, at least the essentials of these conditions must be created—not to speak of the fact, which goes without saying, that parallel to the common school a network of kindergartens and other institutions would develop, in which, even before the school age, children would be habituated to a certain collective discipline and acquire pre-scholastic notions and attitudes. In fact, the common school should be organised like a college, with a collective life by day and by night, freed from the present forms of hypocritical and mechanical discipline; studies should be carried on collectively, with the assistance of the teachers and the best pupils, even during periods of so-called individual study, etc.

The fundamental problem is posed by that phase of the existing school career which is today represented by the *liceo*,[6] and which today does not differ at all, as far as the kind of education is concerned, from the preceding grades—except by the abstract presumption of a greater intellectual and moral maturity of the pupil, matching his greater age and the experience he has already accumulated.

In fact between *liceo* and university, i.e. between the school properly speaking and life, there is now a jump, a real break in continuity, and not a rational passage from quantity (age) to quality (intellectual and moral maturity). From an almost purely dogmatic education, in which learning by heart plays a great part, the pupil passes to the creative phase, the phase of autonomous,

---

[6] Perhaps the nearest English-language equivalents of *ginnasio* and *liceo* are the American junior high school and high school, though in the Italian system they are selective schools (like English grammar schools) leading to a university education.

independent work. From the school, where his studies are subjected to a discipline that is imposed and controlled by authority, the pupil passes on to a phase of study or of professional work in which intellectual self-discipline and moral independence are theoretically unlimited. And this happens immediately after the crisis of puberty, when the ardour of the instinctive and elementary passions has not yet resolved its struggle with the fetters of the character and of moral conscience which are in the process of being formed. Moreover, in Italy, where the principle of 'seminar' work is not widespread in the universities, this passage is even more brusque and mechanical.

By contrast, therefore, the last phase of the common school must be conceived and structured as the decisive phase, whose aim is to create the fundamental values of "humanism", the intellectual self-discipline and the moral independence which are necessary for subsequent specialisation—whether it be of a scientific character (university studies) or of an immediately practical-productive character (industry, civil service, organisation of commerce, etc.). The study and learning of creative methods in science and in life must begin in this last phase of the school, and no longer be a monopoly of the university or be left to chance in practical life. This phase of the school must already contribute to developing the element of independent responsibility in each individual, must be a creative school. A distinction must be made between creative school and active school, even in the form given to the latter by the Dalton method.[7] The entire common school is an active school, although it is necessary to place limits on libertarian ideologies in this field and to stress with some energy the duty of the adult generations, i.e. of the State, to "mould" the new generations. The active school is still in its romantic phase, in which the elements of struggle against the mechanical and Jesuitical school have become

---

[7] The Dalton Method, a development of Montessori's ideas, is described elsewhere by Gramsci (Int., p. 122): "the pupils are free to attend whichever lessons (whether practical or theoretical) they please, provided that by the end of each month they have completed the programme set for them; discipline is entrusted to the pupils themselves. The system has a serious defect: the pupils generally postpone doing their work until the last days of the month, and this detracts from the seriousness of the education and represents a major difficulty for the teachers who are supposed to help them but are overwhelmed with work—whereas in the first weeks of the month they have little or nothing to do. (The Dalton system is simply an extension to the secondary schools of the methods of study which obtain in the Italian universities, methods which leave the student complete freedom in his studies: in certain faculties the students sit twenty examinations and their final degree in the fourth and last year, and the lecturer never so much as knows the student.)"

unhealthily exaggerated—through a desire to distinguish themselves sharply from the latter, and for polemical reasons. It is necessary to enter the "classical", rational phase, and to find in the ends to be attained the natural source for developing the appropriate methods and forms.

The creative school is the culmination of the active school. In the first phase the aim is to discipline, hence also to level out—to obtain a certain kind of "conformism" which may be called "dynamic". In the creative phase, on the basis that has been achieved of "collectivisation" of the social type, the aim is to expand the personality—by now autonomous and responsible, but with a solid and homogeneous moral and social conscience. Thus creative school does not mean school of "inventors and discoverers"; it indicates a phase and a method of research and of knowledge, and not a predetermined "programme" with an obligation to originality and innovation at all costs. It indicates that learning takes place especially through a spontaneous and autonomous effort of the pupil, with the teacher only exercising a function of friendly guide—as happens or should happen in the university. To discover a truth oneself, without external suggestions or assistance, is to create—even if the truth is an old one. It demonstrates a mastery of the method, and indicates that in any case one has entered the phase of intellectual maturity in which one may discover new truths. Hence in this phase the fundamental scholastic activity will be carried on in seminars, in libraries, in experimental laboratories; during it, the organic data will be collected for a professional orientation.

The advent of the common school means the beginning of new relations between intellectual and industrial work, not only in the school but in the whole of social life. The comprehensive principle will therefore be reflected in all the organisms of culture, transforming them and giving them a new content.

IN SEARCH OF THE EDUCATIONAL PRINCIPLE

In the old primary school, there used to be two elements in the educational formation of the children.[8] They were taught the rudiments of natural science, and the idea of civic rights and duties. Scientific ideas were intended to insert the child into the *societas rerum*, the world of things, while lessons in rights and duties were

---

[8] i.e. before the Gentile reform—see introduction to this section, and note 14 on p. 132.

intended to insert him into the State and into civil society. The scientific ideas the children learnt conflicted with the magical conception of the world and nature which they absorbed from an environment steeped in folklore;[9] while the idea of civic rights and duties conflicted with tendencies towards individualistic and localistic barbarism—another dimension of folklore. The school combated folklore, indeed every residue of traditional conceptions of the world. It taught a more modern outlook based essentially on an awareness of the simple and fundamental fact that there exist objective, intractable natural laws to which man must adapt himself if he is to master them in his turn—and that there exist social and state laws which are the product of human activity, which are established by men and can be altered by men in the interests of their collective development. These laws of the State and of society create that human order which historically best enables men to dominate the laws of nature, that is to say which most facilitates their *work*. For work is the specific mode by which man actively participates in natural life in order to transform and socialise it more and more deeply and extensively.

Thus one can say that the educational principle which was the basis of the old primary school was the idea of work. Human work cannot be realised in all its power of expansion and productivity without an exact and realistic knowledge of natural laws and without a legal order which organically regulates men's life in common. Men must respect this legal order through spontaneous assent, and not merely as an external imposition—it must be a necessity recognised and proposed to themselves as freedom, and not simply the result of coercion. The idea and the fact of work (of theoretical and practical activity) was the educational principle latent in the primary school, since it is by means of work that the social and State order (rights and duties) is introduced and identified within the natural order. The discovery that the relations between the social and natural orders are mediated by work, by man's theoretical and practical activity, creates the first elements of an intuition of the world free from all magic and superstition. It provides a basis for the subsequent development of an historical, dialectical conception of the world, which understands movement and change, which appreciates the sum of effort and sacrifice which the present has cost the past and which the future is costing the present, and which conceives the contemporary world as a synthesis

[9] See above, p. 30, for Gramsci's use of the term "folklore". See too, note 5 on p. 326.

of the past, of all past generations, which projects itself into the future. This was the real basis of the primary school. Whether it yielded all its fruits, and whether the actual teachers were aware of the nature and philosophical content of their task, is another question. This requires an analysis of the degree of civic consciousness of the entire nation, of which the teaching body was merely an expression, and rather a poor expression—certainly not an *avant-garde*.

It is not entirely true that "instruction" is something quite different from "education".[10] An excessive emphasis on this distinction has been a serious error of idealist educationalists and its effects can already be seen in the school system as they have reorganised it. For instruction to be wholly distinct from education, the pupil would have to be pure passivity, a "mechanical receiver" of abstract notions—which is absurd and is anyway "abstractly" denied by the supporters of pure educativity precisely in their opposition to mere mechanistic instruction. The "certain" becomes "true" in the child's consciousness.[11] But the child's consciousness is not something "individual" (still less individuated), it reflects the sector of civil society in which the child participates, and the social relations which are formed within his family, his neighbourhood, his village, etc. The individual consciousness of the overwhelming majority of children reflects social and cultural relations which are different from and antagonistic to those which are represented in the school curricula: thus the "certain" of an advanced culture becomes "true" in the framework of a fossilised and anachronistic culture. There is no unity between school and life, and so there is no automatic unity between instruction and education. In the school, the nexus between instruction and education can only be realised by the living work of the teacher. For this he must be aware of the contrast between the type of culture and society which he

---

[10] For this distinction, popular with educational thinkers influenced by Gentile and by Croce, see the introduction to this section.

[11] This distinction was made by Vico, in his *Scienza Nuova* of 1725. Para. 321: "The 'certain' in the laws is an obscurity of judgement backed only by authority, so that we find them harsh in application, yet are obliged to apply them just because they are certain. In good Latin *certum* means particularised, or, as the schools say, individuated; so that, in over-elegant Latin, *certum* and *commune*, the certain and the common, are opposed to each other." Para. 324: "The true in the laws is a certain light and splendour with which natural reason illuminates them; so that jurisconsults are often in the habit of saying *verum est* for *aequum est*." Para. 137: "Men who do not know what is true of things take care to hold fast to what is certain, so that, if they cannot satisfy their intellects by knowledge (*scienza*), their wills at least may rest on consciousness (*coscienza*)." The New Science, trans. Bergin and Fisch, Cornell, 1968.

represents and the type of culture and society represented by his pupils, and conscious of his obligation to accelerate and regulate the child's formation in conformity with the former and in conflict with the latter. If the teaching body is not adequate and the nexus between instruction and education is dissolved, while the problem of teaching is conjured away by cardboard schemata exalting educativity, the teacher's work will as a result become yet more inadequate. We will have rhetorical schools, quite unserious, because the material solidity of what is "certain" will be missing, and what is "true" will be a truth only of words: that is to say, precisely, rhetoric.

This degeneration is even clearer in the secondary school, in the literature and philosophy syllabus. Previously, the pupils at least acquired a certain "baggage" or "equipment" (according to taste) of concrete facts. Now that the teacher must be specifically a philosopher and aesthete, the pupil does not bother with concrete facts and fills his head with formulae and words which usually mean nothing to him, and which are forgotten at once. It was right to struggle against the old school, but reforming it was not so simple as it seemed. The problem was not one of model curricula but of men, and not just of the men who are actually teachers themselves but of the entire social complex which they express. In reality a mediocre teacher may manage to see to it that his pupils become more *informed*, although he will not succeed in making them better educated; he can devote a scrupulous and bureaucratic conscientiousness to the mechanical part of teaching—and the pupil, if he has an active intelligence, will give an order of his own, with the aid of his social background, to the "baggage" he accumulates. With the new curricula, which coincide with a general lowering of the level of the teaching profession, there will no longer be any "baggage" to put in order. The new curricula should have abolished examinations entirely; for to take an examination now must be fearfully more chancy than before. A date is always a date, whoever the examiner is, and a definition is always a definition. But an aesthetic judgement or a philosophical analysis?

The educational efficacy of the old Italian secondary school, as organised by the Casati Act,[12] was not to be sought (or rejected) in its explicit aim as an "educative" system, but in the fact that its structure and its curriculum were the expression of a traditional mode of intellectual and moral life, of a cultural climate diffused

[12] The Casati Act, passed in 1859, remained the basis of the Italian educational system until the Gentile Reform of 1923.

throughout Italian society by ancient tradition. It was the fact that this climate and way of life were in their death-throes, and that the school had become cut off from life, which brought about the crisis in education. A criticism of the curricula and disciplinary structure of the old system means less than nothing if one does not keep this situation in mind. Thus we come back to the truly active participation of the pupil in the school, which can only exist if the school is related to life. The more the new curricula nominally affirm and theorise the pupil's activity and working collaboration with the teacher, the more they are actually designed as if the pupil were purely passive.

In the old school the grammatical study of Latin and Greek, together with the study of their respective literatures and political histories, was an educational principle—for the humanistic ideal, symbolised by Athens and Rome, was diffused throughout society, and was an essential element of national life and culture. Even the mechanical character of the study of grammar was enlivened by this cultural perspective. Individual facts were not learnt for an immediate practical or professional end. The end seemed disinterested, because the real interest was the interior development of personality, the formation of character by means of the absorption and assimilation of the whole cultural past of modern European civilisation. Pupils did not learn Latin and Greek in order to speak them, to become waiters, interpreters or commercial letter-writers. They learnt them in order to know at first hand the civilisation of Greece and of Rome—a civilisation that was a necessary precondition of our modern civilisation: in other words, they learnt them in order to be themselves and know themselves consciously. Latin and Greek were learnt through their grammar, mechanically; but the accusation of formalism and aridity is very unjust and inappropriate. In education one is dealing with children in whom one has to inculcate certain habits of diligence, precision, poise (even physical poise), ability to concentrate on specific subjects, which cannot be acquired without the mechanical repetition of disciplined and methodical acts. Would a scholar at the age of forty be able to sit for sixteen hours on end at his work-table if he had not, as a child, compulsorily, through mechanical coercion, acquired the appropriate psycho-physical habits? If one wishes to produce great scholars, one still has to start at this point and apply pressure throughout the educational system in order to succeed in creating those thousands or hundreds or even only dozens of scholars of the highest quality which are necessary to every civilisation. (Of course, one can improve a great deal in this field by the provision of adequate funds for research, without going back to the educational methods of the Jesuits.)

Latin is learnt (or rather studied) by analysing it down to its smallest parts—analysing it like a dead thing, it is true, but all analyses made by children can only be of dead things. Besides, one must not forget that the life of the Romans is a myth which to some extent has already interested the child and continues to interest him, so that in the dead object there is always present a greater living being. Thus, the language is dead, it is analysed as an inert object, as a corpse on the dissecting table, but it continually comes to life again in examples and in stories. Could one study Italian in the same way? Impossible. No living language could be studied like Latin: it would be and *would seem* absurd. No child knows Latin when he starts to study it by these analytical methods. But a living language can be known and it would be enough for a single child to know it, and the spell would be broken: everybody would be off to the Berlitz school at once. Latin (like Greek) appears to the imagination as a myth, even for the teacher. One does not study Latin in order to learn the language. For a long time, as a result of a cultural and scholarly tradition whose origin and development one might investigate, Latin has been studied as an element in an ideal curriculum, an element which combines and satisfies a whole series of pedagogic and psychological requirements. It has been studied in order to accustom children to studying in a specific manner, and to analysing an historical body which can be treated as a corpse which returns continually to life; in order to accustom them to reason, to think abstractly and schematically while remaining able to plunge back from abstraction into real and immediate life, to see in each fact or datum what is general and what is particular, to distinguish the concept from the specific instance.

For what after all is the educational significance of the constant comparison between Latin and the language one speaks? It involves the distinction and the identification of words and concepts; suggests the whole of formal logic, from the contradiction between opposites to the analysis of distincts;[13] reveals the historical movement of the entire language, modified through time, developing and not static. In the eight years of *ginnasio* and *liceo*[14] the entire history of the real language is studied, after it has first been photo-

---

[13] For Croce's concept of the "analysis of distincts" see Introduction, p. xxiii.
[14] See note 6 on p. 31.

graphed in one abstract moment in the form of grammar. It is studied from Ennius (or rather from the words of the fragments of the twelve tablets) right up to Phaedrus and the Christian writers in Latin: an historical process is analysed from its source until its death in time—or seeming death, since we know that Italian, with which Latin is continually contrasted in school, is modern Latin. Not only the grammar of a certain epoch (which is an abstraction) or its vocabulary are studied, but also, for comparison, the grammar and the vocabulary of each individual author and the meaning of each term in each particular stylistic "period". Thus the child discovers that the grammar and the vocabulary of Phaedrus are not those of Cicero, nor those of Plautus, nor of Lactantius or Tertullian, and that the same nexus of sounds does not have the same meaning in different periods and for different authors. Latin and Italian are continually compared; but each word is a concept, a symbol, which takes on different shades of meaning according to the period and the writer in each of the two languages under comparison. The child studies the literary history of the books written in that language, the political history, the achievements of the men who spoke that language. His education is determined by the whole of this organic complex, by the fact that he has followed that itinerary, if only in a purely literal sense, he has passed through those various stages, etc. He has plunged into history and acquired a historicising understanding of the world and of life, which becomes a second—nearly spontaneous—nature, since it is not inculcated pedantically with an openly educational intention. These studies educated without an explicitly declared aim of doing so, with a minimal "educative" intervention on the part of the teacher: they educated because they gave instruction. Logical, artistic, psychological experience was gained unawares, without a continual self-consciousness. Above all a profound "synthetic", philosophical experience was gained, of an actual historical development. This does not mean—it would be stupid to think so—that Latin and Greek, as such, have intrinsically thaumaturgical qualities in the educational field. It is the whole cultural tradition, which also and particularly lives outside the school, which in a given ambience produces such results. In any case one can see today, with the changes in the traditional idea of culture, the way in which the school is in crisis and with it the study of Latin and Greek.

It will be necessary to replace Latin and Greek as the fulcrum of the formative school, and they will be replaced. But it will not be easy to deploy the new subject or subjects in a didactic form which gives equivalent results in terms of education and general personality-formation, from early childhood to the threshold of the adult choice of career. For in this period what is learnt, or the greater part of it, must be—or appear to the pupils to be—disinterested, i.e. not have immediate or too immediate practical purposes. It must be formative, while being "instructive"—in other words rich in concrete facts. In the present school, the profound crisis in the traditional culture and its conception of life and of man has resulted in a progressive degeneration. Schools of the vocational type, i.e. those designed to satisfy immediate, practical interests, are beginning to predominate over the formative school, which is not immediately "interested". The most paradoxical aspect of it all is that this new type of school appears and is advocated as being democratic, while in fact it is destined not merely to perpetuate social differences but to crystallise them in Chinese complexities.

The traditional school was oligarchic because it was intended for the new generation of the ruling class, destined to rule in its turn: but it was not oligarchic in its mode of teaching. It is not the fact that the pupils learn how to rule there, nor the fact that it tends to produce gifted men, which gives a particular type of school its social character. This social character is determined by the fact that each social group has its own type of school, intended to perpetuate a specific traditional function, ruling or subordinate. If one wishes to break this pattern one needs, instead of multiplying and grading different types of vocational school, to create a single type of formative school (primary-secondary) which would take the child up to the threshold of his choice of job, forming him during this time as a person capable of thinking, studying, and ruling—or controlling those who rule.

The multiplication of types of vocational school thus tends to perpetuate traditional social differences; but since, within these differences, it tends to encourage internal diversification, it gives the impression of being democratic in tendency. The labourer can become a skilled worker, for instance, the peasant a surveyor or petty agronomist. But democracy, by definition, cannot mean merely that an unskilled worker can become skilled. It must mean that every "citizen" can "govern" and that society places him, even if only abstractly, in a general condition to achieve this. Political democracy tends towards a coincidence of the rulers and the ruled (in the sense of government with the consent of the governed), ensuring for each non-ruler a free training in the skills and general technical preparation necessary to that end. But the type of school which is now developing as the school for the people does not tend even to keep up this illusion. For it is organised ever more fully in such a way as to restrict recruitment to the technically qualified governing stratum, in a social and political context which makes it increasingly difficult for "personal initiative" to acquire such skills and technical-political preparation. Thus we are really going back to a division into juridically fixed and crystallised estates rather than moving towards the transcendence of class divisions. The multiplication of vocational schools which specialise increasingly from the very beginning of the child's educational career is one of the most notable manifestations of this tendency. It is noticeable that the new pedagogy has concentrated its fire on "dogmatism" in the field of instruction and the learning of concrete facts—i.e. precisely in the field in which a certain dogmatism is practically indispensable and can be reabsorbed and dissolved only in the whole cycle of the educational process (historical grammar could not be taught in *liceo* classes). On the other hand, it has been forced to accept the introduction of dogmatism *par excellence* in the field of religious thought, with the result that the whole history of philosophy is now implicitly seen as a succession of ravings and delusions.[15] In the philosophy course, the new curriculum impoverishes the teaching and in practice lowers its level (at least for the overwhelming majority of pupils who do not receive intellectual help outside the school from their family or home environment, and who have to form themselves solely by means of the knowledge they receive in the class-room)—in spite of seeming very rational and fine, fine as any utopia. The traditional descriptive philosophy, backed by a course in the history of philosophy and by the reading of a certain number of philosophers, in practice seems the best thing. Descriptive, definitional philosophy may be a dogmatic abstraction, just as grammar and mathematics are, but it is an educational and didactive necessity. "One equals one" is an

---

[15] The Gentile Reform provided for compulsory religious education in Italian schools, and Gentile's justifications of this are criticised by Gramsci in Int., pp. 116–18: "... Gentile's thinking ... is nothing more than an extension of the idea that 'religion is good for the people' (people = child = primitive phase of thought to which religion corresponds, etc.), i.e. a (tendentious) abandonment of the aim of educating the people ... Gentile's historicism is of a very degenerate kind: it is the historicism of those jurists for whom the knout is not a knout when it is an 'historical' knout. Moreover, its ideas are extremely vague and confused. The fact that a 'dogmatic' exposition of scientific ideas and a certain 'mythology' are necessary in the primary school does not mean that the dogma and the mythology have to be precisely those of religion." Etc. See note 14 on p. 132.

abstraction, but it leads nobody to think that one fly equals one elephant. The rules of formal logic are abstractions of the same kind, they are like the grammar of normal thought; but they still need to be studied, since they are not something innate, but have to be acquired through work and reflection. The new curriculum presupposes that formal logic is something you already possess when you think, but does not explain how it is to be acquired, so that in practice it is assumed to be innate. Formal logic is like grammar: it is assimilated in a "living" way even if the actual learning process has been necessarily schematic and abstract. For the learner is not a passive and mechanical recipient, a gramophone record—even if the liturgical conformity of examinations sometimes makes him appear so. The relation between these educational forms and the child's psychology is always active and creative, just as the relation of the worker to his tools is active and creative. A calibre is likewise a complex of abstractions, but without calibration it is not possible to produce real objects—real objects which are social relations, and which implicitly embody ideas.

The child who sweats at *Barbara, Baralipton*[16] is certainly performing a tiring task, and it is important that he does only what is absolutely necessary and no more. But it is also true that it will always be an effort to learn physical self-discipline and self-control; the pupil has, in effect, to undergo a psycho-physical training. Many people have to be persuaded that studying too is a job, and a very tiring one, with its own particular apprenticeship—involving muscles and nerves as well as intellect. It is a process of adaptation, a habit acquired with effort, tedium and even suffering. Wider participation in secondary education brings with it a tendency to ease off the discipline of studies, and to ask for "relaxations". Many even think that the difficulties of learning are artificial, since they are accustomed to think only of manual work as sweat and toil. The question is a complex one. Undoubtedly the child of a traditionally intellectual family acquires this psycho-physical adaptation more easily. Before he ever enters the class-room he has numerous advantages over his comrades, and is already in possession of attitudes learnt from his family environment: he concentrates more easily, since he is used to "sitting still", etc. Similarly, the son of a city worker suffers less when he goes to work in a factory than does a peasant's child or a young peasant already formed by country life. (Even diet has its importance, etc.) This is why many people think

[16] *Barbara, Baralipton*, were mnemonic words used to memorise syllogisms in classical logic.

that the difficulty of study conceals some "trick" which handicaps them—that is, when they do not simply believe that they are stupid by nature. They see the "gentleman"[17]—and for many, especially in the country, "gentleman" means intellectual—complete, speedily and with apparent ease, work which costs their sons tears and blood, and they think there is a "trick". In the future, these questions may become extremely acute and it will be necessary to resist the tendency to render easy that which cannot become easy without being distorted. If our aim is to produce a new stratum of intellectuals, including those capable of the highest degree of specialisation, from a social group which has not traditionally developed the appropriate attitudes, then we have unprecedented difficulties to overcome.

---

[17] *Signore*. On this term, not of course an exact equivalent of "gentleman", see below p. 272.

3
NOTES ON ITALIAN HISTORY

INTRODUCTION

Gramsci planned to organise his notes on Italian history into a study to be entitled "Reformation, Renaissance". Although, in the event, a comparatively small proportion of his historical writing was concerned with the specific historical phenomena normally understood by these designations, nevertheless Gramsci's title does perhaps offer us a starting-point from which to attempt to isolate the basic preoccupations and the basic concepts with which he approached the historical experience of Italy.

Gramsci distinguishes between two quite distinct "Renaissances": ". . . the Renaissance was a vast movement, which started after the year 1000, and of which Humanism and the Renaissance (in the narrow sense of the word) were two closing moments—moments which were primarily located in Italy, whereas the more general historical process was European and not only Italian. Humanism and the Renaissance, as the literary expression of this European historical movement, were located primarily in Italy; but the progressive movement after the year 1000, although an important part of it took place in Italy with the Communes, precisely in Italy degenerated . . . while in the rest of Europe the general movement culminated in the national states and then in the world expansion of Spain, France, England, Portugal. In Italy what corresponded to the national states of these countries was the organisation of the Papacy as an absolute state . . . which divided the rest of Italy, etc. . . . The Renaissance may be viewed as the cultural expression of an historical process in which there was created in Italy a new intellectual class of European dimensions. This class divided into two branches: one exercised a cosmopolitan function in Italy, linked to the Papacy and reactionary in character; the other was formed outside Italy, from political and religious exiles, and exercised a progressive cosmopolitan function in the various countries where it existed, or participated in the organisation of the modern states as a technical element in the armed forces, in politics, in engineering, etc."

Thus contained in the term "Renaissance" are a number of Gramsci's key concerns: the failure of the Italian Communal bourgeoisie (see note 4 on p. 53) to transcend the "economic-corporate" phase and create a national state; the specific historical backwardness of Italy which resulted; the regressive "cosmopolitan" characteristics of the traditional Italian intellectuals, linked to the role of the Papacy, etc.

The term "Reformation" is likewise not a simple, or univocal one for Gramsci. In so far as he used it to stress popular participation, which he saw as a characteristic of Lutheranism and Calvinism in contrast to the Renaissance, it may be questioned to what extent this corresponds to historical reality. Gramsci sees Marxism as involving a "reformation": "The philosophy of praxis corresponds to the nexus Protestant Reformation plus French Revolution: it is a philosophy which is also a politics and a politics which is also a philosophy." (See too "Brief Notes on Machiavelli's Politics" on pp. 132–3.) Here we find one of the couples of opposed but dialectically united concepts which run through Gramsci's work, and whose shifting, and by no means always consistent combinations make it so hard to arrive at any definitive interpretation of his thought. Revolution/Reformation here can be related to the other Gramscian couplets State/civil society, force/consent, domination/leadership, war of manœuvre/war of position, etc. which recur throughout the Prison Notebooks. (See, e.g., p. 170 and note 71 on that page.)

The major focus, in the event, of Gramsci's historical writing was the Risorgimento. He began his analysis by a statement of "the methodological criterion on which our own study must be based . . . that the supremacy of a social group manifests itself in two ways, as "domination" and as "intellectual and moral leadership". The Risorgimento, for Gramsci, was characterised by an absence of the second element, and concretely by an absence of an Italian equivalent of the Jacobins. (What Gramsci meant by "Jacobin" will be discussed more fully in the introduction to "The Modern Prince" below. He saw the essence of "Jacobinism" as the subordination of the "countryside" to the "city" in an organic relationship, i.e. the organising of peasant "consent".)

The basic problem confronting Gramsci was that of identifying the specific weaknesses of the Italian national state which emerged from the Risorgimento—weaknesses which culminated in the advent to power of Fascism sixty years later. His analysis was a complex one, whose point of departure was the question of what the Risorgimento *was not*. Mazzini and the Action Party, the potential "Jacobins", did not make any attempt to rouse the peasantry and draw it into the process of national unification; they did not promote any agrarian reform. Consequently, they failed to give the

Risorgimento any popular dimension or themselves any solid class base. (Incidentally, this aspect of Gramsci's historical writing has given rise to a major historical debate in Italy: see Romario Roseo's thesis—developed in *Risorgimento e capitalismo* (1956–58)—that the absence of an agrarian reform in fact played a "progressive" role in relation to the growth of Italian industrial capitalism, and also the debate between Romeo and Gerschenkron in *La formazione dell'Italia industriale* (1963).) The result was that "what was involved was not a social group which 'led' other groups, but a State [Piedmont] which, even though it had limitations as a power, 'led' the group which should have been 'leading' ". What was involved was a "passive revolution".

Gramsci's use of the term "passive revolution" is one of the cruxes of his political thought. The term originated with Vincenzo Cuoco (see note 11 on p. 59), who used it at first to describe the lack of mass participation in the Neapolitan revolution of 1799 and the latter's "external" origins; subsequently Cuoco came to *advocate* such "passive revolutions" as preferable to violent ones involving the popular masses on the French model. (Incidentally, Lenin also uses the term in *The Crisis of Menshevism* (1906), but there is no evidence that Gramsci knew this text.) Gramsci also uses the expression in two distinct ways: firstly, in something close to Cuoco's original sense, as a revolution without mass participation (and due in large part to outside forces)—e.g. the Risorgimento; secondly, as a "molecular" social transformation which takes place as it were beneath the surface of society, in situations where the progressive class cannot advance openly—e.g. the progress of the bourgeoisie in Restoration France after 1815 ("revolution/restoration": see p. 119), or the development of Christianity within the Roman Empire.

Although Gramsci condemns explicitly any advocacy of "passive revolution" as a programme, his use of the term is often ambiguous. This is especially the case where he tentatively relates it to "war of position", itself by no means a consistent or univocal concept in Gramsci's writing (see introduction to "State and Civil Society"). On the other hand, Gramsci makes use of the notion of "passive revolution" to confront certain of the central problems of revolutionary analysis and strategy. In the two final passages in this section, in which he comments on Croce's historiography and also on his contemporary role, and again in the section entitled "Americanism and Fordism" below, Gramsci relates the concept of passive revolution to the Italian fascist régime. Viewing the latter as a transitional, compromise form comparable in some ways to the rule of Napoleon III, he asks a series of questions. What modification in the fundamental balance of social forces is taking place beneath the surface of fascism? How is Croce organising the long-term "consent" to bourgeois rule? What is the significance of the forms of State intervention in the economy which were common to New Deal America and to Fascist Italy? What are the fundamental economic contradictions under Fascism, and how will these be expressed politically? How can the working class develop and retain some degree of class organisation and consciousness even under the corporate State?

Gramsci does not offer clear answers to all these questions. The sense of the analogy he draws between the post-1815 period in Europe and the period in which he is writing (see final sentences of this section) is simply to reaffirm that even when frontal attack may be impossible, a passive revolution may nonetheless be taking place; that the class struggle continues despite the surface stability of the fascist régime. Yet here we approach one of the supreme paradoxes of Gramsci's thought, a dilemma to which he found no answer. For there is precisely a radical dissimilarity between the situation of the bourgeoisie under feudal or pre-bourgeois forms of State and that of the proletariat under bourgeois rule. In the former case, capitalist relations of production can develop within the feudal State, until at a certain point in time the "carapace" cracks. In the latter case, however, this is not so. It is quite impossible for socialist relations of production to develop "within" capitalism. It is unquestionably for this reason that whenever Gramsci touches on this dilemma—which is also the question of how fascism can be overthrown—he tends to pose questions rather than make assertions. Since no fascist régime has yet been overthrown by internal forces, it is to his credit that he refused any easy, or unilateral formula, but contented himself with rejecting the twin, undialectical deviations of frontal attack and "liquidationism". Clearly these problems are closely related too to Gramsci's statement that "A social group can, and indeed must, already 'lead' [i.e. be hegemonic] before winning governmental power (this indeed is one of the principal conditions for the winning of such power)." For this, see introduction to "State and Civil Society".

OUTLINE CHRONOLOGY OF ITALIAN HISTORY

A.D. 476 Final extinction of the Roman Empire in the West, followed by periods of Ostrogoth and Lombard rule in

	what is now Italy—punctuated by attempts to extend Byzantine power, especially in the South.
Eighth Century	Rise of the Papacy as a territorial power; annexation of the Lombard kingdom by Charlemagne.
800	Charlemagne crowned as Holy Roman Emperor.
912	Otto of Saxony crowned Holy Roman Emperor as Otto I. For the next four centuries and more, Italian history was dominated by the struggle for supremacy between the German Emperors and the Papacy. In the South, Sicily was held by the Arabs (827–1072), then the Normans until 1189, when the Hohenstaufen Emperor Henry VI inherited it by marriage.
Twelfth Century	Emergence in North and Central Italy of the "Communes". The prosperous trading and manufacturing towns which grew up during this period formed self-governing republics which controlled the surrounding *contado*. The German Emperors saw the emergence of these towns as a threat, and supported the feudal
Thirteenth Century	landowners (who were the basis for the Ghibelline party) against them. The Papacy supported the burghers and merchants who constituted the Guelph party. In the internecine struggles between the cities, and within them between the rival parties, the feudal landowning class was effectively wiped out in North and Central Italy by about 1300. It was during the thirteenth century that Italian emerged as a literary language, first in Sicily at the court of Frederick II, and subsequently in Tuscany with Dante (1265–1321).
Fourteenth Century	The mediaeval communes became dominated by their *Signorie* or councils of notables—and in time, in most cases, by one powerful family dynasty. From 1300 onwards, five states were dominant in Italy: Florence, Milan, Venice, the Papal state, and the Kingdom of Naples (ruled by the dynasty of Anjou). Sicily (which had thrown off Angevin rule itself in 1282: the Angevins had acquired the island by marriage in 1265) from 1302 had Aragonese rulers. In 1347–48, a probable third (up to 60 per cent in certain cities) of the population of Italy died in the Black Death.
Fifteenth Century	The family dynasties which dominated the city-states of North and Central Italy were mostly legitimised by

Pope or Emperor: the *Signoria* gave way to the *Principato*. The Renaissance (in the conventional, narrow sense) flowered in Medici Florence, Sforza Milan, Papal Rome, and in a host of smaller cities. Venice remained a republic. In 1442 Alphonse of Aragon succeeded to the Kingdom of Naples (he already ruled Sicily).

1494 Two years after the death of Lorenzo de' Medici, Charles VIII of France invaded Italy to claim the crown of Naples. By 1529, Milan and Naples were under Spanish rule. Machiavelli (1469–1527) wrote precisely during this period of foreign invasions and maximum disunity among the Italian states.

Sixteenth–Eighteenth Centuries Italy was largely under foreign domination or outright occupation. Naples (i.e. virtually the whole of mainland Italy South of Rome) was Spanish until 1713, Austrian until 1735, and was ruled by a Spanish Bourbon dynasty until the approach of Napoleon's armies and the proclamation of the Parthenopean Republic in 1798. Milan was Spanish until 1713, Austrian thereafter until the Napoleonic conquest of 1796. Florence lost its independence in 1532 and was merged into the Grand Duchy of Tuscany, which was effectively an Austrian puppet state from 1737. The Papal State remained formally independent, as did the Venetian Republic, until the advent of Napoleon, in 1797–98. Various other small states existed as independent entities in Central Italy during this period: Parma, Genoa, Lucca, Massa-Carrara, Modena, etc. Sicily was ceded by Spain to the Duke of Savoy in 1713; by Savoy to Austria in 1720; in 1738 it was united with Naples under the Spanish Bourbons. Lastly, Savoy emerged as a powerful state in the seventeenth century; in 1713 the Duke of Savoy acquired Sicily, but in 1720 was forced to exchange the latter for Sardinia—whereafter his realm became known as the Kingdom of Sardinia (although its main territory was in fact what is now Piedmont).

1796–1815 The Napoleonic invasion and occupation temporarily united Italy, and had a lasting impact on the political and social life of the territory.

1815 Congress of Vienna. Austria became the dominant

power throughout the Italian peninsula; she occupied Lombardy, the Veneto and the statelets of central Italy, and protected the restored Bourbons in Naples, the Papacy, and the Kingdom of Sardinia (Sardinia and Piedmont).

1820 Carbonarist risings in Piedmont and Naples were suppressed with Austrian assistance.

1830–31 Risings in Modena, Parma, and especially in the Papal states were suppressed by the Austrians.

1834 Abortive Mazzinian rising, led by Ramorino, at Genoa against the Savoy monarchy of Sardinia and Piedmont.

1848–49 Anti-Austrian risings throughout North and Central Italy. The Piedmont monarchy had by now set its sights on becoming the nucleus and hegemonic force of a united Italy. In March 1848 King Carlo Alberto proclaimed that Italy would "go it alone", and declared war on Austria. In May 1848 the Milanese rose in the "Five Days" insurrection, and drove the Austrians out of the city. A republic was proclaimed once again in Venice, under Manin. In January 1849, a Roman Republic was declared. However, in March 1849 the Piedmontese were defeated by the Austrians at Novara, and in the following months the Austrians re-established total supremacy; Rome fell in June, and Venice in August.

1853 Anti-Austrian rising in Milan suppressed.

1854 Piedmont, under Cavour's ministry, participated somewhat symbolically in the Crimean War on the French side, as the opening move in a determined diplomatic bid for French support.

1858 Alliance signed between France and Piedmont.

1859 War between France and Piedmont on the one hand and Austria on the other. After victories at Magenta and Solferino, Piedmont received Lombardy from Austria, and in turn ceded Nice and Savoy to France.

1860 The Central Italian states (with the exception of the Papal state) joined Piedmont. Garibaldi's expedition to Sicily finally toppled the Bourbon dynasty of the Two Sicilies.

1861 Kingdom of Italy proclaimed, with its capital at Turin, and subsequently (1864) at Florence.

1866 Prussia defeated Austria; Italy, as Prussia's ally, received the Veneto.

1867 French troops prevented Garibaldi from marching on Rome, defeating him at Mentana.

1870 During the Franco-Prussian War, the French troops withdrew and the Piedmontese army occupied Rome, which became the capital of a united Italy. The Pope refused to accept the end of his territorial power or the legitimacy of the new Italian state, and withdrew symbolically into the Vatican.

1885 Italian imperialist expansion into Eritrea and Somalia.

1912 Italian occupation of Libya.

1915 Italy intervened in the First World War on the side of Britain and France; at the end of the war, she was rewarded by the acquisition of Trieste, the Trentino and South Tyrol, at the expense of Austria.

This extremely schematic chronology notably excludes post-Risorgimento, internal Italian politics—which is extensively covered by Gramsci's text, and in the footnotes to it.

NOTES ON ITALIAN HISTORY

HISTORY OF THE SUBALTERN CLASSES: METHODOLOGICAL CRITERIA

The historical unity of the ruling classes is realised in the State, and their history is essentially the history of States and of groups of States. But it would be wrong to think that this unity is simply juridical and political (though such forms of unity do have their importance too, and not in a purely formal sense); the fundamental historical unity, concretely, results from the organic relations between State or political society and "civil society".[1]

The subaltern classes, by definition, are not unified and cannot unite until they are able to become a "State": their history, therefore, is intertwined with that of civil society, and thereby with the history of States and groups of States. Hence it is necessary to study: 1. the objective formation of the subaltern social groups, by the developments and transformations occurring in the sphere of economic production; their quantitative diffusion and their origins in pre-existing social groups, whose mentality, ideology and aims they conserve for a time; 2. their active or passive affiliation to the dominant political formations, their attempts to influence the programmes of these formations in order to press claims of their own, and the consequences of these attempts in determining processes of decomposition, renovation or neo-formation; 3. the birth of new parties of the dominant groups, intended to conserve the assent of the subaltern groups and to maintain control over them; 4. the formations which the subaltern groups themselves produce, in order to press claims of a limited and partial character; 5. those new formations which assert the autonomy of the subaltern groups, but within the old framework; 6. those formations which assert the integral autonomy, . . . etc.[2]

The list of these phases can be broken down still further, with intermediate phases and combinations of several phases. The historian must record, and discover the causes of, the line of development towards integral autonomy, starting from the most primitive phases; he must note every manifestation of the Sorelian "spirit of cleavage".[3] Therefore, the history of the parties of the subaltern groups is very complex too. It must include all the repercussions of

---

[1] For Gramsci's use of the term "civil society", see introduction to *State and Civil Society*, pp. 206–9.

[2] The last three categories refer presumably to trade unions, reformist parties, and communist parties respectively.

[3] See note 4 on p. 126.

party activity, throughout the area of the subaltern groups themselves taken globally, and also upon the attitudes of the dominant group; it must include as well the repercussions of the far more effective actions (effective because backed by the State) of the dominant groups upon the subaltern groups and their parties. Among the subaltern groups, one will exercise or tend to exercise a certain hegemony through the mediation of a party; this must be established by studying the development of all the other parties too, in so far as they include elements of the hegemonic group or of the other subaltern groups which undergo such hegemony.

Numerous principles of historical research can be established by examining the innovatory forces which led the national Risorgimento in Italy: these forces took power and united in the modern Italian State, in struggle against specific other forces and helped by specific auxiliaries or allies. In order to become a State, they had to subordinate or eliminate the former and win the active or passive assent of the latter. A study of how these innovatory forces developed, from subaltern groups to hegemonic and dominant groups, must therefore seek out and identify the phases through which they acquired: 1. autonomy *vis-à-vis* the enemies they had to defeat, and 2. support from the groups which actively or passively assisted them; for this entire process was historically necessary before they could unite in the form of a State. It is precisely by these two yardsticks that the level of historical and political consciousness which the innovatory forces progressively attained in the various phases can be measured—and not simply by the yardstick of their separation from the formerly dominant forces. Usually the latter is the only criterion adopted, and the result is a unilateral history—or sometimes total incomprehension, as in the case of the history of Italy, since the era of the Communes. The Italian bourgeoisie was incapable of uniting the people around itself, and this was the cause of its defeats and the interruptions in its development.[4]

In the Risorgimento too, the same narrow egoism prevented a

---

[4] Clearly the fate of the mediaeval communes in Italy—i.e. the autonomous city-states—and the failure of their bourgeoisies to unite nationally is one of the fundamental problems for Italian historiography, and it recurs throughout the Prison Notebooks, though in particularly fragmentary form, e.g. "This book of Barbadoro's [on the finances of the Florentine Commune] is indispensable for seeing precisely how the communal bourgeoisie did not succeed in transcending the economic-corporate phase, i.e. in creating a State 'with the consent of the governed' and capable of developing. The development of the State proved possible only as a principality, not as a communal republic". (Ris., p. 9). "On the fact that the communal bourgeoisie did not succeed in transcending the corporative phase and hence cannot be said to have created a State, since it was

rapid and vigorous revolution like the French one. This is one of the most important problems, one of the most fertile causes of serious difficulties, in writing the history of the subaltern social groups and hence the (past) history *tout court* of the Italian States.

The history of subaltern social groups is necessarily fragmented

---

rather the Church and the Empire which constituted States, i.e. on the fact that the Communes did not transcend feudalism, it is necessary before writing anything, to read Gioacchino Volpe's book *Il Medioevo*." (Ris., p. 10). "It is necessary to determine what significance the 'State' had in the Communal State: a limited 'corporative' significance, which meant that it was unable to develop beyond middle feudalism, i.e. that which succeeded the absolute feudalism—without a third estate, so to speak—which had existed before the year A.D. 1000, and which was itself succeeded by the absolute monarchy in the fifteenth century, up to the French Revolution. There was an organic transition from the Commune to a system that was no longer feudal in the Low Countries, and there alone. In Italy, the Communes were unable to go beyond the corporative phase, feudal anarchy triumphed in a form appropriate to the new situation and then came the period of foreign domination." (Ris., p. 18). In a note in which Gramsci sketches out a plan of historical research (*Il Risorgimento e la Storia Precedente*, Ris., p. 3), he devotes a section to "Middle Ages, or epoch of the Communes, in which the new urban social groups are formed in molecular fashion, without the process reaching the higher phase of maturation as in France, Spain, etc.". Despite their fragmentary character, Gramsci's notes on "The Mediaeval Commune as the economic-corporative phase of the modern State" are clearly fundamental to his entire analysis of the specificity of Italian historical development. See also, e.g. "A further criterion of research must be borne in mind, in order to emphasise the dangers inherent in the method of historical analogy as an interpretative criterion. In the ancient and mediaeval State alike, centralisation, whether political-territorial or social (and the one is merely a function of the other), was minimal. The State was, in a certain sense, a mechanical bloc of social groups, often of different race: within the circle of political-military compression, which was only exercised harshly at certain moments, the subaltern groups had a life of their own, institutions of their own, etc., and sometimes these institutions had State functions which made of the State a federation of social groups with disparate functions not subordinated in any way—a situation which in periods of crisis highlighted with extreme clarity the phenomenon of 'dual power'. The only group excluded from any organised collective life of its own was that of the slaves (and such proletarians as were not slaves) in the classical world, and is that of the proletarians, the serfs and the peasants in the mediaeval world. However, even though, from many points of view, the slaves of the ancient world and the mediaeval proletariat were in the same conditions, their situation was not identical: the attempted revolt by the Ciompi [in Florence in 1378] certainly did not have the impact that a similar attempt by the slaves of antiquity would have produced (Spartacus demanding to be taken into the government in collaboration with the plebs, etc.). While in the Middle Ages an alliance between proletarians and people, and even more so the support of the proletarians for the dictatorship of a prince, was possible, nothing similar was possible for the slaves of the classical world. The modern State substitutes for the mechanical bloc of social groups their subordination to the active hegemony of the directive and dominant group, hence abolishes certain autonomies, which nevertheless are reborn in other forms, as parties, trade unions, cultural associations. The contemporary dictatorships legally abolish these new forms of autonomy as well, and strive to incorporate them within State activity: the legal centralisation of the entire national life in the hands of the dominant group becomes 'totalitarian'." (Ris., pp. 195–6.)

and episodic. There undoubtedly does exist a tendency to (at least provisional stages of) unification in the historical activity of these groups, but this tendency is continually interrupted by the activity of the ruling groups; it therefore can only be demonstrated when an historical cycle is completed and this cycle culminates in a success. Subaltern groups are always subject to the activity of ruling groups, even when they rebel and rise up: only "permanent" victory breaks their subordination, and that not immediately. In reality, even when they appear triumphant, the subaltern groups are merely anxious to defend themselves (a truth which can be demonstrated by the history of the French Revolution at least up to 1830). Every trace of independent initiative on the part of subaltern groups should therefore be of incalculable value for the integral historian. Consequently, this kind of history can only be dealt with monographically, and each monograph requires an immense quantity of material which is often hard to collect. [1934–35]

THE PROBLEM OF POLITICAL LEADERSHIP IN THE FORMATION AND DEVELOPMENT OF THE NATION AND THE MODERN STATE IN ITALY[5]

The whole problem of the connection between the various political currents of the Risorgimento—of their relations with each other,

---

[5] There is a real problem in translating the Italian "*dirigere*" and its compounds: *direzione*, *dirigente*, *diretto*, *direttivo*, etc. "*Dirigere*" means to "direct, lead, rule"; when, as here, Gramsci counterposes it to "*dominare*" we translate it "to lead". "*Dirigente*" is the present participle of "*dirigere*"—e.g. "*classe dirigente*" is the standard equivalent of "ruling class"—and as a noun is the normal word for (political) "leader"; where Gramsci uses it, as in this passage, in counter-position to "*dominante*" we have translated it as "leading". "*Diretto*" as an adjective means "direct", as a past participle has been translated "led". "*Direttivo*" has been translated "directive", although there is not really any such adjective in English. "*Direzione*" covers the various meanings of the word "direction" in English, but is also the normal word for "leadership", and has usually been translated as such here. It could be argued that a better English version would be achieved, without distorting Gramsci's thought, by regarding "*direzione*" and "*egemonia*" as interchangeable. After all, not only does Gramsci *usually* use them interchangeably; it is also the case that, for example, in the standard English translation of Lenin, e.g. in "Two Tactics of Social-Democracy", the word "hegemony" is used to translate "*rukovodstvo*", which could equally well be translated "leadership", and would certainly normally be translated as "*direzione*" in Italian. However, in view of the importance of these concepts in Gramsci's work, and the variations in his usage of them, we felt it preferable to choose fidelity over good English—despite the awkwardness of "lead" and "leading" in some passages.

Moreover, Gramsci certainly does not *always* use "*egemonia*" interchangeably with "*direzione*"—he sometimes uses it as the equivalent of "*direzione*" plus "*dominazione*", e.g. in the last passage quoted in the preceding note. For Gramsci's more usual use of this important concept, see especially MS. pp. 201–2: "Croces' thought must therefore, at the very least, be appreciated as an instrumental value.

and of their relations with the homogeneous or subordinate social groups existing in the various historical sections (or sectors) of the national territory—can be reduced to the following basic factual

---

Thus it can be said that he has drawn attention energetically to the importance of cultural and intellectual facts in historical development; to the function of great intellectuals in the organic life of civil society and the State; to the moment of hegemony and consent as a necessary form of the concrete historical bloc. That this is not something 'futile' is proved by the fact that, contemporaneously with Croce, the greatest modern theoretician of the philosophy of praxis [Lenin], on the terrain of political struggle and organisation and with a political terminology, gave new weight—in opposition to the various 'economist' tendencies—to the front of cultural struggle, and constructed the doctrine of hegemony as a complement to the theory of the State-as-force, and as the present form of the Forty-Eightist doctrine of 'permanent revolution'. For the philosophy of praxis, the conception of ethical-political history, in as much as it is independent of any realistic conception, can be accepted as an 'empirical canon' of historical research, to be kept continually in mind while studying and analysing historical development, if it is desired to arrive at an integral history and not one that is partial and extrinsic (history of economic forces as such, etc.)." See too LC. pp. 482–83: "My study on intellectuals is a vast project. . . . Moreover, I extend the notion of intellectual considerably, and do not limit myself to the habitual meaning, which refers only to great intellectuals. This study also leads to certain determinations of the concept of State, which is usually understood as political society (or dictatorship; or coercive apparatus to bring the mass of the people into conformity with the specific type of production and the specific economy at a given moment) and not as an equilibrium between political society and civil society (or hegemony of a social group over the entire national society exercised through the so-called private organisations, like the Church, the trade unions, the schools, etc.); it is precisely in civil society that intellectuals operate especially (Benedetto Croce, for example, is a kind of lay pope and an extremely efficient instrument of hegemony—even if at times he may find himself in disagreement with one government or another, etc.). This conception of the function of intellectuals, I believe, throws light on the reason, or one of the reasons, for the fall of the mediaeval communes, i.e. of the rule of an economic class which did not prove able to create its own category of intellectuals and thus exercise a hegemony as well as a dictatorship. The Italian intellectuals did not have a national-popular character, but one that was cosmopolitan on the model of the Church; it was a matter of indifference to Leonardo whether he sold the designs for the fortifications of Florence to Duke Valentino. The Communes were thus a syndicalist state, which did not succeed in transcending this phase and becoming an integral State as Machiavelli vainly urged; the latter attempted, by reorganising the army, to organise the hegemony of the city over the countryside, and he can therefore be called the first Italian Jacobin (the second was Carlo Cattaneo, but he had too many strange fancies in his head). It thus follows that the Renaissance should be considered a reactionary and repressive movement, in contrast to the development of the Communes, etc." See too NM. p. 160: "Hegemony and Democracy. Of the many meanings of democracy, the most realistic and concrete one in my view can be worked out in relation to the concept of 'hegemony'. In the hegemonic system, there exists democracy between the 'leading' group and the groups which are 'led', in so far as the development of the economy and thus the legislation which expresses such development favour the (molecular) passage from the 'led' groups to the 'leading' group. In the Roman Empire there was an imperial-territorial democracy in the concession of citizenship to the conquered peoples, etc. There could be no democracy under feudalism, because of the constitution of the closed groups [i.e. estates, corporations, etc.] etc."

In an earlier draft of 1920–30, this long note on the Risorgimento was entitled

datum. The Moderates[6] represented a relatively homogeneous social group, and hence their leadership underwent relatively limited oscillations (in any case, subject to an organically progressive line of development); whereas the so-called Action Party[7] did not base itself specifically on any historical class, and the oscillations which its leading organs underwent were resolved, in the last analysis, according to the interests of the Moderates. In other words, the Action Party was led historically by the Moderates. The assertion attributed to Victor Emmanuel II that he "had the Action Party in his pocket", or something of the kind, was in practice accurate—not only because of the King's personal contacts with Garibaldi, but because the Action Party was in fact "indirectly" led by Cavour and the King.

The methodological criterion on which our own study must be based is the following: that the supremacy of a social group manifests itself in two ways, as "domination" and as "intellectual and moral leadership". A social group dominates antagonistic groups, which it tends to "liquidate", or to subjugate perhaps even by armed force; it leads kindred and allied groups. A social group can, and indeed must, already exercise "leadership" before winning governmental power (this indeed is one of the principal conditions for the winning of such power); it subsequently becomes dominant when

---

"Class political leadership before and after attaining governmental power". Two of its key passages then read as follows: ". . . a class is dominant in two ways, i.e. 'leading' and 'dominant'. It leads the classes which are its allies, and dominates those which are its enemies. Therefore, even before attaining power a class can (and must) 'lead'; when it is in power it becomes dominant, but continues to 'lead' as well . . . there can and must be a 'political hegemony' even before the attainment of governmental power, and one should not count solely on the power and material force which such a position gives in order to exercise political leadership or hegemony."

[6] The Moderate Party, formally constituted in 1848, had grown out of the neo-Guelph movement (see note 9 on p. 58). Its first document was C. Balbo's *Le speranze d'Italia* (1844), and its ideas inspired the reforms of 1846–47. It stood initially for a confederation of the Italian States, and demanded reforms and written constitutions in each state. It was to some extent eclipsed in 1849, but its influence increased during the ten years from 1849–59, under the leadership of d'Azeglio and Cavour. It abandoned federalism, and was in fact the main instrument, at the level of political institutions, of national unification in 1859–61, and the main beneficiary of the Risorgimento. After Cavour's death in 1861, it became the Right in the Italian parliament, and held power until 1876.

[7] The *Partito d'Azione* was founded by Mazzini in March 1853, after the defeat of the February rising in Milan and the dissolution of the *Associazione Nazionale Italiana*. It was republican, but its ambiguous aims were symbolised by its motto "*Dio e popolo*" (God and the people). After several years of tenuous existence, it was revitalised by Garibaldi's influence in 1859, and played an important role in the organisation of the Sicilian expedition of the Thousand. After the unification of the country, most of its members joined the parliamentary "Left", a minority the tiny Republican Party.

it exercises power, but even if it holds it firmly in its grasp, it must continue to "lead" as well. The Moderates continued to lead the Action Party even after 1870 and 1876, and so-called "transformism"[8] was only the parliamentary expression of this action of intellectual, moral and political hegemony. Indeed one might say that the entire State life of Italy from 1848 onwards has been characterised by transformism—in other words by the formation of an ever more extensive ruling class, within the framework established by the Moderates after 1848 and the collapse of the neo-Guelph[9] and federalist[10] utopias. The formation of this class involved

---

[8] *Trasformismo*. This term was used from the 1880s onwards to describe the process whereby the so-called "historic" Left and Right parties which emerged from the Risorgimento tended to converge in terms of programme during the years which followed, until there ceased to be any substantive difference between them—especially after the "Left" came to power under Depretis in 1876 (see note 23 on p. 227 below) and the latter began to recruit his ministers indiscriminately from both sides of the parliament. The two main parties disintegrated into personal cliques and factions, which characterised Italian parliamentary life until fascism. The emergence of the Socialist Party from the turn of the century onwards did begin a process of polarisation of politics along class lines—a process which was arrested by fascism before the bourgeoisie had created a viable political party of its own (although the Popular Party—see note 14 on p. 62—was an attempt to do this). See too Gramsci's note (Ris. p. 157) entitled *Il trasformismo*: "Transformism as one of the historical forms of what has already been noted about 'revolution-restoration' or 'passive revolution', with respect to the process of formation of a modern State in Italy. Transformism as a 'real historical document' of the real nature of the parties which appeared as extremist in the period of militant activity (*Partito d'Azione*). Two periods of transformism: 1. from 1860 to 1900 'molecular' transformism, i.e. individual political figures formed by the democratic opposition parties are incorporated individually into the conservative-moderate 'political class' (characterised by its aversion to any intervention of the popular masses in state life, to any organic reform which would substitute a 'hegemony' for the crude, dictatorial 'dominance'); 2. from 1900 onwards transformism of entire groups of leftists who pass over to the moderate camp (the first event is the formation of the nationalist party, with ex-syndicalist and anarchist groups, which culminates in the Libyan war in the first instance and subsequently in interventionism). Between the two periods one can discern an intermediate phase (1890–1900) in which a mass of intellectuals joins the parties of the Left—so-called socialist, but in reality simply democratic." See too note 6 on p. 57.

[9] Neo-Guelphism was a liberal catholic movement in Italy in the first half of the nineteenth century. The term was coined by its enemies (the Guelphs had been the Papal party in mediaeval and pre-renaissance Italy), but was accepted by its members—who were quite willing to be identified with the pre-renaissance Papacy, which they saw as symbolising Italian unity and independence. Their aim was an Italian federation under the Pope. Prominent neo-Guelphs included Gioberti (see note 36 on p. 399) and Manzoni, the author of *The Betrothed* (see note 73 on p. 375). The movement's ideals were definitively proved illusory when the Risorgimento created a national Italian state under the Piedmont monarchy, and when the Pope refused to come to terms with that state; most of its members in fact then rallied to the monarchy. It can be seen as a precursor of the Popular Party (see note 14 on p. 62) and hence ultimately of the Christian Democrat Party of today.

[10] There were various federalist tendencies in pre-Risorgimento Italy, in

the gradual but continuous absorption, achieved by methods which varied in their effectiveness, of the active elements produced by allied groups—and even of those which came from antagonistic groups and seemed irreconcilably hostile. In this sense political leadership became merely an aspect of the function of domination—in as much as the absorption of the enemies' *élites* means their decapitation, and annihilation often for a very long time. It seems clear from the policies of the Moderates that there can, and indeed must, be hegemonic activity even before the rise to power, and that one should not count only on the material force which power gives in order to exercise an effective leadership. It was precisely the brilliant solution of these problems which made the Risorgimento possible, in the form in which it was achieved (and with its limitations)—as "revolution" without a "revolution", or as "passive revolution" to use an expression of Cuoco's in a slightly different sense from that which Cuoco intended.[11]

In what forms, and by what means, did the Moderates succeed in establishing the apparatus (mechanism) of their intellectual, moral and political hegemony? In forms, and by means, which may

---

opposition to the unitary conception of the future Italian state held on the one hand by Mazzini and Garibaldi, and on the other by Cavour and the Piedmont monarchy. These tendencies ranged from the neo-Guelph federalism of Gioberti and the moderate liberal federalism of Balbo and d'Azeglio (see foregoing notes) to the radical liberal federalism of Cattaneo (see note 112 on p. 112) and the democratic-republican federalism of Ferrari (see note 23 on p. 65).

[11] Vincenzo Cuoco (1770–1823) was a Neapolitan conservative thinker of great influence in the early stages of the Risorgimento. He played a minor role in the Parthenopean Republic of 1799 (see note 63 on p. 92)—out of a sense of public duty (he was a life-long functionary) rather than out of any particular commitment to its ideals—and was exiled in consequence. In exile he read Burke and De Maistre, and came to the view that revolution must at all costs be avoided, since it was a destroyer of the "traditions" on which civilisation is based. In his "Historical Essay on the Neapolitan Republic of 1799", he described the episode as a passive revolution, because it was the work of an "enlightened" bourgeois class, "abstract rationalists", "Jacobins", imitating French models (and backed by French armies), and involved no mass participation. In the years which followed he came, paradoxically, to argue precisely in favour of such "passive revolutions", in that his main thesis was the need to put through reforms in order to prevent revolution on the French model. He was an enthusiastic supporter of Napoleonic rule, and became a public official under it (1806–15). He can be seen as the theorist of what Gramsci termed (after Edgar Quinet) "revolution-restoration". See MS. pp. 184–85: "One should study the way in which the critical formula of Vincenzo Cuoco on the 'passive revolutions', which when it was formulated (after the tragic experiment of the Parthenopean Republic of 1799) was meant as a warning, to create a national mood of greater energy and popular revolutionary initiative, was converted in the minds of the neo-Guelphs and Moderates, in their state of social panic, into a positive conception, into a political programme . . . the determination to abdicate and capitulate at the first serious threat of an Italian revolution that would be profoundly popular, i.e. radically national."

be called "liberal"—in other words through individual, "molecular", "private" enterprise (i.e. not through a party programme worked out and constituted according to a plan, in advance of the practical and organisational action). However, that was "normal" given the structure and the function of the social groups of which the Moderates were the representatives, the leading stratum, the organic intellectuals.[12]

For the Action Party, the problem presented itself differently, and different systems of organisation should have been adopted. The Moderates were intellectuals already naturally "condensed" by the organic nature of their relation to the social groups whose expression they were. (As far as a whole series of them were concerned, there was realised the identity of the represented and the representative; in other words, the Moderates were a real, organic vanguard of the upper classes, to which economically they belonged. They were intellectuals and political organisers, and at the same time company bosses, rich farmers or estate managers, commercial and industrial entrepreneurs, etc.) Given this organic condensation or concentration, the Moderates exercised a powerful attraction "spontaneously", on the whole mass of intellectuals of every degree who existed in the peninsula, in a "diffused", "molecular" state, to provide for the requirements, however rudimentarily satisfied, of education and administration. One may detect here the methodological consistency of a criterion of historico-political research: there does not exist any independent class of intellectuals, but every social group has its own stratum of intellectuals, or tends to form one; however, the intellectuals of the historically (and concretely) progressive class, in the given conditions, exercise such a power of attraction that, in the last analysis, they end up by subjugating the intellectuals of the other social groups; they thereby create a system of solidarity between all the intellectuals, with bonds of a psychological nature (vanity, etc.) and often of a caste character (technico-juridical, corporate, etc.). This phenomenon manifests itself "spontaneously" in the historical periods in which the given social group is really progressive—i.e. really causes the whole society to move forward, not merely satisfying its own existential requirements, but continuously augmenting its cadres for the conquest of ever new spheres of economic and productive activity. As soon as the dominant social group has exhausted its function, the ideological

---

[12] For the concept of "organic intellectuals", see "The Formation of the Intellectuals" on pp. 5–14 above.

bloc tends to crumble away; then "spontaneity" may be replaced by "constraint" in ever less disguised and indirect forms, culminating in outright police measures and *coups d'état.*

The Action Party not only could not have—given its character—a similar power of attraction, but was itself attracted and influenced: on the one hand, as a result of the atmosphere of intimidation (panic fear of a terror like that of 1793, reinforced by the events in France of 1848–49) which made it hesitate to include in its programme certain popular demands (for instance, agrarian reform); and, on the other, because certain of its leading personalities (Garibaldi) had, even if only desultorily (they wavered), a relationship of personal subordination to the Moderate leaders. For the Action Party to have become an autonomous force and, in the last analysis, for it to have succeeded at the very least in stamping the movement of the Risorgimento with a more markedly popular and democratic character (more than that perhaps it could not have achieved, given the fundamental premisses of the movement itself), it would have had to counterpose to the "empirical" activity of the Moderates (which was empirical only in a manner of speaking, since it corresponded perfectly to the objective) an organic programme of government which would reflect the essential demands of the popular masses, and in the first place of the peasantry. To the "spontaneous" attraction of the Moderates it would have had to counterpose a resistance and a counter-offensive "organised" according to a plan.

As a typical example of spontaneous attraction by the Moderates, one might recall the formation and development of the "liberal-catholic" movement[18] which scared the Papacy so much—partially succeeding in paralysing its movements; demoralising it; in an initial period pushing it too far to the left (with the liberalising measures of Pius IX); in a subsequent period driving it into a more right-wing position than it need have adopted; and in the last analysis being the cause of its isolation in the peninsula and in Europe. The Papacy has since demonstrated that it has learnt its lesson, and has shown itself capable in more recent times of

[18] Liberal catholic movements developed in several European countries—France, Belgium, Italy, England, etc.—in the early and mid-nineteenth century. In Italy they included notably the neo-Guelphs (see note 9 on p. 58). Their common ideological basis was an acceptance of the main body of bourgeois liberal thought at the time. In Italy, after the blow of the Pope's withdrawal to the Lateran in 1870, liberal catholicism more or less disappeared, but as Gramsci points out it can be seen as a precursor of the "Modernist" movement (see following note).

manœuvring brilliantly. Modernism first, and later Popularism,[14] are movements resembling the liberal-catholic movement of the Risorgimento, due in great part to the power of spontaneous attraction exercised on the one hand by the modern historicism of the secular intellectuals of the upper classes, and on the other by the practical movement of the philosophy of praxis.[15] The Papacy combated Modernism as a tendency aimed at reforming the Church and the Catholic religion, but it encouraged Popularism—i.e. the socio-economic basis of Modernism—and today with Pius XI is making it the pivot of its world policies.

But the Action Party lacked even a concrete programme of government. In essence it was always, more than anything else, an agitational and propagandist body in the service of the Moderates. The disagreements and internal conflicts of the Action Party, and the tremendous hatred which Mazzini aroused among the more valiant men of action (Garibaldi, Felice Orsini,[16] etc.) against himself personally and against his activities, were caused by the lack of any firm political leadership. These internal polemics were for the most part as abstract as Mazzini's preaching, but it is possible to draw useful historical indications from them (it is enough to quote the example of Pisacane's[17] writings, despite the

---

[14] Modernism was an intellectual movement which developed among catholics in the late nineteenth and early twentieth centuries. Its proclaimed aims were to bring the Church into harmony with the culture and society of the contemporary world—especially with new developments in scientific and sociological thinking. It was condemned by the Papal decree *Lamentabili* and the Encyclical *Pascendi* in 1907. However, via the work notably of Romolo Murri, it was an important ideological ancestor of contemporary Christian Democracy.

The Popular Party was founded by Luigi Sturzo and others in January 1919. Based on social-christian ideas current throughout Europe at the time, it was encouraged initially by the Papacy (as a political movement directed outwards, and not towards reform of the Church itself like Modernism). It grew swiftly—especially in the agricultural areas of North and Central Italy, where it set up "white" unions whose strength among the small peasants often outstripped that of their "red" rivals. After vacillating in its attitude towards fascism between 1921–25 (Sturzo was not prepared to accept Papal pressure for an accommodation), it was suppressed in 1925–26 like the other opposition parties. After the fall of fascism, it re-emerged as the Christian Democrat Party.

[15] i.e. Modernism and Popularism were a result of—and aimed to counteract—the influence of Croce and Gentile on the one hand, and of socialism on the other.

[16] Felice Orsini (1819–58). After participating in the early stages of the Risorgimento as a follower of Mazzini, he broke with the latter in the mid-50s and made an attempt in 1858 to assassinate Napoleon III, for which he was executed.

[17] Carlo Pisacane (1818–57) was a prominent Risorgimento man of action and military theorist, notable for his advocacy of the creation of peasant armies and a "war of national insurrection". Gramsci commended his perception of the need for a "Jacobin" element in the Risorgimento, but said that he should be compared to the Russian Narodniks. Born in Naples, of aristocratic origins, he became a

fact that he committed irreparable political and military errors, such as opposing Garibaldi's military dictatorship in the Roman Republic). The Action Party was steeped in the traditional rhetoric of Italian literature. It confused the cultural unity which existed in the peninsula—confined, however, to a very thin stratum of the population, and polluted by the Vatican's cosmopolitanism—with the political and territorial unity of the great popular masses, who were foreign to that cultural tradition and who, even supposing that they knew of its existence, couldn't care less about it. A comparison may be made between the Jacobins and the Action Party. The Jacobins strove with determination to ensure a bond between town and country, and they succeeded triumphantly. Their defeat as a specific party was due to the fact that at a certain point they came up against the demands of the Paris workers; but in reality they were perpetuated in another form by Napoleon, and today, very wretchedly, by the radical-socialists of Herriot and Daladier.

In French political literature, the necessity of binding the town (Paris) to the countryside had always been vividly felt and expressed. It is enough to recall the series of novels by Eugène Sue,[18] very widely disseminated in Italy too (Fogazzaro in his novel *Piccolo Mondo Antico* shows Franco Maironi receiving clandestinely from Switzerland the successive episodes of the *Mystères du Peuple*; these were in fact burnt at the hands of the public executioner in certain European cities—Vienna, for example). Sue's novels stress with particular insistence the necessity of having a concern for the peasantry, and of binding it to Paris. And Sue was the popular novelist of the Jacobin political tradition, and a "primary source"

---

military engineer. In 1847 he fled from Naples and joined the Foreign Legion. In 1848 he returned to Italy when fighting broke out in Milan, and arrived in Rome in March 1849 after the proclamation of the republic (see note 90 on p. 102). He became the moving spirit of the city's War Council, and as commander-in-chief organised the city's defences before Mazzini's appointment of General Rosselli (see note 111 on p. 112). After the fall of the republic, he withdrew to Genoa, and published his *Guerra combattuta in Italia negli anni* 1848–49, in which he expressed his disagreements with Garibaldi. He opposed Garibaldi's conception of revolutionary dictatorship as too purely military, and undemocratic since it did not involve the masses. Pisacane committed suicide in 1857 after the failure of a landing at Sapri south of Naples.

[18] Eugène Sue (1804–57) was the author of a series of extremely popular novels of Paris life published by instalments in the 1840s and 1850s, e.g. *Les Mystères de Paris* (1842–43), *Le Juif Errant* (1844–45), *Les Sept Péchés Capitaux* (1847–49), *Les Mystères du Peuple* (1849–57). Set in a popular milieu, they contained a mish-mash of vaguely humanitarian and democratic ideas. *Les Mystères de Paris* and its idealistic interpreters were savagely lampooned by Marx in *The Holy Family*.

for Herriot and Daladier[19] from many points of view (Napoleonic legend, anti-clericalism and anti-Jesuitism, petty bourgeois reformism, penal theories, etc.).

It is true that the Action Party was always implicitly anti-French by virtue of its Mazzinian ideology (compare Omodeo's essay on *French Supremacy and Italian Initiative*, in *Critica*, 1929, pp. 223 ff.), but it found in the history of the peninsula a tradition to which it could go back and attach itself. The history of the mediaeval Communes[20] is rich in relevant experiences: the nascent bourgeoisie seeks allies among the peasants against the Empire and against the local feudalism. (It is true that the question is complicated by the struggle between bourgeoisie and nobles competing for cheap labour. The bourgeoisie needs an abundant supply of labour, which can only be provided by the rural masses—but the nobles want the peasants tied to the soil: flight of the peasants into the cities where the nobles cannot capture them. In any case, even though the situation is different, there is apparent in the development of Communal civilisation the function of the city as a directive element, of the city which deepens the internal conflicts of the countryside and uses them as a politico-military instrument to strike down feudalism.) But the most classic master of the art of politics for the Italian ruling classes, Machiavelli, had also posed the problem—naturally in the terms and with the preoccupations of his time. In his politico-military writings, the need to subordinate the popular masses organically to the ruling strata, so as to create a national militia capable of eliminating the companies of fortune, was quite well understood.[21] Carlo Pisacane should perhaps be connected with this theme in Machiavelli; for him, the problem of satisfying popular demands (after having aroused them by means of propaganda) is seen mainly from the military point of view. With regard to Pisacane, certain contradictions in his conception need to be analysed. Pisacane, a Neapolitan nobleman, had succeeded in acquiring a series of politico-military concepts put into circulation by the military experiences of the French Revolution and of Napoleon, and transplanted to Naples during the reigns of

---

[19] French "Radicals" prominent in the twenties and thirties—both were prime ministers.

[20] See note 4 on p. 53.

[21] For Machiavelli's project for a citizen's militia, see introduction to "The Modern Prince". The companies of fortune were the mercenary armies led by *condottieri* which roved Italy in the fourteenth and fifteenth centuries and in numerous cases took power in the cities which employed them, and founded dynasties.

Joseph Bonaparte and of Joachim Murat[22]—but especially through the direct experience of the Neapolitan officers who had fought with Napoleon.* Pisacane understood that without a democratic policy it is impossible to have national armies with compulsory conscription, but his aversion for Garibaldi's strategy and his mistrust of Garibaldi are inexplicable. He had the same scornful attitude towards Garibaldi that the General Staffs of the *ancien régime* had towards Napoleon.

The other figure who needs to be studied for these problems of the Risorgimento is Giuseppe Ferrari,[23] but not so much for his so-called major works—real hotch-potches of muddle and confusion—as for his occasional pamphlets and letters. Ferrari, however, was to a great extent outside the concrete reality of Italy; he had become too gallicised. Often his judgements appear more acute than they really are, since he applied to Italy French schemas, which represented conditions considerably more advanced than those to be found in Italy. One may say that Ferrari, in relation to Italy, found himself in the position of a "descendant", and that his wisdom was in a certain sense "hindsight". The politician, however, must be an effective man of action, working on the present. Ferrari did not see that an intermediary link was missing between the Italian and French situations, and that it was precisely this link which had to be welded fast for it to be possible to pass on to the next. Ferrari was incapable of "translating" what was French into something Italian, and hence his very "acuteness" became an element of confusion, stimulated new sects and little schools, but did not impinge on the real movement.

If one goes deeper into the question, it appears that from many aspects the difference between many members of the Action Party and the Moderates was more one of "temperament" than of an organically political character. The term "Jacobin" has ended up by taking on two meanings: there is the literal meaning, charac-

---

[22] Joseph Bonaparte, Napoleon's brother, was King of the Two Sicilies from 1806–8; Murat was King from 1808–15.

* In his obituary of Cadorna in *Nuova Antologia*, 1 March 1929, M. Missiroli insists on the importance that this Neapolitan experience and military tradition had, through Pianell for example, in the reorganisation of the Italian army after 1870.

[23] Giuseppe Ferrari (1811–76), philosopher and historian. Living in exile in France from 1838–59, he wrote various works putting forward a democratic-republican federalist point of view. He returned to Italy in 1859, and was active in parliamentary politics until his death, as a more or less isolated radical figure who stood outside the process of transformism which characterised Italian parliamentary life in those years. See pp. 75–6 below.

terised historically, of a particular party in the French Revolution, which conceived of the development of French life in a particular way, with a particular programme, on the basis of particular social forces; and there are also the particular methods of party and government activity which they displayed, characterised by extreme energy, decisiveness and resolution, dependent on a fanatical belief in the virtue of that programme and those methods. In political language the two aspects of Jacobinism were split, and the term "Jacobin" came to be used for a politician who was energetic, resolute and fanatical, because fanatically convinced of the thaumaturgical virtues of his ideas, whatever they might be. This definition stressed the destructive elements derived from hatred of rivals and enemies, more than the constructive one derived from having made the demands of the popular masses one's own; the sectarian element of the clique, of the small group, of unrestrained individualism, more than the national political element. Thus, when one reads that Crispi[24] was a Jacobin, it is in this derogatory sense that the assertion should be understood. In his programme, Crispi was a Moderate pure and simple. His most noble Jacobin "obsession" was the politico-territorial unity of the country. This principle was always the compass by which he took his direction, not only in the period of the Risorgimento, in the strict sense, but in the succeeding period as well, when he was a member of the government. A man of strong passions, he hated the Moderates as individuals: he saw in them the latecomers, the heroes of the eleventh hour; people who would have made peace with the old régimes if these had become constitutional; people like the Tuscan Moderates, who clung to the Grand Duke's coat-tails, afraid that he might run away. He had little trust in a unity achieved by non-unitarians. Hence he tied himself to the monarchy, which he realised would be resolutely unitarian for dynastic reasons, and embraced the principle of Piedmontese hegemony with an energy and ardour which the very Piedmontese politicians themselves

[24] Francesco Crispi (1818–1901). At first a Sicilian autonomist, he became linked with Mazzini and converted to the aim of a unitary post-Risorgimento Italian state. In 1859 he organised an insurrection in Sicily, and played an important part in Garibaldi's expedition of 1860. After the achievement of national unity, he became a parliamentary deputy of the Left. In 1865 he broke with Mazzini and rallied to the monarchy. He was Minister of the Interior and Prime Minister on various occasions between 1876 and 1896, and was the most consistent advocate of Italian colonial expansion, notably into Ethiopia. In 1893–94 he repressed the Sicilian Fasci (see following note) with extreme savagery. In many ways he can be seen as a precursor of the nationalist and fascist movements of the twentieth century.

could not match. Cavour had warned that the South should not be dealt with by placing it under martial law: Crispi on the contrary at once established martial law and set up military courts in Sicily after the Fasci movement,[25] and accused the leaders of the Fasci of plotting with England for the secession of Sicily (pseudo-treaty of Bisacquino).[26] He allied himself closely with the Sicilian latifundists, since their fear of the demands of the peasantry made them the stratum most dedicated to unity, at the same time as overall policy was tending to reinforce Northern industrialism by means of the tariff war against France and customs protectionism. He did not hesitate to plunge the South and the Islands into a terrifying commercial crisis, so long as he was able to reinforce the industry which could give the country a real independence, and which would expand the cadres of the dominant social group: this is the policy of manufacturing the manufacturer. The government of the Right from 1861 to 1876 had merely, and timidly, created the general external conditions for economic development—rationalisation of the government apparatus, roads, railways, telegraph—and had restored to health the country's finances, over-burdened by the wars of the Risorgimento. The Left had attempted to remedy the hatred aroused among the people by the Right's unilateral fiscalism, but it had only succeeded in acting as a safety-valve: it had continued the policies of the Right with a left-wing personnel and phraseology. Crispi, on the other hand, gave the new Italian society a real heave forward: he was the true man of the new bourgeoisie. His figure, however, is characterised by a disproportion between deeds and words, between the repressions and their objects, between the instrument and the blow delivered; he handled a rusty culverin as if it were a piece of modern artillery. Crispi's colonial policy too is connected with his obsession with unity, and in it he proved able to understand the political innocence of the Mezzogiorno. The southern peasant wanted land, and Crispi, who did not want to (or could not) give it to him in Italy itself, who had no wish to go in for "economic Jacobinism", conjured up the mirage of

---

[25] *Fasci dei lavoratori* ("workers' leagues"), led by socialists, spread throughout Sicily in 1892–93. They were basically peasant organisations, and their main aim was the break-up of the big estates and distribution of the land. They had considerable success in securing improved contracts between peasants and landowners in 1893. In 1893–94, under the impact of the economic crisis of that year, the peasantry rose throughout the island, and was repressed with great brutality by Crispi.

[26] It was rumoured that contacts had taken place at Bisacquino, near Palermo, between representatives of the Fasci and the English, with a view to detaching Sicily from Italy and establishing it as an independent state.

colonial lands to be exploited. Crispi's imperialism was passionate, oratorical, without any economic or financial basis. Capitalist Europe, rich in resources and arrived at the point at which the rate of profit was beginning to reveal its tendency to fall,[27] had a need to widen the area of expansion of its income-bearing investments; thus, after 1890, the great colonial empires were created. But the still immature Italy not only had no capital to export, but had to have recourse to foreign capital for its own pressing needs. Hence there was lacking any real drive behind Italian imperialism, and it was substituted for by the strong popular passions of the peasants, blindly intent on possessing land. It was a question of an exigency of internal politics which had to be resolved, and was—by the side-tracking of its solution to infinity. Hence Crispi's policy was opposed by the (northern) capitalists themselves, who would more willingly have seen employed in Italy the huge sums spent in Africa; but in the South Crispi was popular for having created the "myth" of easy land.

Crispi left a profound stamp upon an enormous number of Sicilian intellectuals (these especially, though he influenced all Italian intellectuals, creating the first cells of a national socialism which was later to develop vertiginously).[28] He created that unitarian fanaticism which brought about a permanent atmosphere of suspicion against anything which might have the air of separatism. This, however (understandably), did not prevent the Sicilian latifundists from meeting in Palermo in 1920, and pronouncing a literal ultimatum against the government "of Rome", threatening secession; just as it did not prevent several of these latifundists from continuing to keep Spanish nationality, nor from calling on the Madrid government's diplomatic intervention (case of the Duke of Bivona in 1919) to safeguard their interests, threatened by the agitation of the peasants back from the war. The attitude of the various social groups in the Mezzogiorno from 1919 to 1926 serves to reveal and to emphasise certain weaknesses of the obsessively unitarian approach of Crispi, and to emphasise certain corrections contributed to it by Giolitti. These were very few in reality, since Giolitti essentially kept to the furrow traced by Crispi. For the temperamental Jacobinism of Crispi, Giolitti substituted bureaucratic diligence and continuity; he kept up the "mirage of land" in colonial policy,

---

[27] See *Capital*, Volume III, Section 3, and note 3 on p. 280 below.

[28] i.e. the nationalist party, which as Gramsci showed in *Alcuni temi* was effectively founded by ex-socialists and syndicalists (e.g. Corradini, with his concept of the "proletarian nations"), and fascism, which claimed to be a national socialism.

but he also propped up that policy with a "defensive" military outlook, and with the premise that it was necessary to create the conditions of freedom of expansion for the future. The episode of the Sicilian latifundists' ultimatum in 1920 is not isolated, and another interpretation of it could be suggested—from the precedent of the Lombard upper classes, who on certain occasions threatened to "go it alone" and to reconstitute the ancient Duchy of Milan (a temporary policy of blackmail towards the government)—if the authentic interpretation was not to be found in the campaigns run by the *Mattino* from 1919 until the dismissal of the Scarfoglio brothers.[29] For it would be too ingenuous to think that these campaigns were entirely suspended in mid-air, in other words not related in some way to currents of public opinion and to states of mind which had remained subterranean, latent, potential as a result of the atmosphere of intimidation created by obsessive unitarianism. The *Mattino* on two occasions defended the following thesis: that the Mezzogiorno joined the Italian State on a contractual basis, the Albertine Statute,[30] but that (implicitly) it continues to preserve a real, concrete personality of its own, and has the right to cast off the bonds of the unitary State if the contractual basis is in any way prejudiced, i.e. if the 1848 constitution is modified. This thesis was developed in 1919–20 in the face of a constitutional modification in one direction, and was repeated in 1924–25 against a change in the other direction.[31] One must keep in mind the importance of the *Mattino*'s role in the Mezzogiorno (it was also the newspaper with the widest circulation). The *Mattino* was always pro-Crispi and expansionist, setting the tone for the South's ideology—created by the hunger for land and by the sufferings of emigration, and inclining towards every vague form of settler colonialism. The following points should also be recalled about the *Mattino*: 1. its extremely violent campaign against the North on the occasion of the attempt by the Lombard textile magnates to gain control of certain Southern cotton industries; an attempt which reached the point at which the plant was about to be

---

[29] The brothers Carlo, Paolo and Antonio Scarfoglio inherited *Il Mattino* of Naples from their father, but were ousted by the Bank of Naples in 1928.

[30] Carlo Alberto, King of Sardinia (Piedmont), granted a constitution to Piedmont on 4 March 1848. This "Albertine Statute" provided for a parliament, with ministers responsible to it rather than to the King; it was subsequently extended to the other regions which were annexed to form the Kingdom of Italy.

[31] i.e. in 1919–20 in view of the threat of a socialist revolution, and in 1924–25 in view of the consolidation of fascist power and its progressive replacement of the institutions of bourgeois democracy by its own dictatorial régime.

transported to Lombardy, disguised as scrap metal in order to evade the legislation on industrial zones; an attempt which was precisely foiled by the newspaper, which went so far as to publish a eulogy of the Bourbons and their economic policies (this happened in 1923); 2. the "sorrowful", "nostalgic" commemoration of Maria Sophia[32] published in 1925, which provoked a great fuss and scandal.

To be sure, in order to evaluate this attitude of the *Mattino*, certain qualifications have to be taken into account: the adventurous character and the venality of the Scarfogli,* and their political and ideological dilettantism. But it is necessary to insist on the fact that the *Mattino* was the paper with the largest circulation in the Mezzogiorno, and that the Scarfogli were born journalists, in other words possessed that rapid and "sympathetic" intuition of the deepest currents of popular feeling which makes possible the dissemination of the yellow press.

Another element in evaluating the real significance of the obsessedly unitary policies of Crispi is the complex of feelings created in the North with regard to the Mezzogiorno. The poverty of the Mezzogiorno was historically "inexplicable" for the popular masses in the North; they did not understand that unity had not taken place on a basis of equality, but as hegemony of the North

---

[32] Maria Sophia (1841–1925) was the last Bourbon queen of the Two Sicilies. After the fall of Gaeta in 1861, she and her husband Francesco II fled, first to Rome and then after 1870 to exile in Paris and later Munich. She never ceased to plan the restoration of the Bourbon monarchy.

* It should be recalled that Maria Sophia continually sought to intervene in the internal affairs of Italy, through a thirst for vengeance if not with any hope of restoring the kingdom of Naples—even spending money for that purpose, as seems to be beyond doubt. *Unità*, in 1914 or 1915, published a sharp attack on Errico Malatesta in which it was asserted that the events of June 1914[33] might have been sponsored and financed by the Austrian General Staff through the medium of Zita di Borbone,[34] given the relations of "friendship" seemingly never interrupted between Malatesta and Maria Sophia; in his work *Uomini e cose della vecchia Italia* [Men and things of old Italy], B. Croce refers again to these relations in connection with an attempt to rescue an anarchist who had committed a terrorist attack—an attempt which was followed by diplomatic representations to the French government by that of Italy to stop these activities of Maria Sophia's. The anecdotes about Maria Sophia recounted by Signora B., who used to visit the ex-queen in 1919 to paint her portrait, should also be recalled. When all is said and done, Malatesta never replied to these accusations, as he ought to have done, unless (and this is highly doubtful) it is true that he replied in a letter to a clandestine broadsheet, printed in France by S. Schicchi and called *Il Picconiere*.

[33] i.e. the "Red Week" of Ancona, when troops fired on an anti-war demonstration whose culmination was a rally addressed by Malatesta, killing three people and wounding fifteen more. This led to a general strike and demonstrations throughout the country.

[34] Zita di Borbone was the last Austro-Hungarian Empress.

over the Mezzogiorno in a territorial version of the town-country relationship—in other words, that the North concretely was an "octopus" which enriched itself at the expense of the South, and that its economic-industrial increment was in direct proportion to the impoverishment of the economy and the agriculture of the South. The ordinary man from Northern Italy thought rather that, if the Mezzogiorno made no progress after having been liberated from the fetters which the Bourbon régime placed in the way of a modern development, this meant that the causes of the poverty were not external, to be sought in objective economic and political conditions, but internal, innate in the population of the South—and this all the more since there was a deeply-rooted belief in the great natural wealth of the terrain. There only remained one explanation—the organic incapacity of the inhabitants, their barbarity, their biological inferiority. These already widespread opinions (Neapolitan "vagabondry"[35] is a legend which goes back a long way) were consolidated and actually theorised by the sociologists of positivism (Niceforo, Sergi, Ferri, Orano, etc.),[36] acquiring the strength of "scientific truth" in a period of superstition about science. Thus a polemic arose between North and South on the subject of race, and about the superiority or inferiority of North and South (compare N. Colajanni's books defending the Mezzogiorno in this respect,[37] and the whole series of the *Rivista Popolare*). Meanwhile, in the North there persisted the belief that the Mezzogiorno was a "ball and chain" for Italy, the conviction that the modern industrial civilisation of Northern Italy would have made greater progress without this "ball and chain", etc. The early years of this century then saw the beginnings of a strong Southern reaction on this very subject. In the Sardinian Congress of 1911, held under the presidency of General Rugiu, a calculation was made of how

---

[35] "*Lazzaronismo*", from *lazzaroni* or *lazzari*, from the Spanish *lazaro* = poor (which in turns derives from the Biblical figure of Lazarus the beggar). From the sixteenth century onwards this word was applied by the Spanish rulers to the urban "mob" of Naples (and thence by extension of other cities). In Naples, this sub-proletariat was strongly monarchist, and in 1799 it rose in the *Sanfedista* rising against the bourgeois Jacobin régime of the Parthenopean Republic. It continued to be the bastion of the Bourbons to the end. The term itself was pejorative, stressing the wretched condition of that sub-proletariat and its supposed laziness and dishonesty, and it is these connotations to which Gramsci is referring here.

[36] Alfredo Niceforo, born 1876, was a sociologist and criminologist who wrote numerous studies on poverty, crime, etc., notably in Naples where he held a university post. In *Italiani del Nord e Italiani del Sud* he argued the biological inferiority of Southern Italians. Similar arguments were put forward by Giuseppe Sergi, Enrico Ferri (see note 47 on p. 246) and Paolo Orano.

[37] *Gli avvenimenti di Sicilia e le loro accuse*, and *L'Italia nel 1898: tumulti e reazione*.

many hundreds of millions had been extorted from Sardinia in the first fifty years of the unitary State, to the advantage of the mainland. Then came Salvemini's campaigns[38]—brought to their culmination in the foundation of *Unità*, but already being waged in *Voce* (see the special number of *Voce* on the *Southern Question*, later published as a pamphlet). In Sardinia an autonomist movement started, under the leadership of Umberto Cau, which also had a daily newspaper: *Il Paese*. In those early years of the century a certain "intellectual bloc"—a "pan-Italian" one—was created; it was led by B. Croce and Giustino Fortunato, and sought to pose the Southern Question as a national problem capable of renovating political and parliamentary life.[39] Not simply the influence of Croce and Fortunato, but their contributions, were to be seen in every review of the younger generation which had liberal democratic tendencies and proposed in general to rejuvenate and deprovincialise national life and culture in all fields—in art, in literature, in politics. It was the case with *Voce* and *Unità*, but also with *Patria* from Bologna, *Azione Liberale* from Milan, with the Young Liberal movement led by Giovanni Borelli, etc.[40] The influence of this bloc increased further when it came to determine the political line of Albertini's *Corriere della Sera*; after the war, thanks to the new situation, it appeared in *La Stampa* too (through Cosmo, Salvatorelli, and also through Ambrosini) and in Giolittism with the inclusion of Croce in the last Giolitti government.* The movement developed to its maxi-

---

[38] For Salvemini and the influence of his "southernism" on the young Gramsci, see Introduction, pp. xx, xxvi–vii.

[39] Gramsci develops this analysis of the role played by Croce and Fortunato at greater length in *Alcuni temi*, in MS. p. 173, and below (pp. 93–5) in "The city-countryside relationship . . .". Fortunato, a liberal conservative, was one of the most important of the "southernist" writers, and the author notably of *Il Mezzogiorno e lo Stato italiano*, 1911.

[40] Giovanni Borelli (1869–1932) was the founder of the Young Liberal movement in 1900. Its aim was the re-creation of a "Latin" Mediterranean, and it was in fact monarchist, irredentist and colonialist.

* A tendentious interpretation of this certainly very complex and many-sided movement is also offered today by G. Prezzolini, despite the fact that he himself was a typical incarnation of it. However, as an authentic document, there is still the first edition of *La Coltura Italiana* (1923) by that same Prezzolini—especially in view of its omissions.[41]

[41] Giuseppe Prezzolini (b. 1882) was at first a mystical nationalist close to Enrico Corradini (see note 28 on p. 68), subsequently a Crocean with syndicalist sympathies. From 1908–14 he edited the influential *La Voce*. When the fascists took power he soon adapted himself to the new situation.The first edition of his *La Coltura Italiana* (published in 1923 but written before the fascists came to power) contained many passages—including a relatively complimentary description of the 1919–20 *Ordine Nuovo*—which Prezzolini omitted in later editions, in order to avoid giving offence to the régime.

mum, which was also its point of dissolution. This point was to be identified in the particular stance of Piero Gobetti and in his cultural initiatives.[42] The polemic carried on by Giovanni Ansaldo (and collaborators of his such as "Calcante" [Calchas], otherwise Francesco Ciccotti) against Guido Dorso is the most expressive document of this destination and outcome[43]; the comic aspects

[42] Piero Gobetti (1901–26) founded the fortnightly *Energie Nuove* in 1918, at the age of 17. The son of a Turin grocer, he was at first strongly influenced by Salvemini, but went far beyond the latter's "concretism", i.e. pragmatic liberalism, in his attitude towards the October Revolution, the working-class and Marxism. Although he was explicitly non-socialist, he saluted the October Revolution and the work of Lenin and Trotsky as a gigantic liberation of the Russian people. His positions were extremely confused, and yet brought him near to the revolutionary Left in the years immediately after the war. He wrote, for instance (in 1919): "The Marxist experiment in Russia has certainly failed; the old objections of liberal economics are more powerful than ever against all the proponents of statification—Bolshevism is just a further demonstration of this. . . . But . . . the Russian Revolution is not limited to the socialist experiment. The bases of a new State are being laid there. Lenin and Trotsky are not only Bolsheviks, they are men of action who have awoken a people and are creating a new soul for it. . . . The work of Lenin and Trotsky . . . is basically the negation of socialism and an assertion and exaltation of liberalism . . .". He seems to have been particularly influenced by Trotsky's *Terrorism and Communism: a reply to Kautsky*. His confused positions made him the target of polemics in the pages of *Ordine Nuovo*, from both Gramsci and Togliatti, who attacked his idealism. But he was genuinely concerned, unlike Salvemini, with the theoretical problems raised by the rising tide of working-class revolution in that period, and organised debates in the pages of *Energie Nuove* on socialism, with contributions from, e.g., Croce, Einaudi, Mondolfo, Loria. During 1920 he came closer to the *Ordine Nuovo* group, above all under the influence of the factory council movement, and also because he shared their view that the alliance of workers and peasants was the key to what he saw as the "democratic" revolution in Italy. In January 1921, when *Ordine Nuovo* became a daily, he was asked to become its theatre critic, and he also contributed numerous book reviews. In February 1922 he founded a new weekly *La Rivoluzione Liberale*, whose contributors included Amendola, Pareto, Mosca, Missiroli, Fortunato, Einaudi, Dorso, Lelio Basso, Carlo Levi, Malaparte, Salvatorelli—to name only a few. He made this weekly above all into an organ of bitter opposition to fascism; Gobetti was explicit in his opposition to any illusion that fascism could be somehow contained within the system, or that it would be tamed by coming to terms with it. In his opposition to fascism, Gobetti came very close to Marxism (see, for instance, his *L'ora di Marx*), and his entire position was based on the idea that only the working class could defeat fascism. His activity, including a publishing house founded in 1923 and a new fortnightly *Baretti* in addition to *La Rivoluzione Liberale*, continued despite constant police harassment until the end of 1925, when he was forbidden to edit or publish anything further. He decided to go into exile, and died almost immediately of bronchitis and heart failure. Gramsci analysed the significance of Gobetti in his *Alcuni temi*.

[43] Guido Dorso (see Gramsci's discussion of him in *Alcuni temi*) was the author of *La Rivoluzione Meridionale*, in which he called for the overthrow of the centralised Italian state, and also of the traditional ruling class of the South. Ansaldo and Ciccotti were contributors at this time to Gobetti's *Rivoluzione Liberale* (although Ansaldo later in fact became a fascist, at the time of the Abyssinian campaign), who defended the unity of Italy at any price—raising the bogy of a return of the Bourbons if the unitary link was broken.

which now seem obvious in the gladiatorial and intimidatory attitudes of fanatical unitarianism even help to make it that.*

From this series of observations and analyses of certain elements of Italian history after unity, certain criteria may be drawn for evaluating the position of confrontation between the Moderates and the Action Party, and for investigating the respective political "wisdom" of these two parties and of the various tendencies which contested the political and ideological leadership of the latter of them. It is obvious that, in order to counterpose itself effectively to the Moderates, the Action Party ought to have allied itself with the rural masses, especially those in the South, and ought to have been "Jacobin" not only in external "form", in temperament, but most particularly in socio-economic content. The binding together of the various rural classes, which was accomplished in a reactionary bloc by means of the various legitimist-clerical intellectual strata, could be dissolved, so as to arrive at a new liberal-national formation, only if support was won from two directions: from the peasant masses, by accepting their elementary demands and making these an integral part of the new programme of government; and from the intellectuals of the middle and lower strata, by concentrating them and stressing the themes most capable of interesting them (and the prospect of a new apparatus of government being formed, with the possibilities of employment which it offered, would already have been a formidable element of attraction for them—if that prospect had appeared concrete, because based on the aspirations of the peasantry).

The relation between these two actions was dialectical and reciprocal: the experience of many countries, first and foremost that of France in the period of the great Revolution, has shown that, if the peasants move through "spontaneous" impulses, the intellectuals start to waver; and, reciprocally, if a group of intellectuals situates itself on a new basis of concrete pro-peasant policies, it ends up by drawing with it ever more important elements of the masses.

---

* That Ansaldo, in 1925–26, should have thought he could make people believe in a return of the Bourbons to Naples, would seem inconceivable without a knowledge of all the antecedents of the question and of the subterranean courses taken by the polemics, with their hidden meanings and allusions enigmatic to the non-initiated. However, it is remarkable that even among certain popular elements, who had read Oriani,[44] the fear existed at the time that a Bourbon restoration was possible in Naples, and hence a more extensive dissolution of the unitary State link.

[44] Alfredo Oriani (1852–1909) was a novelist and polemicist whose themes were those of national destiny—as such he was a forerunner of fascism. Gramsci wrote a number of critical notes on him (see LVN. pp. 16–19).

However, one may say that, given the dispersal and the isolation of the rural population and hence the difficulty of welding it into solid organisations, it is best to start the movement from the intellectual groups; however, in general, it is the dialectical relation between the two actions which has to be kept in mind. It may also be said that peasant parties in the strict sense of the word are almost impossible to create. The peasant party generally is achieved only as a strong current of opinion, and not in schematic forms of bureaucratic organisation. However, the existence even of only a skeleton organisation is of immense usefulness, both as a selective mechanism, and for controlling the intellectual groups and preventing caste interests from transporting them imperceptibly onto different ground.

These criteria must be kept in mind when studying the personality of Giuseppe Ferrari, who was the Action Party's unheeded "specialist" on agrarian questions. It is also necessary to study closely Ferrari's attitude towards the agricultural labourers [*bracciantato*], i.e. the landless peasants who live by day-labour. It is on these that he bases a notable part of his ideological positions, for which he is still sought out and read by certain schools of thought (works of Ferrari reprinted by Monanni, with prefatory material by Luigi Fabbri). It must be recognised that the problem of the agricultural labourers is an extremely difficult one, and even today very hard to solve. In general, the following criteria must be borne in mind: the agricultural labourers to this day are for the most part simply peasants without land—(hence were all the more so in the Risorgimento period)—and not the workers of an agricultural industry developed through concentration of capital and the division of labour. Moreover, in the period of the Risorgimento, tied labour [*obbligato*] was considerably more widespread than casual labour [*avventizio*]. Their psychology is therefore, with all due exceptions, the same as that of the farmer and the smallholder.*

The question was posed in acute form not so much in the Mezzo-

---

* It is worth recalling the polemic between Senators Tanari and Bassini in the *Resto del Carlino* and in *Perseveranza*, which took place towards the end of 1917 and in early 1918, concerning the application of the slogan: "the land to the peasants", launched around that time. Tanari was in favour, Bassini against. Bassini based himself on his experience as a big agricultural industrialist, as a proprietor of agricultural concerns in which the division of labour had progressed so far as to render the land indivisible, because of the disappearance of the self-employed peasant and the emergence of the modern worker.

giorno, where the artisanal character of agricultural labour was too obvious, as in the Po valley where it was more disguised. Even in recent times, however, the existence of an acute problem of the agricultural labourers in the Po valley was partly due to extra-economic causes: 1. over-population, which did not find an outlet in emigration as in the South, and was artificially maintained through the policy of public works; 2. policy of the landowners, who did not wish to consolidate the working population into a single class of agricultural labourers and share-croppers [*mezzadri*]; they alternated sharecropping with leaseholding, utilising this alternation in order to bring about a better selection of privileged sharecroppers who would be their allies: in every congress of landowners from the Po region, there was always a discussion on whether sharecropping or direct tenancy was more advantageous, and it was clear that the choice was made for motives of a socio-political character. During the Risorgimento, the problem of the Po agricultural labourers appeared in the guise of a terrible phenomenon of pauperism. It is seen thus by the economist Tullio Martello in his *History of the International*, written in 1871–72, a work which must be borne in mind since it reflects the political passions and the social preoccupations of the preceding period.

Ferrari's position is moreover weakened by his "federalism"; especially in his case—living in France as he did—this appeared all the more like a reflection of the national and State interests of France. Proudhon should be recalled, with his pamphlets against Italian unity—combated from the declared standpoint of French State interest and of democracy. In reality, the principal tendencies of French politics were bitterly opposed to Italian unity. To this day the monarchists (Bainville and Co.) "reproach" retrospectively the two Napoleons with having created the "nationalitarian" myth, and with having helped to secure its realisation in Germany and Italy, thus lowering the relative stature of France, which "ought" to be surrounded by a swarm of little states of the Switzerland type in order to be "secure".

Now the Moderates after 1848 formed a national bloc under their own hegemony—influencing the two supreme leaders of the Action Party, Mazzini and Garibaldi, in different ways and to a different extent. They did this precisely under the slogan of "independence and unity", without taking any account of the concrete political content of such generic formulae. How successful the Moderates had been in their intention of diverting attention from the kernel to the husk is demonstrated, among so many other examples, by this expression of Guerrazzi's in a letter to a Sicilian student*: "Whatever we desire—whether it is despotism or republic or anything else—let us not seek division among ourselves; with this guiding principle, the world can collapse and we will still find the way again." In any case, Mazzini's entire activity was concretely devoted to a continuous and permanent preaching of unity.

On the subject of Jacobinism and the Action Party, an element to be highlighted is the following: that the Jacobins won their function of "leading" [*dirigente*] party by a struggle to the death; they literally "imposed" themselves on the French bourgeoisie, leading it into a far more advanced position than the originally strongest bourgeois nuclei would have spontaneously wished to take up, and even far more advanced than that which the historical premisses should have permitted—hence the various forms of backlash and the function of Napoleon I. This feature, characteristic of Jacobinism (but before that, also of Cromwell and the "Roundheads") and hence of the entire French Revolution, which consists in (apparently) forcing the situation, in creating irreversible *faits accomplis*, and in a group of extremely energetic and determined men driving the bourgeois forward with kicks in the backside, may be schematized in the following way. The Third Estate was the least homogeneous; it had a very disparate intellectual élite, and a group which was very advanced economically but politically moderate. Events developed along highly interesting lines. The representatives of the Third Estate initially only posed those questions which interested the actual physical members of the social group, their immediate "corporate" interests (corporate in the traditional sense, of the immediate and narrowly selfish interests of a particular category). The precursors of the Revolution were in fact moderate reformers, who shouted very loud but actually demanded very little. Gradually a new élite was selected out which did not concern itself solely with "corporate" reforms, but tended to conceive of the bourgeoisie as the hegemonic group of all the popular forces. This selection occurred through the action of two factors: the resistance of the old social forces, and the international threat. The old forces did not wish to concede anything, and if they did concede anything they did it with the intention of gaining time and preparing a counter-offensive. The Third Estate would have fallen into these successive "pitfalls" without the

* Published in the *Archivio Storico Siciliano* by Eugenio Di Carlo, correspondence between F. D. Guerrazzi and the notary Francesco Paolo Sardofontana of Riella, reproduced in *Marzocco* on 24 November 1929.

energetic action of the Jacobins, who opposed every "intermediate" halt in the revolutionary process, and sent to the guillotine not only the elements of the old society which was hard a-dying, but also the revolutionaries of yesterday—today become reactionaries. The Jacobins, consequently, were the only party of the revolution in progress, in as much as they not only represented the immediate needs and aspirations of the actual physical individuals who constituted the French bourgeoisie, but they also represented the revolutionary movement as a whole, as an integral historical development. For they represented future needs as well, and, once again, not only the needs of those particular physical individuals, but also of all the national groups which had to be assimilated to the existing fundamental group. It is necessary to insist, against a tendentious and fundamentally anti-historical school of thought, that the Jacobins were realists of the Machiavelli stamp and not abstract dreamers. They were convinced of the absolute truth of their slogans about equality, fraternity and liberty, and, what is more important, the great popular masses whom the Jacobins stirred up and drew into the struggle were also convinced of their truth. The Jacobins' language, their ideology, their methods of action reflected perfectly the exigencies of the epoch, even if "today", in a different situation and after more than a century of cultural evolution, they may appear "abstract" and "frenetic". Naturally they reflected those exigencies according to the French cultural tradition. One proof of this is the analysis of Jacobin language which is to be found in *The Holy Family*.[45] Another is Hegel's admission,[46] when he places as parallel and reciprocally translatable the juridico-political language of the Jacobins and the concepts of classical German philosophy—which is recognised today to have the maximum of concreteness and which was the source of modern historicism. The first necessity was to annihilate the enemy forces, or at least to reduce them to impotence in order to make a counter-revolution impossible. The second was to enlarge the cadres of the bourgeoisie as such, and to place the latter at the head of all the national forces; this meant identifying the interests and the requirements common to all the national forces, in order to set these forces in motion and lead them into the struggle, obtaining two results: (*a*) that of opposing a wider target to the blows of the enemy, i.e. of creating a politico-military

[45] *The Holy Family*, Lawrence and Wishart, London, 1956, pp. 160–67, in Chapter VI, Section 3(c).

[46] e.g. in Section III, part 3 of his Foreword to the *Phenomenology of the Spirit*, and in his *Lectures on the History of Philosophy*. See MS. pp. 63–71.

relation favourable to the revolution; (*b*) that of depriving the enemy of every zone of passivity in which it would be possible to enrol Vendée-type armies.[47] Without the agrarian policy of the Jacobins, Paris would have had the Vendée at its very doors. The resistance of the Vendée properly speaking is linked to the national question, which had become envenomed among the peoples of Brittany and in general among those alien to the slogan of the "single and indivisible republic" and to the policy of bureaucratic-military centralisation—a slogan and a policy which the Jacobins could not renounce without committing suicide. The Girondins tried to exploit federalism in order to crush Jacobin Paris, but the provincial troops brought to Paris went over to the revolutionaries. Except for certain marginal areas, where the national (and linguistic) differentiation was very great, the agrarian question proved stronger than aspirations to local autonomy. Rural France accepted the hegemony of Paris; in other words, it understood that in order definitively to destroy the old régime it had to make a bloc with the most advanced elements of the Third Estate, and not with the Girondin moderates. If it is true that the Jacobins "forced" its hand, it is also true that this always occurred in the direction of real historical development. For not only did they organise a bourgeois government, i.e. make the bourgeoisie the dominant class—they did more. They created the bourgeois State, made the bourgeoisie into the leading, hegemonic class of the nation, in other words gave the new State a permanent basis and created the compact modern French nation.

That the Jacobins, despite everything, always remained on bourgeois ground is demonstrated by the events which marked their end, as a party cast in too specific and inflexible a mould, and by the death of Robespierre. Maintaining the Le Chapelier law, they were not willing to concede to the workers the right of combination; as a consequence they had to pass the law of the *maximum*.[48] They thus broke the Paris urban bloc: their assault forces, assembled in the Commune, dispersed in disappointment, and Thermidor gained the upper hand. The Revolution had found its widest class limits.

---

[47] From 1793–96 royalist priests and landowners fomented peasant guerrilla warfare against the Republic in the Vendée region in western France.

[48] The Le Chapelier law of June 1791 was brought in to dissolve the craft guilds which had survived from the *ancien régime*. Although it was in conception a "progressive" bourgeois measure, it was used throughout the first half of the nineteenth century to ban workers' associations.

The law of the *maximum* fixed a ceiling for food prices and for wages, and drove a wedge between the Jacobins and the workers.

The policy of alliances and of permanent revolution had finished by posing new questions which at that time could not be resolved; it had unleashed elemental forces which only a military dictatorship was to succeed in containing.[49]

In the Action Party there was nothing to be found which resembled this Jacobin approach, this inflexible will to become the "leading" [*dirigente*] party. Naturally one has to allow for the differences: in Italy the struggle manifested itself as a struggle

---

[49] Gramsci is here referring to what he elsewhere terms the "forty-eightist" slogan of "permanent revolution", since it was first put forward by Marx during the 1848 wave of bourgeois revolutions in the belief that these would lead directly to proletarian revolutions. See notably the 1850 "Address of the Central Committee to the Communist League": "While the democratic petty bourgeoisie wish to bring the revolution to a conclusion as quickly as possible, and with the achievement, at most, of the above demands, it is our interest and our task to make the revolution permanent, until all more or less possessing classes have been forced out of their position of dominance, until the proletariat has conquered state power, . . . Their battle cry must be: 'The Revolution in Permanence'."

See too NM. pp. 102–3: "The development of Jacobinism (of content), and of the formula of Permanent Revolution put into practice in the active phase of the French Revolution, found its juridical-constitutional 'completion' in the parliamentary régime. The latter, in the period in which 'private' energies in society were most plentiful, realised the permanent hegemony of the urban class over the entire population in the Hegelian form of government with permanently organised consent. (However, this organisation of consent was left to private initiative, and was thus of a moral or ethical character, because it was consent 'voluntarily' given in one way or another.) The 'limit' which the Jacobins had come up against in the Le Chapelier law and in the law of the *maximum* was transcended and pushed progressively back in the course of a whole process, in which propagandistic and practical (economic, political-juridical) activity alternated. The economic base was continually enlarged and reinforced through industrial and commercial development. Those social elements which were most highly endowed with energy and spirit of enterprise rose from the lower classes to the ruling classes. The entire society was in a continuous process of formation and dissolution, followed by more complex formations with richer potentialities. This, broadly speaking, lasted until the epoch of imperialism and culminated in the world war. In this process, attempts at insurrection alternated with pitiless repression, enlargements of political suffrage with restrictions, freedom of association with restriction or annulment of that freedom. . . . The 'normal' exercise of hegemony on the now classical terrain of the parliamentary régime is characterised by the combination of force and consent, which balance each other reciprocally, without force predominating excessively over consent. Indeed, the attempt is always made to ensure that force will appear to be based on the consent of the majority, expressed by the so-called organs of public opinion—newspapers and associations—which, therefore, in certain situations, are artificially multiplied. Between consent and force stands corruption/fraud (which is characteristic of certain situations when it is hard to exercise the hegemonic function, and when the use of force is too risky). This consists in procuring the demoralisation and paralysis of the antagonist (or antagonists) by buying its leaders—either covertly, or, in cases of imminent danger, openly—in order to sow disarray and confusion in his ranks. In the period following the World War, cracks opened up everywhere in the hegemonic apparatus, and the exercise of hegemony became permanently difficult and aleatory."

against old treaties and the existing international order, and against a foreign power—Austria—which represented these and upheld them in Italy, occupying a part of the peninsula and controlling the rest. This problem arose in France too, in a certain sense at least, since at a certain point the internal struggle became a national struggle fought at the frontiers. But this only happened after the whole territory had been won for the revolution, and the Jacobins were able to utilise the external threat as a spur to greater energy internally: they well understood that in order to defeat the external foe they had to crush his allies internally, and they did not hesitate to carry out the September massacres.[50] In Italy, although a similar connection, both explicit and implicit, did exist between Austria and at least a segment of the intellectuals, the nobles and the landowners, it was not denounced by the Action Party; or at least it was not denounced with the proper energy and in the most practically effective manner, and it did not become a real political issue. It became transformed "curiously" into a question of greater or lesser patriotic dignity, and subsequently gave rise to a trail of acrimonious and sterile polemics which continued even after 1898.*

---

[50] Between 2 and 5 September 1792, at the insistence notably of Marat, some 1200 royalist prisoners were massacred. They were accused of having by their treachery brought about the defeats suffered by the revolutionary armies prior to the battle of Valmy.

* See the articles of Rerum Scriptor in *Critica Sociale* after the resumption of publication, and the book by Romualdo Bonfadini, *Mezzo secolo di patriottismo* ["Half a century of patriotism"], Milan 1886. The question of the "testimony"[51] of Federico Confalonieri should be recalled in this respect: Bonfadini, in the above-mentioned book, asserts in a note that he has seen the collection of the "testimony" in the State Archives of Milan, and he refers to some 80 dossiers. Others have always denied that this collection of testimony exists in Italy, thus explaining its non-publication. In an article (published in 1925) by Senator Salata, charged with carrying out research in the Viennese archives on documents concerning Italy, it was claimed that the testimony had been traced and would be published. Recall the fact that at a certain time *Civiltà Cattolica* challenged the liberals to publish it, asserting that if it was known it would blow sky high, no less, the unity of the State. In the Confalonieri question, the most remarkable fact is that unlike other patriots pardoned by Austria, Confalonieri, who had been a remarkable politician, withdrew from active life and after his liberation maintained a very reserved bearing. The whole Confalonieri question should be critically re-examined, together with the attitude assumed by him and his companions, and an analysis in depth made of the memoirs written by the individuals involved (when they wrote any). For the polemics which they provoked, the memoirs of the Frenchman Alexandre Andryane are interesting; he treats Confalonieri with great respect and admiration, whereas he attacks Giorgio Pallavicino for his weakness.

[51] "*Costituti*" are more precisely statements made under pre-trial interrogation; the word has no exact English equivalent.

Federico Confalonieri (1785–1846) was a conspirator, inventor and journalist. He was a member of the "*Italici*" in opposition to Napoleon in 1814, and subse-

In connection with the attempts—some even recent—to defend the attitude towards Austria assumed by the Lombard aristocracy, especially after the attempted insurrection at Milan in February 1853 and during the vice-regency of Maximilian,[52] it should be recalled that Alessandro Luzio, whose historical work is always tendentious and acrimonious against the democrats, goes so far as to justify the faithful services rendered to Austria by Salvotti: hardly a Jacobin spirit! The comic note in the discussion is provided by Alfredo Panzini, who, in his *Life of Cavour*, rings all the changes—as affected as they are nauseating and Jesuitical—on a "tiger-skin" displayed from an aristocrat's window during a visit to Milan by Franz Josef![53]

The conceptions of Missiroli, Gobetti, Dorso, etc., on the Italian Risorgimento as a "royal conquest", should be considered from all these points of view.

If in Italy a Jacobin party was not formed, the reasons are to be sought in the economic field, that is to say in the relative weakness of the Italian bourgeoisie and in the different historical climate in Europe after 1815. The limit reached by the Jacobins, in their policy of forced reawakening of French popular energies to be allied with the bourgeoisie, with the Le Chapelier law and that of the *maximum*, appeared in 1848 as a "spectre" which was already threatening—and this was skilfully exploited by Austria, by the old governments and even by Cavour (quite apart from the Pope). The bourgeoisie could not (perhaps) extend its hegemony further over the great popular strata—which it did succeed in embracing in France—(could not for subjective rather than objective reasons); but action directed at the peasantry was certainly always possible. Differences between France, Germany and Italy in the process by which the bourgeoisie took power (and England). It was in France that the process was richest in developments, and in active and

---

quently of the anti-Austrian "*federati*" with wide contacts in French liberal circles. He tried to introduce gas-lighting and river steamboats during this period. In 1821 he plotted a rising in Lombardy to coincide with the Piedmont rising of that year. He was arrested, and his interrogation and trial lasted until 1823, when he was sentenced to death—though this was commuted to life imprisonment, and later to exile.

[52] Arch-duke Maximilian of Austria was vice-regent of Lombardy from 1857 to 1859. The attempted anti-Austrian insurrection of 6 February 1853, involving workers and artisans inspired by Mazzini's ideas, was a failure; the aristocrats did not back it.

[53] Panzini contrasts Cavour's refusal to pay any official respects to the Austrian Emperor when he visited his Italian possessions in 1857 with the attitude of the Lombard aristocracy who paid him homage—including one lady who decorated her balcony with a tiger-skin in his honour.

positive political elements. In Germany, it evolved in ways which in certain aspects resembled what happened in Italy, and in others what happened in England. In Germany, the movement of 1848 failed as a result of the scanty bourgeois concentration (the Jacobin-type slogan was furnished by the democratic Far Left: "permanent revolution"), and because the question of renewal of the State was intertwined with the national question. The wars of 1864, 1866 and 1870[54] resolved both the national question and, in an intermediate form, the class question: the bourgeoisie obtained economic-industrial power, but the old feudal classes remained as the governing stratum of the political State, with wide corporate privileges in the army, the administration and on the land. Yet at least, if these old classes kept so much importance in Germany and enjoyed so many privileges, they exercised a national function, became the "intellectuals" of the bourgeoisie, with a particular temperament conferred by their caste origin and by tradition. In England, where the bourgeois revolution took place before that in France, we have a similar phenomenon to the German one of fusion between the old and the new—this notwithstanding the extreme energy of the English "Jacobins", i.e. Cromwell's "roundheads". The old aristocracy remained as a governing stratum, with certain privileges, and it too became the intellectual stratum of the English bourgeoisie (it should be added that the English aristocracy has an open structure, and continually renews itself with elements coming from the intellectuals and the bourgeoisie).* The explanation given by Antonio Labriola of the fact that the Junkers and Kaiserism continued in power in Germany, despite the great capitalist development, adumbrates the correct explanation: the class relations created by industrial development, with the limits of bourgeois hegemony reached and the position of the progressive classes reversed, have induced the bourgeoisie not to struggle with all its strength against the old régime, but to allow a part of the latter's façade to subsist, behind which it can disguise its own real domination.

---

[54] With Denmark, Austria and France respectively.

* Certain observations contained in the preface to the English translation of *Utopia and Science* should be looked at in this connection. These are worth recalling for the research into intellectuals and their historico-social functions.[55]

[55] The reference is to Engels' *Socialism: Utopian and Scientific*. The major part of the new preface to the English edition of 1892 is relevant to Gramsci's problematic here. See Marx/Engels, *Selected Works*, Vol. II, pp. 105–15, Lawrence and Wishart, London, 1958. See too "Merits of the Ruling Class" on pp. 269–270, and note 6 on p. 216.

These variations in the actual process whereby the same historical development manifests itself in different countries have to be related not only to the differing combinations of internal relations within the different nations, but also to the differing international relations (international relations are usually underestimated in this kind of research). The Jacobin spirit, audacious, dauntless, is certainly related to the hegemony exercised for so long by France in Europe, as well as to the existence of an urban centre like Paris and to the centralisation attained in France thanks to the absolute monarchy. The Napoleonic wars on the other hand, intellectually so fertile for the renovation of Europe, nonetheless through their enormous destruction of manpower—and these were men taken from among the boldest and most enterprising—weakened not only the militant political energy of France but that of other nations as well.

International relations were certainly very important in determining the line of development of the Italian Risorgimento, but they were exaggerated by the Moderate Party, and by Cavour for party reasons. Cavour's case is noteworthy in this connection. Before the Quarto[56] expedition and the crossing of the Straits, he feared Garibaldi's initiative like the devil, because of the international complications which it might create. He was then himself impelled by the enthusiasm created by the Thousand in European opinion to the point where he saw as feasible an immediate new war against Austria. There existed in Cavour a certain professional diplomat's distortion, which led him to see "too many" difficulties, and induced him into "conspiratorial" exaggerations, and into prodigies (which to a considerable extent were simply tightrope-walking) of subtlety and intrigue. In any case Cavour acted eminently as a party man. Whether in fact his party represented the deepest and most durable national interests, even if only in the sense of the widest extension which could be given to the community of interests between the bourgeoisie and the popular masses, is another question.*

In examining the political and military leadership imposed on the national movement before and after 1848, it is necessary to make

---

[56] It was at Quarto, near Genoa, that Garibaldi lived prior to the Sicilian expedition, and from there that the expedition set sail.

* With respect to the "Jacobin" slogan [permanent revolution] formulated in 1848–49, its complex fortunes are worth studying. Taken up again, systematised, developed, intellectualised by the Parvus-Bronstein [Trotsky] group, it proved inert and ineffective in 1905, and subsequently. It had become an abstract thing, belonging in the scientist's cabinet. The [Bolshevik] tendency which opposed it in this literary form, and indeed did not use it "on purpose", applied it in fact in

certain preliminary observations of method and terminology. By military leadership should be understood not only military leadership in the strict, technical sense, i.e. with reference to the strategy and the tactics of the Piedmontese army, or of Garibaldi's troops or of the various militias improvised in the course of local insurrections (Five Days of Milan, defence of Venice, defence of the Roman Republic, Palermo insurrection of 1848, etc.). It should be understood rather in a far wider sense, and one which is more closely connected with political leadership properly speaking. The essential problem which had to be faced from the military point of view was that of expelling from the peninsula a foreign power, Austria, which had at its disposal one of the largest armies in Europe at that time, and whose supporters in the peninsula itself, moreover, even in Piedmont, were neither few nor weak. Consequently, the military problem was the following: how to succeed in mobilising an insurrectional force which was capable not only of expelling the Austrian army from the peninsula, but of preventing it from being able to come back with a counter-offensive—given the fact that the violent expulsion would endanger the complex structure of the Empire, and hence would galvanise all the forces interested in its cohesion for a reconquest.

Numerous abstract solutions to the problem were presented, all of them contradictory and ineffective. "Italy will go it alone" was the Piedmontese slogan of 1848, but it meant catastrophic defeat. The uncertain, ambiguous, timid and at the same time foolhardy policies of the right-wing Piedmontese parties was the principal reason for the defeat. They were capable only of petty cunning. They were the cause of the withdrawal of the armies of the other Italian States, those of Naples and of Rome, when they showed too early that they wanted Piedmontese expansion and not an Italian confederation. They did not favour, but opposed the volunteer movement. They, in short, wanted the only military victors to be the Piedmontese generals, incapable of commanding in so difficult a war. The absence of a popular policy was disastrous. The Lombard and Venetian peasants enrolled by Austria were one of the most effective instruments for suffocating the Vienna revolution, and

---

a form which adhered to actual, concrete, living history, adapted to the time and the place; as something that sprang from all the pores of the particular society which had to be transformed; as the alliance of two social groups [i.e. proletariat and peasantry] with the hegemony of the urban group. In one case, you had the Jacobin temperament without an adequate political content; in the second, a Jacobin temperament and content derived from the new historical relations, and not from a literary and intellectualistic label.

hence also that of Italy. For the peasants the movement in Lombardy-Veneto, like the Viennese movement, was an affair of gentlemen and of students. Whereas the Italian national parties ought to have, by their policies, brought about or assisted the dissolution of the Austrian Empire, in fact by their inertia they saw to it that the Italian regiments were one of the best supports for Austrian reaction. In the struggle between Piedmont and Austria, the strategic objective could not be that of destroying the Austrian army and occupying the enemy's territory, for this would have been an unattainable and utopian objective. But it could have been that of dissolving Austria's internal cohesion, and of assisting the liberals to gain power firmly and change the political structure of the Empire into a federalist one, or at least to create within it a prolonged state of internal struggles which would give a breathing-space to the Italian national forces, and permit them to regroup themselves politically and militarily.*

Having started the war with the slogan "Italy will go it alone", after the defeat, when the entire undertaking was endangered, an attempt was made to gain French assistance. This occurred precisely at the time when, partly as a result of the reinforcement of Austria, the reactionaries had come to power in France—the enemies of a unitary and strong Italian State, and also of Piedmontese expansion.[58] France did not wish to give Piedmont even an experienced general, and the latter had to turn to the Pole Chrzanowski.

Military leadership was a larger question than the leadership of

---

* The same error was committed by Sonnino during the World War, and that in the face of Cadorna's protests. Sonnino did not desire the destruction of the Habsburg Empire, and refused any nationalities policy.[57] Even after Caporetto, a nationalitarian policy was adopted reluctantly and in a Malthusian manner, and therefore did not give the swifter results which it could have given.

[57] i.e., any support for the right of self-determination which might have allowed Italy to forge alliances with the various disaffected ethnic minorities within the Habsburg Empire. Giorgio Sonnino (1847–1924) was a conservative politician, prime minister in 1906 and again in 1909, and foreign minister during the First World War (1915–18). For Cadorna, see note 29 on p. 145.

[58] The Piedmontese under Chrzanowski were defeated by the Austrians at Novara in March 1849. As Marx expressed it in *The Class Struggles in France*: "Piedmont was beaten, Charles-Albert had abdicated and the Austrian army knocked at the gates of France." Marx goes on to describe how the French expedition in Italy, instead of following its proclaimed aim of support for the Italians against Austria, in fact intervened against the Roman Republic. On 11 May the National Assembly rejected a bill of impeachment against Bonaparte and his ministers, and as Marx put it: "the Constituent Assembly . . . admits . . . on 11 May that the bombastically proclaimed passive alliance of the French republic with the struggling peoples means its active alliance with the European counter-revolution".

the army and the working out of the strategic plan which the army was to execute. It included also the politico-insurrectional mobilisation of popular forces who would rise in revolt at the enemy's back and obstruct his movements and logistic services; and the creation of mass auxiliary and reserve forces from which new regiments could be drawn, and which would give to the "technical" army an atmosphere of enthusiasm and ardour.

The policy of popular mobilisation was not carried out even after 1849; indeed stupid quibbles were made about the events of 1849 in order to intimidate the democratic tendencies. The right-wing national policy became involved, during the second period of the Risorgimento, in a search for the assistance of Bonapartist France, and balanced the strength of Austria with the French alliance. The policies of the Right in 1848 delayed the unification of the peninsula by more than two decades.

The uncertainties of political and military leadership, the continual oscillations between despotism and constitutionalism, had their disastrous repercussions within the Piedmontese army too. It may safely be asserted that the more numerous an army is—whether in an absolute sense as a recruited mass, or in a relative sense as a proportion of recruited men to the total population—the more the importance of political leadership increases in comparison with merely technical-military leadership. The combativity of the Piedmontese army was extremely high at the start of the campaign of 1848: the rightists believed that this combativity was an expression of a purely abstract military and dynastic spirit, and began to intrigue to restrain popular freedoms and to tone down expectations of a democratic future. The "morale" of the army fell. Herein lies the entire debate about "fatal Novara". At Novara the army did not want to fight, and therefore was defeated. The "rightists" accused the democrats of having introduced politics into the army and split it: an inept accusation, since constitutionalism precisely "nationalised" the army, made it into an element of general politics, and thereby strengthened it militarily. The accusation is all the more inept in that the army perceives a political change of leadership [*or* direction], without any need for "splitters", from a host of little changes—each one of which might seem insignificant and negligible, but which together form a new, asphyxiating atmosphere. Those who are responsible for the splits are consequently those who have altered the political leadership, without foreseeing the military consequences; those who, in other words, have substituted a bad policy for the previous good one—good, because in conformity with its objective. The army is also an "instrument" for a particular end, but it is made up of thinking men and not of robots who can be utilised to the limits of their mechanical and physical cohesion. Even if one can and must, in this case too, speak in terms of what is expedient and appropriate to the objective, it is nevertheless also necessary to add the qualification: in accordance with the nature of the given instrument. If you hit a nail with a wooden mallet with the same strength with which you would hit it with a steel hammer, the nail will go into the mallet instead of into the wall. Correct political leadership is necessary even with an army of professional mercenaries (even in the companies of fortune there was a minimum of political leadership, apart from of a technical-military kind); it is all the more necessary with a national, conscript army. The question becomes even more complex and difficult in wars of position,[59] fought by huge masses who are only able to endure the immense muscular, nervous and psychic strain with the aid of great reserves of moral strength. Only a very skilful political leadership, capable of taking into account the deepest aspirations and feelings of those human masses, can prevent disintegration and defeat.

Military leadership must always be subordinate to political leadership, or in other words the strategic plan must be the military expression of a particular general policy. Naturally, it may be that in a given situation the politicians are inept, while in the army there are leaders who combine military ability with political ability: it was the case with Caesar and with Napoleon. But we have seen how in Napoleon's case the change of policies, combined with the presumption that he had a military instrument which was military in the abstract, brought about his downfall. Even in those cases in which political and military leadership is united in the same person, it is the political moment which must prevail over the military. Caesar's *Commentaries* are a classical example of the exhibition of an intelligent combination of political art and military art: the soldiers saw in Caesar not only a great military leader but especially their political leader, the leader of democracy. It should be recalled how Bismarck, following Clausewitz, maintained the supremacy of the political moment over the military; whereas Wilhelm II, as Ludwig records, scribbled furious notes on a newspaper in which Bismarck's opinion was quoted. Thus the Germans won almost all the battles brilliantly, but lost the war.

---

[59] See "Political struggle and military war" on pp. 229–39 below, and introduction to "State and Civil Society" pp. 206–9.

There exists a certain tendency to overestimate the contribution of the popular classes to the Risorgimento, stressing especially the phenomenon of volunteers. The most serious and thoughtful things on the subject were written by Ettore Rota in *Nuova Rivista Storica*, in 1928–29. Apart from the observation made in another note[60] about the significance which should be accorded to the volunteers, it should be pointed out that the writings of Rota themselves show how the volunteers were viewed with disfavour and sabotaged by the Piedmontese authorities—which precisely confirms their bad politico-military leadership. The Piedmontese government could forcibly enrol soldiers within its own territory in proportion to its population, just as Austria could in its territory and in proportion to an enormously larger population. An all-out war on these terms would always have been disastrous for Piedmont after a certain time. Given the principle that "Italy goes it alone", it was necessary either to accept immediately a confederation with the other Italian States, or to propose territorial unity on such a radically popular basis that the masses would have been induced to rise up against the other governments, and would have constituted volunteer armies who would have hastened to the support of the Piedmontese. But precisely here lay the problem. The right-wing tendencies in Piedmont either did not want auxiliaries, thinking that they could defeat the Austrians with the regular Piedmontese forces alone (and it is incomprehensible how they could have had such presumption), or else would have liked to have been helped for nothing (and here too it is incomprehensible how serious politicians could have asked such an absurdity). In real life, one cannot ask for enthusiasm, spirit of sacrifice, etc. without giving anything in return, even from the subjects of one's own country; all the less can one ask these things of citizens from outside that country, on the basis of a generic and abstract programme and a blind faith in a far-distant government. This was the drama of 1848 and 1849, but it is certainly not fair therefore to despise the Italian people; the responsibility for the disaster should be attributed either to the Moderates or to the Action Party—in other words, in the last analysis, to the immaturity and the scanty effectiveness of the ruling classes.

These observations concerning the deficiencies of political and military leadership in the Risorgimento might be met with a very trivial and threadbare argument: "those men were not demagogues, they did not go in for demagogy". Another very widespread

---

[60] See "Voluntarism and social masses" on pp. 202–5 below.

triviality used to parry negative judgements on the strategic abilities of the leaders of the national movement consists in repeating in various ways and forms that the national movement's capacity to act was due to the *merit* of the educated classes *solely*. Where the merit lies is hard to see. The merit of an educated class, because it is its historical function, is to lead the popular masses and develop their progressive elements. If the educated class has not been capable of fulfilling its function, one should speak not of merit but of demerit—in other words, of immaturity and intrinsic weakness. Similarly, it is necessary to be clear about the term, and the concept, of demagogy. Those men in effect were not capable of leading the people, were not capable of arousing their enthusiasm and their passion, if one is to take *demagogy* in its original meaning. Did they at least attain the end which they set themselves? They said that they were aiming at the creation of a modern State in Italy, and they in fact produced a bastard. They aimed at stimulating the formation of an extensive and energetic ruling class, and they did not succeed; at integrating the people into the framework of the new State, and they did not succeed. The paltry political life from 1870 to 1900, the fundamental and endemic rebelliousness of the Italian popular classes, the narrow and stunted existence of a sceptical and cowardly ruling stratum, these are all the consequences of that failure. A consequence of it too is the international position of the new State, lacking effective autonomy because sapped internally by the Papacy and by the sullen passivity of the great mass of the people. In reality, furthermore, the rightists of the Risorgimento were great demagogues. They made the people-nation into an instrument, into an object, they degraded it. And therein lies the greatest and most contemptible demagogy, precisely in the sense which the term has assumed on the lips of the right-wing parties when they polemicise against those of the left—although it has always been the right-wing parties who have shown the worst demagogy, and who have often (like Napoleon III in France) appealed to the dregs of society. [1934: 1st version 1929–30.]

THE CITY-COUNTRYSIDE RELATIONSHIP DURING THE RISORGIMENTO AND IN THE NATIONAL STRUCTURE

The relations between urban population and rural population are not of a single, schematic type—especially in Italy. It is therefore necessary to establish what is meant by "urban" and "rural" in modern civilisation, and what combinations may result from the fact that antiquated and retrograde forms continue to exist in the general composition of the population, studied from the viewpoint of its greater or lesser density. Sometimes the paradox occurs that a rural type is more progressive than a self-styled urban type.

An "industrial" city is always more progressive than the countryside which depends organically upon it. But not all Italy's cities are "industrial", and even fewer are typically industrial. Are the "hundred" Italian cities industrial?[61] Does the agglomeration of the population in non-rural centres, which is almost twice as great as in France, demonstrate that Italy's industrialisation is double that of France? Urbanism in Italy is not purely, nor "especially", a phenomenon of capitalistic development or of that of big industry. Naples, which for a long time was the biggest Italian city and which continues to be one of the biggest, is not an industrial city: neither is Rome—at present the largest Italian city. Yet in these mediaeval-type cities too, there exist strong nuclei of populations of a modern urban type; but what is their relative position? They are submerged, oppressed, crushed by the other part, which is not of a modern type, and constitutes the great majority. Paradox of the "cities of silence".[62]

In this type of city there exists, among all social groups, an urban ideological unity against the countryside, a unity which even the most modern nuclei in terms of civil function do not escape (and there are such nuclei). There is hatred and scorn for the "peasant", an implicit common front against the demands of the countryside—which, if realised, would make impossible the existence of this type of city. Reciprocally, there exists an aversion—which, if "generic", is not thereby any less tenacious or passionate—of the country for the city, for the whole city and all the groups which make it up. This general relationship is in reality very complex, and appears in forms which on the surface seem contradictory; it had a primary importance in the course of the struggles for the Risorgimento, when it was even more absolute and operative than it is today.

---

[61] Gramsci defines the "hundred cities" (on PP. p. 98) as "the agglomeration into burgs (cities) of the rural bourgeoisie, and the agglomeration into peasant villages [*borgate*] of great masses of agricultural labourers and landless peasants in areas where extensive *latifundia* exist (Puglie, Sicily)".

[62] D'Annunzio gave the title "Cities of Silence" to a sequence of poems, mainly sonnets, in *Elettra*, the second book of his *Laudi*. These cities—Ferrara, Pisa, Ravenna, Rimini, Assisi, Spoleto, Gubbio, Urbino, Padova, Lucca, Pistoia, Prato, Perugia, Spello, Montefalco, Narni, Todi, Orvieto, Arezzo, Cortona, Bergamo, Carrara, Volterra, Vicenza, Brescia—all had glorious pasts but are now of secondary importance, some little more than villages with magnificent monumental centres as a relic of their bygone splendour.

The first blatant example of these apparent contradictions can be studied in the episode of the Parthenopean Republic of 1799.[63] The city was crushed by the countryside—organised into the gangs of Cardinal Ruffo—for a dual reason. On the one hand the Republic, both in its first aristocratic phase and in its subsequent bourgeois phase, totally neglected the countryside. On the other, by holding out the possibility of a Jacobin upheaval in which landed property, which spent its agrarian income in Naples, would be dispossessed, thus depriving the great mass of the people of their sources of income and livelihood, it left the Neapolitan populace indifferent if not hostile. During the Risorgimento, moreover, there already appeared, embryonically, the historical relationship between North and South, similar to that between a great city and a great rural area. As this relationship was, in fact, not the normal organic one between a province and an industrial capital, but emerged between two vast territories of very different civil and cultural tradition, the features and the elements of a conflict of nationalities were accentuated. What was particularly notable during the period of the Risorgimento was the fact that, in the political crises, it was the South which initiated the action: 1799 Naples, 1820–21 Palermo, 1847 Messina and Sicily, 1847–48 Sicily and Naples. Another notable fact was the particular character which each of these movements assumed in Central Italy, like a middle way between North and South; the period of popular (or relatively popular) initiative lasted from 1815 until 1849, and culminated in Tuscany and the Papal States (Romagna and Lunigiana must always be considered as belonging to the Centre). These peculiarities reoccurred subsequently as well: the events of June 1814 culminated in certain regions of the Centre (Romagna and Marche); the crisis which began in Sicily in 1893, and spread into the Mezzogiorno and Lunigiana, culminated in 1898 at Milan; in 1919 there

---

[63] The Parthenopean Republic was proclaimed at Naples in January 1799, as Napoleon's troops approached. The work of an enlightened, "Jacobin" bourgeoisie, a large section of the city's aristocracy rallied to it (e.g. Cuoco—see note 11 on p. 59). The French troops, however, braked the revolutionary aims of the Neapolitan bourgeoisie, and prevented the measures to destroy feudalism which could have won the countryside. Cardinal Ruffo, with British support, raised the countryside against the town, and when the French were forced by military setbacks in the North to withdraw in March, the Republic's days were numbered. The bourgeois régime was under attack both from outside and from the "*sanfedisti*"—a movement in support of the Bourbons among the lumpen-proletariat—within, and it capitulated in June after a generous amnesty offer by Ruffo. The Bourbons then repudiated this amnesty, and there ensued a pitiless repression, with 129 executions and thousands of imprisonments and exiles, which decimated the Neapolitan intellectuals and destroyed finally any consensual basis for Bourbon rule.

were the invasions of the land in the Mezzogiorno and in Sicily, in 1920 the occupation of the factories in the North.[64] This relative synchronism and simultaneity on the one hand shows the existence, ever since 1815, of a relatively homogeneous politico-economic structure; on the other it shows how in periods of crisis it is the weakest and most marginal sector which reacts first.

The relation of city to countryside pertaining between North and South may also be studied in their differing cultural conceptions and mental attitudes. Allusion has already been made to the fact that B. Croce and G. Fortunato, at the beginning of the century, were at the head of a cultural movement which, in one way or another, counterposed itself to the cultural movement of the North (idealism against positivism, classicism or classicity against futurism).[65] It should be pointed out, however, that Sicily distinguishes itself from the Mezzogiorno—including from a cultural point of view: if Crispi can be seen as the man of Northern industrialism, Pirandello is also generally nearer to futurism. Gentile and actualism are also nearer to the futurist movement (understood in a wide sense, as opposition to traditional classicism; as a form of contemporary romanticism).[66] The intellectual strata of North and South differ in structure and in origin: in the Mezzogiorno the predominant type is still the pettifogging lawyer [*paglietta*], who ensures contact between the peasant masses and the landowners and State apparatus. In the North the dominant type is the factory "technician", who acts as a link between the mass of the workers and the management. The link with the State used to be a function of the

---

[64] The events of June 1814 were a series of bourgeois risings, in connection with an attempt by Murat to unite Italy from his base in Naples. Murat was defeated by the Austrians at Tolentino, and fled to Corsica. The Austrians launched a wave of repression aimed at the bourgeois liberals implicated in the risings.

For the Sicilian Fasci of 1893–94, see note 25 on p. 67. In 1898 the Milan workers demonstrated against rising prices and lack of food, and were bloodily repressed by General Bava Beccaris. For the occupation of the factories in 1920, see Introduction, p. xliii.

[65] See p. 72 and note 39 on p. 72.

[66] Crispi, Pirandello and Gentile were all Sicilians.

The futurist movement was launched by Marinetti in his Futurist Manifesto of 1909, and celebrated the vitality of the modern age, especially in its technical progress which was seen as sweeping away the old order. Gramsci, in a 1922 letter to Trotsky who had requested information on futurism for his "*Literature and Revolution*", described how the workers before the World War "had seen in futurism the elements of a struggle against the old academic culture of Italy, mummified and alien to the popular masses . . .". But during the war the futurists were violent interventionists, and subsequently their positions converged on the one hand with fascism and on the other with d'Annunzio's nationalism. Marinetti stood as a parliamentary candidate on Mussolini's list in 1919.

trade-union and political party organisations, led by a completely new intellectual stratum (the present State syndicalism,[67] whose consequence is the systematic diffusion of this social type on a national scale in a more coherent and thorough way than was possible for the old trade unions, is up to a certain point and in a certain sense an instrument of moral and political unification).

This complex city-countryside relationship can be studied in the general political programmes which were striving to assert themselves before the Fascists achieved governmental power. The programme of Giolitti[68] and the democratic liberals had the aim of creating an "urban" bloc (of industrialists and workers) in the North; this was to be the basis for a protectionist system, and reinforce the economy and Northern hegemony. The Mezzogiorno was reduced to the status of a semi-colonial market, a source of savings and taxes, and was kept "disciplined" by measures of two kinds. First, police measures: pitiless repression of every mass movement, with periodical massacres of peasants.* Second, political-police measures: personal favours to the "intellectual" stratum or *paglietta*—in the form of jobs in the public administration; of licence to pillage the local administration with impunity; and of ecclesiastical legislation less rigidly applied than elsewhere, leaving considerable patrimony at the disposal of the clergy, etc.—i.e. incorporation of the most active Southern elements "individually" into the leading personnel of the State, with particular "judicial" and bureaucratic privileges, etc. Thus the social stratum which could have organised the endemic Southern discontent, instead became an instrument of Northern policy, a kind of auxiliary private police. Southern discontent, for lack of leadership, did not succeed in assuming a normal political form; its manifestations, finding expression only in an anarchic turbulence, were presented as a "matter for the police" and the courts. In reality men like Croce and Fortunato abetted this form of corruption, even if

---

[67] i.e. the "corporations" to which workers had compulsorily to belong in fascist Italy.

[68] Giovanni Giolitti (1842–1928) dominated Italian parliamentary politics between 1900 and 1914, and was prime minister in 1892–93, 1906–09, 1911–14, and 1920–21 (when he encouraged the fascists as a counter-balancing force to the socialists). Gramsci analyses his policy at greater length in *Alcuni temi*.

* In his obituary of Giolitti in *Nuova Antologia*, 1 August 1928, Spectator (Missiroli) expressed surprise that Giolitti was always strenuously opposed to any dissemination of socialism or syndicalism in the South. But in fact the thing is natural and obvious, since a working-class protectionism—reformism, co-operatives, public works—is only possible if partial; in other words, every privilege presupposes somebody being sacrificed and exploited.

passively and indirectly, by means of their fetishistic conception of unity.*

There was also a politico-moral factor which should not be forgotten; this was the campaign of intimidation waged against every assertion, however objective, that there existed motives for conflict between North and South. One might recall the conclusion of the Pais-Serra enquiry into Sardinia, after the commercial crisis of the decade 1890–1900; also the accusation, recalled earlier, which was hurled by Crispi at the Sicilian Fasci, of being sold to the English.[70] This form of hysterical unitarianism was especially prevalent among the Sicilian intellectuals (as a consequence of the formidable peasant pressure on the nobility's land, and also of the local popularity of Crispi); it even revealed itself quite recently in Natoli's attack on Croce for an innocuous reference to Sicilian separatism in relation to the Kingdom of Naples (see Croce's reply in *Critica*).[71]

Giolitti's programme was "upset" by two factors: 1. the coming to the fore of the intransigents in the Socialist Party under the leadership of Mussolini, and their flirtation with the Southernists (free exchange, the Molfetta election, etc.), which destroyed the Northern urban bloc;[72] 2. the introduction of universal suffrage, which enlarged the parliamentary base of the Mezzogiorno to an unprecedented extent, and made individual corruption difficult (too many to be easily corrupted—hence appearance of political thugs). Giolitti changed partners: he replaced the urban bloc by (or rather counterposed to it, in order to prevent its complete

---

* See the Fortunato–Salvemini episode in connection with *Unità*, recounted by Prezzolini in the first edition of *Cultura Italiana*.[69]

[69] For Fortunato, see note 39 on p. 72; for Salvemini, see p. xx ff. Introduction. Salvemini's "*Unità*" was published 1911–15 and 1918–20, and suggested to Gramsci the name for the subsequent official organ of the PCI, founded in 1924. In the first edition of *La Coltura Italiana* (see note 41 on p. 72), Prezzolini wrote of *Unità*: "its title came from senator Fortunato, concerned for that 'unity of Italy' which, to his historian's mind, has always seemed neither entirely nor solidly achieved".

[70] See note 26 on p. 67.

[71] See Luigi Natoli, *Rivendicazioni attraverso le rivoluzioni siciliane del 1848–60*, commented on by Gramsci on PP. pp. 135–36.

[72] For the intransigent wing of the PSI, see General Introduction; they were opposed to any collaboration, however indirect, with the bourgeois government—hence making impossible a continuation of the effective bloc between Giolitti and the reformist leaders of the PSI. Mussolini, as editor of *Avanti!*, was their main spokesman until his defection in 1914. For the Molfetta election of 1913, see following paragraph; as Gramsci explains, it showed the *Corriere della Sera*, the voice of the Lombard industrialists, prospecting a new alliance with a "Southern bloc" in place of the now unviable Giolitti policy of a bloc with the reformist leaders of the Northern working class.

collapse) the "Gentiloni pact".[73] This was ultimately a bloc between Northern industry and the farmers of the "organic and normal" countryside (the Catholic electoral forces coincided geographically with those of the socialists: i.e. they were spread over the North and the Centre); it had additional support in the South as well—at least to an extent immediately sufficient to "rectify" satisfactorily the consequences of the mass electorate's enlargement.

The other programme or general political approach was the one which may be termed that of the *Corriere della Sera*, or of Luigi Albertini;[74] this may be seen as an alliance between a section of the Northern industrialists (headed by the textile, cotton and silk masters—exporters and hence free traders) and the rural bloc of the Mezzogiorno. The *Corriere* supported Salvemini against Giolitti in the Molfetta election of 1913 (Ugo Ojetti's campaign), and it supported first the Salandra Ministry and subsequently that of Nitti[75]—in other words, the first two governments formed by Southern politicians.*

The enlargement of the suffrage in 1913 had already provoked the first signs of that phenomenon which was to have its maximum expression in 1919–20–21 as a consequence of the politico-organisational experience acquired by the peasant masses during the war—i.e. the relative break-up of the Southern rural bloc, and the detachment of the peasants, led by a part of the intellectuals (officers during the war), from the great landowners. So one got

[73] At the elections of 1913—the first under universal suffrage—Giolitti came to an agreement with Count Gentiloni, the president of the Catholic Electoral Union of Italy, whereby Catholic voters would support the governmental candidates in order to check the advance of the socialists.

[74] Luigi Albertini (1871–1941) became editor of *Corriere della Sera* in 1900, and built it up into the major bourgeois newspaper in Italy. He was a liberal-conservative, in favour of intervention in the war but anti-fascist; he was removed from the editorship of the paper in 1925, whereafter the *Corriere* was aligned behind the fascist régime.

[75] Antonio Salandra (1853–1931), a bourgeois politician of the Right, was prime minister in 1914–15; he was forced to resign under neutralist pressure because of his support for intervention in the War, but became prime minister again 1915–16 after the interventionists had won the day.

Francesco Nitti (1868–1953) was an economist and centrist politician, prime minister 1919–20.

* The Sicilians have to be considered separately. They have always had a lion's share in all Ministries from 1860 onwards, and have had several Presidents of the Council—unlike the Mezzogiorno, whose first leader was Salandra. This Sicilian "invasion" is to be explained by the blackmailing policy of the island's parties, who secretly have always maintained a "separatist" spirit in favour of England. Crispi's accusation[76] was, in an ill-considered form, the manifestation of a pre-occupation which really obsessed the most responsible and sensitive national ruling group.

[76] See note 26 on p. 67.

Sardism,[77] one got the Sicilian reformist party (the so-called Bonomi parliamentary group was constituted by Bonomi and 22 Sicilian deputies),[78] with its extreme separatist wing represented by *Sicilia Nuova*; and one got the *Rinnovamento* group in the Mezzogiorno, made up of war-veterans, which attempted to set up regional action parties similar to that of Sardinia.* In this movement, the autonomous importance of the peasant masses decreases progressively from Sardinia via the Mezzogiorno to Sicily, depending on the organised strength, the prestige, and the ideological pressure exercised by the great landowners. In Sicily these are maximally well-organised and united; in Sardinia on the other hand they have relatively small importance. The relative independence of the respective intellectual strata varies in a similar fashion—in inverse proportion, of course, to that of the landowners.**

In order to analyse the socio-political function of the intellectuals, it is necessary to recall and examine their psychological attitude towards the fundamental classes which they put into contact in the various fields.[80] Do they have a "paternalistic" attitude towards the instrumental classes? Or do they think they are an organic expression of them? Do they have a "servile" attitude towards the ruling classes, or do they think that they themselves are leaders, an integral part of the ruling classes? During the Risorgimento, the so-called Action Party had a "paternalistic" attitude; it therefore only succeeded to a very limited extent in bringing the great popular masses into contact with the State. So-called "transformism"[81] was only the parliamentary expression of the fact that the Action Party was incorporated in molecular fashion by the

---

[77] *Sardismo* was a Sardinian autonomist movement which developed after the First World War. The *Partito Sardo d'Azione* was founded in 1920, but split when the fascists came to power. One section joined the fascists, another, led notably by Emilio Lussu, joined the Aventine opposition; its leaders were exiled, but returned to revive the party during the Resistance (1943–5).

[78] Ivanoe Bonomi (1873–1952) was at first a reformist socialist. Expelled from the PSI together with Bissolati in 1912, he remained in parliament as an independent centrist politician, and was prime minister 1921–22.

* See Torraca's review *Volontà*, the transformation of *Popolo Romano*, etc.[79]

[79] Francesco Torraca (1853–1938), Professor of comparative, and later Italian, literature at Naples University, and a senator from 1920.

** By "intellectuals" must be understood not those strata commonly described by this term, but in general the entire social stratum which exercises an organisational function in the wide sense—whether in the field of production, or in that of culture, or in that of political administration. They correspond to the NCOs and junior officers in the army, and also partly to the higher officers who have risen from the ranks.

[80] See "The Formation of the Intellectuals" on pp. 5–14 above.

[81] See note 8 on p. 58 above.

Moderates, and that the popular masses were decapitated, not absorbed into the ambit of the new State.

The relation between city and countryside is the necessary starting-point for the study of the fundamental motor forces of Italian history, and of the programmatic points in the light of which the Action Party's policies during the Risorgimento should be considered and judged. Schematically, one might have this picture: 1. the Northern urban force; 2. the Southern rural force; 3. the Northern-Central rural force; 4. the rural force of Sicily; 5. that of Sardinia. The first of these forces retains its function of "locomotive" in any case; what is needed, therefore, is an examination of the various "most advantageous" combinations for building a "train" to move forward through history as fast as possible. Meanwhile the first force initially has its own problems: internal ones—of organisation, of how to articulate its own homogeneity, of politico-military leadership (Piedmontese hegemony,[82] relations between Milan and Turin, etc.). But it remains a constant that if this force has attained a certain level of unity and combativity, it quite automatically exercises an "indirect" directive function over the others. Moreover, it would appear that its assumption, during the various phases of the Risorgimento, of an intransigent position of struggle against foreign domination had the result of stirring up the progressive forces of the South: hence the relative synchronism, but not simultaneity, of the movements of 1820–21, of 1831, of 1848.[83] In 1859–60, this historico-political "mechanism" operated to maximum effect, since the North initiated the struggle, the Centre came over peacefully (or almost so), and in the South the Bourbon State collapsed under the (relatively weak) thrust of the Garibaldini. This happened because the Action Party (Garibaldi) intervened at the right time, after the Moderates (Cavour) had organised the North and Centre; i.e. it was not the same politico-military leadership (Moderates or Action Party) which organised the relative simultaneity, but the (mechanical) collaboration of the two leaderships, integrating successfully.

The first force therefore had to tackle the problem of organising around itself the urban forces of the other national sectors, and especially of the South. This problem was the most difficult, fraught

---

[82] See "The Function of Piedmont" on pp. 104–106 below.

[83] 1820–21 was the year of the first wave of "carbonarist" revolutions in Italy, France, Spain, Greece, etc. Only the Greek revolution had any durable results, but in various of the Italian states the risings had some initial success, notably in Piedmont, and at Naples. The second wave of carbonarist risings occurred in 1831, affecting notably Modena, Parma and the Papal State.

with contradictions and undercurrents which unleashed torrents of passionate feelings (a farcical solution of these contradictions was the so-called parliamentary revolution of 1876).[84] But its solution, precisely for this reason, was one of the cruxes in the nation's development. The urban forces are socially homogeneous, hence must occupy positions of perfect equality. That was theoretically true, but historically the question posed itself differently: the urban forces of the North were clearly at the head of their national sector, while for the urban forces of the South that was not true, at least not to the same extent. The urban forces of the North had therefore to persuade those of the South that their directive function should be limited to ensuring the "leadership" of North over South in a general relation of city to countryside. In other words, the directive function of the Southern urban forces could not be other than a subordinate moment of the vaster directive function of the North. The most strident contradiction was created by this series of facts. The urban force of the South could not be considered as something on its own, independent of that of the North. To pose the question in such a way would have meant asserting in advance an incurable "national" rift—a rift so serious that not even a federalist solution would have been able to heal it. It would have meant asserting the existence of separate nations, between which all that could have been achieved was a diplomatic-military alliance against the common enemy, Austria. (The sole element of community or solidarity, in short, would have consisted simply in having a "common" enemy.) In reality, however, there existed only certain "aspects" of such a national question, not "all" the aspects nor even the most essential ones. The most serious aspect was the weak position of the Southern urban forces in relation to the rural forces, an unfavourable relation which sometimes took the form of a literal subjugation of the city to the countryside. The close links between the urban forces of North and South gave to the latter the strength which came from representing the prestige of the former, and were destined to help the Southern urban forces to gain their autonomy, to acquire consciousness of their historical leadership function in a "concrete" and not merely theoretical and abstract manner, suggesting the solutions to give to the great regional problems. It was natural that in the South there should be strong forces of opposition to unity. The weightiest task in resolving the situation in any case fell to the urban forces of the North, which not

[84] In 1876 the "Left" in parliament formed a Ministry for the first time.

only had to convince their "brothers" of the South, but had to begin [to convince] themselves of this political system as an entity. In practical terms, therefore, the question posed itself in the existence of a strong centre of political leadership, with which strong and popular personalities from the South and the islands would necessarily have had to collaborate. The problem of creating unity between North and South was closely linked with, and to a great extent absorbed into the problem of creating a cohesion and solidarity among all the national urban forces.*

The Northern-Central rural forces posed in their turn a series of problems which the urban force of the North had to confront in order to establish a normal city-countryside relationship, eliminating interferences and influences extraneous in origin to the development of the new State. In these rural forces, two currents had to be distinguished: the secular, and the clerico-Austrian. The clerical force was strongest in Lombardy–Veneto, as well as in Tuscany and in a part of the Papal State. The secular force was strongest in Piedmont, but had varying influence in the rest of Italy too—not only in the Papal Legations (especially Romagna) but also in the other regions, even including the Mezzogiorno and the Islands. If they had resolved these immediate relations successfully, the Northern urban forces would have set a rhythm for all similar questions on a national scale. On this whole series of problems, the Action Party failed totally. It in fact limited itself to making into a question of principle, and into an essential element of its programme, what was simply a question of the political terrain upon which it might have been possible to focus, and find a legal solution for, such problems: the question of the Constituent Assembly. One cannot say that the Moderate Party failed, since its objectives were the organic expansion of Piedmont, and soldiers for the Piedmontese army rather than insurrections or armies of Garibaldini on too large a scale.

Why did the Action Party not pose the agrarian question globally? That the Moderates would not pose it was obvious: their approach to the national question required a bloc of all the right-wing forces—including the classes of the great landowners—around Piedmont as a State and as an army. Austria's threat to resolve the agrarian question in favour of the peasants—a threat carried out in Galicia against the Polish nobles in favour of the Ruthenian

* The line of argument developed above is in fact valid for all three sectors of the South: Naples and the mainland, Sicily, Sardinia.

peasants[85]—not only threw into confusion those in Italy whose interests would have been touched, and caused all the oscillations of the aristocracy (Milan events of February 1853, and act of homage by the most illustrious Milanese families to Franz Josef on the very eve of the Belfiore hangings);[86] it also paralysed the Action Party itself, which in this field thought like the Moderates, and considered as "national" the aristocracy and the landowners, and not the millions of peasants. Only after February 1853 did Mazzini begin to make the occasional allusion of a substantially democratic kind (see his *Correspondence* for the period), but he was not capable of a decisive radicalisation of his abstract programme. The political conduct of the Garibaldini in Sicily in 1860 should be studied—a political conduct which was dictated by Crispi: the peasant movements of insurrection against the barons were crushed pitilessly, and the anti-peasant National Guard was created. Typical was the repressive expedition of Nino Bixio into the Catania region, where the insurrections were most violent. Yet even in G. C. Abba's *Noterelle* there are elements showing that the agrarian question was the spring to set the great masses in motion: it is enough to recall Abba's conversations with the monk who goes off to meet the Garibaldini immediately after the Marsala landing.[87] In certain of G. Verga's short stories there are picturesque elements from these peasant risings, which the National Guard smothered by means of terror and mass shootings.[88] This aspect of the expedition of the Thousand has never been studied and analysed.

The failure to pose the agrarian question led to the near impossibility of resolving the problem of clericalism and the anti-unitarian

---

[85] In 1845 the nobles and bourgeois of Galicia rose against the Austrians; the latter put down the uprising by mobilising the Ruthenian peasants of the region, promising them land in order to gain their support.

[86] For the Milan insurrection of February 1853, see note 52 on p. 82. Later in the same year the Austrians hanged a number of Mazzini's followers in the valley of Belfiore, near Verona.

[87] In Giuseppe Abba's *Noterelle di uno dei Mille*, the author recounts how a monk came to meet the Garibaldini and informed them eloquently of the peasantry's thirst for land.

[88] Notably in the story *Libertà*, an account of a massacre of local notables by a village population excited by the idea that the Garibaldini had brought them freedom and equality. After the massacre, the peasants find that they can't get on without the "gentlemen"—a characteristic motif of Verga's fundamentally conservative populism—and are then led away to prison in the city, without ever understanding what they have done wrong. The story ends with one of the prisoners saying as he is sentenced: "Where are you taking me? To gaol? Why, why? I never got so much as a square yard of land! Didn't they say that freedom had come?"

attitude of the Pope.[89] In this respect, the Moderates were far more audacious than the Action Party: it is true that they did not distribute ecclesiastical property among the peasants, but they used it to create a new stratum of great and medium landowners tied to the new political situation, and did not hesitate to lay hands on landed property, even if it was only that of the Orders. The Action Party, moreover, was paralysed in its action towards the peasants by Mazzini's wish for a religious reform. This not only was of no interest to the great rural masses, it on the contrary rendered them susceptible to being incited against the new heretics. The example of the French Revolution was there to show that the Jacobins, who had succeeded in crushing all the right-wing parties up to and including the Girondins on the terrain of the agrarian question, who had succeeded not merely in preventing a rural coalition against Paris but in multiplying their supporters in the provinces, were damaged by Robespierre's attempts to instigate a religious reform—although such a reform had, in the real historical process, an immediate significance and concreteness.* [1934; 1st version 1929–30]

THE MODERATES AND THE INTELLECTUALS

Why the Moderates were bound to gain the upper hand as far as the majority of intellectuals were concerned. Gioberti[92] and Mazzini. Gioberti offered the intellectuals a philosophy which appeared original and at the same time national, such as would put Italy at least on the same level as the more advanced nations, and give a new dignity to Italian thought. Mazzini, on the other hand only offered woolly statements, and philosophical allusions which to many intellectuals, especially Neapolitans, must have

---

[89] i.e. the Pope's refusal to accept the end of his temporal power in the Papal States, and his consequent opposition to Italian unity before the Risorgimento, and refusal to come to terms with the post-Risorgimento Italian state—until the Concordat of 1929.

* It would be necessary to study carefully the real agrarian policy of the Roman Republic,[90] and the true character of the repressive mission entrusted by Mazzini to Felice Orsini[91] in the Romagna and the Marche: in this period up to 1870 (and even afterwards), the term "brigandry" almost always meant the chaotic, turbulent movement, punctuated by ferocity, of the peasants trying to gain possession of the land.

[90] The Roman Republic was proclaimed in January 1849, and Mazzini was elected to head the triumvirate which governed it. It fell to the French after a three-month siege in June of the same year.

[91] See note 16 on p. 62.

[92] See note 36 on p. 399.

appeared empty chatter (the Abbé Galiani had taught them to ridicule such ways of thinking and reasoning).[93]

Problem of the school: activity on the part of the Moderates to introduce the pedagogic principle of monitorial teaching (Confalonieri, Capponi, etc.); movement of Ferrante Aporti and the foundling schools, linked to the problem of pauperism.[94] Among the Moderates appeared the only concrete pedagogic movement opposed to the "Jesuitical" school; it could not fail to be effective, both among the lay, to whom it gave a personality of their own within the school, and among the liberalising and anti-Jesuitical clergy (ferocious hostility to Ferrante Aporti, etc.; the sheltering and education of abandoned children was a clerical monopoly, and these initiatives broke the monopoly). Scholastic activities of a liberal or liberalising character have great significance for grasping the mechanism of the Moderates' hegemony over the intellectuals. Scholastic activity, at all its levels, has an enormous importance (economic as well) for intellectuals of all degrees. And at that time it had an even greater importance than it does today, given the narrowness of the social structures and the few roads open to the initiative of the petite bourgeoisie. (Today, journalism, the political parties, industry, a very extensive State apparatus, etc., have broadened the possibilities of employment to an unheard of extent.)

The hegemony of a directive centre over the intellectuals asserts itself by two principal routes: 1. a general conception of life, a

---

[93] The abbé Galiani (1728–1787) was a Neapolitan economist (opposed to free trade and the theories of the physiocrats) and man of letters. Noted as a wit, he was typical of the enlightened, rationalist intellectual stratum of Naples which was to become the "Jacobins" of the Parthenopean Republic of 1799.

[94] The monitor system was devised by Bell and Lancaster in late eighteenth-century England, and Confalonieri (see note 51 on p. 81) made the first attempt to introduce it into Italy in 1819–21.

Gino Capponi (1792–1876), educationalist, historian and politician, was the author of *Frammento sull'educazione* (1841), in which he expressed his scepticism about any attempt on the part of teachers to predetermine "from outside" the development of the "spiritual activity" of children. This type of Rousseauesque, liberal theory of learning is criticised by Gramsci, e.g. Int. p. 115: "it is believed that a child's mind is like a ball of string which the teacher helps to unwind. In reality each generation educates the new generation, i.e. forms it, and education is a struggle against instincts linked to the elementary biological functions, a struggle against nature, to dominate it and create the 'contemporary' man of the epoch."

Ferrante Aporti (1791–1858) was an educationalist, founder of the first infant schools in Italy (Cremona 1829, etc.). The ideology behind these schools derived from Rousseau and Pestalozzi; the first model for them was Owen's 1816 infant school in Scotland. They were opposed strongly by the Church in Italy, both for their liberal ideological connotations and for the challenge they posed to the clerical monopoly.

philosophy (Gioberti), which offers to its adherents an intellectual "dignity" providing a principle of differentiation from the old ideologies which dominated by coercion, and an element of struggle against them; 2. a scholastic programme, an educative principle and original pedagogy which interests that fraction of the intellectuals which is the most homogeneous and the most numerous (the teachers, from the primary teachers to the university professors), and gives them an activity of their own in the technical field.

The Scholars' congresses which were repeatedly organised in the period of the early Risorgimento had a double effect: 1. they regrouped the intellectuals of the highest grade, concentrating them and multiplying their influence; 2. they obtained a more rapid concentration and a more decisive orientation of the intellectuals of the lower grades, who normally tend to follow the university professors and great scholars, through spirit of caste.

The study of encyclopaedic and specialised reviews furnishes another aspect of the Moderates' hegemony. A party like that of the Moderates offered the mass of the intellectuals all the satisfactions for their general needs which can be offered by a government (by a governing party) through the State services. After 1848–49, the Piedmontese State served perfectly as far as this function of Italian governing party was concerned; it welcomed the exiled intellectuals, and provided a model of what a future unified State would do. [1934]

THE FUNCTION OF PIEDMONT

The function of Piedmont in the Italian Risorgimento is that of a "ruling class". In reality, what was involved was not that throughout the peninsula there existed nuclei of a homogeneous ruling class whose irresistible tendency to unite determined the formation of the new Italian national State. These nuclei existed, indubitably, but their tendency to unite was extremely problematic; also, more importantly, they—each in its own sphere—were not "leading".[95] The "leader" presupposes the "led", and who was "led" by these nuclei? These nuclei did not wish to "lead" anybody, i.e. they did not wish to concord their interests and aspirations with the interests

---

[95] This passage presents insuperable translation difficulties (see note 5 on p. 55). Gramsci uses "*dirigente*" here both in its usual sense of "ruling", and in contradistinction to "*dominante*"—when we have translated it "leading". Inevitably good English has had to some extent to be sacrificed here, in the interests of fidelity to Gramsci's original text.

and aspirations of other groups. They wished to "dominate" and not to "lead". Furthermore, they wanted their interests to dominate, rather than their persons; in other words, they wanted a new force, independent of every compromise and condition, to become the arbiter of the Nation: this force was Piedmont and hence the function of the monarchy. Thus Piedmont had a function which can, from certain aspects, be compared to that of a party, i.e. of the leading personnel of a social group (and in fact people always spoke of the "Piedmont party"): with the additional feature that it was in fact a State, with an army, a diplomatic service, etc.

This fact is of the greatest importance for the concept of "passive revolution"[96]—the fact, that is, that what was involved was not a social group which "led" other groups, but a State which, even though it had limitations as a power, "led" the group which should have been "leading" and was able to put at the latter's disposal an army and a politico-diplomatic strength. One may refer to what has been called the function of "Piedmont" in international politico-historical language. Serbia before the war posed as the "Piedmont" of the Balkans. (Moreover France after 1789 and for many years, up to the *coup d'état* of Louis Napoléon, was in this sense the Piedmont of Europe.) That Serbia did not succeed as Piedmont succeeded is due to the fact that after the war there occurred a political awakening of the peasantry such as did not exist after 1848. If one studies closely what is happening in the kingdom of Yugoslavia, one sees that within it the "Serbian" forces or those favourable to Serb hegemony are the forces which oppose agrarian reform. Both in Croatia and in the other non-Serb regions we find that there is an anti-Serb rural intellectual bloc, and that the conservative forces are favourable to Serbia. In this case, too, there do not exist local "hegemonic" groups—they are under the hegemony of Serbia; meanwhile the subversive forces do not have, as a social function, any great importance. Anybody who observes Serb affairs superficially might wonder what would have happened if so-called brigandage of the kind which occurred round Naples and in Sicily from 1860 to 1870 had occurred in Yugoslavia after 1919. Undoubtedly the phenomenon is the same, but the social weight and political experience of the peasant masses are quite different since 1919 from what they were after 1848. The important thing is to analyse more profoundly the significance of a "Piedmont"-type function in passive revolutions—i.e. the fact that a State

[96] See note 11 on p. 59, and pp. 106–120 below.

replaces the local social groups in leading a struggle of renewal. It is one of the cases in which these groups have the function of "domination" without that of "leadership": dictatorship without hegemony. The hegemony will be exercised by a part of the social group over the entire group, and not by the latter over other forces in order to give power to the movement, radicalise it, etc. on the "Jacobin" model.

Studies aimed at capturing the analogies between the period which followed the fall of Napoleon and that which followed the war of 1914–18. The analogies are only seen from two viewpoints: territorial division, and the more conspicuous and superficial one of the attempt to give a stable legal organisation to international relations (Holy Alliance and League of Nations). However, it would seem that the most important characteristic to examine is the one which has been called that of "passive revolution"—a problem whose existence is not manifest, since an external parallelism with the France of 1789–1815 is lacking. And yet, everybody recognises that the war of 1914–18 represents an historical break, in the sense that a whole series of questions which piled up individually before 1914 have precisely formed a "mound", modifying the general structure of the previous process. It is enough to think of the importance which the trade-union phenomenon has assumed, a general term in which various problems and processes of development, of differing importance and significance, are lumped together (parliamentarianism, industrial organisation, democracy, liberalism, etc.), but which objectively reflects the fact that a new social force has been constituted, and has a weight which can no longer be ignored, etc. [1933]

THE CONCEPT OF PASSIVE REVOLUTION

The concept of "passive revolution"[97] must be rigorously derived from the two fundamental principles of political science: 1. that no social formation disappears as long as the productive forces which have developed within it still find room for further forward movement; 2. that a society does not set itself tasks for whose solution the necessary conditions have not already been incubated, etc.[98] It

---

[97] See note 11 on p. 59; also introduction to Notes on Italian History, pp. 44–7.

[98] These principles, here quoted from memory by Gramsci, are taken from Marx's Preface to *The Critique of Political Economy*: "No social order ever perishes before all the productive forces for which there is room in it have developed; and new, higher relations of production never appear before the material conditions of their existence have matured in the womb of the old society itself. Therefore mankind always sets itself only such tasks as it can solve . . ."

goes without saying that these principles must first be developed critically in all their implications, and purged of every residue of mechanicism and fatalism. They must therefore be referred back to the description of the three fundamental moments into which a "situation" or an equilibrium of forces can be distinguished, with the greatest possible stress on the second moment (equilibrium of political forces), and especially on the third moment (politico-military equilibrium).[99]

It may be observed that Pisacane, in his *Essays*, is concerned precisely with this third moment: unlike Mazzini, he understands all the importance of the presence in Italy of a war-hardened Austrian army, always ready to intervene at any point on the peninsula, and with moreover behind it all the military strength of the Habsburg Empire—an ever-ready matrix of new armies of reinforcement. Another historical element to be recalled is the development of Christianity in the bosom of the Roman Empire. Also the current phenomenon of Gandhism in India, and Tolstoy's theory of non-resistance to evil, both of which have so much in common with the first phase of Christianity (before the Edict of Milan).[100] Gandhism and Tolstoyism are naïve theorisations of the "passive revolution" with religious overtones. Certain so-called "liquidationist"[101] movements and the reactions they provoked

---

[99] For the three "moments" to which Gramsci refers, see "Analysis of Situations", on pp. 175–185 below.

[100] The Edict whereby Constantine, in A.D. 313, recognised Christianity as the official religion of the Empire.

[101] This could be a reference to the liquidationist tendency in the Russian Social-Democratic Party during 1908 and in the following years, condemned at the Fifth Party Congress in December 1908 and the subject of numerous attacks by Lenin who identified its essence as the desire for the Party to abandon illegal activity. However, it seems likely that the reference is to more recent events within the PCI. Between 1922 and 1924, the main reason for Gramsci's continued support for Bordiga was his fear of the "liquidationism" of Tasca and the Right, i.e. their readiness to accept an interpretation of the United Front policy (an interpretation which was incidentally also that of the Comintern) which would lead to fusion with the PSI and the effective "liquidation" of the PCI as formed at Livorno. See, for example, exchange of letters between Gramsci and Piero Sraffa, in *Ordine Nuovo*, April 1924. From 1925 on, the Right was incorporated into the leadership, and after Gramsci's arrest the party was in effect led by Togliatti and Tasca together. After the Comintern's left turn in 1929, Tasca—who was close to Bukharin, Humbert-Droz, etc.—was accused like them of "liquidationism", in the "right" period of 1927–28. Gramsci as always is concerned to establish a dialectical position, rejecting both the "liquidationists" who make passive revolution into a programme and abandon the revolutionary perspective, and also those who react against this by a mechanical, and voluntarist, advocacy of frontal attack when this can only lead to defeat. In fact he is faithful to his interpretation of the "dual perspective" of the Fifth World Congress, against both the "right" period of 1927–28 and the "left" period which followed it.

should also be recalled, in connection with the tempo and form of certain situations (especially of the third moment). The point of departure for the study will be Vincenzo Cuoco's work on the subject; but it is obvious that Cuoco's phrase for the Neapolitan revolution of 1799 can be no more than a cue, since the concept has been completely modified and enriched.

Can the concept of "passive revolution", in the sense attributed by Vincenzo Cuoco to the first period of the Italian Risorgimento, be related to the concept of "war of position" in contrast to war of manœuvre?[102] In other words, did these concepts have a meaning after the French Revolution, and can the twin figures of Proudhon and Gioberti be explained in terms of the panic created by the Terror of 1793, as Sorellism can be in terms of the panic following the Paris massacres of 1871? In other words, does there exist an absolute identity between war of position and passive revolution? Or at least does there exist, or can there be conceived, an entire historical period in which the two concepts must be considered identical—until the point at which the war of position once again becomes a war of manœuvre?

The "restorations" need to be judged "dynamically", as a "ruse of providence" in Vico's sense.[103] One problem is the following: in the struggle Cavour–Mazzini, in which Cavour is the exponent of the passive revolution/war of position and Mazzini of popular initiative/war of manœuvre, are not both of them indispensable to precisely the same extent? Yet it has to be taken into account that, whereas Cavour was aware of his role (at least up to a certain point) in as much as he understood the role of Mazzini, the latter does not seem to have been aware either of his own or of Cavour's. If, on the contrary, Mazzini had possessed such awareness—in other words, if he had been a realistic politician and not a visionary apostle (i.e. if he had not been Mazzini)—then the equilibrium which resulted from the convergence of the two men's activities would have been different, would have been more favourable to Mazzinianism. In other words, the Italian State would have been constituted on a less retrograde and more modern basis. And since similar situations

---

[102] See pp. 229–39 below, and introduction to "State and Civil Society", pp. 206–9.

[103] The actual phrase is not Vico's—it is perhaps an echo of Hegel's "ruse of reason"—but the idea is. Vico's theory of divine providence held that men themselves constructed a world according to a divine plan of which they were not aware. "For out of the passions of men each bent on his private advantage, for the sake of which they would live like wild beasts in the wilderness, it [providence] has made the civil institutions by which they may live in human society." Vico, *The New Science*, Cornell, 1968, p. 62.

almost always arise in every historical development, one should see if it is not possible to draw from this some general principle of political science and art. One may apply to the concept of passive revolution (documenting it from the Italian Risorgimento) the interpretative criterion of molecular changes which in fact progressively modify the pre-existing composition of forces, and hence become the matrix of new changes. Thus, in the Italian Risorgimento, it has been seen how the composition of the moderate forces was progressively modified by the passing over to Cavourism (after 1848) of ever new elements of the Action Party, so that on the one hand neo-Guelphism[104] was liquidated, and on the other the Mazzinian movement was impoverished (Garibaldi's oscillations, etc. also belong to this process). This element is therefore the initial phase of the phenomenon which is later called "transformism",[105] and whose importance as a form of historical development has not as yet, it seems, been adequately emphasised.

Pursue further the notion that, while Cavour was aware of his role in as much as he was critically aware of that of Mazzini, the latter, as a consequence of his scanty or non-existent awareness of Cavour's role, had in fact little awareness of his own either. Hence his vacillations (for example at Milan in the period following the Five Days,[106] and on other occasions) and his ill-timed initiatives—which therefore became factors only benefiting the policies of Piedmont. This is an exemplification of the theoretical problem, posed in the *Poverty of Philosophy*, of how the dialectic must be understood.[107] Neither Proudhon nor Mazzini understood the necessity for each member of a dialectical opposition to seek to be itself totally and throw into the struggle all the political and moral "resources" it possesses, since only in that way can it achieve a genuine dialectical "transcendence" of its opponent. The retort will be made that this was not understood by Gioberti or the theoreticians of the passive revolution or "revolution/restoration"* either, but in fact their case is a different one. Their theoretical "incompre-

[104] See note 9 on p. 58.
[105] See note 8 on p. 58.
[106] The insurrection in May 1848 against the Austrians.
[107] See especially chapter II.

* The political literature produced on '48 by Marxist scholars will have to be looked at, but there does not appear to be much to hope for in this direction. What happened in Italy, for instance, was only studied with the help of Bolton King's books, etc.[108]

[108] Bolton King (1860–1937) was an English historian, author of *Life of Mazzini* (1902), *A History of Italian Unity* (1899; Italian translation 1909–10); *Fascism in Italy* (1931).

hension" expressed in practice the necessity for the "thesis" to achieve its full development, up to the point where it would even succeed in incorporating a part of the antithesis itself—in order, that is, not to allow itself to be "transcended" in the dialectical opposition. The thesis alone in fact develops to the full its potential for struggle, up to the point where it absorbs even the so-called representatives of the antithesis: it is precisely in this that the passive revolution or revolution/restoration consists. The problem of the political struggle's transition from a "war of manœuvre" to a "war of position" certainly needs to be considered at this juncture. In Europe this transition took place after 1848, and was not understood by Mazzini and his followers, as it was on the contrary by certain others: the same transition took place after 1871, etc. At the time, the question was hard to understand for men like Mazzini, in view of the fact that military wars had not yet furnished the model—and indeed military theory was developing in the direction of war of movement. One will have to see whether there are any relevant allusions in Pisacane, who was the military theoretician of Mazzinianism.

However, the main reason for studying Pisacane is that he was the only one who tried to give the Action Party a substantive and not merely formal content—as an antithesis transcending traditional positions. Nor can it be said that, for such an historical outcome to be achieved, a popular armed insurrection was an imperative necessity—as Mazzini believed to the point of obsession (i.e. not realistically, but with the fervour of a missionary). The popular intervention which was not possible in the concentrated and instantaneous form of an insurrection, did not take place even in the "diffused" and capillary form of indirect pressure—though the latter would have been possible, and perhaps was in fact the indispensable premiss for the former. The concentrated or instantaneous form was rendered impossible by the military technique of the time—but only partially so; in other words the impossibility existed in so far as that concentrated and instantaneous form was not preceded by long ideological and political preparation, organically devised in advance to reawaken popular passions and enable them to be concentrated and brought simultaneously to detonation point.

After 1848, only the Moderates made a critique of the methods which had led up to the débâcle. (Indeed the entire Moderate movement renewed itself: neo-Guelphism was liquidated, new men occupied the top positions of leadership.) No self-criticism, by contrast, on the part of the Mazzinians—or rather only a self-criticism by liquidation, in the sense that many elements abandoned Mazzini and came to form the left wing of the Piedmontese party. The only "orthodox" attempt—i.e. from within—was Pisacane's essays; but these never became the platform for a new organic policy, notwithstanding the fact that Mazzini himself recognised that Pisacane had a "strategic conception" of the Italian national revolution.

Other aspects of the relation "passive revolution/war of position" in the Italian Risorgimento can be studied too. The most important of these are, on the one hand what can be called the "personnel" aspect, and on the other that of the "revolutionary levy". The "personnel" aspect can precisely be compared to what occurred in the World War, in the relationship on the one hand between career officers and those called up from the reserves, and on the other between conscripts and volunteers/commandos. The career officers corresponded in the Risorgimento to the regular, organic, traditional, etc. political parties, which at the moment of action (1848) revealed themselves inept or almost so, and which in 1848–49 were overtaken by the popular-Mazzinian-democratic tidal wave. This tidal wave was chaotic, formless, "*extempore*" so to speak, but it nonetheless, under an improvised leadership (or nearly so—at any rate not one formed beforehand as was the case with the Moderate party), obtained successes which were indubitably greater than those obtained by the Moderates: the Roman Republic and Venice showed a very notable strength of resistance.[109] In the period after '48 the relation between the two forces—the regular and the "charismatic"—became organised around Cavour and Garibaldi and produced the greatest results (although these results were later confiscated by Cavour).

This "personnel" aspect is related to that of the "levy". It should be observed that the technical difficulty on which Mazzini's initiatives always came to grief was precisely that of the "revolutionary levy". It would be interesting, from this point of view, to study Ramorino's attempt to invade Savoy, together with the attempts of the Bandiera brothers, Pisacane, etc.,[110] and to compare them with the situation which faced Mazzini in '48 at Milan and

[109] The Roman Republic under Garibaldi, and Venice under Manin, held out for several months against the Austrians in 1849—despite the demoralisation following the defeat of the Piedmontese at Novara.

[110] Ramorino tried to invade Savoy in 1834; the Bandiera brothers landed in Calabria in 1844; Pisacane (see note 17 on p. 62) committed suicide after the failure of his landing at Sapri in 1857.

in '49 in Rome—situations which he did not have the capacity to organise.[111] These attempts of a few individuals could not fail to be nipped in the bud; it would have been a miracle indeed if the reactionary forces, concentrated and able to operate freely (i.e. unopposed by any broad movement of the population), had not crushed initiatives of the Ramorino, Pisacane, Bandiera type—even if these had been better prepared than in fact they were. In the second period (1859–60), the "revolutionary levy" (which is what Garibaldi's Thousand in fact was) was made possible firstly by the fact that Garibaldi grafted himself on to the Piedmontese national forces, and secondly by the fact that the English fleet effectively protected the Marsala landing and the capture of Palermo, and neutralised the Bourbon fleet. In Milan after the Five Days and in republican Rome, Mazzini had opportunities to set up recruitment centres for an organic levy, but he had no intention of doing so. This was the source of his conflict with Garibaldi in Rome, and the reason for his ineffectiveness in Milan compared with Cattaneo and the Milanese democratic group.[112]

In any case, although the course of events in the Risorgimento revealed the enormous importance of the "demagogic" mass movement, with its leaders thrown up by chance, improvised, etc., it was nevertheless in actual fact taken over by the traditional organic forces—in other words, by the parties of long standing, with rationally-formed leaders, etc. And identical results occurred in all similar political events. (Examples of this are the preponderance of the Orleanists over the radical-democratic popular forces in France in 1830; and, ultimately, the French Revolution of 1789 too—in which Napoleon represents in the last analysis the triumph of the organic bourgeois forces over the Jacobin petit-bourgeois forces.)

---

[111] In 1848, after the successful "Five Days" insurrection in Milan and the Austrian withdrawal to their "quadrilateral" of fortified towns, Mazzini arrived in Milan and founded *Italia del Popolo*. With this organ, he attempted to combat the notion of a fusion of Piedmont and Lombardy, in favour of his own aim of a united, republican Italy. He failed to gain popular support for his views.

In 1849 (see note 90 on p. 102) Mazzini headed the Roman Republic. His policy of entrusting the city's defences to the regular army rather than attempting to mobilise the entire population was symbolised by his appointment of Rosselli, a regular army general, rather than Garibaldi to command the defence forces.

[112] Carlo Cattaneo (1801–69), sometimes called the first Italian positivist, edited the influential *Il Politecnico*. During the Five Days of Milan (see previous note) he headed the Council of War; at this time he was favourable to the policy of the Piedmontese monarchy. However, he came to oppose the latter fiercely, feeling that the Italian bourgeois revolution was being sacrificed to Piedmontese ambitions. In 1867 he became a deputy in the Italian parliament, but refused to take the oath of loyalty to the throne of Savoy.

Similarly in the World War the victory of the old career officers over the reservists, etc. In any case, the absence among the radical-popular forces of any awareness of the role of the other side prevented them from being fully aware of their own role either; hence from weighing in the final balance of forces in proportion to their effective power of intervention; and hence from determining a more advanced result, on more progressive and modern lines.

Still in connection with the concept of "passive revolution" or "revolution/restoration" in the Italian Risorgimento, it should be noted that it is necessary to pose with great precision the problem which in certain historiographical tendencies is called that of the relations between the objective conditions and the subjective conditions of an historical event. It seems obvious that the so-called subjective conditions can never be missing when the objective conditions exist, in as much as the distinction involved is simply one of a didactic character. Consequently it is on the size and concentration of subjective forces that discussion can bear, and hence on the dialectical relation between conflicting subjective forces.

It is necessary to avoid posing the problem in "intellectualistic" rather than historico-political terms. Naturally it is not disputed that intellectual "clairvoyance" of the terms of the struggle is indispensable. But this clairvoyance is a political value only in as much as it becomes disseminated passion, and in as much as it is the premiss for a strong will. In many recent works on the Risorgimento, it has been "revealed" that there existed individuals who saw everything clearly (recall Piero Gobetti's emphasis on Ornato's[113] significance). But these "revelations" are self-destroying, precisely because they are revelations; they demonstrate that what was involved was nothing more than personal reflections which today represent a form of "hindsight". In fact, they never effected a juncture with actual reality, never became a general and operative national-popular consciousness. Out of the Action Party and the Moderates, which represented the real "subjective forces" of the Risorgimento? Without a shadow of doubt it was the Moderates, precisely because they were also aware of the role of the Action Party: thanks to this awareness, their "subjectivity" was of a superior and more decisive quality. In Victor Emmanuel's crude, sergeant-major's expression "we've got the Action Party in our

113 Luigi Ornato (1787–1842), an obscure Piedmontese thinker, left no published work except a vulgarisation of Marcus Aurelius but enjoyed a high reputation, e.g. with Gioberti. Gobetti saluted him in the Manifesto for the first number of *La Rivoluzione Liberale* as the "philosopher of the risings of 1821", etc.

pocket" there is more historico-political sense than in all Mazzini. [1933]

FIRST EPILOGUE

The thesis of the "passive revolution" as an interpretation of the Risorgimento period, and of every epoch characterised by complex historical upheavals. Utility and dangers of this thesis. Danger of historical defeatism, i.e. of indifferentism, since the whole way of posing the question may induce a belief in some kind of fatalism, etc. Yet the conception remains a dialectical one—in other words, presupposes, indeed postulates as necessary, a vigorous antithesis which can present intransigently all its potentialities for development. Hence theory of the "passive revolution" not as a programme, as it was for the Italian liberals of the Risorgimento, but as a criterion of interpretation, in the absence of other active elements to a dominant extent. (Hence struggle against the political morphinism which exudes from Croce and from his historicism.) (It would seem that the theory of the passive revolution is a necessary critical corollary to the Introduction to the *Critique of Political Economy*.) Revision of certain sectarian ideas on the theory of the party, theories which precisely represent a form of fatalism of a "divine right" type. Development of the concepts of mass party and small élite party, and mediation between the two. (Theoretical and practical mediation: is it theoretically possible for there to exist a group, relatively small but still of significant size, let us say several thousand strong, that is socially and ideologically homogeneous, without its very existence demonstrating a widespread state of affairs and corresponding state of mind which only mechanical, external and hence transitory causes prevent from being expressed?) [1933]

MATERIAL FOR A CRITICAL ESSAY ON CROCE'S TWO HISTORIES, OF ITALY AND OF EUROPE[114]

Historical relationship between the modern French state created by the Revolution and the other modern states of continental Europe. The comparison is vitally important—provided that it is not made on the basis of abstract sociological schemas. It should be based on the study of four elements: 1. revolutionary explosion in France

[114] i.e. *Storia d'Italia dal 1871 al 1915*, and *Storia d'Europa nel secolo decimonono*.

with radical and violent transformation of social and political relations; 2. European opposition to the French Revolution and to any extension of it along class lines; 3. war between France, under the Republic and Napoleon, and the rest of Europe—initially, in order to avoid being stifled at birth, and subsequently with the aim of establishing a permanent French hegemony tending towards the creation of a universal empire; 4. national revolts against French hegemony, and birth of the modern European states by successive small waves of reform rather than by revolutionary explosions like the original French one. The "successive waves" were made up of a combination of social struggles, interventions from above of the enlightened monarchy type, and national wars—with the two latter phenomena predominating. The period of the "Restoration" is the richest in developments of this kind; restoration becomes the first policy whereby social struggles find sufficiently elastic frameworks to allow the bourgeoisie to gain power without dramatic upheavals, without the French machinery of terror. The old feudal classes are demoted from their dominant position to a "governing" one, but are not eliminated, nor is there any attempt to liquidate them as an organic whole; instead of a class they become a "caste" with specific cultural and psychological characteristics, but no longer with predominant economic functions. Can this "model" for the creation of the modern states be repeated in other conditions? Can this be excluded absolutely, or could we say that at least partially there can be similar developments in the form of the appearance of planned economies?[115] Can it be excluded for all states, or only for the large ones? The question is of the highest importance, because the France–Europe model has created a mentality which is no less significant for being "ashamed of itself" or for being an "instrument of government". An important question related to the foregoing is that of the function which the intellectuals thought they fulfilled in this long, submerged process of political and social fragmentation of the restoration. Classical German philosophy was the philosophy of this period, and animated the liberal national movements from 1848 to 1870. Here too is the place to recall the Hegelian parallel (carried over into the philosophy of praxis) between French practice and German speculation.[116] In reality the parallel can be extended: what is practice for the fundamental class becomes "rationality"

---

[115] See "Americanism and Fordism" on pp. 277–318, which opens with a passage which makes clear what Gramsci means by "planned economies". See too "The history of Europe seen as 'passive revolution' " on pp. 118–20.

[116] See note 46 on p. 78.

and speculation for its intellectuals (it is on the basis of these historical relations that all modern philosophical idealism is to be explained).

The conception of the State according to the productive function of the social classes cannot be applied mechanically to the interpretation of Italian and European history from the French revolution throughout the nineteenth century. Although it is certain that for the fundamental productive classes (capitalist bourgeoisie and modern proletariat) the State is only conceivable as the concrete form of a specific economic world, of a specific system of production, this does not mean that the relationship of means to end can be easily determined or takes the form of a simple schema, apparent at first sight. It is true that conquest of power and achievement of a new productive world are inseparable, and that propaganda for one of them is also propaganda for the other, and that in reality it is solely in this coincidence that the unity of the dominant class—at once economic and political—resides.

But the complex problem arises of the relation of internal forces in the country in question, of the relation of international forces, of the country's geo-political position. In reality, the drive towards revolutionary renewal may be initiated by the pressing needs of a given country, in given circumstances, and you get the revolutionary explosion in France, victorious internationally as well. But the drive for renewal may be caused by the combination of progressive forces which in themselves are scanty and inadequate (though with immense potential, since they represent their country's future) with an international situation favourable to their expansion and victory. Raffaele Ciasca's book on "The Origins of the National Programme", while it proved that there existed in Italy the same pressing problems as existed in *ancien régime* France, and a social force which interpreted and represented these problems precisely in the French sense, also proved that these forces were weak and the problems remained at the level of "petty politics".[117] In any case, one can see how, when the impetus of progress is not tightly linked to a vast local economic development which is artificially limited and repressed, but is instead the reflection of international developments which transmit their ideological currents to the periphery—currents born on the basis of the productive development of the

[117] Ciasca's book had been reviewed by Mondolfo in an article on interpretations of the Risorgimento written in 1917, which Gramsci had republished in part in *Il Grido del Popolo*, 16 May 1918. The social force referred to is clearly the PSI and the socialist forces in general.

more advanced countries—then the group which is the bearer of the new ideas is not the economic group but the intellectual stratum, and the conception of the State advocated by them changes aspect; it is conceived of as something in itself, as a rational absolute. The problem can be formulated as follows: since the State is the concrete form of a productive world and since the intellectuals are the social element from which the governing personnel is drawn, the intellectual who is not firmly anchored to a strong economic group will tend to present the State as an absolute; in this way the function of the intellectuals is itself conceived of as absolute and pre-eminent, and their historical existence and dignity are abstractly rationalised. This motive is fundamental for an historical understanding of modern philosophical idealism, and is connected with the mode of formation of the modern States of continental Europe as "reaction—national transcendence" of the French Revolution (a motive which is essential for understanding the concepts of "passive revolution" and "revolution/restoration", and for grasping the importance of the Hegelian comparison between the principles of Jacobinism and classical German philosophy). The observation can be made that certain traditional criteria for historical and cultural evaluation of the Risorgimento period must be modified, and in some cases inverted: 1. the Italian currents which are "branded" for their French rationalism and abstract illuminism are perhaps those which in fact most closely adhere to Italian reality, in so far as in reality they conceive of the State as the concrete form of an Italian economic development in progress; a similar content requires a similar political form; 2. the real "Jacobins" (in the pejorative sense which the term has taken on for certain historiographical currents) are the currents which appear most indigenous in that they seem to develop an Italian tradition.[118] But in reality this current is "Italian" only because culture for many centuries was the only Italian "national" manifestation; this is simply a verbal illusion. Where was the basis for this Italian culture? It was not in Italy; this "Italian" culture is the continuation of the mediaeval cosmopolitanism linked to the tradition of the Empire and the Church. Universal concepts with "geographical" seats in Italy. The Italian intellectuals were functionally a cosmo-

---

[118] These currents are, on the surface of it, the republicans, Mazzinians, etc. (influenced by the ideas of the French Revolution) on the one hand, and the Moderates on the other. However, it is hard not to read into this an indirect comment on the contemporary socialist/communist Left and nationalist/fascist Right respectively. See too 'The Political Party', pp. 147–57.

politan cultural concentration; they absorbed and developed theoretically the reflections of the most solid and indigenous contemporary Italian life. This function can be seen in Machiavelli too, though Machiavelli attempted to turn it to national ends (without success and without any appreciable result). *The Prince*, in fact, was a development of Spanish, French and English experience during the travail of national unification—which in Italy did not command sufficient forces, or even arouse much interest. Since the representatives of the traditional current really wish to apply to Italy intellectual and rational schemas, worked out in Italy it is true, but on the basis of anachronistic experiences rather than immediate national needs, it is they who are the Jacobins in the pejorative sense . . . [1932]

THE HISTORY OF EUROPE SEEN AS "PASSIVE REVOLUTION"

Is it possible to write a history of Europe in the nineteenth century without an organic treatment of the French Revolution and the Napoleonic Wars? And is it possible to write a history of Italy in modern times without the struggles of the Risorgimento? In both cases Croce, for extrinsic and tendentious reasons, excludes the moment of struggle in which the structure is formed and modified, and placidly takes as history the moment of cultural or ethical-political expansion. Does the conception of the "passive revolution" have a "present" significance? Are we in a period of "restoration-revolution" to be permanently consolidated, to be organised ideologically, to be exalted lyrically? Does Italy have the same relation *vis-à-vis* the USSR that the Germany (and Europe) of Kant and Hegel had *vis-à-vis* the France of Robespierre and Napoleon?

Paradigms of ethical-political history. The *History of Europe in the Nineteenth Century* seems to be the work of ethical-political history destined to become the paradigm of Crocean historiography offered to European culture. However, his other studies must be taken into account too: *History of the Kingdom of Naples*; *History of Italy from 1871 to 1915*; *The Neapolitan Revolution of 1799*; and *History of the Baroque Era in Italy*. The most tendentious and revealing, however, are the *History of Europe* and the *History of Italy*. With respect to these two works, the questions at once arise: is it possible to write (conceive of) a history of Europe in the nineteenth century without an organic treatment of the French Revolution and the Napoleonic Wars? And is it possible to write a history of Italy in modern times without a treatment of the struggles of the Risorgimento? In other words: is it fortuitous, or is it for a tendentious motive, that Croce begins his narratives from 1815 and 1871? I.e. that he excludes the moment of struggle; the moment in which the conflicting forces are formed, are assembled and take up their positions; the moment in which one ethical-political system dissolves and another is formed by fire and by steel; the moment in which one system of social relations disintegrates and falls and another arises and asserts itself? Is it fortuitous or not that he placidly takes as history the moment of cultural or ethical-political expansion? One can say, therefore, that the book on the *History of Europe* is nothing but a fragment of history, the "passive" aspect of the great revolution which started in France in 1789 and which spilled over into the rest of Europe with the republican and Napoleonic armies—giving the old régimes a powerful shove, and resulting not in their immediate collapse as in France but in the "reformist" corrosion of them which lasted up to 1870.

The problem arises of whether this Crocean construction, in its tendentious nature, does not have a contemporary and immediate reference. Whether it does not aim to create an ideological movement corresponding to that of the period with which Croce is dealing, i.e. the period of restoration-revolution, in which the demands which in France found a Jacobin–Napoleonic expression were satisfied by small doses, legally, in a reformist manner—in such a way that it was possible to preserve the political and economic position of the old feudal classes, to avoid agrarian reform, and, especially, to avoid the popular masses going through a period of political experience such as occurred in France in the years of Jacobinism, in 1831, and in 1848. But, in present conditions, is it not precisely the fascist movement which in fact corresponds to the movement of moderate and conservative liberalism in the last century?

Perhaps it is not without significance that, in the first years of its development, fascism claimed a continuity with the tradition of the old "historic" Right. It might be one of the numerous paradoxical aspects of history (a ruse of nature, to put it in Vico's language) that Croce, with his own particular preoccupations, should in effect have contributed to a reinforcement of fascism—furnishing it indirectly with an intellectual justification, after having contributed to purging it of various secondary characteristics, of a superficially romantic type but nevertheless irritating to his classical serenity modelled on Goethe. The ideological hypothesis could be presented in the following terms: that there is a passive revolution involved in the fact that—through the legislative intervention of the State, and by means of the corporative organisation—relatively far-reaching modifications are being introduced into the country's economic structure in order to accentuate the "plan of production" element; in other words, that socialisation and co-operation in the sphere of production are being increased, without however touching (or at least not going beyond the regulation and control of) individual and group appropriation of profit. In the concrete framework of Italian social relations, this could be the only solution whereby to develop the productive forces of industry under the direction of the traditional ruling classes, in competition with the more advanced industrial formations of countries which monopolise raw materials and have accumulated massive capital sums.

Whether or not such a schema could be put into practice, and to what extent, is only of relative importance. What is important from the political and ideological point of view is that it is capable of creating—and indeed does create—a period of expectation and hope, especially in certain Italian social groups such as the great mass of urban and rural petit bourgeois. It thus reinforces the hegemonic system and the forces of military and civil coercion at the disposal of the traditional ruling classes.

This ideology thus serves as an element of a "war of position" in the international economic field (free competition and free exchange here corresponding to the war of movement), just as "passive revolution" does in the political field. In Europe from 1789 to 1870 there was a (political) war of movement in the French Revolution and a long war of position from 1815 to 1870. In the present epoch, the war of movement took place politically from March 1917 to March 1921; this was followed by a war of position whose representative—both practical (for Italy) and ideological (for Europe)—is fascism. [1935]

II

NOTES ON POLITICS

I

THE MODERN PRINCE

INTRODUCTION

The concept of "Jacobinism" is perhaps that which establishes most clearly and most succinctly the unifying thread which links all of Gramsci's prison writing on history and on politics. Machiavelli was a "precocious Jacobin"; Mazzini and his followers failed to be the "Jacobins" of the Risorgimento; the "Modern Prince"—i.e. the communist party—must organise and express a national-popular collective will, in other words, must be a "Jacobin" force, binding the peasants beneath the hegemony of the proletariat, and rejecting all forms of economism, syndicalism, spontaneism. What has characterised Italian history hitherto is the fact that "an effective *Jacobin* force was always missing". Now the question is posed of whether the urban proletariat has "attained an adequate development in the field of industrial production and a certain level of historico-political culture". Its historical task can only be accomplished if "the great mass of peasant farmers bursts *simultaneously* into political life". The writings on the communist party grouped in this section aim to define what type of party could play the role of the "Modern Prince".

In an earlier version of the passage here entitled "The Political Party", Gramsci gave what he wrote the heading "Marx and Machiavelli", and began: "This theme can be developed in a two-fold study: a study of the real relations between the two as theorists of militant politics, of action; and a book which would derive from Marxist doctrines an articulated system of contemporary politics of the '*Prince*' type. The theme would be the political party, in its relations with the classes and the State: not the party as a sociological category, but the party which seeks to found the State." Why did Gramsci attach such importance to Machiavelli? Because "Machiavelli was the representative in Italy of the recognition that the Renaissance could not be a real one without the foundation of a national State"; "Machiavelli's political thought was a reaction to the Renaissance [in the narrow sense]; it was an invocation of the political and national necessity of drawing closer to the people as the absolute monarchies of France and Spain had done . . ." Machiavelli did not merely abstractly desire the national unification of Italy; he had a programme, and it was one which revealed his "precocious Jacobinism". He intended through the institution of a citizen militia to bring the great mass of peasant farmers into political life. For Gramsci, he was not simply a precursor of the "historical" Jacobins, but a precursor of the "modern" Jacobins—i.e. the communists—in their task of forging the worker-peasant alliance. In his identification of the communists with Jacobinism, Gramsci was developing and expanding a theme already touched on by Lenin—who wrote in July 1917 that " 'Jacobinism' in Europe or on the boundary line between Europe and Asia in the twentieth century would be the rule of the revolutionary class, of the proletariat, which, supported by the peasant poor and taking advantage of the existing material basis for advancing to socialism, could not only provide all the great, ineradicable, unforgettable things provided by the Jacobins in the eighteenth century, but bring about a lasting world-wide victory for the working people".

The notes grouped in this section approach the problem of the "The Modern Prince" from many angles; they analyse the nature of a political party as such; the relations between party, class and State; the ideological dangers of economism and spontaneism, against which it must struggle; the type of non-bureaucratic internal régime which is necessary if it is to be effective. But if there is one passage which perhaps more than any other encapsulates Gramsci's conception of the revolutionary party, it is the opening sentences of the section entitled "Prediction and Perspective" in which he evokes Machiavelli's Centaur as a symbol of the "dual perspective" which must characterise the revolutionary party (and State). The party must hold together in a dialectical unity the two levels "of force and of consent, authority and hegemony, violence and civilisation, of agitation and of propaganda, of tactics and of strategy". Perhaps one can see here an attempt to theorise the struggle Gramsci had conducted in the PCI against Bordiga on the one hand and Tasca on the other. Bordiga in this schema would represent an undialectical isolation of the moment of force, domination, etc., Tasca a parallel isolation of the moment of consent, hegemony; the short-term and the long-term perspective respectively, mechanically and incorrectly divorced from the other. Gramsci sought to theorise the unity of the two perspectives.

THE MODERN PRINCE

BRIEF NOTES ON MACHIAVELLI'S POLITICS

The basic thing about *The Prince* is that it is not a systematic treatment, but a "live" work, in which political ideology and political science are fused in the dramatic form of a "myth". Before Machiavelli, political science had taken the form either of the Utopia or of the scholarly treatise. Machiavelli, combining the two, gave imaginative and artistic form to his conception by embodying the doctrinal, rational element in the person of a *condottiere*,[1] who represents plastically and "anthropomorphically" the symbol of the "collective will". In order to represent the process whereby a given collective will, directed towards a given political objective, is formed, Machiavelli did not have recourse to long-winded arguments, or pedantic classifications of principles and criteria for a method of action. Instead he represented this process in terms of the qualities, characteristics, duties and requirements of a concrete individual. Such a procedure stimulates the artistic imagination of those who have to be convinced, and gives political passions a more concrete form.*

Machiavelli's *Prince* could be studied as an historical exemplifica-

---

[1] See note 21 on p. 64.

* One will have to look through the political writers who preceded Machiavelli, to see whether there had been other examples of such personification before *The Prince*. The "mythical" character of the book to which I have referred is due also to its conclusion; having described the ideal *condottiere*, Machiavelli here, in a passage of great artistic effect, invokes the real *condottiere* who is to incarnate him historically.[2] This passionate invocation reflects back on the entire book, and is precisely what gives it its dramatic character. L. Russo, in his *Prolegomeni*,[3] calls Machiavelli the artist of politics, and once even uses the word "myth", but not exactly in the sense just indicated.

[2] i.e. Lorenzo de' Medici, to whom "The Prince" is addressed, and who is invited in the famous last chapter of the work to "make Petrarch's words come true: 'Virtù contro a furore prenderà l'arme; e fia el combatter corto, ché l'antico valore nell'italici cor non è ancor morto.' [Virtue will take up arms against fury; and may the fight be brief, since the ancient valour is not yet dead in Italian hearts]".

[3] Luigi Russo: *Prolegomeni a Machiavelli*, included in *Ritratti e disegni storici*, Bari 1937. We have not been able to trace the original place and date of publication. In another note (NM. p. 141) Gramsci writes: "Russo, in his *Prolegomeni*, makes *The Prince* into Machiavelli's treatise on dictatorship (moment of authority and of the individual), and *The Discourses* into his treatise on hegemony (moment of the universal and of liberty). Russo's observation is correct, although there are allusions to the moment of hegemony or consent in *The Prince* too, beside those to authority or force. Similarly, the observation is correct that there is no opposition in principle between *Principato* [see note 51 on p.249] and republic; what is involved is rather the hypostasis of the two moments of authority and of universality." See "Prediction and Perspective" on pp. 169–173.

tion of the Sorelian myth[4]—i.e. of a political ideology expressed neither in the form of a cold utopia nor as learned theorising, but rather by a creation of concrete phantasy which acts on a dispersed and shattered people to arouse and organise its collective will. The utopian character of *The Prince* lies in the fact that the Prince had no real historical existence; he did not present himself immediately and objectively to the Italian people, but was a pure theoretical abstraction—a symbol of the leader and ideal *condottiere*. However, in a dramatic movement of great effect, the elements of passion and of myth which occur throughout the book are drawn together and brought to life in the conclusion, in the invocation of a prince who "really exists". Throughout the book, Machiavelli discusses what the Prince must be like if he is to lead a people to found a new State; the argument is developed with rigorous logic, and with scientific detachment. In the conclusion, Machiavelli merges with the people, becomes the people; not, however, some "generic" people, but the people whom he, Machiavelli, has convinced by the preceding argument—the people whose consciousness and whose expression he becomes and feels himself to be, with whom he feels identified. The entire "logical" argument now appears as nothing other than auto-reflection on the part of the people—an inner

---

[4] Georges Sorel (1847–1922) was the principal theorist of revolutionary syndicalism, and the author notably of *Reflections on Violence* (1906). Influenced above all by Bergson and Marx, he in his turn had an immense influence in France and Italy—e.g. on Mussolini. His work was an amalgam of extremely disparate elements, reflecting the metamorphoses through which he passed—anti-Jacobin moralist, socialist, revolutionary syndicalist, far-right (indeed near-monarchist) preacher of an anti-bourgeois authoritarian moral regeneration, sympathiser with the Bolshevik revolution. In *Reflections on Violence*, Sorel develops the idea of the General Strike as a myth—indeed "the *myth* in which Socialism is wholly comprised, i.e. a body of images capable of evoking instinctively all the sentiments which correspond to the different manifestations of the war undertaken by Socialism against modern society". Myths "enclose within them all the strongest inclinations of a people, of a party, or of a class". He contrasts myth in this sense with utopias "which present a deceptive mirage of the future to the people". (Another example of myth was Mazzini's "mad chimera", which "did more for Italian unity than Cavour and all the politicians of his school"). The idea of the General Strike "destroys all the theoretical consequences of every possible social policy; its partisans look upon even the most popular reforms as having a middle-class character; so far as they are concerned, nothing can weaken the fundamental opposition of the class war." The General Strike thus focuses the "cleavage" between the antagonistic classes, by making every individual outburst of violence into an act in the class war. "Cleavage", for Sorel, is the equivalent of class consciousness, of the class-for-itself; e.g. "When the governing classes, no longer daring to govern, are ashamed of their privileged situation, are eager to make advances to their enemies, and proclaim their horror of all cleavage in society, it becomes much more difficult to maintain in the minds of the proletariat this idea of cleavage without which Socialism cannot fulfil its historical role." *Reflections on Violence*, Collier Books, 1950, pp. 124–26, 133–35, 186.

reasoning worked out in the popular consciousness, whose conclusion is a cry of passionate urgency. The passion, from discussion of itself, becomes once again "emotion", fever, fanatical desire for action. This is why the epilogue of *The Prince* is not something extrinsic, tacked on, rhetorical, but has to be understood as a necessary element of the work—indeed as the element which gives the entire work its true colour, and makes it a kind of "political manifesto".

A study might be made of how it came about that Sorel never advanced from his conception of ideology-as-myth to an understanding of the political party, but stopped short at the idea of the trade union. It is true that for Sorel the "myth" found its fullest expression not in the trade union as organisation of a collective will, but in its practical action—sign of a collective will already operative. The highest achievement of this practical action was to have been the general strike—i.e. a "passive activity", so to speak, of a negative and preliminary kind (it could only be given a positive character by the realisation of a common accord between the various wills involved), an activity which does not envisage an "active and constructive" phase of its own. Hence in Sorel there was a conflict of two necessities: that of the myth, and that of the critique of the myth—in that "every pre-established plan is utopian and reactionary". The outcome was left to the intervention of the irrational, to chance (in the Bergsonian sense of "*élan vital*")[5] or to "spontaneity".*

---

[5] For Henri Bergson's key concept of "*élan vital*" or "vital impulse", see notably the final section of chapter I of his *Creative Evolution*. In contrast to "mechanistic" theories, which "show us the gradual building-up of the machine under the influence of external circumstances", and to "finalist" theories, which say that "the parts have been brought together on a preconceived plan with a view to a certain end", Bergson suggests that there is "an original impetus of life", life being defined as "a tendency to act on inert matter". The implications of this theory were an extreme voluntarism: "Before the evolution of life . . . the portals of the future remain wide open. It is a creation that goes on for ever in virtue of an initial movement." Also an emphasis on chance: "The direction of this action [i.e. action on inert matter] is not predetermined; hence the unforeseeable variety of forms which life, in evolving, sows along its path." *Creative Evolution*, London 1954.

* At this point an implicit contradiction should be noted between on the one hand the manner in which Croce poses his problem of history and anti-history,[6] and on the other hand certain of Croce's other modes of thought: his aversion to "political parties" and the way in which he poses the question of the "predictability" of social facts (see *Conversazioni critiche*, First series, pp. 150–52, review of Ludovico Limentani's book *La previsione dei fatti sociali*, Turin, Bocca, 1907). If social facts cannot be predicted, and the very concept of prediction is meaningless, then the irrational cannot but be dominant, and any organisation of men must be anti-historical—a "prejudice". The only thing left to do is to resolve each

Can a myth, however, be "non-constructive"? How could an instrument conceivably be effective if, as in Sorel's vision of things, it leaves the collective will in the primitive and elementary phase of its mere formation, by differentiation ("cleavage")—even when this differentiation is violent, that is to say destroys existing moral and juridical relations? Will not that collective will, with so rudimentary a formation, at once cease to exist, scattering into an infinity of individual wills which in the positive phase then follow

---

individual, practical problem posed by the movement of history as it comes up, and with extemporaneous criteria; opportunism is the only possible political line. (See Croce's article *Il partito come giudizio e come pregiudizio*, in *Cultura e vita morale*).

[6] For Croce's concept of history and "anti-history", see General Introduction; "Problems of Philosophy and History" below; and note 19 on p. 137. For his "aversion to political parties", see "Politics as an autonomous science", pp. 136–143 below. Gramsci's view was, in fact, that Croce precisely himself fulfilled the function of a "political party" (see especially *Alcuni temi*; and note 39 on p. 150), organising the "leadership" or hegemony of the bourgeoisie at the same time as fascism provided a transitional form of its "domination". Croce in fact supported fascism initially, and continued to do so in the Senate even after Matteotti's murder in 1924—in fact until the banning of the Aventine opposition in 1925. Thereafter he maintained a critical position *vis-à-vis* fascism, but not of a kind to prevent his continuing to live and publish in Italy. At the level of political theory, his essential activity was directed against "the philosophy of praxis", and he contributed in Gramsci's view—whatever his subjective intentions—to the reinforcement of fascism; see for this "The History of Europe seen as 'Passive Revolution' " on pp. 118–120 above. Also *Lettere dal Carcere* pp. 631–33: "I think you exaggerate Croce's present position, and see him as more isolated than he really is . . . Croce has published a considerable proportion of his present views in the review *Politica*, edited by Coppola and Rocco, the Minister [of Justice]; and in my view not just Coppola but many others too are convinced of the usefulness of the position taken up by Croce, which creates a situation in which it becomes possible to give the new ruling groups which have emerged since the war a real education for public life. If you study all Italian history since 1815, you will see that a small ruling group has succeeded in methodically absorbing into its own ambit the entire political personnel thrown up by the various, originally subversive, mass movements. From 1860 to 1876 the Mazzinian and Garibaldine Action Party was absorbed by the Monarchy, leaving only an insignificant residue which lived on as the Republican Party, but whose significance was more folkloristic than historico-political. The phenomenon was called 'transformism', but it was not an isolated phenomenon; it was an organic process which, in the formation of the ruling class, replaced what in France had happened in the Revolution and under Napoleon, and in England under Cromwell. Indeed, even after 1876 the process continued, molecularly. It assumed massive proportions after the War, when the traditional ruling group appeared no longer capable of assimilating and digesting the new forces thrown up by events. But this ruling group is more '*malin*' and capable than one could have imagined: the absorption is difficult and laborious, but takes place nonetheless, by a host of different ways and means. Croce's activity is one of these ways and means; indeed, his teaching produces perhaps the greatest quantity of 'gastric juices' to assist the process of digestion. Set in its historical context, the context of Italian history, Croce's work appears to be the most powerful mechanism for 'conforming' the new forces to its vital interests (not simply its immediate interests, but its future ones as well) that the dominant group today possesses, and I think that the latter has a proper appreciation of his utility, superficial appearances notwithstanding".

separate and conflicting paths? Quite apart from the fact that destruction and negation cannot exist without an implicit construction and affirmation—this not in a "metaphysical" sense but in practice, i.e. politically, as party programme. In Sorel's case it is clear that behind the spontaneity there lies a purely mechanistic assumption, behind the liberty (will—life-force) a maximum of determinism, behind the idealism an absolute materialism.

The modern prince, the myth-prince, cannot be a real person, a concrete individual. It can only be an organism, a complex element of society in which a collective will, which has already been recognised and has to some extent asserted itself in action, begins to take concrete form. History has already provided this organism, and it is the political party—the first cell in which there come together germs of a collective will tending to become universal and total. In the modern world, only those historico-political actions which are immediate and imminent, characterised by the necessity for lightning speed, can be incarnated mythically by a concrete individual. Such speed can only be made necessary by a great and imminent danger, a great danger which precisely fans passion and fanaticism suddenly to a white heat, and annihilates the critical sense and the corrosive irony which are able to destroy the "charismatic" character of the *condottiere* (as happened in the Boulanger adventure).[7] But an improvised action of such a kind, by its very nature, cannot have a long-term and organic character. It will in almost all cases be appropriate to restoration and reorganisation, but not to the founding of new States or new national and social structures (as was at issue in Machiavelli's *Prince*, in which the theme of restoration was merely a rhetorical element, linked to the literary concept of an Italy descended from Rome and destined to restore the order and the power of Rome).* It will be defensive

---

[7] General Boulanger (1837–91) was French Minister of War in 1886. He symbolised the idea of *revanche* (against Germany after the Franco-Prussian War of 1870–71) in the popular consciousness. The government became afraid of his popularity, and of his tractations with monarchist forces. They dismissed him, and posted him to Clermont-Ferrand. He founded a Boulangist party, which called for a new Constituent Assembly, a military regeneration of the nation, and reform of "the abuses of parliamentarism". Elected with a huge majority to the National Assembly, he appeared likely to attempt a *coup*—which could well have succeeded—but in fact hesitated, and subsequently fled the country fearing imminent arrest (1889).

* It is true that Machiavelli was inspired to his political conception of the *necessity* for a unitary Italian State not only by the example and model of the great absolute monarchies of France and Spain, but also by the remembrance of Rome's past. However, it should be emphasised that this is no reason for confusing Machiavelli with the literary-rhetorical tradition. For this element is neither

rather than capable of original creation. Its underlying assumption will be that a collective will, already in existence, has become nerveless and dispersed, has suffered a collapse which is dangerous and threatening but not definitive and catastrophic, and that it is necessary to reconcentrate and reinforce it—rather than that a new collective will must be created from scratch, to be directed towards goals which are concrete and rational, but whose concreteness and rationality have not yet been put to the critical test by a real and universally known historical experience.

The abstract character of the Sorelian conception of the myth is manifest in its aversion (which takes the emotional form of an ethical repugnance) for the Jacobins, who were certainly a "categorical embodiment" of Machiavelli's Prince.[8] *The Modern Prince* must have a part devoted to Jacobinism (in the integral sense which this notion has had historically, and must have conceptually), as an exemplification of the concrete formation and operation of a collective will which at least in some aspects was an original, *ex novo* creation. And a definition must be given of collective will, and of political will in general, in the modern sense: will as operative awareness of historical necessity, as protagonist of a real and effective historical drama.

One of the first sections must precisely be devoted to the "collective will", posing the question in the following terms: "When can the conditions for awakening and developing a national-popular collective will be said to exist?"[9] Hence an historical (economic) analysis of the social structure of the given country and a "dramatic" representation of the attempts made in the course of the centuries to awaken this will, together with the reasons for the successive failures. Why was there no absolute monarchy in Italy in Machiavelli's time? One has to go back to the Roman Empire (the language question, problem of the intellectuals, etc.), and understand the

---

exclusive nor even predominant, nor is the necessity for a great national State argued from it; moreover, this very allusion to Rome is less abstract than it may seem, when it is set in its correct context of the intellectual climate of Humanism and Renaissance. In Book VII of the *Art of War* one finds: "This province (Italy) seems born to bring dead things back to life, as we have seen occur with poetry, with painting and with sculpture"—why then should it not rediscover military skill too? etc. One would have to collect together all the other references of this kind in order to establish their exact character.

[8] For Gramsci's conception of the relation between Machiavelli, Jacobinism and the Communist Party, see introductions to "Notes on Italian History" and to this section (pp. 44–47 and 123–4). See too "Material for a critical essay on Croce's two Histories", on pp. 114–118 above. On Ris. p. 155 Gramsci defines "historical Jacobinism" as "union of city and countryside".

[9] For the concept of national-popular, see note 65 on p. 421.

function of the mediaeval Communes, the significance of Catholicism etc.[10] In short, one has to make an outline of the whole history of Italy—in synthesis, but accurate.

The reason for the failures of the successive attempts to create a national-popular collective will is to be sought in the existence of certain specific social groups which were formed at the dissolution of the Communal bourgeoisie; in the particular character of other groups which reflect the international function of Italy as seat of the Church and depositary of the Holy Roman Empire; and so on. This function and the position which results from it have brought about an internal situation which may be called "economic-corporate"[11]—politically, the worst of all forms of feudal society, the least progressive and the most stagnant. An effective *Jacobin* force was always missing, and could not be constituted; and it was precisely such a Jacobin force which in other nations awakened and organised the national-popular collective will, and founded the modern States. Do the necessary conditions for this will finally exist, or rather what is the present relation between these conditions and the forces opposed to them? Traditionally the forces of opposition have been the landed aristocracy and, more generally, landed property as a whole. Italy's particular characteristic is a special "*rural bourgeoisie*",[12] a legacy of parasitism bequeathed to modern times by the disintegration as a class of the Communal bourgeoisie (the hundred cities, the cities of silence).[13] The positive conditions

[10] For Gramsci's discussion of the "language question", see Int. pp. 21–25, etc. In the Middle Ages, the Catholic Church fought against the use of the vernacular and for the preservation of Latin as the "universal" language, since this was a key element in its own intellectual hegemony. Dante, for example, felt compelled to defend his use of (Florentine) Italian in the Divine Comedy. Gramsci describes the emergence of Florentine dialect as a "noble vernacular". "The flowering of the Communes developed the vernaculars, and the intellectual hegemony of Florence produced a united vernacular, a noble vernacular. . . . The fall of the Communes and the advent of the Princely régime, the creation of a governing caste detached from the people, crystallised this vernacular in the same way as literary Latin had become crystallised. Italian was once again a written and not a spoken language, a language of scholars rather than a language of the nation" The language question was simplified at one level in the nineteenth century, when literary Italian finally defeated Latin as the language of learning, and when it was adopted as the language of the new Italian national state. But it persists in the existence of dialects as the "mother-tongue" in many Italian regions even today, despite the development of the mass media and universal education in this century.
For the Communes, see note 4 on p. 53.

[11] For the concept of economic-corporate, see note 4 on p. 53, and also Notes on Gramsci's Terminology, p. xiii.

[12] On the "rural bourgeoisie", see note 61 on p. 91, and "Subversive", pp. 272–5 below.

[13] See notes 61 and 62 on p. 91.

are to be sought in the existence of urban social groups which have attained an adequate development in the field of industrial production and a certain level of historico-political culture. Any formation of a national-popular collective will is impossible, unless the great mass of peasant farmers bursts *simultaneously* into political life. That was Machiavelli's intention through the reform of the militia, and it was achieved by the Jacobins in the French Revolution. That Machiavelli understood it reveals a precocious Jacobinism that is the (more or less fertile) germ of his conception of national revolution. All history from 1815 onwards shows the efforts of the traditional classes to prevent the formation of a collective will of this kind, and to maintain "economic-corporate" power in an international system of passive equilibrium.

An important part of *The Modern Prince* will have to be devoted to the question of intellectual and moral reform, that is to the question of religion or world-view. In this field too we find in the existing tradition an absence of Jacobinism and fear of Jacobinism (the latest philosophical expression of such fear is B. Croce's Malthusian attitude towards religion).[14] The modern Prince must

[14] Gramsci alludes to Malthus here, as he usually does, simply to indicate fear of, or contempt for, the masses. On MS, pp. 224–29 he discusses Croce's attitude to religion, and the character of the "reformation" which he represents. Gramsci criticises Croce for not understanding that "the philosophy of praxis, with its vast mass movement, has represented and does represent an historical process similar to the Reformation, in contrast with liberalism, which reproduces a Renaissance which is narrowly limited to restricted intellectual groups. . . . Croce is essentially anti-confessional (we cannot call him anti-religious given his definition of religious reality) and for numerous Italian and European intellectuals his philosophy . . . has been a genuine intellectual and moral reform similar to the Renaissance . . . But Croce did not 'go to the people', did not wish to become a 'national' element (just as the men of the Renaissance—unlike the Lutherans and Calvinists—were not 'national' elements), did not wish to create a band of disciples who . . . could have popularised his philosophy and tried to make it into an educative element, starting in the primary school (and hence educative for the simple worker or peasant, i.e. for the simple man of the people). Perhaps this was impossible, but it was worth trying and the fact that it was not tried is certainly significant." Gramsci goes on to criticise Croce's view that religion is appropriate for the masses, while only an élite of superior intellects are capable of a rational conception of the world. Croce was minister of education in Giolitti's 1920–21 government, and introduced a draft bill to reorganise the national educational system; this bill provided for the reintroduction of religious instruction in the primary schools —something which had not existed since the 1859 Casati Act laid the basis for the educational system of post-Risorgimento Italy. In fact, Giolitti withdrew the bill, but the main lines of it were taken up by Gentile when, as minister of education in the first Fascist government of 1922, he drew up the Gentile Act, which was passed in 1923. (See note 15 on p. 41.)

For the concept of "intellectual and moral reform" (taken from Renan), see "Philosophy of Praxis and Modern Culture" on pp. 388–99. It should be noted that the Italian word "*riforma*" translates both "reform" and "reformation" in English.

be and cannot but be the proclaimer and organiser of an intellectual and moral reform, which also means creating the terrain for a subsequent development of the national-popular collective will towards the realisation of a superior, total form of modern civilisation.

These two basic points—the formation of a national-popular collective will, of which the modern Prince is at one and the same time the organiser and the active, operative expression; and intellectual and moral reform—should structure the entire work. The concrete, programmatic points must be incorporated in the first part, that is they should result from the line of discussion "*dramatically*", and not be a cold and pedantic exposition of arguments.

Can there be cultural reform, and can the position of the depressed strata of society be improved culturally, without a previous economic reform and a change in their position in the social and economic fields? Intellectual and moral reform has to be linked with a programme of economic reform—indeed the programme of economic reform is precisely the concrete form in which every intellectual and moral reform presents itself. The modern Prince, as it develops, revolutionises the whole system of intellectual and moral relations, in that its development means precisely that any given act is seen as useful or harmful, as virtuous or as wicked, only in so far as it has as its point of reference the modern Prince itself, and helps to strengthen or to oppose it. In men's consciences, the Prince takes the place of the divinity or the categorical imperative, and becomes the basis for a modern laicism and for a complete laicisation of all aspects of life and of all customary relationships. [1933–34: 1st version 1931–32.]

MACHIAVELLI AND MARX[15]

The basic innovation introduced by the philosophy of praxis into the science of politics and of history is the demonstration that there is no abstract "human nature", fixed and immutable (a concept which certainly derives from religious and transcendentalist thought), but that human nature is the totality of historically determined social relations, hence an historical fact which can, within certain limits, be ascertained with the methods of philology and criticism. Consequently political science, as far as both its concrete content and its logical formulation are concerned, must

[15] This note was given no title in its final version translated here, so we have given it the title used by Gramsci for the first version.

be seen as a developing organism. It must, however, be noted that the way in which Machiavelli posed the problem of politics (i.e. the assertion implicit in his writings that politics is an autonomous activity, with its own principles and laws distinct from those of morality and religion—a proposition with far-reaching philosophical consequences, since it implicitly introduces a new conception of morality and religion, a new world-view) is still questioned and rejected even today, and has not succeeded in becoming "common sense". What does that mean? Does it mean only that the intellectual and moral revolution whose elements are to be found embryonically in Machiavelli's thought has not yet taken place, has not become the public and manifest form of the national culture? Or does it simply have a current political significance; does it serve to indicate the gulf which exists between rulers and ruled, to indicate that there exist two cultures—that of the rulers and that of the ruled—and that the ruling class like the Church has its own attitude towards the common people, dictated by the necessity on the one hand of not becoming detached from them, and on the other of keeping them convinced that Machiavelli is nothing other than the devil incarnate?

Here one comes up against the problem of Machiavelli's significance in his own time, and of the objectives he set himself in writing his books, particularly *The Prince*. Machiavelli's ideas were not, in his own day, purely "bookish", the monopoly of isolated thinkers, a secret memorandum circulating among the initiated. Machiavelli's style is not that of a systematic compiler of treatises, such as abounded during the Middle Ages and Humanism, quite the contrary; it is the style of a man of action, of a man urging action, the style of a party manifesto. The moralistic interpretation offered by Foscolo[16] is certainly mistaken. It is quite true that Machiavelli *revealed* something, and did not merely theorise reality; but what was the aim of his revelation? A moralistic aim or a political one? It is commonly asserted that Machiavelli's standards of political behaviour are practised, but not admitted. Great politicians—it is

---

[16] Foscolo wrote in his famous poem *Dei Sepolcri* [On Tombs]: "*Io quando il monumento vidi ove posa il corpo di quel grande/ che temprando lo scettro a'regnatori/ gli allor ne sfronda, ed alle genti svela/ di che lagrime grondi e di che sangue;*" [When I saw the monument where lies the body of that great man who, even as he strengthens the sceptre of rulers, plucks away the laurel leaves and reveals to their peoples the tears and blood running down it.] In other words Foscolo saw Machiavelli as revealing the tyranny of the rulers even while he strengthened their power. But Gramsci condemns the moralism of this reduction of Machiavelli to little more than an encouragement to "tyrant-haters". For further discussion by Gramsci of Foscolo's and other interpretations of Machiavelli, see NM. pp. 115–19.

said—start off by denouncing Machiavelli, by declaring themselves to be anti-Machiavellian, precisely in order to be able to put his standards "piously" into practice. Was not Machiavelli himself a poor Machiavellian, one of those who "are in the know" and foolishly give the game away, whereas vulgar Machiavellianism teaches one to do just the opposite? Croce asserted that Machiavellianism was a science, serving reactionaries and democrats alike, just as skilful swordplay serves both honest men and brigands, for self-defence and for murder; and that this was the sense in which Foscolo's opinion should be taken. This is true in the abstract. Machiavelli himself remarks that what he is writing about is in fact practised, and has always been practised, by the greatest men throughout history. So it does not seem that he was writing for those who are already in the know; nor is his style that of disinterested scientific activity; nor is it possible to think that he arrived at his theses in the field of political science by way of philosophical speculation—which would have been something of a miracle in that field at the time, when even today he meets with such hostility and opposition.

One may therefore suppose that Machiavelli had in mind "those who are not in the know", and that it was they whom he intended to educate politically. This was no negative political education—of tyrant-haters—as Foscolo seems to have understood it; but a positive education—of those who have to recognise certain means as necessary, even if they are the means of tyrants, because they desire certain ends. Anyone born into the traditional governing stratum acquires almost automatically the characteristics of the political realist, as a result of the entire educational complex which he absorbs from his family milieu, in which dynastic or patrimonial interests predominate. Who therefore is "not in the know"? The revolutionary class of the time, the Italian "people" or "nation", the citizen democracy which gave birth to men like Savonarola and Pier Soderini, rather than to a Castruccio or a Valentino.[17]

[17] Savonarola, Girolamo (1452–98). A Dominican friar who announced the imminent castigation and reform of the Church, he gained immense popular support, notably in Florence—especially when the invasion of Charles VIII in 1492 seemed to fulfil his predictions. He was the leader of a theocratic state in Florence 1495–98. The Papacy tried to stop his preaching by threats of excommunication and bribes of a cardinal's hat, and in 1497 did in fact excommunicate him. The Florentine *Signoria*, who had made use of Savonarola against the Pope, turned against him in the course of a complex faction fight, and he was burned at the stake. He has often been seen as a precursor of the Reformation.

Pier Soderini (1452–1522) was a Florentine politician who, as *gonfaloniere* of the city from 1502–12, instituted a legal reform and supported Machiavelli's idea

It seems clear that Machiavelli wished to persuade these forces of the necessity of having a leader who knew what he wanted and how to obtain it, and of accepting him with enthusiasm even if his actions might conflict or appear to conflict with the generalised ideology of the time—religion.

This position in which Machiavelli found himself politically is repeated today for the philosophy of praxis. Once more there is the necessity to be "anti-Machiavellian", to develop a theory and technique of politics which—however strong the belief that they will in the final resort be especially useful to the side which was "not in the know", since that is where the historically progressive force is to be found—might be useful to both sides in the struggle. In actual fact, one immediate result is achieved, in that the unity based on traditional ideology is broken; until this happens, it is impossible for the new forces to arrive at a consciousness of their own independent personality. Machiavellianism has helped to improve the traditional political technique of the conservative ruling groups, just as the politics of the philosophy of praxis does. That should not disguise its essentially revolutionary character which is still felt today, and which explains all anti-Machiavellianism, from that of the Jesuits to the pietistic anti-Machiavellianism of Pasquale Villari.[18] [1933–34: 1st version 1931–32]

POLITICS AS AN AUTONOMOUS SCIENCE

The first question that must be raised and resolved in a study of Machiavelli is the question of politics as an autonomous science, of the place that political science occupies or should occupy in a systematic (coherent and logical) conception of the world, in a philosophy of praxis.

---

of a militia. Machiavelli, however, had a low opinion of him, and commemorated his death with a savage epigram: "La notte che morì Pier Soderini, L'anima andò dell'inferno alla bocca; Ma Pluto le gridò: anima sciocca! Che inferno! vanne al limbo coi bambini!" [The night that Pier Soderini died, his soul approached the gates of hell; but Pluto cried out: foolish spirit! not hell! off to limbo with the children!] Duke Valentino, better known as Cesare Borgia (1476–1517), was the son of cardinal Rodrigo Borgia, later Pope Alexander VI. A brilliant intriguer and soldier, Machiavelli made him the hero of *The Prince*, seeing him as having created in the Romagna province (around Rimini and Ravenna) the kind of stable state upon which an Italian nation could be based, and depicting him as the perfect *condottiere*. Castruccio Castracani (1281–1328) was also a *condottiere*, who ruled Lucca. Machiavelli celebrated him in his *Vita di Castruccio Castracani da Lucca*.

[18] Pasquale Villari (1826–1917), historian and politician, wrote books on Savonarola and Machiavelli (*Niccolò Machiavelli e i suoi tempi*, 1877–82). His treatment of Machiavelli was naïvely and heavily moralistic.

The progress brought about by Croce in this respect in the study of Machiavelli and in political science consists mainly (as in other fields of Croce's critical activity) in the dissolution of a series of false, non-existent or wrongly formulated problems.[19] Croce based himself on his distinction of the moments of the spirit, and on his affirmation of a moment of practice, of a practical spirit, autonomous and independent though linked in a circle to all reality by the dialectic of distincts. In a philosophy of praxis, the distinction will certainly not be between the moments of the absolute Spirit, but between the levels of the superstructure. The problem will therefore be that of establishing the dialectical position of political activity (and of the corresponding science) as a particular level of the superstructure. One might say, as a first schematic approximation, that political activity is precisely the first moment or first level; the moment in which the superstructure is still in the unmediated phase of mere wishful affirmation, confused and still at an elementary stage.

In what sense can one identify politics with history, and hence all of life with politics? How then could the whole system of superstructures be understood as distinctions within politics, and the introduction of the concept of distinction into a philosophy of praxis hence be justified? But can one really speak of a dialectic of distincts, and how is the concept of a circle joining the levels of the superstructure to be understood? Concept of "historical bloc", i.e. unity between nature and spirit (structure and superstructure), unity of opposites and of distincts.

Can one introduce the criterion of distinction into the structure too? How is structure to be understood? How, in the system of social relations, will one be able to distinguish the element "technique", "work", "class", etc., understood in an historical and not in a metaphysical sense? Critique of Croce's position; for polemical

---

[19] Croce notably attacked any moralistic interpretation of Machiavelli (as he did of Marx), for instance that of Villari, "for whom Machiavelli's great defect is that he fails to see the moral problem . . . Machiavelli starts by establishing a fact: the conditions of struggle in which society finds itself. He then gives rules in accordance with this objective condition. Why . . . should he concern himself with the ethics of the struggle?"

The paragraphs which follow discuss some of the more technical aspects of Croce's philosophy. For the "dialectic of distincts" see Introduction, p. xxiii. For Croce's concept of politics as passion, see note 35 on p. 349. The discussion of superstructure and structure, and of "appearances", relates to Croce's speech on "Anti-history" to the Oxford Philosophical Congress in 1930, when he attacked what he understood as Marxism—and what Gramsci points out frequently is in fact vulgar Marxism—for reducing the "superstructure" to a mere "appearance" (phenomenon), etc. (See MS. p. 229, etc.). For Kant's *Noumenon*, see pp. 367-8.

ends, he represents the structure as a "hidden god", a "noumenon", in contrast to the "appearances" of the superstructure. "Appearances" both metaphorically and literally. How "historically", and as a fact of speech, was the notion of "appearances" arrived at?

It is interesting to establish how Croce developed his own individual theory of error and of the practical origin of error from this general conception. For Croce, error has its origin in an immediate "passion"—one, that is, of an individual or group character. But what will produce the "passion" of more far-reaching historical importance, the passion as a category? The passion/immediate interest which is the origin of error is the moment which in the Theses on Feuerbach is called *schmutzig-jüdisch.* But just as the passion/*schmutzig-jüdisch* interest determines immediate error, so does the passion of the larger social group determine the philosophical error, while between the two is the error/ideology, which Croce deals with separately. In this series: "egoism (immediate error)—ideology—philosophy", it is the common term "error" which is important. This is linked to the various levels of passion, and must be understood not in a moralistic or scholastic sense, but in the purely historical and dialectical sense of "that which is historically decayed, and deserves to fall"—in the sense of the non-definitive character of all philosophy, of the "death/life", "being/non-being", i.e. of the term of the dialectic which the latter must transcend in its forward movement.

The terms "apparent" and "appearance" mean precisely this and nothing else, and are justifiable despite dogmatic opposition. They are the assertion of the perishable nature of all ideological systems, side by side with the assertion that all systems have an historical validity, and are necessary ("Man acquires consciousness of social relations in the field of ideology":[20] is not this an assertion of the necessity and the validity of "appearances"?) [1933–34: 1st version 1932–33.]

Croce's conception of politics/passion excludes parties, since it is not possible to think of an organised and permanent passion. Permanent passion is a condition of orgasm and of spasm, which means operational incapacity. It excludes parties, and excludes

[20] The exact quotation, from Marx' Preface to *The Critique of Political Economy*, is: "a distinction should always be made between the material transformation of the economic conditions of production, which can be determined with the precision of natural science, and the legal, political, religious, aesthetic or philosophic—in short, ideological forms in which men become conscious of this conflict [i.e. that between the material productive forces of society and the existing relations of production] and fight it out".

every plan of action worked out in advance. However, parties exist and plans of action are worked out, put into practice, and are often successful to a remarkable extent. So there is a flaw in Croce's conception. Nor is it enough to say that, even if parties exist, that has little theoretical importance, because at the moment of action the party in operation is not the same thing as the "party" which existed previously. There may be a partial truth in this, but the points of coincidence between the two "parties" are such that one may really be said to be dealing with the same organism.

But for Croce's conception to be valid, it would have to be possible to apply it also to war, and hence to explain the fact of standing armies, military academies, officer corps. War in progress too is "passion", the most intense and febrile of all passions; it is a moment of political life; it is the continuation in other forms of a given policy. It is necessary therefore to explain how passion can become moral "duty"—duty in terms not of political morality but of ethics.

On political plans, which are related to the parties as permanent formations, recall what Moltke[21] said of military plans; that they cannot be worked out and finalised in advance in every particular, but only in so far as their nucleus and central design is concerned, since the details of the action depend to a certain extent on the moves of the adversary. It is precisely in the details that passion manifests itself, but it does not appear that Moltke's principle is such as to justify Croce's conception. There would still remain to be explained the kind of passion of the General Staff which worked out the plan in the light of cold reason, and "dispassionately". [1933–34: 1st version 1931–32.]

If the Crocean concept of passion as a moment of politics comes up against the difficulty of explaining and justifying the permanent political formations, such as the parties and still more the national armies and General Staffs, since it is impossible to conceive of a passion being organised permanently without its becoming rationality and deliberate reflection and hence no longer passion, the solution can only be found in the identification of politics and economics. Politics becomes permanent action and gives birth to permanent organisations precisely in so far as it identifies itself with

[21] General Moltke (the younger, 1848–1916) was German Chief of Staff, 1906–14 and the successor of Schlieffen. His modifications of the famous "Schlieffen Plan" for war against France were blamed for the German failure to defeat the French decisively in 1914, and led to his removal. In fact, modern historiography (and the unearthing of the original Schlieffen Plan) make it clear that he was a scapegoat, sacrificed to an unmerited myth of Schlieffen's infallibility.

economics. But it is also distinct from it, which is why one may speak separately of economics and politics, and speak of "political passion" as of an immediate impulse to action which is born on the "permanent and organic" terrain of economic life but which transcends it, bringing into play emotions and aspirations in whose incandescent atmosphere even calculations involving the individual human life itself obey different laws from those of individual profit, etc. [1931–32]

Beside the merits of modern Machiavelli studies derived from Croce, the exaggerations and distortions which they have inspired should also be noted. The habit has been formed of considering Machiavelli too much as the man of politics in general, as the "scientist of politics", relevant in every period.

Machiavelli should be considered more as a necessary expression of his time, and as closely tied to the conditions and exigencies of his time, which were the result: 1. of the internal struggles of the Florentine republic, and of the particular structure of the State, which was unable to free itself from the residues of commune and municipality—i.e. from a form of feudalism which had become a hindrance; 2. of the struggles between the Italian states for a balance of power throughout Italy—which was obstructed by the existence of the Papacy and the other feudal and municipalistic residues of forms of state based on city rather than on territory; 3. of the struggles of the Italian states, more or less united, for a European balance of power—or, put in another way, of the contradictions between the requirements of an internal balance of power in Italy and the exigencies of the European states struggling for hegemony.

Machiavelli is influenced by the examples of France and Spain, which have achieved as states a strong territorial unity; he makes an "elliptic comparison" (to use Croce's expression) and deduces the rules for a strong State in general and a strong Italian State in particular. Machiavelli is a man wholly of his period; his political science represents the philosophy of the time, which tended to the organisation of absolute national monarchies—the political form which permitted and facilitated a further development of bourgeois productive forces. In Machiavelli one may discover in embryonic form both the separation of powers and parliamentarianism (the representative régime). His "ferocity"[22] is turned against the

[22] *Ferocia.* Machiavelli wrote: "Cesare Borgia was considered cruel: yet that cruelty of his had restored Romagna, united it, rendered it peaceful and loyal. . . . Thus a prince must not mind if he has a reputation for cruelty."

residues of the feudal world, not against the progressive classes. The Prince is to put an end to feudal anarchy; and that is what Valentino does in Romagna, basing himself on the support of the productive classes, merchants and peasants. Given the military-dictatorial character of the head of state, such as is needed in a period of struggle for the installation and consolidation of a new form of power, the class references contained in the *Art of War* must be taken as referring as well to the general structure of the State: if the urban classes wish to put an end to internal disorder and external anarchy, they must base themselves on the mass of the peasants, and constitute a reliable and loyal armed force of a kind totally different from the companies of fortune.[23] One may say that the essentially political conception is so dominant in Machiavelli that it makes him commit errors in the military field. He gives most thought to the infantry, who can be recruited *en masse* through political action, and as a result he misjudges the significance of artillery. [1933–4: 1st version 1929–30.]

Russo (in *Prolegomeni a Machiavelli*) remarks correctly that the *Art of War* contains *The Prince* within it, but he fails to draw all the conclusions from his observation. Even in the *Art of War*, Machiavelli must be seen as a man of politics who has to concern himself with military theory. His one-sidedness (together with other idiosyncrasies such as the phalanx theory, which give rise to facile sallies of wit, the best-known of which originated with Bandello)[24] comes from the fact that the centre of his interest and of his thought does not lie in the question of military technique, which he deals with only in so far as it is necessary for his political edifice. Moreover, not only the *Art of War* but also the *History of Florence* must be related to *The Prince*; this was precisely intended to serve as an analysis of the real conditions in Italy and in Europe from which the immediate demands contained in *The Prince* spring. [1933–4]

A secondary consequence of a conception of Machiavelli which takes more fully into account the period in which he lived is a more

---

[23] See note 21 on p. 64.

[24] Bandello (1480–1562), was the author of a popular collection of stories. One was dedicated to Giovanni de' Medici, better known as Giovanni delle Bande Nere, the famous *condottiere*. In his dedication, Bandello recalls somewhat maliciously how one day "Messire Niccolò [i.e. Machiavelli] kept us that day over two hours in the sun while he was about setting three thousand foot-soldiers into the order of which he had written—without ever succeeding in so ordering them". Whereupon, at Bandello's own suggestion, Giovanni had called Machiavelli back, and had himself drawn up the troops "in the twinkling of an eye". See for this NM. 122–3. Machiavelli's phalanx theory was developed in his *Art of War*.

historicist evaluation of the so-called anti-Machiavellians, or at least of the most "ingenuous" of them. They are not really so much anti-Machiavellians as politicians who express exigencies of their time or of conditions different from those which affected Machiavelli; the polemical form is nothing but a contingent literary device. The typical example it seems to me of these anti-Machiavellians is Jean Bodin (1530–96), who was a delegate to the Estates General of Blois in 1576 and there persuaded the Third Estate to refuse the subsidies requested for the civil war.*

During the civil wars in France, Bodin is the exponent of the third party—the so-called politicians' party—which defends the viewpoint of national interest, that is to say of an internal balance of classes in which hegemony belongs to the Third Estate through the monarchy. It seems evident to me that classifying Bodin among the anti-Machiavellians is an absolutely irrelevant and superficial question. Bodin lays the foundations of political science in France on a terrain which is far more advanced and complex than that which Italy offered to Machiavelli. For Bodin the question is not that of founding the territorially united (national) State—i.e. of going back to the time of Louis XI—but of balancing the conflicting social forces within this already strong and well-implanted State. Bodin is interested in the moment of consent, not in the moment of force. With Bodin there is a tendency to develop the absolute monarchy: the Third Estate is so aware of its strength and its dignity, it knows so well that the fortunes of the absolute monarchy are linked to its own fortunes and its own development, that *it poses conditions for its loyalty*, it presents demands, tends to limit absolutism. In France Machiavelli was already at the service of reaction, since he could serve to justify maintaining the world perpetually in the "cradle" (in Bertrando Spaventa's expression);[25] hence it was necessary to be polemically anti-Machiavellian.

It should be noted that in the Italy studied by Machiavelli there

---

* Bodin's works: *Methodus ad facilem historiarum cognitionem* (1566), in which he shows the influence of climate on forms of State, hints at an idea of progress, etc.; *République* (1576), in which he expresses the opinions of the Third Estate on absolute monarchy and its relations with the people; *Heptaplomeres* (unpublished until the modern era), in which he compares all religions and justifies them as different expressions of natural religion which alone is reasonable, and as all equally worthy of respect and tolerance.

[25] Bertrando Spaventa (1817–83), a philosopher influenced by German idealism and above all Hegel, did much to introduce the latter into Italy and was an important precursor of Croce and Gentile. Critical of the provincialism of Italian intellectuals, he was particularly hostile to Gioberti and Catholic thought in general. He was a senator (of the Right) until 1876.

existed no representative institutions already developed and significant in national life like the Estates General in France. When in modern times it is suggested tendentiously that parliamentary institutions in Italy were imported from abroad,[26] it is not realised that this fact only reflects a condition of backwardness and of stagnation of Italian political and social history from 1500 until 1700—a condition which was to a great extent due to the preponderance of international relations over internal ones, which were paralysed and congealed. Is it really a national "originality", destroyed by the importation of parliamentary forms, that the State structure in Italy, as a result of foreign dominance, should have remained in the semi-feudal phase of an object of foreign suzerainty? In fact parliamentary institutions give a form to the process of national liberation, and to the transition to a modern (independent and national) territorial State. Moreover, representative institutions did exist, especially in the South and in Sicily, but of a far more limited kind than in France, for the Third Estate was little developed in these regions, and hence the Parliaments were instruments for upholding the anarchy of the barons against the innovating attempts of the monarchy, which in the absence of a bourgeoisie had to base itself on the support of the mob.*[27] That Machiavelli should only have been able to express his programme and his tendency to relate city to countryside in military terms is understandable if one reflects that French Jacobinism would be inexplicable without the presupposition of Physiocrat culture, with its demonstration of the economic and social importance of the peasant proprietor. Machiavelli's economic theories have been studied by Gino Arias (in the *Annali d' Economia* of the Bocconi University in Milan), but it might be queried whether Machiavelli really had any economic theories. One will have to see whether Machiavelli's essentially political language can be translated into economic terms, and to which economic system it could be reduced. See whether Machiavelli living in the mercantilist period was politically in advance of his time, and anticipated certain demands which later found expression in the Physiocrats.**

[1933–34: 1st version 1931–32]

---

[26] i.e. by fascist spokesmen, justifying the abolition of parliamentary institutions.

* Recall Antonio Panella's study of the anti-Machiavellians published in *Marzocco* in 1927 (or even in 1926?), in eleven articles: see how Bodin is judged in it compared with Machiavelli, and how the problem of anti-Machiavellianism is posed in general.

[27] *lazzari*, see note 35 on p. 71.

** Would Rousseau have been possible either, without Physiocrat culture? It does not seem to me correct to claim that the Physiocrats merely represented

ELEMENTS OF POLITICS

It really must be stressed that it is precisely the first elements, the most elementary things, which are the first to be forgotten. However, if they are repeated innumerable times, they become the pillars of politics and of any collective action whatsoever.

The first element is that there really do exist rulers and ruled, leaders and led. The entire science and art of politics are based on this primordial, and (given certain general conditions)[28] irreducible fact. The origins of this fact are a problem apart, which will have to be studied separately (at least one could and should study how to minimise the fact and eliminate it, by altering certain conditions which can be identified as operating in this sense), but the fact remains that there do exist rulers and ruled, leaders and led. Given this fact, it will have to be considered how one can lead most effectively (given certain ends); hence how the leaders may best be prepared (and it is more precisely in this that the first stage of the art and science of politics consists); and how, on the other hand, one can know the lines of least resistance, or the most rational lines along which to proceed if one wishes to secure the obedience of the led or ruled. In the formation of leaders, one premiss is fundamental: is it the intention that there should always be rulers and ruled, or is the objective to create the conditions in which this division is no longer necessary? In other words, is the initial premiss the perpetual division of the human race, or the belief that this division is only an historical fact, corresponding to certain conditions? Yet it must be clearly understood that the division between rulers and ruled—though in the last analysis it has its origin in a division between social groups—is in fact, things being as they are, also to be found within the group itself, even where it is a socially homogeneous one. In a certain sense it may be said that this division is created by the division of labour, is merely a technical fact, and

---

agrarian interests, and that the interests of urban capitalism were not asserted before classical economics. The Physiocrats represent the break with mercantilism and with the guild system, and are a stage on the way to classical economics. But it seems to me that precisely for that reason they represent a far more complex future society than the one against which they are fighting, and even than the one which immediately derives from their affirmations. Their language is too much linked to their time, and expresses the immediate contrast between city and countryside, but it permits an expansion of capitalism into agriculture to be foreseen. The formula of "*laissez-faire, laissez-passer*", that is to say of free industry and free enterprise, is certainly not linked to agrarian interests.

[28] i.e. under the conditions of class society. For Gramsci's "first element" here, see Hegel: *Philosophy of History*, Dover 1956, p. 44: "The primary consideration is, then, the distinction between the governing and the governed . . .".

those who see everything purely in terms of "technique", "technical" necessity, etc., speculate on this coexistence of different causes in order to avoid the fundamental problem.

Since the division between rulers and ruled exists even within the same group, certain principles have to be fixed upon and strictly observed. For it is in this area that the most serious "errors" take place, and that the most criminal weaknesses and the hardest to correct are revealed. For the belief is common that obedience must be automatic, once it is a question of the same group; and that not only must it come about without any demonstration of necessity or rationality being needed, but it must be unquestioning. (Some believe, and what is worse act in the belief, that obedience "will come" without being solicited, without the path which has to be followed being pointed out.) Thus it is difficult to cure leaders completely of "Cadornism"[29] or the conviction that a thing will be done because the leader considers it just and reasonable that it should be done: if it is not done, the blame is put on those who "ought to have . . .", etc. Thus too it is hard to root out the criminal habit of permitting useless sacrifices through neglect. Yet common sense shows that the majority of collective (political) disasters occur because no attempt has been made to avoid useless sacrifice, or because manifestly no account has been taken of the sacrifices of others and their lives have been gambled with. Everyone has heard officers from the front recount how the soldiers were quite ready to risk their lives when necessary, but how on the other hand they would rebel when they saw themselves overlooked. For example: a company would be capable of going for days without food because it could see that it was physically impossible for supplies to get through; but it would mutiny if a single meal was missed as a result of neglect or bureaucratism, etc.

This principle extends to all actions demanding sacrifices. Hence, after every disaster, it is necessary first of all to enquire into the responsibility of the leaders, in the most literal sense. (For example: a front is made up of various sectors, and each sector has its leaders; it is possible that the leaders of one sector are more responsible for a particular defeat than those of another; but it is purely a question of degree—never of anybody being exempt from responsibility.)

---

[29] Luigi Cadorna (1850–1928) was commander-in-chief of the Italian armed forces until the defeat at Caporetto in 1917, for which he was held responsible. The war was widely unpopular by 1917, and the Italian soldiers' disaffection was certainly an important factor in the defeat. Cadorna was taken by Gramsci as the symbol of the authoritarian leader who makes no attempt to win the "consent" of those he is leading.

The principle once posed that there are leaders and led, rulers and ruled, it is true that parties have up till now been the most effective way of developing leaders and leadership. (Parties may present themselves under the most diverse names, even calling themselves the anti-party or the "negation of the parties"; in reality, even the so-called "individualists" are party men, only they would like to be "party chiefs" by the grace of God or the idiocy of those who follow them.)[30]

Development of the general concept contained in the expression "State spirit".[31] This expression has a quite precise, historically determinate meaning. But the problem is raised: does there exist something similar to what is called "State spirit" in every serious movement, that is to say in every movement which is not the arbitrary expression of more or less justified individualisms? Meanwhile "State spirit" presupposes "continuity", either with the past, or with tradition, or with the future; that is, it presupposes that every act is a moment in a complex process, which has already begun and which will continue. The responsibility for this process, of being actors in this process, of being in solidarity with forces which are materially "unknown" but which nevertheless feel themselves to be active and operational—and of which account is taken, as if they were physically "material" and present—is precisely in certain cases called "State spirit". It is obvious that such awareness of "duration" must be concrete and not abstract, that is to say in a certain sense must not go beyond certain limits. Let us say that the narrowest limits are a generation back and a generation to come. This represents no short period, since generations cannot be calculated simply as thirty years each—the last thirty and the next thirty respectively. They have to be calculated organically, which

---

[30] The fascists often described their party as an "anti-party", and Mussolini liked to expatiate on his own "individualism".

[31] Term used by Hegel, e.g. in his *Philosophy of History*: "This Spirit of a People is a *determinate* and particular Spirit, and is, as just stated, further modified by the degree of its historical development. This Spirit, then, constitutes the basis and substance of those other forms of a nation's consciousness, which have been noticed. . . . In virtue of the original identity of their essence, purport, and object, these various forms are inseparably united with the Spirit of the State. Only in connection with this particular religion can this particular political constitution exist; just as in such or such a State, such or such a Philosophy or order of Art." Hegel, *op cit.*, p. 53.

The notion of a "State spirit" was adopted by fascism, see e.g. Mussolini, Speech to the Chamber of Deputies, 13 May 1929: "What would the State be if it did not have a spirit, a morality, which is what gives the strength to its laws, and through which it succeeds in securing the obedience of its citizens?" I is not entirely clear exactly what Gramsci has in mind here, when he refers to the "precise, historically determinate meaning" of the expression.

at least as far as the past is concerned is easy to understand: we feel ourselves linked to men who are now extremely old, and who represent for us the *past* which still lives among us, which we need to know and to settle our accounts with, which is one of the elements of the present and one of the premisses of the future. We also feel ourselves linked to our children, to the generations which are being born and growing up, and for which we are responsible. (The *cult* of tradition, which has a tendentious value, is something different; it implies a choice and a determinate goal—that is to say, it is the basis for an ideology.) However, if it can be said that a "State spirit" in this sense is to be found in everybody, it is necessary from time to time to combat distortions of it or deviations from it.

"The act for the act's sake", struggle for the sake of struggle, etc., and especially mean, petty individualism, which is anyway merely an arbitrary satisfying of passing whims, etc. (In reality, the question is still that of Italian "apoliticism",[32] which takes on these various picturesque and bizarre forms.) Individualism is merely brutish apoliticism; sectarianism is apoliticism, and if one looks into it carefully is a form of personal following [*clientela*], lacking the party spirit which is the fundamental component of "State spirit". The demonstration that party spirit is the basic component of "State spirit" is one of the most critically important assertions to uphold. Individualism on the other hand is a brutish element, "admired by foreigners", like the behaviour of the inmates of a zoological garden. [1933]

THE POLITICAL PARTY

It has already been said that the protagonist of the new Prince could not in the modern epoch be an individual hero, but only the political party. That is to say, at different times, and in the various internal relations of the various nations, that determinate party which has the aim of founding a new type of State (and which was rationally and historically created for that end).

It should be noted that in those régimes which call themselves totalitarian,[33] the traditional function of the institution of the Crown is in fact taken over by the particular party in question,

---

[32] See PP. pp. 11–12.

[33] It is important to realise that Gramsci does not use this word in the pejorative sense which it has acquired in bourgeois ideology today—it is a quite neutral term for him, meaning approximately "all-embracing and unifying". We have sometimes translated it by "global".

which indeed is totalitarian precisely in that it fulfils this function. Although every party is the expression of a social group, and of one social group only, nevertheless in certain given conditions certain parties represent a single social group precisely in so far as they exercise a balancing and arbitrating function between the interests of their group and those of other groups, and succeed in securing the development of the group which they represent with the consent and assistance of the allied groups—if not out and out with that of groups which are definitely hostile. The constitutional formula of the king, or president of the republic, who "reigns but does not govern" is the juridical expression of this function of arbitration, the concern of the constitutional parties not to "unmask" the Crown or the president. The formulae stating that it is not the head of State who is responsible for the actions of the government, but his ministers, are the casuistry behind which lies the general principle of safeguarding certain conceptions—the unity of the State; the consent of the governed to State action—whatever the current personnel of the government, and whichever party may be in power.

With the totalitarian party, these formulae lose their meaning; hence the institutions which functioned within the context of such formulae become less important. But the function itself is incorporated in the party, which will exalt the abstract concept of the "State", and seek by various means to give the impression that it is working actively and effectively as an "impartial force". [1933–34: 1st version 1930–32.]

Is political action (in the strict sense) necessary, for one to be able to speak of a "political party"? It is observable that in the modern world, in many countries, the organic[34] and fundamental parties have been compelled by the exigencies of the struggle or for other reasons to split into fractions—each one of which calls itself a "party" and even an independent party. Hence the intellectual General Staff of the organic party often does not belong to any of these fractions, but operates as if it were a directive force standing on its own, above the parties, and sometimes is even believed to be such by the public. This function can be studied with greater precision if one starts from the point of view that a newspaper too (or group of newspapers), a review (or group of reviews), is a "party" or "fraction of a party" or "a function of a particular party". Think of the role of *The Times* in England; or that which

[34] For Gramsci's use of the term "organic", see e.g. "The Formation of the Intellectuals" on pp. 5–14 above.

Corriere della Sera[35] used to have in Italy; or again of the role of the so-called "informational press"[36] with its claim to be "apolitical"; or even of that of the sporting and technical press. Moreover, the phenomenon reveals interesting aspects in countries where there is a single, totalitarian, governing party. For the functions of such a party are no longer directly political, but merely technical ones of propaganda and public order, and moral and cultural influence. The political function is indirect. For, even if no other legal parties exist, other parties in fact always do exist and other tendencies which cannot be legally coerced; and, against these, polemics are unleashed and struggles are fought as in a game of blind man's buff. In any case it is certain that in such parties cultural functions predominate, which means that political language becomes jargon. In other words, political questions are disguised as cultural ones, and as such become insoluble.

But there is one traditional party too with an essentially "indirect" character—which in other words presents itself explicitly as purely "educative" (*lucus*, etc.),[37] moral, cultural (sic). This is the anarchist movement. Even so-called direct (terrorist) action is conceived of as "propaganda" by example. This only further confirms the judgement that the anarchist movement is not autonomous, but exists on the margin of the other parties, "to educate them". One may speak of an "anarchism" inherent in every organic party. (What are the "intellectual or theoretical anarchists" except an aspect of this "marginalism" in relation to the great parties of the dominant social groups?) The "economists' sect"[38] itself was an historical aspect of this phenomenon.

Thus there seem to be two types of party which reject the idea of immediate political action as such. Firstly, there is that which is constituted by an élite of men of culture, who have the function of

---

[35] The *Corriere*, under the editorship of Albertini (see note 74 on p. 96), had been built up as the principal ideological expression of the Milan industrialists, and the nearest thing to a national organ of the Italian bourgeoisie, prior to fascism. Under fascism, it was aligned with the régime, but has since reassumed its former role.

[36] Literally *news*papers. On Int. p. 152, Gramsci writes: "A distinction is made between the so-called informational or 'non-party' paper (without an explicit party) and the official organ of a particular party; between the paper for the popular masses or 'popular' paper and that which is aimed at a necessarily restricted public."

[37] *Lucus a non lucendo*: a famous example of mediaeval false etymology, meaning "a wood (*lucus*) is so called because it gives no light (*lux*)". i.e. the anarchists claim to be educators, and Gramsci suggests ironically that this is perhaps because they are nothing of the sort.

[38] i.e. the Physiocrats in eighteenth-century France.

providing leadership of a cultural and general ideological nature for a great movement of interrelated parties (which in reality are fractions of one and the same organic party). And secondly, in the more recent period, there is a type of party constituted this time not by an élite but by masses—who as such have no other political function than a generic loyalty, of a military kind, to a visible or invisible political centre. (Often the visible centre is the mechanism of command of forces which are unwilling to show themselves in the open, but only operate indirectly, through proxies and a "proxy ideology").[39] The mass following is simply for "manœuvre", and is kept happy by means of moralising sermons, emotional stimuli, and messianic myths of an awaited golden age, in which all present contradictions and miseries will be automatically resolved and made well. [1933]

To write the history of a political party, it is necessary in reality to confront a whole series of problems of a much less simple kind than Robert Michels,[40] for example, believes—though he is considered an expert on the subject. In what will the history of a party consist? Will it be a simple narrative of the internal life of a political organisation? How it comes into existence, the first groups which constitute it, the ideological controversies through which its programme and its conception of the world and of life are formed? In such a case, one would merely have a history of certain intellectual groups, or even sometimes the political biography of a single personality. The study will therefore have to have a vaster and more comprehensive framework.

The history will have to be written of a particular mass of men who have followed the founders of the party, sustained them with their trust, loyalty and discipline, or criticised them "realistically"

---

[39] This second type of party must refer to fascism. The first type of "party" is probably a reference to the role of Croce; see MS. p. 172: "The party as general ideology, superior to the various more immediate groupings. In reality the liberal party in Italy after 1876 was characterised by the way in which it presented itself to the country as a number of national and regional fractions and groups 'in open order'. All of the following were fractions of political liberalism: the liberal catholicism of the Popular Party; nationalism (Croce was a contributor to *Politica*, the journal of A. Rocco and F. Coppola); the monarchist unions; the Republican Party; a great part of socialism; the democratic radicals; the conservatives; Sonnino and Salandra; Giolitti, Orlando, Nitti and Co. Croce was the theorist of what all these groups, grouplets, *camarillos* and *mafias* had in common; the head of a central propaganda office which benefited all these groups and which they all made use of; the national leader of the cultural movements which arose to renovate the old political forms." See too "The History of Europe seen as 'Passive Revolution' " on pp. 118–20 above.

[40] See note 79 on p. 430.

by dispersing or remaining passive before certain initiatives. But will this mass be made up solely of members of the party? Will it be sufficient to follow the congresses, the votes, etc., that is to say the whole nexus of activities and modes of existence through which the mass following of a party manifests its will? Clearly it will be necessary to take some account of the social group of which the party in question is the expression and the most advanced element. The history of a party, in other words, can only be the history of a particular social group. But this group is not isolated; it has friends, kindred groups, opponents, enemies. The history of any given party can only emerge from the complex portrayal of the totality of society and State (often with international ramifications too). Hence it may be said that to write the history of a party means nothing less than to write the general history of a country from a monographic viewpoint, in order to highlight a particular aspect of it. A party will have had greater or less significance and weight precisely to the extent to which its particular activity has been more or less decisive in determining a country's history.

We may thus see that from the way in which the history of a party is written there emerges the author's conception of what a party is and should be. The sectarian will become excited over petty internal matters, which will have an esoteric significance for him, and fill him with mystical enthusiasm. The historian, though giving everything its due importance in the overall picture, will emphasise above all the real effectiveness of the party, its determining force, positive and negative, in having contributed to bringing certain events about and in having prevented other events from taking place. [1933–4: 1st version 1932.]

The problem of knowing when a party was actually formed, i.e. undertook a precise and permanent task, gives rise to many arguments and often too, unfortunately, to a kind of conceit which is no less absurd and dangerous than the "conceit of nations"[41] of which Vico speaks. It is true that one may say that a party is never complete and fully-formed, in the sense that every development creates new tasks and functions, and in the sense that for certain

---

[41] "On the conceit of nations, there is a golden saying of Diodorus Siculus. Every nation, according to him, whether Greek or barbarian, has had the same conceit that it before all other nations invented the comforts of human life and that its remembered history goes back to the very beginning of the world." *The New Science of Giambattista Vico*, Cornell, 1968, p. 61. When Gramsci speaks of "party conceit" he may also have in mind a phrase of Zinoviev's at the Fourth World Congress, directed in particular against the PCI. Zinoviev referred to the danger of "*Kom-tchvanstvo*" = communist boastfulness or conceit.

parties the paradox is true that they are complete and fully-formed only when they no longer exist—i.e. when their existence has become historically redundant. Thus, since every party is only the nomenclature for a class, it is obvious that the party which proposes to put an end to class divisions will only achieve complete self-fulfilment when it ceases to exist because classes, and therefore their expressions, no longer exist. But here I wish to refer to a particular moment of this process of development, the moment succeeding that in which something may either exist or not exist—in the sense that the necessity for it to exist has not yet become "imperative", but depends to a great extent on the existence of individuals of exceptional will-power and of exceptional will.

When does a party become historically necessary? When the conditions for its "triumph", for its inevitable progress to State power, are at least in the process of formation, and allow their future evolution—all things going normally—to be foreseen. But when can one say, given such conditions, that a party cannot be destroyed by normal means? To give an answer, it is necessary to develop the following line of reasoning: for a party to exist, three fundamental elements (three groups of elements) have to converge:

1. A mass element, composed of ordinary, average men, whose participation takes the form of discipline and loyalty, rather than any creative spirit or organisational ability. Without these the party would not exist, it is true, but it is also true that neither could it exist with these alone. They are a force in so far as there is somebody to centralise, organise and discipline them. In the absence of this cohesive force, they would scatter into an impotent diaspora and vanish into nothing. Admittedly any of these elements might become a cohesive force, but I am speaking of them precisely at the moment when they are not this nor in any condition to become it—or if they are, it is only in a limited sphere, politically ineffectual and of no consequence.

2. The principal cohesive element, which centralises nationally and renders effective and powerful a complex of forces which left to themselves would count for little or nothing. This element is endowed with great cohesive, centralising and disciplinary powers; also—and indeed this is perhaps the basis for the others—with the power of innovation (innovation, be it understood, in a certain direction, according to certain lines of force, certain perspectives, even certain premisses). It is also true that neither could this element form the party alone; however, it could do so more than could the first element considered. One speaks of generals without an army,

but in reality it is easier to form an army than to form generals. So much is this true that an already existing army is destroyed if it loses its generals, while the existence of a united group of generals who agree among themselves and have common aims soon creates an army even where none exists.

3. An intermediate element, which articulates the first element with the second and maintains contact between them, not only physically but also morally and intellectually. In reality, for every party there exist "fixed proportions"[42] between these three elements, and the greatest effectiveness is achieved when these "fixed proportions" are realised.

In view of these considerations, it is possible to say when it is that a party cannot be destroyed by normal means. The second element must necessarily be in existence (if it is not, discussion is meaningless); its appearance is related to the existence of objective material conditions, even if still in a fragmented and unstable state. The moment when it becomes impossible to destroy a party by normal means is reached when the two other elements cannot help being formed—that is, the first element, which in its turn necessarily forms the third as its continuation and its means of expressing itself.

For that to happen, the iron conviction has to have been formed that a particular solution of the vital problems is necessary. Without this conviction the second element will not be formed. This element can the more easily be destroyed in that it is numerically weak, but it is essential that if it is destroyed it should leave as its heritage a ferment from which it may be recreated. And where could this ferment better be formed and subsist than in the first and third elements, which, obviously, are the nearest in character to the second? The activity of the second element towards creating this ferment is therefore fundamental. The criteria by which the second element should be judged are to be sought; 1. in what it actually does; 2. in what provision it makes for the eventuality of its own destruction. It is difficult to say which of these two facts is the more important. Since defeat in the struggle must always be envisaged, the preparation of one's own successors is as important as what one does for victory.

With regard to party conceit, this may be said to be worse than the national conceit of which Vico speaks. Why? Because a nation cannot help existing; and in the fact that it exists it is always possible—maybe with a little goodwill and an invocation of the

---

[42] See "The Theorem of Fixed Proportions" on pp. 190–2.

texts—to discover that its existence is pregnant with destiny and significance. A party on the other hand may not exist by virtue of its own strength. It should *never* be forgotten that, in the struggle between the nations, it is in the interest of each one of them that the other should be weakened by internal struggles—and the parties are precisely the elements of internal struggle. Hence it is always possible to pose the question of whether the parties exist by virtue of their own strength, as their own necessity, or whether rather they only exist to serve the interests of others (and indeed in polemics this point is never overlooked, in fact it is even a recurring theme, especially when the answer is not in doubt—so that it takes hold and creates doubts). Naturally, anybody who allowed himself to be torn apart by such doubts would be a fool. Politically the question has only an ephemeral relevance. In the history of the so-called principle of nationality, foreign interventions in favour of national parties which trouble the internal order of enemy States are innumerable; so much so that when one speaks, for example, of Cavour's "Eastern" policy,[43] one wonders if it was really a question of a "policy", a permanent line of action, or not rather a stratagem of the moment to weaken Austria before 1859 and 1866. Similarly, in the Mazzinian movements of the early eighteen-seventies (the Barsanti affair, for instance)[44] one can discern the intervention of Bismarck, who with his eyes on the war with France and the danger of a Franco-Italian alliance thought to weaken Italy through internal conflict. Similarly, in the events of June 1914[45] some see the intervention of the Austrian General Staff with a view to the coming war. As can be seen, the list of examples is a long one, and it is essential to have clear ideas on the subject. Given that whatever one does one is always playing somebody's game, the important thing is to seek in every way to play one's own game with success—in other words, to win decisively. At all events, party conceit is to be despised, and replaced by concrete facts. Anyone who reinforces conceit, or prefers it to concrete facts, is certainly not be to taken seriously. It is unnecessary to add that it is essential for parties to avoid even the "justified" appearance of playing somebody else's game, especially

[43] i.e. The policy whereby Piedmont allied itself with England and France and sent troops to fight in the Crimean War against Russia (1855).

[44] On 24 May 1870 Pietro Barsanti, a Mazzinian corporal, attacked a barracks in Pavia with forty republican followers, shouting "Long live Rome! Long live the Republic! Down with the monarchy!". He was arrested and shot on 27 August 1870.

[45] See note 33 on p. 70.

if the somebody is a foreign State. But nobody can prevent speculations from being made.

It is difficult to deny that all political parties (those of subordinate as well as ruling groups) also carry out a policing function—that is to say, the function of safeguarding a certain political and legal order. If this were conclusively demonstrated, the problem would have to be posed in other terms; it would have to bear, in other words, on the means and the procedures by which such a function is carried out. Is its purpose one of repression or of dissemination; in other words, does it have a reactionary or a progressive character? Does the given party carry out its policing function in order to conserve an outward, extrinsic order which is a fetter on the vital forces of history; or does it carry it out in the sense of tending to raise the people to a new level of civilisation expressed programmatically in its political and legal order? In fact, a law finds a lawbreaker: 1. among the reactionary social elements whom it has dispossessed; 2. among the progressive elements whom it holds back; 3. among those elements which have not yet reached the level of civilisation which it can be seen as representing. The policing function of a party can hence be either progressive or regressive. It is progressive when it tends to keep the dispossessed reactionary forces within the bounds of legality, and to raise the backward masses to the level of the new legality. It is regressive when it tends to hold back the vital forces of history and to maintain a legality which has been superseded, which is anti-historical, which has become extrinsic. Besides, the way in which the party functions provides discriminating criteria. When the party is progressive it functions "democratically" (democratic centralism); when the party is regressive it functions "bureaucratically" (bureaucratic centralism). The party in this second case is a simple, unthinking executor. It is then technically a policing organism, and its name of "political party" is simply a metaphor of a mythological character. [1933]

The problem arises of whether the great industrialists have a permanent political party of their own. It seems to me that the reply must be in the negative. The great industrialists utilise all the existing parties turn by turn, but they do not have their own party. This does not mean that they are in any way "agnostic" or "apolitical". Their interest is in a determinate balance of forces, which they obtain precisely by using their resources to reinforce one party or another in turn from the varied political checkerboard (with the exception, needless to say, only of the enemy party, whose reinforcement cannot be assisted even as a tactical move). It is certain, however, that if this is what happens in "normal" times, in extreme cases—which are those which count (like war in the life of a nation)—the party of the great industrialists is that of the landowners, who for their part do have their own permanent party. The exemplification of this note may be seen in England, where the Conservative Party has swallowed up the Liberal Party, although the latter had traditionally appeared to be the party of the industrialists.

The English situation, with its great Trade Unions, explains this fact. In England, admittedly, there does not exist formally a party on the grand scale which is the enemy of the industrialists.[46] But there do exist mass organisations of the working-class, and it has been noted how at certain decisive moments they transform their constitution from top to bottom, shattering the bureaucratic carapace (for example, in 1919 and 1926). On the other hand the landowners and the industrialists have permanent interests which bind them together (especially now that protectionism has become general, covering both agriculture and industry); and it is undeniable that the landowners are "politically" far better organised than the industrialists, attract more intellectuals than they do, are more "permanent" in the directives they give, etc. The fate of the traditional "industrial" parties, like the English "liberal-radicals",[47] the (very different) French radicals, and even the late, lamented "Italian radicals",[48] is of considerable interest. What did they represent? A nexus of classes, great and small, rather than a single, great class. This is the cause of their various histories and their various ends. Their combat troops were provided by the petite bourgeoisie, which found itself in ever-changing conditions within the nexus until its total transformation. Today it provides the troops of the "demagogic parties",[49] and it is not hard to understand why this should be.

In general it may be said that, in this history of the parties, comparison between different countries is highly instructive and

---

[46] i.e. there is no mass Communist Party. Gramsci, of course, did not consider the Labour Party as an enemy of the industrialists.

[47] i.e. the Liberal Party of the latter half of the nineteenth century, with its radical wing, and perhaps especially with reference to the period after 1870 when the Radicals under Chamberlain, Dilke and Bradlaugh were republican and influenced by socialist ideas.

[48] The Italian Radical Party was a small offshoot of the *Partito d'Azione*, which campaigned for social legislation, notably on working conditions, in the 1880s. It thereafter declined, and became a minor component of Giolitti's political bloc.

[49] i.e. the fascist parties.

indeed decisive in the search for the origin of the causes of transformation. It is true, too, of the polemics between parties in the "traditionalist" countries—where "remainders" are found from the entire historical "catalogue".

CONCEPTIONS OF THE WORLD AND PRACTICAL STANCES: GLOBAL[50] AND PARTIAL

A prime criterion for judging either conceptions of the world or, especially, practical stances is the following: can the conception of the world or the practical action in question be conceived of as "isolated", "independent", bearing entire responsibility for the collective life? Or is that impossible, and must it be conceived of as "integration" or perfecting of—or counterweight to—another conception of the world or practical attitude? Upon reflection, it can be seen that this criterion is decisive for an ideal judgement on both ideal and practical changes, and it can also be seen that it has no small practical implications.

One of the commonest totems is the belief about everything that exists, that it is "natural" that it should exist, that it could not do otherwise than exist, and that however badly one's attempts at reform may go they will not stop life going on, since the traditional forces will continue to operate and precisely will keep life going on. There is some truth, certainly, in this way of thinking; it would be disastrous if there were not. All the same, beyond certain limits, this way of thinking becomes dangerous (certain cases of "*politique du pire*"),[51] and in any case, as has already been said, the criterion subsists for a philosophical, political and historical judgement. It is certain that, if one looks into it closely, certain movements conceive of themselves as being only marginal; that is, they presuppose a major movement onto which they graft themselves in order to reform certain presumed or real evils. In other words, certain movements are purely reformist.

This principle has political importance, because the theoretical truth that every class has a single party is demonstrated, at the decisive turning-points, by the fact that various groupings, each of which had up till then presented itself as an "independent" party, come together to form a united bloc. The multiplicity which previously existed was purely "reformist" in character, that is to say it was concerned with partial questions. In a certain sense, it

---

50 "Global" has been used here to translate "*totalitari*", see note 33 on p. 147.
51 i.e. the idea that "the worse things get, the better that will be".

was a political division of labour (useful, within its limits). But each part presupposed the other, so much so that at the decisive moments —in other words precisely when fundamental questions were brought into play—the unity was formed, the bloc came into existence. Hence the conclusion that in building a party, it is necessary to give it a "monolithic" character rather than base it on secondary questions; therefore, painstaking care that there should be homogeneity between the leadership and the rank and file, between the leaders and their mass following. If, at the decisive moments, the leaders pass over to their "true party", the rank and file militants are left suspended, paralysed and ineffective. One may say that no real movement becomes aware of its global character all at once, but only gradually through experience—in other words, when it learns from the facts that nothing which exists is natural (in the non-habitual sense of the word), but rather exists because of the existence of certain conditions, whose disappearance cannot remain without consequences. Thus the movement perfects itself, loses its arbitrary, "symbiotic" traits, becomes truly independent, in the sense that in order to produce certain results it creates the necessary preconditions, and indeed devotes all its forces to the creation of these preconditions. [1933]

SOME THEORETICAL AND PRACTICAL ASPECTS OF "ECONOMISM"

Economism—theoretical movement for Free Trade—theoretical syndicalism.[52] It should be considered to what degree theoretical

---

[52] Economism was defined in various ways by Lenin, especially in *What is to be Done?*, e.g. "the fundamental political tendency of Economism—let the workers carry on the economic struggle (it would be more correct to say the trade-unionist struggle, because the latter also embraces specifically working-class politics) and let the Marxist intelligentsia merge with the liberals for the political 'struggle'." Lenin opposed to economism the theory of a vanguard party which would unite intellectuals and workers, and bring socialist theory "from outside" to the proletariat—which in the course of its own, spontaneous activity can only develop "trade-union consciousness".

By "theoretical syndicalism", Gramsci means what is in English known simply as "syndicalism"—the Italian word "*sindacalismo*" means both "syndicalism" and "trade-unionism". There was a strong syndicalist tradition in the Italian working-class, notably among the anarchists and anarcho-syndicalists. Anarchist workers played a leading part in many of the great industrial struggles of the war and immediate post-war years, especially in Turin, where Gramsci during the *Ordine Nuovo* period repeatedly attacked the sectarianism of many socialists towards them. On the other hand, the anarcho-syndicalist leaders, typified by Arturo Labriola, were politically ambiguous to say the least. Labriola was an inter-

syndicalism derives originally from the philosophy of praxis, and to what degree from the economic doctrines of Free Trade—i.e. in the last analysis from liberalism. Hence it should be considered whether economism, in its most developed form, is not a direct descendant of liberalism, having very little connection with the philosophy of praxis even in its origins—and what connection it had only extrinsic and purely verbal.

From this point of view one should study the polemic between Einaudi and Croce over the new (1917) preface to Croce's "Historical Materialism".[53] The need, spoken of by Einaudi, to take into account the literature of economic history inspired by English classical economics, may be satisfied in the following sense. The literature in question, through a superficial contamination with the philosophy of praxis, gave rise to economism; hence when Einaudi criticises (very imprecisely, to tell the truth) certain economistic degenerations, he forgets the old adage that those who live in glass houses should not throw stones. The nexus between free-trade ideology and theoretical syndicalism is particularly evident in Italy, where the admiration of syndicalists like Lanzillo & Co. for Pareto is well known.[54] The significance of the two tendencies, however, is very different. The former belongs to a dominant and directive social group; the latter to a group which is still subaltern, which has not yet gained consciousness of its strength, its possibilities, of how it is to develop, and which therefore does not know how to escape from the primitivist phase.

The ideas of the Free Trade movement are based on a theoretical error whose practical origin is not hard to identify; they are based

---

ventionist in 1915, and although he was later an anti-fascist, many of the other anarcho-syndicalist leaders rallied via nationalism to fascism, in a process which Gramsci related to the "transformism" of the bourgeois politicians following the Risorgimento. (See note 8 on p. 58 and *Alcuni temi*.)

[53] Luigi Einaudi (1874–1961) was a prominent liberal politican and economist, who participated in the Aventine opposition to fascism in 1924–25, and who after the fall of fascism became Governor of the Bank of Italy, and subsequently President of the Republic (1948–55). Croce's *Materialismo storico ed economia marxistica* was first published in 1900, but in 1917 Croce added a new preface to the third edition in which he explained his reasons for having written the book: what he saw as the beneficent effects of Marxism on Italian intellectual life in the decade 1890–1900, notably in its impact on historical studies. Einaudi's comments were published in *Riforma Sociale*, July–August 1918, p. 415.

[54] Agostino Lanzillo (1886–1952) was an anarcho-syndicalist, author of a book on Sorel, who rallied to fascism and became a member of the National Council of the fascist corporations in 1931. Gramsci analysed the process whereby many anarcho-syndicalists rallied to nationalism and fascism in his *Alcuni temi*. (See too note 8 on p. 58.) Pareto is best known today for his theory of élites, but he was also a prominent economist and theorist of Free Trade.

on a distinction between political society and civil society,[55] which is made into and presented as an organic one, whereas in fact it is merely methodological. Thus it is asserted that economic activity belongs to civil society, and that the State must not intervene to regulate it. But since in actual reality civil society and State are one and the same, it must be made clear that *laissez-faire* too is a form of State "regulation", introduced and maintained by legislative and coercive means. It is a deliberate policy, conscious of its own ends, and not the spontaneous, automatic expression of economic facts. Consequently, *laissez-faire* liberalism is a political programme, designed to change—in so far as it is victorious—a State's leading personnel, and to change the economic programme of the State itself—in other words the distribution of the national income.

The case of theoretical syndicalism is different. Here we are dealing with a subaltern group, which is prevented by this theory from ever becoming dominant, or from developing beyond the economic-corporate stage and rising to the phase of ethical-political hegemony in civil society, and of domination in the State. In the case of *laissez-faire* liberalism, one is dealing with a fraction of the ruling class which wishes to modify not the structure of the State, but merely government policy; which wishes to reform the laws controlling commerce, but only indirectly those controlling industry (since it is undeniable that protection, especially in countries with a poor and restricted market, limits freedom of industrial enterprise and favours unhealthily the creation of monopolies). What is at stake is a rotation in governmental office of the ruling-class parties, not the foundation and organisation of a new political society, and even less of a new type of civil society. In the case of the theoretical syndicalist movement the problem is more complex. It is undeniable that in it, the independence and autonomy of the subaltern group which it claims to represent are in fact sacrificed to the intellectual hegemony of the ruling class, since precisely theoretical syndicalism is merely an aspect of *laissez-faire* liberalism—justified with a few mutilated (and therefore banalised) theses from the philosophy of praxis. Why and how does this "sacrifice" come about? The transformation of the subordinate group into a dominant one is excluded, either because the problem is not even considered (Fabianism, De Man,[56] an important part

---

[55] See introduction to "State and Civil Society" on pp. 206–9.

[56] Henri de Man (1885–1953) was a Belgian social-democrat, author notably of the work of revisionism "*Au delà du marxisme*" (1929). In 1934 he wrote a programme of peaceful transition to socialism, known as the "De Man Plan",

of the Labour Party), or because it is posed in an inappropriate and ineffective form (social-democratic tendencies in general), or because of a belief in the possibility of leaping from class society directly into a society of perfect equality with a syndical economy.

The attitude of economism towards expressions of political and intellectual will, action or initiative is to say the least strange—as if these did not emanate organically from economic necessity, and indeed were not the only effective expression of the economy. Thus it is incongruous that the concrete posing of the problem of hegemony should be interpreted as a fact subordinating the group seeking hegemony. Undoubtedly the fact of hegemony presupposes that account be taken of the interests and the tendencies of the groups over which hegemony is to be exercised, and that a certain compromise equilibrium should be formed—in other words, that the leading group should make sacrifices of an economic-corporate kind. But there is also no doubt that such sacrifices and such a compromise cannot touch the essential; for though hegemony is ethical-political, it must also be economic, must necessarily be based on the decisive function exercised by the leading group in the decisive nucleus of economic activity.

Economism appears in many other guises besides *laissez-faire* liberalism and theoretical syndicalism. All forms of electoral abstentionism belong to it (a typical example is the abstentionism of the Italian Clericals after 1870, which became ever more attenuated after 1900 until 1919 and the formation of the Popular Party;[57] the organic distinction which the Clericals made between the real Italy and the legal Italy was a reproduction of the distinction between economic world and politico-legal world); and there are many such forms, in the sense that there can be semi-abstentionism, 25 per cent abstentionism, etc. Linked with abstentionism is the formula "the worse it gets, the better that will be", and also the formula of the so-called parliamentary "intransigence" of certain groups of deputies.[58] Economism is not always opposed to political action and to the political party, but the latter is seen merely as an educational organism similar in kind to a trade union.

---

and was a minister from 1935 to 1938. In 1946 he was sentenced to prison for collaboration with the Germans during the occupation of Belgium.

[57] See notes 14 on p. 62, 73 on p. 96 and 89 on p. 102.

[58] For the "intransigents" see note 72 on p. 95 and General Introduction. Some of the old intransigent wing of the PSI helped to form the Communist Party in 1921, others remained in the "maximalist" majority faction of the PSI. This passage, however, seems clearly directed more specifically against Bordiga, his abstentionism, etc.

One point of reference for the study of economism, and for understanding the relations between structure and superstructure, is the passage in *The Poverty of Philosophy* where it says that an important phase in the development of a social class is that in which the individual components of a trade union no longer struggle solely for their own economic interests, but for the defence and the development of the organisation itself.* In this connection Engels' statement too should be recalled, that the economy is only the mainspring of history "in the last analysis" (to be found in his two letters on the philosophy of praxis also published in Italian);[61] this statement is to be related directly to the passage in the preface to the *Critique of Political Economy* which says that it is on the level of ideologies that men become conscious of conflicts in the world of the economy.

At various points in these notes it is stated that the philosophy of praxis is far more widely diffused than is generally conceded. The assertion is correct if what is meant is that historical economism, as Professor Loria[62] now calls his more or less incoherent theories, is widely diffused, and that consequently the cultural environment has completely changed from the time in which the philosophy of praxis began its struggles. One might say, in Crocean terminology, that the greatest heresy which has grown in the womb of the "religion of freedom" has itself too like orthodox religion degenerated, and has become disseminated as "superstition"—in other words, has combined with *laissez-faire* liberalism and produced economism. However, it remains to be seen whether—in contrast to orthodox religion, which has by now quite shrivelled up—this heretical superstition has not in fact always maintained a ferment which will cause it to be reborn as a higher form of religion; in other words, if the dross of superstition is not in fact easily got rid of.

---

* See the exact statement.[59] *The Poverty of Philosophy* is an essential moment in the formation of the philosophy of praxis. It can be considered as a development of the *Theses on Feuerbach*, while *The Holy Family*—an occasional work—is a vaguely intermediate stage, as is apparent from the passages devoted to Proudhon and especially to French materialism. The passage on French materialism is more than anything else a chapter of cultural history—not a theoretical passage as it is often interpreted as being—and as cultural history it is admirable. Recall the observation that the critique of Proudhon and of his interpretation of the Hegelian dialectic contained in *The Poverty of the Philosophy* may be extended to Gioberti and to the Hegelianism of the Italian moderate liberals in general.[60] The parallel Proudhon–Gioberti, despite the fact that they represent non-homogeneous politico-historical phases, indeed precisely for that reason, can be interesting and productive.

[59] *Poverty of Philosophy*, Lawrence and Wishart, London, 1956, pp. 194–95.

[60] See note 36 on p. 399.

[61] See note 74 on p. 427.

[62] See note 108 on p. 458.

A few characteristics of historical economism: 1. in the search for historical connections it makes no distinction between what is "relatively permanent" and what is a passing fluctuation, and by an economic fact it means the self-interest of an individual or small group, in an immediate and "dirty-Jewish" sense. In other words, it does not take economic class formations into account, with all their inherent relations, but is content to assume motives of mean and usurious self-interest, especially when it takes forms which the law defines as criminal; 2. the doctrine according to which economic development is reduced to the course of technical change in the instruments of work. Professor Loria has produced a splendid demonstration of this doctrine in application, in his article on the social influence of the aeroplane published in *Rassegna Contemporanea* in 1912; 3. the doctrine according to which economic and historical development are made to depend directly on the changes in some important element of production—the discovery of a new raw material or fuel, etc.—which necessitate the application of new methods in the construction and design of machines. In recent times there has been an entire literature on the subject of petroleum: Antonio Laviosa's article in *Nuova Antologia* of 16 May 1929 can be read as a typical example. The discovery of new fuels and new forms of energy, just as of new raw materials to be transformed, is certainly of great importance, since it can alter the position of individual states; but it does not determine historical movement, etc.

It often happens that people combat historical economism in the belief that they are attacking historical materialism. This is the case, for instance, with an article in the Paris *Avenir* of 10 October 1930 (reproduced in *Rassegna Settimanale della Stampa Estera* [Weekly Review of the Foreign Press] of 21 October 1930, pp. 2303–4), which can be quoted as typical: "We have been hearing for some time, especially since the war, that it is self-interest which governs nations and drives the world forward. It was the Marxists who invented this thesis, to which they give the somewhat doctrinaire title of 'Historical Materialism'. In pure Marxism, men taken as a mass obey economic necessity and not their own emotions. Politics is emotion; patriotism is emotion; these two imperious goddesses merely act as a façade in history. In reality, the history of peoples throughout the centuries is to be explained by a changing, constantly renewed interplay of material causes. Everything is economics. Many 'bourgeois' philosophers and economists have taken up this refrain. They pretend to be able to explain high international politics to us by the current price of grain, oil or rubber. They use all their ingenuity to prove that diplomacy is entirely governed by questions of custom tariffs and cost prices. These explanations enjoy a high esteem. They have a modicum of scientific appearance, and proceed from a sort of superior scepticism which would like to pass for the last word in elegance. Emotions in foreign policy? Feelings in home affairs? Enough of that! That stuff is all right for the common people. The great minds, the initiates, know that everything is governed by debits and credits. Now this is an absolute pseudo-truth. It is utterly false that peoples only allow themselves to be moved by considerations of self-interest, and it is entirely true that they are above all motivated by desire for, and ardent belief in, prestige. Anyone who does not understand this, does not understand anything." The article (entitled *The Desire for Prestige*) goes on to cite the examples of German and Italian politics, which it claims are governed by considerations of prestige, and not dictated by material interests. In short, it includes most of the more banal polemical gibes that are directed against the philosophy of praxis; but the real target of the polemic is crude economism of Loria's kind. However, the author is not very strong in argument in other respects either. He does not understand that "feelings" may be simply a synonym for economic interests, and that it is difficult to maintain that political activity is a permanent state of raw emotion and of spasm. Indeed he himself presents French politics as systematic and coherent "rationality", i.e. purged of all emotional elements, etc.

In its most widespread form as economistic superstition, the philosophy of praxis loses a great part of its capacity for cultural expansion among the top layer of intellectuals, however much it may gain among the popular masses and the second-rate intellectuals, who do not intend to overtax their brains but still wish to appear to know everything, etc. As Engels wrote, many people find it very convenient to think that they can have the whole of history and all political and philosophical wisdom in their pockets at little cost and no trouble, concentrated into a few short formulae. They forget that the thesis which asserts that men become conscious of fundamental conflicts on the level of ideology is not psychological or moralistic in character, but structural and epistemological; and they form the habit of considering politics, and hence history, as a continuous *marché de dupes*, a competition in conjuring and sleight of hand. "Critical" activity is reduced to the exposure of swindles, to creating scandals, and to prying into the pockets of public figures.

It is thus forgotten that since "economism" too is, or is presumed to be, an objective principle of interpretation (objective-scientific), the search for direct self-interest should apply to all aspects of history, to those who represent the "thesis" as well as to those who represent the "antithesis". Furthermore, another proposition of the philosophy of praxis is also forgotten: that "popular beliefs" and similar ideas are themselves material forces. The search for "dirty-Jewish" interests has sometimes led to monstrous and comical errors of interpretation, which have consequently reacted negatively on the prestige of the original body of ideas. It is therefore necessary to combat economism not only in the theory of historiography, but also and especially in the theory and practice of politics. In this field, the struggle can and must be carried on by developing the concept of hegemony—as has been done in practice in the development of the theory of the political party,[63] and in the actual history of certain political parties (the struggle against the theory of the so-called Permanent Revolution—to which was counterposed the concept of revolutionary-democratic dictatorship;[64] the extent of

[63] By Lenin, *What is to be done?* etc.

[64] Trotsky's theory of permanent revolution was not really developed before his "Balances and Prospects" of 1906. However, in 1905 he had published a pamphlet called "The period up to 9 January" which was published with a preface by Parvus which stated that "The Revolutionary Provisional Government of Russia will be the government of a workers' democracy . . . a coherent government with a social-democratic majority". This position differed both from that of the Mensheviks, who believed that the revolution was necessarily bourgeois in character and that the social-democrats should adopt an abstentionist attitude, and from that of the Bolsheviks, who stood precisely for a "revolutionary-democratic dictatorship of workers and peasants". Lenin's two main texts (prior to his "*Two Tactics of Social-Democracy*") developing the latter concept: "Social-Democracy and the Provisional Revolutionary Government", and "The Revolutionary-democratic Dictatorship of the Proletariat and the Peasantry" are polemics against the Mensheviks, but the former includes a section commending Parvus' text, but warning against certain errors contained in it, notably the statement that the revolutionary provisional government would be a Social-Democratic government. "This is impossible", Lenin wrote, ". . . because only a revolutionary dictatorship supported by the vast majority of the people can be at all durable. . . . The Russian proletariat, however, is at present a minority of the population in Russia. It can become the great, overwhelming majority only if it combines with the mass of semi-proletarians, semi-proprietors, i.e. with the mass of the petty-bourgeois urban and rural poor. Such a composition of the social basis of the possible and desirable revolutionary-democratic dictatorship will, of course, affect the composition of the revolutionary government and inevitably lead to the participation, or even predominance, within it of the most heterogeneous representatives of revolutionary democracy." The slogan of the revolutionary-democratic dictatorship was of course dropped by Lenin and the Bolsheviks after the February Revolution in 1917, but it was revived in the inner-party debates of the mid-twenties, especially with reference to Poland and to the Chinese Revolution.

the support given to constituentist ideologies,[65] etc.). A study could be made of how certain political movements were judged during the course of their development. One could take as a model the Boulangist movement (from 1886 to 1890 approximately)[66] or the Dreyfus trial or even the coup d'état of 2nd December (one would analyse the classic work on the subject[67] and consider how much relative importance is given on the one hand to immediate economic factors, and on the other to the concrete study of "ideologies"). Confronted with these events, economism asks the question: "who profits directly from the initiative under consideration?", and replies with a line of reasoning which is as simplistic as it is fallacious: the ones who profit directly are a certain fraction of the ruling class. Furthermore, so that no mistake shall be made, the choice falls on that fraction which manifestly has a progressive function, controlling the totality of economic forces. One can be certain of not going wrong, since necessarily, if the movement under consideration comes to power, sooner or later the progressive fraction of the ruling group will end up by controlling the new government, and by making it its instrument for turning the State apparatus to its own benefit.

This sort of infallibility, therefore, comes very cheap. It not only has no theoretical significance—it has only minimal political implications or practical efficacy. In general, it produces nothing but moralistic sermons, and interminable questions of personality. When a movement of the Boulangist type occurs, the analysis realistically should be developed along the following lines: 1. social content of the mass following of the movement; 2. what function did this mass have in the balance of forces—which is in process of transformation, as the new movement demonstrates by its very coming into existence? 3. what is the political and social significance of those of the demands presented by the movement's leaders which find general assent? To what effective needs do they correspond? 4. examination of the conformity of the means to the proposed end; 5. only in the last analysis, and formulated in political not moralistic terms, is the *hypothesis* considered that such a movement will necessarily be perverted, and serve quite different ends from those which the mass of its followers expect. But economism

---

[65] i.e. the huge weight of the "mass of the petit-bourgeois urban and rural poor", referred to in the passage from Lenin quoted in the preceding note, in the existing balance of social forces in Russia. These strata had democratic or "constituentist" objectives, i.e. they wanted a Constituent Assembly and put their faith in constitutional reforms. See too Lenin's article "Constitutional Illusions" of July 1917.

[66] See note 7 on p. 129.

[67] i.e. Marx's *Eighteenth Brumaire of Louis Bonaparte*.

puts forward this hypothesis in advance, when no concrete fact (that is to say, none which appears as such to the evidence of common sense—rather than as a result of some esoteric "scientific" analysis) yet exists to support it. It thus appears as a moralistic accusation of duplicity and bad faith, or (in the case of the movement's followers), of naiveté and stupidity. Thus the political struggle is reduced to a series of personal affairs between on the one hand those with the genie in the lamp who know everything and on the other those who are fooled by their own leaders but are so incurably thick that they refuse to believe it. Moreover, until such movements have gained power, it is always possible to think that they are going to fail—and some indeed have failed (Boulangism itself, which failed as such and then was definitively crushed with the rise of the Dreyfusard movement; the movement of Georges Valois; that of General Gajda).[68] Research must therefore be directed towards identifying their strengths and weaknesses. The "economist" hypothesis asserts the existence of an immediate element of strength—i.e. the availability of a certain direct or indirect financial backing (a large newspaper supporting the movement is also a form of indirect financial backing)—and is satisfied with that. But it is not enough. In this case too, an analysis of the balance of forces—at all levels—can only culminate in the sphere of hegemony and ethico-political relations. [1933–34: 1st version 1930–32.]

One point which should be added as an example of the so-called intransigence theories is the rigid aversion on principle to what are termed compromises[69]—and the derivative of this, which can be termed "fear of dangers". It is clear that this aversion on principle

---

[68] Georges Valois was a French fascist thinker, who early in this century formed the "*Cercle Proudhon*", of which Sorel was a member. After the World War he organised a movement aimed at "national revolution", based on ex-servicemen and inspired by Mussolini; it was equally hostile to "bolshevism" and "plutocracy". In the 'thirties he espoused a form of "convergence" theory, seeing both the USA and the USSR as evolving towards a highly technological, syndical form of society.

General Rudolf Gajda, commander of the Czech Legion under Kolchak during the Civil War in Russia, discharged from the Czech army for plotting a military putsch in the 'twenties, formed a fascist League for Electoral Reform which won three seats in the 1929 elections in Czechoslovakia. When the Nazis entered the country, he hoped to become their puppet ruler, but they no doubt mistrusted his nationalist past since his hopes were frustrated.

[69] In his comments on "intransigents" (see note 58 on p. 161) Gramsci often appears, as here, to be referring also—or even especially—to the positions of Amadeo Bordiga (see General Introduction). Bordiga was among those communists criticised in Lenin's *Left-wing Communism—an infantile disorder*, whose eighth chapter was entitled, ironically, "No compromises?".

to compromise is closely linked to economism. For the conception upon which the aversion is based can only be the iron conviction that there exist objective laws of historical development similar in kind to natural laws, together with a belief in a predetermined teleology like that of a religion: since favourable conditions are inevitably going to appear, and since these, in a rather mysterious way, will bring about palingenetic events, it is evident that any deliberate initiative tending to predispose and plan these conditions is not only useless but even harmful. Side by side with these fatalistic beliefs however, there exists the tendency "thereafter" to rely blindly and indiscriminately on the regulatory properties of armed conflict. Yet this too is not entirely without its logic and its consistency, since it goes with a belief that the intervention of will is useful for destruction but not for reconstruction (already under way in the very moment of destruction). Destruction is conceived of mechanically, not as destruction/reconstruction. In such modes of thinking, no account is taken of the "time" factor, nor in the last analysis even of "economics". For there is no understanding of the fact that mass ideological factors always lag behind mass economic phenomena, and that therefore, at certain moments, the automatic thrust due to the economic factor is slowed down, obstructed or even momentarily broken by traditional ideological elements—hence that there must be a conscious, planned struggle to ensure that the exigencies of the economic position of the masses, which may conflict with the traditional leadership's policies, are understood. An appropriate political initiative is always necessary to liberate the economic thrust from the dead weight of traditional policies—i.e. to change the political direction of certain forces which have to be absorbed if a new, homogeneous politico-economic historical bloc, without internal contradictions, is to be successfully formed. And, since two "similar" forces can only be welded into a new organism either through a series of compromises or by force of arms, either by binding them to each other as allies or by forcibly subordinating one to the other, the question is whether one has the necessary force, and whether it is "productive" to use it. If the union of two forces is necessary in order to defeat a third, a recourse to arms and coercion (even supposing that these are available) can be nothing more than a methodological hypothesis; the only concrete possibility is compromise. Force can be employed against enemies, but not against a part of one's own side which one wishes rapidly to assimilate, and whose "good will" and enthusiasm one needs. [1933–34: 1st version 1932.]

PREDICTION AND PERSPECTIVE

Another point which needs to be defined and developed is the "dual perspective"[70] in political action and in national life. The dual perspective can present itself on various levels, from the most elementary to the most complex; but these can all theoretically be reduced to two fundamental levels, corresponding to the dual nature

---

[70] As explained in the following passage, this notion means for Gramsci the dialectical unity of the moments of force and consent in political action. The term "*doppia prospettiva*" goes back to the Fifth World Congress of the Comintern. The Congress followed a long series of defeats for the revolution internationally, culminating in the German October of 1923. Zinoviev, who had succeeded in placing his protégés Fischer and Maslov at the head of the German Party and in laying the blame for the defeat at the door of Brandler, who was ousted from the leadership, was anxious to present the entire episode as not being of critical importance, and the German revolution as still being on the cards in the immediate future. Trotsky and Radek were arguing that the European bourgeoisie was moving in the direction of a "labourist" resolution of its post-war political crisis, witness events in England and France. Under Zinoviev's guidance, the Congress in effect adopted a compromise solution, allowing both for the imminence of revolution and for a generalisation of the "labourist" solution. Section XIII of the Theses on Tactics was entitled "Two Perspectives". It stated:

"The epoch of international revolution has commenced. The rate of its development as a whole or partially, the rate of development of revolutionary events in any particular continent or in any particular country, cannot be foretold with precision. The whole situation is such that two perspectives are open: (*a*) a possible slow and prolonged development of the proletarian revolution, and (*b*) on the other hand, that the ground under capitalism has been mined to such an extent and that the contradictions of capitalism as a whole have developed so rapidly, that the solution in one country or another may come in the not distant future.

"The Comintern must base its tactics upon the possibility of both perspectives. The manœuvres of the Comintern must be so arranged as to be able rapidly to adapt oneself to the changing rate of development, and in any case even with a prolonged rate of development of events, to remain the irreconcilable mass Communist Party of proletarian revolution which attracts the masses and trains them for the revolutionary struggle."

This dual perspective continued to characterise Comintern strategy in the following years; Zinoviev reaffirmed it, for instance, at the Sixth Plenum in early 1926. Although its original formulation by Zinoviev was due to mainly tactical considerations, Gramsci seems to have continued to see it as preferable to the "right" line of 1926–28 and the "left" line of the Third Period, and to have felt that its directives could be generalised for all periods when "frontal attack" was not immediately possible. According to Athos Lisa (see General Introduction), Gramsci spoke of the "two perspectives" during the discussions which took place among the prisoners at Turi. He said that of the two, the more likely was that of some form of transitional stage intervening between the fall of fascism and the dictatorship of the proletariat, and that the party's tactics should take this into account. On the other hand, his criticisms here of those who "have reduced the theory of the 'dual perspective' to . . . nothing but two forms of 'immediacy', etc." are directed against any strategy which separates the moment of force from the moment of consent.

of Machiavelli's Centaur[71]—half-animal and half-human. They are the levels of force and of consent, authority and hegemony, violence and civilisation, of the individual moment and of the universal moment ("Church" and "State"), of agitation and of propaganda, of tactics and of strategy, etc. Some have reduced the theory of the "dual perspective" to something trivial and banal, to nothing but two forms of "immediacy" which succeed each other mechanically in time, with greater or less "proximity". In actual fact, it often happens that the more the first "perspective" is "immediate" and elementary, the more the second has to be "distant" (not in time, but as a dialectical relation), complex and ambitious. In other words, it may happen as in human life, that the more an individual is compelled to defend his own immediate physical existence, the more will he uphold and identify with the highest values of civilisation and of humanity, in all their complexity. [1933–34: 1st version 1931–32.]

It is certain that prediction only means seeing the present and the past clearly as movement. Seeing them clearly: in other words, accurately identifying the fundamental and permanent elements of

---

[71] "You should understand, therefore, that there are two ways of fighting: by law or by force. The first way is natural to men, and the second to beasts. But as the first way often proves inadequate one must needs have recourse to the second. So a prince must understand how to make a nice use of the beast and the man. The ancient writers taught princes about this by an allegory, when they described how Achilles and many other princes of the ancient world were sent to be brought up by Chiron, the centaur, so that he might train them his way. All the allegory means, in making the teacher half beast and half man, is that a prince must know how to act according to the nature of both, and that he cannot survive otherwise." Machiavelli, *The Prince*, Penguin, 1961, p. 99. See too NM. pp. 121–2: "Guicciardini's assertion that two things are absolutely necessary for the life of a State: arms and religion. Guicciardini's formula can be translated by various other, less drastic formulae: force and consent; coercion and persuasion; State and Church; political society and civil society; politics and morality (Croce's ethical-political history); law and freedom; order and self-discipline; or (with an implicit judgement of somewhat libertarian flavour) violence and fraud. In any case, in the political conception of the Renaissance, religion was consent and the Church was civil society, the hegemonic apparatus of the ruling group. For the latter did not have its own apparatus, i.e. did not have its own cultural and intellectual organisation, but regarded the universal ecclesiastical organisation as being that. The only way in which this differed from the Middle Ages was the fact that religion was openly conceived of and analysed as an *instrumentum regni*. It is from this point of view that the Jacobin attempt to institute a cult of the 'Supreme Being' should be studied. This appears to be an attempt to create an identity between State and civil society; to unify in a dictatorial way the constitutive elements of the State (in the organic, wider sense of the State proper + civil society), in a desperate endeavour to keep a hold on all of popular and national life. But it appears too as the first root of the modern lay State, independent of the Church, which seeks and finds in itself, in its own complex life, all the elements of its historical personality."

the process. But it is absurd to think of a purely "objective" prediction. Anybody who makes a prediction has in fact a "programme" for whose victory he is working, and his prediction is precisely an element contributing to that victory. This does not mean that prediction need always be arbitrary and gratuitous, or simply tendentious. Indeed one might say that only to the extent to which the objective aspect of prediction is linked to a programme does it acquire its objectivity: 1. because strong passions are necessary to sharpen the intellect and help make intuition more penetrating; 2. because reality is a product of the application of human will to the society of things (the machine-operator's to his machine); therefore if one excludes all voluntarist elements, or if it is only other people's wills whose intervention one reckons as an objective element in the general interplay of forces, one mutilates reality itself. Only the man who wills something strongly can identify the elements which are necessary to the realisation of his will.

Hence to believe that one particular conception of the world, and of life generally, in itself possesses a superior predictive capacity is a crudely fatuous and superficial error. Certainly a conception of the world is implicit in every prediction, and therefore whether the latter is a random series of arbitrary notions or a rigorous and coherent vision is not without its importance; but it precisely acquires that importance in the living brain of the individual who makes the prediction, and who by the strength of his will makes it come true. This can be clearly seen in the case of predictions made by people who claim to be "impartial": they are full of idle speculation, trivial detail, and elegant conjectures. When a particular programme has to be realised, it is only the existence of somebody to "predict" it which will ensure that it deals with what is essential—with those elements which, being "organisable" and susceptible of being directed or deflected, are in reality alone predictable. This is in contrast with the habitual way of looking at the problem. For it is generally thought that every act of prediction presupposes the determination of laws of regularity similar to those of the natural sciences. But since these laws do not exist in the absolute or mechanical sense that is imagined, no account is taken of the will of others, nor is its application "predicted". Consequently everything is built on an arbitrary hypothesis and not on reality. [1933]

"Too much" (therefore superficial and mechanical) political realism often leads to the assertion that a statesman should only work within the limits of "effective reality"; that he should not interest himself in what "ought to be" but only in what "is". This would mean that he should not look farther than the end of his own nose. This misunderstanding led Paolo Treves to see in Guicciardini rather than in Machiavelli the "true politician".[72]

A distinction must be made not only between "diplomat" and "politician", but also between political scientist and active politician. The diplomat inevitably will move only within the bounds of effective reality, since his specific activity is not the creation of some new equilibrium, but the maintenance of an existing equilibrium within a certain juridical framework. Similarly, the political scientist has to keep within the bounds of effective reality in so far as he is merely a scientist. But Machiavelli is not merely a scientist: he is a partisan, a man of powerful passions, an active politician, who wishes to create a new balance of forces and therefore cannot help concerning himself with what "ought to be" (not of course in a moralistic sense). Hence the question cannot be posed in these terms, it is more complex. It is one, that is to say, of seeing whether what "ought to be" is arbitrary or necessary; whether it is concrete will on the one hand or idle fancy, yearning, daydream on the other. The active politician is a creator, an initiator; but he neither creates from nothing nor does he move in the turbid void of his own desires and dreams. He bases himself on effective reality, but what is this effective reality? Is it something static and immobile, or is it not rather a relation of forces in continuous motion and shift of equilibrium? If one applies one's will to the creation of a new equilibrium among the forces which really exist and are operative—basing oneself on the particular force which one believes to be progressive and strengthening it to help it to victory—one still moves on the terrain of effective reality, but does so in order to dominate and transcend it (or to contribute to this). What "ought to be" is therefore concrete; indeed it is the only realistic and historicist interpretation of reality, it alone is history in the making and philosophy in the making, it alone is politics.

The opposition between Savonarola and Machiavelli is not an opposition between what is and what ought to be (Russo's whole paragraph on this point is pure *belles-lettres*),[73] but one between two

---

[72] Gramsci is referring to the article *Il realismo politico di Francesco Guicciardini*, in *Nuova Rivista Storica*, November/December 1930. See too "Economic-Corporate Phase of the State" on p. 173. Guicciardini (1483–1540) was a Florentine diplomat and historian, a friend of Machiavelli's and often contrasted with him; he was an altogether more conservative figure. See too note 90 on p. 193.

[73] Russo, *op. cit.*, see note 3 on p. 125. He wrote: "Savonarola is pure religion, Machiavelli science, technique, pure politics." For Savonarola, see note 17 on p. 135.

concepts of what ought to be: the abstract and phantasmagorical concept of Savonarola, and the realistic concept of Machiavelli—realistic even if it did not in fact become direct reality, since one cannot expect an individual or a book to change reality but only to interpret it and to indicate the possible lines of action. Machiavelli was limited or narrow only in as much as he was a "private individual", a writer, and not the leader of a State or an army; the latter too is a single individual, but has at his disposal the forces of his State or army and not merely armies of words. But one cannot therefore say that Machiavelli himself was a "prophet unarmed" too: it would be too easy a witticism. Machiavelli never says that he has any thought or intention of himself changing reality—only of showing concretely how the historical forces ought to have acted in order to be effective. [1933–34: 1st version 1931–32.]

ECONOMIC-CORPORATE PHASE OF THE STATE

Guicciardini represents a step backwards in political science with respect to Machiavelli. This is all that Guicciardini's greater "pessimism" means. Guicciardini regressed to a purely Italian political thought, whereas Machiavelli had attained a European thought. It is impossible to understand Machiavelli without taking into account the fact that he subsumed Italian experience into European (in his day synonymous with international) experience: his "will" would have been utopian, were it not for the European experience. The same conception of "human nature" thus becomes different in the two cases. Machiavelli's "human nature" embraces "European man", who in France and Spain has effectively transcended the phase of the break-up of feudalism by means of the system of absolute monarchy: hence the creation of a unitary absolute monarchy in Italy is prevented not by "human nature" but by transitory conditions which the will can overcome. Machiavelli is "pessimistic" (or better realistic) when he regards men, and the motives of their actions: Guicciardini is not pessimistic, but sceptical and petty. Paolo Treves* commits a host of errors in his judgement of Guicciardini and Machiavelli; he does not make a clear distinction between "politics" and "diplomacy", and it is precisely this which is the cause of his mistaken evaluations. In politics, in fact, will has a far greater importance than in diplomacy. Diplomacy sanctions, and tends to conserve, situations created by

* See *Il realismo politico di Francesco Guicciardini*, in *Nuova Rivista Storica*, November/December 1930.

the clash of policies of different States; it is only creative metaphorically, or by philosophical convention ("all human activity is creative"). International relations deal with a balance of forces in which any single State component has only a very limited weight. Florence, for instance, might have had a certain weight if it had become stronger; but such a growth of its strength, even if it had improved its position in the Italian and European balance of forces, certainly could not have been thought of as decisive for a wholesale transformation of the balance itself. Therefore diplomacy, through the very habits of the profession, tends to scepticism and to conservative narrowness of mind.

In the internal relations of a State, the situation is incomparably more favourable to central initiative, to what Machiavelli understood as a will to command. De Sanctis' judgement of Guicciardini is far more realistic than Treves thinks.[74] It should be asked why De Sanctis was better prepared than Treves to provide this historically and scientifically more accurate judgement. De Sanctis participated in a creative moment of Italian political history, a moment in which the effectiveness of the political will—turned to awakening new and original forces rather than merely to calculating on the traditional ones, which were seen as incapable of being developed and reorganised (Guicciardinesque political scepticism)—had revealed all its potentiality not only in the art of founding a State from within, but also in that of mastering international relations, rejuvenating the professional and customary methods of diplomacy (with Cavour). The cultural atmosphere was propitious to a more comprehensively realistic conception of the science and art of politics. But, supposing there had not been this atmosphere, would it have been impossible for De Sanctis to understand Machiavelli? The atmosphere provided by the historical moment enriches De Sanctis' essays with a sentimental *pathos* which renders the argument more sympathetic and moving, the scientific exposition more artistically expressive and captivating; but the logical, political-scientific content could have been thought out even in periods of blackest reaction. Is not reaction too perhaps a constructive act of will? And is not conservation a deliberate act? Why then should Machiavelli's will be "utopian", and why revolutionary and not utopian the will of someone who wants to conserve what exists, and to prevent the creation and organisation of new forces which would disturb and transform the traditional equilibrium? Political

---

[74] De Sanctis condemned Guicciardini's "egoism"—see note 90 on p. 193.

science abstracts the element "will", and does not take account of the end to which a particular will is applied. The attribute "utopian" does not apply to political will in general, but to specific wills which are incapable of relating means to end, and hence are not even wills, but idle whims, dreams, longings, etc.

Guicciardini's scepticism (not pessimism of the intelligence, which can be combined with an optimism of the will in active and realistic politicians)[75] has other sources: 1. diplomatic habit: i.e. the habit of a subordinate, subaltern activity (executive-bureaucratic) which has to accept a will (the political will of the diplomat's government or sovereign) which is extraneous to the diplomat's individual convictions. (He may, it is true, feel it as his own, in so far as it is in line with his own convictions: but he may also not do so. The fact that diplomacy has of necessity become a specialised profession has led to this consequence, of allowing the diplomat to become independent of the policies of changing governments, etc.). The result is scepticism and, in scientific discussion, extra-scientific prejudices; 2. the actual convictions of Guicciardini, who, in the general context of Italian politics, was a conservative, and hence theorises his own opinions, his own political position, etc.

Guicciardini's writings are more of a period piece than they are political science, and that is De Sanctis' judgement. Just as Paolo Treves' work too is more of a period piece than it is history of political science. [1930–32]

ANALYSIS OF SITUATIONS. RELATIONS OF FORCE

The study of how "situations" should be analysed, in other words how to establish the various levels of the relations of force, offers an opportunity for an elementary exposition of the science and art of politics—understood as a body of practical rules for research and of detailed observations useful for awakening an interest in effective reality and for stimulating more rigorous and more vigorous

[75] See PP. p. 6: "On daydreams and fantasies. They show lack of character and passivity. One imagines that something has happened to upset the mechanism of necessity. One's own initiative has become free. Everything is easy. One can do whatever one wants, and one wants a whole series of things which at present one lacks. It is basically the present turned on its head which is projected into the future. Everything repressed is unleashed. On the contrary, it is necessary to direct one's attention violently towards the present as it is, if one wishes to transform it. Pessimism of the intelligence, optimism of the will." [1932] Romain Rolland's maxim "Pessimism of the intelligence, optimism of the will" was made by Gramsci into something of a programmatic slogan as early as 1919, in the pages of *Ordine Nuovo*.

political insights. This should be accompanied by the explanation of what is meant in politics by strategy and tactics, by strategic "plan", by propaganda and agitation, by command structure[76] or science of political organisation and administration.

The elements of empirical observation which are habitually included higgledy-piggledy in works of political science (G. Mosca's *Elementi di scienza politica* may be taken as typical) ought, in so far as they are not abstract and illusory, to be inserted into the context of the relations of force, on one level or another. These levels range from the relations between international forces (one would insert here the notes written on what a great power is, on the combinations of States in hegemonic systems, and hence on the concept of independence and sovereignty as far as small and medium powers are concerned)[77] to the objective relations within society—in other words, the degree of development of productive forces; to relations of political force and those between parties (hegemonic systems within the State); and to immediate (or potentially military) political relations.

Do international relations precede or follow (logically) fundamental social relations? There can be no doubt that they follow. Any organic innovation in the social structure, through its technical-military expressions, modifies organically absolute and relative relations in the international field too. Even the geographical position of a national State does not precede but follows (logically) structural changes, although it also reacts back upon them to a certain extent (to the extent precisely to which superstructures react upon the structure, politics on economics, etc.). However, international relations react both passively and actively on political relations (of hegemony among the parties). The more the immediate economic life of a nation is subordinated to international relations, the more a particular party will come to represent this situation and to exploit it, with the aim of preventing rival parties gaining the upper hand (recall Nitti's famous speech on the *technical* impossibility of revolution in Italy). From this series of facts one may conclude that often the so-called "foreigner's party"[78] is not really

---

[76] *Organica* has no exact equivalent in English—it means the organisation of armed forces, their division into different arms and corps, their system of ranks, etc.

[77] See NM. pp. 141 and 167 ff.

[78] Term used especially of communist parties by the nationalist Right, and, in an earlier period, of parties influenced by the ideas of the French Revolution. The latter—Mazzini's Action Party is a good example—did in fact often have links with liberals in other countries.

the one which is commonly so termed, but precisely the most nationalistic party—which, in reality, represents not so much the vital forces of its own country, as that country's subordination and economic enslavement to the hegemonic nations or to certain of their number.* [1933–34: 1st version 1931–32.]

It is the problem of the relations between structure and superstructure which must be accuratcly posed and resolved if the forces which are active in the history of a particular period are to be correctly analysed, and the relation between them determined. Two principles must orient the discussion: 1. that no society sets itself tasks for whose accomplishment the necessary and sufficient conditions do not either already exist or are not at least beginning to emerge and develop; 2. that no society breaks down and can be replaced until it has first developed all the forms of life which are implicit in its internal relations.** From a reflection on these two principles, one can move on to develop a whole series of further principles of historical methodology. Meanwhile, in studying a structure, it is necessary to distinguish organic movements (relatively permanent) from movements which may be termed "conjunctural" (and which appear as occasional, immediate, almost accidental).[79] Conjunctural phenomena too depend on organic movements to be sure, but they do not have any very far-reaching historical significance; they give rise to political criticism of a minor, day-to-day character, which has as its subject top political leaders and personalities with direct governmental responsibilities. Organic phenomena

---

* An allusion to this international element which "represses" domestic energies can be found in G. Volpe's articles published in *Corriere della Sera*, on 22 and 23 March 1932.

** "No social order ever perishes before all the productive forces for which there is room in it have developed; and new, higher relations of production never appear before the material conditions for their existence have matured in the womb of the old society. Therefore mankind always sets itself only such tasks as it can solve; since, looking at the matter more closely, it will always be found that the task itself arises only when the material conditions for its solution already exist or are at least in the process of formation." Marx, Preface to the *Critique of Political Economy*.

[79] On PP. pp. 148–49 Gramsci wrote: "The conjuncture can be defined as the set of circumstances which determine the market in a given phase, provided that these are conceived of as being in movement, i.e. as constituting a process of ever-changing combinations, a process which is the economic cycle . . . In Italian the meaning of 'favourable or unfavourable economic situation (*occasione*)' remains attached to the word 'conjuncture'. Difference between 'situation' and 'conjuncture': the conjuncture is the set of immediate and ephemeral characteristics of the economic situation . . . Study of the conjuncture is thus more closely linked to immediate politics, to 'tactics' and agitation, while the 'situation' relates to 'strategy' and propaganda, etc."

on the other hand give rise to socio-historical criticism, whose subject is wider social groupings—beyond the public figures and beyond the top leaders. When an historical period comes to be studied, the great importance of this distinction becomes clear. A crisis occurs, sometimes lasting for decades. This exceptional duration means that incurable structural contradictions have revealed themselves (reached maturity), and that, despite this, the political forces which are struggling to conserve and defend the existing structure itself are making every effort to cure them, within certain limits, and to overcome them. These incessant and persistent efforts (since no social formation will ever admit that it has been superseded) form the terrain of the "conjunctural", and it is upon this terrain that the forces of opposition organise. These forces seek to demonstrate that the necessary and sufficient conditions already exist to make possible, and hence imperative, the accomplishment of certain historical tasks (imperative, because any falling short before an historical duty increases the necessary disorder, and prepares more serious catastrophes). (The demonstration in the last analysis only succeeds and is "true" if it becomes a new reality, if the forces of opposition triumph; in the immediate, it is developed in a series of ideological, religious, philosophical, political, and juridical polemics, whose concreteness can be estimated by the extent to which they are convincing, and shift the previously existing disposition of social forces.)

A common error in historico-political analysis consists in an inability to find the correct relation between what is organic and what is conjunctural. This leads to presenting causes as immediately operative which in fact only operate indirectly, or to asserting that the immediate causes are the only effective ones. In the first case there is an excess of "economism", or doctrinaire pedantry; in the second, an excess of "ideologism". In the first case there is an overestimation of mechanical causes, in the second an exaggeration of the voluntarist and individual element. The distinction between organic "movements" and facts and "conjunctural" or occasional ones must be applied to all types of situation; not only to those in which a regressive development or an acute crisis takes place, but also to those in which there is a progressive development or one towards prosperity, or in which the productive forces are stagnant. The dialectical nexus between the two categories of movement, and therefore of research, is hard to establish precisely. Moreover, if error is serious in historiography, it becomes still more serious in the art of politics, when it is not the reconstruction of past history but the construction of present and future history which is at stake.* One's own baser and more immediate desires and passions are the cause of error, in that they take the place of an objective and impartial analysis—and this happens not as a conscious "means" to stimulate to action, but as self-deception. In this case too the snake bites the snake-charmer—in other words the demagogue is the first victim of his own demagogy.

These methodological criteria will acquire visibly and didactically their full significance if they are applied to the examination of concrete historical facts. This might usefully be done for the events which took place in France from 1789 to 1870. It seems to me that for greater clarity of exposition it is precisely necessary to take in the whole of this period. In fact, it was only in 1870–71, with the attempt of the Commune, that all the germs of 1789 were finally historically exhausted. It was then that the new bourgeois class struggling for power defeated not only the representatives of the old society unwilling to admit that it had been definitively superseded, but also the still newer groups who maintained that the new structure created by the 1789 revolution was itself already outdated; by this victory the bourgeoisie demonstrated its vitality *vis-à-vis* both the old and the very new.

Furthermore, it was in 1870–71 that the body of principles of political strategy and tactics engendered in practice in 1789, and developed ideologically around '48, lost their efficacy. (I am referring to those which can be resumed in the formula of "Permanent Revolution"; it would be interesting to study how much of this formula passed into Mazzini's strategy—for example, in the Milan insurrection of 1853—and whether this happened consciously or not.) One piece of evidence for the correctness of this point of view is the fact that historians are by no means of one mind (and it is impossible that they should be) in fixing the limits of the group

* Failure to consider the immediate moment of "relations of force" is linked to residues of the vulgar liberal conception—of which syndicalism is a manifestation which thought itself more advanced when in reality it was taking a step backward. In fact the vulgar liberal conception, stressing relations between political forces organised in the various forms of party (newspaper readerships, parliamentary and local elections, the mass organisations of parties and trade unions in the strict sense), was more advanced than syndicalism, which gave primordial importance to the fundamental socio-economic relation and only to that. The vulgar liberal conception took implicit account of this socio-economic relation too (as many signs clearly indicate), but it insisted besides on the relation of political forces—which was an expression of the former and in reality contained it. These residues of the vulgar liberal conception can be traced in a whole series of works purporting to be connected with the philosophy of praxis, and have given rise to infantile forms of optimism and folly.

of events which constitutes the French Revolution. For some (Salvemini, for instance) the Revolution was complete at Valmy: France had created its new State and had shown itself capable of organising the politico-military force necessary to assert and to defend its territorial sovereignty. For others the Revolution continues until Thermidor—indeed they speak of various revolutions (10 August[80] is a separate revolution, etc.).* The interpretation of Thermidor and of the work of Napoleon provokes the sharpest disagreements. Was it revolution or counter-revolution? For others the history of the Revolution continues until 1830, 1848, 1870 and even until the World War of 1914. All these views are partially true. In reality the internal contradictions which develop after 1789 in the structure of French society are resolved to a relative degree only with the Third Republic; and France has now enjoyed sixty years of stable political life only after eighty years of convulsions at ever longer intervals: 1789, 1794, 1799, 1804, 1815, 1830, 1848, 1870. It is precisely the study of these "intervals" of varying frequency which enables one to reconstruct the relations on the one hand between structure and superstructure, and on the other between the development of organic movement and conjunctural movement in the structure. One might say in the meantime that the dialectical mediation between the two methodological principles formulated at the beginning of this note is to be found in the historico-political formula of Permanent Revolution.

The question of so-called relations of force is an aspect of the same problem. One often reads in historical narratives the generic expression: "relation of forces favourable, or unfavourable, to this or that tendency". Thus, abstractly, this formulation explains nothing, or almost nothing—since it merely repeats twice over the fact which needs to be explained, once as a fact and once as an abstract law and an explanation. The theoretical error consists therefore in making what is a principle of research and interpretation into an "historical cause".

Meanwhile, in the "relation of forces" various moments or levels must be distinguished, and they are fundamentally the following:

1. A relation of social forces which is closely linked to the structure, objective, independent of human will, and which can be measured with the systems of the exact or physical sciences. The level of development of the material forces of production provides a basis for the emergence of the various social classes, each one of which

---

[80] On 10 August 1792 the Tuileries Palace was stormed and the Monarchy fell.

* See *La Révolution française* by A. Mathiez, in the A. Colin series.

represents a function and has a specific position within production itself. This relation is what it is, a refractory reality: nobody can alter the number of firms or their employees, the number of cities or the given urban population, etc. By studying these fundamental data it is possible to discover whether in a particular society there exist the necessary and sufficient conditions for its transformation—in other words, to check the degree of realism and practicability of the various ideologies which have been born on its own terrain, on the terrain of the contradictions which it has engendered during the course of its development.

2. A subsequent moment is the relation of political forces; in other words, an evaluation of the degree of homogeneity, self-awareness, and organisation attained by the various social classes. This moment can in its turn be analysed and differentiated into various levels, corresponding to the various moments of collective political consciousness, as they have manifested themselves in history up till now. The first and most elementary of these is the economic-corporate level: a tradesman feels *obliged* to stand by another tradesman, a manufacturer by another manufacturer, etc., but the tradesman does not yet feel solidarity with the manufacturer; in other words, the members of the professional group are conscious of its unity and homogeneity, and of the need to organise it, but in the case of the wider social group this is not yet so. A second moment is that in which consciousness is reached of the solidarity of interests among all the members of a social class—but still in the purely economic field. Already at this juncture the problem of the State is posed—but only in terms of winning politico-juridical equality with the ruling groups: the right is claimed to participate in legislation and administration, even to reform these—but within the existing fundamental structures. A third moment is that in which one becomes aware that one's own corporate interests, in their present and future development, transcend the corporate limits of the purely economic class, and can and must become the interests of other subordinate groups too. This is the most purely political phase, and marks the decisive passage from the structure to the sphere of the complex superstructures; it is the phase in which previously germinated ideologies become "party", come into confrontation and conflict, until only one of them, or at least a single combination of them, tends to prevail, to gain the upper hand, to propagate itself throughout society—bringing about not only a unison of economic and political aims, but also intellectual and moral unity, posing all the questions around which the struggle

rages not on a corporate but on a "universal" plane, and thus creating the hegemony of a fundamental social group over a series of subordinate groups. It is true that the State is seen as the organ of one particular group, destined to create favourable conditions for the latter's maximum expansion. But the development and expansion of the particular group are conceived of, and presented, as being the motor force of a universal expansion, of a development of all the "national" energies. In other words, the dominant group is coordinated concretely with the general interests of the subordinate groups, and the life of the State is conceived of as a continuous process of formation and superseding of unstable equilibria (on the juridical plane) between the interests of the fundamental group and those of the subordinate groups—equilibria in which the interests of the dominant group prevail, but only up to a certain point, i.e. stopping short of narrowly corporate economic interest.

In real history these moments imply each other reciprocally—horizontally and vertically, so to speak—i.e. according to socio-economic activity (horizontally) and to country (vertically), combining and diverging in various ways. Each of these combinations may be represented by its own organised economic and political expression. It is also necessary to take into account the fact that international relations intertwine with these internal relations of nation-states, creating new, unique and historically concrete combinations. A particular ideology, for instance, born in a highly developed country, is disseminated in less developed countries, impinging on the local interplay of combinations.* This relation between international forces and national forces is further complicated by the existence within every State of several structurally diverse territorial sectors, with diverse relations of force at all levels (thus the Vendée[81] was allied with the forces of international reaction, and represented them in the heart of French territorial unity; similarly Lyons in the French Revolution represented a particular knot of relations, etc.).

---

* Religion, for example, has always been a source of such national and international ideological-political combinations, and so too have the other international organisations—Freemasonry, Rotarianism, the Jews, career diplomacy. These propose political solutions of diverse historical origin, and assist their victory in particular countries—functioning as international political parties which operate within each nation with the full concentration of the international forces. A religion, freemasonry, Rotary, Jews, etc., can be subsumed into the social category of "intellectuals", whose function, on an international scale, is that of mediating the extremes, of "socialising" the technical discoveries which provide the impetus for all activities of leadership, of devising compromises between, and ways out of, extreme solutions.

[81] See note 47 on p. 79.

3. The third moment is that of the relation of military forces, which from time to time is directly decisive. (Historical development oscillates continually between the first and the third moment, with the mediation of the second.) But this too is not undifferentiated, nor is it susceptible to immediate schematic definition. Here too, two levels can be distinguished: the military level in the strict or technical military sense, and the level which may be termed politico-military. In the course of history these two levels have appeared in a great variety of combinations. A typical example, which can serve as a limiting case, is the relation involved in a State's military oppression of a nation seeking to attain its national independence. The relation is not purely military, but politico-military; indeed this type of oppression would be inexplicable if it were not for the state of social disintegration of the oppressed people, and the passivity of the majority among them; consequently independence cannot be won with purely military forces, it requires both military and politico-military. If the oppressed nation, in fact, before embarking on its struggle for independence, had to wait until the hegemonic State allowed it to organise its own army in the strict and technical sense of the word, it would have to wait quite a while. (It may happen that the claim to have its own army is conceded by the hegemonic nation, but this only means that a great part of the struggle has already been fought and won on the politico-military terrain.) The oppressed nation will therefore initially oppose the dominant military force with a force which is only "politico-military", that is to say a form of political action which has the virtue of provoking repercussions of a military character in the sense: 1. that it has the capacity to destroy the war potential of the dominant nation from within; 2. that it compels the dominant military force to thin out and disperse itself over a large territory, thus nullifying a great part of its war potential. In the Italian Risorgimento the disastrous absence of politico-military leadership may be noted, especially in the Action Party (through congenital incapacity), but also in the Piedmontese Moderate Party, both before and after 1848, not to be sure through incapacity but through "politico-economic Malthusianism"—in other words, because they were unwilling even to hint at the possibility of an agrarian reform, and because they had no desire to see a national constituent assembly convoked, but merely waited for the Piedmont monarchy, free from any conditions or limitations of popular origin, to extend its rule to the whole of Italy—sanctioned only by regional plebiscites.

A further question connected with the foregoing is whether the fundamental historical crises are directly determined by economic crises. The answer is contained implicitly in the foregoing paragraphs, where problems have been considered which are only another way of presenting the one now under consideration. Nevertheless it is still necessary, for didactic reasons, given the particular public which is being aimed at, to examine each of the ways in which a single question may present itself as if it were a new and independent problem. It may be ruled out that immediate economic crises of themselves produce fundamental historical events; they can simply create a terrain more favourable to the dissemination of certain modes of thought, and certain ways of posing and resolving questions involving the entire subsequent development of national life. Moreover, all assertions concerning periods of crisis or of prosperity may give rise to unilateral judgements. In his historical outline of the French Revolution, Mathiez, in opposition to the vulgar traditional history which aprioristically "discovers" a crisis coinciding with every major rupture of social equilibrium, asserts that towards 1789 the economic situation was in an immediate sense rather good, so that it cannot be said that the downfall of the absolute State was due to a crisis of impoverishment. It should be observed that the State was in the throes of a mortal financial crisis and considering which of the privileged social orders would have to bear the sacrifices and burdens necessary for the State and Royal finances to be put back in order. Furthermore, if the economic position of the bourgeoisie was flourishing, the situation of the popular classes was certainly not good either in the towns or, especially, on the land—where they suffered from endemic poverty. In any case, the rupture of the equilibrium of forces did not occur as the result of direct mechanical causes—i.e. the impoverishment of the social group which had an interest in breaking the equilibrium, and which did in fact break it. It occurred in the context of conflicts on a higher plane than the immediate world of the economy; conflicts related to class "prestige" (future economic interests), and to an inflammation of sentiments of independence, autonomy and power. The specific question of economic hardship or well-being as a cause of new historical realities is a partial aspect of the question of the relations of force, at the various levels. Changes can come about either because a situation of well-being is threatened by the narrow self-interest of a rival class, or because hardship has become intolerable and no force is visible in the old society capable of mitigating it and of re-establishing normality by legal means. Hence it may be said that all these elements are the concrete manifestation of the conjunctural fluctuations of the totality of social relations of force, on whose terrain the passage takes place from the latter to political relations of force, and finally to the military relation which is decisive.

If this process of development from one moment to the next is missing—and it is essentially a process which has as its actors men and their will and capability—the situation is not taken advantage of, and contradictory outcomes are possible: either the old society resists and ensures itself a breathing-space, by physically exterminating the élite of the rival class and terrorising its mass reserves; or a reciprocal destruction of the conflicting forces occurs, and a peace of the graveyard is established, perhaps even under the surveillance of a foreign guard. [1933–34: 1st version 1930–32.]

But the most important observation to be made about any concrete analysis of the relations of force is the following: that such analyses cannot and must not be ends in themselves (unless the intention is merely to write a chapter of past history), but acquire significance only if they serve to justify a particular practical activity, or initiative of will. They reveal the points of least resistance, at which the force of will can be most fruitfully applied; they suggest immediate tactical operations; they indicate how a campaign of political agitation may best be launched, what language will best be understood by the masses, etc. The decisive element in every situation is the permanently organised and long-prepared force which can be put into the field when it is judged that a situation is favourable (and it can be favourable only in so far as such a force exists, and is full of fighting spirit). Therefore the essential task is that of systematically and patiently ensuring that this force is formed, developed, and rendered ever more homogeneous, compact, and self-aware. This is clear from military history, and from the care with which in every period armies have been prepared in advance to be able to make war at any moment. The great Powers have been great precisely because they were at all times prepared to intervene effectively in favourable international conjunctures—which were precisely favourable because there was the concrete possibility of effectively intervening in them. [1933–34: 1st version 1931–32.]

ON BUREAUCRACY

1. As political and economic forms develop historically, a new type of functionary is increasingly being produced—what could be

described as "career" functionaries, technically trained for bureaucratic work (civil and military). This is a fact of prime significance for political science, and for any history of the forms taken by the State. Has this process been a necessary one, or, as the "pure" liberals claim, a degeneration in respect of the ideal of *self-government*?[82] Certainly every type of society and State has had its own problem of functionaries, which it has formulated and resolved in its own way; every society has had its own system of selection, and its own type of functionary to be trained. The reconstruction of how all these elements have evolved is of capital importance. The problem of functionaries partly coincides with that of the intellectuals. However, though it is true that every new form of society and State has required a new type of functionary, it is also true that new ruling groups have never been able, at least initially, to ignore tradition or established interests—i.e. the categories of functionary (especially in the ecclesiastical and military spheres) who already existed and had been constituted before they came to power. Unity of manual and intellectual work, and closer links between legislative and executive power (so that elected functionaries concern themselves not merely with the control of State affairs but also with their execution), may be motives of inspiration for a new approach in solving the problem of the intellectuals as well as the problem of functionaries.

2. Connected with the question of the bureaucracy and its "optimum" organisation is the debate about so-called "organic

---

[82] Gramsci gives the English term in parenthesis in his original text. He appears to mean by it the phenomenon whereby, notably in England, certain functions elsewhere carried out by the State are devolved onto formally autonomous local bodies or institutions. On PP. pp. 163–64, in the note "*Self-government e burocrazia*", Gramsci writes: "Self-government is an institution or a political and administrative usage which presupposes quite specific conditions: the existence of a social stratum which lives off rent, which by tradition is experienced in public affairs, and enjoys a certain prestige among the popular masses for its rectitude and impartiality (and also for certain psychological qualities, such as its ability to exercise authority with dignified firmness, but without haughtiness or arrogant detachment). It is thus understandable that self-government has only been possible in England, where the class of landowners, in addition to its condition of economic independence, had never been in savage conflict with the population (as happened in France) and had not had great corporate military traditions (as in Germany), with the separateness and the authoritarian attitude which derive from these. Change of meaning of self-government in non-Anglo-Saxon countries: struggle against the centralism of the high government bureaucracy, but institutions entrusted to a bureaucracy controlled directly from below. Bureaucracy become necessity: the question must be raised of forming an honest and impartial bureaucracy, which does not abuse its function to make itself independent of the control of the representativ' system. It can be said that every form of society has its approach or solution to the problem of bureaucracy, these must inevitably vary."

centralism" and "democratic centralism" (which despite its name has nothing to do with abstract democracy, in as much as the French Revolution and Third Republic developed form of organic centralism unknown either to the absolute monarchy or to Napoleon I).[83] One will have to seek out and study the real economic and political relations which find their organisational form, their articulation and their functionality in the various manifestations of organic and democratic centralism in all fields: in State life (unitary State, federation, union of federated States, federation of States or federal State, etc.); in interstate life (alliances, various forms of

---

[83] On "organic centralism", see NM. p. 113: "So-called 'organic centralism' is based on the principle that a political group is selected by 'cooptation' around an 'infallible bearer of truth', one who is 'enlightened by reason', who has found the infallible natural laws of historical evolution, infallible even if only in the long term, and if present events 'seem' to disprove them." And NM. pp. 157–58: "A collective organism is made up of single individuals, who form the organism in as much as they have given themselves, and actively accept, a particular hierarchy and leadership. If each of the individual members sees the collective organism as an entity external to himself, it is evident that this organism no longer in fact exists, it becomes a phantasm of the mind, a fetish . . . What is astonishing, and typical, is that fetishism of this kind occurs too in 'voluntary' organisms, not of a 'public' or State character, like parties and trade unions. The tendency is to see the relationship between the individual and the organism as a dualism; it is towards an external, critical attitude of the individual towards the organism (if the attitude does not consist of an enthusiastic, acritical admiration). In any case a fetishistic relationship. The individual expects the organism to act, even if he does not do anything himself, and does not reflect that precisely because his attitude is very widespread, the organism is necessarily inoperative. Furthermore, it should be recognised that, since a deterministic and mechanical conception of history is very widespread (a common-sense conception which is related to the passivity of the great popular masses), each individual, seeing that despite his non-intervention something still does happen, tends to think that there indeed exists, over and above individuals, a phantasmagorical being, the abstraction of the collective organism, a kind of autonomous divinity, which does not think with any concrete brain but still thinks, which does not move with specific human legs but still moves, etc.

"It might seem that certain ideologies, such as that of present-day idealism (Ugo Spirito's), which identify the individual and the State, ought to re-educate the individual consciousness; but it does not seem that this in fact happens, because this identification is merely verbal and verbalistic. The same can be said of every form of so-called 'organic centralism', which is based on the presupposition—true only at exceptional moments, when popular passions are aflame—that the relationship between ruler and ruled is determined by the fact that the rulers satisfy the interests of the ruled and thus 'must' have their consent, i.e. the individual must identify with the whole—which (whatever the organism involved) is represented by the rulers." See too PP. pp. 65–66. It should also be noted that Bordiga and the Left in 1925–26, and notably in their theses for the Congress of Lyons, had spoken of the need for the Comintern and the individual communist parties to "realize an organic centralism", and had counterposed this to existing party practice and in particular to bolshevisation. However, it is clear that Gramsci uses the concept of "organic centralism" as a general category of political organisation, as in this passage with reference to the French Revolution and the Third Republic.

international political "constellation"); in the life of political and cultural associations (Freemasonry, Rotary Club, Catholic Church) and of trade-union and economic ones (cartels, trusts); in the same country, in different countries, etc.

Polemics from the past (pre-1914) on the subject of German predominance in the life of high culture, and in that of certain international political forces: was this predominance in fact real, and in what did it really consist?[84] It may be said: (*a*) that no organic or disciplinary bonds ensured this supremacy, which was therefore merely a phenomenon of abstract cultural influence and of highly unstable prestige; (*b*) that such cultural influence in no way affected real activity, which was on the contrary fragmented, localised, and without overall direction. Thus one cannot speak of any kind of centralism here—neither organic nor democratic, nor of any other kind, nor a mixture of these. The influence was felt and experienced by a handful of intellectual groups, who had no links with the popular masses; and it was precisely the absence of any such links which characterised the situation. Nevertheless, such a state of affairs is worth studying, since it helps to explain the process which led to the formulation of the theories of organic centralism. These are precisely a one-sided and intellectualistic critique of that disorder and dispersal of forces.

Meanwhile, it is necessary to distinguish among the theories of organic centralism. One the one hand there are those which conceal a precise programme of real predominance of one part over the whole (whether the part consists of a stratum such as the intellectuals, or of a "privileged" territorial group). On the other there are those which are purely and simply the one-sided perspectives of sectarians or fanatics, and which, although capable of concealing a programme of predominance (usually of a single individual, such as the infallible Pope—whereby Catholicism has become transformed into a sort of cult of the Pope), do not seem in the immediate consciously to conceal any such programme. The most accurate name would be bureaucratic centralism. "Organicity" can only be found in democratic centralism, which is so to speak a "centralism" in movement—i.e. a continual adaptation of the organisation to the real movement, a matching of thrusts from below with orders from above, a continuous insertion of elements thrown up from the depths of the rank and file into the solid framework of the leadership

---

[84] Presumably a reference to the influence of Hegel and German idealism on the Italian idealists (Croce and Gentile), and to that of the German Social-Democratic Party within the Second International.

apparatus which ensures continuity and the regular accumulation of experience. Democratic centralism is "organic" because on the one hand it takes account of movement, which is the organic mode in which historical reality reveals itself, and does not solidify mechanically into bureaucracy; and because at the same time it takes account of that which is relatively stable and permanent, or which at least moves in an easily predictable direction, etc. This element of stability within the State is embodied in the organic development of the leading group's central nucleus, just as happens on a more limited scale within parties. The prevalence of bureaucratic centralism in the State indicates that the leading group is saturated, that it is turning into a narrow clique which tends to perpetuate its selfish privileges by controlling or even by stifling the birth of oppositional forces—even if these forces are homogeneous with the fundamental dominant interests (e.g. in the ultra-protectionist systems struggling against economic liberalism). In parties which represent socially subaltern classes, the element of stability is necessary to ensure that hegemony will be exercised not by privileged groups but by the progressive elements—organically progressive in relation to other forces which, though related and allied, are heterogeneous and wavering.

In any case, it needs to be stressed that the unhealthy manifestations of bureaucratic centralism occurred because of a lack of initiative and responsibility at the bottom, in other words because of the political immaturity of the peripheral forces, even when these were homogeneous with the hegemonic territorial group (phenomenon of Piedmontism[85] in the first decades of Italian unity). The creation of such situations can be extremely damaging and dangerous in international bodies (League of Nations).

Democratic centralism offers an elastic formula, which can be embodied in many diverse forms; it comes alive in so far as it is interpreted and continually adapted to necessity. It consists in the critical pursuit of what is identical in seeming diversity of form and on the other hand of what is distinct and even opposed in apparent uniformity, in order to organise and interconnect closely that which is similar, but in such a way that the organising and the interconnecting appear to be a practical and "inductive" necessity, experimental, and not the result of a rationalistic, deductive, abstract process—i.e. one typical of pure intellectuals (or pure asses). This continuous effort to separate out the "international"

[85] The transposition of Piedmontese institutions wholesale to the other Italian regions after the unification of the country.

and "unitary" element in national and local reality is true concrete political action, the sole activity productive of historical progress. It requires an organic unity between theory and practice, between intellectual strata and popular masses, between rulers and ruled. The formulae of unity and federation lose a great part of their significance from this point of view, whereas they retain their sting in the bureaucratic conception, where in the end there is no unity but a stagnant swamp, on the surface calm and "mute", and no federation but a "sack of potatoes",[86] i.e. a mechanical juxtaposition of single "units" without any connection between them. [1933–34: 1st version 1932.]

THE THEOREM OF FIXED PROPORTIONS[87]

This theorem can usefully be employed to clarify—and to bring out the general applicability of—many propositions concerning the science of organisations (the study of the administrative apparatus, of demographic composition, etc.) and also concerning general politics (in analyses of situations or of relations of force, in the problem of the intellectuals, etc.). Of course it must always be borne in mind that a recourse to the theory of fixed proportions has only a schematic and metaphoric value. In other words, it cannot be applied mechanically, since in human collectivities the qualitative element (or that of the technical and intellectual capacity of the individual components) is predominant, and this cannot be measured mathematically. Hence one may say that every human collectivity has its own specific *optimum* principle of fixed proportions.

The science of organisations in particular can usefully have recourse to this theorem, and this becomes apparent in the case of the army. But every form of society has its own type of army, and every type of army has its own principle of fixed proportions, which moreover also changes from one arm of the service or specialised corps to the next. There is a specific relation between privates, NCOs, subalterns, junior officers, senior officers, General

---

[86] In *The Eighteenth Brumaire of Louis Bonaparte*, Marx had written: "Each individual peasant family is almost self-sufficient; it itself directly produces the major part of its consumption and thus acquires its means of life more through exchange with nature than in intercourse with society. A smallholding, a peasant and his family; alongside them another smallholding, another peasant and another family. A few score of these make up a village, and a few score of villages make up a Department. In this way, the great mass of the French nation is formed by simple addition of homologous magnitudes, much as potatoes in a sack form a sack of potatoes." *Marx/Engels Selected Works*, Moscow 1958, Vol. I, p. 334.

[87] See p. 191.

Staff, Combined General Staff, etc. There is a relation between the various arms and corps among themselves, etc. Each change in a single part necessitates a new equilibrium with the whole, etc.

The theorem can be seen in application politically in parties, trade unions or factories. It is also possible to see how each social group has its own law of fixed proportions, which varies according to the level of its culture, independence of mind, spirit of initiative and sense of responsibility, and according to the degree of discipline of its most backward and peripheral members.

The law of fixed proportions is resumed by Pantaleoni in his *Principles of Pure Economics*:[88] "Bodies combine chemically only in fixed proportions, and any quantity of an element which is in excess of the quantity required for a combination with other elements, which are themselves present in the amounts as defined, remains free; if the quantity of an element is insufficient in relation to the quantities of the other elements present, the combination can only take place to the extent to which the quantity of the element which is present in a smaller quantity than the others suffices." One might make use of this law metaphorically to understand how a "movement" or current of opinion becomes a party—i.e. a political force which is effective from the point of view of the exercise of governmental power: precisely to the extent to which it possesses (has developed within itself) cadres at the various levels, and to the extent to which the latter have acquired certain capabilities. The historical "automatism" of certain premisses (the existence of certain objective conditions) is potentialised politically by parties and by men of ability: absence or inadequacy (quantitative and qualitative) of these neutralises the "automatism" itself (which anyway is not really automatic): the premisses exist abstractly, but the consequences are not realised because the human factor is missing. Hence parties may be said to have the task of forming capable leaders; they are the mass function which selects, develops, and multiplies the leaders which are necessary if a particular social group (which is a "fixed" quantity, since it can be established how many members there are of any social group) is to become articulated, and be transformed from turbulent chaos into an organically prepared political army. When the total vote for a particular party oscillates between apparently strange and arbitrary maximums and minimums in successive elections, whether at the same level or at different levels (for instance, in pre-Hitler

---

[88] Maffeo Pantaleoni, *Principi di economia pura*, Milan 1931.

Germany, elections for the President of the Republic, for the Reichstag, for the diets of the Länder, for the communal councils, and so on right down to the factory committees), it may be deduced that that party's cadres are inadequate both in quantity and quality, or else in quantity though not in quality (relatively), or else in quality though not in quantity. A party which wins a lot of votes in local elections, but fewer in those of greater political importance, is certainly qualitatively deficient in its central leadership: it possesses numerous, or at any rate sufficient, junior cadres, but not a General Staff adequate for that country and its position in the world, etc. [1933–34: 1st version 1932.]

NUMBER AND QUALITY IN REPRESENTATIVE SYSTEMS OF GOVERNMENT

One of the most banal commonplaces which get repeated against the elective system of forming State organs is the following: that in it numbers decide everything,[89] and that the opinions of any idiot who knows how to write (or in some countries even of an illiterate) have exactly the same weight in determining the political course of the State as the opinions of somebody who devotes his best energies to the State and the nation, etc.* But the fact is that it is not true, in any sense, that numbers decide everything, nor that the opinions of all electors are of "exactly" equal weight. Numbers, in this case too, are simply an instrumental value, giving a measure and a relation and nothing more. And what then is measured? What is measured is precisely the effectiveness, and the expansive and persuasive capacity, of the opinions of a few individuals, the active minorities, the élites, the avant-gardes, etc.—i.e. their rationality, historicity or concrete functionality. Which means it is untrue that all individual opinions have "exactly" equal weight. Ideas and opinions are not spontaneously "born" in each individual brain: they have had a centre of formation, of irradiation, of dissemination, of persuasion—a group of men, or a single individual even, which has developed them and presented them in the political form of

---

[89] See, for example, Mussolini "The war was 'revolutionary' in the sense that it liquidated—in rivers of blood—the century of democracy, the century of number, of majority, of quantity", in *Which way is the world going?*, 1922; or again, "Fascism is against democracy which levels the people down to the largest number, bringing it down to the level of the majority", in *The Doctrine of Fascism*, 1932.

* There are numerous formulations of this, some more felicitous than the one quoted—which is due to Mario de Silva, in *Critica Fascista*, 15 August 1932. But the content is always the same.

current reality. The counting of "votes" is the final ceremony of a long process, in which it is precisely those who devote their best energies to the State and the nation (when such they are) who carry the greatest weight. If this hypothetical group of worthy men, notwithstanding the boundless material power which they possess, do not have the consent of the majority, they must be judged either as inept, or as not representative of "national" interests—which cannot help being decisive in inflecting the national will in one direction rather than in another. "Unfortunately" everyone tends to confound his own "private interest"[90] with that of the nation, and hence to find it "dreadful", etc. that it should be the "law of numbers" which decides; it is better of course to become an élite by decree. Thus it is not a question of the people who "have the brains" feeling that they are being reduced to the level of the lowest illiterate, but rather one of people who think they are the ones with the brains wanting to take away from the "man in the street" even that tiniest fraction of power of decision over the course of national life which he possesses.

These banal assertions have been extended from a critique (of oligarchic rather than élitist origin)[91] of the parliamentary system of government (it is strange that it should not be criticised because the historical rationality of numerical consensus is systematically falsified by the influence of wealth) to a critique of all representative systems—even those which are not parliamentary and not fashioned according to the canons of formal democracy.[92] These assertions are even less accurate. In these other systems of government, the people's consent does not end at the moment of voting, quite the contrary. That consent is presumed to be permanently active; so much so that those who give it may be considered as "functionaries" of the State, and elections as a means of voluntary enrolment of State functionaries of a certain type—a means which in a certain sense may be related to the idea of *self-government* (though on a different level). Since elections are held on the basis not of vague, generic programmes, but of programmes of immediate, concrete work, anyone who gives his consent commits himself to do something more than the simple, juridical citizen towards their realisa-

[90] The Italian word here is "*particulare*", a term used by Guicciardini, who suggested that the best refuge from the trials of public life was one's own "*particulare*" or private interest. De Sanctis criticised this "egoism".

[91] i.e. of conservative origin (concerned to restrict political power to a traditional ruling stratum—Mosca's "political class"), rather than élitist in the strict sense of the word (élite = chosen)—i.e. meritocratic, Pareto, fascist ideology, etc.)

[92] i.e, presumably, soviets

tion—i.e. to be a vanguard of active and responsible work. The "voluntary" element in the whole undertaking could not be stimulated in any other way as far as the broader masses are concerned; and when these are not made up of amorphous citizens, but of skilled productive elements, then one can understand the importance that the demonstration of the vote may have.* [1933–34]

The proposition that society does not pose itself problems for whose solution the material preconditions do not already exist.[93] This proposition immediately raises the problem of the formation of a collective will. In order to analyse critically what the proposition means, it is necessary to study precisely how permanent collective wills are formed, and how such wills set themselves concrete short-term and long-term ends—i.e. a line of collective action. It is a question of more or less long processes of development, and rarely of sudden, "synthetic" explosions. Synthetic "explosions" do occur, but if they are looked at closely it can be seen that they are more destructive than reconstructive; they remove mechanical and external obstacles in the way of an indigenous and spontaneous development. Thus the Sicilian Vespers[94] can be taken as typical.

It would be possible to study concretely the formation of a collective historical movement, analysing it in all its molecular phases—a thing which is rarely done, since it would weigh every treatment down. Instead, currents of opinion are normally taken as already constituted around a group or a dominant personality. This is the problem which in modern times is expressed in terms of the party, or coalition of related parties: how a party is first set up, how its organisational strength and social influence are developed, etc. It requires an extremely minute, molecular process of exhaustive analysis in every detail, the documentation for which is made up of an endless quantity of books, pamphlets, review and newspaper articles, conversations and oral debates repeated countless times, and which in their gigantic aggregation represent this long labour which gives birth to a collective will with a certain degree of homogeneity—with the degree necessary and sufficient to achieve an action which is coordinated and simultaneous in the time and the geographical space in which the historical event takes place.

Importance of utopias and of confused and rationalistic ideologies

* These observations could be developed more amply and organically, stressing other differences as well between the various types of elective systems, according to changes in general social and political relations: the relation between elected and career functionaries, etc.

[93] See note 98 on p. 106.

[94] See note 102 on p. 199.

in the initial phase of the historical processes whereby collective wills are formed. Utopias, or abstract rationalism, have the same importance as old conceptions of the world which developed historically by the accumulation of successive experience. What matters is the criticism to which such an ideological complex is subjected by the first representatives of the new historical phase. This criticism makes possible a process of differentiation and change in the relative weight that the elements of the old ideologies used to possess. What was previously secondary and subordinate, or even incidental, is now taken to be primary—becomes the nucleus of a new ideological and theoretical complex. The old collective will dissolves into its contradictory elements since the subordinate ones develop socially, etc.

After the formation of the party system—an historical phase linked to the standardisation of broad masses of the population (communications, newspapers, big cities, etc.)—the molecular processes take place more swiftly than in the past, etc. [1931–32]

CONTINUITY AND TRADITION

An aspect of the question alluded to elsewhere of "Dilettantism and Discipline",[95] from the point of view of the organising centre of a grouping is that of the "continuity" which tends to create a "tradition"—understood of course in an active and not a passive sense: as continuity in continuous development, but "organic development". This problem contains in a nutshell the entire "juridical problem", i.e. the problem of assimilating the entire grouping to its most advanced fraction; it is a problem of education of the masses, of their "adaptation" in accordance with the requirements of the goal to be achieved. This is precisely the function of law in the State and in society; through "law" the State renders the ruling group "homogeneous", and tends to create a social conformism which is useful to the ruling group's line of development. The general activity of law (which is wider than purely State and governmental activity and also includes the activity involved in directing civil society, in those zones which the technicians of law call legally neutral—i.e. in morality and in custom generally) serves to understand the ethical problem better, in a concrete sense. In practice, this problem is the correspondence "spontaneously and freely accepted" between the acts and the admissions of each indivi-

[95] See Int., pp. 139–41.

dual, between the conduct of each individual and the ends which society sets itself as necessary—a correspondence which is coercive in the sphere of positive law technically understood, and is spontaneous and free (more strictly ethical) in those zones in which "coercion" is not a State affair but is effected by public opinion, moral climate, etc. The "juridical" continuity of the organised centre must be not of a Byzantine/Napoleonic type, i.e. according to a code conceived of as perpetual, but Roman/Anglo-Saxon—that is to say, a type whose essential characteristic consists in its method, which is realistic and always keeps close to concrete life in perpetual development. This organic continuity requires a good archive, well stocked and easy to use, in which all past activity can be reviewed and "criticised". The most important manifestations of this activity are not so much "organic decisions" as explicative and reasoned (educative) circulars.

There is a danger of becoming "bureaucratised", it is true; but every organic continuity presents this danger, which must be watched. The danger of discontinuity, of improvisation, is still greater. Organ: the "Bulletin", which has three principal sections: 1. directive articles; 2. decisions and circulars; 3. criticism of the past, i.e. continual reference back from the present to the past, to show the differentiations and the specifications, and to justify them critically. [1930–32]

SPONTANEITY AND CONSCIOUS LEADERSHIP

The term "spontaneity" can be variously defined, for the phenomenon to which it refers is many-sided. Meanwhile it must be stressed that "pure" spontaneity does not exist in history: it would come to the same thing as "pure" mechanicity. In the "most spontaneous" movement it is simply the case that the elements of "conscious leadership" cannot be checked, have left no reliable document. It may be said that spontaneity is therefore characteristic of the "history of the subaltern classes", and indeed of their most marginal and peripheral elements; these have not achieved any consciousness of the class "for itself", and consequently it never occurs to them that their history might have some possible importance, that there might be some value in leaving documentary evidence of it.

Hence in such movements there exist multiple elements of "conscious leadership", but no one of them is predominant or transcends the level of a given social stratum's "popular science"—

its "common sense" or traditional conception of the world.[96] This is precisely what De Man,[97] empirically, counterposes to Marxism; but he does not realise (apparently) that he is falling into the position of somebody who, after describing folklore, witchcraft, etc., and showing that these conceptions have sturdy historical roots and are tenaciously entwined in the psychology of specific popular strata, believed that he had "transcended" modern science—taking as "modern science" every little article in the popular scientific journals and periodicals. This is a real case of intellectual teratology, of which there are other examples: precisely, the admirers of folklore, who advocate its preservation; the "magicalists" connected with Maeterlinck, who believe it is necessary to take up anew the thread—snapped by violence—of alchemy and witchcraft, so that science may be put back onto a course more fertile in discoveries, etc. However, De Man does have one incidental merit: he demonstrates the need to study and develop the elements of popular psychology, historically and sociologically, actively (i.e. in order to transform them, by educating them, into a modern mentality) and descriptively as he does. But this need was at least implicit (perhaps even explicitly stated) in the doctrine of Ilitch [Lenin]—something of which De Man is entirely ignorant. The fact that every "spontaneous" movement contains rudimentary elements of conscious leadership, of discipline, is indirectly demonstrated by the fact that there exist tendencies and groups who extol spontaneity as a method. Here one must distinguish between the realm of pure "ideology" and that of practical action, between scholars who argue that spontaneity is the immanent and objective "method" of the historical process, and political adventurers who argue for it as a "political" method. With the former it is a question of a mistaken conception, whereas with the latter what is involved is an immediate and vulgar contradiction which betrays its manifest practical origin—i.e. the immediate desire to replace a given leadership by a different one. Even in the case of the scholars the error does have a practical origin, but it is not an immediate one as in the latter case. The apoliticism of the French syndicalists before the war contained both these elements: there was a theoretical error and a contradiction (there was the "Sorelian" element, and the elements of rivalry between the anarcho-syndicalist political tendency and that of the socialists). That apoliticism was still a

[96] See introduction to "The Study of Philosophy", on pp. 321–22 below. Also the essays in the section "On Education" pp. 26–43.

[97] See note 56 on p. 160.

consequence of the terrible events of 1871 in Paris: the continuation, with new methods and a brilliant theory, of the thirty years of passivity (1870–1900) of the French working class. The purely "economic" struggle was not to the distaste of the ruling class—on the contrary. The same may be said of the Catalan movement,[98] which if it "displeased" the Spanish ruling class did so only because it objectively reinforced Catalan republican separatism, producing a real republican industrial bloc against the latifundists, the petite bourgeoisie and the royal army. The Turin movement was accused simultaneously of being "spontaneist" and "voluntarist" or Bergsonian.[99] This contradictory accusation, if one analyses it, only testifies to the fact that the leadership given to the movement was both creative and correct. This leadership was not "abstract"; it neither consisted in mechanically repeating scientific or theoretical formulae, nor did it confuse politics, real action, with theoretical disquisition. It applied itself to real men, formed in specific historical relations, with specific feelings, outlooks, fragmentary conceptions of the world, etc., which were the result of "spontaneous" combinations of a given situation of material production with the "fortuitous" agglomeration within it of disparate social elements. This element of "spontaneity" was not neglected and even less despised. It was *educated*, directed, purged of extraneous contaminations; the aim was to bring it into line with modern theory[100]—but in a living and historically effective manner. The leaders themselves spoke of the "spontaneity" of the movement, and rightly so. This assertion was a stimulus, a tonic, an element of unification in depth; above all it denied that the movement was arbitrary, a cooked-up venture, and stressed its historical necessity. It gave the masses a "theoretical" consciousness of being creators of *historical* and institutional *values*, of being founders of a State. This unity between "spontaneity" and "conscious leadership" or "discipline" is precisely the real political action of the subaltern classes, in so far as this is mass politics and not merely an adventure by groups claiming to represent the masses.

At this point, a fundamental theoretical question is raised: can modern theory be in opposition to the "spontaneous" feelings of the masses? ("Spontaneous" in the sense that they are not the result of any systematic educational activity on the part of an already

---

[98] i.e. the syndicalist struggle in Barcelona between 1916 and 1923.

[99] For Trozzi's accusation, subsequently often repeated, that Gramsci and the *Ordine Nuovo* group were "Bergsonian", see note 28 on p. 343.

[100] i.e. Marxism.

conscious leading group, but have been formed through everyday experience illuminated by "common sense", i.e. by the traditional popular conception of the world—what is unimaginatively called "instinct", although it too is in fact a primitive and elementary historical acquisition.) It cannot be in opposition to them. Between the two there is a "quantitative" difference of degree, not one of quality. A reciprocal "reduction" so to speak, a passage from one to the other and vice versa, must be possible. (Recall that Immanuel Kant believed it important for his philosophical theories to agree with common sense; the same position can be found in Croce. Recall too Marx's assertion in *The Holy Family* that the political formulae of the French Revolution can be reduced to the principles of classical German philosophy.)[101] Neglecting, or worse still despising, so-called "spontaneous" movements, i.e. failing to give them a conscious leadership or to raise them to a higher plane by inserting them into politics, may often have extremely serious consequences. It is almost always the case that a "spontaneous" movement of the subaltern classes is accompanied by a reactionary movement of the right-wing of the dominant class, for concomitant reasons. An economic crisis, for instance, engenders on the one hand discontent among the subaltern classes and spontaneous mass movements, and on the other conspiracies among the reactionary groups, who take advantage of the objective weakening of the government in order to attempt *coups d'état*. Among the effective causes of the *coups* must be included the failure of the responsible groups to give any conscious leadership to the spontaneous revolts or to make them into a positive political factor. N.B. the example of the Sicilian Vespers,[102] and the arguments among historians about whether this was a spontaneous movement or one planned in advance. In my view the two elements were combined in the case of the Vespers. On the one hand, a spontaneous rising of the Sicilian people against their Provençal rulers which spread so rapidly that it gave the impression of simultaneity and hence of preconcertation; this rising was the result of an oppression which

---

[101] See chapter VI.

[102] On 31 March 1282, the population of Palermo rose against the government of Charles of Anjou. The uprising, which came to be known as the Sicilian Vespers, spread rapidly throughout the island, and the French were expelled in less than a month. The throne was subsequently given to Frederick of Aragon. The rising had been the result of a combination of popular discontent and the plans of pro-Aragonese elements among the nobility, e.g. Giovanni da Procida (1210 approx.—1282), who became chancellor of the Kingdom after the rising had succeeded.

had become intolerable throughout the national territory. On the other hand, there was the conscious element, of varying importance and effectiveness, and the success of Giovanni da Procida's plot with the Aragonese. Other examples can be drawn from all past revolutions in which several subaltern classes were present, with a hierarchy determined by economic position and internal homogeneity. The "spontaneous" movements of the broader popular strata make possible the coming to power of the most progressive subaltern class as a result of the objective weakening of the State. This is still a "progressive" example; but, in the modern world, the regressive examples are more frequent.

There exists a scholastic and academic historico-political outlook which sees as real and worthwhile only such movements of revolt as are one hundred per cent conscious, i.e. movements that are governed by plans worked out in advance to the last detail or in line with abstract theory (which comes to the same thing). But reality produces a wealth of the most bizarre combinations. It is up to the theoretician to unravel these in order to discover fresh proof of his theory, to "translate" into theoretical language the elements of historical life. It is not reality which should be expected to conform to the abstract schema. This will never happen, and hence this conception is nothing but an expression of passivity. (Leonardo was able to discern number in all the manifestations of cosmic life, even where profane eyes only saw blind chance and chaos.) [1930]

AGAINST BYZANTINISM

One may term "Byzantinism" or "scholasticism" the regressive tendency to treat so-called theoretical questions as if they had a value in themselves, independently of any specific practice. A typical example of Byzantinism were the so-called Rome Theses,[103]

[103] The "Rome Theses" were the fundamental policy document of the first years of the PCI. Passed at the Rome Congress of 20 March 1922 (the founding congress of January 1921 immediately after the split from the PSI was simply a demonstration, and a provisional settlement of organisational questions), they consisted of theses on tactics drafted by Bordiga and Terracini—it is these which are normally referred to as the "Rome Theses"—on the agrarian question by Sanna and Graziadei, and on the trade unions by Gramsci and Tasca. In the perspective of Bordiga's theses on tactics, the main danger was seen as a social-democratic resolution of the crisis of the Italian State. The phenomenon of fascism (the March on Rome was to occur within six months, and the fascist squads had been active for almost two years) was seen as an organic development of the bourgeois parliamentary régime; it was necessary to combat it, but only with the minimum of means necessary to contain it—it was not to be made the main enemy. When the Comintern considered these theses, Trotsky and Radek proposed that they

in which a kind of mathematical method was applied to each issue, as in pure economics. The problem arises of whether a theoretical truth, whose discovery corresponded to a specific practice, can be generalised and considered as universal for a historical epoch. The proof of its universality consists precisely 1. in its becoming a stimulus to know better the concrete reality of a situation that is different from that in which it was discovered (this is the principal measure of its fecundity); 2. when it has stimulated and helped this better understanding of concrete reality, in its capacity to incorporate itself in that same reality as if it were originally an expression of it. It is in this incorporation that its real universality lies, and not simply in its logical or formal coherence, or in the fact that it is a useful polemical tool for confounding the enemy. In short, the principle must always rule that ideas are not born of other ideas, philosophies of other philosophies; they are a continually renewed expression of real historical development. The unity of history (what the idealists call unity of the spirit) is not a presupposition, but a continuously developing process. Identity in concrete reality determines identity of thought, and not vice versa. It can further be deduced that every truth, even if it is universal, and even if it can be expressed by an abstract formula of a mathematical kind (for the sake of the theoreticians), owes its effectiveness to its being expressed in the language appropriate to specific concrete situations. If it cannot be expressed in such specific terms, it is a byzantine and scholastic abstraction, good only for phrasemongers to toy with. [1932]

THE COLLECTIVE WORKER

In a critical account of the post-war events, and of the constitutional (organic) attempts to escape from the prevailing state of disorder

should simply be rejected—this was prior to the congress itself. They were finally presented to the congress as a contribution to the preparation of the Fourth World Congress of the Comintern, due in December, and in this way it was intended to avoid breaking Comintern discipline. At the congress the theses were attacked by the Comintern representatives, notably Kolarov, who harshly criticised their rejection of the United Front slogan. They were defended not only by Bordiga and Terracini, but also by Gramsci, who spoke of the "peasant" character of the PSI and expressed fears that a united front would lead to the drowning of the revolutionary party in a peasant context. Kolarov's speech had a considerable effect on the delegates, and provoked the emergence of a minority opposition, led notably by Tasca. It appears that one of the main reasons for Gramsci's continued support for the Bordiga leadership at this time was his fear that if Bordiga was removed only Tasca and the Right could replace him. For all this see General Introduction. It was only at the Lyons Congress of January 1926 that the Rome Theses were finally replaced by a document of similar stature—the Lyons Theses.

and dispersal of forces, show how the movement to valorise the factory by contrast with (or rather independently of) craft organisation[104] corresponded perfectly to the analysis of how the factory system developed given in the first volume of the Critique of Political Economy.[105] An increasingly perfect division of labour objectively reduces the position of the factory worker to increasingly "analytical" movements of detail, so that the complexity of the collective work passes the comprehension of the individual worker; in the latter's consciousness, his own contribution is devalued to the point where it seems easily replaceable at any moment. At the same time, work that is concerted and well organised gives a better "social" productivity, so that the entire work-force of a factory should see itself as a "collective worker". These were the premisses of the factory movement, which aimed to render "subjective" that which is given "objectively". What does objective mean in this instance? For the individual worker, the junction between the requirements of technical development and the interests of the ruling class is "objective". But this junction, this unity between technical development and the interests of the ruling class is only a historical phase of industrial development, and must be conceived of as transitory. The nexus can be dissolved; technical requirements can be conceived in concrete terms, not merely separately from the interests of the ruling class, but in relation to the interests of the class which is as yet still subaltern. A compelling proof that such a "split" and new synthesis is historically mature is constituted by the very fact that such a process is understood by the subaltern class—which precisely for that reason is no longer subaltern, or at least is demonstrably on the way to emerging from its subordinate position. The "collective worker" understands that this is what he is, not merely in each individual factory but in the broader spheres of the national and international division of labour. It is precisely in the organisms which represent the factory as a producer of real objects and not of profit that he gives an external, political demonstration of the consciousness he has acquired. [1932]

VOLUNTARISM AND SOCIAL MASSES

In a whole series of problems—problems arising both in the reconstruction of past history and in historico-political analysis of the present—no account is taken of the following factor: that the

---

104 i.e. the factory council movement animated by *Ordine Nuovo*.

105 i.e. *Capital* (Volume I, chapters XIV and XV).

actions and organisations of "volunteers'[106] must be distinguished from the actions and organisations of homogeneous social blocs, and judged by different criteria. (Obviously, "volunteers" should be taken as meaning not the *élite* when this is an organic expression of the social mass, but rather those who have detached themselves from the mass by arbitrary individual initiative, and who often stand in opposition to that mass or are neutral with respect to it.)

This factor is especially important in the case of Italy: 1. on account of the traditional apoliticism and passivity of the great popular masses; the relative ease with which "volunteers are recruited" is a natural reaction to these phenomena; 2. on account of the social composition of Italy, one of whose features is the unhealthy quantity of rural (or rural-type) middle and petits bourgeois, who produce a large number of dissatisfied intellectuals—hence ready "volunteers" for any enterprise (even the most bizarre) which is vaguely subversive (to the Right or to the Left); 3. on account of the mass of rural wage-labourers and of *Lumpenproletariat* —called in Italy by the picturesque name of "*morti di fame*".[107] When one analyses the Italian political parties, one can see that they have always been parties of "volunteers", and in a certain sense of *déclassés*; they have never or almost never represented

---

[106] The notion that modern Italian history was the creation of "volunteers" was a typical fascist theme. On PP. p. 165, Gramsci quotes the fascist deputy Balbo as stating: "The original creations of Italian history and civilisation, from the day in which the country reawoke from its secular lethargy until today, are due to the voluntary action of the youth. The holy rabble of Garibaldi, the heroic interventionism of 1915, the Black Shirts of the Fascist Revolution have given unity and power to Italy, have welded a divided people into a nation." Gramsci comments: "The assertion that modern Italy was characterised by volunteer action is correct (commandos in the war could be added to the list), but it must be stressed that this volunteer action, despite its undeniable historical merit, has been a surrogate for popular intervention, and in this sense is a solution of compromise with the passivity of the masses of the nation. Volunteer action and passivity go together more than is thought. The solution involving volunteer action is a solution of authority, from the top down, formally legitimised by the consent, it is claimed, of the 'best' elements. But to construct a lasting history the 'best elements' are not enough; the vaster and more numerous national-popular energies are needed." And in another oblique comment on fascism, in the course of a note on various interpretations of the Risorgimento (Ris. p. 60), Gramsci refers to the fact that "an organic adhesion of the national-popular masses to the State is replaced by a selection of 'volunteers' of the 'nation' abstractly conceived. Nobody has realised that precisely the problem posed by Machiavelli when he proclaimed the necessity of replacing the untrustworthy, provisional mercenaries by national militia cannot be resolved until 'voluntarism' has been superseded by mass 'national-popular' action, since voluntarism is an intermediate, equivocal solution, as dangerous as the phenomenon of mercenaries."

[107] For the concept of "*morto di fame*" see the note entitled "Subversive", pp. 272–5 below.

homogeneous social blocs. One exception was the Cavourian historic Right, and that was what constituted its organic and permanent superiority over the so-called Action Party of Mazzini and Garibaldi.[108] The latter was the prototype for subsequent "mass" parties in Italy—which were not really mass parties at all (i.e. they did not organise homogeneous social groups), but the political equivalent of gypsy bands or nomads. Only one such analysis exists (and that imprecise and gelatinous, written solely from a "statistical-sociological" point of view); this is in Roberto Michels' *Il proletariato e la borghesia nel movimento socialista italiano*, Torino, Bocca 1908.

The position of Gottlieb[109] was precisely similar to that of the Action Party, i.e. of a gypsy or nomad kind. His interest in the trade unions was extremely superficial, and polemical in origin—not systematic, not organic and coherent, not directed towards social homogeneity but paternalistic and formalistic.

A distinction must be made between two kinds of voluntarism or Garibaldism. On the one hand there is that which theorises itself as an organic form of historico-political activity, and celebrates itself in terms which are purely and simply a transposition of the language of the individual superman to an ensemble of "supermen" (celebration of active minorities as such, etc.). On the other hand there is voluntarism or Garibaldism conceived as the initial moment of an organic period which must be prepared and developed; a period in which the organic collectivity, as a social bloc, will participate fully. "Vanguards" without armies to back them up, "commandos" without infantry or artillery, these too are transpositions from the language of rhetorical heroism—though vanguard and commandos as specialised functions within complex and regular organisms are quite another thing. The same distinction can be made between the notion of intellectual *élites* separated from the masses, and that of intellectuals who are conscious of being linked organically to a national-popular mass. In reality, one has to struggle against the above-mentioned degenerations, the false heroisms and pseudo-aristocracies, and stimulate the formation of

---

[108] For the Cavourian Right and the Action Party, see "The Problem of Political Leadership in the Formation and Development of the Nation and the Modern State in Italy", on pp. 55–90 above.

[109] Literally translated, Gottlieb = Amadeo [Bordiga]. For Gramsci's analysis of Bordiga, see General Introduction. The rather odd designation of Bordiga as "gypsy" can be taken to mean that in Gramsci's view Bordiga's conception of the party involved no organic relationship with the proletariat, but made it into a kind of "volunteer" organisation, unattached to any class.

homogeneous, compact social blocs, which will give birth to their own intellectuals, their own commandos, their own vanguard—who in turn will react upon those blocs in order to develop them, and not merely so as to perpetuate their gypsy domination. Romanticism's Paris *bohème* too was intellectually at the root of many contemporary modes of thought which appear nonetheless to deride those *bohémiens*. [1933–34]

2
STATE AND CIVIL SOCIETY

INTRODUCTION

The notes grouped in this section include some of the most crucial to an understanding of Gramsci's political thought. They deal with the nature of fascism, the revolutionary strategy appropriate in the West (or in the epoch in which Gramsci is writing—see below), and the theory of the State. They can perhaps best be approached via the three related concepts of Caesarism, war of position, and civil society.

"Caesarism", for Gramsci, is a concept which does not merely refer to fascism, but can have a wider application—e.g. to the British National Government of 1931, etc.; it is thus not identical to Marx's concept of "Bonapartism", although it is clearly related to it. "Caesarism" represents a compromise between two "fundamental" social forces, but 1. "The problem is to see whether in the dialectic 'revolution/restoration' it is revolution or restoration which predominates", and 2. "It would be an error of method to believe that in Caesarism . . . the entire new historical phenomenon is due to the equilibrium of the 'fundamental' forces. It is also necessary to see the interplay of relations between the principal groups . . . of the fundamental classes and the auxiliary forces directed by, or subjected to, their hegemonic influence." Thus, in the specific case of the fascist régime in Italy, the problem, in Gramsci's eyes, is 1. to analyse the "passive revolution" which fascism perhaps represents, and 2. to analyse the specificity of the social forces which produced it—i.e. rejecting absolutely the crude equation fascism = capitalism.

In "The Concept of 'Passive Revolution' " (pp. 106–14), Gramsci tentatively related "passive revolution" to "war of position". The difficulty of this latter concept is that Gramsci uses it in two partially conflicting senses. Sometimes it is the form of political struggle which alone is possible in periods of relatively stable equilibrium between the fundamental classes, i.e. when frontal attack, or war of manoeuvre, is impossible. It is in such periods that Gramsci poses the question "does there exist an absolute identity between war of position and passive revolution? Or at least does there exist, or can there be conceived, an entire historical period in which the two concepts must be considered identical—until the point at which the war of position again becomes a war of manœuvre?" Here, clearly, war of position will give way to war of manœuvre at a certain point in the historical development, and then it will once again be possible to carry out "frontal attacks" on the State. However, in "Political Struggle and Military War" (pp. 229–38), war of position is related to the West, where there is a "proper relation between State and civil society", unlike the East (Russia), where war of manœuvre was appropriate. The two conceptions of "war of position" are only reconciled in one passage, and that with considerable qualifications, where Gramsci suggests that in the West civil society resists, i.e. must be conquered, before the frontal assault on the State. This notion can of course be related to the thesis put forward in "The Problem of Political Leadership . . ." above, where Gramsci says that "A social group can, and indeed must, already exercise 'leadership' [i.e. be hegemonic] before winning governmental power (this indeed is one of the principal conditions for the winning of such power)".

Clearly this thesis is open to reformist interpretations, involving an under-estimate of the problem of the State in revolutionary strategy. But there is little justification for imputing any such illusion to Gramsci himself. The fact that, more than any other great revolutionary Marxist thinker, he concerned himself with the sphere of "civil society" and of "hegemony", in his prison writings, cannot be taken to indicate a neglect of the moment of political society, of force, of domination. On the contrary, his entire record shows that this was not the case, and that his constant preoccupation was to avoid any undialectical separation of "the ethical-political aspect of politics or theory of hegemony and consent" from "the aspect of force and economics". What is, however, true is that Gramsci did not succeed in finding a single, wholly satisfactory conception of "civil society" or the State. This is not the place to attempt a discussion of his theory of the State. (Those interested should see, in particular, the important exchange between Norberto Bobbio and Jacques Texier in *Gramsci e la cultura contemporanea*, Editori Riuniti, 1969.) But the diversity of his attempts to formulate his position must be briefly indicated.

In the passage referred to above, civil society resists *before* the frontal assault on the State. Yet, in another of the notes grouped under the title "Political Struggle and Military War", Gramsci describes the State in the West as "an outer ditch, behind which there stand a powerful system of fortresses and earthworks"—i.e. in precisely the opposite way. The State is elsewhere defined as "political society + civil society", and elsewhere again as a balance between political society and civil society. In yet another passage, Gramsci stresses that "in concrete reality, civil society and State are one and the same".

To these variations in Gramsci's conception of the State there correspond analogous variations in his conception of civil society. (See too notes 4, 5 and 49 on pp. 55, 55 and 80 respectively, and note 71 on p. 170.) On PP, p. 164, Gramsci writes: "A distinction must be made between civil society as understood by Hegel, and as often used in these notes (i.e. in the sense of political and cultural hegemony of a social group over the entire society, as ethical content of the State), and on the other hand civil society in the sense in which it is understood by catholics, for whom civil society is instead political society of the State, in contrast with the society of family and that of the Church." In this "Hegelian" usage, State/political society is contrasted to civil society as moments of the superstructure. Yet in Hegel's Philosophy of Right, civil society includes economic relations—and it is in this sense that the term is used by Marx, for example in *The Jewish Question*. And Gramsci too at times adopts this usage, e.g. on MS, pp. 266–67: "Every social form has its *homo oeconomicus*, i.e. its own economic activity. To maintain that the concept of *homo oeconomicus* has no scientific value is merely a way of maintaining that the economic structure and the economic activity appropriate to it are radically changed, in other words that the economic structure is so changed that the mode of economic behaviour must necessarily change too in order to become appropriate to the new structure. But precisely here lies the disagreement, and a disagreement which is not so much objective and scientific as political. What, anyway, would a scientific recognition that the economic structure has changed, and that economic behaviour must change to conform to the new structure, mean? It would have the significance of a political stimulus, nothing more. Between the economic structure and the State with its legislation and its coercion stands civil society, and the latter must be radically transformed, in a concrete sense and not simply on the statute-book or in scientific books. The State is the instrument for conforming civil society to the economic structure, but it is necessary for the State to 'be willing' to do this; i.e. for the representatives of the change that has taken place in the economic structure to be in control of the State. To expect that civil society will conform to the new structure as a result of propaganda and persuasion, or that the old *homo oeconomicus* will disappear without being buried with all the honours it deserves, is a new form of economic rhetoric, a new form of empty and inconclusive economic moralism." Here civil society is in effect equated with "the mode of economic behaviour".

STATE AND CIVIL SOCIETY

OBSERVATIONS ON CERTAIN ASPECTS OF THE STRUCTURE OF POLITICAL PARTIES IN PERIODS OF ORGANIC CRISIS

At a certain point in their historical lives, social classes become detached from their traditional parties. In other words, the traditional parties in that particular organisational form, with the particular men who constitute, represent, and lead them, are no longer recognised by their class (or fraction of a class) as its expression. When such crises occur, the immediate situation becomes delicate and dangerous, because the field is open for violent solutions, for the activities of unknown forces, represented by charismatic "men of destiny".

These situations of conflict between "represented and representatives" reverberate out from the terrain of the parties (the party organisations properly speaking, the parliamentary-electoral field, newspaper organisation) throughout the State organism, reinforcing the relative power of the bureaucracy (civil and military), of high finance, of the Church, and generally of all bodies relatively independent of the fluctuations of public opinion. How are they created in the first place? In every country the process is different, although the content is the same. And the content is the crisis of the ruling class's hegemony, which occurs either because the ruling class has failed in some major political undertaking for which it has requested, or forcibly extracted, the consent of the broad masses (war, for example), or because huge masses (especially of peasants and petit-bourgeois intellectuals) have passed suddenly from a state of political passivity to a certain activity, and put forward demands which taken together, albeit not organically formulated, add up to a revolution. A "crisis of authority"[1] is spoken of: this is precisely the crisis of hegemony, or general crisis of the State.

The crisis creates situations which are dangerous in the short run, since the various strata of the population are not all capable of orienting themselves equally swiftly, or of reorganizing with the same rhythm. The traditional ruling class, which has numerous trained cadres, changes men and programmes and, with greater speed than is achieved by the subordinate classes, reabsorbs the control that was slipping from its grasp. Perhaps it may make sacrifices, and expose itself to an uncertain future by demagogic promises; but it retains power, reinforces it for the time being, and

---

[1] See " 'Wave of Materialism' and 'Crisis of Authority' ", on pp. 275–6.

uses it to crush its adversary and disperse his leading cadres, who cannot be very numerous or highly trained. The passage of the troops of many different parties under the banner of a single party, which better represents and resumes the needs of the entire class, is an organic and normal phenomenon, even if its rhythm is very swift—indeed almost like lightning in comparison with periods of calm. It represents the fusion of an entire social class under a single leadership, which alone is held to be capable of solving an overriding problem of its existence and of fending off a mortal danger. When the crisis does not find this organic solution, but that of the charismatic leader, it means that a static equilibrium exists (whose factors may be disparate, but in which the decisive one is the immaturity of the progressive forces); it means that no group, neither the conservatives nor the progressives, has the strength for victory, and that even the conservative group needs a master. [1932–1934: 1st version 1930–1932.] See *The Eighteenth Brumaire of Louis Bonaparte*. This order of phenomena is connected to one of the most important questions concerning the political party—i.e. the party's capacity to react against force of habit, against the tendency to become mummified and anachronistic. Parties come into existence, and constitute themselves as organisations, in order to influence the situation at moments which are historically vital for their class; but they are not always capable of adapting themselves to new tasks and to new epochs, nor of evolving *pari passu* with the overall relations of force (and hence the relative position of their class) in the country in question, or in the international field. In analysing the development of parties, it is necessary to distinguish: their social group; their mass membership; their bureaucracy and General Staff. The bureaucracy is the most dangerously hidebound and conservative force; if it ends up by constituting a compact body, which stands on its own and feels itself independent of the mass of members, the party ends up by becoming anachronist and at moments of acute crisis it is voided of its social content and left as though suspended in mid-air. One can see what has happened to a number of German parties as a result of the expansion of Hitlerism. French parties are a rich field for such research: they are all mummified and anachronistic—historico-political documents of the various phases of past French history, whose outdated terminology they continue to repeat; their crisis could become even more catastrophic than that of the German parties. [1932–34: 1st version 1930–32.]

In examining such phenomena people usually neglect to give due importance to the bureaucratic element, both civil and military; furthermore they forget that not only actual military and bureaucratic elements, but also the social strata from which, in the particular national structure, the bureaucracy is traditionally recruited, must be included in such analyses. A political movement can be of a military character even if the army as such does not participate in it openly; a government can be of a military character even if the army as such does not take part in it. In certain situations it may happen that it suits better not to "reveal" the army, not to have it cross the bounds of what is constitutional, not to introduce politics into the ranks, as the saying goes—so that the homogeneity between officers and other ranks is maintained, on a terrain of apparent neutrality and superiority to the factions; yet it is nonetheless the army, that is to say the General Staff and the officer corps, which determines the new situation and dominates it. However, it is not true that armies are constitutionally barred from making politics; the army's duty is precisely to defend the Constitution—in other words the legal form of the State together with its related institutions. Hence so-called neutrality only means support for the reactionary side; but in such situations, the question has to be posed in such terms to prevent the unrest in the country being reproduced within the army, and the determining power of the General Staff thus evaporating through the disintegration of its military instrument. Obviously, none of these observations is absolute; at various moments of history and in various countries they have widely differing significance.

The first problem to be studied is the following: does there exist, in a given country, a widespread social stratum in whose economic life and political self-assertion (effective participation in power, even though indirectly, by "blackmail") the bureaucratic career, either civil or military, is a very important element? In modern Europe this stratum can be identified in the medium and small rural bourgeoisie, which is more or less numerous from one country to another—depending on the development of industrial strength on the one hand, and of agrarian reform on the other. Of course the bureaucratic career (civil and military) is not the monopoly of this social stratum; however, it is particularly well suited to the social function which this stratum carries out, and to the psychological tendencies which such a function produces or encourages. These two elements impart to the entire social stratum a certain homogeneity and energy in its aims—and hence a political value, and an often decisive function within the entire social organism. The members of this stratum are accustomed to direct command over nuclei of men, however tiny, and to commanding "politically", not "economically". In other words, their art of command implies no aptitude for ordering "things", for ordering "men and things" into an organic whole, as occurs in industrial production—since this stratum has no economic functions in the modern sense of the word. It has an income, because legally it is the owner of a part of the national soil, and its function consists in opposing "politically" the attempts of the peasant farmer to ameliorate his existence—since any improvement in the relative position of the peasant would be catastrophic for its social position. The chronic poverty and prolonged labour of the peasant, with the degradation these bring, are a primordial necessity for it. This is the explanation for the immense energy it shows in resisting and counterattacking whenever there is the least attempt at autonomous organisation of peasant labour, or any peasant cultural movement which leaves the bounds of official religion. This social stratum finds its limits, and the reasons for its ultimate weakness, in its territorial dispersal and in the "non-homogeneity" which is intimately connected to this dispersal. This explains some of its other characteristics too: its volubility, the multiplicity of ideological systems it follows, even the bizarre nature of the ideologies it sometimes follows. Its will is directed towards a specific end—but it is retarded, and usually requires a lengthy process before it can become politically and organisationally centralised. This process accelerates when the specific "will" of this stratum coincides with the will and the immediate interests of the ruling class; not only that, but its "military strength" then at once reveals itself, so that sometimes, when organised, it lays down the law to the ruling class, at least as far as the "form" of solution is concerned, if not the content. The same laws can be seen functioning here as have been observed in relations between town and countryside in the case of the subordinate classes.[2] Power in the towns automatically becomes power in the countryside. But the absence of economic margins and the normally heavier repression exercised from the top downwards in the countryside cause conflicts there immediately to assume an acute and "personal" form, so that counterattacks have to be more rapid and determined. The stratum under consideration understands and sees that the origin of its troubles is in the towns, in urban power; it therefore understands that it "must" dictate a

[2] See "The City-Countryside Relationship" on pp. 90–102 above.

solution to the urban ruling classes, so that the principal hot-bed will be extinguished—even if this does not immediately suit the urban ruling classes themselves, either because it is too costly, or because it is dangerous in the long term (these classes see longer cycles of development, in which it is possible to manoeuvre, instead of simply following "material" interests). It is in that sense, rather than in an absolute one, that the function of this stratum should be seen as directive;[3] all the same, it is no light matter.* It must be noted how this "military" character of the social group in question—traditionally a spontaneous reaction to certain specific conditions of its existence—is now consciously cultivated and organically formed in anticipation. To this conscious process belong the systematic efforts to create and reinforce various associations of reservists and ex-combatants from the various corps and branches of the services, especially of officers. These associations are linked to the respective General Staffs, and can be mobilised when required, without the need to mobilise the conscript army. The latter can thus preserve its character of a reserve force—forewarned, reinforced, and immunised from the political gangrene by these "private" forces which cannot fail to influence its morale, sustaining and stiffening it. It could be said that the result is a movement of the "cossack" type—with its formations ranged not along the frontiers of nationality, as was the case with the Tsarist cossacks, but along the "frontiers" of the social class.

In a whole series of countries, therefore, military influence in national life means not only the influence and weight of the military in the technical sense, but the influence and weight of the social

---

[3] See note 5 on p. 55. Gramsci's argument here is that the North Italian capitalists might have preferred to continue with Giolitti's strategy of alliance with the reformist working-class leaders after 1920, but that they were "led" by their landlord allies to switch to a policy of total repression of the organized working class. (It is true that "agrarian fascism" did precede urban repression.) "Absolute" hegemony within the ruling-class bloc, however, remained of course with the urban bourgeoisie.

* A reflection of this stratum can be seen in the ideological activity of the conservative intellectuals of the Right. Gaetano Mosca's book *Teorica dei governi e governo parlamentare* (second edition 1925, first edition 1883) is typical in this respect;[4] even in 1883 Mosca was terrified at the possibility of a contact between the towns and the countryside. Mosca, because of his defensive position (of counterattack), understood the political technique of the subaltern classes better in 1883 than the representatives of those same classes, even in the towns, understood it themselves even several decades later.

[4] Mosca (1858–1941) was together with Pareto and Michels an originator of the sociological theory of "*élites*". His basic concept was that of the "political class", and his main object of attack was the Marxist theory of class struggle and concept of "ruling class". (See NM. p. 140, etc.)

stratum from which the latter (especially the junior officers) mostly derives its origin. This series of observations is indispensable for any really profound analysis of the specific political form usually termed Caesarism or Bonapartism—to distinguish it from other forms in which the technical military element as such predominates, in conformations perhaps still more visible and exclusive.

Spain and Greece offer two typical examples, with both similar and dissimilar characteristics. In Spain it is necessary to take certain peculiarities into account: the size of the national territory, and the low density of the peasant population. Between the latifundist aristocrat and the peasant there does not exist a numerous rural bourgeoisie; hence, minor importance of the junior officer corps as a force in itself. (On the other hand, a certain oppositional importance was possessed by the officers of the technical corps—artillery and engineers; these, of urban bourgeois origin, opposed the generals and attempted to have a policy of their own.) Hence military governments in Spain are governments of "great" generals. Passivity of the peasant masses, as citizens and as soldiers. If political disintegration occurs in the army, it does so in a vertical rather than a horizontal sense, through rivalries between cliques at the top: the rank and file splits up behind the various competing leaders. Military government is a parenthesis between two constitutional governments. The military are the permanent reserves of order and conservation; they are a political force which comes into action "publicly" when "legality" is in danger. The course of events is similar in Greece, with the difference that Greek territory is scattered over a whole system of islands, and that a part of its more energetic and active population is always at sea, which makes military intrigue and conspiracy easier. The peasantry is passive in Greece as in Spain; but in the context of the total population—the most energetic and active Greeks being sailors, and almost always far from the centre of their political life—the general passivity must be analysed differently in each case, nor can the solution to the problem be the same in both countries. When the members of a deposed government were shot in Greece some years ago,[5] this was probably to be explained as an outburst of rage on

[5] In 1920, Greece was torn between two ruling class factions. On the one hand the supporters of the deposed King Constantine, who leaned towards Germany. On the other the "liberals" headed by Venizelos, supported by the British. After several alternations in power, an attempt was made to assassinate Venizelos—who was Prime Minister at the time—in August 1920, and its failure was followed by savage reprisals. Among those massacred was the royalist ex-minister Dragoumis.

the part of the energetic and active element referred to above, with the intention of imparting a bloody lesson. The most important observation to be made is that neither in Greece nor in Spain has the experience of military government created a permanent, and formally organic, political and social ideology—as does on the other hand occur in those countries which are, so to speak, potentially Bonapartist. The general historical conditions of the two types are the same: an equilibrium of the conflicting urban classes, which obstructs the mechanism of "normal" democracy—i.e. parliamentarism. But the influence of the countryside in this equilibrium is diverse in the two cases. In countries like Spain, the total passivity of the countryside enables the generals of the landowning aristocracy to utilise the army politically to restabilise the threatened equilibrium—in other words the supremacy of the ruling classes. In other countries the countryside is not passive, but the peasant movement is not coordinated politically with the urban movement: here the army has to remain neutral (up to a certain point, of course), since otherwise it might split horizontally; instead the bureacratic military class comes into action. This class, by military means, stifles the (more immediately dangerous) movement in the countryside. In this struggle, it finds a certain political and ideological unification; it finds allies in the urban middle classes (middle in the Italian sense)[6]—reinforced by students of rural origin now living in the towns; and it imposes its political methods on the upper classes, which are compelled to make numerous concessions to it, and to allow some legislation favourable

[6] On NM. pp. 148–49, Gramsci writes: "The meaning of the expression 'middle class' changes from country to country. . . . The term came from English social development. It seems that in England the bourgeoisie was never conceived of as an integral part of the people, but always as an entity separate from the latter: it thus came to pass, in English history, that instead of the bourgeoisie leading the people and winning the latter's support to abolish feudal privileges, the nobility (or a fraction of it) formed the national-popular bloc first against the Crown and later against the industrial bourgeoisie. English tradition of a popular "Toryism" (Disraeli, etc.). After the great liberal reforms, which brought the State into conformity with the interests and needs of the middle class, the two basic parties of English political life were differentiated on internal questions regarding the same class; the nobility increasingly acquired the specific character of a "bourgeois aristocracy" tied to certain functions of civil society and of political society (the State)—concerning tradition, the education of the ruling stratum, the preservation of a particular mentality which protects the system from sudden upheavals, etc., the consolidation of the imperial structure, etc. . . . In Italy, where the feudal aristocracy was destroyed by the mediaeval Communes (physically destroyed in the civil wars, except in Southern Italy and Sicily), since the traditional 'high' class is missing, the term 'middle' has gone down a rung. 'Negatively,' middle class means non-popular, i.e. those not workers or peasants; positively, it means the intellectual strata, the professional strata, the public employees."

to its interests. In short, continuing to maintain itself under arms amidst the general disarmament, and brandishing the danger of a civil war between its own troops and the regular, conscripted army if the ruling class shows too great an itch for resistance, it succeeds in permeating the State with its interests, up to a certain point, and in replacing a part of the leading personnel. These observations must not be conceived of as rigid schemata, but merely as practical criteria of historical and political interpretation. In concrete analyses of real events, the historical forms are individualised and can almost be called "unique". Caesar represents a very different combination of real circumstances from that represented by Napoleon I, as does Primo de Rivera from that of Živkovič, etc.[7] [1933–34: 1st version 1930–32]

In analysing the third level or moment of the system of relations of force which exists in a given situation,[8] one may usefully have recourse to the concept which in military science is called the "strategic conjuncture"—or rather, more precisely, the level of strategic preparation of the theatre of struggle. One of the principal factors of this "strategic conjuncture" consists in the qualitative condition of the leading personnel, and of what may be called the "front-line" (and assault) forces. The level of strategic preparation can give the victory to forces which are "apparently" (i.e. quantitatively) inferior to those of the enemy. It could be said that strategic preparation tends to reduce to zero the so-called "imponderable factors"—in other words, the immediate, unpremeditated reactions at a given moment of the traditionally inert and passive forces. Among the factors involved in the preparation of a favourable strategic conjuncture, there must precisely be included those already studied in our earlier observations on the existence and organisation of a military social stratum, side by side with the national army in the technical sense.*

---

[7] Primo de Rivera (1870–1930) was dictator of Spain 1923–30, with the support of the monarchy. Petar Živkovič (1879–1947) was Yugoslav prime minister 1929–32, and the instrument of King Alexander's dictatorial rule during those years.

[8] See "Analysis of Situations" above, pp. 175–185.

* In connection with the "military stratum", what T. Tittoni writes in *Ricordi personali di politica interna* (Nuova Antologia, 1–16 April 1929) is interesting. Tittoni recounts how he meditated on the fact that, in order to assemble the forces of order required to confront disturbances which had broken out in one place, it was necessary to plunder other regions. During the Red Week of June 1914, in order to repress the troubles in Ancona, Ravenna was plundered in this way; and subsequently the Prefect of Ravenna, deprived of his forces of order, was obliged to shut himself up in the Prefecture, abandoning the city to the rebels. "Several times I wondered what the government could have done if a

Further points could be developed out of the following extract from the speech which General Gazzera, Minister of War, delivered in the Senate on 19 May 1932 (see *Corriere della Sera*, 20 May): "The disciplinary régime obtaining in our army thanks to Fascism, today sets a guiding norm valid for the entire nation. Other armies have had, and still retain, a formal and rigid discipline. We keep the principle constantly before us that the army is made for war, and that it is for war that it must prepare; peacetime discipline must be the same as wartime discipline, and it is in peacetime that the latter must find its spiritual foundations. Our discipline is based on a spirit of cohesion between leaders and followers which is a spontaneous product of the system adopted. This system resisted magnificently throughout a long and very hard war until the final victory; it is the merit of the Fascist régime to have extended to the entire Italian people so distinguished a disciplinary tradition. It is on individual discipline that the outcome of strategic conceptions and of tactical operations depends. War has taught us many things, among them that there is a deep gulf between peacetime preparation and wartime reality. It is certain that, whatever preparations may have been made, the initial operations of a campaign place the belligerents before new problems, which produce surprises on both sides. It should not for that reason be concluded that it is useless to have any *a priori* conceptions, and that no lessons can be derived from past wars. A theory of war can in fact be extracted from them, a theory which must be understood through intellectual discipline—understood as a means for promoting modes of reasoning which are not discordant, and uniformity of language such as will enable all to understand and make themselves understood. If, on occasions, theoretical unity has threatened to degenerate into schematism, there has at once been a prompt reaction, enforcing a rapid renovation of tactics—also made necessary by technical advances. Such a system of rules is therefore not static and traditional, as some people think. Tradition is considered only as a force, and the rules are constantly in the process of revision —not simply for the sake of change, but in order to fit them to reality." (An example of "preparation of the strategic conjuncture" is to be found in Churchill's *Memoirs*, where he speaks of the battle of Jutland.) [1933–34: 1st version 1932]

---

movement of revolt had broken out simultaneously all over the peninsula." Tittoni proposed to the government that it should enrol ex-combatants under the command of retired officers as "public order volunteers". His project seemed to merit consideration, but it was not followed up.

CAESARISM[9]

Caesar, Napoleon I, Napoleon III, Cromwell, etc. Compile a catalogue of the historical events which have culminated in a great "heroic" personality.

Caesarism can be said to express a situation in which the forces in conflict balance each other in a catastrophic manner; that is to say, they balance each other in such a way that a continuation of the conflict can only terminate in their reciprocal destruction. When the progressive force A struggles with the reactionary force B, not only may A defeat B or B defeat A, but it may happen that neither A nor B defeats the other—that they bleed each other mutually and then a third force C intervenes from outside, subjugating what is left of both A and B. In Italy, after the death of Lorenzo il Magnifico, this is precisely what occurred.[10]

But Caesarism—although it always expresses the particular solution in which a great personality is entrusted with the task of "arbitration" over a historico-political situation characterised by an equilibrium of forces heading towards catastrophe—does not in all cases have the same historical significance. There can be both progressive and reactionary forms of Caesarism; the exact significance of each form can, in the last analysis, be reconstructed only through concrete history, and not by means of any sociological rule of thumb. Caesarism is progressive when its intervention helps the progressive force to triumph, albeit with its victory tempered by certain compromises and limitations. It is reactionary when its intervention helps the reactionary force to triumph—in this case too with certain compromises and limitations, which have, however, a different value, extent, and significance than in the former. Caesar and Napoleon I are examples of progressive Caesarism. Napoleon III and Bismarck of reactionary Caesarism.

The problem is to see whether in the dialectic "revolution/restoration" it is revolution or restoration which predominates; for it is certain that in the movement of history there is never any

---

[9] As is clear from another note (PP, p. 189) this term was suggested to Gramsci by the analogy commonly drawn in fascist Italy between Caesar and Mussolini. Gramsci pours scorn on the "theory of Caesarism", on the idea that Caesar "transformed Rome from a city-state into the capital of the Empire"—and by implication on the idea that Mussolini had effected a similar transformation in the status of modern Italy.

[10] The death of Lorenzo in 1492 marked the end of the internal balance of power between the Italian states, and the beginning of the period of foreign domination which was to last until the Risorgimento.

turning back, and that restorations *in toto* do not exist. Besides, Caesarism is a polemical-ideological formula, and not a canon of historical interpretation. A Caesarist solution can exist even without a Caesar, without any great, "heroic" and representative personality. The parliamentary system has also provided a mechanism for such compromise solutions. The "Labour" governments of MacDonald were to a certain degree solutions of this kind; and the degree of Caesarism increased when the government was formed which had MacDonald as its head and a Conservative majority.[11] Similarly in Italy from October 1922 until the defection of the "Popolari", and then by stages until 3 January 1925, and then until 8 November 1926,[12] there was a politico-historical movement in which various gradations of Caesarism succeeded each other, culminating in a more pure and permanent form—though even this was not static or immobile. Every coalition government is a first stage of Caesarism, which either may or may not develop to more significant stages (the common opinion of course is that coalition governments, on the contrary, are the most "solid bulwark" against Caesarism). In the modern world, with its great economic-trade-union and party-political coalitions, the mechanism of the Caesarist phenomenon is very different from what it was up to the time of Napoleon III. In the period up to Napoleon III, the regular military forces or soldiers of the line were a decisive element in the advent of Caesarism, and this came about through quite precise *coups d'état*, through military actions, etc. In the modern world trade-union and political forces, with the limitless financial means which may be at the disposal of small groups of citizens, complicate the problem. The functionaries of the parties and economic unions can be corrupted or terrorised, without any need for military action in the grand style—of the Caesar or 18 Brumaire type. The same situation recurs in this field as was examined in connection with the Jacobin/Forty-eightist formula of the so-called "Permanent Revolution".[13] Modern political tech-

---

[11] i.e. the formation of the National Government after MacDonald's abandonment of the Labour Party in 1931.

[12] October 1922 was the date of the March on Rome. The Popular Party (see note 14 on p. 62 above) at first supported the fascists in parliament and joined the government. In the summer of 1923, however, it split on the issue of policy towards the fascists, and in the elections of January 1924 it presented its own list of candidates. After the elections it refused to join a common front of opposition parties. On 3 January 1925, the fascist government suppressed freedom of the press. On 8 November 1926 the opposition parties were formally dissolved, and non-fascist deputies were declared to be stripped of their mandates—Gramsci among them (he was arrested on the same day).

[13] See note 49 on p. 80.

nique became totally transformed after Forty-eight; after the expansion of parliamentarism and of the associative systems of union and party, and the growth in the formation of vast State and "private" bureaucracies (i.e. politico-private, belonging to parties and trade unions); and after the transformations which took place in the organisation of the forces of order in the wide sense—i.e. not only the public service designed for the repression of crime, but the totality of forces organised by the State and by private individuals to safeguard the political and economic domination of the ruling classes. In this sense, entire "political" parties and other organisations—economic or otherwise—must be considered as organs of political order, of an investigational and preventive character. The generic schema of forces A and B in conflict with catastrophic prospects—i.e. with the prospect that neither A nor B will be victorious, in the struggle to constitute (or reconstitute) an organic equilibrium, from which Caesarism is born (can be born)—is precisely a generic hypothesis, a sociological schema (convenient for the art of politics). It is possible to render the hypothesis ever more concrete, to carry it to an ever greater degree of approximation to concrete historical reality, and this can be achieved by defining certain fundamental elements.

Thus, in speaking of A and B, it has merely been asserted that they are respectively a generically progressive, and a generically reactionary, force. But one might specify the type of progressive and reactionary force involved, and so obtain closer approximations. In the case of Caesar and of Napoleon I, it can be said that A and B, though distinct and in conflict, were nevertheless not such as to be "absolutely" incapable of arriving, after a molecular process, at a reciprocal fusion and assimilation. And this was what in fact happened, at least to a certain degree (sufficient, however, for the historico-political objectives in question—i.e. the halting of the fundamental organic struggle, and hence the transcendence of the catastrophic phase). This is one element of closer approximation. Another such element is the following: the catastrophic phase may be brought about by a "momentary" political deficiency of the traditional dominant force, and not by any necessarily insuperable organic deficiency. This was true in the case of Napoleon III. The dominant force in France from 1815 up to 1848 had split politically (factiously) into four camps: legitimists, Orleanists, Bonapartists, Jacobin-republicans. The internal faction struggle was such as to make possible the advance of the rival force B (progressive) in a precocious form; however, the existing social form had not yet exhausted its possibilities for development, as subsequent history abundantly demonstrated. Napoleon III represented (in his own manner, as fitted the stature of the man, which was not great) these latent and immanent possibilities: his Caesarism therefore has a particular coloration. The Caesarism of Caesar and Napoleon I was, so to speak, of a quantitative/qualitative character; in other words it represented the historical phase of passage from one type of State to another type—a passage in which the innovations were so numerous, and of such a nature, that they represented a complete revolution. The Caesarism of Napoleon III was merely, and in a limited fashion, quantitative; there was no passage from one type of State to another, but only "evolution" of the same type along unbroken lines.

In the modern world, Caesarist phenomena are quite different, both from those of the progressive Caesar/Napoleon I type, and from those of the Napoleon III type—although they tend towards the latter. In the modern world, the equilibrium with catastrophic prospects occurs not between forces which could in the last analysis fuse and unite—albeit after a wearying and bloody process—but between forces whose opposition is historically incurable and indeed becomes especially acute with the advent of Caesarist forms. However, in the modern world Caesarism also has a certain margin—larger or smaller, depending on the country and its relative weight in the global context. For a social form "always" has marginal possibilities for further development and organisational improvement, and in particular can count on the relative weakness of the rival progressive force as a result of its specific character and way of life. It is necessary for the dominant social form to preserve this weakness: this is why it has been asserted that modern Caesarism is more a police than a military system. [1933–34: 1st version 1932]

It would be an error of method (an aspect of sociological mechanicism) to believe that in Caesarism—whether progressive, reactionary, or of an intermediate and episodic character—the entire new historical phenomenon is due to the equilibrium of the "fundamental" forces. It is also necessary to see the interplay of relations between the principal groups (of various kinds, socio-economic and technical-economic) of the fundamental classes and the auxiliary forces directed by, or subjected to, their hegemonic influence. Thus it would be impossible to understand the *coup d'état* of 2 December[14]

---

[14] i.e. the *coup d'état* whereby Louis Napoleon came to power.

without studying the function of the French military groups and peasantry.

A very important historical episode from this point of view is the so-called Dreyfus affair in France. This too belongs to the present series of observations, not because it led to "Caesarism", indeed precisely for the opposite reason: because it prevented the advent of a Caesarism in gestation, of a clearly reactionary nature. Nevertheless, the Dreyfus movement is characteristic, since it was a case in which elements of the dominant social bloc itself thwarted the Caesarism of the most reactionary part of that same bloc. And they did so by relying for support not on the peasantry and the countryside, but on the subordinate strata in the towns under the leadership of reformist socialists (though they did in fact draw support from the most advanced part of the peasantry as well). There are other modern historico-political movements of the Dreyfus type to be found, which are certainly not revolutions, but which are not entirely reactionary either—at least in the sense that they shatter stifling and ossified State structures in the dominant camp as well, and introduce into national life and social activity a different and more numerous personnel.[15] These movements too can have a relatively "progressive" content, in so far as they indicate that there were effective forces latent in the old society which the old leaders did not know how to exploit—perhaps even "marginal forces". However, such forces cannot be absolutely progressive, in that they are not "epochal". They are rendered historically effective by their adversary's inability to construct, not by an inherent force of their own. Hence they are linked to a particular situation of equilibrium between the conflicting forces—both incapable in their respective camps of giving autonomous expression to a will for reconstruction. [1933]

THE FABLE OF THE BEAVER

(The beaver, pursued by trappers who want his testicles from which medicinal drugs can be extracted, to save his life tears off his own testicles.) Why was there no defence? Because the parties had

---

[15] This passage appears to refer to fascism again—particularly if it is related to the passage on "Self-criticism and the Hypocrisy of Self-criticism" on pp. 254–7 below, where Gramsci makes similar points about the non-"epochal" character of the régime, and about its "relatively" progressive character *vis-à-vis* the preceding bourgeois régime. In the other passage, Gramsci is careful to stress that it is important in making any such judgement "to exclude the slightest appearance of support for the 'absolutist' tendency, and that can be achieved by insisting on the 'transitory' character of the phenomenon . . .".

little sense of human or political dignity? But such factors are not natural phenomena, deficiencies inherent in a people as permanent characteristics. They are "historical facts", whose explanation is to be found in past history and in the social conditions of the present. *Apparent contradictions*: there predominated a fatalistic and mechanistic conception of history (Florence, 1917, accusation of Bergsonianism),[16] and yet positions taken up were characterised by a formalistic, crude and superficial voluntarism. For example, the 1920 plan to establish an urban council in Bologna, restricted to organised elements.[17] This would only have created a useless duplicate, replacing an organism with historical roots in the masses like the *Camera del Lavoro* by an organism of a purely abstract and bookish kind. Did the plan at least have the political aim of transferring hegemony to the urban element [the proletariat]? (The latter, with the establishment of the council, would have acquired a centre of its own—given that the *Camera del Lavoro* was organised on a provincial basis.) There was no question of any intention of this kind, and in any case the project was never carried out.

Treves' "expiation" speech:[18] this speech is fundamental for understanding the political confusion and polemical dilettantism of the leaders. Such skirmishes concealed these leaders' fear of concrete responsibilities, and that fear in turn concealed the absence of any unity with the class they represented, any comprehension of its fundamental needs, its aspirations, its latent energies. Paternalistic party, of petits bourgeois with an inflated idea of their own importance.[19] Why no defence? The notion of war psychosis,

---

[16] See note 28 on p. 343. This passage analyses the suicidal passivity of Italian maximalism and reformism before fascism.

[17] There was a prolonged polemic in 1919–20 between the *Ordine Nuovo* conception of factory councils as organs of the entire working class (including those not organised in the socialist party or in trade unions) and the majority opinion in the PSI which was horrified at this notion. The *Ordine Nuovo* group would certainly have applied similar criteria to the formation of other forms of council, such as the territorial "soviet" mentioned here.

[18] Claudio Treves (1869–1933) was together with Turati the main leader of the reformist wing of the PSI, and, after their expulsion in 1922, of the reformist PSUI, until he went into exile in 1926. On 30 March 1920 he made what became known as his "expiation" speech, in which he described the tragic situation, the expiation, of the ruling classes in a situation in which the bourgeoisie was powerless to carry on effectively, while the proletariat was not yet ready to exercise power. See also note 20 on p. 225.

[19] In Italian *che fanno le mosche cocchiere*, an allusion to La Fontaine's fable *Le Coche et la Mouche*, which recounts the story of a fly who thinks that it is due to his efforts that a coach drawn by six horses succeeds in ascending a steep hill; the poem ends: "Ainsi certaines gens, faisant les empressés, S'introduisent dans les affaires: Ils font partout les nécessaires, Et, partout importuns, devraient être chassés."

and the belief that a civilised country cannot "allow" certain violences to take place.

These generalities too were masks for other, deeper motives (besides, they were in contradiction with what was repeated each time a massacre occurred: We have always said, for our part, that the ruling class is reactionary!), whose core once again was the fact of separation from the class, i.e. the existence of "two classes". There was a failure to grasp what would happen if reaction triumphed, because the real struggle was not lived—only the struggle as a doctrinal "principle". A further contradiction with respect to voluntarism: if one is against voluntarism, one ought to appreciate "spontaneity". But in fact the opposite was the case: what was "spontaneous" was inferior, not worth considering, not even worth analysing. In reality, the "spontaneous" was the most crushing proof of the party's ineptitude, because it demonstrated the gulf between the fine-sounding programmes and the wretched deeds. But in the meantime the "spontaneous" events occurred (1919–20), damaged interests, disturbed settled positions, aroused terrible hatreds even among peaceful folk, brought out of their passivity social strata which had been stagnating in putridity.[20] They created, precisely because of their "spontaneity" and because they were disavowed, the generic "panic", the "great fear" which could not fail to unify the forces of repression which would crush them without pity.

The so-called pact of alliance between Confederation and Party,[21]

---

[20] In other words, the "spontaneous" activity of the Italian working class and peasantry in 1919–20 provoked a back-lash among the traditionally "apolitical" petit-bourgeois strata. Gramsci analyses this apoliticism elsewhere (PP, pp. 11–12). See too PP, p. 54, where he wrote: "Treves' 'expiation' speech and the obsession with interventionism are closely linked: what is involved is a policy of avoiding the basic problem, the problem of power, and of diverting the attention and the passions of the masses on to secondary objectives; of hypocritically concealing the historical and political responsibility of the ruling class, channelling popular anger against material and often unconscious instruments of ruling-class policies; in essence, this policy was a continuation of that of Giolitti. . . . It was obvious that the war, with the immense economic and psychological upheaval which it had brought about—especially among the petty intellectuals and the petits bourgeois—was going to radicalise these strata. The party turned them gratuitously into enemies, instead of making allies of them, i.e. it threw them back towards the ruling class." (The party alluded to is, of course, the PSI—the PCI was not founded until 1921—and the obsession with interventionism to which Gramsci refers was the tendency of the socialists in the post-war period to use as the basic criterion for all political judgements the stance taken up in 1914–15 on the question of Italian intervention in the war.)

[21] i.e. the agreement of 29 September 1918, whereby the PSI and the CGL defined their respective fields of activity: e.g. the party would direct all political strikes, the CGL all economic ones "without obstructing each other".

which can be compared to a concordat between State and Church, constitutes an exceptional document of this gulf between represented and representatives. The party, which is an embyronic State structure, can allow no division of its political powers. It cannot permit a part of its members to claim rights equal to its own, to pose as allies of the "whole"—just as a State cannot allow a part of its subjects to make (via a foreign power) a special contract, over and above the general laws, governing their relations with it, i.e. with the very State to which they belong. To admit such a situation would imply the subordination *de facto* and *de jure* of the State and of the party to the so-called majority of the represented: in reality, to a group which poses itself as anti-State and anti-party and which ends up by indirectly exercising power. In the case of the pact of alliance it was clear that power did not lie with the party.

The curious relations obtaining between party and parliamentary group likewise corresponded to the pact of alliance; these too took the form of an alliance with equal rights. This system of relations meant that the party had no concrete existence as an independent organism, but merely as one constitutive element of a more complex organism which had all the characteristics of a labour party—without a centre, without any unitary will, etc. Must the unions therefore be subordinated to the party? This is not the right way to pose the question. The problem must be posed in the following terms: every member of the party, whatever his position or his responsibilities, is still a member of the party and subordinate to its leadership. There cannot be subordination between union and party: if the union has spontaneously chosen as its leader a member of the party, that means that the union freely accepts the directives of the party, hence freely accepts (indeed desires) control by the party over its officials. This problem was not posed correctly in 1919, although there existed a great and instructive precedent, that of June 1914.[22] For in reality, the fractions had no policy, and hence neither did the party. [1930]

---

[22] In June 1914, after the massacre of workers at Ancona (see note 33 on p. 70), the General Strike called by the PSI was briefly and reluctantly supported, and subsequently sabotaged, by the CGL. Gramsci points out that, despite this, the PSI in 1919 had not learnt its lesson with reference to the CGL. In August 1920, on the eve of the factory occupations, Gramsci had in fact written in *Ordine Nuovo*: "Today . . . at a moment when the revolutionary period may impel the Party into action from one moment to the next, the Italian movement is in a situation where not only it has not resolved in practice the problem of the relations between party and trade union, but it has not even raised the question. The Italian proletarian movement is the field of activity of two political parties: the official one and the *de facto* one constituted by the trade-union leaders."

AGITATION AND PROPAGANDA

The weakness of the Italian political parties (excepting to some extent the Nationalist party) throughout their period of activity, from the Risorgimento onwards, has consisted in what one might call an imbalance between agitation and propaganda—though it can also be termed lack of principle, opportunism, absence of organic continuity, imbalance between tactics and strategy, etc. The principal reason why the parties are like this is to be sought in the deliquescence of the economic classes, in the gelatinous economic and social structure of the country—but this explanation is somewhat fatalistic. In fact, if it is true that parties are only the nomenclature for classes, it is also true that parties are not simply a mechanical and passive expression of those classes, but react energetically upon them in order to develop, solidify and universalise them. This precisely did not occur in Italy, and the result of this "omission" is precisely the imbalance between agitation and propaganda—or however else one wishes to term it.

The State/government has a certain responsibility in this state of affairs: one can call it a responsibility, in so far as it prevented the strengthening of the State itself, i.e. demonstrated that the State/government was not a national factor. The government in fact operated as a "party". It set itself over and above the parties, not so as to harmonise their interests and activities within the permanent framework of the life and interests of the nation and State, but so as to disintegrate them, to detach them from the broad masses and obtain "a force of non-party men linked to the government by paternalistic ties of a Bonapartist-Caesarist type". This is the way in which the so-called *dictatorships* of Depretis, Crispi and Giolitti, and the parliamentary phenomenon of transformism,[23] should be analysed. Classes produce parties, and parties form the personnel of State and government, the leaders of civil and political society. There must be a useful and fruitful relation in these manifestations and functions. There cannot be any formation of leaders without the theoretical, doctrinal activity of parties,

---

[23] For "*trasformismo*", see note 8 on p. 58; for Crispi, note 24 on p. 66; for Giolitti, note 68 on p. 94. Agostino Depretis (1813–87) was at first a Mazzinian; later, in Sicily with Garibaldi, he was in fact working for Cavour. In 1876 he became the first "Left" prime minister, and dominated parliamentary life until his death. He chose his ministers from both sides of the parliament, in the process which became known as transformism; Crispi called this means of securing his personal power a "parliamentary dictatorship", but did the same himself when in power.

without a systematic attempt to discover and study the causes which govern the nature of the class represented and the way in which it has developed. Hence, scarcity of State and government personnel; squalor of parliamentary life; ease with which the parties can be disintegrated, by corruption and absorption of the few individuals who are indispensable. Hence, squalor of cultural life and wretched inadequacy of high culture. Instead of political history, bloodless erudition; instead of religion, superstitition; instead of books and great reviews, daily papers and broadsheets; instead of serious politics, ephemeral quarrels and personal clashes. The universities, and all the institutions which develop intellectual and technical abilities, since they were not permeated by the life of the parties, by the living realities of national life, produced apolitical national cadres, with a purely rhetorical and non-national mental formation. Thus the bureaucracy became estranged from the country, and via its administrative positions became a true political party, the worst of all, because the bureaucratic hierarchy replaced the intellectual and political hierarchy. The bureaucracy became precisely the State/Bonapartist party.* [1930]

THE "PHILOSOPHY OF THE EPOCH"

The discussion on force and consent has shown that political science is relatively advanced in Italy, and is treated with a certain frankness of expression—even by individuals holding responsible positions in the State. The discussion in question is the debate about the "philosophy of the epoch", about the central theme in the lives of the various states in the post-war period. How to reconstruct the hegemonic apparatus of the ruling group, an apparatus which disintegrated as a result of the war, in every state throughout the world? Moreover, why did this apparatus disintegrate? Perhaps because a strong antagonistic[24] collective political will developed? If this were the case, the question would have been resolved in favour of such an antagonist. In reality, it disintegrated under the impact of purely mechanical causes, of various kinds: 1. because great masses, previously passive, entered into movement—but into

* See the books which after 1919 criticised a "similar" state of affairs (but far richer in terms of the life of "civil society") in the Kaiser's Germany, for example Max Weber's book *Parliament and Government in the German New Order: a Political Critique of Bureaucracy and Party Life*. Translation and preface by Enrico Ruta, pp. xvi, 200—the translation is very imperfect and imprecise.

[24] i.e. antagonistic to the existing capitalist and bourgeois order.

a chaotic and disorganised movement, without leadership, i.e. without any precise collective political will; 2. because the middle classes, who during the war held positions of command and responsibility, when peace came were deprived of these and left unemployed—precisely after having learned how to command, etc.; 3. because the antagonistic forces proved to be incapable of organising this situation of disorder to their own advantage. The problem was to reconstruct a hegemonic apparatus for these formerly passive and apolitical elements. It was impossible to achieve this without the use of force—which could not be "legal" force, etc. Since the complex of social relations was different in each state, the political methods of using force and the ways in which legal and illegal forces were combined had to be equally diverse. The greater the mass of the apolitical, the greater the part played by illegal forces has to be. The greater the politically organised and educated forces, the more it is necessary to "cover" the legal State, etc. [1930–32]

POLITICAL STRUGGLE AND MILITARY WAR

In military war, when the strategic aim—destruction of the enemy's army and occupation of his territory—is achieved, peace comes. It should also be observed that for war to come to an end, it is enough that the strategic aim should simply be achieved potentially: it is enough in other words that there should be no doubt that an army is no longer able to fight, and that the victorious army "could" occupy the enemy's territory. Political struggle is enormously more complex: in a certain sense, it can be compared to colonial wars or to old wars of conquest—in which the victorious army occupies, or proposes to occupy, permanently all or a part of the conquered territory. Then the defeated army is disarmed and dispersed, but the struggle continues on the terrain of politics and of military "preparation".

Thus India's political struggle against the English (and to a certain extent that of Germany against France, or of Hungary against the Little Entente) knows three forms of war: war of movement, war of position, and underground warfare. Gandhi's passive resistance is a war of position, which at certain moments becomes a war of movement, and at others underground warfare. Boycotts are a form of war of position, strikes of war of movement, the secret preparation of weapons and combat troops belongs to underground warfare. A kind of commando tactics[25] is also to be found, but it can only be utilised with great circumspection. If the English believed that a great insurrectional movement was being prepared, destined to annihilate their present strategic superiority (which consists, in a certain sense, in their ability to manoeuvre through control of the internal lines of communication, and to concentrate their forces at the "sporadically" most dangerous spot) by mass suffocation—i.e. by compelling them to spread out their forces over a theatre of war which had simultaneously become generalised—then it would suit them to *provoke* a premature outbreak of the Indian fighting forces, in order to identify them and decapitate the general movement. Similarly it would suit France if the German Nationalist Right were to be involved in an adventurist *coup d'état*; for this would oblige the suspected illegal military organisation to show itself prematurely, and so permit an intervention which from the French point of view would be timely. It is thus evident that in these forms of mixed struggle—fundamentally of a military character, but mainly fought on the political plane (though in fact every political struggle always has a military substratum)—the use of commando squads requires an original tactical development, for which the experience of war can only provide a stimulus, and not a model.

The question of the Balkan *comitadjis*[26] requires separate treat-

---

[25] "*Arditismo.*" During the First World War, the "*arditi*" were volunteer commando squads in the Italian army. The term was adopted by d'Annunzio for his nationalist volunteer "legions", and was also used by the "*arditi del popolo*", formed to combat the fascist squads in the summer of 1921. This latter organisation emerged outside the left parties, but the mass of its local leaders and members were communist or socialist. The PSI (who signed a "concilation pact" with the fascists at this time) condemned the organisation; they advocated a policy of non-resistance. The PCI also condemned the organisation, for sectarian reasons, preferring to concentrate on its own, purely communist, defence squads. Gramsci had written and published articles welcoming the organisation before the official condemnation, and even afterwards did so obliquely, by criticising the PSI's attitude. However, as his comments later in this note indicate, he did not feel that working-class "*arditi*" could in fact hope to stand up to the fascist squads, who enjoyed the connivance of the State. It was only *mass* as opposed to *volunteer* action which could provide a viable response.

[26] In the late nineteenth century, Turkey still occupied large parts of the Balkans—what are now Albania, Northern Greece, Southern Yugoslavia and Southern Bulgaria—including the whole of the area traditionally known as Macedonia (now divided between Yugoslavia, Greece and to a lesser extent Bulgaria). In 1893 a revolutionary Macedonian committee was set up in Sophia by the Macedonian nationalists Delcev and Gruev, and this committee began to send armed bands (*comitadjis*) across the border into Turkish territory. Their aim—strongly opposed by the Young Turks—was at least some measure of Macedonian autonomy. All the surrounding countries—Bulgaria, Serbia and

ment; they are related to particular conditions of the region's geophysical environment, to the particular formation of the rural classes, and also to the real effectiveness of the governments there. The same is true with the Irish bands,[27] whose form of warfare and of organisation was related to the structure of Irish society. The *comitadjis*, the Irish, and the other forms of partisan warfare have to be separated from the question of commandos, although they appear to have points of contact. These forms of struggle are specific to weak, but restive, minorities confronted by well-organised majorities: modern commandos on the contrary presuppose a large reserve-force, immobilised for one reason or another but potentially effective, which gives them support and sustenance in the form of individual contributions.

The relationship which existed in 1917–18 between the commando units and the army as a whole can lead, and has led, political leaders to draw up erroneous plans of campaign. They forget: 1. that the commandos are simple tactical units, and do indeed presuppose an army which is not very effective—but not one which is completely inert. For even though discipline and fighting spirit have slackened to the point where a new tactical deployment has become advisable, they still do exist to a certain degree—a degree to which the new tactical formation precisely corresponds. Otherwise there could only be rout, and headlong flight; 2. that the phenomenon of commandos should not be considered as a sign of the general combativity of the mass of the troops, but, on the contrary, as a sign of their passivity and relative demoralisation. But in saying all this, the general criterion should be kept in mind that comparisons between military art and politics, if made, should always be taken *cum grano salis* [with a pinch of salt]—in other words, as stimuli to thought, or as terms in a *reductio ad absurdum*. In actual fact, in the case of the political militia there is neither any implacable penal sanction for whoever makes a mistake or does not obey an order exactly, nor do courts-martial exist—quite apart from the fact that the line-up of political forces is not even remotely comparable to the line-up of military forces.

In political struggle, there also exist other forms of warfare—apart from the war of movement and siege warfare or the war of

---

Greece—formed their own armed bands (*čete*) in the years that followed (as did the Vlachs), to protect their own interests in the area. These bands fought each other at the same time as they fought the Turks.

[27] Presumably a reference to the Fenian bands, who rose against British rule unsuccessfully in 1867 and continued sporadic activity during the latter years of the century.

position. True, i.e. modern, commandos belong to the war of position, in its 1914–18 form. The war of movement and siege warfare of the preceding periods also had their commandos, in a certain sense. The light and heavy cavalry, crack rifle corps,[28] etc.—and indeed mobile forces in general—partly functioned as commandos. Similarly the art of organising patrols contained the germ of modern commandos. This germ was contained in siege warfare more than in the war of movement: more extensive use of patrols, and particularly the art of organising sudden sorties and surprise attacks with picked men.

Another point to be kept in mind is that in political struggle one should not ape the methods of the ruling classes, or one will fall into easy ambushes. In the current struggles this phenomenon often occurs. A weakened State structure is like a flagging army; the commandos—i.e. the private armed organisations—enter the field, and they have two tasks: to make use of illegal means, while the State appears to remain within legality, and thus to reorganise the State itself. It is stupid to believe that when one is confronted by illegal private action one can counterpose to it another similar action—in other words, combat commando tactics by means of commando tactics. It means believing that the State remains perpetually inert, which is never the case—quite apart from all the other conditions which differ. The class factor leads to a fundamental difference: a class which has to work fixed hours every day cannot have permanent and specialised assault organisations—as can a class which has ample financial resources and all of whose members are not tied down by fixed work. At any hour of day or night, these by now professional organisations are able to strike decisive blows, and strike them unawares. Commando tactics cannot therefore have the same importance for some classes as for others. For certain classes a war of movement and manœuvre is necessary—because it is the form of war which belongs to them; and this, in the case of political struggle, may include a valuable and perhaps indispensable use of commando tactics. But to fix one's mind on the military model is the mark of a fool: politics, here too, must have priority over its military aspect, and only politics creates the possibility for manœuvre and movement.

From all that has been said it follows that in the phenomenon of military commandos, it is necessary to distinguish between the technical function of commandos as a special force linked to the

---

[28] "*Bersaglieri*"—an élite corps of the Italian army, founded by Lamarmora in 1836.

modern war of position, and their politico-military function. As a special force commandos were used by all armies in the World War. But they have only had a politico-military function in those countries which are politically enfeebled and non-homogeneous, and which are therefore represented by a not very combative national army, and a bureaucratised General Staff, grown rusty in the service. [1929–30]

On the subject of parallels between on the one hand the concepts of war of manœuvre and war of position in military science, and on the other the corresponding concepts in political science, Rosa [Luxemburg]'s little book, translated (from French) into Italian in 1919 by C. Alessandri, should be recalled.[29]

In this book, Rosa—a little hastily, and rather superficially too—theorised the historical experiences of 1905. She in fact disregarded the "voluntary" and organisational elements which were far more extensive and important in those events than—thanks to a certain "economistic" and spontaneist prejudice—she tended to believe. All the same, this little book (like others of the same author's essays) is one of the most significant documents theorizing the war of manœuvre in relation to political science. The immediate economic element (crises, etc.) is seen as the field artillery which in war opens a breach in the enemy's defences—a breach sufficient for one's own troops to rush in and obtain a definitive (strategic) victory, or at least an important victory in the context of the strategic line. Naturally the effects of immediate economic factors in historical science are held to be far more complex than the effects of heavy artillery in a war of manœuvre, since they are conceived of as having a double effect: 1. they breach the enemy's defences, after throwing him into disarray and causing him to lose faith in himself, his forces, and his future; 2. in a flash they organise one's own troops and create the necessary cadres—or at least in a flash they put the existing cadres (formed, until that moment, by the general historical process) in positions which enable them to encadre one's scattered forces; 3. in a flash they bring about the necessary ideological concentration on the common objective to be achieved. This view was a form of iron economic determinism, with the aggravating factor that it was conceived of as operating with lightning speed in time and in space. It was thus out and out historical mysticism, the awaiting of a sort of miraculous illumination.

---

[29] Rosa Luxemburg: *The General Strike—the party and the unions*. The Italian edition was published by *Società Editrice "Avanti!"* in Milan, 1919.

General Krasnov asserted (in his novel)[30] that the Entente did not wish for the victory of Imperial Russia (for fear that the Eastern Question would be definitively resolved in favour of Tsarism), and therefore obliged the Russian General Staff to adopt trench warfare (absurd, in view of the enormous length of the Front from the Baltic to the Black Sea, with vast marshy and forest zones), whereas the only possible strategy was a war of manœuvre. This assertion is merely silly. In actual fact, the Russian Army did attempt a war of manœuvre and sudden incursion, especially in the Austrian sector (but also in East Prussia), and won successes which were as brilliant as they were ephemeral. The truth is that one cannot choose the form of war one wants, unless from the start one has a crushing superiority over the enemy. It is well known what losses were caused by the stubborn refusal of the General Staffs to recognise that a war of position was "imposed" by the overall relation of the forces in conflict. A war of position is not, in reality, constituted simply by the actual trenches, but by the whole organisational and industrial system of the territory which lies to the rear of the army in the field. It is imposed notably by the rapid fire-power of cannons, machine-guns and rifles, by the armed strength which can be concentrated at a particular spot, as well as by the abundance of supplies which make possible the swift replacement of material lost after an enemy breakthrough or a retreat. A further factor is the great mass of men under arms; they are of very unequal calibre, and are precisely only able to operate as a mass force. It can be seen how on the Eastern Front it was one thing to make an incursion in the Austrian Sector, and quite another in the German Sector; and how even in the Austrian Sector, reinforced by picked German troops and commanded by Germans, incursion tactics ended in disaster. The same thing occurred in the Polish campaign of 1920; the seemingly irresistible advance was halted before Warsaw by General Weygand, on the line commanded by French officers.[31] Even those military experts whose minds are now fixed on the war of position, just as they were

---

[30] P. N. Krasnov, *From Two-headed Eagle to Red Flag*, Berlin, 1921. Italian edition, Florence, 1928.

[31] The Red Army under Tukhachevsky was halted at the gates of Warsaw in August 1920, in its counter-offensive following Pilsudski's invasion of the Soviet Union. The defeat was followed by controversy both concerning the viability of the entire attempt to "export revolution" without the support of the local population, and concerning the specific responsibilities for the defeat (Budyenny and Egorov, supported by Stalin, had not followed the orders of S. Kamenev, the commander-in-chief, and had marched on Lvov instead of linking up with Tukhachevsky before Warsaw).

previously on that of manœuvre, naturally do not maintain that the latter should be considered as expunged from military science. They merely maintain that, in wars among the more industrially and socially advanced States, the war of manœuvre must be considered as reduced to more of a tactical than a strategic function; that it must be considered as occupying the same position as siege warfare used to occupy previously in relation to it.

The same reduction must take place in the art and science of politics, at least in the case of the most advanced States, where "civil society" has become a very complex structure and one which is resistant to the catastrophic "incursions" of the immediate economic element (crises, depressions, etc.). The superstructures of civil society are like the trench-systems of modern warfare. In war it would sometimes happen that a fierce artillery attack seemed to have destroyed the enemy's entire defensive system, whereas in fact it had only destroyed the outer perimeter; and at the moment of their advance and attack the the assailants would find themselves confronted by a line of defence which was still effective. The same thing happens in politics, during the great economic crises. A crisis cannot give the attacking forces the ability to organise with lightning speed in time and in space; still less can it endow them with fighting spirit. Similarly, the defenders are not demoralised, nor do they abandon their positions, even among the ruins, nor do they lose faith in their own strength or their own future. Of course, things do not remain exactly as they were; but it is certain that one will not find the element of speed, of accelerated time, of the definitive forward march expected by the strategists of political Cadornism.[32]

The last occurrence of the kind in the history of politics was the events of 1917. They marked a decisive turning-point in the history of the art and science of politics. Hence it is a question of studying "in depth" which elements of civil society correspond to the defensive systems in a war of position. The use of the phrase "in depth" is intentional, because 1917 has been studied—but only either from superficial and banal viewpoints, as when certain social historians study the vagaries of women's fashions, or from a "rationalistic" viewpoint—in other words, with the conviction that certain phenomena are destroyed as soon as they are "realistically" explained, as if they were popular superstitions (which anyway are not destroyed either merely by being explained).

The question of the meagre success achieved by new tendencies

---

[32] See note 29 on p. 145.

in the trade-union movement should be related to this series of problems.[33] One attempt to begin a revision of the current tactical methods was perhaps that outlined by L. Dav. Br. [Trotsky] at the fourth meeting, when he made a comparison between the Eastern and Western fronts.[34] The former had fallen at once, but unprecedented struggles had then ensued; in the case of the latter, the struggles would take place "beforehand". The question, therefore, was whether civil society resists before or after the attempt to seize power; where the latter takes place, etc. However, the question was outlined only in a brilliant, literary form, without directives of a practical character. [1933–34: 1st version 1930–32.]

It should be seen whether Bronstein's famous theory about the *permanent* character of the movement[35] is not the political reflection of the theory of war of manœuvre (recall the observation of the cossack general Krasnov)—i.e. in the last analysis, a reflection of the general-economic-cultural-social conditions in a country in which the structures of national life are embryonic and loose, and incapable of becoming "trench or fortress". In this case one might

---

[33] This is presumably a reference to the failure of communists in Italy between 1921 and 1926 to win more than a minority position within the trade-union movement, despite the betrayals of the CGL's reformist leaders.

[34] The "fourth meeting" is the Fourth World Congress of the Comintern, at which Gramsci was present. Trotsky gave the report on NEP, in the course of which he said: ". . . it will hardly be possible to catch the European bourgeoisie by surprise as we caught the Russian bourgeoisie. The European bourgeoisie is more intelligent, and more farsighted; it is not wasting time. Everything that can be set on foot against us is being mobilised by it right now. The revolutionary proletariat will thus encounter on its road to power not only the combat vanguards of the counter-revolution but also its heaviest reserves. Only by smashing, breaking up and demoralising these enemy forces will the proletariat be able to seize state power. By way of compensation, after the proletarian overturn, the vanquished bourgeoisie will no longer dispose of powerful reserves from which it could draw forces for prolonging the civil war. In other words, after the conquest of power, the European proletariat will in all likelihood have far more elbow room for its creative work in economy and culture than we had in Russia on the day after the overturn. The more difficult and gruelling the struggle for state power, all the less possible will it be to challenge the proletariat's power after the victory." Trotsky, *The First Five Years of the Communist International*, Vol. II, pp. 221–22, Pioneer, New York 1953.

[35] i.e. Trotsky's theory of Permanent Revolution. Paradoxically, in view of Gramsci's analogy here, in the military debate of 1920–21 Trotsky was the main *opponent* of war of manœuvre, or the tactic of the revolutionary offensive, which was put forward by those civil war generals who supported the idea of a "proletarian military science"—Frunze, Budyenny and also Tukhachevsky. Moreover, he also delivered the main attack at the Third Comintern Congress on the "theory of the offensive" in the political sphere; its main supporters were the PCI (see General Introduction), the Left in the German party, and Bela Kun. It should also perhaps be noted that the reference to Foch's unified command being a possible military equivalent of the "united front" in politics was hardly a happy analogy, since Foch in fact had leanings towards Napoleonic offensive tactics.

say that Bronstein, apparently "Western", was in fact a cosmopolitan—i.e. superficially national and superficially Western or European. Ilitch [Lenin] on the other hand was profoundly national and profoundly European.

Bronstein in his memoirs recalls being told that his theory had been proved true . . . fifteen years later, and replying to the epigram with another epigram.[36] In reality his theory, as such, was good neither fifteen years earlier nor fifteen years later. As happens to the obstinate, of whom Guicciardini speaks,[37] he guessed more or less correctly; that is to say, he was right in his more general practical prediction. It is as if one was to prophesy that a little four-year-old girl would become a mother, and when at twenty she did so one said: "I guessed that she would"—overlooking the fact, however, that when she was four years old one had tried to rape the girl, in the belief that she would become a mother even then. It seems to me that Ilitch understood that a change was necessary from the war of manœuvre applied victoriously in the East in 1917, to a war of position which was the only form possible in the West—where, as Krasnov observes, armies could rapidly accumulate endless quantities of munitions, and where the social structures were of themselves still capable of becoming heavily-armed fortifications. This is what the formula of the "United Front"[38] seems to me to

---

[36] In *My Life*, pp. 157–58, Trotsky wrote: "Writing afterward in the inexact and slovenly manner which is peculiar to him, Lunacharsky described my revolutionary concept as follows: 'Comrade Trotsky held in 1905 that the two revolutions (the bourgeois and socialist), although they do not coincide, are bound to each other in such a way that they make a permanent revolution. After they have entered upon the revolutionary period through a bourgeois political revolution, the Russian section of the world, along with the rest, will not be able to escape from this period until the Social Revolution has been completed. It cannot be denied that in formulating this view Comrade Trotsky showed great insight and vision, albeit he erred to the extent of fifteen years.' The remark about my error of fifteen years does not become any more profound through its later repetition by Radek. All our estimates and slogans of 1905 were based on the assumption of a victorious revolution, and not of a defeat. We achieved then neither a republic nor a transfer of land, nor even an eight-hour day. Does it mean that we erred in putting these demands forward? The defeat of the revolution blanketed all prospects—not merely those which I had been expounding. The question was not of the dates of revolution but of the analysis of its inner forces and of foreseeing its progress as a whole."

[37] See *Ricordi*, Series II, No. 1: "He who therefore has faith becomes obstinate in what he believes and goes on his way intrepid and resolute, scorning difficulties and dangers. . . . Whence it comes to pass that, since worldly affairs are subjected to a thousand hazards and accidents, in the course of time there are many ways in which unhoped for help may come to whoever has persevered in his obstinacy. . .".

[38] For the united front policy, launched by the Comintern Executive in December 1921, see General Introduction.

mean, and it corresponds to the conception of a single front for the Entente under the sole command of Foch.

Ilitch, however, did not have time to expand his formula—though it should be borne in mind that he could only have expanded it theoretically, whereas the fundamental task was a national one; that is to say it required a reconnaissance of the terrain and identification of the elements of trench and fortress represented by the elements of civil society, etc. In Russia the State was everything, civil society was primordial and gelatinous; in the West, there was a proper relation between State and civil society, and when the State trembled a sturdy structure of civil society was at once revealed. The State was only an outer ditch, behind which there stood a powerful system of fortresses and earthworks: more or less numerous from one State to the next, it goes without saying—but this precisely necessitated an accurate reconnaissance of each individual country.

Bronstein's theory can be compared to that of certain French syndicalists on the General Strike, and to Rosa [Luxemburg]'s theory in the work translated by Alessandri. Rosa's book and theories anyway influenced the French syndicalists, as is clear from some of Rosmer's[39] articles on Germany in *Vie Ouvrière* (first series in pamphlet form). It partly depends too on the theory of spontaneity. [1930–32]

THE TRANSITION FROM THE WAR OF MANŒUVRE (FRONTAL ATTACK) TO THE WAR OF POSITION—IN THE POLITICAL FIELD AS WELL

This seems to me to be the most important question of political theory that the post-war period has posed, and the most difficult to solve correctly. It is related to the problems raised by Bronstein [Trotsky], who in one way or another can be considered the political theorist of frontal attack in a period in which it only leads to defeats. This transition in political science is only indirectly (mediately) related to that which took place in the military field, although certainly a relation exists and an essential one. The war of position demands enormous sacrifices by infinite masses of people. So an unprecedented concentration of hegemony is necessary, and hence a more "interventionist" government, which will take the

[39] Alfred Rosmer was a revolutionary syndicalist during the First World War, and edited *La Vie Ouvrière* together with Pierre Monatte. They were both among the first leaders of the PCF, and Rosmer was editor of *Humanité* from 1923 to 1924. He was expelled in 1926 for supporting the Joint Opposition in the Russian Party.

offensive more openly against the oppositionists and organise permanently the "impossibility" of internal disintegration—with controls of every kind, political, administrative, etc., reinforcement of the hegemonic "positions" of the dominant group, etc. All this indicates that we have entered a culminating phase in the political-historical situation, since in politics the "war of position", once won, is decisive definitively. In politics, in other words, the war of manœuvre subsists so long as it is a question of winning positions which are not decisive, so that all the resources of the State's hegemony cannot be mobilised. But when, for one reason or another, these positions have lost their value and only the decisive positions are at stake, then one passes over to siege warfare; this is concentrated, difficult, and requires exceptional qualities of patience and inventiveness. In politics, the siege is a reciprocal one, despite all appearances, and the mere fact that the ruler has to muster all his resources demonstrates how seriously he takes his adversary. [1930–32]

"A resistance too long prolonged in a besieged camp is demoralising in itself. It implies suffering, fatigue, loss of rest, illness and the continual presence not of the acute danger which tempers but of the chronic danger which destroys." Karl Marx: Eastern Question. 14 September 1855.

POLITICS AND MILITARY SCIENCE

Tactic of great masses, and immediate tactic of small groups. Belongs to the discussion about war of position and war of movement, in so far as this is reflected in the psychology both of great leaders (strategists) and of their subordinates. It is also (if one can put it like that) the point of connection between strategy and tactics, both in politics and in military science. Individuals (even as components of vast masses) tend to conceive war instinctively as "partisan warfare" or "Garibaldine warfare" (which is a higher form of "partisan warfare"). In politics the error occurs as a result of an inaccurate understanding of what the State (in its integral meaning: dictatorship + hegemony) really is. In war a similar error occurs, transferred to the enemy camp (failure to understand not only one's own State but that of the enemy as well). In both cases, the error is related to individual particularism—of town or region; this leads to an underestimation of the adversary and his fighting organisation. [1930–32]

INTERNATIONALISM AND NATIONAL POLICY

A work (in the form of questions and answers) by Joseph Vissarionovitch [Stalin] dating from September 1927: it deals with certain key problems of the science and art of politics.[40] The problem which seems to me to need further elaboration is the following: how, according to the philosophy of praxis (as it manifests itself politically)—whether as formulated by its founder [Marx] or particularly as restated by its most recent great theoretician [Lenin] —the international situation should be considered in its national aspect. In reality, the internal relations of any nation are the result of a combination which is "original" and (in a certain sense) unique: these relations must be understood and conceived in their originality and uniqueness if one wishes to dominate them and direct them. To be sure, the line of development is towards internationalism, but the point of departure is "national"—and it is from this point of departure that one must begin. Yet the perspective is international and cannot be otherwise. Consequently, it is necessary to study accurately the combination of national forces which the international class [the proletariat] will have to lead and develop, in accordance with the international perspective and directives [i.e. those of the Comintern]. The leading class is in fact only such if it accurately interprets this combination—of which it is itself a component and precisely as such is able to give the movement a certain direction, within certain perspectives. It is on this point, in my opinion, that the fundamental disagreement between Leo Davidovitch [Trotsky] and Vissarionovitch [Stalin] as interpreter of the majority movement [Bolshevism] really hinges. The accusations of nationalism are inept if they refer to the nucleus of

---

[40] This has usually been taken as a reference to Stalin's interview of September 1927 with the first American Labour Delegation. However, that interview contains nothing that seems likely to have suggested to Gramsci the reflections in this note; moreover, it is difficult to believe that he could have had any opportunity of reading a text of Stalin's which appeared after his arrest. He did have, on the other hand, among his books before his arrest an Italian translation, in pamphlet form, of Stalin's June 1925 text entitled "Questions and Answers" (a speech given at Sverdlov University), which perhaps appeared in Italian in September. It seems certain that this is the text to which Gramsci is referring. In it Stalin notably spoke of two forms of "liquidationist" danger in the Russian Party: 1. those who felt that there was no chance of building socialism in such a *backward* country as Russia; 2. those who felt that the fate of the Russian Revolution was entirely dependent on the *international* revolution. Stalin went on to speak of a "nationalist" danger caused by the pressure of the bourgeoisie in the field of foreign policy, and by lack of confidence in the international proletarian revolution, on the part of "the people who are handling our foreign policy".

the question. If one studies the majoritarians' [Bolsheviks'] struggle from 1902 up to 1917, one can see that its originality consisted in purging internationalism of every vague and purely ideological (in a pejorative sense) element, to give it a realistic political content. It is in the concept of hegemony that those exigencies which are national in character are knotted together; one can well understand how certain tendencies either do not mention such a concept, or merely skim over it. A class that is international in character has—in as much as it guides social strata which are narrowly national (intellectuals), and indeed frequently even less than national: particularistic and municipalistic (the peasants)—to "nationalise" itself in a certain sense. Moreover, this sense is not a very narrow one either, since before the conditions can be created for an economy that follows a world plan, it is necessary to pass through multiple phases in which the regional combinations (of groups of nations) may be of various kinds. Furthermore, it must never be forgotten that historical development follows the laws of necessity until the initiative has decisively passed over to those forces which tend towards construction in accordance with a plan of peaceful and solidary division of labour [i.e. to the socialist forces]. That non-national concepts (i.e. ones that cannot be referred to each individual country) are erroneous can be seen *ab absurdo*: they have led to passivity and inertia in two quite distinct phases: 1. in the first phase, nobody believed that they ought to make a start—that is to say, they believed that by making a start they would find themselves isolated; they waited for everybody to move together, and nobody in the meantime moved or organised the movement; 2. the second phase is perhaps worse, because what is being awaited is an anachronistic and anti-natural form of "Napoleonism" (since not all historical phases repeat themselves in the same form).[41] The theoretical weaknesses of this modern form of the old mechanicism are masked by the general theory of permanent revolution, which is nothing but a generic forecast presented as a dogma, and which demolishes itself by not in fact coming true. [1933]

---

[41] The first phase to which Gramsci refers is clearly that of the pre-war Second International. The second is presumably a reference to the internationalism increasingly invoked by Trotsky after 1924, and against the notion of Socialism in One Country; Gramsci is arguing that this implies an expectation of the revolution spreading out from Russia in the way that Napoleon's armies carried certain of the ideas and achievements of the French Revolution outside the borders of France and throughout Europe.

PROBLEM OF THE "COLLECTIVE MAN" OR OF "SOCIAL CONFORMISM"[42]

Educative and formative role of the State. Its aim is always that of creating new and higher types of civilisation; of adapting the "civilisation" and the morality of the broadest popular masses to the necessities of the continuous development of the economic apparatus of production; hence of evolving even physically new types of humanity. But how will each single individual succeed in incorporating himself into the collective man, and how will educative pressure be applied to single individuals so as to obtain their consent and their collaboration, turning necessity and coercion into "freedom"? Question of the "Law": this concept will have to be extended to include those activities which are at present classified as "legally neutral", and which belong to the domain of civil society; the latter operates without "sanctions" or compulsory "obligations", but nevertheless exerts a collective pressure and obtains objective results in the form of an evolution of customs, ways of thinking and acting, morality, etc.

Political concept of the so-called "Permanent Revolution", which emerged before 1848 as a scientifically evolved expression of the

---

[42] See too NM. pp. 150–51: "Tendency to conformism in the contemporary world, more widespread and deeper than in the past: the standardisation of thought and action assumes national or even continental proportions. The economic basis of the 'collective man': big factories, Taylorisation, rationalisation, etc. . . . On social 'conformism', it should be stressed that the problem is not a new one, and that the alarm expressed by certain intellectuals is merely comic. Conformism has always existed: what is involved today is a struggle between 'two conformisms', i.e. a struggle for hegemony, a crisis of civil society. The old intellectual and moral leaders of society feel the ground slipping from under their feet; they perceive that their 'sermons' have become precisely mere 'sermons', i.e. external to reality, pure form without any content, shades without a spirit. This is the reason for their reactionary and conservative tendencies; for the particular form of civilisation, culture and morality which they represented is decomposing, and they loudly proclaim the death of all civilisation, all culture, all morality; they call for repressive measures by the State, and constitute resistance groups cut off from the real historical process, thus prolonging the crisis, since the eclipse of a way of living and thinking cannot take place without a crisis. The representatives of the new order in gestation, on the other hand, inspired by 'rationalistic' hatred for the old, propagate utopias and fanciful schemes. What is the point of reference for the new world in gestation? The world of production; work. The greatest utilitarianism must go to found any analysis of the moral and intellectual institutions to be created and of the principles to be propagated. Collective and individual life must be organised with a view to the maximum yield of the productive apparatus. The development of economic forces on new bases and the progressive installation of the new structure will heal the contradictions which cannot fail to exist, and, when they have created a new 'conformism' from below, will permit new possibilities for self-discipline, i.e. for freedom, including that of the individual."

Jacobin experience from 1789 to Thermidor.[43] The formula belongs to an historical period in which the great mass political parties and the great economic trade unions did not yet exist, and society was still, so to speak, in a state of fluidity from many points of view: greater backwardness of the countryside, and almost complete monopoly of political and State power by a few cities or even by a single one (Paris in the case of France); a relatively rudimentary State apparatus, and greater autonomy of civil society from State activity; a specific system of military forces and of national armed services; greater autonomy of the national economies from the economic relations of the world market, etc. In the period after 1870, with the colonial expansion of Europe, all these elements change: the internal and international organisational relations of the State become more complex and massive, and the Forty-Eightist formula of the "Permanent Revolution" is expanded and transcended in political science by the formula of "civil hegemony". The same thing happens in the art of politics as happens in military art: war of movement increasingly becomes war of position, and it can be said that a State will win a war in so far as it prepares for it minutely and technically in peacetime. The massive structures of the modern democracies, both as State organisations, and as complexes of associations in civil society, constitute for the art of politics as it were the "trenches" and the permanent fortifications of the front in the war of position: they render merely "partial" the element of movement which before used to be "the whole" of war, etc.

This question is posed for the modern States, but not for backward countries or for colonies, where forms which elsewhere have been superseded and have become anachronistic are still in vigour. The question of the value of ideologies must also be studied in a treatise of political science. [1933–34]

SOCIOLOGY AND POLITICAL SCIENCE

The rise of sociology is related to the decline of the concept of political science and the art of politics which took place in the nineteenth century (to be more accurate, in the second half of that century, with the success of evolutionary and positivist theories). Everything that is of real importance in sociology is nothing other than political science. "Politics" became synonymous with parlia-

---

[43] See note 49 on p. 80.

mentary politics or the politics of personal cliques. Conviction that the constitutions and parliaments had initiated an epoch of "natural" "evolution", that society had discovered its definitive, because rational, foundations, etc. And, lo and behold, society can now be studied with the methods of the natural sciences! Impoverishment of the concept of the State which ensued from such views. If political science means science of the State, and the State is the entire complex of practical and theoretical activities with which the ruling class not only justifies and maintains its dominance, but manages to win the active consent of those over whom it rules, then it is obvious that all the essential questions of sociology are nothing other than the questions of political science. If there is a residue, this can only be made up of false problems, i.e. frivolous problems. The question therefore which faced Bukharin when he wrote his *Popular Manual*[44] was that of determining what status could be accorded to political science in relation to the philosophy of praxis: whether the two are identical (something impossible to maintain, except from the most crudely positivist viewpoint); or whether political science is the body of empirical or practical principles which are deduced from a vaster conception of the world or philosophy properly speaking; or whether this philosophy is only the science of the concepts or general categories created by political science, etc.

If it is true that man cannot be conceived of except as historically determined man—i.e. man who has developed, and who lives, in certain conditions, in a particular social complex or totality of social relations—is it then possible to take sociology as meaning simply the study of these conditions and the laws which regulate their development? Since the will and initiative of men themselves cannot be left out of account, this notion must be false. The problem of what "science" itself is has to be posed. Is not science itself "political activity" and political thought, in as much as it transforms men, and makes them different from what they were before? If everything is "politics", then it is necessary—in order to avoid lapsing into a wearisome and tautological catalogue of platitudes—to distinguish by means of new concepts between on the one hand the politics which corresponds to that science which is traditionally called "philosophy", and on the other the politics which is called political science in the strict sense. If science is the "discovery" of formerly unknown reality, is this reality not conceived

[44] See note 63 on p. 419.

of in a certain sense as transcendent? And is it not thought that there still exists something "unknown" and hence transcendent? And does the concept of science as "creation" not then mean that it too is "politics"? Everything depends on seeing whether the creation involved is "arbitrary", or whether it is rational—i.e. "useful" to men in that it enlarges their concept of life, and raises to a higher level (develops) life itself.*

HEGEMONY (CIVIL SOCIETY) AND SEPARATION OF POWERS

The separation of powers,[46] together with all the discussion provoked by its realisation and the legal dogmas which its appearance brought into being, is a product of the struggle between civil society and political society in a specific historical period. This period is characterised by a certain unstable equilibrium between the classes, which is a result of the fact that certain categories of intellectuals (in the direct service of the State, especially the civil and military bureaucracy) are still too closely tied to the old dominant classes. In other words, there takes place within the society what Croce calls the "perpetual conflict between Church and State", in which the Church is taken as representing the totality of civil society (whereas in fact it is only an element of diminishing importance within it), and the State as representing every attempt to crystallise permanently a particular stage of development, a particular situation. In this sense, the Church itself may become State, and the conflict may occur between on the one hand secular (and secularising) civil society, and on the other State/Church (when the Church has become an integral part of the State, of political society monopolised by a specific privileged group, which absorbs the Church in order the better to preserve its monopoly with the support of that zone of "civil society" which the Church represents).

Essential importance of the separation of powers for political and economic liberalism; the entire liberal ideology, with its strengths

---

* In connection with the *Popular Manual* and its appendix *Theory and Practice*, the philosophical review by Armando Carlini (*Nuova Antologia*, 16 March 1933) should be consulted; it appears from this that the equation "Theory: practice = pure mathematics: applied mathematics" was formulated by an Englishman (Wittaker, I think).[45]

[45] Sir Edmund Whittaker (1873–1956), physicist and mathematician.

[46] The doctrine developed by Montesquieu in his *Esprit des Lois*—on the basis of the contemporary bourgeois political system in England as he saw it—whereby executive, legislative and judiciary functions are exercised independently of each other. The principle inspired the American Constitution and others modelled on it.

and its weaknesses, can be encapsulated in the principle of the separation of powers, and the source of liberalism's weakness then becomes apparent: it is the bureaucracy—i.e. the crystallisation of the leading personnel—which exercises coercive power, and at a certain point it becomes a caste. Hence the popular demand for making all posts elective—a demand which is extreme liberalism, and at the same time its dissolution (principle of the permanent Constituent Assembly, etc.; in Republics, the election at fixed intervals of the Head of State gives the illusion of satisfying this elementary popular demand).

Unity of the State in the differentiation of powers: Parliament more closely linked to civil society; the judiciary power, between government and Parliament, represents the continuity of the written law (even against the government). Naturally all three powers are also organs of political hegemony, but in different degrees: 1. Legislature; 2, Judiciary; 3. Executive. It is to be noted how lapses in the administration of justice make an especially disastrous impression on the public: the hegemonic apparatus is more sensitive in this sector, to which arbitrary actions on the part of the police and political administration may also be referred. [1930–32]

THE CONCEPTION OF LAW

A conception of the Law which must be an essentially innovatory one is not to be found, integrally, in any pre-existing doctrine (not even in the doctrine of the so-called positive school, and notably that of Ferri).[47] If every State tends to create and maintain a certain type of civilisation and of citizen (and hence of collective life and of individual relations), and to eliminate certain customs and attitudes and to disseminate others, then the Law will be its instrument for this purpose (together with the school system, and other institutions and activities). It must be developed so that it is suitable for such a purpose—so that it is maximally effective and productive of positive results.

The conception of law will have to be freed from every residue of transcendentalism and from every absolute; in practice, from every moralistic fanaticism. However, it seems to me that one cannot

[47] Enrico Ferri (1856–1929), penologist and politician, began his political career as a socialist (editor of *Avanti!* 1900–1905), but rallied to fascism in 1922. He was the most prominent member of the so-called positive school of penology, and the founder of Italian criminology. The main idea behind his penal theories was the rejection of any idea of moral retribution in the punishment of crimes, in favour of the notion of punishment as a deterrent.

start from the point of view that the State does not "punish" (if this term is reduced to its human significance), but only struggles against social "dangerousness". In reality, the State must be conceived of as an "educator", in as much as it tends precisely to create a new type or level of civilisation. Because one is acting essentially on economic forces, reorganising and developing the apparatus of economic production, creating a new structure, the conclusion must not be drawn that superstructural factors should be left to themselves, to develop spontaneously, to a haphazard and sporadic germination. The State, in this field, too, is an instrument of "rationalisation", of acceleration and of Taylorisation.[48] It operates according to a plan, urges, incites, solicits, and "punishes"; for, once the conditions are created in which a certain way of life is "possible", then "criminal action or omission" must have a punitive sanction, with moral implications, and not merely be judged generically as "dangerous". The Law is the repressive and negative aspect of the entire positive, civilising activity undertaken by the State. The "prize-giving"[49] activities of individuals and groups, etc., must also be incorporated in the conception of the Law; praiseworthy and meritorious activity is rewarded, just as criminal actions are punished (and punished in original ways, bringing in "public opinion" as a form of sanction).

[1933–34: 1st version 1931–32.]

POLITICS AND CONSTITUTIONAL LAW

In *Nuova Antologia*, 16 December 1929, there is published a brief note by a certain M. Azzalini, *La politica, scienza ed arte di Stato*, which may be of interest as a presentation of the elements among which scientific schematism flounders.

Azzalini begins by affirming that it was a "dazzling" glory on Machiavelli's part "to have circumscribed the ambit of politics within the State". What Azzalini means is not easy to grasp: he quotes from Chapter III of *The Prince* the passage: "When the Cardinal of Rouen said to me that the Italians understood nothing of war, I replied that the French understood nothing of the State", and on this single quotation he bases his assertion that "hence" for Machiavelli "politics must be understood as a science, and as the science of the State, and that was his glory, etc." (the term

---

[48] See "Americanism and Fordism" on pp. 301–8.

[49] "*premiatrici*".

"science of the State" for "politics" was it seems used, in the correct modern sense, only by Marsilio of Padua[50] before Machiavelli). Azzalini is fairly lightweight and superficial. The anecdote of the Cardinal of Rouen, torn from its context, means nothing. In its context it takes on a meaning which does not lend itself to scientific deductions: it was clearly just a witty epigram, a spontaneous retort. The Cardinal of Rouen had asserted that the Italians understood nothing of war; in retaliation, Machiavelli replies that the French understand nothing of the State, because otherwise they would not have allowed the Pope to extend his power in Italy, against the interests of the French State. Machiavelli was in fact very far from thinking that the French understood nothing of the State; on the contrary he admired the manner in which the monarchy (Louis XI) had welded France into a unitary State, and he used the actions of the French State as a term of comparison for Italy. This conversation of his with the Cardinal of Rouen is "political action" and not "political science"; for, according to him, if it was damaging to French "foreign policy" that the Pope should grow stronger, it was even more damaging to the domestic affairs of Italy.

The strange thing is that, taking this incongruous quotation as his cue, Azzalini goes on to say that "despite the assertion that this science studies the State, a totally imprecise (!) definition (!?) is given of it—since there is no indication of the criterion with which the object of the enquiry is to be examined. And the imprecision is absolute, in view of the fact that all the legal sciences in general, and constitutional law in particular, refer indirectly and directly to the State."

What does all this mean, applied to Machiavelli? Less than nothing: mental confusion. Machiavelli wrote books of "immediate political action", and not utopias—which express the longing for a ready-made State, with all its functions and elements ready-made too. In his treatment, in his critique of the present, he expressed general concepts—presented, however, in aphoristic rather than in systematic form—and an original conception of the world. This conception of the world too could be called "philosophy of praxis", or "neo-humanism", in as much as it does not recognise transcendent or immanent (in the metaphysical sense) elements, but

---

[50] Marsilio of Padua (1275–1342), author of *Defensor Pacis*. He ascribed the continual wars in northern Italy to the temporal claims of the Papacy, and said that the Church ought to be subordinated to the State. He stood for a general restriction of Church powers, and influenced Reformation thinkers like Luther.

bases itself entirely on the concrete action of man, who, impelled by historical necessity, works and transforms reality. It is not true, as Azzalini seems to believe, that in Machiavelli no account is taken of "constitutional law", since general principles of constitutional law can be found scattered throughout Machiavelli's work. Indeed he quite clearly asserts the necessity for the State to be ruled by law, by fixed principles, which virtuous citizens can follow in the certainty of not being destroyed by the blows of blind fate. But what Machiavelli does do is to bring everything back to politics—i.e. to the art of governing men, of securing their permanent consent, and hence of founding "great States". (It must be remembered that, in Machiavelli's opinion, neither the Commune, nor the Republic, nor the communal *Signoria*[51] was a State, since they lacked not only a sizeable territory but also a population capable of supporting the military force required for an autonomous international policy. In his opinion, there was still a situation of non-State in Italy, with the Papacy, and this would last until religion too became a "policy" of the State, and ceased to be the Pope's policy for preventing the formation of strong States in Italy—a policy which involved intervention in the internal affairs of peoples not under his temporal domination, in the pursuit of interests which were not those of the States in question, and which hence were troublesome and disruptive.)

One could find in Machiavelli the confirmation of what I have noted elsewhere: that the Italian mediaeval bourgeoisie could not pass from the corporate to the political phase, because it was unable to free itself completely from the mediaeval cosmopolitan conception represented by the Pope, the clergy and also by the lay intellectuals (humanists)—in other words, it was unable to create an autonomous State, but remained within the mediaeval framework, feudal and cosmopolitan.

Azzalini writes that "Ulpian's[52] definition on its own, or better still the examples he gives in his *Digest*, are sufficient to reveal the extrinsic identity (and so what?) of the object of the two sciences. '*Ius publicum ad statum rei (publicae) romanae spectat.—Publicum ius, in*

---

[51] The "*Signoria*" or council of notables became the effective power in the Italian city states in the fourteenth century, replacing the "communal" democracy of their earlier development and representing a transitional phase before the emergence, in most cases, of a single dominant family dynasty. Such dynasties were legitimised in the fifteenth century by Pope or Emperor, as the *Principato* or Princely régime.

[52] Ulpian was a Roman jurist, who died in A.D. 228.

sacris, in sacerdotibus, in magistratibus consistit'![53] Hence there is an identity of object in constitutional law and in political science, but not a substantive one; for the criteria with which the two sciences treat the same material are totally different. In fact, the spheres of the juridical order and the political order are different. And, in reality, while the first observes the public organism from a static perspective, as the natural product of a particular historical evolution, the second observes that same organism from a dynamic perspective, as a product whose virtues and whose defects can be evaluated, and which consequently must be modified in the light of new requirements and later developments." Hence one might say that "the juridical order is ontological and analytical, since it studies and analyses the various public institutions in their real essence", while "the political order is deontological and critical, since it studies the various institutions not as they are, but as they ought to be, that is to say with evaluative criteria and considerations of expediency which are not, and cannot be, juridical".

And this wiseacre considers himself an admirer of Machiavelli, a disciple—indeed he even thinks that he has perfected Machiavelli's thought!

"It follows from this that, despite the formal identity described above, there exists a substantive diversity so profound and striking that it perhaps invalidates the opinion pronounced by one of the greatest contemporary publicists, that it is difficult if not impossible to create a political science entirely distinct from constitutional law. It seems to us that that opinion is true only if the analysis of the juridical and political aspects stops there—but not if it goes further, defining that further area which belongs to the exclusive competence of political science. The latter, in fact, does not confine itself to studying the organisation of the State with a criterion which is deontological and critical, and therefore different from that used by constitutional law for the same object; instead it extends its sphere to a field which is proper to it, investigating the laws which regulate the rise, evolution and decline of States. Nor can it be asserted that such a study belongs to history (!) understood in a general sense (!). For—even if it is admitted that the search for causes, effects, and the mutual bonds of interdependence of the natural laws governing the nature and the evolution of States, constitutes an historical enquiry—the search for appropriate means to control in practice the overall political strategy will always

[53] "Public law concerns the state of the Roman republic. Public law consists in rites, priests, and magistrates."

remain of exclusively political competence, not historical and hence not juridical. The function which Machiavelli promised once more to carry out, and synthesised, when he said: 'I will argue how these princedoms can be ruled and held', is such, both by the intrinsic importance of the problem and by definition, that it not only legitimises the autonomy of politics, but it also allows, at least from the point of view last outlined, even a formal distinction between itself and constitutional law." And that is what is meant by *autonomy* of politics!

But—says Azzalini—there exists an art as well as a science of politics. "There exist men who draw, or drew, from personal intuition their vision of the needs and interests of the country they govern; who, in their governmental activity, realised that vision of personal intuition in the external world. By this we certainly do not mean that intuitive, and hence artistic, activity is the only, or the predominant, activity of the Statesman; we only mean that, side by side with practical, economic and moral activities, he must also preserve the above-mentioned theoretical activity (whether in the subjective form of intuition, or the objective (!) form of expression); and that if such requisites are missing, the politician cannot exist, and even less (!) can the statesman—whose eminence is characterised precisely by this faculty, which cannot be learnt (?). Thus in the political field, too, in addition to the man of science in whom cognitive theoretical activity predominates, there subsists the artist, in whom intuitive theoretical activity predominates. Nor does that entirely exhaust the sphere of action of the art of politics; for this may be seen not only in terms of the statesman who, through the practical functions of government, externalises the vision that intuition creates internally, but can also be evaluated in terms of the writer who realises in the external world (!) the political truth which he intuits—realises it not through political action, but through works and writings which translate the author's intution. This is the case with the Indian Kamandaka (third century A.D.), with Petrarch in the *Trattarello pei Carraresi*, with Botero in the *Ragion di Stato*, and, from certain points of view, with Machiavelli and Mazzini."

This all really is a fine hotch-potch—worthy not so much of Machiavelli as, more than anything else, of Tittoni, editor of *Nuova Antologia*. Azzalini is incapable of finding his way about either in philosophy or in political science. But I wanted to take all these notes, in order to try to disentangle his plot, and see if I could arrive at clear concepts for my own sake.

For instance, it is necessary to disembroil what "intuition" might mean in politics, and also the expression "art" of politics, etc. Certain points from Bergson should be recalled at this juncture: "Of life (reality in movement), intelligence offers us only a translation in terms of inertia. It circles around, taking the greatest possible number of external views of the object, which, instead of penetrating, it draws towards itself. But it is intuition which will lead us into the very interior of life: by that I mean instinct which has become disinterested." "Our eye perceives the traits of the living being, but juxtaposed to each other rather than organically related. The purpose of life, the simple movement which runs through the lineaments, which links them together and gives them a meaning, escapes it; and it is this purpose that the artist tends to capture, situating himself within the object by a kind of sympathy, breaking down by an effort of intuition the barrier which space places between him and his model. However, it is true that aesthetic intuition only captures that which is individual." "Intelligence is characterised by a natural incomprehensibility of life, since it represents clearly only the discontinuous and the immobile."[54]

Divergence, in the meantime, between political intuition and aesthetic, lyric or artistic intuition; only by metaphor does one speak of the art of politics. Political intuition is not expressed through the artist, but through the "leader"; and "intuition" must be understood to mean not "knowledge of men", but swiftness in connecting seemingly disparate facts, and in conceiving the means adequate to particular ends—thus discovering the interests involved, and arousing the passions of men and directing them towards a particular action. The "expression" of the "leader" is his "action" (in a positive or a negative sense, of launching or preventing a particular action, which is consistent or inconsistent with the end which one wishes to attain). However, the "leader" in politics may be an individual, but also be a more or less numerous political body: in the latter case, unity of purpose will be achieved by an individual (or by a small inner group, and within that small group by an individual) who may change from time to time even though the group remains united and consistent in its on-going activity.

If one had to translate the notion "Prince", as used in Machiavelli's work, into modern political language, one would have to make a series of distinctions: the "Prince" could be a Head

---

[54] Henri Bergson, *Creative Evolution*, London, 1954, passim.

of State, or the leader of a government, but it could also be a political leader whose aim is to conquer a State, or to found a new type of State; in this sense, "Prince" could be translated in modern terms as "political party". In certain States, the "Head of State"—in other words, the element which balances the various interests struggling against the predominant (but not absolutely exclusivistic) interest—is precisely the "political party". With the difference, however, that in terms of traditional, constitutional law it juridically neither rules nor governs. It has "*de facto* power", and exercises the hegemonic function and hence that of holding the balance between the various interests in "civil society"; the latter, however, is in fact intertwined with political society to such an extent that all the citizens feel that the party on the contrary both rules and governs. It is not possible to create a constitutional law of the traditional type on the basis of this reality, which is in continuous movement; it is only possible to create a system of principles asserting that the State's goal is its own end, its own disappearance, in other words the re-absorption of political society into civil society. [1930]

PARLIAMENT AND THE STATE[55]

Professor Julius Miskolczy, the director of the Hungarian Academy in Rome, has written in *Magyar Szemle* that in Italy "Parliament, which used formerly to be so to speak outside the State, has now, despite the valuable contribution which it continues to make, become inserted in the State and has undergone a basic change in its composition . . ."

The notion that Parliament may have become "inserted" into the State is a discovery in the science and art of politics that is worthy of the Christopher Columbuses of contemporary Reaction. All the same, the assertion is interesting as evidence of the way in which many politicians conceive the State in practice. For the question does indeed have to be asked: do parliaments, even in those countries where apparently they have most real power, in fact constitute a part of the State structure? In other words, what is their real function? Furthermore, if the answer is affirmative, in what way do they constitute a part of the State, and how do they carry out their particular function? On the other hand, even if parliaments do not constitute an organic part of the State, is their

---

[55] This title has been added by the editors—Gramsci's note originally had no title.

existence of no significance for the State? And what grounds are there for the accusations made against parliamentarianism and against the party system—which is inseparable from parliamentarianism? (Objective grounds, naturally—i.e. ones related to the fact that the existence of Parliament, in itself, hinders and delays the *technical* actions of the government.)

That the representative system may politically "be a nuisance" for the career bureaucracy is understandable; but this is not the point. The point is to establish whether the representative and party system, instead of being a suitable mechanism for choosing elected functionaries to integrate and balance the appointed civil servants and prevent them from becoming ossified, has become a hindrance and a mechanism which operates in the reverse direction—and, if so, for what reasons. Moreover, even an affirmative reply to these questions does not exhaust the problem. For even allowing (as it must be allowed) that parliamentarianism has become inefficient and even harmful, it is not necessary to conclude that the bureaucratic system must be rehabilitated and praised. It has to be considered whether parliamentarianism and representative system are synonymous, and whether a different solution is not possible—both for parliamentarianism and for the bureaucratic system—with a new type of representative system. [1933]

SELF-CRITICISM AND THE HYPOCRISY OF SELF-CRITICISM

It is clear that self-criticism has become a fashionable word.[56] The stated claim is that an equivalent has been found to the criticism represented by the "free" political struggle of a representative

[56] We have been unable to track down any example of the use of this word in fascist Italy, but it seems clear that it must have been used, in arguments destined to counter the charge that opposition parties were necessary to ensure criticism—and hence efficiency. Precisely this kind of argument occurs in one of Mussolini's speeches on 26 May 1927: "Here the problem arises: but how do you manage to do without an opposition? . . . Opposition is not necessary to the functioning of a healthy political régime. Opposition is stupid, superfluous in a totalitarian régime like the Fascist régime. Opposition is useful in easy times, academic times, as was the case before the war, when there were discussions in the Assembly about if, how and when socialism would be achieved, and indeed a whole debate about this—though this was clearly not serious, despite the men who took part in it. But *we* have the opposition within ourselves, dear sirs, we are not old nags who need a touch of the spur. We keep a strict check on ourselves . . ."

The term "self-criticism" was of course already current in the communist movement, and especially in the Soviet Union, by the late twenties. Tasca was expelled from the PCI for refusing to criticise himself for his positions in 1927–28; the Italian delegates to the Tenth Plenum in July 1929 had to criticise their party's 1927–28 policies, and also the "softness" shown towards Tasca by the

system—an equivalent which, in fact, if it is seriously applied, is more effective and fruitful than the original. But this is the nub of the matter: that the surrogate should be applied seriously, that the self-criticism should be operative and "pitiless"—since its effectiveness lies precisely in its being pitiless. In reality it has turned out that self-criticism offers an opportunity for fine speeches and pointless declarations, and for nothing else; self-criticism has been "parliamentarised". For it has not yet been remarked that it is not so easy to destroy parliamentarism as it seems. "Implicit" and "tacit" parliamentarism is far more dangerous than the explicit variety, since it has all its defects without its positive values. There often exists a "tacit" party system, i.e. a "tacit" and "implicit" parliamentarism where one would least think it. It is obvious that it is impossible to abolish a "pure" form, such as parliamentarism, without radically abolishing its content, individualism, and this in its precise meaning of "individual appropriation" of profit and of economic initiative for capitalist and individual profit. Hypocritical self-criticism is precisely a feature of such situation. Beside statistics give an index of the real position. Unless it is claimed that criminality has disappeared—which in any case other statistics disprove (and how!).

The entire subject needs re-examining, especially with respect to the "implicit" party system and parliamentarism, i.e. that which functions like "black markets" and "illegal lotteries" where and when the official market and the State lottery are for some reason kept closed. Theoretically the important thing is to show that between the old defeated absolutism of the constitutional régimes and the new absolutism there is an essential difference, which means that it is not possible to speak of a regression; not only this, but also to show that such "black parliamentarism" is a function of present historical necessities, is "a progress" in its way, that the return to traditional "parliamentarism" would be an anti-historical regression, since even where this "functions" publicly, the effective parliamentarism is the "black" one. Theoretically it seems to me that one can explain the phenomenon with the concept of "hegemony", with a return to "corporativism"—not in the *ancien régime* sense, but in the modern sense of the word, in which the

---

party leadership; the "three" began their opposition during the same year by calling for "serious self-criticism" (notably by Togliatti and Grieco) for the 1927–28 line. However, it seems difficult to interpret this note of Gramsci's as a reference to the communist usage of the term, and at all events it is clear that what follows refers to fascism in Italy.

"corporation" cannot have closed and exclusivistic limits as was the case in the past. (Today it is corporativism of "social function", without hereditary or any other restriction—which was anyway only relative in the past too, when its most obvious feature was that of "legal privilege"). In discussing this subject, care must be taken to exclude the slightest appearance of support for the "absolutist" tendency, and that can be achieved by insisting on the "transitory" character of the phenomenon (in the sense that it does not constitute an epoch, not in the sense of its "short duration").[57] (With respect to this, it should be noted that the fact of "not constituting an epoch" is too often confused with brief "temporal" duration: it is possible to "last" a long time, relatively, and yet not "constitute an epoch": the viscous forces of certain régimes are often unsuspected, especially if they are "strong" as a result of the weakness of others (including where this has been procured): with respect to this, the opinions of Cesarino Rossi[58] should be recalled; these were certainly mistaken "in the last resort", but they really did contain a certain effective realism). "Black" parliamentarism appears to be a theme which should be developed quite extensively; it also offers an opportunity to define the political concepts which constitute the "parliamentary" conception. (Comparisons with other countries, in this respect, are interesting: for example, is not the liquidation of Leone Davidovi [Trotsky] an episode of the liquidation "also" of the "black" parliamentarism which existed after the abolition of the "legal" parliament?) Real fact and legal fact. System of forces in unstable equilibrium which find on the parliamentary terrain the "legal" terrain of their "more economic" equilibrium; and abolition of this legal terrain, because it becomes a source of organisation and of reawakening of latent and slumbering social forces. Hence this abolition is a symptom (and prediction) of intensifications of struggles and not vice versa. When a struggle

---

[57] See note 15 on p. 223. The Italian "*far epoca*" has no exact English translation (although the English "epoch-making" does exist, with a rather different meaning).

[58] Cesare Rossi (b. 1887) was one of Mussolini's closest lieutenants in the early days of the fascist movement, and in charge of his Press bureau until the Matteotti murder of 1924. He was made the scapegoat for this, and broke with Mussolini and fascism in consequence. He wrote a famous "Memorandum" on Mussolini's involvement in a number of the most notorious fascist outrages of the period 1920–24, and gave this to the opposition parties; it was published by the liberal Amendola in *Il Mondo* in 1925. It is difficult to be sure which "opinions" Gramsci is referring to here, but they might perhaps be the idea expressed in his "Memorandum" that "the general atmosphere of illegality and cowardice" was "created by the weakness of the Fascist régime".

can be resolved legally, it is certainly not dangerous; it becomes so precisely when the legal equilibrium is recognised to be impossible. (Which does not mean that by abolishing the barometer one can abolish bad weather.) [1933]

THE STATE

In the new "juridical" tendencies represented by the *Nuovi Studi* of Volpicelli and Spirito, the confusion between the concept of class-State and the concept of regulated society[59] should be noted, as a critical point of departure. This confusion is especially noteworthy in the paper on *Economic Freedom* presented by Spirito at the Nineteenth Congress of the Society for Scientific Progress held at Bolzano in September 1930, and published in *Nuovi Studi* in the 1930 September–October issue.

As long as the class-State exists the regulated society cannot exist, other than metaphorically—i.e. only in the sense that the class-State too is a regulated society. The utopians, in as much as they expressed a critique of the society that existed in their day, very well understood that the class-State could not be the regulated society. So much is this true that in the types of society which the various utopias represented, economic equality was introduced as

[59] Spirito and Volpicelli were the principal theorists of the "corporate economy' in fascist Italy. They claimed that corporativism represented a "post-capitalist" economy, and that it had abolished the anarchy of liberal capitalism. Gramsci here refers to the confusion involved in the idea that a "regulated" society could co-exist with capitalism—the class-State. Elsewhere Gramsci uses "regulated society" to mean Communism (see "Statement of the Problem" in "Some Problems in the Study of the Philosophy of Praxis', on pp. 381–2 below). The concept is probably a reference to the concluding passage of "*Socialism: Utopian and Scientific*" where Engels discusses the withering away of the State. He writes: "With the seizing of the means of production by society, production of commodities is done away with, and, simultaneously, the mastery of the product over the producer. Anarchy in social production is replaced by *systematic, definite organisation*" (our italics). Spirito and Volpicelli claimed that the corporate economy had achieved order and harmony. Gramsci comments, in effect, that this will only be possible under Communism; until then, there will continue to be a class-State, and hence no "regulated" society. See too the discussion of Spirito's theories on PP. pp. 79–82, especially: "Fundamental question: the utopia of Spirito and Volpicelli consists in confusing the State with the regulated society, a confusion which occurs by way of a purely 'rationalistic' concatenation of concepts: individual = society (the individual is not an 'atom' but the historical individuation of the entire society), society = State, hence individual = State. The feature which differentiates this 'utopia' from the traditional utopias and from attempts in general to find the 'best possible State' is the fact that Spirito and Volpicelli claim that this 'fantastic' entity of theirs already exists . . . For political reasons the masses have been told: 'What you were awaiting, and what was promised you by charlatans (i.e. the socialists and communists) already exists', i.e. the regulated society, economic equality, etc."

a necessary basis for the projected reform. Clearly in this the utopians were not utopians, but concrete political scientists and consistent critics. The utopian character of some of them was due to the fact that they believed that economic equality could be introduced by arbitrary laws, by an act of will, etc. But the idea that complete and perfect political equality cannot exist without economic equality (an idea to be found in other political writers, too, even right-wing ones—i.e. among the critics of democracy, in so far as the latter makes use of the Swiss or Danish model to claim that the system is a reasonable one for all countries) nevertheless remains correct. This idea can be found in the writers of the seventeenth century too, for example in Ludovico Zuccolo and in his book *Il Belluzzi*, and I think in Machiavelli as well. Maurras believes that in Switzerland that particular form of democracy is possible precisely because there is a certain common averageness of economic fortunes, etc.

The confusion of class-State and regulated society is peculiar to the middle classes and petty intellectuals, who would be glad of any regularisation that would prevent sharp struggles and upheavals. It is a typically reactionary and regressive conception. [1930–32]

In my opinion, the most reasonable and concrete thing that can be said about the ethical State,[60] the cultural State, is this: every State is ethical in as much as one of its most important functions is to raise the great mass of the population to a particular cultural and moral level, a level (or type) which corresponds to the needs of the productive forces for development, and hence to the interests of the ruling classes. The school as a positive educative function, and the courts as a repressive and negative educative function, are the most important State activities in this sense: but, in reality, a multitude of other so-called private initiatives and activities tend to the same end—initiatives and activities which form the apparatus of the political and cultural hegemony of the ruling classes. Hegel's conception belongs to a period in which the spreading development of the bourgeoisie could seem limitless,

[60] The idea of the "ethical" State is associated with Croce. For the latter, the two moments of the State were the "ethical" and the "political" (or the "moral" and the "useful"); he saw these as being in perpetual dialectical contradiction—a conflict which he represented symbolically as that between Church and State. The term was also adopted by fascism, see e.g. Mussolini, in "*The Doctrine of Fascism*", 1932: "The fascist State has its own consciousness, its own will, and for that reason is called an 'ethical' State. In 1929 . . . I said 'For fascism the State is not the night-watchman . . . it is a spiritual and moral fact . . . it educates the citizens to civil virtue . . .'," etc.

so that its ethicity or universality could be asserted: all mankind will be bourgeois. But, in reality, only the social group that poses the end of the State and its own end as the target to be achieved can create an ethical State—i.e. one which tends to put an end to the internal divisions of the ruled, etc., and to create a technically and morally unitary social organism. [1931–32]

Hegel's doctrine of parties and associations as the "private" woof of the State. This derived historically from the political experiences of the French Revolution, and was to serve to give a more concrete character to constitutionalism. Government with the consent of the governed—but with this consent organised, and not generic and vague as it is expressed in the instant of elections. The State does have and request consent, but it also "educates" this consent, by means of the political and syndical associations; these, however, are private organisms, left to the private initiative of the ruling class. Hegel, in a certain sense, thus already transcended pure constitutionalism and theorised the parliamentary State with its party system. But his conception of association could not help still being vague and primitive, halfway between the political and the economic; it was in accordance with the historical experience of the time, which was very limited and offered only one perfected example of organisation—the "corporative" (a politics grafted directly on to the economy). Marx was not able to have historical experiences superior (or at least much superior) to those of Hegel; but, as a result of his journalistic and agitational activities, he had a sense for the masses. Marx's concept of organisation remains entangled amid the following elements: craft organisation; Jacobin clubs; secret conspiracies by small groups; journalistic organisation.

The French Revolution offered two prevalent types. There were the "clubs"—loose organisations of the "popular assembly" type, centralised around individual political figures. Each had its newspaper, by means of which it kept alive the attention and interest of a particular clientèle that had no fixed boundaries. This clientèle then upheld the theses of the paper in the club's meetings. Certainly, among those who frequented the clubs, there must have existed tight, select groupings of people who knew each other, who met separately and prepared the climate of the meetings, in order to support one tendency or another—depending on the circumstances and also on the concrete interests in play.

The secret conspiracies, which subsequently spread so widely in Italy prior to 1848, must have developed in France after Thermidor among the second-rank followers of Jacobinism: with great difficulty in the Napoleonic period on account of the vigilant control of the police; with greater facility from 1815 to 1830 under the Restoration, which was fairly liberal at the base and was free from certain preoccupations. In this period, from 1815 to 1830, the differentiation of the popular political camp was to occur. This already seemed considerable during the "glorious days" of 1830,[61] when the formations which had been crystallising during the preceding fifteen years now came to the surface. After 1830 and up to 1848, this process of differentiation became perfected, and produced some quite highly-developed specimens in Blanqui and Filippo Buonarroti.

It is unlikely that Hegel could have had first-hand knowledge of these historical experiences, which are, however, more vivid in Marx.*

The revolution which the bourgeois class has brought into the conception of law, and hence into the function of the State, consists especially in the will to conform (hence ethicity of the law and of the State). The previous ruling classes were essentially conservative in the sense that they did not tend to construct an organic passage from the other classes into their own, i.e. to enlarge their class sphere "technically" and ideologically: their conception was that of a closed caste. The bourgeois class poses itself as an organism in continuous movement, capable of absorbing the entire society, assimilating it to its own cultural and economic level. The entire function of the State has been transformed; the State has become an "educator", etc.

How this process comes to a halt, and the conception of the State as pure force is returned to, etc. The bourgois class is "saturated": it not only does not expand—it starts to disintegrate; it not only does not assimilate new elements, it loses part of itself (or at least its losses are enormously more numerous than its assimilations). A class claiming to be capable of assimilating the whole of society, and which was at the same time really able to express such a process, would perfect this conception of the State and of law, so as to conceive the end of the State and of law—rendered useless since they will have exhausted their function and will have been absorbed by civil society. [1931–32]

That the everyday concept of State is unilateral and leads to

---

[61] The three days in which the people of Paris rose and drove out Charles X.

* For this series of facts, see as primary material the publications of Paul Louis and Maurice Block's *Political Dictionary*; for the French Revolution, see especially Aulard; see too Andler's notes to the *Manifesto*. For Italy, see Luzio's book on Masonry and the Risorgimento—highly tendentious.

grotesque errors can be demonstrated with reference to Danièl Halévy's recent book *Décadence de la liberté*, of which I have read a review in *Nouvelles Littéraires*. For Halévy, "State" is the representative apparatus; and he discovers that the most important events of French history from 1870 until the present day have not been due to initiatives by political organisms deriving from universal suffrage, but to those either of private organisms (capitalist firms, General Staffs, etc.) or of great civil servants unknown to the country at large, etc. But what does that signify if not that by "State" should be understood not only the apparatus of government, but also the "private" apparatus of "hegemony" or civil society? It should be noted how from this critique of the State which does not intervene, which trails behind events, etc., there is born the dictatorial ideological current of the Right, with its reinforcement of the executive, etc. However, Halévy's book should be read to see whether he too has taken this path: it is not unlikely in principle, given his antecedents (sympathies for Sorel, for Maurras, etc.). [1930–32]

Curzio Malaparte, in the introduction to his little volume on the *Technique of the Coup d'Etat*, seems to assert the equivalence of the formula: "Everything within the State, nothing outside the State, nothing against the State" with the proposition: "Where there is freedom, there is no State". In the latter proposition, the term "freedom" cannot be taken in its ordinary meaning of "political freedom, freedom of the press, etc.", but as counterposed to "necessity"; it is related to Engels' proposition on the passage from the rule of necessity to the rule of freedom.[62] Malaparte has not caught even the faintest whiff of the significance of the proposition.

[1931–32]

In the (anyway superficial) polemic over the functions of the State (which here means the State as a politico-juridical organisation in the narrow sense), the expression "the State as *veilleur de nuit*" corresponds to the Italian expression "the State as policeman"[63] and means a State whose functions are limited to the safeguarding of public order and of respect for the laws. The fact is glossed over that in this form of régime (which anyway has never existed except on paper, as a limiting hypothesis) hegemony over its historical development belongs to private forces, to civil society—which is "State" too, indeed is the State itself.

---

[62] At the end of his *Socialism: Utopian and Scientific*.

[63] *Veilleur de nuit* means "night-watchman", see below. The Italian expression referred to is "*Stato-carabiniere*".

It seems that the expression *veilleur de nuit*, which should have a more sarcastic ring than "the State as policeman", comes from Lassalle. Its opposite should be "ethical State" or "interventionist State" in general, but there are differences between the two expressions. The concept of ethical State is of philosophical and intellectual origin (belonging to the intellectuals: Hegel), and in fact could be brought into conjunction with the concept of State-*veilleur de nuit*; for it refers rather to the autonomous, educative and moral activity of the secular State, by contrast with the cosmopolitanism and the interference of the religious-ecclesiastical organisation as a mediaeval residue. The concept of interventionist State is of economic origin, and is connected on the one hand with tendencies supporting protection and economic nationalism, and on the other with the attempt to force a particular State personnel, of landowning and feudal origin, to take on the "protection" of the working classes against the excesses of capitalism (policy of Bismarck and of Disraeli).[64]

These diverse tendencies may combine in various ways, and in fact have so combined. Naturally liberals ("economists") are for the "State as *veilleur de nuit*", and would like the historical initiative to be left to civil society and to the various forces which spring up there—with the "State" as guardian of "fair play" and of the rules of the game. Intellectuals draw very significant distinctions as to when they are liberals and when they are interventionists (they may be liberals in the economic field and interventionists in the cultural field, etc.). The catholics would like the State to be interventionist one hundred per cent in their favour; failing that, or where they are in a minority, they call for a "neutral" State, so that it should not support their adversaries. [1935: 1st version 1930]

The following argument is worth reflecting upon: is the conception of the *gendarme*-nightwatchman State (leaving aside the polemical designation: *gendarme*, nightwatchman, etc.) not in fact the only conception of the State to transcend the purely "economic-corporate" stages?

We are still on the terrain of the identification of State and government—an identification which is precisely a representation of the economic-corporate form, in other words of the confusion between civil society and political society. For it should be

---

[64] Bismarck put through legislation providing for sickness and old age pensions; Disraeli denounced certain of the worst excesses of mid-Victorian capitalism in his novels, and his ministry (1874–80) limited the working day for women and children, passed the Combination Act of 1875 giving limited recognition to trade unions, and put through the Public Health Act and the Artisans' Dwelling Act in the same year, etc.

remarked that the general notion of State includes elements which need to be referred back to the notion of civil society (in the sense that one might say that State = political society + civil society, in other words hegemony protected by the armour of coercion). In a doctrine of the State which conceives the latter as tendentially capable of withering away and of being subsumed into regulated society, the argument is a fundamental one. It is possible to imagine the coercive element of the State withering away by degrees, as ever-more conspicuous elements of regulated society (or ethical State or civil society) make their appearance.

The expressions "ethical State" or "civil society" would thus mean that this "image" of a State without a State was present to the greatest political and legal thinkers, in so far as they placed themselves on the terrain of pure science (pure utopia, since based on the premise that all men are really equal and hence equally rational and moral, i.e. capable of accepting the law spontaneously, freely, and not through coercion, as imposed by another class, as something external to consciousness).

It must be remembered that the expression "nightwatchman" for the liberal State comes from Lassalle, i.e. from a dogmatic and non-dialectical statalist (look closely at Lassalle's doctrines on this point and on the State in general, in contrast with Marxism). In the doctrine of the State as regulated society, one will have to pass from a phase in which "State" will be equal to "government", and "State" will be identified with "civil society", to a phase of the State as nightwatchman—i.e. of a coercive organisation which will safeguard the development of the continually proliferating elements of regulated society, and which will therefore progressively reduce its own authoritarian and forcible interventions. Nor can this conjure up the idea of a new "liberalism", even though the beginning of an era of organic liberty be imminent. [1930–32]

If it is true that no type of State can avoid passing through a phase of economic-corporate primitivism, it may be deduced that the content of the political hegemony of the new social group which has founded the new type of State must be predominantly of an economic order: what is involved is the reorganisation of the structure and the real relations between men on the one hand and the world of the economy or of production on the other. The superstructural elements will inevitably be few in number, and have a character of foresight and of struggle, but as yet few "planned" elements. Cultural policy will above all be negative, a critique of the past; it will be aimed at erasing from the memory and at destroying. The lines of construction will as yet be "broad lines", sketches, which might (and should) be changed at all times, so as to be consistent with the new structure as it is formed. This precisely did not happen in the period of the mediaeval communes; for culture, which remained a function of the Church, was precisely anti-economic in character (i.e. against the nascent capitalist economy); it was not directed towards giving hegemony to the new class, but rather to preventing the latter from acquiring it. Hence Humanism and the Renaissance were reactionary, because they signalled the defeat of the new class, the negation of the economic world which was proper to it, etc. [1931–32]

Another element to examine is that of the organic relations between the domestic and foreign policies of a State. Is it domestic policies which determine foreign policy, or vice versa? In this case too, it will be necessary to distinguish: between great powers, with relative international autonomy, and other powers; also, between different forms of government (a government like that of Napoleon III had two policies, apparently—reactionary internally, and liberal abroad).

Conditions in a State before and after a war. It is obvious that, in an alliance, what counts are the conditions in which a State finds itself at the moment of peace. Therefore it may happen that whoever has exercised hegemony during the war ends up by losing it as a result of the enfeeblement suffered in the course of the struggle, and is forced to see a "subordinate" who has been more skilful or "luckier" become hegemonic. This occurs in "world wars" when the geographic situation compels a State to throw all its resources into the crucible: it wins through its alliances, but victory finds it prostrate, etc. This is why in the concept of "great power" it is necessary to take many elements into account, and especially those which are "permanent"—i.e. especially "economic and financial potential" and population. [1932–32]

ORGANISATION OF NATIONAL SOCIETIES

I have remarked elsewhere that in any given society nobody is disorganised and without party, provided that one takes organisation and party in a broad and not a formal sense. In this multiplicity of private associations (which are of two kinds: natural, and contractual or voluntary) one or more predominates relatively or absolutely—constituting the hegemonic apparatus of one social group over the rest of the population (or civil society): the basis for the State in the narrow sense of the governmental-coercive apparatus.

It always happens that individuals belong to more than one private association, and often to associations which are objectively in contradiction to one another. A totalitarian[65] policy is aimed precisely: 1. at ensuring that the members of a particular party find in that party all the satisfactions that they formerly found in a multiplicity of organisations, i.e. at breaking all the threads that bind these members to extraneous cultural organisms; 2. at destroying all other organisations or at incorporating them into a system of which the party is the sole regulator. This occurs: 1. when the given party is the bearer of a new culture—then one has a progressive phase; 2. when the given party wishes to prevent another force, bearer of a new culture, from becoming itself "totalitarian"—then one has an objectively regressive and reactionary phase, even if that reaction (as invariably happens) does not avow itself, and seeks itself to appear as the bearer of a new culture.

Luigi Einaudi, in *Riforma Sociale* for May–June 1931, reviews a French work *Les sociétés de la nation, Etude sur les éléments constitutifs de la nation française*, by Etienne Martin Saint-Léon (volume of 415 pages, éd. Spes, Paris, 1930), in which some of these organisations are studied—but only those which exist formally. (For example, do the readers of a newspaper form an organisation, or not?, etc.) In any case, in as much as the subject was dealt with, see the book and Einaudi's review as well. [1930–32]

WHO IS A LEGISLATOR?

The concept of "legislator" must inevitably be identified with the concept of "politician". Since all men are "political beings", all are also "legislators". But distinctions will have to be made. "Legislator" has a precise juridical and official meaning—i.e. it means those persons who are empowered by the law to enact laws. But it can have other meanings too.

Every man, in as much as he is active, i.e. living, contributes to modifying the social environment in which he develops (to modifying certain of its characteristics or to preserving others); in other words, he tends to establish "norms", rules of living and of behaviour. One's circle of activity may be greater or smaller, one's awareness of one's own action and aims may be greater or smaller; furthermore, the representative power may be greater or smaller, and will

[65] See note 33 on p. 147.

be put into practice to a greater or lesser extent in its normative, systematic expression by the "represented". A father is a legislator for his children, but the paternal authority will be more or less conscious, more or less obeyed and so forth.

In general, it may be said that the distinction between ordinary men and others who are more specifically legislators is provided by the fact that this second group not only formulates directives which will become a norm of conduct for the others, but at the same time creates the instruments by means of which the directives themselves will be "imposed", and by means of which it will verify their execution. Of this second group, the greatest legislative power belongs to the State personnel (elected and career officials), who have at their disposal the legal coercive powers of the State. But this does not mean that the leaders of "private" organisms and organisations do not have coercive sanctions at their disposal too, ranging even up to the death penalty. The maximum of legislative capacity can be inferred when a perfect formulation of directives is matched by a perfect arrangement of the organisms of execution and verification, and by a perfect preparation of the "spontaneous" consent of the masses who must "live" those directives, modifying their own habits, their own will, their own convictions to conform with those directives and with the objectives which they propose to achieve. If everyone is a legislator in the broadest sense of the concept, he continues to be a legislator even if he accepts directives from others—if, as he carries them out, he makes certain that others are carrying them out too; if, having understood their spirit, he propagates them as though making them into rules specifically applicable to limited and definite zones of living. [1933]

RELIGION, STATE, PARTY

In *Mein Kampf*, Hitler writes: "The founding or the destruction of a religion is an action of immeasurably greater importance than the founding or the destruction of a State: not to speak of a party..." Superficial and acritical. The three elements—religion (or "active" conception of the world), State, party—are indissoluble, and in the real process of historico-political development there is a necessary passage from one to the other.

In Machiavelli, in the ways and language of the time, an understanding of this necessary homogeneity and interrelation of the three elements can be observed. To lose one's soul in order to save one's country or State is an element of absolute laicism, of positive and negative conception of the world (against religion, or the dominant conception). In the modern world, a party is such—integrally, and not, as happens, a fraction of a larger party—when it is conceived, organised and led in ways and in forms such that it will develop integrally into a State (an integral State, and not into a government technically understood) and into a conception of the world. The development of the party into a State reacts upon the party and requires of it a continuous reorganisation and development, just as the development of the party and State into a conception of the world, i.e. into a total and molecular (individual) transformation of ways of thinking and acting, reacts upon the State and the party, compelling them to reorganise continually and confronting them with new and original problems to solve. It is evident that such a conception of the world is hindered in its practical development by blind, unilateral "party" fanaticism (in this case that of a sect, of a fraction of a larger party, within which the struggle takes place), i.e. by the absence either of a State conception or of a conception of the world capable of developing because historically necessary.

The political life of today furnishes ample evidence of these mental limitations and deficiencies, which, besides, provoke dramatic struggles—for they are themselves the means by which historical development in practice occurs. But the past, and the Italian past which interests us most, from Machiavelli onwards, is no less rich in experiences; for all of history bears witness to the present. [1933]

STATE AND PARTIES

The function of hegemony or political leadership exercised by parties can be estimated from the evolution of the internal life of the parties themselves. If the State represents the coercive and punitive force of juridical regulation of a country, the parties—representing the spontaneous adhesion of an élite to such a regulation, considered as a type of collective society to which the entire mass must be educated—must show in their specific internal life that they have assimilated as principles of moral conduct those rules which in the State are legal obligations. In the parties necessity has already become freedom, and thence is born the immense political value (i.e. value for political leadership) of the internal discipline of a party, and hence the value as a criterion of such discipline in estimating the growth potential of the various parties. From this point of view the parties can be considered as schools of State life. Elements of party life: character (resistance to the pressures of surpassed cultures), honour (fearless will in maintaining the new type of culture and life), dignity (awareness of operating for a higher end), etc. [1930–32]

STATOLATRY

Attitude of each particular social group towards its own State. The analysis would not be accurate if no account were taken of the two forms in which the State presents itself in the language and culture of specific epochs, i.e. as civil society and as political society. The term "statolatry" is applied to a particular attitude towards the "government by functionaries" or political society, which in everyday language is the form of State life to which the term of State is applied and which is commonly understood as the entire State. The assertion that the State can be identified with individuals (the individuals of a social group), as an element of active culture (i.e. as a movement to create a new civilisation, a new type of man and of citizen), must serve to determine the will to construct within the husk of political society a complex and well-articulated civil society, in which the individual can govern himself without his self-government thereby entering into conflict with political society—but rather becoming its normal continuation, its organic complement. For some social groups, which before their ascent to autonomous State life have not had a long independent period of cultural and moral development on their own (as was made possible in mediaeval society and under the absolute régimes by the juridical existence[66] of the privileged Estates or orders), a period of statolatry is necessary and indeed opportune. This "statolatry" is nothing other than the normal form of "State life", or at least of initiation to autonomous State life and to the creation of a "civil society" which it was not historically possible to create before the ascent to independent State life. However, this kind of "statolatry" must not be abandoned to itself, must not, especially, become theoretical fanaticism or be conceived of as "perpetual". It must be criticised, precisely in order to develop and produce new forms of State life, in which the initiative of individuals and groups will have a "State" character,

---

[66] The Einaudi edition gives *esigenza* = "need", instead of Gramsci's original *esistenza* = "existence".

even if it is not due to the "government of the functionaries" (make State life become "spontaneous"). [1931–32]

"MERITS" OF THE RULING CLASSES

In view of the fact that the identity State/class is not easy to understand, there is something strange about the way in which a government (State) is able to reflect back upon the class it represents, as a merit and a source of prestige, the fact that it has finally done what should have been done for fifty years and more—and which should therefore be a demerit and a source of shame.[67] One lets a man starve until he is fifty; when he is fifty, one finally notices him. In private life, such behaviour would warrant a good kicking. In the case of the State, it appears to be a "merit". Not merely that, but the fact that one "washes oneself" at the age of fifty appears to be a sign of superiority over other men of fifty who have always washed. One hears this kind of thing said about drainage schemes, public works, roads, etc., i.e. about a country's basic social equipment. The fact that a country provides itself with this equipment, with which others have provided themselves in their day, is loudly acclaimed and trumpeted forth, and the others are told: do as much, if you can. But the others cannot, because they have already done so in their day, and this is presented as a sign of their "impotence".

At all events, the fact that the State/government, conceived as an autonomous force, should reflect back its prestige upon the class upon which it is based, is of the greatest practical and theoretical importance, and deserves to be analysed fully if one wants a more realistic concept of the State itself. Moreover, this phenomenon is not something exceptional, or characteristic of one kind of State only. It can, it seems, be incorporated into the function of élites or vanguards, i.e. of parties, in relation to the class which they represent. This class, often, as an economic fact (which is what every class is essentially) might not enjoy any intellectual or moral prestige, i.e. might be incapable of establishing its hegemony, hence of founding a State. Hence the function of monarchies, even in the modern era; hence, too, in particular, the phenomenon (especially in England and in Germany) whereby the leading

---

[67] A clear reference to fascist propaganda extolling the régime's achievements in the field of public works, etc. In England in the 'thirties, approval for fascist Italy often took the form of "at least Mussolini has got the trains to run on time", etc.

personnel of the bourgeois class organised into a State can be constituted by elements of the old feudal classes, who have been dispossessed of their traditional economic predominance (Junkers and Lords), but who have found new forms of economic power in industry and in the banks, and who have not fused with the bourgeoisie but have remained united to their traditional social group.[68] [1933]

HISTORICAL BELLES-LETTRES

The position taken up in practice by Croce is an essential element of any analysis or critique of his philosophical position, indeed it is the fundamental element. In Croce, philosophy and "ideology" finally become identical, and philosophy is revealed as nothing other than a "practical instrument" for organisation and action—for organising a party, indeed an international of parties, and for a course of action in practice. Croce's speech to the Oxford philosophical congress[69] was in fact a political manifesto, for an international union of the great intellectuals of all nations—especially those of Europe. Moreover, this undeniably might become an important party, with a considerable role to play.

Broadly speaking, one can already discern in the world of today a phenomenon which resembles the rift between "spiritual" and "temporal" in the Middle Ages—but a phenomenon that is far more complex than its predecessor, to the extent that modern life itself is more complex. To an ever-increasing extent, regressive and conservative social groupings are being reduced to their initial economic-corporate stage, while the progressive and innovatory groupings are still in their initial, precisely economic-corporate phase. The traditional intellectuals are detaching themselves from the social grouping to which they have hitherto given the highest and most comprehensive form—hence the most extensive and perfect consciousness of the modern State. In so doing, they are accomplishing an act of incalculable historical significance; they are marking and ratifying the crisis of the State in its decisive form. But these intellectuals neither have the organisation which the Church possessed, nor anything comparable to it, and in that respect the crisis of today is more acute than that of the Middle Ages; the latter lasted several centuries, up to the French Revolu-

---

[68] See note 6 on p. 216.

[69] Croce addressed the Seventh International Philosophy Congress at Oxford in September 1930 on "Anti-History". See note 19 on p. 137.

tion, when the social grouping that had been economically the motor force in Europe throughout the millennium was able to present itself as an integral "State", possessing all the intellectual and moral forces it needed to organise a complete and perfect society. Today, the "spiritual" which is detaching itself from the "temporal", and distinguishing itself as autonomous of the latter, is something disorganic, lacking a centre, an unstable diaspora of great cultural personalities, "without a Pope" and without a territory. This process of disintegration of the modern State is, however, far more catastrophic than the mediaeval historical process, which was disintegrative and integrative at the same time, given the particular grouping which was the motor of the historical process itself, and given the type of State which had existed since the beginning of the millennium in Europe—a State which was innocent of the centralisation of today, and which could be called "federative of the dominant classes" rather than the State of a single dominant class.

It is worth considering the extent to which Gentile's "actualism"[70] corresponds to the positive phase of the State, whereas Croce provides the opposition to this. The concept of "unity in the act" allows Gentile to recognise as "history" what is anti-history for Croce.[71] For Gentile history is entirely State history, while for Croce it is "ethical-political". In other words, Croce seeks to maintain a distinction between civil society and political society, between hegemony and dictatorship; the great intellectuals exercise hegemony, which presupposes a certain collaboration, i.e. an active and voluntary (free) consent, i.e. a liberal, democratic régime. Gentile sees the economic-corporate phase as an ethical phase within the historical act: hegemony and dictatorship are indistinguishable, force and consent are simply equivalent; one cannot distinguish political society from civil society; only the State, and of course the State-as-government, exists, etc.

The same conflicting positions which emerge in the philosophical sphere, between Croce and Gentile, appear again in the field of political economy, between Einaudi and the followers of Gentile.* Spirito's[72] concept of citizen as State functionary derives directly from the absence of separation between political and civil society, between political hegemony and State-political government. In

---

[70] See note 70 on p. 424.
[71] See note 6 on p. 128.
* See the Einaudi–Benini–Spirito polemic in *Nuovi Studi*, 1930.
[72] See notes 59 on p. 257 and 120 on p. 470.

other words, it derives from the anti-historicity or ahistoricity of the conception of the State that is implicit in Spirito's position, despite his peremptory assertions and polemical rantings. Spirito refuses to recognise that, since every form of property is linked to the State, even for the classical economists the latter intervenes at every moment of economic life—which is a continuous web of transfers of property. Spirito's position, concretely, represents a return to the pure economicity of which he accuses his opponents. It is interesting to note that this position contains the essence of "Americanism",[73] since America has not yet emerged from the economic-corporate phase which Europe passed through in the Middle Ages—in other words, has not yet created a conception of the world or a group of great intellectuals to lead the people within the ambit of civil society. In this sense it is true that America is under the influence of Europe, and of European history. (This question of the basic form of the State in the U.S.A. is a very complex one, but the kernel of the question seems to me to be precisely this.) [1930–32]

"SUBVERSIVE"

The purely Italian concept of "subversive"[74] can be explained as follows: a negative rather than a positive class position—the "people" is aware that it has enemies, but only identifies them empirically as the so-called *signori*.[75] Contained in the concept of *signore* there is much of the old dislike of country for town; dress is a fundamental element of distinction. There is also dislike of officialdom—the only form in which the State is perceived. The peasant, and even the small farmer, hates the civil servant; he does not hate the State, for he does not understand it. He sees the civil servant as a "*signore*", even if he is himself in fact better off economically; hence the apparent contradiction whereby the *signore* is often at the same time a *morto di fame*[76] as far as the peasant is

[73] See "Americanism and Fordism" on pp. 277–318.

[74] The term *sovversivo* was used by both socialists and fascists to describe themselves, as well as by others to describe them—which gives an idea of the difference between it and the English equivalent "subversive". See, for example, Gramsci's article in *Ordine Nuovo*, 22 June 1921, "*Sovversismo Reazionario*", in which he comments sarcastically on Mussolini's motives for stressing his "subversive" past in a speech to the Chamber of Deputies, and suggests that Mussolini was never so very subversive in reality.

[75] "Gentleman" would be the nearest English equivalent of *signore*, but since this note is directly on the concept itself, the word has been left in the Italian.

[76] Literally "starveling", the term has overtones of both pity and contempt. See following paragraph.

concerned. This "generic" hatred is still "semi-feudal" rather than modern in character, and cannot be taken as evidence of class consciousness—merely as the first glimmer of such consciousness, in other words, merely as the basic negative, polemical attitude. Not only does the people have no precise consciousness of its own historical identity, it is not even conscious of the historical identity or the exact limits of its adversary. The lower classes, historically on the defensive, can only achieve self-awareness via a series of negations, via their consciousness of the identity and class limits of their enemy; but it is precisely this process which has not yet come to the surface, at least not nationally.

A further element towards understanding the concept of "subversive" is furnished by the stratum known typically as the *morti di fame*. The *morti di fame* are not a homogeneous stratum, and serious mistakes can be made if they are identified abstractly. In the village, and in the small urban centres of certain agricultural regions, there exist two distinct strata of *morti di fame*: the day-labourers, and the petty intellectuals. The essential characteristic of the day-labourers is not their economic situation but their intellectual and moral condition. The typical peasant of these regions is the smallholder or the more primitive share-cropper (whose rent takes the form of a third, half, or even two-thirds of his crop, depending on the fertility and location of his holding), who owns a few tools, a pair of oxen, and a cottage which he has often built himself on days when he is not working, and who has obtained the necessary capital either by emigrating for a few years, or by spending a few years "down the pits" or serving in the *carabinieri*,[77] etc., or as a servant for a big landowner—i.e. by "contriving" and saving. The day-labourer on the other hand, unable or unwilling to "contrive", possesses nothing, is a *morto di fame*, because day labour is scarce and irregular.

The petit-bourgeois *morto di fame* came originally from the rural bourgeoisie. Property gets broken up among large families until it vanishes altogether, but the members of this class are not prepared to work with their hands. In this way there is formed a famished stratum of aspirants to minor municipal appointments, as clerks, messengers, etc. This stratum constitutes a disruptive element in the life of the countryside, always thirsting for changes (elections,

---

[77] The *carabinieri*, founded in Piedmont in 1814 as a military force for maintaining internal security, after the Risorgimento became a national police force, organised on a military footing and independent from the ordinary police. This is still the case today.

etc.), and furnishes the local "subversive"; since it is fairly numerous, it has a certain importance. It allies itself especially with the rural bourgeoisie against the peasantry, and organises the *morti di fame* to serve its interests. These strata exist in every region, and have ramifications in the towns, too, where they merge into the criminal underworld or into the shifting milieu which surrounds it. Many petty clerks in the towns originate socially from these strata, and conserve the arrogant mentality of the impoverished nobleman, of the landowner who endures work under compulsion. The "subversivism" of these strata has two faces, one turned to the left and one to the right, but the left face is simply a means of blackmail; at the decisive moments they always move to the right, and their desperate "courage" always prefers to have the *carabinieri* on their side.

A further element to examine is the so-called "internationalism" of the Italian people, which is linked to the concept of "subversivism". In reality, this is a kind of vague "cosmopolitanism", related to certain easily identifiable historical phenomena: to the cosmopolitanism and the universalism of the Catholic Middle Ages, centred on Italy and preserved through the absence of any Italian "political and national history". Little national or State consciousness in the modern sense. I have noted elsewhere[78] that there has existed, and still exists, a particular form of Italian chauvinism, more widespread than might at first appear. The two observations are not contradictory. In Italy, political, territorial and national unity enjoy a scanty tradition (or perhaps no tradition at all, since before 1870 Italy was never a unified entity, and even the name Italy, which in Roman times meant Southern and Central Italy up to the Magra and the Rubicon, during the Middle Ages lost ground to the name of Longobardia: see the study by C. Cipolla on the name "Italia", published in the *Atti dell'Accademia di Torino*). However, Italy did have, and preserve, a cultural tradition going back to the period 1300–1700—not, however, to classical antiquity, although humanism and renaissance both claimed a continuity with the classical era. This cultural unity was the basis, and a very weak one at that, of the Risorgimento and of national unity; it served to group the most active and intelligent strata of the population around the bourgeoisie, and it is still the substratum of popular nationalism. As a consequence of the absence in this sentiment of politico-military or politico-

[78] In a note on d'Annunzio, PP, p. 13.

economic elements, i.e. of the elements which are at the basis of French, German or American nationalist psychology, it comes about that many so-called "subversives" and "internationalists" are "chauvinists" in this sense, without being aware of any contradiction. What one has to note if one wants to understand the virulence which this cultural chauvinism sometimes assumes is the following: the fact that in Italy a great scientific, artistic and literary flowering coincided with the period of political, military and State decadence. (Sixteenth and seventeenth centuries. Explain this phenomenon. Noble, courtly culture, i.e. when the bourgeoisie of the Communes was already decadent, and wealth had become usurial rather than productive, with concentrations of "luxury", the prelude to total economic decadence.) The concept of revolutionary and of internationalist, in the modern sense of the word, is correlative with the precise concept of State and of class: little understanding of the State means little class consciousness (and understanding of the State exists not only when one defends it, but also when one attacks it in order to overthrow it); hence low level of effectiveness of the parties, etc. Gypsy bands or political nomadism are not dangerous phenomena,[79] and similarly Italian subversivism and internationalism were not dangerous. Popular "subversivism" correlates with "subversivism" at the top, i.e. with the fact of there never having existed a "rule of law", but only a politics characterised by absolute power and by cliques around individuals or groups.

All these observations, naturally, cannot be taken as categorical or absolute: they constitute an attempt to describe certain aspects of a situation. Firstly, in order to be able the better to evaluate the activity undertaken to change it (or the non-activity, i.e. the failure to understand one's own task). Secondly, in order to give greater prominence to those groups which rose above it, as a result of having understood the situation and modified it within their own ranks. [1930]

"WAVE OF MATERIALISM" AND "CRISIS OF AUTHORITY"

That aspect of the modern crisis which is bemoaned as a "wave of materialism" is related to what is called the "crisis of authority". If the ruling class has lost its consensus, i.e. is no longer "leading"[80]

---

[79] For the term "gypsy" see "Voluntarism and Social Masses" on pp. 202–4 and note 109 on p. 204.

[80] See note 5 on p. 55.

but only "dominant", exercising coercive force alone, this means precisely that the great masses have become detached from their traditional ideologies, and no longer believe what they used to believe previously, etc. The crisis consists precisely in the fact that the old is dying and the new cannot be born; in this interregnum a great variety of morbid symptoms appear. N.B. this paragraph should be completed by some observations which I made on the so-called "problem of the younger generation"[81]—a problem caused by the "crisis of authority" of the old generations in power, and by the mechanical impediment that has been imposed on those who could exercise hegemony, which prevents them from carrying out their mission.

The problem is the following: can a rift between popular masses and ruling ideologies as serious as that which emerged after the war be "cured" by the simple exercise of force, preventing the new ideologies from imposing themselves? Will the interregnum, the crisis whose historically normal solution is blocked in this way, necessarily be resolved in favour of a restoration of the old? Given the character of the ideologies, that can be ruled out—yet not in an absolute sense. Meanwhile physical depression will lead in the long run to a widespread scepticism, and a new "arrangement" will be found—in which, for example, catholicism will even more become simply Jesuitism, etc.

From this too one may conclude that highly favourable contions are being created for an unprecedented expansion of historical materialism. The very poverty which at first inevitably characterises historical materialism as a theory diffused widely among the masses will help it to spread. The death of the old ideologies takes the form of scepticism with regard to all theories and general formulae; of application to the pure economic fact (earnings, etc.), and to a form of politics which is not simply realistic in fact (this is always the case) but which is cynical in its immediate manifestation (remember the story of the *Prelude to Machiavelli*,[82] written perhaps under the influence of Professor Rensi, which at a certain moment—in 1921 or 1922—extolled slavery as a modern means of political economy).

But this reduction to economics and to politics means precisely a reduction of the highest superstructures to the level of those which adhere more closely to the structure itself—in other words, the possibility and necessity of creating a new culture. [1930]

---

[81] PP., pp. 104–7.

[82] By Mussolini.

3
AMERICANISM AND FORDISM

INTRODUCTION

Americanism and Fordism is unique among Gramsci's prison writings, The problems it sets out to analyse were contemporary ones, brought into prominence by events that had taken place since his imprisonment—the development of the corporate (fascist) economy, the depression, the first Soviet Five Year Plan. Yet, despite his isolation, he nevertheless succeeds in this essay in laying the groundwork for a persuasive analysis of trends in social and economic development which had passed by most of his active contemporaries and whose importance is only now becoming clear.

The basic question Gramsci asks himself in *Americanism and Fordism* is this: were the changes taking place within the world of production at the time he was writing of such importance as to constitute the beginnings of a new historical epoch, or were they merely a conjunction of events of no lasting significance? No definitive answer is offered, nor could one be demanded, but it is clear from the way he approaches the question, linking together features of the superstructures such as prohibition or the regulation of sexuality with changes in the socio-economic base, projecting each trend into the future as well as examining its roots in the past, that he regarded "Americanism" as a symptom of an historical development within the relations of production of the utmost importance, from which there could be no turning back.

The starting-point of *Americanism and Fordism* is the impact of America and American productive methods on Europe after the First World War. The fact that America had never known a feudal phase and was therefore free of parasitic residues of older modes of production has always intrigued European Marxists, ever since the days of Marx himself. In the early days of the Soviet Union much attention was paid to the American phenomenon, to the efficiency of American productive technique and even to the apparent democracy of American enterprise. There was also a general interest in the Soviet Union in the possibility of applying American ideas, notably those of Frederick Taylor on "Scientific Management", under Socialist relations of production. For Gramsci, the full-scale introduction of Americanism into Italy would have a different significance. It would represent a high point of capitalist development, the abolition of the last residues of feudalism.

Opposition to Americanism, as he saw it, came mostly from backward economic groups such as the "rural bourgeoisie" of petty landowners and their attendant parasites, but also from a reactionary intelligentsia, stuffed with myths about its cultural heritage and unable to accept its own uselessness and impending supercession by more vital forces. The working class, by contrast, he saw as not opposed to Americanism as such, nor even to its attendant effects in social life, but rather to the specific form it would take in conditions of intensified economic exploitation and authoritarian cultural repression. The victory of Americanism might also affect the political superstructures of fascism, now more and more embroiled (since the Concordat) with the Catholic Church, and increasingly torn between notions of a new order and a commitment to the most retrograde elements of culture and society.

An essential, though unspoken, premiss of *Americanism and Fordism* is that the revolutionary working-class movement was in a phase of retrenchment and defeat throughout the capitalist world. In the absence of an antagonistic revolutionary force any changes taking place within the mode of production could at most constitute what Gramsci, here and elsewhere in the *Quaderni*, terms a "passive revolution". Changes would take place, leading to the suppression of certain contradictions. But new contradictions would appear in their place. Not the least of the merits of *Americanism and Fordism* lies in its recognition of the fluidity of the situation and the complexity of the contradictions generated. Although in general it foresees a development, already prefigured in fascist Italy, in the direction of a more achieved form of state monopoly capitalism, it emphatically rejects any undialectical pessimism and leaves open the question of how the contradictions that this new development of capitalism will bring about will themselves be contested in their turn.

AMERICANISM AND FORDISM

A series of problems requires to be examined under the general and somewhat conventional heading "Americanism and Fordism". But first of all one should take account of the basic fact that solutions to these problems must necessarily be put forward within the contradictory conditions of modern society, which create complications, absurd positions, and moral and economic crises often tending towards catastrophe.

In generic terms one could say that Americanism and Fordism derive from an inherent necessity to achieve the organisation of a planned economy, and that the various problems examined here should be the links of the chain marking the passage from the old economic individualism to the planned economy. Problems arise from the various forms of resistance to this evolution encountered by the process of development, the source of the problems being difficulties inherent in both the *societas rerum* and the *societas hominum*.[1]

The fact that a progressive initiative has been set in train by a particular social force is not without fundamental consequences: the "subaltern" forces, which have to be "manipulated" and rationalised to serve new ends, naturally put up a resistance. But resistance is also offered by certain sectors of the dominant forces, or at least by forces which are allied to those which are dominant. Prohibition, which in the United States was a necessary condition for developing a new type of worker suitable to "Fordised" industry, has failed as a result of the opposition of marginal and still backward forces and certainly not because of the opposition of either the industrialists or the workers (etc.).

A catalogue of some of the essentially most important or interesting problems, even if at first sight they do not appear to be in the forefront:

1. The replacement of the present plutocratic stratum by a new mechanism of accumulation and distribution of finance capital based directly on industrial production.

2. The question of sex.

3. The question of whether Americanism can constitute an historical "epoch", that is, whether it can determine a gradual evolution of the same type as the "passive revolution" examined

[1] "The society of things and the society of men": i.e. the natural and human worlds.

elsewhere and typical of the last century,[2] or whether on the other hand it does not simply represent the molecular accumulation of elements destined to produce an "explosion", that is, an upheaval on the French pattern.

4. The question of the "rationalisation" of the demographic composition of Europe.

5. The question of whether this evolution must have its starting-point within the industrial and productive world, or whether it can come from the outside, through the cautious but massive construction of a formal juridical arm which can guide from the outside the necessary evolution of the productive apparatus.

6. The question of the so-called "high wages" paid by Fordised and rationalised industry.

7. Fordism as the ultimate stage in the process of progressive attempts by industry to overcome the law of the tendency of the rate of profit to fall.[3]

8. Psychoanalysis and its enormous diffusion since the war, as the expression of the increased moral coercion exercised by the apparatus of State and society on single individuals, and of the pathological crisis determined by this coercion.

9. Rotary Clubs and Free Masonry.

RATIONALISATION OF THE DEMOGRAPHIC COMPOSITION OF EUROPE

In Europe the various attempts which have been made to introduce certain aspects of Americanism and Fordism have been due to the old plutocratic stratum which would like to reconcile what, until proved to the contrary, appear to be irreconcilables: on the one hand the old, anachronistic, demographic social structure of Europe, and on the other hand an ultra-modern form of production

---

[2] "Passive revolution." For Gramsci's development of this concept, see pp. 106–114.

[3] "Law of the Tendency", etc. See Marx, *Capital*, Vol. III, Chaps. 13–15. In Marxist economic analysis, the rate of profit is determined by the rate of exploitation (the ratio of unpaid, surplus labour to paid, necessary labour) and by the organic composition of capital (the ratio of capital expended on materials, use of machinery, etc., to capital expended on wages). As the rate of exploitation rises the rate of profit tends to rise, but as the organic composition of capital rises the rate of profit tends to fall. In *Capital*, Vol. III, Marx argues that the long-run tendency of capitalist accumulation is to raise the organic composition of capital to such an extent that the rate of profit will fall even if the rate of exploitation is rising. Attempts to overcome the tendency require therefore a very considerable rise in the rate of exploitation, which Gramsci sees as happening through "Fordist" methods of intensification and rationalisation of labour.

and of working methods—such as is offered by the most advanced American variety, the industry of Henry Ford.

For this reason, the introduction of Fordism encounters so much "intellectual" and "moral" resistance, and takes place in particularly brutal and insidious forms, and by means of the most extreme coercion. To put it crudely, Europe would like to have a full barrel and a drunken wife, to have all the benefits which Fordism brings to its competitive power while retaining its army of parasites who, by consuming vast sums of surplus value, aggravate initial costs and reduce competitive power on the international market. The reaction of Europe to Americanism merits, therefore, close examination. From its analysis can be derived more than one element necessary for the understanding of the present situation of a number of states in the old world and the political events of the post-war period.

Americanism, in its most developed form, requires a preliminary condition which has not attracted the attention of the American writers who have treated the problems arising from it, since in America it exists quite "naturally". This condition could be called "a rational demographic composition" and consists in the fact that there do not exist numerous classes with no essential function in the world of production, in other words classes which are purely parasitic. European "tradition", European "civilisation", is, conversely, characterised precisely by the existence of such classes, created by the "richness" and "complexity" of past history. This past history has left behind a heap of passive sedimentations produced by the phenomenon of the saturation and fossilisation of civil-service personnel and intellectuals, of clergy and landowners, piratical commerce and the professional (and later conscript, but for the officers always professional) army. One could even say that the more historic a nation the more numerous and burdensome are these sedimentations of idle and useless masses living on "their ancestral patrimony", pensioners of economic history. Statistics of these economically passive elements (in a social sense) are very hard to work out because it is impossible to find a "heading" under which they can be defined for the purposes of immediate research. But useful indications can be derived indirectly, for example, from the existence of specific forms of national life. The considerable number of large, medium-sized (or even small) agglomerations of an urban type with no industry (with no factories) is one such indication and one of the most significant.

On the so-called "mystery of Naples": it is worth recalling the observations made by Goethe about Naples and the "consoling moral conclusions" which Giustino Fortunato drew from them.[4] Goethe was right to demolish the legend of the organic vagabondry [*lazzaronismo*]* of the Neapolitans, and to point out that, on the contrary, they are very active and industrious. But the question consists in examining the actual result of their industry. It is not in itself productive, nor is it directed towards satisfying the needs and demands of the productive classes. Naples is the city where the majority of Southern landowners, whether members of the nobility or not, spend the income from their estates. Around some tens of thousands of these landowning families, of greater or lesser importance, together with their immediate retinues of servants and lackeys, is organised the practical life of a large part of the city, its artisanal industries, its itinerant trades and the incredible way in which the immediate supply of goods and services is split up among the multitude of layabouts who hang around the streets. Another important part of the city is organised around transport and the wholesale trade, "Productive" industry, in the sense of one that creates and accumulates new goods, is relatively small despite the fact that in the official statistics Naples is classified as the fourth industrial city of Italy, after Milan, Turin and Genoa.

This socio-economic structure of Naples (on which it is now possible to have reasonably exact information, thanks to the activities of the provincial councils of the corporate economy)[6] explains a great deal of the history of the city of Naples, so full of apparent contradictions and thorny political problems. The phenomenon of

---

[4] Johann Wolfgang Goethe, *Italienische Reise*. The "conclusions" drawn by Giustino Fortunato (1848–1932), a noted "meridionalist" intellectual and politician, are to be found in Fortunato's translation of the Neapolitan section (*Lettere da Napoli, di Volfgango Goethe, tradotte da GF*, Naples, 1917).

* Fortunato's short work on Goethe and his judgement on the Neapolitans has been republished by the Bibliografia Editrice di Rieti in the collection "Quaderni Critici" directed by Domenico Petrini. On Fortunato's short work, worth reading is Luigi Einaudi's review in *La Riforma Sociale*, perhaps 1912.[5]

[5] Actually 1918. Subsequently reprinted in *Le Lotte del Lavoro*, Turin, 1924, pp. 267–76.

[6] Corporate here is more or less a synonym (or euphemism) for fascist, the Italian economy having been organised from 1926 in "Corporations", including labour corporations which effectively took the place of the trade unions. Elsewhere in this text when Gramsci speaks about the "corporate trend" (*indirizzo corporativo*) he is sometimes referring not to Fascism as such but to the organised ideology of corporatism which was already a major force in pre-fascist Italy, having supporters among progressive Catholics and reformist Socialists as well as among rationalising elements of Italian capitalism. Needless to say the form the corporate economy took under Mussolini, particularly after 1930, was not altogether that intended by the movement's non-fascist originators.

Naples is repeated on a large scale in Palermo and Rome, and also in a number of cities (the famous hundred cities)[7] not only in Southern Italy and the islands, but in Central and even in Northern Italy (Bologna, to a certain extent, Parma, Ferrara, etc.). For much of the population of cities of this type, one can recall the proverb: "Where a horse shits a hundred sparrows feed."

The fact that has not yet been properly studied is this: that the ownership of medium-sized and small property in the rural areas is not in the hands of the peasant cultivators but of a small-town bourgeoisie and that the land is given over to primitive share-cropping [*mezzadria*], that is, rented in exchange for natural goods and services, or is leased against rent [*enfiteusi*]. This means that there exists, in proportion to gross landed income, an enormous bulk of petty and middle bourgeoisie living on "pensions" and "rents", which has created, in a species of economic literature truly worthy of *Candide*, the monstrous figure of the so-called "producers of savings", an economically unproductive stratum which not only extracts its own sustenance from the primitive labour of a specific number of peasants, but also manages to save. This is the most hideous and unhealthy means of capital accumulation, because it is founded on the iniquitous usurial exploitation of a peasantry kept on the verge of malnutrition, and because it is inordinately expensive, since the small saving of capital is offset by the incredible expenditure which is often necessary to maintain a high standard of living for such a great mass of absolute parasites. (The historical phenomenon whereby, in the Italian peninsula, since the fall of the mediaeval Communes and the decline of the spirit of capitalist initiative among the urban bourgeoisie, this abnormal and stagnation-creating situation has grown up, wave by wave, has been described by the historian Niccolò Rodolico as a "return to the earth", and has even been taken as an index of healthy national progress, such is the power of catch-phrases to annul the critical sense.)

Another source of absolute parasitism has always been the State administration. Renato Spaventa has reckoned that in Italy one tenth of the population (four million inhabitants) live off the state budget. Even today it happens that men who are still relatively young, not much above forty, in excellent health and at the height of their physical and intellectual capacities, after twenty-five years of state service cease to devote themselves to any productive activity

---

[7] "Hundred Cities". See note 61 on p. 91.

but make do with more or less substantial pensions. However, a worker can only enjoy his pension from the age of sixty-five, and for a peasant there is no limit to the age up to which he may continue to work. (One result of this is that the average Italian is surprised when he hears it said that an American multi-millionaire continues to be active right up to the last day of his conscious life.) If in any family a priest becomes a canon, immediately, for the entire clan, "manual labour" becomes a "disgrace": the most one should do is to engage in commerce.

The composition had already been rendered "unhealthy" by long-term emigration and by the low rate of employment of women in work productive of new goods. The relationship between "potentially" active and passve population was one of the most unfavourable in Europe.* It is even more unfavourable if one takes into account the following:

1. Endemic diseases (malaria, etc.) which reduce the average work potential of the labour force.

2. The chronic state of malnutrition of many of the lower strata of the peasantry (as documented in the researches of Professor Mario Camis published in *La Riforma Sociale* in 1926).[8] National averages of living standards should be broken down into class averages: if the national average hardly attains the standard scientifically established as indispensable, it follows obviously that a not inconsiderable stratum of the population lives in a state of chronic mulnutrition. In the Senate discussion on the budget for 1929/30, Senator Mussolini affirmed that in some regions people live exclusively on wild plants and vegetables for whole seasons of the year.**

3. The endemic unemployment which exists in a number of agricultural regions and does not figure in official reports.

4. The really remarkable segment of the population which is absolutely parasitic and which requires for its service the labour of another immense and indirectly parasitic mass; and the semi-parasitic segment, which is so because it multiplies to an abnormal and unhealthy degree subordinate economic activities like commerce and intermediary functions in general.

---

* Cf. the research into this subject by Professor Mortara, for example, in *Prospettive Economiche* of 1922.

[8] M. Camis, *Intorno alle condizioni economiche del popolo italiano.* "La Riforma Sociale", June 1926.

** Cf. the *Atti Parlamentari* for the session, and the speech by Senator Ugo Ancona, whose reactionary fancies were smartly slapped down by the head of the Government [Mussolini].

This situation is not unique to Italy; to a greater or lesser extent it exists also in all countries of Old Europe and it exists in an even worse form in India and China, which explains the historical stagnation of those countries and their politico-military impotence. (In the examination of this problem, what is immediately in question is not the form of economico-social organisation, but the rationality of the proportional relationships between the various sectors of the population in the existing social system. Every system has its own law of fixed proportions[9] in its demographic composition, its own "optimum" equilibrium and forms of disequilibrium which, if not redressed, by appropriate legislation, can be catastrophic in themselves in that, apart from any other disintegrative element, they dry up the sources of economic life.)

America does not have "great historical and cultural traditions"; but neither does it have this leaden burden to support. This is one of the main reasons (and certainly more important than its so-called natural wealth) for its formidable accumulation of capital which has taken place in spite of the superior living standard enjoyed by the popular classes compared with Europe. The non-existence of viscous parasitic sedimentations left behind by past phases of history has allowed industry, and commerce in particular, to develop on a sound basis. It also allows a continual reduction of the economic function of transport and trade to the level of a genuinely subaltern activity of production. Indeed, it has led to the attempt to absorb these activities into productive activity itself. Recall here the experiments conducted by Ford and to the economies made by his firm through direct management of transport and distribution of the product. These economies affected production costs and permitted higher wages and lower selling prices. Since these preliminary conditions existed, already rendered rational by historical evolution, it was relatively easy to rationalise production and labour by a skilful combination of force (destruction of working-class trade unionism on a territorial basis) and persuasion (high wages, various social benefits, extremely subtle ideological and political propaganda) and thus succeed in making the whole life of the nation revolve around production. Hegemony here is born in the factory and requires for its exercise only a minute quantity of professional political and ideological intermediaries. The phenomenon of the "masses" which so struck Romier[10] is nothing but

---

[9] "Fixed proportions." See p. 191.

[10] Lucien Romier, *Qui sera le maître, Europe ou Amérique?* Paris, 1927.

the form taken by this "rationalised" society in which the "structure" dominates the superstructures more immediately and in which the latter are also "rationalised" (simplified and reduced in number).

Rotary Clubs and Free Masonry: Rotary is a Free Masonry without the petits bourgeois and without the petit-bourgois mentality. America has Rotary and the YMCA; Europe has Free Masonry and the Jesuits. Attempts to introduce the YMCA into Italy; help given by Italian industry to these attempts (financial aid from Agnelli and the violent reactions of the Catholics); Agnelli's attempts to absorb the *Ordine Nuovo* group[11] which upheld its own type of "Americanism" in a form acceptable to the workers.

In America rationalisation has determined the need to elaborate a new type of man suited to the new type of work and productive process. This elaboration is still only in its initial phase and therefore (apparently) still idyllic. It is still at the stage of psycho-physical adaptation to the new industrial structure, aimed for through high wages. Up to the present (until the 1929 crash) there has not been, except perhaps sporadically, any flowering of the "superstructure". In other words, the fundamental question of hegemony has not yet been posed. The struggle is conducted with arms taken from the old European arsenal, bastardised and therefore anachronistic compared with the development of "things." The struggle taking place in America, as described by Philip,[12] is still in defence of craft rights against "industrial liberty". In other words, it is similar to the struggle that took place in Europe in the eighteenth century, although in different conditions. American workers unions are, more than anything else, the corporate expression of the rights of qualified crafts and therefore the industrialists' attempts to curb them have a certain "progressive" aspect. The absence of the European historical phase, marked even in the economic field by the French

[11] Giovanni Agnelli, the "progressive" head of FIAT, made various attempts in the immediately post-war years to buy off the intense militancy of the workers and enlist support for the rationalisation and intensification of production in the FIAT works in Turin. In October 1920, after the occupation of the factories, he went so far as to put forward a scheme of co-operative management, which was decisively rejected by the workers under Communist leadership. The Communist workers, centred around the "Ordine Nuovo", had been in the forefront of the struggle setting up the Workers' Councils which took over the running of the factory during the September occupation, and it was Agnelli's hope that the Ordine Nuovo group could be won over to his own class-collaborationist version of the councils. (Gramsci's account of the Agnelli episode is to be found in *Alcuni Temi della Questione Meridionale* (1926, GF, pp. 804–809). See also the article in *Avanti!*, 5 February 1919, GF, pp. 357–359.)

[12] André Philip. *Le Problème ouvrier aux Etats-Unis*, Paris, 1929.

Revolution, has left the American popular masses in a backward state. To this should be added the absence of national homogeneity, the mixture of race-cultures, the negro question.

In Italy there have been the beginnings of a Fordist fanfare: exaltation of big cities, overall planning for the Milan conurbation, etc.; the affirmation that capitalism is only at its beginnings and that it is necessary to prepare for it grandiose patterns of development (on this see some articles by Schiavi in *La Riforma Sociale*). But afterwards came a conversion to ruralism,[13] the disparagement of the cities typical of the Enlightenment, exaltation of the artisanat and of idyllic patriarchalism, reference to craft rights and a struggle against industrial liberty. All the same, even though the development is slow and full of understandable caution, one cannot say that the conservative side, the side that represents old European culture with all its train of parasites, has not encountered opposition. (Interesting from this point of view is the tendency represented by *Nuovi Studi* and *Critica Fascista* and by the intellectual centre for corporate studies organised at the University of Pisa.) De Man's book[14] is also in its way an expression of these problems which are disturbing the old European bone-structure, but it is an expression without greatness and is unattached to any of the major historical forces which are striving for mastery of the world.

SUPER-CITY and SUPER-COUNTRY[15]

Excerpts from *La Fiera Letteraria* of 15 January 1928. From Giovanni Papini:[16]

"The city does not create, but consumes. Just as it is the emporium where congregate the goods seized from the country-

[13] "Ruralism." A notion which became current after Mussolini's call in 1927 to "ruralise [*ruralizzare*] Italy".

[14] Henri De Man. *Au delà du Marxisme*, Paris, 1924. The title "Beyond Marxism" is deceptive. As Gramsci points out, De Man's book is little more than a return to pre-Marxian humanism, with positivistic accretions and propped up by reference to the "psychological and ethical values" of the working-class movement (MS, pp. 110–114. See also p. 430 of this volume and notes 74 on p. 376 and 56 on p. 160.

[15] Super-City and Super-Country (*Stracittà e Strapaese*). This mainly literary polemic in the 1920's opposed (among others) Massimo Bontempelli and Corrado Alvaro, on the side of urbanism and cosmopolitanism, to Curzio Malaparte, Giuseppe Ungaretti and Giovanni Papini, on the side of nationalism and ruralism. As Benjamin Crémieux pointed out at the time, these conflicting attitudes can in a sense be seen as two sides of the coin of fascist imperialism (*Panorama de la littérature italienne contemporaine*. Paris, 1928. Quoted in OC).

[16] Giovanni Papini, ex-Futurist, converted to Catholicism and to a cult of austerity and simple values.

side and the mines, so it is to the city that there flow the freshest minds from the provinces and the ideas of great solitary men. The city is like a pyre which gives light because it is burning what was created far away from it and many times against it. All cities are sterile. Proportionately few children are born there, and genius almost never. In the city there is enjoyment, but no creation; there is love but no generation, consumption but no production."

Apart from the "absolute" idiocies here, one should point out that Papini has in mind the "relative" model of the city non-city, the Koblenz of the consumers of landed income and tolerated houses.[17] In the same number of *La Fiera Letteraria* the following item may be read:

"Our super-country recipe has these characteristics: decisive aversion to all those forms of civilisation which are not compatible with ours or which ruin, through being indigestible, the classical gifts of the Italians. Then, guardianship of the universal sense of the country, which is, spelt out, the natural and immanent relationship between the individual and his land. Finally, exaltation of our own native characteristics in every field and activity of life, that is to say: Catholic foundation, religious sense of the world, fundamental simplicity and sobriety, closeness to reality, control of fantasy, equilibrium between spirit and matter."

(Note: how would Italy of today, the Italian nation, have come into existence without the formation and development of cities and without the unifying influence of cities. "Supercountrymanism" in the past would have meant municipalism, just as it meant popular disarray and foreign rule. And would Catholicism itself have developed if the Pope, instead of residing in Rome, had taken up residence in Scaricalasino?)[18]

Or take this judgment of Francesco Meriano (from *L'Assalto*, Bologna):

"In the philosophical field I claim to discover on the other hand a real antithesis, which is an antithesis more than a hundred

---

[17] Koblenz, a city in the Rhineland, here used proverbially as a centre of parasitic consumption and legalised prostitution.

[18] *Scaricalasino*, literally "unload-the-donkey", in the sense of a tiny village at the back of beyond.

years old but always reappearing in a new outward guise: between voluntarism, pragmatism and activism, identifiable in Supercity, and enlightenment, rationalism and historicism, identifiable in Supercountry."

(In other words the immortal principles have taken refuge in Supercountry.) In any case it is worth noting that the "literary" polemic between Supercountry and Supercity was nothing but the froth on top of the polemic between parasitic conservatism and the innovating tendencies of Italian society. In *La Stampa*, 4 May 1929, Mino Maccari writes:

> "When Supercountry opposes modernistic importations, its opposition is aimed at preserving the right to select from them with a view to preventing harmful contacts, mixed with those which could be useful, from corrupting the integrity of the nature and character proper to Italian civilisation, quintessentialised over the ages and now yearning (!) after a unifying synthesis."

(Already "quintessentialised" but not "synthesised" and "unified" ! ! !)

FINANCIAL AUTARKY[19] OF INDUSTRY

A noteworthy article by Carlo Pagni, *A proposito di un tentativo di teoria pura del corporativismo* (*La Riforma Sociale*, September/October 1929) examines Massimo Fovel's book *Economia e corporativismo* (Ferrara, S.A.T.E., 1929) and refers to another work of the same author *Rendita e salario nello Stato Sindacale* (Rome, 1928). But he does not realise, or does not point out explicitly, that Fovel in his writings conceives of "corporatism" as the premiss for the introduction into Italy of the most advanced American systems of production and labour. It would be interesting to know whether Fovel is writing "out of his head" or whether he has behind him specific social forces (practically speaking and not just in general) which back him and urge him on. Fovel has never been a "pure scientist", since all intellectuals, however "pure", are always expressive of certain tendencies. In many ways he belongs to the Cicotti, Naldi, Bazzi, Preziosi, etc., coterie, but he is more complex, because of his undeniable intellectual quality. Fovel has always harboured the aspiration of becoming a great political *leader*,[20] but he has never

[19] Autarky: i.e. self-sufficiency, particularly in the sense of self-financing.
[20] *Leader*. In English in the text.

managed it because he lacks certain basic gifts—a force of will directed to a single end and a freedom from Missiroli's type of intellectual volubility. Furthermore, he is all too often clearly connected with shady petty interests.

He began as a "young radical"[21] before the war. He wanted to rejuvenate the traditional democratic movement by giving it a more concrete and modern content, and flirted a bit with the Republicans, especially with the federalist and regionalist trends (Oliviero Zuccarini's *Critica Politica*). During the war he was a Giolittian neutralist: in 1919 he joined the Socialist Party in Bologna, but never wrote for *Avanti!* Before the armistice he made several excursions to Turin. The Torinese industrialists had acquired the old and infamous *Gazzetta di Torino* in order to transform it and make it their own direct mouthpiece. Fovel aspired to become editor-in-chief of the new combination and was certainly in contact with industrial circles. But Tommaso Borelli, a "young liberal" was chosen instead, and was shortly succeeded by Italo Minunni of the *Idea Nazionale*. However, *La Gazzetta di Torino* did not flourish, even under the name of *Paese*, despite the sums expended on its development, and was closed down by its promoters.

A curious letter came from Fovel in 1919: he wrote that he "felt a "duty" to collaborate on the weekly *Ordine Nuovo*. We sent a reply establishing the limits of any possible contribution by him, after which the "voice of duty" was suddenly silent. Fovel joined up with the Passigli, Montelli, Gardenghi crowd, which had made out of the *Lavoratore* in Trieste a pretty lucrative business affair, and which must have had contacts with the Torinese industrial world. An attempt was made by Passigli to transport *L'Ordine Nuovo* to Trieste with a "commercially" profitable management (the date can be checked against the subscription of 100 lire made by Passigli who had come to Turin for direct talks).[22] The question arose of whether a "gentleman" could collaborate on *Il Lavoratore*. In 1921 certain papers belonging to Fovel and Gardenghi were found in the *Lavoratore* offices, from which it emerged that the two colleagues were speculating in cotton shares on the Stock Exchange during the strike led by the syndicalists of Nicola Vecchi, and were

[21] The curious biographical note which follows, about the apparently insignificant figure of Massimo Fovel, is interesting for the light it throws on part of the intellectual fringe of the Italian labour movement in the period immediately following the First World War and on the facility with which certain Social Democrats and "Radicals" passed into active complicity with the socio-economic manifestations of fascism.

[22] Passigli's subscription is recorded in *L'Ordine Nuovo*, 27 March 1920.

running the paper according to the interests of their speculations. After Livorno[23] Fovel was not heard of for some time. He reappeared in 1925, as a collaborator on *Avanti!* with Nenni[24] and Gardenghi, and set up a campaign in favour of the vassalage of Italian industry to American finance, a campaign which was instantly exploited (but there must have been an agreement in advance) by the *Gazzetta del Popolo*, connected with Ponti of S.I.P. [Piedmont Hydro-Electrics]. In 1925–26 Fovel was a frequent contributor to *La Voce Repubblicana*. Today (1929) he upholds corporatism as a premiss for an Italian form of Americanisation, collaborates on the Ferrara *Corriere Padano*,[25] on *Nuovi Studi*, *Nuovi Problemi* and *Problemi del Lavoro* and teaches (so it appears) at Ferrara University.

What would appear significant in Fovel's thesis, as summarised by Pagni, is his conception of the corporation as an autonomous industrial productive bloc destined to resolve in a modern and increasingly capitalist direction the problem of further development of the Italian economic apparatus. This is opposed to the semi-feudal and parasitic elements of society which appropriate an excessive tithe of surplus value and to the so-called "producers of savings". The production of savings should become an internal (more economical) function of the productive bloc itself, with the help of a development of production at diminishing costs which would allow, in addition to an increase of surplus value, higher salaries as well. The result of this would be a larger internal market, a certain level of working-class saving and higher profits. In this way one should get a more rapid rhythm of capital accumulation within the enterprise rather than through the intermediary of the "producers of savings" who are really nothing other than predators of surplus value. Within the industrial-productive bloc, the technical element, management and workers, should be more important than the "capitalistic" element in the petty sense of the word. The alliance of captains of industry and petit-bourgeois savers should be replaced by a bloc consisting of all the elements which are directly operative in production and which are the only ones capable of combining in a union and thus constituting the productive corporation. (Whence the extreme conclusion drawn by Spirito, of the corporation as property.)[26]

---

[23] The Congress of Livorno of January 1920, at which the Communist fraction definitively split from the Socialist Party and formed the Communist Party of Italy.

[24] Pietro Nenni, later to become leader of the Socialist Party.

[25] *Corriere Padano*. The paper of Italo Balbo, one of the leaders of Mussolini's March on Rome in October 1922.

[26] See note 120 on p. 470.

Pagni's objection to Fovel is that his treatment is not a new political economy but just a new economic policy. This is a purely formal objection, which could be important in a certain context but does not touch the core of the argument. The other objections, in concrete terms, are nothing other than the observation that there exist various aspects of the Italian situation which are backward in relation to the "organisational" upheaval of the economic machine. Fovel's greatest weaknesses consist in his having neglected the economic function which the state has always had in Italy because of the diffident attitude of small savers towards the industrialists, and in having neglected the fact that the corporative trend did not originate from the need for changes in the technical conditions of industry, or even from that of a new economic policy, but rather from the need for economic policing, a need which was aggravated by the 1929 crisis which is still going on.

In reality skilled workers in Italy have never, as individuals or through union organisations, actively or passively opposed innovations leading towards lowering of costs, rationalisation of work or the introduction of more perfect forms of automation and more perfect technical organisation of the complex of the enterprise. On the contrary. However, this has happened in America and has resulted in the semi-liquidation of the free trade unions and their replacement by a system of mutually isolated factory-based workers' organisations. In Italy on the other hand even the slightest and most cautious attempt to make the factory the centre of the trade union organisation (recall the question of the "shop stewards")[27] has been bitterly contested and resolutely crushed. A careful analysis of Italian history before 1922, or even up to 1926, which does not allow itself to be distracted by external trappings but manages to seize on the essential moments of the working-class struggle, must objectively come to the conclusion that it was precisely the workers who brought into being newer and more modern industrial requirements and in their own way upheld these strenuously. It could also be said that some industrialists understood this movement and tried to appropriate it to themselves. This explains Agnelli's attempt to absorb the *Ordine Nuovo* and its school into the FIAT complex and thus to institute a school of workers and technicians qualified for industrial change and for work with "rationalised" systems. The YMCA tried to open courses of abstract "Americanism", but despite all the money spent they were not a success.

---

[27] "*fiduciari d'azienda.*"

The considerations apart, a further series of questions is raised. The corporative movement exists. It is also true that in some ways the juridical changes which have already taken place have created the formal conditions within which major technical-economic change can happen on a large scale, because the workers are not in a position either to oppose it or to struggle to become themselves the standard-bearers of the movement. Corporative organisation could become the form of the new change, but one asks onself: shall we experience one of Vico's "ruses of providence"[28] in which men, without either proposing or willing it, are forced to obey the imperatives of history? For the moment one is more inclined to be dubious. The negative element of "economic policing" has so far had the upper hand over the positive element represented by the requirements of a new economic policy which can renovate, by modernising it, the socio-economic structure of the nation while remaining within the framework of the old industrialism.

The juridical form possible is one of the conditions required, but not the only one or even the most important: it is only the most important of the immediate conditions. Americanisation requires a particular environment, a particular social structure (or at least a determined intention to create it) and a certain type of State. This State is the liberal State, not in the sense of free-trade liberalism or of effective political liberty, but in the more fundamental sense of free initiative and of economic individualism which, with its own means, on the level of "civil society", through historical development, itself arrives at a régime of industrial concentration and monopoly. The disappearance of the semi-feudal type of *rentier* is in Italy one of the major conditions of an industrial revolution (and, in part, the revolution itself) and not a consequence. The economic and financial policy of the state is the instrument of their disappearance through the amortisation of the national debt, compulsory registration of shares, and by giving a greater weight to direct rather than indirect taxation in the governmental budget. But it does not seem that this has been or is going to become the trend of financial policy. Indeed, the State is creating new *rentiers*, that is to say it is promoting the old forms of parasitic accumulation of savings and tending to create closed social forma-

---

[28] "*astuzie della Provvidenza.*" In Vico's *Scienza Nuova,* Divine Providence, which is conceived as an immanent rather than a transcendental force and is broadly identifiable with Reason or History in later idealist writers, is seen as capable of overriding the contingent vagaries of human wills and redirecting the path of history by covert means. But see also note 103 on p. 108.

tions. In reality the corporative trend has operated to shore up crumbling positions of the middle classes and not to eliminate them, and is becoming, because of the vested interests that arise from the old foundations, more and more a machinery to preserve the existing order just as it is rather than a propulsive force. Why is this? Because the corporative trend is also dependent on unemployment. It defends for the employed a certain minimum standard which, if there were free competition, would likewise collapse and thus provoke serious social disturbances; and it creates new forms of employment, organisational and not productive, for the unemployed of the middle classes. But there still remains a way out: the corporative trend, born in strict dependence on such a delicate situation whose essential equilibrium must at all costs be maintained if monstrous catastrophe is to be averted, could yet manage to proceed by very slow and almost imperceptible stages to modify the social structure without violent shocks: even the most tightly swathed baby manages nevertheless to develop and grow. This is why it would be interesting to know whether Fovel is speaking just for himself or whether he is the representative of economic forces which are looking for a way forward at all costs. In any case, the process would be so long and encounter so many difficulties that new interests could grow up in the meanwhile and once again oppose its development so tenaciously as to crush it entirely.

SOME ASPECTS OF THE SEXUAL QUESTION

Obsession with the sexual question and dangers of that obsession. All the promoters of "blueprints" for society[29] put the sexual question in the forefront and resolve it "frankly".

It is worth noting that in "Utopias" the sexual question plays a large and often dominant part. (Croce's observation that Campanella's solutions in *La Città del Sole*[30] are inexplicable in terms of the sexual needs of Calabrian peasants is just inept.) Sexual instincts are those that have undergone the greatest degree of repression from society in the course of its development. "Regulation" of sexual instincts, because of the contradictions it creates and the perversions that are attributed to it, seems particularly "unnatural". Hence the frequency of appeals to "nature" in this area. "Psycho-analytical"

---

[29] "*progettisti.*"

[30] Tommaso Campanella (1568–1639), heretical Dominican monk, was the author of a famous early Utopia, *La Città del Sole* (The City of the Sun), which put forward a theocratic-communistic ideal of social organisation including a form of sexual communism.

literature is also a kind of criticism of the regulation of sexual instincts in a form which often recalls the Enlightenment, as in its creation of a new myth of the "savage" on a sexual basis (including relations between parents and children).

There is a split, in this field, between city and country, but with no idyllic bias in favour of the country, where the most frequent and the most monstrous sexual crimes take place and where bestiality and sodomy are widespread. In the parliamentary enquiry on the South in 1911 it is stated that in Abruzzo and the Basilicata, which are the regions where there is most religious fanaticism and patriarchalism and the least influence of urban ideas (to such an extent that, according to Serpieri, in the years 1919–20 there was not even any peasant unrest in those areas) there is incest in 30 per cent of families. And it does not appear that the situation has changed since then.

Sexuality as reproductive function and as sport: The "aesthetic" ideal of woman oscillates between the conceptions of "brood mare" and of "dolly". But it is not only in the cities that sexuality has become a "sport". The popular proverbs, "man is a hunter, woman a temptress", "the man who has no choice goes to bed with his wife", etc., show how widespread the conception of sex as sport is even in the countryside and in sexual relations between members of the same class.

The economic function of reproduction. This is not only a general fact which concerns the whole of society in its totality, because society demands a certain proportion between age-groups for purposes of production and of supporting the section of the population that for normal reasons (age, illness, etc.) is passive. It is also a "molecular" fact which operates within the smallest economic units, such as the family. The expression about the "staff of old age" demonstrates an instinctive consciousness of the economic need for there to be a certain ratio of young to old over the entire area of society. The sight of the maltreatment meted out in country villages to old people without a family encourages couples to want to have children. (The proverb to the effect that "a mother may raise a hundred sons, but a hundred sons do not support a mother", shows another side to this question.) Among the people old men without children are treated in the same way as bastards. Medical advance, which has raised the average expectancy of human life, is making the sexual question increasingly important as a fundamental and autonomous aspect of the economic, and this sexual aspect raises, in its turn, complex problems of a "superstructural" order. The increase of life-expectancy in France, where the birth-rate is low and where there is a rich and complex productive apparatus to be kept going, has already given rise to a number of problems connected with the national question. The older generations are finding themselves in an increasingly abnormal relationship with the younger generations of the same national culture, and the working masses are being swollen by immigrant elements from abroad which modify the base. The same phenomenon is happening there as in America, that of a certain division of labour, with the native population occupying the qualified trades and, of course, the functions of direction and organisation, and the immigrants the unskilled work.

In a number of states a similar relationship, with important negative economic consequences, exists between industrial cities with a low birth-rate and a prolific countryside. Life in industry demands a general apprenticeship, a process of psycho-physical adaptation to specific conditions of work, nutrition, housing, customs, etc. This is not something "natural" or innate, but has to be acquired, and the urban characteristics thus acquired are passed on by heredity or rather are absorbed in the development of childhood and adolescence. As a result the low birth-rate in the cities imposes the need for continual massive expenditure on the training of a continual flow of new arrivals in the city and brings with it a continual change in the socio-political composition of the city, thus continually changing the terrain on which the problem of hegemony is to be posed.

The formation of a new feminine personality is the most important question of an ethical and civil order connected with the sexual question. Until women can attain not only a genuine independence in relation to men but also a new way of conceiving themselves and their role in sexual relations, the sexual question will remain full of unhealthy characteristics and caution must be exercised in proposals for new legislation. Every crisis brought about by unilateral coercion in the sexual field unleashes a "romantic" reaction which could be aggravated by the abolition of organised legal prostitution. All these factors make any form of regulation of sex and any attempt to create a new sexual ethic suited to the new methods of production and work extremely complicated and difficult. However, it is still necessary to attempt this regulation and to attempt to create a new ethic. It is worth drawing attention to the way in which industrialists (Ford in particular) have been concerned with the sexual affairs of their employees and with their family arrangements in general. One should not be misled, any more than in the case of prohibition, by the "puritanical" appearance assumed by this concern. The truth is that the new type of man demanded by the rationalisation of production and work cannot be developed until the sexual instinct has been suitably regulated and until it too has been rationalised.

FEMINISM AND "MASCULINISM"

From the review which A. De Pietri Tonelli has published in the *Rivista di politica economica* (February 1930) of the book by Anthony M. Ludovici, *Woman. A Vindication* (2nd edition, London, 1921):

> "When things are going badly in the social structure of a nation because of the decadence of the fundamental capacities of its men", Ludovici claims, "two distinct tendencies seem always to assert themselves: on the one hand to interpret as symptoms of progress changes which are purely and simply signs of decadence and ruin of old and healthy (!) institutions; and the second, which is due to a justified loss of confidence in the governing class, is to give to everyone, whether or not they have the qualities required, the certainty of being chosen to make an effort in the direction of putting things right".

(The translation is manifestly uncertain and inaccurate.)[31] The author regards feminism as an expression of the second tendency and demands a resurgence of "masculinism". Apart from any other considerations on the subject, difficult to make because the text printed by De Pietri Tonelli is so uncertain, this anti-feminist and "masculinist" tendency is worth drawing attention to. One should also study the origins of the legislation in the Anglo-Saxon countries[32] which is so favourable to women in a

---

[31] Anthony Mario Ludovici, *Woman. A Vindication*, London, 1923. We have been unable to trace any corresponding passage in the original, and have simply retranslated the "manifestly uncertain and inaccurate Italian". The anti-feminist, anti-democratic tone of the passage is however quite typical of the author, amateur sexologist and translator of Nietzsche.

[32] Exactly what legislation Gramsci had in mind here is uncertain, but it is worth pointing out that in both England and America legislation in regard to divorce and custody of the children of separated parents was far in advance of that in Italy. The "unhealthy 'feministic' deviations" referred to immediately below would seem to be connected with an upper-class American phenomenon of sexual liberation achieved on the basis of economic independence obtained through a favourable divorce settlement.

whole series of questions relating to "sentimental" or pseudo-sentimental conflicts. This represents an attempt to regulate the sexual question, and to treat it seriously, but it doesn't seem to have accomplished its purpose. It has made way for unhealthy "feministic" deviations in the worst sense of the word, and has created for women (of the upper classes) a paradoxical social position.

"ANIMALITY" AND INDUSTRIALISM

The history of industrialism has always been a continuing struggle (which today takes an even more marked and vigorous form) against the element of "animality" in man. It has been an uninterrupted, often painful and bloody process of subjugating natural (i.e. animal and primitive) instincts to new, more complex and rigid norms and habits of order, exactitude and precision which can make possible the increasingly complex forms of collective life which are the necessary consequence of industrial development. This struggle is imposed from outside, and the results to date, though they have great immediate practical value, are to a large extent purely mechanical: the new habits have not yet become "second nature". But has not every new way of life, in the period in which it was forced to struggle against the old, always been for a certain time a result of mechanical repression? Even the instincts which have to be overcome today because they are too "animal" are really a considerable advance on earlier, even more primitive instincts. Who could describe the "cost" in human lives and in the grievous subjugation of instinct involved in the passage from nomadism to a settled agricultural existence? The process includes the first forms of rural serfdom and trade bondage, etc. Up to now all changes in modes of existence and modes of life have taken place through brute coercion, that is to say through the dominion of one social group over all the productive forces of society. The selection or "education" of men adapted to the new forms of civilisation and to the new forms of production and work has taken place by means of incredible acts of brutality which have cast the weak and the non-conforming into the limbo of the lumpen-classes or have eliminated them entirely.

With the appearance of new types of civilisation, or in the course of their development, there have always been crises. But who has been involved in these crises? Not so much the working masses as the middle classes and a part even of the ruling class which had undergone the process of coercion which was necessarily being exercised over the whole area of society. Crises of *libertinism* have been many, and there has been one in every historical epoch.

When the pressure of coercion is exercised over the whole complex of society (and this has taken place in particular since the fall of slavery and the coming of Christianity) puritan ideologies develop which give an external form of persuasion and consent to the intrinsic use of force. But once the result has been achieved, if only to a degree, the pressure is fragmented. Historically this fragmentation has assumed many different forms, which is to be expected, since the pressure itself has always taken original and often personal forms—it has been identified with a religious movement, it has created an apparatus of its own incarnated in particular strata or castes, it has taken the name of a Cromwell or a Louis XV as the case may be. It is at this point that the crisis of libertinism ensues. The French crisis following the death of Louis XV, for example, cannot be compared with the crisis in America following the appearance of Roosevelt, nor does prohibition, with its consequent gangsterism, etc., have any parallel in preceding epochs. But the crisis does not affect the working masses except in a superficial manner, or it can affect them indirectly, in that it depraves their women folk. These masses have either acquired the habits and customs necessary for the new systems of living and working, or else they continue to be subject to coercive pressure through the elementary necessities of their existence. Opposition to prohibition was not wanted by the workers, and the corruption brought about by bootlegging and gangsterism was widespread amongst the upper classes.

In the post-war period there has been a crisis of morals of unique proportions, but it took place in opposition to a form of coercion which had not been imposed in order to create habits suited to forms of work but arose from the necessities, admitted as transitory, of wartime life and life in the trenches. This pressure involved a particular repression of sexual instincts, even the most normal, among great masses of young people, and the crisis which broke out with the return to normal life was made even more violent by the disappearance of so many young men and by a permanent disequilibrium in the numerical proportions of individuals of the two sexes. The institutions connected with sexual life were profoundly shaken and new forms of enlightened utopias developed around the sexual question. The crisis was made even more violent, and still is, by the fact that it affected all strata of the population and came into conflict with the necessities of the new methods of work which were meanwhile beginning to impose themselves. (Taylorism and rationalisation in general.) These new methods demand a rigorous discipline of the sexual instincts (at the level of the nervous system) and with it a strengthening of the "family" in the wide sense (rather than a particular form of the familial system) and of the regulation and stability of sexual relations.

It is worth insisting on the fact that in the sexual field the most depraving and "regressive" ideological factor is the enlightened and libertarian conception proper to those classes which are not tightly bound to productive work and spread by them among the working classes. This element becomes particularly serious in a state where the working masses are no longer subject to coercive pressure from a superior class and where the new methods of production and work have to be acquired by means of reciprocal persuasion and by convictions proposed and accepted by each individual. A two-fold situation can then create itself in which there is an inherent conflict between the "verbal" ideology which recognises the new necessities and the real "animal" practice which prevents physical bodies from effectively acquiring the new attitudes. In this case one gets the formation of what can be called a situation of totalitarian social hypocrisy. Why totalitarian? In other situations the popular strata are compelled to practise "virtue". Those who preach it do not practice it, although they pay it verbal homage.[33] The hypocrisy is therefore a question of strata: it is not total. This is a situation which cannot last, and is certain to lead to a crisis of libertinism, but only when the masses have already assimilated "virtue" in the form of more or less permanent habits, that is with ever-decreasing oscillations. On the other hand, in the case where no coercive pressure is exercised by a superior class, "virtue" is affirmed in generic terms but is not practised either through conviction or through coercion, with the result that the psycho-physical attitudes necessary for the new methods of work are not acquired. The crisis can become "permanent"—that is, potentially catastrophic—since it can be resolved only by coercion. This coercion is a new type, in that it is exercised by the *élite* of a class over the rest of that same class. It can also only be self-coercion and therefore self-discipline (like Alfieri tying himself to the chair).[34]

---

[33] Cf. the famous "Maxim" of La Rochefoucauld (n. CCXVIII): "hypocrisy is a homage which vice pays to virtue".

[34] Vittorio Alfieri (1749–1803), the Italian poet and dramatist, recounts in his autobiography (V. Alfieri, *Vita*, Epoca Terza, cap. XV) how in his determina-

In any case in the sphere of sexual relations what can be opposed to this function of the *élites* is the enlightened and libertarian mentality. The struggle against the libertarian conception means therefore precisely creating the *élites* necessary for the historical task, or at least developing them so that their function is extended to cover all spheres of human activity.

RATIONALISATION OF PRODUCTION AND WORK

The tendency represented by Lev Davidovitch [Trotsky] was closely connected to this series of problems, a fact which does not seem to me to have been fully brought out. Its essential content, from this point of view, consisted in an "over"-resolute (and therefore not rationalised) will to give supremacy in national life to industry and industrial methods, to accelerate, through coercion imposed from the outside, the growth of discipline and order in production, and to adapt customs to the necessities of work. Given the general way in which all the problems connected with this tendency were conceived, it was destined necessarily to end up in a form of Bonapartism. Hence the inexorable necessity of crushing it. The preoccupations were correct, but the practical solutions were profoundly mistaken, and in this imbalance between theory and practice there was an inherent danger—the same danger, incidentally, which had manifested itself earlier, in 1921. The principle of coercion, direct or indirect, in the ordering of production and work, is correct: but the form which it assumed was mistaken. The military model had become a pernicious prejudice and the militarisation of labour was a failure.[35]

---

tion to stop wasting his life and dedicate himself wholeheartedly to poetry he used to get his servant Elia to tie him to a chair at his desk, thus giving him no choice but to carry on working.

[35] The militarisation of labour was a labour policy which operated for a short time in the Soviet Union during the period of War Communism. Adopted at the IXth Party Congress in 1920, it met with growing opposition from the Trades Unions particularly after the end of the Civil War. It was most closely associated with the figure of Trotsky who, at the IXth Congress, put the policy in these terms:

> "Militarisation is unthinkable without the militarisation of the Trades Unions as such, without the establishment of a régime in which every worker feels himself a soldier of labour, who cannot dispose of himself freely; if the order is given to transfer him, he must carry it out; if he does not carry it out, he will be a deserter who is punished. Who looks after this? The Trade Union. It creates the new régime. This is the militarisation of the working class."

The policy was implicitly defeated, with the rejection of the Trotsky–Bukharin theses on the Trades Unions, at the Xth Congress in 1921. The adoption of the

Interest of Lev Davidovitch in Americanism. He wrote articles, researched into the "byt" [БЫТ = mode of living] and into literature. These activities were less disconnected than might appear, since the new methods of work are inseparable from a specific mode of living and of thinking and feeling life. One cannot have success in one field without tangible results in the other. In America rationalisation of work and prohibition are undoubtedly connected. The enquiries conducted by the industrialists into the workers' private lives and the inspection services created by some firms to control the "morality" of their workers are necessities of the new methods of work. People who laugh at these initiatives (failures though they were) and see in them only a hypocritical manifestation of "puritanism" thereby deny themselves any possibility of understanding the importance, significance and objective import of the American phenomenon, which is *also* the biggest collective effort to date to create, with unprecedented speed, and with a consciousness of purpose unmatched in history, a new type of worker and of man. The expression "consciousness of purpose" might appear humorous to say the least to anyone who recalls Taylor's phrase about the "trained gorilla".[36] Taylor is in fact expressing with brutal cynicism the purpose of American society—developing in the worker to the highest degree automatic and mechanical attitudes, breaking up the old psycho-physical nexus of qualified professional work, which demands a certain active participation of intelligence, fantasy and initiative on the part of the worker, and reducing productive operations exclusively to the mechanical, physical aspect. But these things, in reality, are not original or novel: they represent simply the most recent phase of a long process which began with industrialism itself. This phase is more intense than preceding phases, and manifests itself in more brutal forms, but it is a phase which will itself be superseded by the creation of a

---

New Economic Policy rendered the methods of War Communism redundant. However, it has been argued that a close resemblance can be found between the "militarisation of labour" and the labour policy of the period of the Five Year Plans.

[36] This phrase, whose revealing "tactlessness" instantly attracted the attention of commentators, occurs on p. 40 of Frederick Taylor's *The Principles of Scientific Management* (1911), where the author writes: "This work [pig-iron handling] is so crude and elementary in its nature that the writer firmly believes that it would be possible to train an intelligent gorilla so as to become a more efficient pig-iron handler than any man could be." Frederick Taylor (1856–1915) was an American engineer and pioneer of scientific management.

For Gramsci's analysis of the significance of "Taylorism", see also pp. 308–10 below and Introduction to this Section, pp. 277–8.

psycho-physical nexus of a new type, both different from its predecessors and undoubtedly *superior*. A forced selection will ineluctably take place; a part of the old working class will be pitilessly eliminated from the world of labour, and perhaps from the world *tout court*.

It is from this point of view that one should study the "puritanical" initiative of American industrialists like Ford. It is certain that they are not concerned with the "humanity" or the "spirituality" of the worker, which are immediately smashed. This "humanity and spirituality" cannot be realised except in the world of production and work and in productive "creation". They exist most in the artisan, in the "demiurge",[37] when the worker's personality was reflected whole in the object created and when the link between art and labour was still very strong. But it is precisely against this "humanism" that the new industrialism is fighting. "Puritanical" initiatives simply have the purpose of preserving, outside of work, a certain psycho-physical equilibrium which prevents the physiological collapse of the worker, exhausted by the new method of production. This equilibrium can only be something purely external and mechanical, but it can become internalised if it is proposed by the worker himself, and not imposed from the outside, if it is proposed by a new form of society, with appropriate and original methods. American industrialists are concerned to maintain the continuity of the physical and muscular-nervous efficiency of the worker. It is in their interests to have a stable, skilled labour force, a permanently well-adjusted complex, because the human complex (the collective worker) of an enterprise is also a machine which cannot, without considerable loss, be taken to pieces too often and renewed with single new parts.

The element of so-called high wages also depends on this necessity. It is the instrument used to select and maintain in stability a skilled labour force suited to the system of production and work. But high wages are a double-edged weapon. It is necessary for the worker to spend his extra money "rationally" to maintain, renew and, if possible, increase his muscular-nervous efficiency and not to corrode or destroy it. Thus the struggle against alcohol, the most dangerous agent of destruction of labouring power, becomes a function of the state. It is possible for other "puritanical" struggles as well to become functions of the state if the private initiative of the industrialists proves insufficient or if a moral crisis breaks out among the

[37] "demiurge": from the Greek, meaning a handicraftsman, but with the extended sense, in Platonic philosophy, of "creator of the world".

working masses which is too profound and too widespread, as might happen as a result of a long and widespread crisis of unemployment.

The sexual question is again connected with that of alcohol. Abuse and irregularity of sexual functions is, after alcoholism, the most dangerous enemy of nervous energies, and it is commonly observed that "obsessional" work provokes alcoholic and sexual depravation. The attempts made by Ford, with the aid of a body of inspectors, to intervene in the private lives of his employees and to control how they spent their wages and how they lived is an indication of these tendencies. Though these tendencies are still only "private" or only latent, they could become, at a certain point, state ideology, inserting themselves into traditional puritanism and presenting themselves as a renaissance of the pioneer morality and as the "true" America (etc.). The most noteworthy fact in the American phenomenon in relation to these manifestations is the gap which has been formed and is likely to be increasingly accentuated, between the morality and way of life of the workers and those of other strata of the population.

Prohibition has already given an example of this gap. Who drank the alcohol brought into the United States by the bootleggers? Alcohol became a luxury product and even the highest wages were not enough to enable it to be consumed by large strata of the working masses. Someone who works for a wage, with fixed hours, does not have time to dedicate himself to the pursuit of drink or to sport or evading the law. The same observation can be made about sexuality. "Womanising" demands too much leisure. The new type of worker will be a repetition, in a different form, of peasants in the villages. The relative stability of sexual unions among the peasants is closely linked to the system of work in the country. The peasant who returns home in the evening after a long and hard day's work wants the "*venerem facilem parabilemque*"[38] of Horace. It is not his style. He loves his own woman, sure and unfailing, who is free from affectation and doesn't play little games about being seduced or raped in order to be possessed. It might seem that in this way the sexual function has been mechanised, but in reality we are dealing with the growth of a new form of sexual union shorn of the bright and dazzling colour of the romantic tinsel typical of the petit bourgeois and the Bohemian layabout. It seems clear that the new industrialism wants monogamy: it wants the man as worker not to squander his nervous energies in the disorderly

---

[38] "Easy and accessible love." Cf. Horace, *Satires*, I, ii, 119, ". . . namque parabilem amo venerem facilemque".

and stimulating pursuit of occasional sexual satisfaction. The employee who goes to work after a night of "excess" is no good for his work. The exaltation of passion cannot be reconciled with the timed movements of productive motions connected with the most perfected automatism. This complex of direct and indirect repression and coercion exercised on the masses will undoubtedly produce results and a new form of sexual union will emerge whose fundamental characteristic would apparently have to be monogamy and relative stability.

It would be interesting to know the statistical occurrence of deviation from the sexual behaviour officially propagandised in the United States, broken down according to social group.

It will show that in general divorce is particularly frequent among the upper classes. This demonstrates the moral gap in the United States between the working masses and the ever more numerous elements of the ruling classes. This moral gap seems to me one of the most interesting phenomena and one which is most rich in consequences. Until recently the American people was a working people. The "vocation of work" was not a trait inherent only in the working class but it was a specific quality of the ruling classes as well. The fact that a millionaire continued to be practically active until forced to retire by age or illness and that his activity occupied a very considerable part of his day, is a typically American phenomenon. This, for the average European, is the weirdest American extravagance. We have noted above that this difference between Americans and Europeans is determined by the absence of "tradition" in the United States, in so far as tradition also means passive residues of all the social forms eclipsed by past history. In the United States, on the other hand, there is a recent "tradition" of the pioneers, the tradition of strong individual personalities in whom the vocation of work had reached its greatest intensity and strength, men who entered directly, not by means of some army of servants and slaves, into energetic contact with the forces of nature in order to dominate them and exploit them victoriously. In Europe it is the passive residues that resist Americanism (they "represent quality", etc.) because they have the instinctive feeling that the new forms of production and work would sweep them away implacably. But if it is true that in Europe the old but still unburied residues are due to be definitively destroyed, what is beginning to happen in America itself? The moral gap mentioned above shows that ever wider margins of social passivity are in the process of being created. It would appear that women have a particularly important role here. The male industrialist continues to work even if he is a millionaire, but his wife and daughters are turning, more and more, into "luxury mammals". Beauty competitions, competitions for new film actresses (recall the 30,000 Italian girls who sent photographs of themselves in bathing costumes to Fox in 1926), the theatre, etc., all of which select the feminine beauty of the world and put it up for auction, stimulate the mental attitudes of prostitution, and "white slaving" is practised quite legally among the upper classes. The women, with nothing to do, travel; they are continually crossing the ocean to come to Europe, escaping prohibition in their own country and contracting "marriages" for a season. (It is worth recalling that ship's captains in the United States have been deprived of their right to celebrate marriages on board ship, since so many couples get married on leaving Europe and divorced again before disembarking in America.) Prostitution in a real sense is spreading, in a form barely disguised by fragile legal formulae.

These phenomena proper to the upper classes will make more difficult any coercion on the working masses to make them conform to the needs of the new industry. In any case they are determining a psychological split and accelerating the crystallisation and saturation of the various social groups, thereby making evident the way that these groups are being transformed into castes just as they have been in Europe.

TAYLOR AND AMERICANISM

Eugenio Giovannetti has written an article in *Pegasos*, May 1929, on Frederick Taylor and Americanism, in which he says:

> "Literary energy, abstract and nourished on the rhetoric of generalisation, is no longer in a position to understand technical energy, which is increasingly sharp and individual, a highly original fabric of singular will and specialised education. The literature of energy is still at the stage of its Prometheus Unbound—far too facile an image. The hero of technical civilisation is not a man unchained: he is a man of silence, who can carry his iron chains up to the heavens. He is not an ignorant fool whiling away his time: he is a man of study in the finest classical sense, in that *studium* used to mean '*punta viva*'.[39] While technical

[39] "*punta viva.*" The expression is obscure. What is probably meant is concentration and enthusiasm, which is the original etymological meaning of *studium*.

or mechanicist civilisation, whichever you prefer, is silently elaborating its new type of incisive hero, the literary cult of energy only succeeds in creating an airy-fairy good-for-nothing, a breathless fool reaching after the clouds."

It is worth pointing out that no attempt has been made to apply to Americanism Gentile's little formula about "philosophy which is not expressed in verbal formulations, but is affirmed in action". This fact is instructive and significant, because if the formula has any value at all, it is precisely in Americanism that it finds its justification. On the contrary, in any discussion of Americanism it is claimed that it is "mechanicist", crude, brutal—"pure action" in other words—and it is contrasted with tradition, etc. But why is this tradition not taken up as the basis of a philosophy or as the verbally formulated philosophy of those movements for which, conversely, "philosophy is affirmed in action"? This contradiction can explain many things: for example, the difference between real action on the one hand, which modifies in an essential way both man and external reality (in other words, real culture) and which is Americanism, and on the other hand the gladiatorial futility which is self-declared action but modifies only the word, not things, the external gesture and not the man inside. The former is creating a future which is intrinsic to its objective activity and which it prefers to keep quiet about. The second only creates a superior kind of puppet, modelled on a basis of rhetorical predicates, which will collapse into nothingness the moment the strings are cut which give from outside the appearance of motion and of life.

QUANTITY AND QUALITY

In the world of production these words mean nothing more than "inexpensive" and "expensive"—i.e. satisfaction or failure to satisfy the basic needs of the popular classes and a tendency respectively to raise or to lower their standard of living. All the rest is just an ideological serial story, of which Guglielmo Ferrero has written the first episode. In a nation-enterprise which has at its disposal a large labour force and a small amount of raw materials (which is a dubious hypothesis, since every nation-enterprise can "create" its own raw materials) the term "quality" simply means the intention of employing a lot of labour on a little material, perfecting the product to the maximum. In other words, it means specialisation for a luxury market. But is this possible for an entire, very populous nation? Where plenty of raw materials exist both alternatives are possible, the qualitative and the quantitative, but the same does not hold good for the so-called poor countries. Quantitative production can also be qualitative, in the sense that it can compete with purely qualitative industry at least among that part of the class of consumers of "distinct" objects which is not traditionalistic because it is a recent formation.

These observations are valid if one accepts the commonly put forward criterion of "quality", which is not however a rational criterion. In reality one should speak of quality only for works of art which are individual and not susceptible of reproduction. Everything that is susceptible of reproduction belongs to the realm of quantity, and can be mass produced.

One can further observe this: if a nation specialises in "qualitative" production, what industry provides the consumer goods for the poorer classes? Does this mean promoting a system of international division of labour? The whole thing is nothing more than a formula for idle men of letters and for politicians whose demagogy consists in building castles in the air. Quality should be attributed to men, not to things; and human quality is raised and refined to the extent that man can satisfy a greater number of needs and thus make himself independent of them. The high price of bread, due to a desire to keep a greater quantity of people tied to a specific activity, leads to malnutrition. A policy of quality almost always determines its opposite: dis-qualified quantity.

TAYLORISM AND THE MECHANISATION OF THE WORKER

Taylorism supposedly produces a gap between manual labour and the "human content" of work. On this subject some useful observations can be made on the basis of past history and specifically of those professions thought of as amongst the most intellectual, that is to say the professions connected with the reproduction of texts for publication or other forms of diffusion and transmission: the scribes of the days before the invention of printing, compositors on hand presses, linotype operators, stenographers and typists. If one thinks about it, it is clear that in these trades the process of adaptation to mechanisation is more difficult than elsewhere. Why? Because it is so hard to reach the height of professional qualification when this requires of the worker that he should "forget" or not think about the intellectual content of the text he is reproducing: this in order to be able, if he is a scribe, to fix his attention exclusively on the calligraphic form of the single letters; or to be able to break down phrases into "abstract" words and then words into characters, and rapidly select the pieces of lead in the cases; or to be able to break down not single words but groups of words, in the context of discourse, and group them mechanically into shorthand notation; or to acquire speed in typing, etc. The worker's interest in the intellectual content of the text can be measured from his mistakes. In other words, it is a professional failing. Conversely his qualification is commensurate with his lack of intellectual interest, i.e. the extent to which he has become "mechanised". The mediaeval copyist who was interested in the text changed the spelling, the morphology and the syntax of the text he was copying; he missed out entire passages which because of his meagre culture he could not understand; the train of thoughts aroused in his mind by his interest in the text led him to interpolate glosses and observations; if his language or dialect was different from that of the text he would introduce nuances deriving from his own speech: he was a bad scribe because in reality he was "remaking" the text. The slow speed of the art of writing in the Middle Ages explains many of these weaknesses: there was too much time in which to reflect, and consequently "mechanisation" was more difficult. The compositor has to be much quicker; he has to keep his hands and eyes constantly in movement, and this makes his mechanisation easier. But if one really thinks about it, the effort that these workers have to make in order to isolate from the often fascinating intellectual content of a text (and the more fascinating it is the less work is done and the less well) its written symbolisation, this perhaps is the greatest effort that can be required in any trade. However it is done, and it is not the spiritual death of man. Once the process of adaptation has been completed, what really happens is that the brain of the worker, far from being mummified, reaches a state of complete freedom. The only thing that is completely mechanicised is the physical gesture; the memory of the trade, reduced to simple gestures repeated at an intense rhythm, "nestles" in the muscular and nervous centres and leaves the brain free and unencumbered for other occupations. One can walk without having to think about all the movements needed in order to move, in perfect synchronisation, all the parts of the body, in the specific way that is necessary for walking. The same thing happens and will go on happening in industry with the basic gestures of the trade. One walks automatically, and at the same time thinks about whatever one chooses. American industrialists have understood all too well this dialectic inherent in the new industrial methods. They have understood that "trained gorilla" is just a phrase, that "unfortunately" the worker remains a man and even that during his work he thinks more, or at least has greater opportunities for thinking, once he has overcome the crisis of adaptation without being eliminated: and not only does the worker think, but the fact that he gets no immediate satisfaction from his work and realises that they are trying to reduce him to a trained gorilla, can lead him into a train of thought that is far from conformist. That the industrialists are concerned about such things is made clear from a whole series of cautionary measures and "educative" initatives which are well brought out in Ford's books and the work of Philip.[40]

HIGH WAGES

It is an obvious reflection that so-called high wages are a transitory form of remuneration. Adaptation to the new methods of production and work cannot take place simply through social compulsion. This is a "prejudice" which is widespread in Europe and even more so in Japan, which cannot fail before long to have serious consequences for the physical and psychic health of the workers. It is, furthermore, a prejudice which has its roots only in the endemic unemployment which has been a feature of the post-war period. If the situation were "normal", the apparatus of coercion needed to obtain the desired result would involve more than just high wages. Coercion has therefore to be ingeniously combined with persuasion and consent. This effect can be achieved, in forms proper to the society in question, by higher remuneration such as to permit a particular living standard which can maintain and restore the strength that has been worn down by the new form of toil. But no sooner have the new methods of work and production been generalised and diffused, the new type of worker been created universally and the apparatus of material production further perfected, no sooner has this happened than the excessive "turnover" has automatically to be restricted by widespread unemployment, and high wages disappear. In reality American high-wage industry is still exploiting a monopoly granted to it by

---

[40] Henry Ford (with Samuel Crowther), *My Life and Work*, Garden City and London, 1922: and *Today and Tomorrow*, Garden City. André Philip, *Le Problème ouvrier*, cit.

The "educative initiatives" referred to are presumably institutions like the Henry Ford Trade School, created in 1916 for the further education of workers.

the fact that it has the initiative with the new methods. Monopoly wages correspond to monopoly profits. But the monopoly will necessarily be first limited and then destroyed by the further diffusion of the new methods both within the United States and abroad (compare the Japanese phenomenon of low-priced goods), and high wages will disappear along with enormous profits. Also it is well known that high wages are of necessity connected with a labour aristocracy and are not granted to all American workers.

The whole Fordian ideology of high wages is a phenomenon derived from an objective necessity of modern industry when it has reached a certain stage of development. It is not a primary phenomenon—which does not however exonerate one from studying its importance and the repercussions that the ideology can have on its own account. Meanwhile, what is meant by "high wages"? Are the wages paid by Ford high only in relation to the average American wage? Or are they high as a price to be paid for the labouring power expended by Ford's employees in production and with those methods of work? It doesn't seem that any systematic research has been done on this, but that alone could provide a conclusive answer. The research is difficult, but the reasons why it is difficult are in themselves an indirect answer to the problem. The answer is difficult because the skilled labour force at Ford is extremely unstable and as a result it is not possible to establish an average for "rational" turnover among Ford workers for the purpose of comparison with the average in other industries. But why is it unstable? Why on earth should a worker prefer lower wages than those paid by Ford? Does this not mean that the so-called "high wages" are less capable of reconstituting the labour power expended than the lower wages paid by other firms? The instability of the labour force demonstrates that as far as Ford's is concerned the normal conditions of workers' competition for jobs (wage differentials) are effective only to a limited degree. The different level of average wages is not effective, nor is the pressure of the reserve army of the unemployed. This means that in dealing with Ford a new element must be looked for, and this new element will be the origin both of the high wages and of the other phenomena referred to (instability, etc.). The new element must be looked for in this fact alone: that Ford's industry requires a discrimination, a qualification, in its workers, which other industries do not yet call for, a new type of qualification, a form of consumption of labour power and a quantity of power consumed in average hours which are the same numerically but which are more wearying and exhausting than elsewhere and which, in the given conditions of society as it is, the wages are not sufficient to recompense and make up for.

Once these reasons have been established, the problem arises: whether the type of industry and organisation of work and production typical of Ford is rational; whether, that is, it can and should be generalised, or whether, on the other hand, we are not dealing with a malignant phenomenon which must be fought against through trade-union action and through legislation? In other words, whether it is possible, with the material and moral pressure of society and of the State, to lead the workers as a mass to undergo the entire process of psycho-physical transformation so that the average type of Ford worker becomes the average type of worker in general? Or whether this is impossible because it would lead to physical degeneration and to deterioration of the species, with the consequent destruction of all labour power? It seems possible to reply that the Ford method is rational, that is, that it should be generalised; but that a long process is needed for this, during which a change must take place in social conditions and in the way of life and the habits of individuals. This, however, cannot take place through coercion alone, but only through tempering compulsion (self-discipline) with persuasion. Persuasion should also take the form of high wages, which offer the possibility of a better standard of living, or more exactly perhaps, the possibility of realising a standard of living which is adequate to the new methods of production and work which demand a particular degree of expenditure of muscular and nervous energy.

To a limited but none the less important degree, phenomena similar to those created on a large scale by Fordism have been and still are occurring in certain branches of industry and in certain not yet "Fordised" establishments. To build up an organic and well-articulated skilled labour force in a factory or a team of specialised workers, has never been easy. Once the labour force or the team has been built up, its components, or a part of them, sometimes not only finish up enjoying monopoly wages but are not dismissed from work in the event of a temporary check in production. It would be uneconomic to allow the elements of an organic whole so laboriously built up to be dispersed, because it would be almost impossible to bring them together again, while on the other hand reconstructing it with new elements, chosen haphazardly, would involve not inconsiderable effort and expense. This is a limitation on the law of competition determined by the reserve army and by unemployment, and this limitation has always been at the origin of the formation of privileged labour aristocracies. Since there has never functioned and does not function any law of perfect parity of systems and production and work methods valid for all firms in a specific branch of industry, it follows that every firm is, to a greater or less degree, "unique" and will form a labour force with qualifications proper to its own particular requirements. Little manufacturing and working secrets, or "fiddles", practised by this labour force, which in themselves seem insignificant, can, when repeated an infinite number of times, assume immense economic importance. A particular case of this can be observed in the organisation of work in the docks, particularly in ports where there is an imbalance between loading and unloading of goods or where seasonal pile-ups of goods alternate with seasons which are entirely dead. There has to be a skilled labour force which is permanently available (which does not absent itself from the place of work) to deal with the minimum of seasonal or other work, and this leads to the formation of a kind of closed shop with high wages and other privileges, opposed to the mass of "casual" workers. The same thing happens in agriculture, in the relationship between tenant farmers and "*braccianti*"[41] and also in many industries which have "dead" seasons, either for reasons inherent in the industry itself (as with the clothing industry) or because of the inefficient organisation of the wholesale trade which does its buying according to a pattern of its own which is not properly geared to the pattern of production.

SHARES, DEBENTURES AND GOVERNMENT BONDS

What radical change will be brought about in the area of small and medium savings by the present economic depression, if, as seems probable, it continues for some time to come? It can be observed that the slump in the stock market has produced an enormous shift of wealth and a phenomenon of "simultaneous" expropriation of the savings of vast masses of the population almost everywhere, but in America most of all. Thus the malignant processes which had grown up as a result of inflation just after the war have started up again in a number of countries and have begun to operate in countries which did not experience inflation in the

[41] "*braccianti*": landless agricultural labourers, who are not fixed wage earners but are hired by the day according to the work to be done. The problems of organising in a single movement "braccianti" and small tenant farmers, with their obviously conflicting immediate interests, were particularly acute in the Romagna and the Po Valley. See also p. 75.

earlier period. The system whose application the Italian government has intensified in the last few years (continuing a tradition which already existed, though on a smaller scale) appears the most organic and rational, at least for a certain group of countries. But what are its consequences likely to be?

Difference between ordinary and preference shares, between these and debentures, and between shares and debentures on the free market and government bonds.

The mass of savers is trying to get rid of shares of every kind, which have been devalued to an unprecedented degree. It prefers debentures to shares, but it prefers government bonds to any other form of investment. It could be said that the mass of savers wants to break off any direct connection with the *ensemble* of private. capitalism, but that it does not refuse its confidence to the State, It wants to take part in economic activity, but through the State, which can guarantee a modest but sure return on investment. The State thus finds itself invested with a primordial function in the capitalist system, both as a company (state holdings) which concentrates the savings to be put at the disposal of private industry and activity, and as a medium and long-term investor (creation in Italy of various mortgage houses, industrial reconstruction, etc., transformation of the Banca Commerciale,[42] consolidation of the savings banks, creation of new forms of Post-Office savings, etc.). But once, through unavoidable economic necessity, the State has assumed this function, can it fail to interest itself in the organisation of production and exchange? Will it leave it, as before, up to the initiative of competition and private initiative? If this were to happen, the crisis of confidence that has struck private industry and commerce would overwhelm the State as well. The formation of a situation which obliged the State to devalue its bonds, either through inflation or otherwise, in the same way as private shares have been devalued, would become catastrophic for the *ensemble* of socio-economic organisation. The State is therefore led necessarily to intervene in order to check whether the investments which have taken place through State means are properly administered. This

---

[42] Mortgage houses. The most important of these was the Istituto Mobiliare Italiano, formed in November 1931, during the Great Depression, which issued Government guaranteed bonds and provided investment loans to small and medium-sized commercial and industrial enterprises. The transformation of the Banca Commerciale took place at the same time, the Bank receiving Government help when it was in danger of collapse.

In this passage the words "holding", "deficit" and "dumping" are all in English in the text.

explains at least one aspect of the theoretical discussion about the corporate regime. But control by itself is not sufficient. It is not just a question of preserving the productive apparatus just as it is at a given moment. It is a matter of reorganising it in order to develop it in parallel with the increase in the population and in collective needs. It is in these nccessary developments that private initiative is involved in the greatest risks, and here therefore that State intervention should be even greater, not that it is entirely free from dangers itself, indeed far from it.

These elements are emphasised, as being the most organic and essential. But there are also other elements which are leading towards State intervention, or provide a theoretical justification for it—increasing protectionism and autarkic tendencies, investment premiums, dumping, salvaging of large enterprises which are in the process, or in danger of going bankrupt; in other words, as the phase goes, the "nationalisation of losses and industrial deficits" (etc.).

If the State were proposing to impose an economic direction by which the production of savings ceased to a "function" of a parasitic class and became a function of the productive organism itself, such a hypothetical development would be progressive, and could have its part in a vast design of integral rationalisation. But for that it would be necessary to promote both agrarian reform (involving the abolition of landed income of a non-working class, and its incorporation into the productive organism in the form of collective savings to be dedicated to reconstruction and further progress), and an industrial reform. One could thus reduce all income to the status of technico-industrial functional necessities and no longer keep them as the juridical consequences of pure property rights.

This complex of demands, not always acknowledged, is at the origin of the historical justification of the so-called corporate trends, which manifest themselves for the most part in the form of an exaltation of the State in general, conceived as something absolute, and in the form of diffidence and aversion to the traditional forms of capitalism. The result of these phenomena is that in theory the State appears to have its socio-political base among the ordinary folk and the intellectuals, while in reality its structure remains plutocratic and it is impossible for it to break its links with big finance capital. Besides, it is the State itself which becomes the biggest plutocratic organism, the *holding* of the masses of savings of the small capitalists. (The Jesuit state of Paraguay could be usefully recalled as a model for a number of contemporary tendencies. That a State can exist politically based simultaneously on the plutocracy and on the "ordinary folk" is not in any case entirely contradictory, as is proved by the example of France, where the rule of finance capital could not be explained without the political base of a democracy of petit-bourgeois and peasant *rentiers*. For complex reasons, however, France still has a relatively healthy social composition, since there exists there a broad base of small and medium-sized farming properties. In other countries, on the other hand, the savers are cut off from the world of production and work. Saving in these countries has too high a social cost, as it is obtained with a level of existence for industrial and especially agricultural workers which is far too low. If the new structure of credit were to consolidate this situation, in reality it would be a turn for the worse. If parasitic savings, thanks to State guarantees, were to be rendered exempt even from the general hazards of the normal market, then on the one hand parasitic landed property would be strengthened and on the other hand industrial debentures, with legally determined dividends, would undoubtedly impose an even more crushing burden on labour.

AMERICAN AND EUROPEAN CIVILISATION

In an interview given to Corrado Alvaro (*L'Italia Letteraria*, 14 April 1929) Luigi Pirandello declares: "Americanism is swamping us. I think that a new beacon of civilisation has been lit over there." "The money that runs through the world is American (?!), and behind the money (?!) runs the way of life and the culture." (This is true only of the scum of society, and it is this cosmopolitan scum that Pirandello, and many others with him, thinks makes up the whole "world".) "Does America have a culture?" (It would be more to the point to say: does it have a unitary and centralised culture, i.e. is America a nation of the French, German or English type?) "It has books and customs(?). Its customs are its new literature, which penetrates through the best fortified and defended doors. In Berlin you do not feel the gap between the old and the new Europe, because the structure of the city itself offers no resistance." (Today Pirandello could no longer say the same thing, so it is to be understood that he is referring to the Berlin of the night clubs.) "In Paris, where there is an historical and artistic structure, where the evidence of an indigenous civilisation is present, Americanism is as strident and jarring as the make-up on the face of an aging *femme du monde*."

The problem is not whether in America there exists a new

civilisation, a new culture, even if only as a "beacon", and whether it is invading or has invaded Europe. If the problem were to be posed in that way, the answer would be simple: no, it does not exist, and indeed all that they do in America is to remasticate the old European culture. The problem is rather this; whether America, through the implacable weight of its economic production (and therefore indirectly), will compel or is already compelling Europe to overturn its excessively antiquated economic and social basis. This would have happened anyway, though only slowly. In the immediate perspective it is presented as a repercussion of American super-power. In other words, whether we are undergoing a transformation of the material bases of European civilisation, which in the long run (though not all that long, since in the contemporary period everything happens much faster than in the past ages) will bring about the overthrow of the existing forms of civilisation and the forced birth of a new.

The elements of a "new culture" and "new way of life" which are being spread around under the American label, are still just tentative feelers. They are not due to a new "order" deriving from a new basis, because that has not yet been formed, but are due to the superficial apish initiative of elements which are beginning to feel themselves socially displaced by the operation (still destructive and dissolutive) of the new basis in the course of formation. What is today called "Americanism" is to a large extent an advance criticism of old strata which will in fact be crushed by any eventual new order and which are already in the grips of a wave of social panic, dissolution and despair. It is an unconscious attempt at reaction on the part of those who are impotent to rebuild and who are emphasising the negative aspects of the revolution. But it is not from the social groups "condemned" by the new order that reconstruction is to be expected, but from those on whom is imposed the burden of creating with their own suffering the material bases of the new order. It is they who "must" find for themselves an "original", and not Americanised, system of living, to turn into "freedom" what today is "necessity".

The criterion then is that both the intellectual and moral reactions against the establishment of the new methods of production, and the superficial praises of Americanism, are due to the remains of old, disintegrating strata, and not to groups whose destiny is linked to the further development of the new method. This criterion is extremely important, and explains how it is that some elements in responsible positions in modern politics, who base their fortunes on the organisation of middle strata of the population as a whole, do not wish to take up a position but remain "theoretically" neutral, and resolve practical problems by the traditional methods of empiricism and opportunism. (Compare the various interpretations of ruralism given by Ugo Spirito, who wants to "urbanise" the countryside, and by other writers blowing on their panpipes.)

In the case of Americanism, understood not only as a form of café life but as an ideology of the kind represented by Rotary Clubs, we are not dealing with a new type of civilisation. This is shown by the fact that nothing has been changed in the character of and the relationships between fundamental groups. What we are dealing with is an organic extension and an intensification of European civilisation, which has simply acquired a new coating in the American climate. Pirandello's observation on the opposition that Americanism encounters in Paris (but in Le Creusot?) and on the immediate welcome that it supposedly had in Berlin proves, in any case, that the difference between it and "Europeanism" is not one of nature but of degree. In Berlin the middle classes had already been ruined by the war and by inflation, and Berlin industry has very different characteristics overall from that of Paris. The French middle classes did not undergo either occasional crises, like the inflation in Germany, nor did they suffer the organic crisis of 1929 with the same intensity as Germany. For this reason it is true that in Paris Americanism can appear like a form of make-up, a superficial foreign fashion.

III

THE PHILOSOPHY OF PRAXIS

I

THE STUDY OF PHILOSOPHY

INTRODUCTION

This section of Gramsci's philosophical notebooks is in two parts. The first part, *Some Preliminary Points of Reference*, starts by suggesting the terms of a Marxist historicist approach to philosophical activity, seeing it as organised critical reflection on existing forms of thought and their relation to the actual world which produced them. The premiss behind this approach is that philosophy is not just the abstract cogitation of a few professional intellectuals but a concrete social activity in which, implicitly, all men are engaged. If this is the starting-point from which the Marxist philosopher determines his own critique of philosophy, it follows that Marxist philosophy itself must be seen as a collective activity, involving not only the dissemination of ideas from above but also the extension of critical intellectual activity, in close links with the political practice of the movement, among ever-broadening sections of the population. In this way ideas are not only corrected and made adequate to the situation but become, in the phrase of Marx frequently quoted by Gramsci, "a material force".

The second part, *Problems of Philosophy and History*, consists of a number of notes from the *Quaderni* dealing with the application of Gramsci's theory of philosophy as a "critico-practical activity" to problems thrown up by the philosophy of the time at which Gramsci was writing. The problematic which Gramsci is criticising is mainly idealistic, and at first sight it may seem that what he does is to take this problematic and modify or invert its terms in a Marxist direction. If this were the case there would be some substance in the point of view that Gramsci's philosophy fails to escape from the idealist matrix provided by the culture of his time. Such an impression is strengthened by the fragmentary and elliptical character of many of the notes, which often fail to make explicit the real connection between the subject treated and the "philosophy of praxis". In point of fact, however, Gramsci's procedure is more radical than it looks. He is not juggling abstractly with the ideas he criticises, but always sets them in an implied or explicit historical perspective. Essential to Gramsci's approach is the notion that an intellectual revolution is not performed by simply confronting one philosophy with another. It is not just the ideas that require to be confronted but the social forces behind them and, more directly, the ideology these forces have generated and which has become part of what Gramsci calls "common sense". This last term is used by Gramsci to mean the uncritical and largely unconscious way of perceiving and understanding the world that has become "common" in any given epoch. (Correspondingly he uses the phrase "good sense" to mean the practical, but not necessarily rational or scientific attitude that in English is usually called common sense.) The critique of "common sense" and that of "the philosophy of the philosophers" are therefore complementary aspects of a single ideological struggle. This struggle must be waged, as Gramsci himself wages it, with the utmost intensity, but its ultimate resolution lies on another terrain, that of "revolutionising praxis", which alone can determine the forms of thought appropriate to the new age.

THE STUDY OF PHILOSOPHY

SOME PRELIMINARY POINTS OF REFERENCE

It is essential to destroy the widespread prejudice that philosophy is a strange and difficult thing just because it is the specific intellectual activity of a particular category of specialists or of professional and systematic philosophers. It must first be shown that all men are "philosophers", by defining the limits and characteristics of the "spontaneous philosophy" which is proper to everybody. This philosophy is contained in: 1. language itself, which is a totality of determined notions and concepts and not just of words grammatically devoid of content; 2. "common sense" and "good sense";[1] 3. popular religion and, therefore, also in the entire system of beliefs, superstitions, opinions, ways of seeing things and of acting, which are collectively bundled together under the name of "folklore".

Having first shown that everyone is a philosopher, though in his own way and unconsciously, since even in the slightest manifestation of any intellectual activity whatever, in "language", there is contained a specific conception of the world, one then moves on to the second level, which is that of awareness and criticism. That is to say, one proceeds to the question—is it better to "think", without having a critical awareness, in a disjointed and episodic way? In other words, is it better to take part in a conception of the world mechanically imposed by the external environment, i.e. by one of the many social groups in which everyone is automatically involved from the moment of his entry into the conscious world (and this can be one's village or province; it can have its origins in the parish and the "intellectual activity" of the local priest or aging patriarch whose wisdom is law, or in the little old woman who has inherited the lore of the witches or the minor intellectual soured by his own stupidity and inability to act)? Or, on the other hand, is it better to work out consciously and critically one's own conception of the world and thus, in connection with the labours of one's own brain, choose one's sphere of activity, take an active part in the creation of the history of the world, be one's own guide, refusing to accept

---

[1] The meaning that Gramsci gives to these two terms is explained in the paragraphs which follow. Broadly speaking, "common sense" means the incoherent set of generally held assumptions and beliefs common to any given society, while "good sense" means practical empirical common sense in the English sense of the term. See also introduction to this section.

passively and supinely from outside the moulding of one's personality?

Note I. In acquiring one's conception of the world one always belongs to a particular grouping which is that of all the social elements which share the same mode of thinking and acting. We are all conformists of some conformism or other, always man-in-the-mass or collective man. The question is this: of what historical type is the conformism, the mass humanity to which one belongs? When one's conception of the world is not critical and coherent but disjointed and episodic, one belongs simultaneously to a multiplicity of mass human groups. The personality is strangely composite: it contains Stone Age elements and principles of a more advanced science, prejudices from all past phases of history at the local level and intuitions of a future philosophy which will be that of a human race united the world over. To criticise one's own conception of the world means therefore to make it a coherent unity and to raise it to the level reached by the most advanced thought in the world. It therefore also means criticism of all previous philosophy, in so far as this has left stratified deposits in popular philosophy. The starting-point of critical elaboration is the consciousness of what one really is, and is "knowing thyself"[2] as a product of the historical process to date which has deposited in you an infinity of traces, without leaving an inventory.

Note II. Philosophy cannot be separated from the history of philosophy, nor can culture from the history of culture. In the most immediate and relevant sense, one cannot be a philosopher, by which I mean have a critical and coherent conception of the world, without having a consciousness of its historicity, of the phase of development which it represents and of the fact that it contradicts other conceptions or elements of other conceptions. One's conception of the world is a response to certain specific problems posed by reality, which are quite specific and "original" in their immediate relevance. How is it possible to consider the present, and quite specific present, with a mode of thought elaborated for a past which is often remote and superseded? When someone does this, it means that he is a walking anachronism, a fossil, and not living in the modern world, or at the least that he is strangely composite. And it is in fact the case that social groups which in some ways express the most developed

[2] "Know thyself" was the inscription written above the gate of the Oracle at Delphi, and became a principle of Socratic philosophy.

modernity, lag behind in other respects, given their social position, and are therefore incapable of complete historical autonomy.

Note III. If it is true that every language contains the elements of a conception of the world and of a culture, it could also be true that from anyone's language one can assess the greater or lesser complexity of his conception of the world. Someone who only speaks dialect, or understands the standard language incompletely, necessarily has an intuition of the world which is more or less limited and provincial, which is fossilised and anachronistic in relation to the major currents of thought which dominate world history. His interests will be limited, more or less corporate or economistic,[3] not universal. While it is not always possible to learn a number of foreign languages in order to put oneself in contact with other cultural lives, it is at the least necessary to learn the national language properly. A great culture can be translated into the language of another great culture, that is to say a great national language with historic richness and complexity, and it can translate any other great culture and can be a world-wide means of expression. But a dialect cannot do this.

Note IV. Creating a new culture does not only mean one's own individual "original" discoveries. It also, and most particularly, means the diffusion in a critical form of truths already discovered, their "socialisation" as it were, and even making them the basis of vital action,[4] an element of co-ordination and intellectual and moral order. For a mass of people to be led to think coherently and in the same coherent fashion about the real present world, is a "philosophical" event far more important and "original" than the discovery by some philosophical "genius" of a truth which remains the property of small groups of intellectuals.

Connection between "common sense", religion and philosophy

Philosophy is intellectual order, which neither religion nor common sense can be. It is to be observed that religion and common sense do not coincide either, but that religion is an element of fragmented common sense. Moreover common sense is a collective noun, like religion: there is not just one common sense, for that too is a product

---

[3] See note on Gramsci's terminology, pp. xiii–xiv.

[4] "vital action." The concept here would appear to derive from Bergson, some of whose ideas were filtered to Gramsci through Sorel and in a sense provided him with a psychological antidote to the fatalism of Austro-Marxism. There is no question, however, of Bergson having had a systematic influence on Gramsci's "philosophy of praxis" as such.

of history and a part of the historical process.[5] Philosophy is criticism and the superseding of religion and "common sense". In this sense it coincides with "good" as opposed to "common" sense.

Relation between science, religion and common sense

Religion and common sense cannot constitute an intellectual order, because they cannot be reduced to unity and coherence even within an individual consciousness, let alone collective consciousness. Or rather they cannot be so reduced "freely"—for this may be done by "authoritarian" means, and indeed within limits this has been done in the past.

Note the problem of religion taken not in the confessional sense but in the secular sense of a unity of faith between a conception of the world and a corresponding norm of conduct. But why call this unity of faith "religion" and not "ideology", or even frankly "politics"?[6]

Philosophy in general does not in fact exist. Various philosophies or conceptions of the world exist, and one always makes a choice between them. How is this choice made? Is it merely an intellectual event, or is it something more complex? And is it not frequently the case that there is a contradiction between one's intellectual choice and one's mode of conduct? Which therefore would be the real conception of the world: that logically affirmed as an intellectual choice? or that which emerges from the real activity of each man, which is implicit in his mode of action? And since all action is political, can one not say that the real philosophy of each man is contained in its entirety in his political action?

This contrast between thought and action, i.e. the co-existence of two conceptions of the world, one affirmed in words and the other displayed in effective action, is not simply a product of self-

---

[5] "part of the historical process." In the original "*un divenire storico*"—historical becoming. For this aspect of common sense see Int., p. 144: "Every social stratum has its own 'common sense' and its own 'good sense', which are basically the most widespread conception of life and of man. Every philosophical current leaves behind a sedimentation of 'common sense': this is the document of its historical effectiveness. Common sense is not something rigid and immobile, but is continually transforming itself, enriching itself with scientific ideas and with philosophical opinions which have entered ordinary life. 'Common sense' is the folklore of philosophy, and is always half-way between folklore properly speaking and the philosophy, science, and economics of the specialists. Common sense creates the folklore of the future, that is as a relatively rigid phase of popular knowledge at a given place and time."

[6] For Gramsci's uses of "ideology" in its various senses see pp. 375–77.

By "politics" Gramsci means conscious action (praxis) in pursuit of a common social goal.

deception [*malafede*]. Self-deception can be an adequate explanation for a few individuals taken separately, or even for groups of a certain size, but it is not adequate when the contrast occurs in the life of great masses. In these cases the contrast between thought and action cannot but be the expression of profounder contrasts of a social historical order. It signifies that the social group in question may indeed have its own conception of the world, even if only embryonic; a conception which manifests itself in action, but occasionally and in flashes—when, that is, the group is acting as an organic totality. But this same group has, for reasons of submission and intellectual subordination, adopted a conception which is not its own but is borrowed from another group; and it affirms this conception verbally and believes itself to be following it, because this is the conception which it follows in "normal times"[7]—that is when its conduct is not independent and autonomous, but submissive and subordinate. Hence the reason why philosophy cannot be divorced from politics. And one can show furthermore that the choice and the criticism of a conception of the world is also a political matter.

What must next be explained is how it happens that in all periods there co-exist many systems and currents of philosophical thought, how these currents are born, how they are diffused, and why in the process of diffusion they fracture along certain lines and in certain directions. The fact of this process goes to show how necessary it is to order in a systematic, coherent and critical fashion one's own intuitions of life and the world, and to determine exactly what is to be understood by the word "systematic", so that it is not taken in the pedantic and academic sense. But this elaboration must be, and can only be, performed in the context of the history of philosophy, for it is this history which shows how thought has been elaborated over the centuries and what a collective effort has gone into the creation of our present method of thought which has subsumed and absorbed all this past history, including all its follies and mistakes. Nor should these mistakes themselves be neglected, for, although made in the past and since corrected, one cannot be sure that they will not be reproduced in the present and once again require correcting.

What is the popular image of philosophy? It can be reconstructed by looking at expressions in common usage. One of the most usual

---

[7] "normal times": as opposed to the exceptional (and hence potentially revolutionary) moments in history in which a class or group discovers its objective and subjective unity in action.

is "being philosophical about it", which, if you consider it, is not to be entirely rejected as a phrase. It is true that it contains an implicit invitation to resignation and patience, but it seems to me that the most important point is rather the invitation to people to reflect and to realise fully that whatever happens is basically rational and must be confronted as such, and that one should apply one's power of rational concentration and not let oneself be carried away by instinctive and violent impulses. These popular turns of phrase could be compared with similar expressions used by writers of a popular stamp—examples being drawn from a large dictionary—which contain the terms "philosophy" or "philosophically". One can see from these examples that the terms have a quite precise meaning: that of overcoming bestial and elemental passions through a conception of necessity which gives a conscious direction to one's activity. This is the healthy nucleus that exists in "common sense", the part of it which can be called "good sense" and which deserves to be made more unitary and coherent. So it appears that here again it is not possible to separate what is known as "scientific" philosophy from the common and popular philosophy which is only a fragmentary collection of ideas and opinions.

But at this point we reach the fundamental problem facing any conception of the world, any philosophy which has become a cultural movement, a "religion", a "faith", any that has produced a form of practical activity or will in which the philosophy is contained as an implicit theoretical "premiss". One might say "ideology" here, but on condition that the word is used in its highest sense of a conception of the world that is implicitly manifest in art, in law, in economic activity and in all manifestations of individual and collective life. This problem is that of preserving the ideological unity of the entire social bloc which that ideology serves to cement and to unify. The strength of religions, and of the Catholic church in particular, has lain, and still lies, in the fact that they feel very strongly the need for the doctrinal unity of the whole mass of the faithful and strive to ensure that the higher intellectual stratum does not get separated from the lower. The Roman church has always been the most vigorous in the struggle to prevent the "official" formation of two religions, one for the "intellectuals" and the other for the "simple souls". This struggle has not been without serious disadvantages for the Church itself, but these disadvantages are connected with the historical process which is transforming the whole of civil society and which contains overall a corrosive critique of all religion, and they only serve to emphasise the organisational capacity of the clergy in the cultural sphere and the abstractly rational and just relationship which the Church has been able to establish in its own sphere between the intellectuals and the simple. The Jesuits have undoubtedly been the major architects of this equilibrium, and it order to preserve it they have given the Church a progressive forward movement which has tended to allow the demands of science and philosophy to be to a certain extent satisfied. But the rhythm of the movement has been so slow and methodical that the changes have passed unobserved by the mass of the simple, although they appear "revolutionary" and demagogic to the "integralists".[8]

One of the greatest weaknesses of immanentist[9] philosophies in general consists precisely in the fact that they have not been able to create an ideological unity between the bottom and the top, between the "simple" and the intellectuals. In the history of Western civilisation the fact is exemplified on a European scale, with the rapid collapse of the Renaissance and to a certain extent also the Reformation faced with the Roman church. Their weakness is demonstrated in the educational field, in that the immanentist philosophies have not even attempted to construct a conception which could take the place of religion in the education of children. Hence the pseudo-historicist sophism whereby non-religious, non-confessional, and in reality atheist, educationalists justify allowing the teaching of religion on the grounds that religion is the philosophy of the infancy of mankind renewed in every non-metaphorical infancy. Idealism has also shown itself opposed to cultural movements which "go out to the people", as happened with the so-called "Popular Universities"[10] and similar institutions. Nor was the objection solely to the worst aspects of the institutions, because in that case they could simply have tried to improve them. And yet these movements were worthy of attention, and deserved study. They enjoyed a certain success, in the sense that they demonstrated on

---

[8] "integralists." See note 13 on p. 332.

[9] By "immanentist philosophies" Gramsci normally means Italian idealism of the beginning of the century (Croce, Gentile, etc.), one of whose features was its rejection of Catholic transcendentalism; but he uses the term here also to characterise much of the philosophical thought of, for example, the Renaissance, which was in a similar way hermetic and incapable of extending its influence beyond elite circles. It should be noted however that Gramsci also describes the philosophy of praxis as in a different sense "immanentist", in that it offers the most consistent rejection of any form of transcendence.

[10] "Popular Universities"—*Università Popolari*. Independent institutes of adult education, more or less equivalent in scope, though not in extension, to the English W.E.A.

the part of the "simple" a genuine enthusiasm and a strong determination to attain a higher cultural level and a higher conception of the world. What was lacking, however, was any organic quality either of philosophical thought or of organisational stability and central cultural direction. One got the impression that it was all rather like the first contacts of English merchants and the negroes of Africa: trashy baubles were handed out in exchange for nuggets of gold. In any case one could only have had cultural stability and an organic quality of thought if there had existed the same unity between the intellectuals and the simple as there should be between theory and practice. That is, if the intellectuals had been organically the intellectuals of those masses, and if they had worked out and made coherent the principles and the problems raised by the masses in their practical activity, thus constituting a cultural and social bloc. The question posed here was the one we have already referred to, namely this: is a philosophical movement properly so called when it is devoted to creating a specialised culture among restricted intellectual groups, or rather when, and only when, in the process of elaborating a form of thought superior to "common sense" and coherent on a scientific plane, it never forgets to remain in contact with the "simple" and indeed finds in this contact the source of the problems it sets out to study and to resolve? Only by this contact does a philosophy become "historical", purify itself of intellectualistic elements of an individual character and become "life".*

A philosophy of praxis[11] cannot but present itself at the outset in a polemical and critical guise, as superseding the existing mode of thinking and existing concrete thought (the existing cultural world). First of all, therefore, it must be a criticism of "common sense", basing itself initially, however, on common sense in order to demonstrate that "everyone" is a philosopher and that it is not a question of introducing from scratch a scientific form of thought

---

* Perhaps it is useful to make a "practical" distinction between philosophy and common sense in order to indicate more clearly the passage from one moment to the other. In philosophy the features of individual elaboration of thought are the most salient: in common sense on the other hand it is the diffuse, unco-ordinated features of a generic form of thought common to a particular period and a particular popular environment. But every philosophy has a tendency to become the common sense of a fairly limited environment (that of all the intellectuals). It is a matter therefore of starting with a philosophy which already enjoys, or could enjoy, a certain diffusion, because it is connected to and implicit in practical life, and elaborating it so that it becomes a renewed common sense possessing the coherence and the sinew of individual philosophies. But this can only happen if the demands of cultural contact with the "simple" are continually felt.

11 "philosophy of praxis." See Introduction, p. xxi.

into everyone's individual life, but of renovating and making "critical" an already existing activity. It must then be a criticism of the philosophy of the intellectuals out of which the history of philosophy developed and which, in so far as it is a phenomenon of individuals (in fact it develops essentially in the activity of single particularly gifted individuals) can be considered as marking the "high points" of the progress made by common sense, or at least the common sense of the more educated strata of society but through them also of the people. Thus an introduction to the study of philosophy must expound in synthetic form the problems that have grown up in the process of the development of culture as a whole and which are only partially reflected in the history of philosophy. (Nevertheless it is the history of philosophy which, in the absence of a history of common sense, impossible to reconstruct for lack of documentary material, must remain the main source of reference.) The purpose of the synthesis must be to criticise the problems, to demonstrate their real value, if any, and the significance they have had as superseded links of an intellectual chain, and to determine what the new contemporary problems are and how the old problems should now be analysed.

The relation between common sense and the upper level of philosophy is assured by "politics", just as it is politics that assures the relationship between the Catholicism of the intellectuals and that of the simple. There are, however, fundamental differences between the two cases. That the Church has to face up to a problem of the "simple" means precisely that there has been a split in the community of the faithful. This split cannot be healed by raising the simple to the level of the intellectuals (the Church does not even envisage such a task, which is both ideologically and economically beyond its present capacities), but only by imposing an iron discipline on the intellectuals so that they do not exceed certain limits of differentiation and so render the split catastrophic and irreparable. In the past such divisions in the community of the faithful were healed by strong mass movements which led to, or were absorbed in, the creation of new religious orders centred on strong personalities (St. Dominic, St. Francis).*

* The heretical movements of the Middle Ages were a simultaneous reaction against the politicking of the Church and against the scholastic philosophy which expressed this. They were based on social conflicts determined by the birth of the Communes, and represented a split between masses and intellectuals within the Church. This split was "stitched over" by the birth of popular religious movements subsequently reabsorbed by the Church through the formation of the mendicant orders and a new religious unity.

But the Counter-Reformation has rendered sterile this upsurge of popular forces. The Society of Jesus is the last of the great religious orders. Its origins were reactionary and authoritarian, and its character repressive and "diplomatic".[12] Its birth marked the hardening of the Catholic organism. New orders which have grown up since then have very little religious significance but a great "disciplinary" significance for the mass of the faithful. They are, or have become, ramifications and tentacles of the Society of Jesus, instruments of "resistance" to preserve political positions that have been gained, not forces of renovation and development. Catholicism has become "Jesuitism". Modernism[13] has not created "religious orders", but a political party—Christian Democracy.*

The position of the philosophy of praxis is the antithesis of the Catholic. The philosophy of praxis does not tend to leave the "simple" in their primitive philosophy of common sense, but rather to lead them to a higher conception of life. If it affirms the need for contact between intellectuals and simple it is not in order to restrict scientific activity and preserve unity at the low level of the masses, but precisely in order to construct an intellectual-

---

[12] "diplomatic." In a disparaging sense, common in Italian as applied to the superficial machinations of Italian bourgeois politics from Cavour to Giolitti.

[13] "Modernism." A product of the challenge of Socialism among the masses, Modernism aimed to revitalise the Church as a social force at the end of the nineteenth century and to counteract the effects of its refusal to allow Catholics to participate in the affairs of the Italian state. Modernism's concern was with the relationship of the Church to state and society rather than with theological questions as such, and its main ideological contribution was the theory of "Christian Democracy"—a term which is, for this period, to be understood literally. The Modernist/Christian-Democrat movement was suppressed under the pontificate of Pius X (1903–14) but re-emerged with Sturzo and the Partito Popolare in 1918. The reaction to Modernism connected with Pius X goes under the name of Integralism and was a theological movement aimed at reasserting Church authority against secularisation. Integralism, although ostensibly purely doctrinal, had in practice reactionary social effects, and Christian Democracy was for a long time a progressive trend within the Church. The *Partito Popolare* adopted an ambiguous attitude to fascism at the outset, but was nevertheless eventually banned, along with the other parties, by the regime; it re-emerged during the resistance, as Christian Democracy. The present-day role of Christian Democracy as a mass political organisation dominated by big capital and the Church hierarchy dates effectively from 1945–47.

* Recall the anecdote, recounted by Steed in his Memoirs,[14] about the Cardinal who explains to the pro-Catholic English Protestant that the miracles of San Gennaro [St. Januarius] are an article of faith for the ordinary people of Naples, but not for the intellectuals, and that even the Gospels contain "exaggerations", and who answers the question "But aren't we Christians?" with the words "We are the 'prelates', that is the 'politicians', of the Church of Rome".

[14] "Steed's memoirs." *Through Thirty Years*, London, 1924, by Henry Wickham Steed, a former editor of *The Times*.

moral bloc which can make politically possible the intellectual progress of the mass and not only of small intellectual groups.

The active man-in-the-mass has a practical activity, but has no clear theoretical consciousness of his practical activity, which nonetheless involves understanding the world in so far as it transforms it.[15] His theoretical consciousness can indeed be historically in opposition to his activity. One might almost say that he has two theoretical consciousnesses (or one contradictory consciousness): one which is implicit in his activity and which in reality unites him with all his fellow-workers in the practical transformation of the real world; and one, superficially explicit or verbal, which he has inherited from the past and uncritically absorbed. But this verbal conception is not without consequences. It holds together a specific social group, it influences moral conduct and the direction of will, with varying efficacity but often powerfully enough to produce a situation in which the contradictory state of consciousness does not permit of any action, any decision or any choice, and produces a condition of moral and political passivity. Critical understanding of self takes place therefore through a struggle of political "hegemonies" and of opposing directions, first in the ethical field and then in that of politics proper, in order to arrive at the working out at a higher level of one's own conception of reality. Consciousness of being part of a particular hegemonic force (that is to say, political consciousness) is the first stage towards a further progressive self-consciousness in which theory and practice will finally be one. Thus the unity of theory and practice is not just a matter of mechanical fact, but a part of the historical process, whose elementary and primitive phase is to be found in the sense of being "different" and "apart", in an instinctive feeling of independence, and which progresses to the level of real possession of a single and coherent conception of the world. This is why it must be stressed that the political development of the concept of hegemony represents a great philosophical advance as well as a politico-practical one.[16] For it necessarily supposes an intellectual unity and an ethic in conformity with a conception of reality that has gone beyond common

---

[15] A reference to the 11th of Marx's *Theses on Feuerbach*, which Gramsci interprets as meaning that philosophy (and, in particular, the philosophy of praxis) is a socio-practical activity, in which thought and action are reciprocally determined.

[16] The reference here is not only to Marx's argument about "ideas becoming a material force", but also to Lenin and the achievement of proletarian hegemony through the Soviet revolution (see below pp. 381–82).

sense and has become, if only within narrow limits, a critical conception.

However, in the most recent developments of the philosophy of praxis the exploration and refinement of the concept of the unity of theory and practice is still only at an early stage. There still remain residues of mechanicism, since people speak about theory as a "complement" or an "accessory" of practice, or as the handmaid of practice.[17] It would seem right for this question too to be considered historically, as an aspect of the political question of the intellectuals. Critical self-consciousness means, historically and politically, the creation of an *élite*[18] of intellectuals. A human mass does not "distinguish" itself, does not become independent in its own right without, in the widest sense, organising itself; and there is no organisation without intellectuals, that is without organisers and leaders,[19] in other words, without the theoretical aspect of the theory-practice nexus being distinguished concretely by the existence of a group of people "specialised" in conceptual and philosophical elaboration of ideas. But the process of creating intellectuals is long, difficult, full of contradictions, advances and retreats, dispersals and regroupings, in which the loyalty of the masses is often sorely tried. (And one must not forget that at this early stage loyalty and discipline are the ways in which the masses participate and collaborate in the development of the cultural movement as a whole.)

The process of development is tied to a dialectic between the intellectuals and the masses. The intellectual stratum develops both quantitatively and qualitatively, but every leap forward towards a new breadth and complexity of the intellectual stratum is tied to an analogous movement on the part of the mass of the "simple", who raise themselves to higher levels of culture and at the same time extend their circle of influence towards the stratum of specialised intellectuals, producing outstanding individuals and groups of

---

[17] The notion of the subservience of theory to practice, neatly summed up in this adaptation of the mediaeval adage *philosophia ancilla theologiae* (philosophy the handmaid of theology) has been widespread in the Marxist movement, in forms as diverse as Stalin's formulation "theory must serve practice" (Works, Vol. VI, p. 88) and Rosa Luxemburg's argument (in *Stillstand und Fortschritt im Marxismus*) that theory only develops to the extent that the need for it is created by the practice of the movement.

[18] "*élite.*" As is made clear later in the text, Gramsci uses this word (in French in the original) in a sense very different from that of the reactionary post-Pareto theorists of "political *élites*". The *élite* in Gramsci is the revolutionary vanguard of a social class in constant contact with its political and intellectual base. (But see also note 79 on p. 430.)

[19] "*dirigenti.*" See notes on Gramsci's terminology, p. xiii.

greater or less importance. In the process, however, there continually recur moments in which a gap develops between the mass and the intellectuals (at any rate between some of them, or a group of them), a loss of contact, and thus the impression that theory is an "accessory", a "complement" and something subordinate. Insistence on the practical element of the theory-practice nexus, after having not only distinguished but separated and split the two elements (an operation which in itself is merely mechanical and conventional), means that one is going through a relatively primitive historical phase, one which is still economic-corporate, in which the general "structural" framework is being quantitatively transformed and the appropriate quality-superstructure is in the process of emerging, but is not yet organically formed. One should stress the importance and significance which, in the modern world, political parties have in the elaboration and diffusion of conceptions of the world, because essentially what they do is to work out the ethics and the politics corresponding to these conceptions and act as it were as their historical "laboratory". The parties recruit individuals out of the working mass, and the selection is made on practical and theoretical criteria at the same time. The relation between theory and practice becomes even closer the more the conception is vitally and radically innovatory and opposed to old ways of thinking. For this reason one can say that the parties are the elaborators of new integral and totalitarian intelligentsias[20] and the crucibles where the unification of theory and practice, understood as a real historical process, takes place. It is clear from this that the parties should be formed by individual memberships and not on the pattern of the British Labour Party, because, if it is a question of providing an organic leadership for the entire economically active mass, this leadership should not follow old schemas but should innovate. But innovation cannot come from the mass, at least at the beginning, except through the mediation of an *élite* for whom the conception implicit in human activity has already become to a certain degree a coherent and systematic ever-present awareness and a precise and decisive will.

One of these phases can be studied by looking at the recent discussion in which the latest developments of the philosophy of praxis are brought out, and which has been summarised in an

---

[20] "*intellettualità totalitarie.*" It seems certain that *intellettualità* here is a concrete noun meaning "intelligentsia" rather than the abstract "intellectual conception". "Totalitarian" is to be understood not in its modern sense, but as meaning simultaneously "unified" and "all-absorbing".

article by D. S. Mirsky, a collaborator on *La Cultura*.[21] One can see from this that a change has taken place from a mechanistic and purely external conception to one which is activist and, as has been pointed out, closer to a correct understanding of the unity of theory and practice, although it has not yet attained the full synthetic meaning of the concept. It should be noted how the deterministic, fatalistic and mechanistic element has been a direct ideological "aroma" emanating from the philosophy of praxis, rather like religion or drugs (in their stupefying effect). It has been made necessary and justified historically by the "subaltern"[23] character of certain social strata.

When you don't have the initiative in the struggle and the struggle itself comes eventually to be identified with a series of defeats, mechanical determinism becomes a tremendous force of moral resistance, of cohesion and of patient and obstinate perseverance. "I have been defeated for the moment, but the tide of history is working for me in the long term." Real will takes on the garments of an act of faith in a certain rationality of history and in a primitive and empirical form of impassioned finalism[24] which appears in the role of a substitute for the Predestination or Providence of confessional religions. It should be emphasised, though, that a strong activity of the will is present even here, directly intervening in the "force of circumstance", but only implicitly, and in a veiled and, as it were, shamefaced manner. Consciousness here, therefore, is contradictory and lacking critical unity, etc. But when the "subaltern" becomes directive and responsible for the economic activity of the masses, mechanicism at a certain point becomes an imminent danger and a revision must take place in modes of thinking because a change has taken place in the social mode of existence.[25] The boundaries and the dominion of the "force of

---

[21] The article referred to is probably D. S. Mirsky, *Demokratie und Partei im Bolschewismus*, in *Demokratie und Partei*, ed. P. R. Rohden, Vienna, 1932. A different article of Mirsky had appeared in *La Cultura* in 1931, and it is possible that Gramsci refers to this magazine in order to quiet the suspicions of the censor, alerted by the Russian name.

[23] "subaltern." See note on Gramsci's terminology, p. xiii.

[24] "finalism": the notion that history is always working towards a determined end. The idea that Gramsci is attacking is that of historical inevitability, and in particular of the "inevitable" spontaneous collapse of capitalism and its replacement by the socialist order.

[25] This is an echo of Marx's statement (Preface to *A Contribution to the Critique of Political Economy*) that it is not consciousness which determines being but man's social being which determines his consciousness. This conception is very important to Gramsci and constantly recurs in his prison writings, as do other ideas from the same Preface.

circumstance" become restricted. But why? Because, basically, if yesterday the subaltern element was a thing, today it is no longer a thing but an historical person, a protagonist; if yesterday it was not responsible, because "resisting" a will external to itself, now it feels itself to be responsible because it is no longer resisting but an agent, necessarily active and taking the initiative.

But even yesterday was it ever mere "resistance", a mere "thing", mere "non-responsibility"? Certainly not. Indeed one should emphasise how fatalism is nothing other than the clothing worn by real and active will when in a weak position. This is why it is essential at all times to demonstrate the futility of mechanical determinism: for, although it is explicable as a naïve philosophy of the mass and as such, but only as such, can be an intrinsic element of strength, nevertheless when it is adopted as a thought-out and coherent philosophy on the part of the intellectuals, it becomes a cause of passivity, of idiotic self-sufficiency. This happens when they don't even expect that the subaltern will become directive and responsible. In fact, however, some part of even a subaltern mass is always directive and responsible, and the philosophy of the part always precedes the philosophy of the whole, not only as its theoretical anticipation but as a necessity of real life.

That the mechanicist conception has been a religion of the subaltern is shown by an analysis of the development of the Christian religion. Over a certain period of history in certain specific historical conditions religion has been and continues to be a "necessity", a necessary form taken by the will of the popular masses and a specific way of rationalising the world and real life, which provided the general framework for real practical activity. This quotation from an article in *La Civiltà Cattolica* (*Individualismo pagano e individualismo cristiano*: issue of 5 March 1932) seems to me to express very well this function of Christianity:

> "Faith in a secure future, in the immortality of the soul destined to beatitude, in the certainty of arriving at eternal joy, was the force behind the labour for intense interior perfection and spiritual elevation. True Christian individualism found here the impulse that led it to victory. All the strength of the Christian was gathered around this noble end. Free from the flux of speculation which weakens the soul with doubt, and illuminated by immortal principles, man felt his hopes reborn; sure that a superior force was supporting him in the struggle against Evil, he did violence to himself and conquered the world."

But here again it is naïve Christianity that is being referred to: not Jesuitised Christianity, which has become a pure narcotic for the popular masses.

The position of Calvinism, however, with its iron conception of predestination and grace, which produces a vast expansion of the spirit of initiative (or becomes the form of this movement) is even more revealing and significant.*

What are the influential factors in the process of diffusion (which is also one of a substitution of the old conception, and, very often, of combining old and new), how do they act, and to what extent? Is it the rational form in which the new conception is expounded and presented? Or is it the authority (in so far as this is recognised and appreciated, if only generically) of the expositor and the thinkers and experts whom the expositor calls in in his support? Or the fact of belonging to the same organisation as the man who upholds the new conception (assuming, that is, that one has entered the organisation for other reasons than that of already sharing the new conception)?

In reality these elements will vary according to social groups and the cultural level of the groups in question. But the enquiry has a particular interest in relation to the popular masses, who are slower to change their conceptions, or who never change them in the sense of accepting them in their "pure" form, but always and only as a more or less heterogeneous and bizarre combination. The rational and logically coherent form, the exhaustive reasoning which neglects no argument, positive or negative, of any significance, has a certain importance, but is far from being decisive. It can be decisive, but in a secondary way, when the person in question is already in a state of intellectual crisis, wavering between the old and the new, when he has lost his faith in the old and has not yet come down in favour of the new, etc.

One could say this about the authority of thinkers and experts: it is very important among the people, but the fact remains that every conception has its thinkers and experts to put forward, and authority does not belong to one side; further, with every thinker

---

* On this question see: Max Weber, *L'etica protestante e lo spirito del capitalismo*; published in *Nuovi Studi*, volume for 1931 *et seq.* [*Die protestantische Ethik und der Geist des Capitalismus*; first published in the *Archiv für Sozialwissenschaft und Sozialpolitik*, Vols. XX and XXI, 1904 and 1905. English translation (by Talcott Parsons) *The Protestant Ethic and the Spirit of Capitalism*, London, Allen and Unwin, 1930.] And see Groethuysen's book on the religious origins of the bourgeoisie in France. [*Origines de l'esprit bourgeois en France*, Vol. I. *L'Eglise et la bourgeoisie*, Paris, 1927.]

it is possible to make distinctions, to cast doubt on whether he really said such and such a thing, etc.

One can conclude that the process of diffusion of new conceptions takes place for political (that is, in the last analysis, social) reasons; but that the formal element, that of logical coherence, the element of authority and the organisational element have a very important function in this process immediately after the general orientation has been reached, whether by single individuals or groups of a certain size. From this we must conclude, however, that in the masses *as such*, philosophy can only be experienced as a faith.

Imagine the intellectual position of the man of the people: he has formed his own opinions, convictions, criteria of discrimination, standards of conduct. Anyone with a superior intellectual formation with a point of view opposed to his can put forward arguments better than he and really tear him to pieces logically and so on. But should the man of the people change his opinions just because of this? Just because he cannot impose himself in a bout of argument? In that case he might find himself having to change every day, or every time he meets an ideological adversary who is his intellectual superior. On what elements, therefore, can his philosophy be founded? and in particular his philosophy in the form which has the greatest importance for his standards of conduct?

The most important element is undoubtedly one whose character is determined not by reason but by faith. But faith in whom, or in what? In particular in the social group to which he belongs, in so far as in a diffuse way it thinks as he does. The man of the people thinks that so many like-thinking people can't be wrong, not so radically, as the man he is arguing against would like him to believe; he thinks that, while he himself, admittedly, is not able to uphold and develop his arguments as well as the opponent, in his group there is someone who could do this and could certainly argue better than the particular man he has against him; and he remembers, indeed, hearing expounded, discursively, coherently, in a way that left him convinced, the reasons behind his faith. He has no concrete memory of the reasons and could not repeat them, but he knows that reasons exist, because he has heard them expounded, and was convinced by them. The fact of having once suddenly seen the light and been convinced is the permanent reason for his reasons persisting, even if the arguments in its favour cannot be readily produced.

These considerations lead, however, to the conclusion that new conceptions have an extremely unstable position among the popular masses; particularly when they are in contrast with orthodox convictions (which can themselves be new) conforming socially to the general interests of the ruling classes. This can be seen if one considers the fortunes of religions and churches. Religion, or a particular church, maintains its community of faithful (within the limits imposed by the necessities of general historical development) in so far as it nourishes its faith permanently and in an organised fashion, indefatigably repeating its apologetics, struggling at all times and always with the same kind of arguments, and maintaining a hierarchy of intellectuals who give to the faith, in appearance at least, the dignity of thought. Whenever the continuity of relations between the Church and the faithful has been violently interrupted, for political reasons, as happened during the French Revolution, the losses suffered by the Church have been incalculable. If the conditions had persisted for a long time in which it was difficult to carry on practising one's own religion, it is quite possible that these losses would have been definitive, and a new religion would have emerged, as indeed one did emerge in France in combination with the old Catholicism. Specific necessities can be deduced from this for any cultural movement which aimed to replace common sense and old conceptions of the world in general:

1. Never to tire of repeating its own arguments (though offering literary variation of form): repetition is the best didactic means for working on the popular mentality.

2. To work incessantly to raise the intellectual level of ever-growing strata of the populace, in other words, to give a personality to the amorphous mass element. This means working to produce *élites* of intellectuals of a new type which arise directly out of the masses, but remain in contact with them to become, as it were, the whalebone in the corset.[26]

This second necessity, if satisfied, is what really modifies the "ideological panorama" of the age. But these *élites* cannot be formed or developed without a hierarchy of authority and intellectual competence growing up within them. The culmination of this process can be a great individual philosopher. But he must be capable of re-living concretely the demands of the massive ideological community and of understanding that this cannot have the flexibility of movement proper to an individual brain, and must succeed in giving formal elaboration to the collective doctrine in

---

[26] For Gramsci's theory of the "organic" intellectuals see the essay "The Formation of the Intellectuals", pp. 5–14.

the most relevant fashion, and the one most suited to the modes of thought of a collective thinker.

It is evident that this kind of mass creation cannot just happen "arbitrarily", around any ideology, simply because of the formally constructive will of a personality or a group which puts it foward solely on the basis of its own fanatical philosophical or religious convictions. Mass adhesion or non-adhesion to an ideology is the real critical test of the rationality and historicity of modes of thinking. Any arbitrary constructions are pretty rapidly eliminated by historical competition, even if sometimes, through a combination of immediately favourable circumstances, they manage to enjoy popularity of a kind; whereas constructions which respond to the demands of a complex organic period of history always impose themselves and prevail in the end, even though they may pass through several intermediary phases during which they manage to affirm themselves only in more or less bizarre and heterogeneous combinations.

These developments pose many problems, the most important of which can be subsumed in the form and the quality of the relations between the various intellectually qualified strata; that is, the importance and the function which the creative contribution of superior groups must and can have in connection with the organic capacity of the intellectually subordinate strata to discuss and develop new critical concepts. It is a question, in other words, of fixing the limits of freedom of discussion and propaganda, a freedom which should not be conceived of in the administrative and police sense, but in the sense of a self-limitation which the leaders impose on their own activity, or, more strictly, in the sense of fixing the direction of cultural policy. In other words—who is to fix the "rights of knowledge" and the limits of the pursuit of knowledge? And can these rights and limits indeed be fixed? It seems necessary to leave the task of researching after new truths and better, more coherent, clearer formulations of the truths themselves to the free initiative of individual specialists, even though they may continually question the very principles that seem most essential. And it will in any case not be difficult to expose the fact whenever such proposals for discussion arise because of interested and not scientific motives. Nor is it inconceivable that individual initiatives should be disciplined and subject to an ordered procedure, so that they have to pass through the sieve of academies or cultural institutes of various kinds and only become public after undergoing a process of selection.

It would be interesting to study concretely the forms of cultural organisation which keep the ideological world in movement within a given country, and to examine how they function in practice. A study of the numerical relationship between the section of the population professionally engaged in active cultural work in the country in question and the population as a whole, would also be useful, together with an approximate calculation of the unattached forces. The school, at all levels, and the Church, are the biggest cultural organisations in every country, in terms of the number of people they employ. Then there are newspapers, magazines and the book trade and private educational institutions, either those which are complementary to the state system, or cultural institutions like the Popular Universities. Other professions include among their specialised activities a fair proportion of cultural activity. For example, doctors, army officers, the legal profession. But it should be noted that in all countries, though in differing degrees, there is a great gap between the popular masses and the intellectual groups, even the largest ones, and those nearest to the peripheries of national life, like priests and school teachers. The reason for this is that, however much the ruling class may affirm to the contrary, the State, as such, does not have a unitary, coherent and homogeneous conception, with the result that intellectual groups are scattered between one stratum and the next, or even within a single stratum. The Universities, except in a few countries, do not exercise any unifying influence: often an independent thinker has more influence than the whole of university institutions, etc.

With regard to the historical role played by the fatalistic conception of the philosophy of praxis one might perhaps prepare its funeral oration, emphasising its usefulness for a certain period of history, but precisely for this reason underlining the need to bury it with all due honours. Its role could really be compared with that of the theory of predestination and grace for the beginnings of the modern world, a theory which found its culmination in classical German philosophy and in its conception of freedom as the consciousness of necessity.[27] It has been a replacement in the popular consciousness for the cry of " 'tis God's will", although even on this primitive, elementary plane it was the beginnings of a more modern and fertile conception than that contained in the expression " 'tis God's will" or in the theory of grace. Is it possible that a "formally" new conception can present itself in a guise other than the crude, unsophisticated version of the populace? And yet the

[27] "the consciousness of necessity." This notion, which originated with Spinoza, plays a particularly important role in Hegelian philosophy.

historian, with the benefit of all necessary perspective, manages to establish and to understand the fact that the beginnings of a new world, rough and jagged though they always are, are better than the passing away of the world in its death-throes and the swan-song that it produces.*

PROBLEMS OF PHILOSOPHY AND HISTORY

Scientific discussion

In the formulation of historico-critical problems it is wrong to conceive of scientific discussion as a process at law in which there is an accused and a public prosecutor whose professional duty it is to demonstrate that the accused is guilty and has to be put out of

---

* The fading away of "fatalism" and "mechanicism" marks a great historical turning-point: hence the great impression of Mirsky's résumé. Memories that it has raised: I remember in Florence in November 1917, a discussion with Mario Trozzi, and the first mention of Bergsonism, voluntarism, etc.[28] One could make a semi-serious sketch of how this conception presented itself in reality. I also remember a discussion with Professor Presutti in Rome in June 1924. Comparison with Capt. Giulietti made by G. M. Serrati, which was for him decisive and conferred a death sentence. For Serrati, Giulietti was like the Confucian to the Taoist, like the southern Chinese, the busy and active merchant, in the eyes of the mandarin scholar from the North, who looks down with the supreme contempt of the enlightened sage for whom life holds no more mysteries, on the southern mannikins who hope, with their busy, ant-like movements to capture "the way". Speech by Claudio Treves on expiation. This speech had something of the spirit of an Old Testament prophet. Those who had wanted and had made the war, who had torn the world from its hinges and were therefore responsible for post-war disorder, had to expiate their sins and bear the responsibility for the disorder; they were guilty of "voluntarism" and had to be punished for their sin, etc. There was a certain priestly grandeur about this speech, a crescendo of maledictions which should have petrified us with terror but were instead a great consolation, because they showed that the undertaker was not yet ready and that Lazarus could still rise again.

[28] The meeting in question took place between various leaders and adherents of the "intransigent" current of the Socialist Party on the night of 18 November 1917. It was mainly concerned with preparing a document criticising the reformist wing of the Party for its attitude to the war. In the course of the discussion Trozzi appears to have taken Gramsci to task for Bergsonian voluntarism. That Gramsci's views at the time were decidedly unorthodox by the standards of the Second International, is shown by his famous article saluting the Soviet revolution, *La Rivoluzione contro il 'Capitale'*, published in *Avanti!* a week after the meeting with Trozzi and others, which was subsequently widely criticised for apparently counterposing "Leninist" revolutionism to "Marxist" passivity and determinism. Gramsci, in fact, as he makes clear here in the *Quaderni*, did not know Bergson's writing at the time. Bergson had, however, influenced Sorel, who in turn had influenced Gramsci in an early period. The result of Trozzi's charge was to lead Gramsci to a re-examination and criticism of idealistic and Bergsonian influences in Sorel's work.

circulation. In scientific discussion, since it is assumed that the purpose of discussion is the pursuit of truth and the progress of science, the person who shows himself most "advanced" is the one who takes up the point of view that his adversary may well be expressing a need which should be incorporated, if only as a subordinate aspect, in his own construction. To understand and to evaluate realistically one's adversary's position and his reasons (and sometimes one's adversary is the whole of past thought) means precisely to be liberated from the prison of ideologies in the bad sense of the word—that of blind ideological fanaticism. It means taking up a point of view that is "critical", which for the purpose of scientific research is the only fertile one.

Philosophy and History

Question of what should be understood by philosophy, or by philosophy in a particular epoch, and of what is the importance and the significance of philosophers' philosophy in each of these historical epochs.

Accepting Croce's definition of religion as a conception of the world which has become a norm of life[29] (since the term norm of life is understood here not in a bookish sense but as being carried out in practical life) it follows that the majority of mankind are philosophers in so far as they engage in practical activity and in their practical activity (or in their guiding lines of conduct) there is implicitly contained a conception of the world, a philosophy. The history of philosophy as it is generally understood, that is as the history of philosophers' philosophies, is the history of attempts made and ideological initiatives undertaken by a specific class of people to change, correct or perfect the conceptions of the world that exist in any particular age and thus to change the norms of conduct that go with them; in other words, to change practical activity as a whole.

From our point of view, studying the history and the logic of the various philosophers' philosophies is not enough. At least as a methodological guide-line, attention should be drawn to the other parts of the history of philosophy; to the conceptions of the world held by the great masses, to those of the most restricted ruling (or intellectual) groups, and finally to the links between these various

[29] *norma di vita.* Croce's own word was "ethics" (*etica*), which Gramsci has adapted to emphasise the connection between ethical standards and practical life, implicitly denied in the Crocean system.

cultural complexes and the philosophy of the philosophers. The philosophy of an age is not the philosophy of this or that philosopher, of this or that group of intellectuals, of this or that broad section of the popular masses. It is a process of combination of all these elements, which culminates in an overall trend, in which the culmination becomes a norm of collective action and becomes concrete and complete (integral) "history".

The philosophy of an historical epoch is, therefore, nothing other than the "history" of that epoch itself, nothing other than the mass of variations that the leading group has succeeded in imposing on preceding reality. History and philosophy are in this sense indivisible: they form a bloc. But the philosophical elements proper can be "distinguished", on all their various levels: as philosophers' philosophy and the conceptions of the leading groups (philosophical culture) and as the religions of the great masses. And it can be seen how, at each of these levels, we are dealing with different forms of ideological "combination".

"Creative" philosophy

What is philosophy? Is it a purely receptive or, at the very most, ordering activity? Or is it an absolutely creative activity? One must first define what is meant by "receptive", "ordering" and "creative". "Receptive" implies the certainty of an external world which is absolutely immutable, which exists "in general", objectively in the vulgar sense. "Ordering" is similar to "receptive". Although it implies an activity of thought, this activity is limited and narrow. But what does "creative" mean? Should it mean that the external world is created by thought? But what thought and whose? There is a danger of falling into solipsism,[30] and in fact every form of idealism necessarily does fall into solipsism. To escape simultaneously from solipsism and from mechanicist conceptions implicit in the concept of thought as a receptive and ordering activity, it is necessary to put the question in an "historicist" fashion, and at the same time to put the "will" (which in the last analysis equals practical or political activity) at the base of philosophy. But it must be a rational, not an arbitrary, will, which is realised in so far as it corresponds to objective historical necessities, or in so far as it is universal history itself in the moment of its progressive actualisation. Should this will be represented at the beginning by a single indi-

[30] Solipsism: the form of subjective idealism which maintains that the self is the only object of knowledge.

vidual, its rationality will be documented by the fact that it comes to be accepted by the many, and accepted permanently: that is, by becoming a culture, a form of "good sense", a conception of the world with an ethic that conforms to its structure. Until classical German philosophy, philosophy was conceived as a receptive, or at the most an ordering activity, i.e. as knowledge of a mechanism that functioned objectively outside man. Classical German philosophy introduced the concept of "creativity" of thought, but in an idealistic and speculative sense.

It seems that the philosophy of praxis alone has been able to take philosophy a step forward, basing itself on classical German philosophy but avoiding any tendency towards solipsism, and historicising thought in that it assumes it in the form of a conception of the world and of "good sense" diffused among the many (a diffusion which precisely would be inconceivable without rationality or historicity) and diffused in such a way as to convert itself into an active norm of conduct. Creative, therefore, should be understood in the "relative" sense, as thought which modifies the way of feeling of the many and consequently reality itself, which cannot be thought without this many.[31] Creative also in the sense that it teaches that reality does not exist on its own, in and for itself, but only in an historical relationship with the men who modify it, etc.

Historical Importance of a Philosophy

A great deal of research and study on the historical significance of different philosophies is utterly sterile and fanciful because it fails to take account of the fact that many philosophical systems are exclusively, or almost exclusively, individual expressions and that that part of them which can be called historical is often minimal and swamped in a complex of abstractions whose origins are purely and abstractly ratiocinative. One could say that the historical value of a philosophy can be calculated from the "practical" efficacity it has acquired for itself, understanding "practical" in the widest sense. If it is true that every philosophy is the expression of a society, it should react back on that society and produce certain effects, both positive and negative. The extent to which precisely it reacts back is the measure of its historical importance, of its not being individual "elucubration" but "historical fact".

---

[31] i.e. our capacity to think and act on the world is dependent on other people who are themselves also both subjects and objects of history.

The Philosopher

The principle must first be established that all men are "philosophers", that is, that between the professional or "technical" philosophers and the rest of mankind, the difference is not one of "quality" but only of "quantity". (The term "quantity" is being used here in a special sense, which is not to be confused with its meaning in arithmetic, since what it indicates is greater or lesser degrees of "homogeneity", "coherence", "logicality", etc.; in other words, quantity of qualitative elements.) But having established this it still remains to be seen exactly what the difference consists in. Thus it would not be exact to call by the name of "philosophy" every tendency of thought, every general orientation, etc., nor even every "conception of the world and of life". The philosopher can be called a "specialised worker" by comparison with the unskilled labourer, but this isn't exact either, since in industry, in addition to the labourer and the specialised worker there also exists the engineer, who not only knows the trade from the practical angle, but knows it theoretically and historically. The professional or technical philosopher does not only "think" with greater logical rigour, with greater coherence, with more systematic sense than do other men, but he knows the entire history of thought. In other words, he is capable of accounting for the development of thought up to his own day and he is in a position where he can take up a problem from the point which it has reached after having undergone every previous attempt at a solution. He has the same function in the field of thought that specialists have in their various scientific fields.

However, there is a difference between the specialised philosopher and other specialists, which is that the specialist philosopher is much more similar to the rest of mankind than are other specialists. The specialised philosopher has been represented as a figure similar to the specialists of other branches of science and this has been responsible for his caricatured image. There can be specialists in entomology, without everybody else having to be an empirical entomologist, or specialists in trigonometry without the majority of people having to be concerned with trigonometry. One can find extremely refined, extremely specialised sciences which are necessary, but are not for that reason common. But it is not possible to conceive of any man who is not also a philosopher, who doesn't think, because thought is proper to man as such, or at least to any man who is not a pathological cretin.

"Language", Languages and Common Sense

In what exactly does the merit of what is normally termed "common sense" or "good sense" consist? Not just in the fact that, if only implicitly, common sense applies the principle of causality, but in the much more limited fact that in a whole range of judgments common sense identifies the exact cause, simple and to hand, and does not let itself be distracted by fancy quibbles and pseudo-profound, pseudo-scientific metaphysical mumbo-jumbo. It was natural that "common sense" should have been exalted in the seventeenth and eighteenth centuries, when there was a reaction against the principle of authority represented by Aristotle and the Bible. It was discovered indeed that in "common sense" there was a certain measure of "experimentalism" and direct observation of reality, though empirical and limited. Even today, when a similar state of affairs exists, we find the same favourable judgment on common sense, although the situation has in fact changed and the "common sense" of today has a much more limited intrinsic merit.

We have established that philosophy is a conception of the world and that philosophical activity is not to be conceived solely as the "individual" elaboration of systematically coherent concepts, but also and above all as a cultural battle to transform the popular "mentality" and to diffuse the philosophical innovations which will demonstrate themselves to be "historically true" to the extent that they become concretely—i.e. historically and socially—universal. Given all this, the question of language in general and of languages in the technical sense[32] must be put in the forefront of our enquiry. What the pragmatists[33] wrote about this question merits re-examination.*

---

[32] The English word language does the work of two Italian words here: *lingua* ("languages in the technical sense"), meaning a particular system of verbal signs, as it were the English or Italian language; and *linguaggio* ("language in general"), in the generic sense of the faculty to transmit messages, verbal or otherwise, by means of a common code. In modern linguistics (and Gramsci studied linguistics at the very beginning of the modern period) *lingua* ("la langue") usually means the code, and *linguaggio* ("le langage"), besides its generic sense, also refers to the set of messages transmitted, i.e. the concretisation of the abstract rules of a *lingua*.

[33] "pragmatists": adherents of the philosophical theory of pragmatism, which originated in America and is connected with the names of William James and C. S. Peirce. Pragmatism enjoyed a certain vogue in Italy as an off-shoot and partial reaction against the positivist movement. Its most noteworthy exponent was Giovanni Vailati (1863–1909), also a distinguished mathematician and logician. The sociologist Pareto was also influenced by pragmatism.

* Cf. the *Scritti* [Writings] of G. Vailati (Florence, 1911), among which the essay *Il linguaggio come ostacolo alla eliminazione di contrasti illusori*. [Language as an obstacle to the elimination of illusory conflicts.]

In the case of the pragmatists, as generally with any attempt to systematise philosophy in an organic fashion, it is not made clear whether the reference is to the system in its entirety or just to its essential nucleus. It seems to me safe to say that the conception of language held by Vailati and other pragmatists is not acceptable. But it also seems that they felt real needs and "described" them with an exactness that was not far off the mark, even if they did not succeed in posing the problems fully or in providing a solution. It seems that one can say that "language"[34] is essentially a collective term which does not presuppose any single thing existing in time and space. Language also means culture and philosophy (if only at the level of common sense) and therefore the fact of "language" is in reality a multiplicity of facts more or less organically coherent and co-ordinated. At the limit it could be said that every speaking being has a personal language of his own, that is his own particular way of thinking and feeling. Culture, at its various levels, unifies in a series of strata, to the extent that they come into contact with each other, a greater or lesser number of individuals who understand each other's mode of expression in differing degrees, etc. It is these historico-social distinctions and differences which are reflected in common language and produce those "obstacles" and "sources of error" which the pragmatists have talked about.

From this one can deduce the importance of the "cultural aspect", even in practical (collective) activity. An historical act can only be performed by "collective man", and this presupposes the attainment of a "cultural-social" unity through which a multiplicity of dispersed wills, with heterogeneous aims, are welded together with a single aim, on the basis of an equal and common conception of the world, both general and particular, operating in transitory bursts (in emotional ways) or permanently (where the intellectual base is so well rooted, assimilated and experienced that it becomes passion.[35] Since this is the way things happen, great importance is assumed by the general question of language, that is, the question of collectively attaining a single cultural "climate".

This problem can and must be related to the modern way of

---

[34] *linguaggio*. See note 32 above.

[35] "passion:" a Crocean term, denoting active as well as passive subjective emotionality. Croce generally uses the term disparagingly, arguing for example that politics is mere "passion", and not, as Gramsci was to maintain, the active centre of human life. Gramsci tends to follow the Crocean usage and devotes a lot of space to arguing (see, for example, pp. 138–40) that politics is precisely not passion in the Crocean sense. Here, however, the word has an approving sense of a strongly-felt internalised commitment to an objective goal.

considering educational doctrine and practice, according to which the relationship between teacher and pupil is active and reciprocal so that every teacher is always a pupil and every pupil a teacher.[36] But the educational relationship should not be restricted to the field of the strictly "scholastic" relationships by means of which the new generation comes into contact with the old and absorbs its experiences and its historically necessary values and "matures" and develops a personality of its own which is historically and culturally superior. This form of relationship exists throughout society as a whole and for every individual relative to other individuals. It exists between intellectual and non-intellectual sections of the population, between the rulers and the ruled, *élites* and their followers, leaders [*dirigenti*] and led, the vanguard and the body of the army. Every relationship of "hegemony" is necessarily an educational relationship and occurs not only within a nation, between the various forces of which the nation is composed, but in the international and world-wide field, between complexes of national and continental civilisations.

One could say therefore that the historical personality of an individual philosopher is also given by the active relationship which exists between him and the cultural environment he is proposing to modify. The environment reacts back on the philosopher and imposes on him a continual process of self-criticism. It is his "teacher". This is why one of the most important demands that the modern intelligentsias have made in the political field has been that of the so-called "freedom of thought and of the expression of thought" ("freedom of the press", "freedom of association"). For the relationship between master and disciple in the general sense referred to above is only realised where this political condition exists, and only then do we get the "historical" realisation of a new type of philosopher, whom we could call a "democratic philosopher" in the sense that he is a philosopher convinced that his personality is not limited to himself as a physical individual but is an active social relationship of modification of the cultural environment. When the "thinker" is content with his own thought, when he is "subjectively", that is abstractly, free, that is when he nowadays becomes a joke. The unity of science and life is precisely an active unity, in which alone liberty of thought can be realised; it is a master-pupil relationship, one between the philosopher and the

[36] This point is also made elsewhere by Gramsci, and further extended to cover the whole relationship of man to his environment in the sense of Marx's Theses on Feuerbach ("the educator must be educated.").

cultural environment in which he has to work and from which he can draw the necessary problems for formulation and resolution. In other words, it is the relationship between philosophy and history.

What is Man?

This is the primary and principal question that philosophy asks. How is it to be answered? The definition can be found in man himself, that is, in each individual man. But is it correct? In every individual man one can discover what every "individual man" is. But we are not interested in what every individual man is, which then comes to mean what every individual man is at every individual moment. Reflecting on it, we can see that in putting the question "what is man?" what we mean is: what can man become? That is, can man dominate his own destiny, can he "make himself", can he create his own life? We maintain therefore that man is a process, and, more exactly, the process of his actions. If you think about it, the question itself "what is man?" is not an abstract or "objective" question. It is born of our reflection about ourselves and about others, and we want to know, in relation to what we have thought and seen, what we are and what we can become; whether we really are, and if so to what extent, "makers of our own selves", of our life and of our destiny. And we want to know this "today", in the given conditions of today, the conditions of our daily life, not of any life or any man.

The question is born and receives its content from special, that is, specific ways of considering life and man. The most important of these is religion, and a specific religion, which is Catholicism. In reality, when we ask ourselves "what is man?", what importance do his will and his concrete activity have in creating himself and the life he lives? what we mean is: is Catholicism a correct conception of the world and of life? As Catholics, making Catholicism a norm of life, are we making a mistake or are we right? Everyone has a vague intuitive feeling that when they make Catholicism a norm of life they are making a mistake, to such an extent that nobody attaches himself to Catholicism as a norm of life, even when calling himself a Catholic. An integral Catholic, one, that is, who applied the Catholic norms in every act of his life, would seem a monster. Which, when you come to think about it, is the severest and most peremptory criticism of Catholicism itself.

Catholics would say that no other conception is followed punctiliously either, and they would be right. But all this shows is that there does not exist, historically, a way of seeing things and of acting which is equal for all men, no more no less. It is not a reason in favour of Catholicism, although for centuries the Catholic way of seeing things and of acting has been organised around this very end, which has not been the case with any other religion possessed of the same means, of the same systematic spirit, of the same continuity and centralisation. From the "philosophical" point of view, what is unsatisfactory in Catholicism is the fact that, in spite of everything, it insists on putting the cause of evil in the individual man himself, or in other words that it conceives of man as a defined and limited individual. It could be said of all hitherto existing philosophies that they reproduce this position of Catholicism, that they conceive of man as an individual limited to his own individuality and of the spirit as being this individuality. It is on this point that it is necessary to reform the concept of man. I mean that one must conceive of man as a series of active relationships (a process) in which individuality, though perhaps the most important, is not, however, the only element to be taken into account. The humanity which is reflected in each individuality is composed of various elements: 1. the individual; 2. other men; 3. the natural world. But the latter two elements are not as simple as they might appear. The individual does not enter into relations with other men by juxtaposition, but organically, in as much, that is, as he belongs to organic entities which range from the simplest to the most complex. Thus Man does not enter into relations with the natural world just by being himself part of the natural world, but actively, by means of work and technique. Further: these relations are not mechanical. They are active and conscious. They correspond to the greater or lesser degree of understanding that each man has of them. So one could say that each one of us changes himself, modifies himself to the extent that he changes and modifies the complex relations of which he is the hub. In this sense the real philosopher is, and cannot be other than, the politician, the active man who modifies the environment, understanding by environment the *ensemble* of relations which each of us enters to take part in. If one's own individuality is the *ensemble* of these relations,[37] to create one's personality means to acquire consciousness of them and to modify one's own personality means to modify the *ensemble* of these relations.

---

[37] Cf. the sixth of Marx's *Theses on Feuerbach*: "The human essence is no abstraction inherent in each single individual. In its reality it is the *ensemble* of social relations. . . ."

But these relations, as we have said, are not simple. Some are necessary, others are voluntary. Further, to be conscious of them, to whatever degree of profundity (that is, to know, in varying degrees, how to modify them) already modifies them. Even the necessary relations, in so far as they are known to be necessary, take on a different aspect and importance. In this sense, knowledge is power. But the problem is complex in another way as well. It is not enough to know the *ensemble* of relations as they exist at any given time as a given system. They must be known genetically, in the movement of their formation. For each individual is the synthesis not only of existing relations, but of the history of these relations. He is a précis of all the past. It will be said that what each individual can change is very little, considering his strength. This is true up to a point. But when the individual can associate himself with all the other individuals who want the same changes, and if the changes wanted are rational, the individual can be multiplied an impressive number of times and can obtain a change which is far more radical than at first sight ever seemed possible.

The "societies" in which a single individual can take part are very numerous, more than would appear. It is through these "societies" that the individual belongs to the human race. Thus the ways in which the single individual enters into relation with nature are many and complex, since by technique one should understand not only the *ensemble* of scientific ideas applied industrially (which is the normal meaning of the word) but also the "mental" instruments, philosophical knowledge.

That man cannot be conceived other than as living in society is a commonplace.[38] But not all the necessary consequences have been drawn from this, even on an individual level. That a specific human society presupposes a specific "society of things", and that human society is possible only in so far as there exists a specific society of things, is also a commonplace. It is true that up to now the significance attributed to these supra-individual organisms (both the *societas hominum* and the *societas rerum*)[39] has been mechanistic and determinist: hence the reaction against it. It is necessary to elaborate a doctrine in which these relations are seen as active and in movement, establishing quite clearly that the source of this

---

[38] This notion derives from Aristotle's "Man is a political animal", taken up in scholastic philosophy and again in the Renaissance, and perhaps more deeply engrained in Italian philosophical culture than in that of any other country.

[39] The society of men and the society of things: i.e. the human and natural worlds.

activity is the consciousness of the individual man who knows, wishes, admires, creates (in so far as he does know, wish, admire, create, etc.) and conceives of himself not as isolated but rich in the possibilities offered him by other men and by the society of things of which he cannot help having a certain knowledge. Just as every man is a philosopher, every man is a man of science (etc.).

Taken in itself, Feuerbach's assertion "Man is what he eats"[40] can be interpreted in various ways. Crude and stupid interpretation: man is at any time what he eats materially, i.e. food has an immediate and determining influence on the way of thinking. Recall Amadeo [Bordiga]'s remark to the effect that if one knew what a man had eaten before making a speech, for example, one would be in a better position to interpret the speech itself. A childish remark, and not even in conformity with positive scientific data, because the brain is not nourished on beans and truffles but rather the food manages to reconstitute the molecules of the brain once it has been turned into homogeneous and assimilable substances, which have potentially the "same nature", as the molecules of the brain. If this assertion were true, then the determining matrix of history would be the kitchen and revolutions would coincide with radical changes in the diet of the masses. Historically the contrary is true. It is revolutions and the complex development of history which have modified diet and created the successive "tastes" in the choice of food. It wasn't the regular sowing of wheat that brought nomadism to an end, but vice versa. The emergence of conditions hostile to nomadism provided an impetus to regular sowing.*

On the other hand it is also true that "man is what he eats", in so far as diet is one of the expressions of social relations taken as a whole, and every social group has its own basic form of diet. But one might equally well say that "man is his clothing", "man is his housing" or "man is his particular way of reproducing himself, that is, his family". For, together with diet, housing, clothing and reproduction are among the elements of social life

---

[40] The original German is in the form of a pun, "*der Mensch ist* [is] *was er isst* [eats]". Gramsci's hostility to philosophical materialism of the Feuerbachian non-dialectical type involves him here also in some superficial point-scoring against Bordiga.

* Compare Feuerbach's assertion with Marinetti's campaign against spaghetti and Bontempelli's polemical defence of it, all in 1930 at the height of the world crisis.[41]

[41] F. T. Marinetti, futurist poet and propagandist, and author of a curious work on gastronomy entitled *La Cucina Futurista*, attributed the degeneration of Italy to the Germanic importation of noodles in the Middle Ages.

in which social relations as a whole are manifested in the most evident and widespread (i.e. mass) fashion.

The problem of what is man is always therefore the so-called problem of "human nature" or that of so-called "man in general". It is thus an attempt to create a science of man (a philosophy) which starts from an initially "unitary"[42] concept, from an abstraction in which everything that is "human" can be contained. But is the "human" a starting-point or a point of arrival, as a concept and as a unitary fact? Or might not the whole attempt, in so far as it posits the human as a starting-point, be a "theological" or "metaphysical" residue? Philosophy cannot be reduced to a naturalistic "anthropology": the nature of the human species is not given by the "biological" nature of man.

The differences in man which count in history are not the biological—race, shape of the cranium, colour of skin, etc. (For it is to these that the affirmation "man is what he eats" can be reduced—he eats wheat in Europe, rice in Asia, etc.—and it could indeed be further reduced to the affirmation "man is the country where he lives", since most of diet is in general connected with the land inhabited.) Nor has "biological unity" ever counted for very much in history: man is the animal which has eaten himself precisely when he was nearest to the "state of nature" and when he could not artificially multiply the production of natural goods. Nor yet have the "faculty of reason" or "the mind" created unity, and they cannot be recognised as a "unitary" fact as they represent a purely formal and categorical concept.[43] It is not "thought" but what people really think that unites or differentiates mankind.

That "human nature" is the "complex of social relations"[44] is the most satisfactory answer, because it includes the idea of becoming (man "becomes", he changes continuously with the changing of social relations) and because it denies "man in general". Indeed social relations are expressed by various groups of men which each presuppose the others and whose unity is dialectical, not formal. Man is aristocratic in so far as man is a serf, etc.[45] One could also say that the nature of man is "history" (and, in this sense, given history as equal to spirit, that the nature of man is spirit if one gives to history precisely this significance of

---

[42] "unitary": in the sense of establishing a concrete principle of unity.

[43] "categorical": i.e. non-historical and non-dialectical.

[44] See note 37 on p. 352.

[45] *servo della gleba*. The concept here is that of the unity of opposites. Aristocracy by definition presupposes the existence of another class, the serfs, in relation to which it acquires its particular defining characteristics.

"becoming" which takes place in a "*concordia discors*" [discordant concord] which does not start from unity, but contains in itself the reasons for a possible unity. For this reason "human nature" cannot be located in any particular man but in the entire history of the human species (and the fact that we use the word "species", which is a naturalistic word, is itself significant)[46] while in each single individual there are to be found characteristics which are put in relief by being in contradiction with the characteristics of others. Both the conception of "spirit" found in traditional philosophy and that of "human nature" found in biology should be explained as "scientific utopias" which took the place of the greater utopia of a human nature to be sought for in God (and in men as sons of God) and they serve to indicate the continual travail of history, an aspiration of a rational and sentimental kind, etc. It is also true that both the religions which affirm the quality of man as the sons of God and the philosophies which affirm the equality of man as participants in the faculty of reason have been expressions of complex revolutionary movements (respectively the transformation of the classical world and the transformation of the medieval world) which laid the most powerful links of the chain of historical development.

The idea that the Hegelian dialectic has been the last reflection of these great historical nexuses, and that the dialectic, from being the expression of social contradictions, should become, with the disappearance of these contradictions, a pure conceptual dialectic, would appear to be at the root of those recent philosophies, like that of Croce, which have a utopistic basis.

In history real "equality", that is the degree of "spirituality" reached by the historical process of "human nature" is to be identified in the system of "private and public" "explicit and implicit" associations whose threads are knotted together in the "State" and in the world political system. We are dealing here with "equalities" experienced as such between the members of an association, and "inequalities" experienced between one association and another. These are equalities and inequalities which are valid in so far as people, individually or as a group, are conscious of them. In this way we arrive also at the equality of, or equation between, "philosophy and politics", thought and action, that is,

---

[46] Naturalistic in the sense of derived from natural history. Gramsci in fact uses the phrase "*genere umano*", but we have preferred to translate "species" in accordance with normal English usage, and also with Feuerbach, whose conception of "*die Gattung*", normally translated "species", is here being criticised.

at a philosophy of praxis. Everything is political, even philosophy or philosophies (cf. the notes on the character of ideologies)[47] and the only "philosophy" is history in action, that is, life itself. It is in this sense that one can interpret the thesis of the German proletariat as the heir of classical German philosophy—and one can affirm that the theorisation and realisation of hegemony carried out by Ilich [Lenin] was also a great "metaphysical" event.

Progress and Becoming

Are these two different things or different aspects of one and the same concept? Progress is an ideology: becoming is a philosophical conception. "Progress" depends on a specific mentality, in the constitution of which are involved certain historically determined cultural elements: "becoming" is a philosophical concept from which "progress" can be absent. In the idea of progress is implied the possibility of quantitative and qualitative measuring, of "more" and "better". A "fixed", or fixable, yardstick must therefore be supposed, but this yardstick is given by the past, by a certain phase of the past or by certain measurable aspects, etc. (Not that one should think of a metric system of progress.)

How was the idea of progress born? Does its birth represent a fundamental and epoch-making cultural event? It seems that it does. The birth and the development of the idea of progress correspond to a widespread consciousness that a certain relationship has been reached between society and nature (including in the concept of nature those of chance and "irrationality") such that as a result mankind as a whole is more sure of its future and can conceive "rationally" of plans through which to govern its entire life. In order to combat the idea of progress, Leopardi[48] had to have recourse to volcanic eruptions, that is to those natural phenomena which are still irresistible and irremediable. But in the past there were far more irresistible forces, famines, epidemics, etc., which, within certain limits, have now been overcome.

There can be no doubt that progress has been a democratic ideology. Nor is there any doubt that it has had a political function in the formation of modern constitutional states, etc. It is also certain that it is no longer at its zenith. But in what sense is this

---

[47] See in particular "The Concept of Ideology" on pp. 375–377.

[48] Giacomo Leopardi (1798–1837). The reference is to his great poem *La Ginestra*, written in 1836, in which he derides the optimism of progress ("*le magnifiche sorti e progressive*") and counterposes the advance of civilisation to the threat of an eruption of Vesuvius.

the case? Not in the sense that the faith in the possibility of rationally dominating nature and chance has been lost, but in the sense that it is "democratic". In other words, the official "standard bearers" of progress have become incapable of this domination, because they have brought into being in the present destructive forces like crises and unemployment, etc., every bit as dangerous and terrifying as those of the past. (The past forces meanwhile have now been "socially" forgotten, though not by all elements of society: the peasants continue not to understand "progress"; they think of themselves as being, and still are all too much, in the hands of natural forces and of chance, and therefore retain a "magical", mediaeval and religious mentality.) The crisis of the idea of progress is not therefore a crisis of the idea itself, but a crisis of the standard bearers of the idea, who have in turn become a part of "nature" to be dominated. In this situation attacks on the idea of progress are very tendentious and interest-motivated.

Can the idea of progress be kept apart from that of becoming? It would appear not. They were born at the same time, as politics (France) and as philosophy (in Germany: subsequently developed in Italy). In the idea of "becoming" there has been an attempt to save the most concrete aspect of "progress"—movement, and indeed dialectical movement. This also represents a development in depth, since progress tends to be linked with the vulgar notion of evolution.

From a little article by Aldo Capasso in *L'Italia letteraria* of 4 December 1932, I quote one or two extracts which present common doubts on these problems:

> "Even here a derisive attitude is common towards the humanitarian and democratic optimism of a nineteenth-century type, and Leopardi is not alone when he talks of 'progressive lot'.[49] But an astute disguise has been devised for 'progress' in the form of the idealistic 'becoming', an idea which will remain in history, in our opinion, more as Italian than as German. But what sense can there be in a becoming that is pursued *ad infinitum*, an improvement which can never be compared to a physical good? In the absence of a criterion of a 'final' stable step, the unity of measurement of this 'improvement' also lacking. Furthermore, we cannot even reach the point of luxuriating in the confidence of being—we real living men—better than, say,

[49] See preceding note.

the Romans or the early Christians, because, with improvement being understood in a purely ideal sense, it is quite possible for us all to be 'decadent', whereas in those days they could almost all have been complete men or even saints. So that, from an ethical point of view, the idea of an ascent *ad infinitum* which is implicit in the concept of Becoming remains to a certain degree unjustifiable, given that ethical 'improvement' is an individual fact and that on the individual plane it is quite possible to conclude, proceeding from individual case to individual case, that the whole latter epoch is worse . . . And then the optimistic concept of becoming proves as elusive on the ideal as on the real plane. . . It is well known that Croce denied any value as a thinker to Leopardi, maintaining that pessimism and optimism are sentimental and not philosophical attitudes. But the pessimist could observe that, for its part, the idealist conception of Becoming is a matter of optimism and sentiment, since pessimism and optimism (if not animated by any faith in the Transcendent) conceive of History in the same way: as the flow of a river that has no mouth and then they place the emphasis either on the word 'river' or on the words 'that has no mouth' according to their state of mind. One side says: there is no mouth, but, as in a harmonious river, there is the continuity of the waves and the survival, in a developed form, of yesterday in today . . . And on the other side: there is the continuity of a river, but there is no river mouth . . . In brief, let us not forget that optimism is sentiment, no less than pessimism. It remains the fact that every philosophy cannot but form its attitudes sentimentally, 'as pessimism or as optimism', etc."

Capasso's thought is not very coherent, but his way of thinking is expressive of a widespread state of mind, very snobbish and unsure, very disconnected and superficial and often without much intellectual honesty and loyalty and without the necessary formally logical character.

The question is still the same: what is man? what is human nature? If man is defined as an individual, psychologically and speculatively, these problems of progress and becoming are insoluble or remain purely verbal. But if man is conceived as the *ensemble* of social relations, it then appears that every comparison between men, over time, is impossible, because one is dealing with different, if not heterogenous, objects. Moreover, since man is also the *ensemble* of his conditions of life, one can provide a quantitative measurement of the difference between past and present, since one can measure the extent to which man dominates nature and chance. Possibility is not reality: but it is in itself a reality. Whether a man can or cannot do a thing has its importance in evaluating what is done in reality. Possibility means "freedom". The measure of freedom enters into the concept of man. That the objective possibilities exist for people not to die of hunger and that people do die of hunger, has its importance, or so one would have thought. But the existence of objective conditions, of possibilities or of freedom is not yet enough: it is necessary to "know" them, and know how to use them. And to want to use them. Man, in this sense, is concrete will, that is, the effective application of the abstract will or vital impulse[50] to the concrete means which realise such a will. Men create their own personality, 1. by giving a specific and concrete ("rational") direction to their own vital impulse or will; 2. by identifying the means which will make this will concrete and specific and not arbitrary; 3. by contributing to modify the *ensemble* of the concrete conditions for realising this will to the extent of one's own limits and capacities and in the most fruitful form. Man is to be conceived as an historical bloc of purely individual and subjective elements and of mass and objective or material elements with which the individual is in an active relationship. To transform the external world, the general system of relations, is to potentiate oneself and to develop oneself. That ethical "improvement" is purely individual is an illusion and an error: the synthesis of the elements constituting individuality is "individual", but it cannot be realised and developed without an activity directed outward, modifying external relations both with nature and, in varying degrees, with other men, in the various social circles in which one lives, up to the greatest relationship of all, which embraces the whole human species. For this reason one can say that man is essentially "political" since it is through the activity of transforming and consciously directing other men that man realises his "humanity", his "human nature".

---

[50] The conceptual vocabulary here is drawn in part from Bergson, introduced in order to fill a gap felt by Gramsci to exist in traditional Marxist theories of social and individual praxis. More than anything else it is these importations from non-Marxist philosophies that have caused Gramsci to be taxed with idealism by more "orthodox" Marxists. It should, however, be noted that in an earlier passage Gramsci defines "will" in a very non-Bergsonian sense as equalling, in the last analysis, practical or political activity, and in general he does not hesitate consciously to use words from an earlier philosophical tradition while endowing them with a new content determined by their context within a Marxist discourse. (See below, "Questions of Nomenclature and Content", pp. 452 ff.

Individualism

On the question of so-called "individualism", that is the attitude that every historical period has adopted towards the position of the individual in the world and in historical life: what is today called "individualism" had its origins in the cultural revolution that came after the Middle Ages (Renaissance and Reformation) and indicates a specific position adopted towards the problem of divinity and therefore of the Church; it is the passage from transcendental thought to immanentism.[51]

Prejudices against individualism, taken to the point of Jeremiads, rather than criticisms of Catholic and reactionary thought; the form of "individualism" that today has become anti-historical is that manifested in the individual appropriation of wealth while the production of wealth has been progressively socialised. That the Catholics are the least qualified to moan about individualism can be deduced from the fact that, politically, they have always recognised a political personality only in property, implying in other words that man is not worthy for his own sake but insofar as he is completed by material goods. What is the meaning of the fact that people became electors though paying a census tax and that one could belong to as many politico-administrative communities as one possessed property in, if not a devaluation of the "spirit" before "matter"? If only a man with possessions is conceived of as "man", and if it has become impossible for all to have possessions, why should it be anti-spiritual to look for a form of property in which material forces complete and contribute to the constitution of all personalities? In reality, though, it was implicitly admitted that human "nature" was not within the individual but in the unity of man and material forces. Therefore, the conquest of material forces is one way, and indeed the most important, of conquest of personality.*

---

[51] i.e. to a form of thought which finds the principles governing the historical world within the world itself, without recourse to any external philosophical principle or motive force. Within the limits of this definition Gramsci sees immanentism as a progressive development, while insisting that in its idealistic formulation it is unacceptable and that it has value only when thoroughly historicised and based on the concrete and material development of history.

* Recently a lot of praise has been showered on a book by the young French Catholic writer Daniel Rops, *Le Monde sans âme* (Paris, Plon, 1932), also translated in Italy. It is important to examine, in this connection, a whole series of concepts through which, by a form of sophistry, positions of the past are revived as if they had contemporary importance.

Examination of the concept of human nature

Origins of the feeling of "equality": religion with its idea of God-as-Father and Man-as-Sons and therefore equal: philosophy according to the aphorism "*Omnis enim philosophia, cum ad communem hominum cogitandi facultatem revocet, per se democratica est; ideoque ab optimatibus non iniuria sibi exstimatur perniciosa*". [For every philosophy, since it refers to the common human faculty of thought, is democratic *per se*; therefore the aristocracy is not wrong in estimating it pernicious to itself.] Biological science which affirms the "natural" (psycho-physical) equality of all the individual elements of the human "species"; everyone is born in the same way, etc.: Man is mortal: John is a man: John is mortal. John equals all mankind. Hence the empirical-scientific (folkloristic empirical science) origin of the formula "we are all born naked".

Recall Chesterton's story in *The Innocence of Father Brown*[52] about the postman and the little man who constructed prodigious machines. In the story there is an observation of this type: "An old lady lives in a castle with twenty servants. Another lady visits, and she says to the visitor 'I am always so alone'. The doctor informs here that the plague is spreading, that there is a danger of infection, etc., and then she says 'There are so many of us here'." (Chesterton uses this as a basis simply for purely novelistic plot effects.)

Philosophy and Democracy

One can observe the parallel evolution of modern democracy and of specific forms of metaphysical materialism and idealism. Equality is sought for by the French materialists of the eighteenth century in the reduction of man to a category of natural history, an individual of a biological species, distinguished not by social and historical qualifications but by natural gifts, and in any case, essentially equal to his kind. This conception has passed into

---

[52] In the story "The Invisible Man", where Father Brown, *à propos* the postman, makes this observation: "Have you ever noticed this—that people never answer what you say? They answer what you mean—or what they think you mean. Suppose one lady says to another, in a country house, 'is anybody staying with you?', the lady doesn't answer 'yes; the butler, the three footmen, the parlourmaid and so on', though the parlourmaid may be in the room, or the butler behind her chair. She says 'there is nobody staying with us', meaning nobody of the sort you mean. But suppose a doctor enquiring into an epidemic asks 'who is staying in the house?' then the lady will remember the butler, the parlourmaid and the rest."

conventional common sense, where we find the popular affirmation "we are all born naked" (unless of course the commonsense affirmation doesn't precede the ideological discussion of the intellectuals). In idealism we find the affirmation that philosophy is the democratic science *par excellence* in so far as it refers to the reasoning faculty common to all mankind—a fact which explains the hatred of the aristocracy for philosophy and the legal prohibitions on teaching and culture imposed by the classes of the *ancien régime*.

Quantity and quality

Since there cannot exist quantity without quality or quality without quantity (economy without culture, practical activity without the intelligence and vice versa) any opposition of the two terms is, rationally, a nonsense. And, indeed, when we get the opposition of quantity and quality with all the idiotic variations on the theme practised by Guglielmo Ferrero and Co., what are really being opposed are one form of quality and another form of quality, one form of quantity and another form of quantity. In other words, a matter of politics and not a philosophical proposition. If the quantity-quality nexus is indivisible the question is posed thus: where is it more useful to apply the force of one's will, to develop quantity or quality? Which of the two aspects is more easily controlled? Which is more easily measurable? On the basis of which can one make predictions and construct work plans? The answer appears to be in no doubt and to be the quantitative aspect. But to affirm that one wants to work on quantity, that one wants to develop the "bodily" aspect of reality does not mean that one intends to neglect "quality" but rather that one intends to pose the problem of quality in the most concrete and realistic form, in other words, to develop quality in the only way in which this development is controllable and measurable.

This question is connected with the other question expressed in the proverb "*Primum vivere deinde philosophari*" [Live first and philosophise afterwards]. In reality it is not possible to separate living from philosophising, but nonetheless the proverb has a practical meaning—living means concerning oneself in particular with practical economic activity; philosophising means concerning oneself with the intellectual activities of *otium litteratum* [learned leisure]. However, there are people who just "live" and are forced to undertake servile and exhausting labour without which others would not have the chance to be exonerated from economic activity in order to philosophise. To back "quality" against quantity means simply this: to maintain intact specific conditions of social life in which some people are pure quantity and others quality. And how pleasant it is to think of oneself as one of the licensed representatives of quality, beauty, thought and the like. There is hardly a lady in the fashionable world who doesn't imagine she is performing this function of preserving quality and beauty upon earth!

Theory and practice

It is worth searching for, analysing and criticising the various forms in which the concept of the unity of theory and practice has been presented in the history of ideas, since it appears without doubt that every conception of the world and every philosophy has been concerned with this problem. Affirmation of Aquinas and Scholasticism: "*Intellectus speculativus extensione fit practicus*" (Theory by simple extension becomes practice—in other words, the affirmation of the necessary connection between the order of ideas and that of action). Aphorism of Leibniz, so often repeated by the Italian idealists, "*Quo magis speculativa, magis practica*" [The more speculative, the more practical], in connection with science. The proposition of G. B. Vico, "*verum ipsum factum*" [true is what is done],[53] so much discussed and variously interpreted (see Croce's book on Vico and other polemical writings by Croce himself) and which Croce develops in the idealistic sense that knowledge is a form of doing and that one knows that which one does. ("To do" here has a particular meaning, so particular in fact that it finally means nothing more than "to know" and the phrase resolves itself into a tautology. This conception should, however, be considered in relation to the conception held by the philosophy of praxis.)

Since every action is the result of various wills, with a varying degree of intensity and awareness and of homogeneity with the entire complex of the collective will, it is clear that also the theory corresponding to it and implicit in it will be a combination of beliefs and points of view which are equally disordered and heterogeneous. However, in these terms and within these limits,

---

[53] The principle of *verum-factum* is one of the cornerstones of Vico's theory of knowledge. It is perhaps best understood not so much in the interpretation that Gramsci attributes here to Croce that knowledge is a form of doing, as in its inverse, that doing is a means of knowing. Contrary to the prevailing Cartesianism, Vico maintained that only the object of human action ("factum") could be truly known in that there was here an identity of subject and object absent in our dealings with the world of natural science.

the adhesion of theory to practice exists. If the problem of the identification of theory and practice is to be raised, it can be done in this sense, that one can construct, on a specific practice, a theory which, by coinciding and identifying itself with the decisive elements of the practice itself, can accelerate the historical process that is going on, rendering practice more homogeneous, more coherent, more efficient in all its elements, and thus, in other words, developing its potential to the maximum: or alternatively, given a certain theoretical position one can organise the practical element which is essential for the theory to be realised. The identification of theory and practice is a critical act, through which practice is demonstrated rational and necessary, and theory realistic and rational. This is why the problem of the identity of theory and practice is raised especially in the so-called transitional moments of history, that is, those moments in which the movement of transformation is at its most rapid. For it is then that the practical forces unleashed really demand justification in order to become more efficient and expansive; and that theoretical programmes multiply in number, and demand in their turn to be realistically justified, to the extent that they prove themselves assimilable into practical movements, thereby making the latter yet more practical and real.

Structure and Superstructure

The proposition contained in the "Preface to a Contribution to the Critique of Political Economy"[54] to the effect that men acquire consciousness of structural conflicts on the level of ideologies should be considered as an affirmation of epistemological and not simply psychological and moral value. From this, it follows that the theoretical-practical principle of hegemony has also epistemological significance, and it is here that Ilich [Lenin]'s greatest theoretical contribution to the philosophy of praxis should be sought. In these terms one could say that Ilich advanced philosophy as philosophy in so far as he advanced political doctrine and practice. The realisation of a hegemonic apparatus, in so far as it creates a new ideological terrain, determines a reform of consciousness and of methods of knowledge: it is a fact of knowledge, a philosophical

[54] Cf. Marx, Preface to *A Contribution to the Critique of Political Economy*: "In considering such [revolutionary] transformations a distinction should always be made between the material transformation of the economic conditions of production, which can be determined with the precision of natural science, and the legal, political, religious, aesthetic or philosophic—in short, ideological forms in which men become conscious of this conflict and fight it out."

fact. In Crocean terms: when one succeeds in introducing a new morality in conformity with a new conception of the world, one finishes by introducing the conception as well; in other words, one determines a reform of the whole of philosophy.

Structures and superstructures form an "historical bloc". That is to say the complex, contradictory and discordant *ensemble* of the superstructures is the reflection of the *ensemble* of the social relations of production. From this, one can conclude: that only a totalitarian[55] system of ideologies gives a rational reflection of the contradiction of the structure and represents the existence of the objective conditions for the revolutionising of praxis.[56] If a social group is formed which is one hundred per cent homogeneous on the level of ideology, this means that the premisses exist one hundred per cent for this revolutionising: that is that the "rational" is actively and actually real.[57] This reasoning is based on the necessary reciprocity between structure and superstructure, a reciprocity which is nothing other than the real dialectical process.

The term "catharsis"

The term "catharsis" can be employed to indicate the passage from the purely economic (or egoistic-passional) to the ethico-political moment,[58] that is the superior elaboration of the structure into superstructure in the minds of men. This also means the

---

[55] totalitarian: in the sense, also on p. 335 (see note 20), of "unified" and "all absorbing".

[56] *rovesciamento della prassi*. Syntactically this phrase is obscure, since it could either mean "the revolutionising *of* praxis" or "the revolution *through* praxis". It seems best to take it as an Italian rendering of Marx's phrase "*umwälzende Praxis*" (revolutionising praxis) in the 3rd thesis on Feuerbach.

[57] *il reale è "razionale" attuosamente e attualmente*. The notion that the rational is real and the real is rational, whose interpretation is much disputed, derives from Hegel's Philosophy of Right. Gramsci uses it here not as a general principle but to describe a particular moment of unity of structure and superstructure and of thought and action.

[58] Terminology derived from the Crocean system, according to which the categories of Logic and Ethics are "universal" elaborations of the "particular" categories of Aesthetics and Economics. Gramsci occasionally makes instrumental use of this classification, particularly as regards the passage from the particular ("economic" or "corporate") to the universal ("hegemonic"); but it should be noted that for him Politics plays a far more important role than it did for Croce and one which effectively subverts the system of Crocean categories for which Politics is either down-graded to the level of individual passion or subsumed under Ethics.

The highly original use here of the word "catharsis" to indicate (roughly speaking) the acquisition of revolutionary consciousness was perhaps suggested to Gramsci by his mental habit of selecting terminology unlikely to alert the suspicions of the censor.

passage from "objective to subjective" and from "necessity to freedom".[59] Structure ceases to be an external force which crushes man, assimilates him to itself and makes him passive; and is transformed into a means of freedom, an instrument to create a new ethico-political form and a source of new initiatives. To establish the "cathartic" moment becomes therefore, it seems to me, the starting-point for all the philosophy of praxis, and the cathartic process coincides with the chain of syntheses which have resulted from the evolution of the dialectic.*

The Kantian "Noumenon"

The question of the "external objectivity of the real"[61] in so far as it is connected with the concept of the "thing in itself" and of

---

[59] Gramsci's treatment of the notion of the passage from the realm of necessity to the realm of freedom differs slightly from that of Marx. Whereas Gramsci develops the notion in terms of the free movement of thought untrammelled either by tendentious ideology or by the need for thought to take as its basis contradictions engendered in the world of material production, with the result that the philosophy of a future communist society could well be a form of what would now be regarded as idealism; Marx is more cautious, emphasising (*Capital*, Vol. III, Chapter 48) that "the true realm of freedom . . . can blossom forth only with this realm of necessity [the appropriation from nature of man's material wants] as its basis".

* One must keep permanently in mind the two points between which this process oscillates: that no society poses for itself problems the necessary and sufficient conditions for whose solution do not already exist or are coming into being; and that no society comes to an end before it has expressed all its potential content.[60]

[60] A reference to Marx's Preface to *A Contribution to the Critique of Political Economy:*

"No social order ever perishes before all the productive forces for which there is room in it have been developed; and new, higher relations of production never appear before the material conditions of their existence have matured in the womb of the old society itself. Therefore mankind always sets itself only such tasks as it can solve; since, looking at the matter more closely, it will always be found that the task itself arises only when the material conditions for its solution already exist or at at least in the process of formation."

[61] The question of the external objectivity of the real is dealt with more specifically, in relation to the distinction between mechanical and dialectical materialism, in Gramsci's *Critical Notes on Bukharin's Popular Manual* (see below, pp. 440–448). Here Gramsci is concerned with a slightly different problem, that of the Kantian "noumenon" or the "*ding an sich*" (i.e. the reality of things as distinct from the "phenomenon" through which we have knowledge of them). Despite the obvious differences between "Graeco-Christian" philosophy (the Aristotelian and Scholastic tradition) and Kantianism, Gramsci discerns in both currents an underlying similarity—their assumption that the whole of reality is not contained within the phenomenal world alone. Even more remarkably, in his attempt to establish the difference between the "philosophy of praxis" and other philosophies, he assimilates much of positivist thought to the same transcendentalist matrix.

the Kantian "noumenon". It seems difficult to exclude the assumption that the "thing in itself" is a derivation from the "external objectivity of the real" and from so-called Graeco-Christian realism (Aristotle, Aquinas). This derivation can also be seen in the fact that an entire tendency of vulgar materialism and positivism has given rise to the neo-Kantian and neo-critical school.

If reality is as we know it and if our knowledge changes continually—if, that is, no philosophy is definitive but all are historically determined—it is hard to imagine that reality changes objectively with changes in ourselves. Not only common sense but scientific thought as well make this difficult to accept. In the *Holy Family*[62] it is said that the whole reality is in phenomena and that beyond phenomena there is nothing, and this is certainly correct. But it is not easy to demonstrate. What are phenomena? Are they something objective, existing in and for themselves, or are they qualities which man has isolated in consequence of his practical interests (the construction of his economic life) and his scientific interests (the necessity to discover an order in the world and to describe and classify things, a necessity which is itself connected to mediated and future practical interests).

Accepting the affirmation that our knowledge of things is nothing other than ourselves, our needs and interests, that is that our knowledge is superstructure (or non-definitive philosophy), it is difficult not to think in terms of something real beyond this knowledge—not in the metaphysical sense of a "noumenon", an "unknown God" or an "unknowable", but in the concrete sense of a "relative" ignorance of reality, of something still unknown, which will however be known one day when the "physical" and intellectual instruments of mankind are more perfect, when, that is, the technical and social conditions of mankind have been changed in a progressive direction. We are then making an historical prediction which consists simply in an act of thought that projects into the future a process of development similar to that which has taken place from the past until today. In any case one should study Kant and re-examine his concepts exactly.

---

[62] Karl Marx and Frederick Engels, *The Holy Family*. We have not been able to trace such a statement in the text. It would appear in any case to be a slight distortion of the actual position of Marx and Engels. In *Capital* Marx clearly distinguishes the reality of the content from the phenomenal form [*Erscheinungsform*] of things, while maintaining that this reality can only be derived from the phenomena and can have no separate existence apart from them. It should be noted, however, that Gramsci tends in general to underplay the element of "abstraction" inherent in Marx's method, attributing it to simple "pedagogic" necessities.

History and Anti-History

It is worth observing that the present debate between "history and anti-history" is nothing other than a repetition, in the language of modern philosophical culture, of the debate that took place at the end of the last century, in the language of naturalism and positivism, about whether nature and history proceed by "leaps" or only by gradual and progressive evolution. The same debate can be seen to have been engaged in by earlier generations, whether in the field of natural science (the doctrines of Cuvier) or in that of philosophy (where it can be found in Hegel). The history of this problem should be dealt with in all its concrete and significant manifestations. One would find that it has always been contemporary, since at all times there have been conservatives and Jacobins, progressives and reactionaries. But the "theoretical" significance of this debate seems to me to consist in this: that it marks the "logical" point at which every conception of the world makes the passage to the morality appropriate to it, when contemplation becomes action and every philosophy becomes the political action dependent on it. In other words, it is the point at which the conception of the world, contemplation, philosophy become "real", since they now aim to modify the world and to revolutionise praxis. One could say therefore that this is the central nexus of the philosophy of praxis, the point at which it becomes actual and lives historically (that is socially and no longer just in the brains of individuals), when it ceases to be arbitrary and becomes necessary—rational—real.

The problem is precisely that of seeing things historically. That all those Nietzschean charlatans in verbal revolt against all that exists, against conventionality, etc., should have ended up by accepting it after all, and have thus made certain attitudes seem quite unserious, may well be the case, but it is not necessary to let oneself be guided in one's own judgments by charlatans. In opposition to fashionable titanism, to a taste for wishful thinking and abstraction, one must draw attention to a need for "sobriety" in words and in external attitudes, precisely so that there should be more strength in one's character and concrete will. But this is a question of style, not "theory".

The classical form of these passages from conception of the world to practical norm of conduct seems to me to be that through which out of Calvinist predestination there arose one of the greatest impulses to practical initiative the world has ever known. Similarly, every other form of determinism has at a certain point developed into a spirit of initiative and into an extreme tension of collective will.

Speculative Philosophy

It would be wrong to conceal the difficulties presented by the discussion and criticism of the "speculative" character of certain philosophical systems and by the theoretical "negation" of the "speculative form" of philosophical conceptions.

The following questions are raised: 1. Is the "speculative" element proper to every philosophy and is it the form itself which every theoretical construction as such must assume? That is to say, is "speculation" synonymous with philosophy and with theory? 2. Or is the question to be put an "historical" one? Is the problem only an historical, and not a theoretical one, in the sense that every conception of the world, at a specific phase of its history, assumes a "speculative" form which represents its apogee and the beginning of its dissolution?

Analogy and connection with the development of the State, which passes from the "economic-corporate" phase to the "hegemonic" (that of active consent). One could say, that is, that every culture has its speculative and religious moment, which coincides with the period of complete hegemony of the social group of which it is the expression and perhaps coincides exactly with the moment in which the real hegemony disintegrates at the base, molecularly: but precisely because of this disintegration, and to react against it, the system of thought perfects itself as dogma and becomes a transcendental "faith". For this reason one can observe that every so-called decadent epoch (in which a disintegration of the old world takes place) is characterised by a refined and highly "speculative" form of thought.

Criticism however must resolve speculation into its real terms as a political ideology and an instrument of practical action. But the critique itself will have its own speculative phase, which marks its apogee. The question is this: whether this apogee cannot be the beginning of an historical phase of a new type in which necessity and freedom have organically interpenetrated and there will be no more social contradictions, so that the only dialectic will be that of the idea, a dialectic of concepts and no longer of historical forces.

The passage in the *Holy Family*[63] on French materialism in the eighteenth century describes quite well and quite clearly the genesis

[63] *Holy Family* (*cit.*) VI, 3(d).

of the philosophy of praxis. It is "materialism" perfected by the work of speculative philosophy itself and fused with humanism. It is also true that with this perfecting of the old materialism there remains only philosophical realism.

Another point worth meditating on is this: whether the conception of "spirit" in speculative philosophy is not a transformed and updated version of the old concept of "human nature" which is proper both to the philosophies of transcendence and to vulgar materialism; whether that is, the conception of "spirit" is anything other than the old "Holy Spirit" made speculative. If this is true, one could then say that idealism is intrinsically theological.

Has not "speculation" (in the idealistic sense) introduced a new type of transcendence into the reform of philosophy characterised by immanentist conceptions? It seems as if the philosophy of praxis is the only consistent "immanentist" conception. It is particularly worth re-examining and criticising all historicist theories of a speculative character. A new *Anti-Dühring*[64] could be written, which from this point of view would be an "Anti-Croce", and which brought together not only the polemic against speculative philosophy but also that against positivism, mechanicism and degenerate forms of the philosophy of praxis itself.

"*Objectivity*" *of Knowledge*

For Catholics ". . . the whole theory of idealism is based on the denial of the objectivity of all our knowledge and on the idealistic monism of 'spirit' (a monism which, as such, is equivalent to the positivistic monism of 'matter'). In this conception, the very foundation of religion, God, does not exist objectively outside of ourselves, but is a creation of the intellect. Idealism, therefore, no less than materialism, is radically contrary to religion."*

The question of the "objectivity of knowledge, according to the philosophy of praxis, can be treated by starting from the proposition contained in the Preface to *A Contribution to the Critique of Political Economy* that "men become conscious (of the conflict between the material forces of production) on the ideological level" of juridical, political, religious, artistic and philosophical forms.[65] But is this

---

[64] *Anti-Dühring* [*Herrn Eugen Dührings Umwälzung der Wissenschaft*]: polemic by Engels which also provides the most systematic exposition of the philosophy of Marxism. For Gramsci's ideas on the need to contest in a similar way the philosophy of Croce, see General Introduction.

* Cf. the article by Father Mario Barbera in *La Civiltà Cattolica*, 1 June 1929.

[65] See above, note 54 on p. 365.

consciousness limited to the conflict between the material forces of production and the relations of production—according to the letter of the text—or does it refer to all conscious knowledge? This is the point to consider and which can be treated along with the whole *ensemble* of the philosophical doctrine of the value of the superstructures. In such a case, what will be the meaning of the term "monism"? It will certainly not be idealistic or materialistic monism, but rather the identity of contraries in the concrete historical act, that is in human activity (history-spirit) in the concrete, indissolubly connected with a certain organised (historicised) "matter" and with the transformed nature of man. Philosophy of the act (praxis, development), but not of the "pure" act,[66] but rather of the real "impure" act, in the most profane and worldly sense of the word.

Pragmatism and Politics

It would seem that "pragmatism" (as in James, etc.) cannot be criticised without taking account of the Anglo-Saxon historical context in which it was born and developed. If it is true that every philosophy is a "politics", and that every philosopher is essentially a politician, this is doubly true for the pragmatist who constructs philosophy in a way which is in an immediate sense "utilitarian". Such a thing is unthinkable (as a movement) in Catholic countries, where religion and cultural life have been split since the days of the Renaissance and Counter-Reformation, whereas it is thinkable in Anglo-Saxon countries, where religion is closely bound up with everyday cultural life and is neither bureacratically centralised nor intellectually dogmatised. In any case pragmatism escapes from the positive religious sphere and tends to create a secular morality (though not of the French type); it tends to create a "popular philosophy" superior to common sense, and it is an immediate "ideological party"[67] rather than a system of philosophy.

Take the pragmatist principle as expounded by James: "The best way of discussing the various points of any theory is to start by establishing what practical difference would result if one or

---

[66] A reference to Gentile and to his *Teoria dello Spirito come atto puro* (Theory of the Spirit as Pure Act. 1916) which exalts the "act" as such, unaccompanied by any objective consciousness or self-reflection.

[67] "ideological party": i.e. an ideological grouping or alignment, similar in its organisation and function to a Party in the political sphere.

other of the alternatives were the true one."[68] One can see from this the immediacy of the philosophical politicism of the pragmatists. The "individual" philosopher of the Italian or German type is tied to "practice" in a mediated way, and there are often many rings on the chain of mediations. The pragmatist on the other hand wishes to tie himself immediately to practice. It would appear, however, that the Italian or German type of philosopher is more "practical" than the pragmatist who judges from immediate reality, often at the most vulgar level, in that the German or Italian has a higher aim, sets his sights higher and tends (if he tends in any direction) to raise the existing cultural level. Hegel can be considered as the theoretical precursor of the liberal revolutions of the nineteenth century. The pragmatists, at the most, have contributed to the creation of the Rotary Club movement and to the justification of conservative and reactionary movements—and to their justification in a real sense, and not just, as happened with Hegel and the Prussian State, as a result of polemical distortion.[69]

Ethics

Kant's maxim "Act in such a way that your conduct can become a norm for all men in similar conditions"[70] is less simple and obvious than it appears at first sight. What is meant by "similar conditions"? The immediate conditions in which one is operating, or the complex and organic general conditions, knowledge of which requires long and critically elaborated research? (Foundation of the Socratic ethic, in which the "moral" will has its base in the intellect, in wisdom, so that wrong-doing is due to ignorance and the search for critical knowledge is the basis of superior morality or of morality *tout court*.)

---

[68] For this principle Gramsci gives a reference to an Italian translation of *The Varieties of Religious Experience* (*Le varie forme dell'esperienza religiosa*, translated by G. C. Ferrari and M. Calderoni, 1904, p. 382). It would appear to be a summary of James's exposition of Peirce (*The Varieties of Religious Experience*, London and New York, 1902, pp. 444–45).

[69] This distortion is particularly current in England, where it has been sanctified by the authority, amongst others, of Bertrand Russell. Marx himself was more just, describing Hegel's Philosophy of Right as "... at once the critical analysis of the modern state and of the reality connected with it, and the definitive negation of all past forms of consciousness in German jurisprudence and politics". (*Contribution to the Critique of Hegel's Philosophy of Right*. In Karl Marx, *Early Writings*, ed. Bottomore, p. 51.)

[70] Kant's maxim is expressed, without the rider about "similar conditions" as the categorical imperative: "Act only on that maxim whereby you can at the same time will that it should become a universal law" (*Fundamental Principles of the Metaphysic of Morals* [*Grundlegung*], standard edition, p. 47).

Kant's maxim can be considered as a truism, since it is hard to find anyone who does not act in the belief that in the conditions he is in everyone else would act in the same way. A man who steals for hunger maintains that hungry people steal; a man who kills his unfaithful wife maintains that all betrayed husbands should kill, etc. It is only "madmen" in the clinical sense who act without believing themselves to be in the right. This question is connected with others: 1. Everyone is indulgent towards himself, because when one acts in a "non-conformist" fashion one knows the mechanism of one's own sensations and judgments and of the chain of cause and effect which has led one to act as one did; but one is much more severe with others because one does not know their inner life. 2. Everyone acts according to his culture, that is the culture of his environment, and as far as one is concerned "all men" means one's environment, people who think like oneself. Kant's maxim presupposes a single culture, a single religion, a "world-wide" conformism.

The objection which would not seem right is this: that "similar conditions" do not exist because among the conditions one must include the agent, his individuality, etc. What one can say is that Kant's maxim is connected with his time, with the cosmopolitan enlightenment and the critical conception of the author. In brief, it is linked to the philosophy of the intellectuals as a cosmopolitan stratum. Therefore the agent is the bearer of the "similar conditions" and indeed their creator. That is, he "must" act according to a "model" which he would like to see diffused among all mankind, according to a type of civilisation for whose coming he is working or for whose preservation he is "resisting" the forces that threaten its disintegration.

Scepticism

The common-sense objection that one can make against scepticism is this: that to be consistent with himself the sceptic should do nothing else but live like a vegetable, without involving himself in the business of ordinary life. If the sceptic takes part in the debate, it means that he thinks that he can convince people. That is, he is no longer a sceptic, but represents a specific positive opinion, which is usually bad and can triumph only by convincing the community that other opinions are even worse, because useless. Scepticism is connected with vulgar materialism and positivism. Interesting in this connection is an excerpt from Roberto Ardigò,[71] in which he says that one should admire Bergson for his voluntarism. But what does this mean? Is it not a confession of the incapacity of one's own philosophy to explain the world if one has to turn to an opposite system in order to find the element necessary for practical life? This point of Ardigò's (contained in his *Scritti Vari*, collected and arranged by G. Marchesini, Florence, Le Monnier, 1922) should be confronted with Marx's theses on Feuerbach[72] and goes to show precisely the extent to which Marx had got beyond the philosophical position of vulgar materialism.

The Concept of "Ideology"

"Ideology" was an aspect of "sensationalism", i.e. eighteenth-century French materialism. Its original meaning was that of "science of ideas", and since analysis was the only method recognised and applied by science it means "analysis of ideas", that is, "investigation of the origin of ideas". Ideas had to be broken down into their original "elements", and these could be nothing other than "sensations". Ideas derived from sensations. But sensationalism could be associated, without too much difficulty, with religious faith and with the most extreme beliefs in the "power of the Spirit" and its "immortal destinies", so that Manzoni,[73] even after his conversion and return to Catholicism, even at the time when he wrote the *Inni sacri*, continued to adhere in principle to the theory of sensationalism, until he learnt about the philosophy of Rosmini.*

---

[71] Roberto Ardigò (1828–1920), leading Italian positivist philosopher.

[72] See in particular the first five of the *Theses*, in which Marx criticises Feuerbach for epistemologically separating theory from practice, contemplation from action, etc.

[73] Alessandro Manzoni (1785–1873), Italian novelist and poet, brought up on the ideas of the French and Italian Enlightenment but converted to Catholicism in or about 1810. His major work is the historical novel *I promessi sposi* (The Betrothed) (1827: revised and partly rewritten 1840) in which Enlightenment ideas co-exist uneasily with Catholic Quietism. The *Inni sacri* (Sacred Hymns, or Songs) date from 1812–22.

* The most effective literary propagator of ideology was Destutt de Tracy (1754–1836), because of the ease and popularity of his exposition. Another was Dr. Cabanis with his *Rapport du Physique et du Moral*. (Condillac, Helvétius, etc., are more strictly speaking philosophers.) Link between Catholicism and ideology: Manzoni, Cabanis, Bourget, Taine (Taine is the *chef d'école* for Maurras and others of a Catholic tendency); also the "psychological novel" (Stendhal was a pupil of De Tracy, etc.). Destutt de Tracy's main work is the *Eléments d'Idéologie* (Paris, 1817–18). The Italian translation is more complete (*Elementi di Ideologia del Conte Destutt de Tracy*, translated by G. Compagnoni, Milan, Stamperia di Giambattista Sonzogno, 1819). In the French text a whole section is missing, I think the one on Love, which Stendhal knew and used from the Italian translation.

How the concept of Ideology passed from meaning "science of ideas" and "analysis of the origin of ideas" to meaning a specific "system of ideas" needs to be examined historically. In purely logical terms the process is easy to grasp and understand.

It could be asserted that Freud is the last of the Ideologues, and that De Man is also an "ideologue". This makes the "enthusiasm" of Croce and the Croceans for De Man even more curious—or would if there wasn't a "practical" justification for their enthusiasm.[74] One should examine the way in which the author of the *Popular Manual* [Bukharin][75] has remained trapped in Ideology; whereas the philosophy of praxis represents a distinct advance and historically is precisely in opposition to Ideology. Indeed the meaning which the term "ideology" has assumed in Marxist philosophy implicitly contains a negative value judgment and excludes the possibility that for its founders the origin of ideas should be sought for in sensations, and therefore, in the last analysis, in physiology. "Ideology" itself must be analysed historically, in the terms of the philosophy of praxis, as a superstructure.

It seems to me that there is a potential element of error in assessing the value of ideologies, due to the fact (by no means casual) that the name ideology is given both to the necessary superstructure of a particular structure and to the arbitrary elucubrations of particular individuals. The bad sense of the word has become widespread, with the effect that the theoretical analysis of the concept of ideology has been modified and denatured. The process leading up to this error can be easily reconstructed:

1. ideology is identified as distinct from the structure, and it is asserted that it is not ideology that changes the structures but vice versa;

2. it is asserted that a given political solution is "ideological"—i.e. that it is not sufficient to change the structure, although it thinks that it can do so; it is asserted that it is useless, stupid, etc.;

3. one then passes to the assertion that every ideology is "pure" appearance, useless, stupid, etc.

One must therefore distinguish between historically organic ideologies, those, that is, which are necessary to a given structure,

---

[74] Henri De Man, Belgian Social-Democrat, was the author of a book *Au delà du Marxisme* ("Beyond Marxism"), frequently referred to and criticised in the *Quaderni* (see in particular MS, pp. 111–114). Croce's "practical" reason for enthusiasm for De Man lies in their shared opposition to revolutionary Marxism, although strictly speaking Crocean philosophy denies a serious theoretical role to ideological and instrumental thought such as De Man's.

[75] For Gramsci's criticism of Bukharin's *Popular Manual*, see below pp. 419–472.

and ideologies that are arbitrary, rationalistic, or "willed". To the extent that ideologies are historically necessary they have a validity which is "psychological"; they "organise" human masses, and create the terrain on which men move, acquire consciousness of their position, struggle, etc. To the extent that they are arbitrary they only create individual "movements", polemics and so on (though even these are not completely useless, since they function like an error which by contrasting with truth, demonstrates it).

It is worth recalling the frequent affirmation made by Marx on the "solidity of popular beliefs" as a necessary element of a specific situation. What he says more or less is "when this way of conceiving things has the force of popular beliefs", etc. Another proposition of Marx is that a popular conviction often has the same energy as a material force or something of the kind, which is extremely significant. The analysis of these propositions tends, I think, to reinforce the conception of *historical bloc* in which precisely material forces are the content and ideologies are the form, though this distinction between form and content has purely didactic value, since the material forces would be inconceivable historically without form and the ideologies would be individual fancies without the material forces.

2

PROBLEMS OF MARXISM

INTRODUCTION

In this section we have included some basic texts from the Prison Notebooks dealing with problems of Marxism itself. The first part, *Some Problems in the Study of the Philosophy of Praxis*, has the same fragmentary character as the *Problems of Philosophy and History* (pp. 343–77), and like that text is the result of some re-ordering of Gramsci's MS by the original Italian editors. Two basic themes underlie the notes. One is the need for a reconstruction of the origins of Marxism, beginning with the works of Marx and Engels themselves. The second concerns the liberation of the Marxist tradition from various accretions of a positivist and/or neo-Kantian order, characteristic of much of orthodox Marxism since the death of Engels. In the notes Gramsci stresses Marx's debt to English political economy and to the idealist tradition in German philosophy, culminating in Hegel, seeing Marxism as a synthesis of these two trends with the political heritage of the French Revolution. The originality of Marxism, in this perspective, lies in its definitive rejection of any form of transcendentalism, rather than in its materialism. This leads Gramsci to a reformulation of the critique of idealism. Although he argues the need to combat directly the theories of Croce and devotes large sections of his Notebooks (MS. pp. 171–254, not reproduced in this volume) to precisely this task, he locates the main enemy of the philosophy of praxis not in idealism as such but in transcendence and metaphysics, focusing his attention on the neo-Kantian deviations of the Austro-Marxism of Adler and Hilferding and on the "materialist" orthodoxy of Plekhanov and Bukharin.

The second part of the section consists of Gramsci's *Critical Notes on an Attempt at Popular Sociology*, which provide a sustained critique of the "vulgar materialist" aspect of Marxist orthodoxy. Nikolai Bukharin's *The Theory of Historical Materialism, A Manual of Popular Sociology* was first published in Moscow in 1921, where it went through several editions. An English translation, based on the third Russian edition, was published by Allen and Unwin in 1926, under the title *Historical Materialism, A System of Sociology*, and there was a French edition in the following year, which was probably the one known to Gramsci. (For reasons which will appear, we have preferred, in our translation of Gramsci's text, to stick to the original title as used by Gramsci.) Various criticisms were made of the book, on grounds of positivism and vulgar materialism, initially by Lukács (see *New Left Review*, No. 39) but also by Soviet philosophers. Lenin had observed, in his "Testament", that Bukharin was a brilliant theoretician but "ignorant of the dialectic", a criticism which was to gain force with the revival of interest in the dialectic following the publication in the Soviet Union of Lenin's *Philosophical Notebooks*. In the face of criticism Bukharin made attempts to modify his point of view. Gramsci refers in this connection to a paper given by Bukharin at the London Congress of the History of Science in June–July 1931, which unfortunately we have been unable to trace. There is no doubt, though, that the text he wrote for the Academy of Sciences of the USSR in 1933 (published in *Marxism and Modern Thought*, by N. Bukharin and others, edited by Ralph Fox, London 1935) represents a last-ditch attempt to reconcile the positions of the 1921 *Manual* with the criticisms levelled against it—and not only from the "idealist" standpoint of Deborin and Lukács. By that time however Bukharin's days were numbered, politically as well as philosophically. He had been under fire for his opposition to the first Five Year Plan and the collectivisation of agriculture and was put on trial for his part in a supposed "conspiracy" and executed in 1938.

The interest and importance of Gramsci's critique are two-fold. In the first place Bukharin, despite his subsequent disgrace, represented an influential current within orthodox Marxism. He was in many ways the inheritor of a materialist tradition which flourished as much in Social-Democratic circles as within the Communist movement and whose influence has survived to this day. Gramsci's exposure, from an alternative Marxist standpoint, of the crudity and banality of a style of thinking of which the *Manual* is a prime representative has therefore more than academic and historical interest. More important still is the fact that, in the course of his demolition of the vulgar materialist position of the *Manual*, Gramsci in the *Critical Notes* comes closer than anywhere else to a systematic *exposé* of the principles underlying his own approach to the problems of Marxist theory. Gramsci's Marxism was essentially critical. For that reason he could not be content with any doctrine which attempted to reduce Marxism to the status of a positive science—in Bukharin's case a "sociology"—separating the thing known from the process whereby knowledge is acquired. And, by reason of this same critical method, it is through his analysis of the errors of the *Manual*—sociologism, vulgar materialism, philistinism, ignorance of the dialectic—that he himself most clearly expresses the dialectical historicism which is the hallmark of his own genius.

PROBLEMS OF MARXISM

SOME PROBLEMS IN THE STUDY OF THE PHILOSOPHY OF PRAXIS

Statement of the problem

Production of new *Weltanschauungen* [world outlooks] to fertilise and nourish the culture of an historical epoch, and philosophically directed production according to the original *Weltanschauungen*. Marx is the creator of a *Weltanschauung*. But what is Ilich [Lenin]'s position? Is it purely subordinate and subaltern? The explanation is to be found in Marxism itself as both science and action.

The passage from utopia to science and from science to action. The foundation of a directive class [*classe dirigente*] (i.e. of a State) is equivalent to the creation of a *Weltanschauung*. How is the statement that the German proletariat is the heir of classical German philosophy to be understood? Surely what Marx[1] wanted to indicate was the historical function of his philosophy when it became the theory of a class which was in turn to become a State? With Ilich this really came about in a particular territory. I have referred elsewhere[2] to the philosophical importance of the concept and the fact of hegemony, for which Ilich is responsible. Hegemony realised means the real critique of a philosophy, its real dialectic. Compare here what Graziadei* writes in the introduction to *Prezzo e sopraprezzo*:[4] he puts forward Marx as a unit in a series of great men of

---

[1] The statement that the German proletariat is the heir of classical German philosophy is not in Marx but is the final sentence of Engels' *Ludwig Feuerbach and the End of Classical German Philosophy*.

[2] See pp. 333, 357 and 365 above. The "fact of hegemony" referred to is of course the Soviet Revolution. The attribution of the "concept of hegemony" to Lenin is more difficult to interpret, since the word hegemony as such does not figure prominently in Lenin's work. It seems most likely that what Gramsci has in mind are aspects of Lenin's general theory of proletarian revolution as they evolved in the struggle against economism and as they are expressed for example in *Two Tactics of Social Democracy* (1905).

* Graziadei is backward in comparison with Monsignor Olgiati,[3] who, in his volume on Marx, finds no comparison possible except with Jesus—a comparison which, coming from a prelate, is really the most extreme concession, given that he believes in the divine nature of Christ.

[3] F. Olgiati, *Carlo Marx*, Milan, 1918.

[4] *Prezzo e sopraprezzo nell'economia capitalistica* [Price and surplus price in capitalist economy], subtitled "A Critique of Marx's theory of value" and first published by Edizioni Avanti, Milan, 1923. Count Antonio Graziadei (1873–1953) joined the PCI at Livorno, wrote the theses on the agrarian question for the 1922 Rome Congress, and became one of the main leaders of the Right after the congress. At the Fourth World Congress, he was the principal spokesman for the

science. Fundamental error: none of the others has produced an original and integral conception of the world. Marx initiates intellectually an historical epoch which will last in all probability for centuries, that is, until the disappearance of political society and the coming of a regulated society.[5] Only then will his conception of the world be superseded, when the conception of necessity is superseded by the conception of freedom.

To make a comparison between Marx and Ilich in order to create a hierarchy is stupid and useless. They express two phases: science and action, which are homogeneous and heterogeneous at the same time.

Thus, historically, a parallel between Christ and St. Paul would be absurd. Christ—*Weltanschauung*, and St. Paul—organiser, action, expansion of the *Weltanschauung*—are both necessary to the same degree and therefore of the same historical stature. Christianity could be called historically "Christianity-Paulinism", and this would indeed be a more exact title. (It is only the belief in the divinity of Christ which has prevented this from happening, but the belief is itself an historical and not a theoretical element.)

Questions of Method

If one wishes to study the birth of a conception of the world which has never been systematically expounded by its founder (and one furthermore whose essential coherence is to be sought not in each individual writing or series of writings but in the whole development of the multiform intellectual work in which the elements of the conception are implicit) some preliminary detailed philological work has to be done. This has to be carried out with the most scrupulous accuracy, scientific honesty and intellectual loyalty and without any preconceptions, apriorism or *parti pris*. It is necessary, first of all, to reconstruct the process of intellectual development of the thinker in question in order to identify those elements which were to become stable and "permanent"—in other words those

---

minority in the Italian party, arguing for a full acceptance of the united front policy. Coopted into the CC after the wave of arrests of communist leaders in early 1923, he was violently attacked by Zinoviev at the Fifth World Congress for his revision of Marxism—in the book referred to here by Gramsci. After the incorporation of Tasca into the PCI leadership, the Right ceased to exist in any organised form; Graziadei remained as an isolated figure on the extreme right of the party until he was expelled in 1928.

[5] i.e. Communism. See note 59 on p. 257. For the notion that with the coming of Communism and of the "reign of freedom" Marxism itself will be superseded, see p. 404 and note 59 on p. 367.

which were taken up as the thinker's own thought, distinct from and superior to the "material" which he had studied earlier and which served as a stimulus to him. It is only the former elements which are essential aspects of the process of development. This selection can be made for periods of varying length, determined by intrinsic factors and not by external evidence (though that too can be utilised) and it results in a series of "discards", that is to say of partial doctrines and theories for which the thinker may have had a certain sympathy, at certain times, even to the extent of having accepted them provisionally and of having availed himself of them for his work of criticism and of historical and scientific creation.

It is a matter of common observation among all scholars, from personal experience, that any new theory studied with "heroic fury"[6] (that is, studied not out of mere external curiosity but for reasons of deep interest) for a certain period, especially if one is young, attracts the student of its own accord and takes possession of his whole personality, only to be limited by the study of the next theory, until such a time as a critical equilibrium is created and one learns to study deeply but without succumbing to the fascination of the system and the author under study. These observations are all the more valid the more the thinker in question is endowed with a violent impetus, has a polemical character and is lacking in *esprit de système*, or when one is dealing with a personality in whom theoretical and practical activity are indissolubly intertwined and with an intellect in a process of continual creation and perpetual movement, with a strong and mercilessly vigorous sense of self-criticism.

Given these premisses, the work should be conducted on the following lines:

1. Reconstruction of the author's biography, not only as regards his practical activity, but also and above all as regards his intellectual activity.

2. A catalogue of all his works, even those most easily overlooked, in chronological order, divided according to intrinsic criteria—of intellectual formation, maturity, possession and application of the new way of thinking and of conceiving life and the world. Search for the *Leitmotiv*,[7] for the rhythm of the thought as it develops,

[6] The reference is to the *Dell'eroico furore* (1585) of Giordano Bruno (1548–1600), in which a distinction is made between knowledge as contemplation and as active striving or "heroic fury".

[7] Guiding (or leading) motif. The term is most commonly used in connection with music, in particularly with Wagner.

should be more important than that for single casual affirmations and isolated aphorisms.

This preliminary work is needed to make any further research possible. A distinction should further be made within the work of the thinker under consideration between those works which he has carried through to the end and published himself or those which remain unpublished, because incomplete, and those which were published by a friend or disciple, but not without revisions, re-writings, cuts, etc., or in other words not without the active intervention of a publisher or editor. It is clear that the content of posthumous works has to be taken with great discretion and caution, because it cannot be considered definitive but only as material still being elaborated and still provisional. One should not exclude the possibility that these works, particularly if they have been a long time in the making and if the author never decided to finish them, might have been repudiated or deemed unsatisfactory in whole or in part by the author.

In the specific case of the founder of the philosophy of praxis [Marx], the literary work can be distinguished into two categories:

1. Works published under the direct responsibility of the author: among these one should reckon, generally speaking, not only those materially handed over for printing but all those "published" or put into circulation in any way by the author, things like letters, circulars, etc. (a typical example would be the *Notes on the Gotha Programme*, and the Correspondence).

2. Works printed not under the direct responsibility of the author, but posthumously by others: for these works it is as well to have a diplomatic text,[8] as indeed is already being done, or at least a minute description of the original text made according to scientific criteria.

Both sections should be reconstructed according to chronological-critical periods, so that it is possible to establish valid comparisons and not purely mechanical and arbitrary ones.

Minute study and analysis should be devoted to the work of

---

[8] A diplomatic edition is one which reproduces exactly the literal text of what an author wrote, as opposed to a critical edition which attempts to produce the best text, emending or correcting the manuscript where necessary. The importance of issuing a diplomatic edition of Marx's work lies in the fact that many of his most important writings, including the second and third volumes of *Capital*, were left in fragmentary or unfinished form at the time of his death. Although Engels at least was a very scrupulous editor, the fact remains, as Gramsci points out below, that he was not Marx and even the best emendations to a manuscript are no substitute for the original itself.

elaboration carried out by the author on the material of the works subsequently printed by the author himself. At the least this study would provide indications and criteria to enable one to evaluate critically the reliability of edited versions of posthumous works compiled by others. The further the preparatory material for the works published by the author is from the definitive text as revised by himself, the less reliable the revision by another hand of similar material. A work can never be identified with the raw material collected for its compilation. It is the definitive choice, the way the component elements are disposed, the greater or lesser importance given to this or that element of those collected in the preparatory phase, which are precisely what constitute the effective work.

Even a study of the correspondence should be carried out with certain precautions: a confident assertion made in a letter would perhaps not be repeated in a book. The stylistic vivacity of the letters, though often artistically more effective than the more measured and considered style of a book, can sometimes lead to weaknesses in the argument. In letters, as in speeches or in conversations, *logical errors* occur more frequently: the greater rapidity of thought is often achieved at the expense of its solidity.

Only at the secondary level, in the study of an original and innovating form of thought, should one consider the contribution of other people to its documentation. It is in this way, at least as a general principle and as method, that the question of the relationship of homogeneity between the two founders of the philosophy of praxis [Marx and Engels] should be posed. When one or other makes an affirmation on their reciprocal agreement, this affirmation is valid only for the subject in question. Even the fact that one of them has written some chapters for a book written by the other is not an absolute reason why the book should be considered the result of a perfect agreement. There is no need to underrate the contribution of the second [Engels] but there is no need either to identify the second with the first [Engels with Marx] nor should one think that everything attributed by [Engels] to [Marx] is absolutely authentic and free from infiltration. It is certain that [Engels] demonstrates a disinterest and a lack of personal vanity which are unique in the history of literature, but this is not the point: nor is it a question of doubting [Engels's] absolute scientific honesty. The point is that [Engels] is not [Marx], and that if one wants to know [Marx] one must look for him above all in his authentic works, those published under his direct responsibility. From these observations there derive a number of warnings about method and some indications for related research. For example, what would be the value of Rodolfo Mondolfo's book[9] on the historical materialism of F[rederick] E[ngels], published by Formaggini in 1912? In a letter to Croce, Sorel expresses doubts whether, given Eng[els]'s scant capacities as an original thinker, such a subject can be studied, and he frequently repeats that one should not confuse the two authors. Apart from the question raised by Sorel, it would seem that for the very reason that (apparently) it is asserted that the second of the two friends has scant capacities as a theoretician (or at least occupies a subaltern position in relation to the first), it is indispensable to study who is responsible for the original thought. In reality, apart from Mondolfo's book, no systematic research of this type has been undertaken in the world of culture. Indeed, [Engels's] expositions, some of which are relatively systematic, have by now been given a position in the front rank as an authentic source, and indeed as the only authentic source. For this reason Mondolfo's volume seems very useful, at least for the guiding line which it traces.

Antonio Labriola[10]

One very useful thing would be an objective and systematic *résumé* (even of a scholastic-analytical kind) of all the publications of Antonio Labriola on the philosophy of praxis to replace the volumes no longer available. A work of this kind is a necessary preliminary for any initiative aimed at putting back into circulation Labriola's philosophical position, which is very little known outside a restricted circle. It is amazing that Leo Bronstein [Trotsky] in his memoirs[11] should speak of Labriola's "dilettantism". This judgment is incomprehensible (unless it is a reference to the gap between theory and practice in Labriola as a person, which would not appear to be the case) except as an unconscious reflection of the pseudo-scientific pedantry of the German intellectual group that was so influential in Russia. In reality Labriola, who affirms that the

[9] Roberto Mondolfo, *Il materialismo storico in Federico Engels*, Genoa, 1912. For a possible influence of Mondolfo's Hegelian-Marxist theory of praxis on Gramsci's "philosophy of praxis" see General Introduction.

[10] For a discussion of Antonio Labriola (1843–1904), the most important of early Italian Marxists and a vital influence on Gramsci's philosophical thought, see General Introduction.

[11] The reference to Labriola comes in *My Life* (1930), a book which Gramsci was able to read in prison only because it was written after Trotsky's expulsion from the Soviet Union and therefore, apparently, did not come into the forbidden category of "political agitation".

philosophy of praxis is independent of any other philosophical current, is self-sufficient and is the only man who has attempted to build up the philosophy of praxis scientifically.

The dominant tendency manifested itself in two main currents:

1. The so-called orthodox tendency, represented by Plekhanov[12] (cf. his Fundamental Problems [of Marxism]), who, in reality, despite his assertions to the contrary, relapses into vulgar materialism. The problem of the "origins" of Marx's thought has not been properly considered: a detailed study of his philosophical culture (and of the general philosophical environment in which he was formed directly and indirectly) is certainly necessary, but only as the premiss for a far more important study, that of his own "original" philosophy, which cannot be exhausted by study of a few "sources" or his personal "culture". It is necessary, first of all, to take account of his creative and constructive activity. The way in which Plekhanov poses the problem is typical of the positivist method, and demonstrates his meagre speculative and historiographical ability.

2. The orthodox tendency has determined the growth of its opposite: the tendency to connect the philosophy of praxis to Kantianism and to other non-positivist and non-materialist philosophical tendencies. This reached its "agnostic" conclusion with Otto Bauer,[13] who writes in his book on religion that Marxism can be supported and integrated by any philosophy, even Thomism.[14] This second tendency is not really a tendency in the strict sense, buf an *ensemble* of all the tendencies—including even the Freudianism ot De Man—that do not accept the so-called "orthodoxy" of Germanic pedantry.

Why is it that Labriola and his way of posing the philosophical problem has enjoyed such a limited fortune? One could repeat here what Rosa [Luxemburg] said about critical economy [*Capital*] and its most refined problems:[15] in the romantic period of struggle, the

---

[12] Georgy Valentinovich Plekhanov (1857–1918), Marxist philosopher, active in the Russian Social-Democratic movement in the latter years of the nineteenth century and then after 1903 aligned with the Menshevik faction. As a philosopher Plekhanov continued to be esteemed by the Bolsheviks, both before and after the Revolution, and he represents an essential link in the chain of orthodox materialist thought which Gramsci is combating. *The Fundamental Problems of Marxism*, called by Lenin the finest exposition of Marxism, was first published in 1908.

[13] Otto Bauer (1882–1938) was an Austrian Social Democrat and a leading exponent of the tendency known as Austro-Marxism (see note 19 on p. 389). His views on the compatibility of Marxist economics with Thomist epistemology are to be found in the volume *Sozialdemokratie, Religion und Kirche* (1927).

[14] Thomism: i.e. the scholastic philosophy of St. Thomas Aquinas (1224–74).

[15] In the article *Stagnation and Progress in Marxism* (see note 25 on p. 392).

period of popular *Sturm und Drang*,[16] all interest is focussed on the most immediate weapons and on tactical problems in the political field and on minor cultural problems in the philosophical field. But from the moment in which a subaltern group becomes really autonomous and hegemonic, thus bringing into being a new form of State, we experience the concrete birth of a need to construct a new intellectual and moral order, that is, a new type of society, and hence the need to develop more universal concepts and more refined and decisive ideological weapons. That is why it is necessary to bring Labriola back into circulation and to make his way of posing the philosophical problem predominant. One can thus open the struggle for an autonomous and superior culture, the positive part of the struggle whose negative and polemical manifestations bear names with "*a*-"privative and "*anti*-"—a-theism, anti-clericalism etc. One thus gives a modern and contemporary form to the traditional secular humanism which must be the ethical basis of the new type of State.*

The Philosophy of Praxis and Modern Culture

The philosophy of praxis has been a "moment"[17] of modern culture. To a certain extent it has determined or enriched certain cultural currents. Study of this fact, which is very important and full of significance, has been neglected or quite simply ignored by the so-called orthodoxy, and for this reason: the most important philosophical combination that has taken place has been between the philosophy of praxis and various idealistic tendencies, a fact which, to the so-called orthodoxy, essentially bound to a particular cultural current of the last quarter of the last century (positivism, scientism), has seemed an absurdity if not actually a piece of chicanery. (In Plekhanov's essay on *Fundamentals* the fact is, admittedly, referred to, but it is hardly touched upon and with no attempt at a critical explanation.) For this reason it would appear necessary to re-evaluate the consideration of the problem as attempted by Antonio Labriola.

---

[16] *Sturm und Drang* (literally "storm and stress"): a German pre-Romantic literary movement, hence by extension any turbulent period in cultural life.

* An analytical and systematic treatment of Antonio Labriola's philosophical conception could become the philosophical part of an ordinary magazine (*Voce*, *Leonardo*, *Ordine Nuovo*). An international bibliography on Labriola (*Neue Zeit*, etc.) should also be compiled.

[17] As frequently in Gramsci, the word "moment" [*momento*] is here being used in a sense that combines the temporal "moment of time" with the ideas of "aspect" or "feature", and of "motive force". (See also Note on Gramsci's Terminology, p. xiii.)

What happened is this: the philosophy of praxis has undergone in reality a double revision, that is to say it has been subsumed into a double philosophical combination. On the one hand, certain of its elements, explicitly or implicitly, have been absorbed and incorporated by a number of idealist currents (one need mention only Croce, Gentile, Sorel, Bergson even, pragmatism).[18] On the other hand, the so-called orthodoxy, concerned to find a philosophy which, according to their extremely limited viewpoint, was more comprehensive than just a "simple" interpretation of history, have believed themselves orthodox in identifying this philosophy fundamentally with traditional materialism. Another current has gone back to Kantianism (here one can mention, apart from Professor Max Adler[19] in Vienna, the Italian professors Alfredo Poggi and Adelchi Baratono).[20] It can be observed, in general terms, that the currents which have attempted combinations of the philosophy of praxis with idealist tendencies consist for the most part of "pure" intellectuals, whereas the current which has constituted the orthodoxy consisted of intellectual personalities more markedly dedicated to practical activity and therefore more closely linked (with more or less extrinsic links) to the great popular masses (a fact which,

---

[18] For the influence of Marxism on Croce, initially considerable, then reduced to that of a "simple canon of historical research", see B. Croce, *Materialismo storico ed economia marxistica* (first published 1900: Volume II, 4 of Collected Works). For Gentile see *La filosofia di Marx, Studi critici*, Pisa, 1899, in which Gentile shows himself a devotee of the Young Marx, interpreted in a very idealist fashion. As for Sorel, the Marxist residues, implicit and explicit, in his later syndicalist theory are fairly transparent, even when he is at his most polemical. Such cannot be claimed, however, for either Bergson or the Pragmatists, in whose writings Marxism appears, if at all, only as part of a general heritage of current ideas.

[19] Max Adler (1873–1937), Austrian sociologist and Social Democrat theoretician, together with Otto Bauer (see note 13 above) and Rolf Hilferding one of the leading exponents of Austro-Marxism (from 1904). The Austro-Marxists, who represented the "orthodox" thinking of the Second International, in opposition both to Lenin and to the revisionism of Bernstein, laid particular stress on the scientific aspects of Marx's work, at the expense of the element of revolutionary praxis. Having found in Marx only the objective laws of the development of society, in a strictly value-free sense, they tended to look for their values and for reasons for political choices, not in the immanent laws of the dialectic itself, but in the transcendental ethics of Kant.

[20] Social-Democratic theoreticians. Of Baratono (1875–1947), the more important of the two and once defined by the Reformist Socialist leader Turati as "the philosopher of the leadership of our Party", Gramsci wrote (*Ordine Nuovo*, 17 January 1922): "The revolutionary verbalism of the Rt. Hon. Adelchi Baratono has no parallel except in the philosophical verbalism of Professor Adelchi Baratono, pedagogue. . . . Baratono's interior life, his capacity for understanding, the activity of his imagination, show him as nothing other than the tape-worm of a political and philosophical culture that he has absorbed as a reader of books and newspapers."

however, has not prevented the majority of them from performing somersaults of no small historico-political consequence).

The distinction has considerable importance. The "pure" intellectuals, acting as the elaborators of the most widespread ideologies of the dominant classes and as *leaders*[21] of the intellectual groups in their countries, could not fail to make use of at least some elements of the philosophy of praxis, to give strength to their conceptions and moderate an excess of speculative philosophism with the historicist realism of the new theory and to provide new arms for the arsenal of the social group with which they were linked. The orthodox tendency, on the other hand, found itself involved in a struggle against the ideology most widespread amongst the popular masses, religious transcendentalism, and reckoned to overcome this only with the crudest and most banal materialism. But this materialism was itself a far from indifferent stratum of common sense, kept alive, to a much greater degree than was thought then or is thought today, by religion itself, which has its expression among the people in a low and trivial form, full of superstition and witchcraft, in which matter plays no small role.

Labriola distinguishes himself from both currents by his affirmation (not always, admittedly, unequivocal) that the philosophy of praxis is an independent and original philosophy which contains in itself the elements of a further development, so as to become, from an interpretation of history, a general philosophy. This is the direction in which one must work, developing Antonio Labriola's position, which Rodolfo Mondolfo's books (as far as I remember) do not seem to develop coherently.*

Why has the philosophy of praxis had this fate of having served to form combinations between its principal elements and either idealism or philosophical materialism? Research into this cannot but be complex and delicate; it requires a lot of finesse in analysis and intellectual sobriety. For it is very easy to be deceived by external similarities and not to see hidden similarities and necessary but camouflaged connections. The identification of the concepts which the philosophy of praxis has "yielded up" to traditional philosophies, and thanks to which these latter have enjoyed a brief moment of

---

[21] In English in the text.

* It seems that Mondolfo has never completely abandoned the fundamentally positivist point of view of a pupil of Roberto Ardigò. The book by Mondolfo's disciple, Diambrini Palazzi (with preface by Mondolfo) on the philosophy of Antonio Labriola,[22] is evidence of the poverty of concepts and guidelines of Mondolfo's own university teaching.

[22] S. Diambrini Palazzi, *Il pensiero filosofico di Antonio Labriola*, Bologna s.d. [1923]

rejuvenation, must be made with great critical caution, and it means no more nor less than writing the history of modern culture since the activity of its founders [Marx and Engels].

Clearly, explicit absorption is not hard to track down, though that too must be critically analysed. A classical example is that represented by the Crocean reduction of the philosophy of praxis to an empirical canon of historical research. This concept, which has penetrated even among the Catholics (cf. Monsignor Olgiati's book) has contributed to the creation of the economico-juridical school of Italian historiography,[23] which has spread beyond the frontiers of Italy. But the most difficult and delicate research is that into implicit and unacknowledged absorption, which has taken place precisely because the philosophy of praxis has been a moment of modern culture, a diffuse atmosphere, which has modified old ways of thinking through actions and reactions which are neither apparent nor immediate. A study of Sorel is particularly interesting from this point of view, because through Sorel and his fortunes one can obtain many relevant indications. The same could be said for Croce. But the most important study, it seems to me, should be that of Bergsonian philosophy and of pragmatism, in order to find out to what extent certain of their positions would be inconceivable without the historical link of the philosophy of praxis.

Another aspect of the question is the practical lesson in the science of politics which the philosophy of praxis has given even to those of its opponents who contest it bitterly on principle, just as the Jesuits contested Machiavelli in theory while remaining in practice his best disciples. In an "Opinion" published in *La Stampa* at the time when he was its Rome correspondent (about 1925), Mario Missiroli[24] writes more or less that it would be interesting to know whether in their heart of hearts the more intelligent industrialists were not convinced that the "Critical Economy" [*Capital*] contained very good insights into their affairs, and

---

[23] Members of this school included Gaetano Salvemini, Gioacchino Volpe, Niccolò Rodolico and Romolo Caggese. With the victory of fascism the school broke up, Salvemini, a Socialist, going into exile and Volpe becoming an historian of the régime.

[24] The figure of Mario Missiroli (b. 1886), historian, journalist and editor, appears to have exercised a peculiar fascination on Gramsci and references to him abound throughout the *Quaderni*. In a sense Gramsci sees him as the type-figure of the bourgeois Italian intellectual, prevented by a natural facility and superficiality and by the general conditions of Italian intellectual life from any consistent application of his considerable talent, and a willing victim, despite his brilliance, of intellectual and political fashions. (See, in particular the short text entitled *Gli intellettuali: la decadenza di Mario Missiroli*, PP. pp. 110–12.)

whether they do not take advantage of the lessons thus acquired. This would not be in any way surprising, for if [Marx] has analysed reality exactly then he has done nothing other than systematise rationally and coherently what the historical agents of this reality felt and still feel in a confused and instinctive way, and of which they have a clearer consciousness as a result of the hostile critique.

A further aspect of the question is even more interesting. Why is it that even the so-called orthodoxy has combined the philosophy of praxis with other philosophies, and prevalently with one in particular rather than with others? In fact the one that counts is the combination with traditional materialism; the combination with Kantianism has had only a limited success and only among certain restricted intellectual groups. On this question it is worth looking at Rosa [Luxemburg]'s essay on progress and stagnation in the development of the philosophy of praxis,[25] where she notes how the constituent parts of this philosophy have developed in varying degrees, but always following the necessities of practical activity. This implies that the founders of the new philosophy were a long way ahead of the necessities of their period and even of the period that followed, and that they created an arsenal stocked with weapons which were still not ready for use, because ahead of their time, and which were to be ready for service only some time later. The explanation is somewhat arbitrary in that to a large extent all it does is to present an abstract formulation of the fact to be explained as an explanation of the fact itself. None the less it contains a nugget of truth which is worth exploring in depth. One of the historical reasons can, it seems to me, be looked for in the fact that the philosophy of praxis has been forced to ally itself with extraneous tendencies in order to combat the residues of the pre-capitalist world that still exist among the popular masses, especially in the field of religion.

The philosophy of praxis had two tasks to perform: to combat modern ideologies in their most refined form, in order to be able to constitute its own group of independent intellectuals; and to educate the popular masses, whose culture was medieval. This second task, which was fundamental, given the character of the new philosophy, has absorbed all its strength, not only in quantitative but also in qualitative terms. For "didactic" reasons, the new philosophy was combined into a form of culture which was a

---

[25] Rosa Luxemburg, *Stillstand und Fortschritt im Marxismus*, first published in *Vorwärts* on 14 March 1903, on the occasion of the 20th anniversary of Marx' death.

little higher than the popular average (which was very low) but was absolutely inadequate to combat the ideologies of the educated classes. And yet the new philosophy was born precisely to supersede the highest cultural manifestation of the age, classical German philosophy, and to create a group of intellectuals specific to the new social group whose conception of the world it was. On the other side, modern culture, especially that marked by idealism, does not manage to elaborate a popular culture or to give a moral and scientific content to its own school programmes, which remain abstract and theoretical schemas.[26] It remains the culture of a restricted intellectual aristocracy, which exercises a hold on youth only rarely and to the extent that it becomes immediate (and occasional)[27] politics.

It remains to be seen whether this form of cultural alignment of forces might not be an historical necessity, and whether one would not find similar alignments in past history, allowing for particular circumstances of time and place. The classical example, previous to the modern period, is undoubtedly that of the Renaissance in Italy and the Reformation in the Protestant countries. On Page 11 of his book *Storia dell'età barocca in Italia*[28] Croce writes:

> "The movement of the Renaissance remained an aristocratic movement and one of élite circles, and even in Italy, which was both mother and nurse to the movement, it did not escape from courtly circles, it did not penetrate to the people or become custom and 'prejudice', in other words collective persuasion and faith. The Reformation, on the other hand, did indeed possess this efficacity of popular penetration, but it paid for it with a retarding of its intrinsic development, with the slow and often interrupted maturation of its vital germ."

And again on Page 8:

> "Luther, like those humanists, deplores sadness and celebrates gaiety, he condemns idleness and commands work: but, on the

---

[26] Gramsci would appear here particularly to have in mind the reform of the Italian school system carried out under the aegis of the idealist philosopher and Fascist Minister of Education, Giovanni Gentile, in 1923. A major feature of the *riforma Gentile* as it affected humanistic education in secondary schools was its attempt to provide a rapid synthesis of the whole of Italian "high culture", seen in the light of the development of the national ideal. (See also introduction to "On Education", p. 24.)

[27] *occasionale*: meaning, as often in Gramsci, "occasional" not in the temporal sense but in that of "inorganic" or "peripheral".

[28] B. Croce, *Storia dell'età barocca in Italia* (first published 1929: Volume III, 23 of Collected Works). In the Collected Works edition the quotation given by Gramsci as on p. 11 is in fact on p. 12.

other hand, he is led to an attitude of diffidence and hostility towards letters and study, so that Erasmus could say '*ubicumque regnat lutheranismus, ibi literarum est interitus*' [wherever Lutheranism reigns, there is the death of letters]. Certainly, if not just as the effect solely of the aversion adopted by its founder, German protestantism was for a couple of centuries all but sterile in the field of study, criticism, and philosophy. The Italian reformers, notably those of the circle of Juan de Valdés and their friends, managed however, to combine without stress humanism and mysticism, the cult of study and moral austerity. Calvinism, with its harsh conception of Grace and its harsh discipline, did not favour the free search for knowledge and the cult of beauty either, but it acquired the role, by interpreting, developing and adapting the concept of Grace into that of vocation, of energetically promoting economic life, production and the increase of wealth."

The Lutheran Reformation and Calvinism created a vast national-popular movement through which their influence spread: only in later periods did they create a higher culture. The Italian reformers were infertile of any major historical success.[29] It is true that even the Reformation, in its higher phase, necessarily adopted the style of the Renaissance and as such spread even in non-protestant countries where the movement had not had a popular incubation. But the phase of popular development enabled the protestant countries to resist the crusade of the Catholic armies tenaciously and victoriously. Thus there was born the German nation as one of the most vigorous in modern Europe. France was lacerated by the wars of religion leading to an apparent victory of Catholicism, but it experienced a great popular reformation in the eighteenth century with the Enlightenment, Voltairianism and the Encyclopaedia. This reformation preceded and accompanied the Revolution of 1789. It really was a matter here of a great intellectual and moral reformation of the French people, more complete than the German Lutheran Reformation, because it also embraced the great peasant masses in the countryside and had a distinct secular basis and attempted to replace religion with a completely secular ideology

[29] For this thesis compare what Gramsci writes elsewhere (Ris. pp. 33–34) on the subject of the Reformation in Italy: "It must be observed that in Italy, unlike other countries, not even religion acted as an element of cohesion between people and intellectuals, and that for this very reason the philosophical crisis of the intellectuals did not extend to the people, because it did not originate from the people and there did not exist a 'national-popular bloc' in the religious field."

represented by the national and patriotic bond. Not even this reformation had an immediate flowering of high culture, except in political science in the form of the positive science of right.*

A conception of the philosophy of praxis as a modern popular reformation (since those people who expect a religious reformation in Italy, a new Italian edition of Calvinism, like Missiroli and Co., are living in cloud-cuckooland) was perhaps hinted at by Georges Sorel, but his vision was fragmentary and intellectualistic, because of his kind of Jansenist fury against the squalor of parliamentarism and political parties. Sorel has taken from Renan the concept of the necessity of an intellectual and moral reformation; he has affirmed (in a letter to Missiroli) that great historical movements are often represented by a modern culture, etc. It seems to me, though, that a conception of this kind is implicit in Sorel when he uses primitive Christianity as a touchstone, in a rather literary way it is true, but nevertheless with more than a grain of truth; with mechanical and often contrived references, but nevertheless with occasional flashes of profound intuition.

The philosophy of praxis presupposes all this cultural past: Renaissance and Reformation, German philosophy and the French Revolution, Calvinism and English classical economics, secular liberalism and this historicism which is at the root of the whole modern conception of life. The philosophy of praxis is the crowning point of this entire movement of intellectual and moral reformation, made dialectical in the contrast between popular culture and high culture. It corresponds to the nexus Protestant Reformation plus French Revolution: it is a philosophy which is also politics, and a politics which is also philosophy. It is still going through its populist[31] phase: creating a group of independent intellectuals is not an easy thing; it requires a long process, with actions and reactions, coming

* Compare here the comparison made by Hegel of the particular national forms assumed by the same culture in France and Germany in the period of the French Revolution: this Hegelian conception, at the end of a rather long chain, led to the famous verses of Carducci: "... *con opposta fé/Decapitaro, Emmanuel Kant, Iddio/Massimilian Robespierre, il re*". [With opposing faiths/Immanuel Kant cut off the head of God/and Maximilian Robespierre, that of the King].[30]

[30] In the poem *Versaglia*, vv. 50–2 (G. Carducci, *Giambi ed Epodi*). See also MS. p. 65, where Gramsci claims that Carducci drew the idea from Heine, but that it originated earlier, with Hegel; and the letter to Tatiana Schucht of 30 May 1932 (LC, p. 629), where he writes: "Thus, in his Lectures on the History of Philosophy, he [Hegel] discovered a nexus between the French Revolution and the philosophy of Kant, Fichte and Schelling."

[31] The Italian word here is *popolaresco*, which is a derivative of *popolare* ("popular") and does not quite correspond to "populist", e.g. as applied to the Narodniks, for which the Italian word is *populista*.

together and drifting apart and the growth of very numerous and complex new formations. It is the conception of a subaltern social group, deprived of historical initiative, in continuous but disorganic expansion, unable to go beyond a certain qualitative level, which still remains below the level of the possession of the State and of the real exercise of hegemony over the whole of society which alone permits a certain organic equilibrium in the development of the intellectual group. The philosophy of praxis has itself become "prejudice" and "superstition". As it stands, it is the popular aspect of modern historicism, but it contains in itself the principle through which this historicism can be superseded. In the history of culture, which is much broader than the history of philosophy, every time that there has been a flowering of popular culture because a revolutionary phase was being passed through and because the metal of a new class was being forged from the ore of the people, there has been a flowering of "materialism": conversely, at the same time the traditional classes clung to philosophies of the spirit. Hegel, half-way between the French Revolution and the Restoration, gave dialectical form to the two moments of the life of thought, materialism and spiritualism, but his synthesis was "a man walking on his head".[32] Hegel's successors destroyed this unity and there was a return to materialist systems on the one side and spiritualist on the other. The philosophy of praxis, through its founder, relived all this experience of Hegelianism, Feuerbachianism and French materialism, in order to reconstruct the synthesis of dialectical unity, "the man walking on his feet". The laceration which happened to Hegelianism has been repeated with the philosophy of praxis. That is to say, from dialectical unity there has been a regress to philosophical materialism on the one hand, while on the other hand modern idealist high culture has tried to incorporate that part of the philosophy of praxis which was needed in order for it to find a new elixir.

"Politically" the materialist conception is close to the people, to "common sense". It is closely linked to many beliefs and prejudices, to almost all popular superstitions (witchcraft, spirits, etc.). This can be seen in popular Catholicism, and, even more so, in Byzantine orthodoxy. Popular religion is crassly materialistic, and yet the

---

[32] The image of the Hegelian dialectic as a man "standing on his head" is frequent in Marx and Engels (Marx, Afterword to the Second German Edition of *Capital Vol. I*, and, earlier, *Holy Family* VIII, 4: Engels, *Ludwig Feuerbach*, 4), and is in fact a turning against Hegel of a phrase used by Hegel himself in the Preface to the *Phenomenology of Spirit*.

official religion of the intellectuals attempts to impede the formation of two distinct religions, two separate strata, so as not to become officially, as well as in reality, an ideology of restricted groups. But from this point of view it is important not to confuse the attitude of the philosophy of praxis with that of Catholicism. Whereas the former maintains a dynamic contact and tends continually to raise new strata of the population to a higher cultural life, the latter tends to maintain a purely mechanical contact, an external unity based in particular on the liturgy and on a cult visually imposing to the crowd. Many heretical movements were manifestations of popular forces aiming to reform the Church and bring it closer to the people by exalting them. The reaction of the Church was often very violent: it has created the Society of Jesus; it has clothed itself in the protective armour of the Council of Trent; although it has organised a marvellous mechanism of "democratic" selection of its intellectuals, they have been selected as single individuals and not as the representative expression of popular groups.

In the history of cultural developments, it is important to pay special attention to the organisation of culture and the personnel through whom this organisation takes concrete form. G. De Ruggiero's volume on Renaissance and Reformation[33] brings out the attitude of very many intellectuals, with Erasmus[34] at their head: they gave way in the face of persecution and the stake. The bearer of the Reformation was therefore the German people itself in its totality, as undifferentiated mass, not the intellectuals. It is precisely this desertion of the intellectuals in the face of the enemy which explains the "sterility" of the Reformation in the immediate sphere of high culture, until, by a process of selection, the people, which remained faithful to the cause, produced a new group of intellectuals culminating in classical philosophy.

Something similar has happened up to now with the philosophy of praxis. The great intellectuals formed on the terrain of this philosophy, besides being few in number, were not linked with the people, they did not emerge from the people, but were the expression of traditional intermediary classes, to which they returned at the great "turning points" of history. Some remained, but rather to subject the new conception to a systematic revision than to advance

[33] Guido De Ruggiero, *Rinascimento, riforma, controriforma*, Bari, 1930.

[34] Erasmus of Rotterdam (1465–1536), Dutch humanist and reformer, shared with the Lutherans a moral and theological critique of Catholic institutions, but was not prepared, whether for reasons of principle or personal safety, to commit himself totally to the reforming camp.

its autonomous development. The affirmation that the philosophy is a new, independent and original conception, even though it is also a moment of world historical development, is an affirmation of the independence and originality of a new culture in incubation, which will develop with the development of social relations. What exists at any given time is a variable combination of old and new, a momentary equilibrium of cultural relations corresponding to the equilibrium of social relations. Only after the creation of the new State does the cultural problem impose itself in all its complexity and tend towards a coherent solution. In any case the attitude to be taken up before the formation of the new State can only be critico-polemical, never dogmatic; it must be a romantic attitude, but of a romanticism which is consciously aspiring to its classical synthesis.

Note I. One should study the period of the Restoration[35] as the period of the elaboration of all modern historicist doctrines, including the philosophy of praxis, which is their crowning point and which was in any case elaborated just on the eve of 1848, when Restoration was crumbling on every side and the Holy Alliance was falling to pieces. It is well known that restoration is only a metaphorical expression; in reality there was no effective restoration of the *ancien régime*, but only a new alignment of forces through which the revolutionary conquests of the middle classes were limited and codified. The King in France and the Pope in Rome became heads of their respective parties and no longer the unquestioned representatives of France or of Christianity. The position of the Pope was particularly shaken. In this period begins the formation of permanent organisms of "militant Catholics", which, after sundry intermediary stages—1848–49, 1861, (year of the first disintegration of the Papal State with the annexation of the Emilian Legations), 1870 and the post-war period—were to become the powerful organisation of Catholic Action, powerful but in a defensive position. The historicist theories of the Restoration opposed the eighteenth century ideologies, abstract and utopistic, which remain alive as proletarian philosophy, ethics and politics, particularly widespread in France up to 1870. The philosophy of praxis was opposed to these eighteenth century popular conceptions as a mass philosophy, in all their forms, from the most infantile to that of Proudhon. (Proudhon's conception underwent a certain grafting of conservative historicism,

[35] i.e. the period of European history that goes from the fall of Napoleon and the Congress of Vienna in 1815 up to the time of the 1848 revolutions.

and he can perhaps be called the French Gioberti,[36] but from the popular classes—Italian history being backward in relation to French, as can be seen from the period of 1848.) If the conservative historicists, theorists of the old, are well placed to criticise the utopian character of the mummified Jacobin ideologies, philosophers of praxis are better placed to appreciate the real and not abstract value that Jacobinism had as an element in the creation of the new French nation (that is to say as a fact of circumscribed activity in specific circumstances and not as something ideologised) and are better placed also to appreciate the historical role of the conservatives themselves, who were in reality the shame-faced children of the Jacobins, who damned their excesses while carefully administering their heritage. The philosophy of praxis not only claimed to explain and to justify all the past, but to explain and justify historically itself as well. That is, it was the greatest form of "historicism", total liberation from any form of abstract "ideologism", the real conquest of the historical world, the beginnings of a new civilisation.

Speculative Immanence and Historicist or Realist Immanence

It is affirmed that the philosophy of praxis was born on the terrain of the highest development of culture in the first half of the nineteenth century, this culture being represented by classical German philosophy, English classical economics and French political literature and practice. These three cultural movements are at the origin of the philosophy of praxis.[37] But in what sense is the affirmation to be understood? That each of these movements has

---

[36] Vincenzo Gioberti (1801–52) was a leading moderate during the Risorgimento, and the parallel with Proudhon, which is a favourite one with Gramsci (see, for example, p. 108 of this volume), is at first sight surprising. As is made clear however elsewhere (MS. p. 185) the parallel relates to their positions within the French working-class movement and the "more backward" Italian liberal-national movement respectively. Within this context Gioberti appears, in a curious way, as the more radical figure. Whereas in Proudhon the conservative element gradually comes to take precedence over the Jacobin (to use Gramsci's term), with Gioberti the process is reversed. In his *Rinnovamento civile dell'Italia* (1851), written towards the end of his life and just after the abortive revolutions of 1848 and the consequent blood-bath of repression, Gioberti comes to take up position in favour of a massive renewal of the popular forces in alliance with the liberal bourgeois intellegentsia, a position far more advanced in relation to its time and place than Proudhon's hardly dialectical oscillations between utopian socialism and acceptance of the bourgeois order.

[37] Cf. Lenin's *The Three Sources and Three Component Parts* (1913): "The Marxian doctrine . . . is the legitimate successor of the best that was created by humanity in the nineteenth century in the shape of German philosophy, English political economy and French socialism."

contributed respectively to the elaboration of the philosophy, the economics and the politics of the philosophy of praxis? Or that the philosophy of praxis has synthesised the three movements, that is, the entire culture of the age, and that in the new synthesis, whichever "moment" one is examining, the theoretical, the economic, or the political, one will find each of the three movements present as a preparatory "moment"? This is what seems to me to be the case. And it seems to me that the unitary "moment" of synthesis is to be identified in the new concept of immanence, which has been translated from the speculative form, as put forward by classical German philosophy, into a historicist form with the aid of French politics and English classical economics.

As far as concerns the substantial identity between German philosophical language and French political language, see the notes above.[38] But it seems to me that one of the most interesting and fecund subjects for research yet to be carried out concerns the relationship between German philosophy, French politics and English classical economics. One could say in a sense, I think, that the philosophy of praxis equals Hegel plus David Ricardo.[39] The

---

[38] See the section *Traducibilità dei linguaggi scientifici e filosofici*, MS. pp. 63–71.

[39] David Ricardo (1772–1823), celebrated English political economist much admired but also severely criticised by Marx, notably in *Capital*. In the *Theories on Surplus Value* Marx sums up the importance of Ricardo's discoveries under two main heads, the theory that value is determined by labour time and his demonstration of the economic roots of the class struggle. What interests Gramsci, however, here and below (p. 412) is less Ricardo's conclusions than his methodological innovations. But, as he admits in the letter to Tatiana of 30 May 1932 (cited above: LC. p. 629), he is here following an intuition rather than a certainty, and it is in fact doubtful whether either the "law of tendency" (see next note) or the concepts of *homo oeconomicus* (economic man) and "determined market" should properly be attributed to Ricardo at all. As far as the latter concepts are concerned, it seems better to situate them, as Gramsci implicitly does on other occasions (in his *Noterelle di economia*, MS. pp. 259–83), in the context of the debate between "critical" (i.e. Marxist) economy and the "pure" economics of the turn of the century. On MS. p. 266 Gramsci defines economic man as "the abstraction of the economic activity of a particular form of society, that is of a particular economic structure", and he goes on to say (MS. p. 267): "it can be said that such an abstraction is by no means necessarily extra-historical and is by no means of the same nature as economic abstractions. *Homo oeconomicus* is the abstraction of the needs and of the economic operations of a particular form of society, just as the *ensemble* of hypotheses put forward by economists in their scientific work is nothing other than the *ensemble* of premisses that are at the base of a particular form of society." And on "determined market" (*mercato determinato*) (MS. p. 269): "Determined market in pure economics is an arbitrary abstraction, which has a purely conventional value for the purposes of a pedantic and scholastic analysis. For critical economy on the other hand it should be the *ensemble* of the concrete economic activities of a determined social form, activities subsumed according to their laws of uniformity which are abstract laws but not such that the abstraction ceases to be historically determined."

problem should be presented thus at the outset: are the new methodological canons introduced by Ricardo in the science of economics to be considered as merely instrumental values (alternatively as a new chapter of formal logic), or do they have a significance as a philosophical innovation? The discovery of the formal logical principle of the "law of tendency"[40] which leads to the scientific definition of the fundamental economic concepts of *homo oeconomicus* and of the "determined market", was this not also a discovery of epistemological value as well? Does it not precisely imply a new "immanence", a new conception of "necessity" and of freedom, etc.? Translation into these terms seems to me precisely the achievement of the philosophy of praxis, which has universalised Ricardo's discoveries, extending them in an adequate fashion to the whole of history and thus drawing from them, in an original form, a new conception of the world.

A whole series of questions will have to be studied:

1. to summarise Ricardo's formal scientific principles in their form of empirical canons.

2. to look for the historical origin of these Ricardian principles, which are connected with the rise of economic science itself, that is, to the development of the bourgeoisie as a "concrete world class" and to the subsequent formation of a world market which was already sufficiently "dense" in complex movements for it to be possible to isolate and study necessary laws of regularity. (It should be said that these are laws of tendency which are not laws in the naturalistic sense or that of speculative determinism, but in a "historicist" sense, valid, that is, to the extent that there exists the "determined market" or in other words an environment which is organically alive and interconnected in its movements of development. Economics studies these laws of tendency in so far as they are quantitative expressions of phenomena; in the passage from economics to general history the concept of quantity is integrated with that of quality and of the dialectic quality-that-becomes-quality).*

---

[40] For Gramsci's analysis of laws of tendency as having "a real 'historical' and not just a methodological character", see his note on the Tendency of the Rate of Profit to Fall on MS. pp. 211–15. Here Gramsci also criticises Croce for giving an "absolute" rather than a dialectical historical value to the law—a criticism which, curiously, parallels Marx's criticism of Ricardo in *Capital* (III, 15). See too note 3 on p. 280.

* *Quantity—Necessity: Quality—Freedom*. The dialectic (the dialectical nexus) of Quantity—Quality is identical with that of necessity—freedom.

3. to establish the connection of Ricardo with Hegel and Robespierre.

4. to consider how the philosophy of praxis has arrived, from the synthesis of the three living currents to the new conception of immanence, purified of any trace of transcendence and theology.

Alongside the research outlined above must be put that concerning the attitude of the philosophy of praxis towards the contemporary continuations of classical German philosophy as represented by the modern Italian idealist philosophy of Croce and Gentile. How are we to understand Engels' proposition on the inheritance of classical German philosophy?[41] Is it to be understood as a historical circle already completed, in which the vital part of Hegelianism has already been definitively absorbed once and for all; or should it rather be understood as a historical process still in motion in which the necessity for a philosophical cultural synthesis is being renewed? To me the second answer seems correct. In reality the reciprocally unilateral position contrasting materialism and idealism, criticised in the first thesis on Feuerbach,[42] is being repeated, and now, as then, though at a more advanced moment of history, a synthesis remains necessary at a higher level of development of the philosophy of praxis.

Unity in the Constituent Elements of Marxism

Unity is given by the dialectical development of the contradictions between man and matter (nature—material forces of production). In economics the unitary centre is value, alias the relationship between the worker and the industrial productive forces (those who deny the theory fall into crass vulgar materialism by posing machines in themselves—as constant and technical capital—as producers of value independent of the man who runs them). In philosophy [it

---

[41] In his *Ludwig Feuerbach*. See note 1 on p. 381.

[42] Karl Marx, *Theses on Feuerbach*: "The chief defect of all hitherto existing materialism—including that of Feuerbach—is that the thing, reality, sensuousness, is grasped only under the form of the *object* or of *contemplation*; but not as *human sensuous activity*, as *praxis*, not subjectively. Thus it happened that the *active* side, rather than by materialism, was developed by idealism—but only abstractly since naturally idealism does not know real, sensuous activity as such. Feuerbach wants sensuous objects, really distinct from the objects of thought; but he does not grasp human activity itself as *objective* activity. Therefore, in his *Essence of Christianity*, he regards the theoretical attitude as the only genuine human attitude, while praxis is conceived and fixed only in its dirty-judaical manifestation. He therefore does not grasp the meaning of 'revolutionary', 'practico-critical' activity."

is] praxis, that is, the relationship between human will (superstructure) and economic structure. In politics [it is] the relationship between the State and civil society, that is, the intervention of the State (centralised will) to educate the educator, the social environment in general. (Question to be gone into in depth and stated in more exact terms.)

Philosophy—Politics—Economics

If these three activities are the necessary constituent elements of the same conception of the world, there must necessarily be, in their theoretical principles, a convertibility from one to the others and a reciprocal translation into the specific language proper to each constituent element. Any one is implicit in the others, and the three together form a homogeneous circle.*

From these propositions (still in need of elaboration) there derive for the historian of culture and of ideas a number of research criteria and critical canons of great significance. It can be that a great personality expresses the more fecund aspects of his thought not in the section which, or so it would appear from the point of view of external classification, ought to be the most logical, but elsewhere, in a part which apparently could be judged extraneous. A man of politics writes about philosophy: it could be that his "true" philosophy should be looked for rather in his writings on politics. In every personality there is one dominant and predominant activity: it is here that his thought must be looked for, in a form that is more often than not implicit and at times even in contradiction with what is professly expressed. Admittedly such a criterion of historical judgment contains many dangers of dilettantism and it is necessary to be very cautious in applying it, but that does not deprive it of its capacity to generate truth.

In reality the occasional "philosopher" can succeed only with difficulty in making abstractions from the currents dominant in his age and from interpretations of a certain conception of the world that have become dogmatic (etc.). As a scientist of politics on the other hand he feels himself free from these idols of his age and of his group and treats the same conception with more immediacy and with total originality; he penetrates to its heart and develops it in a vital way. Here again the thought expressed by [Rosa] Luxemburg remains useful and suggestive when she writes about the impossibility

* Compare the notes above on the reciprocal translatability of scientific languages. [MS. pp. 63–67]

of treating certain questions of the philosophy of praxis in so far as they have not yet become *actual* for the course of history in general or that of a given social grouping. To the economico-corporate phase, to the phase of struggle for hegemony in civil society and to the phase of State power there correspond specific intellectual activities which cannot be arbitrarily improvised or anticipated. In the phase of struggle for hegemony it is the science of politics which is developed; in the State phase all the superstructures must be developed, if one is not to risk the dissolution of the State.

Historicity of the Philosophy of Praxis

That the philosophy of praxis thinks of itself in a historicist manner, that is, as a transitory phase of philosophical thought, is not only implicit in its entire system, but is made quite explicit in the well-known thesis that historical development will at a certain point be characterised by the passage from the reign of necessity to the reign of freedom.[43] All hitherto existing philosophies (philosophical systems) have been manifestations of the intimate contradictions by which society is lacerated. But each philosophical system taken by itself has not been the conscious expression of these contradictions, since this expression could be provided only by the *ensemble* of systems in conflict with each other. Every philosopher is, and cannot but be, convinced that he expresses the unity of the human spirit, that is, the unity of history and nature. Indeed, if such a conviction did not exist, men would not act, they would not create new history, philosophies would not become ideologies and would not in practice assume the fanatical granite compactness of the "popular beliefs" which assume the same energy as "material forces".[44]

In the history of philosophical thought Hegel represents a chapter on his own, since in his system, in one way or another, even in the form of a "philosophical romance", one manages to understand what reality is. That is to say, one finds, in a single system and in a single philosopher, that consciousness of contradictions which one previously acquired from the *ensemble* of systems and of philosophers in polemic and contradiction with each other.

In a sense, moreover, the philosophy of praxis is a reform and a development of Hegelianism; it is a philosophy that has been liberated (or is attempting to liberate itself) from any unilateral

---

[43] See note 59 on p. 367.
[44] In Marx's *Critique of Hegel's Philosophy of Right—Introduction.*

and fanatical ideological elements; it is consciousness full of contradictions, in which the philosopher himself, understood both individually and as an entire social group, not only grasps the contradictions, but posits himself as an element of the contradiction and elevates this element to a principle of knowledge and therefore of action. "Man in general", in whatever form he presents himself, is denied and all dogmatically "unitary" concepts are spurned and destroyed as expressions of the concept of "man in general" or of "human nature" immanent in every man.

But even the philosophy of praxis is an expression of historical contradictions, and indeed their most complete, because most conscious, expression; this means that it too is tied to "necessity" and not to a "freedom" which does not exist and, historically, cannot yet exist. If, therefore, it is demonstrated that contradictions will disappear, it is also demonstrated implicitly that the philosophy of praxis too will disappear, or be superseded. In the reign of "freedom" thought and ideas can no longer be born on the terrain of contradictions and the necessity of struggle. At the present time the philosopher—the philosopher of praxis—can only make this generic affirmation and can go no further; he cannot escape from the present field of contradictions, he cannot affirm, other than generically, a world without contradictions, without immediately creating a utopia.

This is not to say that utopia cannot have a philosophical value, for it has a political value and every politics is implicitly a philosophy, even if disconnected and crudely sketched. In this sense religion is the most gigantic utopia, that is the most gigantic "metaphysics", that history has ever known, since it is the most grandiose attempt to reconcile, in mythological form, the real contradictions of historical life. It affirms, in fact, that mankind has the same "nature", that man in general exists, in so far as created by God, son of God, therefore brother of other men, equal to other men, and free amongst and as other men; and that he can conceive of himself as such, mirrored in God, who is the "self-consciousness" of humanity; but it also affirms that all this is not of this world, but of another (the utopia). Thus do ideas of equality, fraternity and liberty ferment among men, among those strata of mankind who do not see themselves as equals nor as brothers of other men, nor as free in relation to them. Thus it has come about that in every radical stirring of the multitude, in one way or another, with particular forms and particular ideologies, these demands have always been raised.

At this point one can insert an element proposed by Vilich [Lenin]. The April 1917 programme,[45] in the section devoted to the common school,[46] and more exactly in the explanatory note to that section (see the Geneva edition of 1918) refers to the chemist and educationalist Lavoisier,[47] guillotined under the Terror, who had put forward the concept of the common school, and had done so in accord with the popular sentiments of his age, which saw in the democratic movement of 1789 a developing reality and not just an ideology used as an instrument of government and which drew from this concrete egalitarian consequences. In Lavoisier this was still a utopian element (an element which crops up more or less in all cultural currents that presuppose the singleness of human "nature"), whereas for Vilich it had the demonstrative-theoretical significance of a political principle.

If the philosophy of praxis affirms theoretically that every "truth" believed to be eternal and absolute has had practical origins and has represented a "provisional" value (historicity of every conception of the world and of life), it is still very difficult to make people grasp "practically" that such an interpretation is valid also for the philosophy of praxis itself, without in so doing shaking the convictions that are necessary for action. This is, moreover, a difficulty that recurs for every historicist philosophy; it is taken advantage of by cheap polemicists (particularly Catholics) in order to contrast within the same individual the "scientist" and the "demagogue", the philosopher and the man of action, and to deduce that historicism leads necessarily to moral scepticism and depravity. From this difficulty arise many dramas of conscience in little men, and in great men the "Olympian" attitude *à la* Goethe. This is the reason why the proposition about the passage from the reign of necessity to that of freedom must be analysed and elaborated with subtlety and delicacy.

As a result even the philosophy of praxis tends to become an

---

[45] See the *Draft of the Revised Party Programme*, prepared by Lenin in April-May 1917, §14: "Free and compulsory general and polytechnical education . . . for all children of both sexes up to the age of sixteen: training of children to be closely integrated with socially productive work." Explanatory notes to the draft were prepared by N. Krupskaya and presumably published, but we have been unable to trace a copy.

[46] *Scuola unitaria.*

[47] Antoine-Laurent Lavoisier (1743–94), French chemist, described by Engels as "the first to place all chemistry, which in its phlogistic form had stood on its head, squarely on its feet". Lavoisier was executed, not for his ideas, but because in order to finance his experiments he had obtained the hated post of *fermier-général* of taxes.

ideology in the worst sense of the word, that is to say a dogmatic system of eternal and absolute truths. This is particularly true when, as happens in the "Popular Manual",[48] it is confused with vulgar materialism, with its metaphysics of "matter" which is necessarily eternal and absolute.

It is also worth saying that the passage from necessity to freedom takes place through the society of men and not through nature (although it may have effects on our intuition of nature, on scientific opinions, etc.). One can go so far as to affirm that, whereas the whole system of the philosophy of praxis may fall away in a unified world, many idealist conceptions, or at least certain aspects of them which are utopian during the reign of necessity, could become "truth" after the passage. One cannot talk of the "spirit" when society is divided into groups without necessarily concluding that this "spirit" is just "*esprit de corps*"! (This fact is implicitly recognised when it is said, as is done by Gentile in his book on modernism,* following Schopenhauer, that religion is the philosophy of the multitude, whereas philosophy is the religion of the elect, that is of the great intellectuals.) But it will be possible to talk in these terms after the unification has taken place (etc.).

Economy and Ideology

The claim, presented as an essential postulate of historical materialism, that every fluctuation of politics and ideology can be presented and expounded as an immediate expression of the structure, must be contested in theory as primitive infantilism, and combated in practice with the authentic testimony of Marx, the author of concrete political and historical works. Particularly important from this point of view are *The 18th Brumaire* and the writings on the Eastern Question, but also other writings (*Revolution and Counter-Revolution in Germany*, *The Civil War in France* and lesser works). An analysis of these works allows one to establish better the Marxist historical methodology, integrating, illuminating and interpreting the theoretical affirmations scattered throughout his works.

One will be able to see from this the real precautions introduced by Marx into his concrete researches, precautions which could have

---

[48] N. Bukharin, *The Theory of Historical Materialism. A Popular Manual of Marxist Sociology*. See introduction to this section, p. 378.

* G. Gentile, *Il modernismo e i rapporti tra religione e filosofia*, Bari, Laterza, 1909.

no place in his general works.* Among these precautions the following examples can be enumerated:

1. The difficulty of identifying at any given time, statically (like an instantaneous photographic image) the structure. Politics in fact is at any given time the reflection of the tendencies of development in the structure, but it is not necessarily the case that these tendencies must be realised. A structural phase can be concretely studied and analysed only after it has gone through its whole process of development, and not during the process itself, except hypothetically and with the explicit proviso that one is dealing with hypotheses.

2. From this it can be deduced that a particular political act may have been an error of calculation on the part of the leaders [*dirigenti*] of the dominant classes, an error which historical development, through the parliamentary and governmental "crises" of the directive [*dirigenti*] classes, then corrects and goes beyond. Mechanical historical materialism does not allow for the possibility of error, but assumes that every political act is determined, immediately, by the structure, and therefore as a real and permanent (in the sense of achieved) modification of the structure. The principle of "error" is a complex one: one may be dealing with an individual impulse based on mistaken calculations or equally it may be a manifestation of the attempts of specific groups or sects to take over hegemony within the directive grouping, attempts which may well be unsuccessful.

3. It is not sufficiently borne in mind that many political acts are due to internal necessities of an organisational character, that is they are tied to the need to give coherence to a party, a group, a society. This is made clear for example in the history of the Catholic Church. If, for every ideological struggle within the Church one wanted to find an immediate primary explanation in the structure one would really be caught napping: all sorts of politico-economic romances have been written for this reason. It is evident on the contrary that the majority of these discussions are connected with sectarian and organisational necessities. In the discussion between

---

* They could have a place only in a systematic and methodical exposition such as that of Bernheim,[49] and Bernheim's book can be held up as a "model" for a scholastic or "popular manual" of historical materialism, in which, apart from the philological and scholarly method (which Bernheim holds to as a matter of principle, although in his treatment there is implicit a conception of the world) the Marxist conception of history should be explicitly treated.

[49] E. Bernheim, *Lehrbuch der historischen Methode*, considered in more detail by Gramsci on p. 415.

Rome and Byzantium on the Procession of the Holy Spirit,[50] ti would be ridiculous to look in the structure of the European East for the claim that it proceeds only from the Father, and in that of the West for the claim that it proceeds from the Father and the Son. The two Churches, whose existence and whose conflict is dependent on the structure and on the whole of history, posed questions which are principles of distinction and internal cohesion for each side, but it could have happened that either of the Churches could have argued what in fact was argued by the other. The principle of distinction and conflict would have been upheld all the same, and it is this problem of distinction and conflict that constitutes the historical problem, and not the banner that happened to be hoisted by one side or the other.

Note II. The author of ideological serial stories in *Problemi del Lavoro* (who must be none other than the notorious Franz Weiss), during his farcical fairy tale "Russian dumping and its historical significance", speaking about precisely these controversies in early Christian times, asserts that they are tied to the immediate material conditions of the age, and that if we do not succeed in identifying this immediate link it is because the facts are so distant from us or because of some other intellectual weakness. The position is a convenient one, but scientifically insignificant. In fact every real historical phase leaves traces of itself in succeeding phases, which then become in a sense the best document of its existence. The process of historical development is a unity in time through which the present contains the whole of the past and in the present is realised that part of the past which is "essential"—with no residue of any "unknowable" representing the true "essence". The part which is lost, i.e. not transmitted dialectically in the historical process, was in itself of no import, casual and contingent "dross", chronicle and not history, a superficial and negligible episode in the last analysis.

Moral Science and Historical Materialism

The scientific base for a morality of historical materialism is to be looked for, in my opinion, in the affirmation that "society does not

---

[50] This debate, which lasted until the fifteenth century, centred around the so-called *filioque* clause in the Creed, in other words the argument whether the Holy Spirit proceeds "from the Father and from the Son" (*patro filioque*) as the Western Church maintained, or, as the Byzantines held, only from the Father.

pose for itself tasks the conditions for whose resolution do not already exist".[51] Where these conditions exist "the solution of the tasks *becomes* 'duty', 'will' *becomes* free".[52] Morality would then become a search for the conditions necessary for the freedom of the will in a certain sense, aimed at a certain end, and the demonstration that these conditions exist. It should be a question also not of a hierarchy of ends but of a gradation of the ends to be attained, granted that what one wants to "moralise" is not just each individual taken singly but also a whole society of individuals.

Regularity and Necessity

How did the founder of the philosophy of praxis arrive at the concept of regularity and necessity in historical development? I do not think that it can be thought of as a derivation from natural science but rather as an elaboration of concepts born on the terrain of political economy, particularly in the form and with the methodology that economic science acquired from David Ricardo. Concept and fact of determined market: i.e. the scientific discovery that specific decisive and permanent forces have risen historically and that the operation of these forces presents itself with a certain "automatism" which allows a measure of "predictability" and certainty for the future of those individual initiatives which accept these forces after having discerned and scientifically established their nature. "Determined market" is therefore equivalent to "determined relation of social forces in a determined structure of the productive apparatus", this relationship being guaranteed (that is, rendered permanent) by a determined political, moral and juridical superstructure. After having established the character of these decisive and permanent forces and their spontaneous automatism (i.e. their relative independence from individual choices and from arbitrary government interventions), the scientist has, by way of hypothesis, rendered the automatism absolute; he has isolated the merely economic facts from the combinations of varying importance in which they present themselves in reality; he has established relations of cause and effect, of premisses and conclusions; and he has thus produced an abstract scheme of a determined economic society. (On this realistic and concrete scientific construct there has subsequently been imposed a new, more

[51] Karl Marx, Preface to *A Contribution to the Critique of Political Economy*. See note 60 on p. 367.

[52] This phrase, which is somewhat obscure, is perhaps best taken as a gloss on the above quotation from the Preface to the *Contribution*.

generalised abstraction of "man" as such, "historical" and generic, and it is this abstraction that has come to be seen as "true" economic science.)[53]

Given these conditions in which classical economics was born, in order to be able to talk about a new science or a new conception of economic science (which is the same thing), it would be necessary to have demonstrated that new relations of forces, new conditions, new premisses, have been establishing themselves, in other words that a new market has been "determined" with a new "automatism" and phenomenism of its own, which present themselves as something "objective", comparable to the automatism of natural phenomena. Classical economics has given rise to a "critique of political economy" but it does not seem to me that a new science or a new conception of the scientific problem has yet been possible. The "critique" of political economy[54] starts from the concept of the historical character of the "determined market" and of its "automatism", whereas pure economists conceive of these elements as "eternal" and "natural"; the critique analyses in a realistic way the relations of forces determing the market, it analyses in depth their contradictions, evaluates the possibilities of modification connected with the appearance and strengthening of new elements and puts forward the "transitory" and "replaceable" nature of the science being criticised; it studies it as life but also as death and finds at its heart the elements that will dissolve it and supersede it without fail, and it puts forward the "inheritor", the heir presumptive who must yet give manifest proof of his vitality (etc.).

It is true that in modern economic life the "arbitrary" element, whether at individual, consortium or State level, has acquired an importance it previously did not have and has profoundly disturbed the traditional automatism: but this fact is not sufficient in itself

---

[53] This abstraction is also referred to by Gramsci as the concept of *homo oeconomicus* or economic man. See note 39 on p. 400.

[54] "Critique of Political Economy" (*Kritik der politischen Ökonomie*) was, as is well known, the title or sub-title given by Marx to all his major economic writings from the *Grundrisse* onwards, and Gramsci also uses the phrase "Critical Economy" as a euphemism for *Capital*. The opposition between "pure" and "critical" economy, however, tends to occur in the *Quaderni* in relation to a later debate, between Marxists and modern bourgeois economists. What is not clear in this passage is whether Gramsci is referring directly to Marx and to *Capital* or to Marxist economics in general. The problem is further aggravated by the fact Gramsci is applying his own set of concepts and criteria (in part suggested to him by Croce), which though interesting in their own right do not respect the historical order of the development of economic thought and are based on a rather summary knowledge of Marx's economic writings and in particular of *Capital* itself.

to justify the conception of new scientific problems, precisely because these interventions are arbitrary, vary in scale, and are unpredictable. It could justify the affirmation that economic life has been modified, that there is a "crisis", but this is obvious. Besides, it is not claimed that the old "automatism" has disappeared; it only asserts itself on a scale larger than before, at the level of major economic phenomena, while individual facts have "gone wild".

It is from these considerations that one must start in order to establish what is meant by "regularity", "law", "automatism" in historical facts. It is not a question of "discovering" a metaphysical law of "determinism", or even of establishing a "general" law of causality. It is a question of bringing out how in historical evolution relatively permanent forces are constituted which operate with a certain regularity and automatism. Even the law of large numbers,[55] although very useful as a model of comparison, cannot be assumed as the "law" of historical events. In order to establish the historical origin of the philosophy of praxis (an element which is nothing less than its particular way of conceiving "immanence"), it will be necessary to study the conception of economic laws put forward by David Ricardo. It is a matter of realising that Ricardo was important in the foundation of the philosophy of praxis not only for the concept of "value" in economics, but was also "philosophically" important and has suggested a way of thinking and intuiting history and life. The method of "supposing that . . .", of the premiss that gives a certain conclusion, should it seems to me, be identified as one of the starting points (one of the intellectual stimuli) of the philosophical experience of the founders of the philosophy of praxis. It is worth finding out if Ricardo has ever been studied from this point of view.*

It would appear that the concept of "necessity" in history is closely connected to that of "regularity" and "rationality". "Necessity" in the "speculative-abstract" and in the "historical-concrete" sense: necessity exists when there exists an efficient and active

---

[55] The law of large numbers is a statistical theorem broadly to the effect that the greater the number of samples the more likely they are to average out to the mean of the "population" from which they are drawn. In economics this means that the random variations of individual cases will tend "on average" to express the underlying law.

* One should also consider in this light the philosophical concept of "chance" and "law": the concept of a "rationality" or "providence" through which one ends up in transcendental, if not transcendent, teleologism; and that of "chance", as in the metaphysical materialism that "ascribes the world to chance".[56]

[56] The phrase comes from Dante's description (*Inferno* IV, 136) of the Ancient Greek materialist philosopher Democritus "*che il mondo a caso pone*".

premiss, consciousness of which in people's minds has become operative, proposing concrete goals to the collective consciousness and constituting a complex of convictions and beliefs which acts powerfully in the form of "popular beliefs". In the *premiss* must be contained, already developed or in the process of development, the necessary and sufficient material conditions for the realisation of the impulse of collective will; but it is also clear that one cannot separate from this "material" premiss, which can be quantified, a certain level of culture, by which we mean a complex of intellectual acts and, as a product and consequence of these, a certain complex of overriding passions and feelings, overriding in the sense that they have the power to lead men on to action "at any price".

As we have said, this is the only way through which one can reach a historicist and not speculative-abstract conception of "rationality" (and therefore irrationality) in history.

Concepts of "providence" and "fortune", in the sense in which they are employed (speculatively) by Italian idealist philosophers and particularly Croce: one should look at Croce's book on Giambattista Vico,[57] in which the concept of "providence" is translated into speculative terms and in which is to be found the beginnings of the idealist interpretation of Vico's philosophy. For the meaning of "fortune" in Machiavelli, one should look at Luigi Russo's writings.[58] According to Russo, "fortune" has a double meaning for Machiavelli, objective and subjective. "Fortune" is the natural force of circumstances (i.e. the causal nexus) the chance concurrence of events, what providence is in the works of Vico; it can also be that transcendent power (i.e. God) mythologised in old mediaeval doctrine, but for Machiavelli this is then nothing other than individual "*virtù*"[59] itself and its power is rooted in

---

[57] *La filosofia di Giambattista Vico*, first published 1911: Vol. II, 2 of Collected Works.

[58] Gramsci refers in a footnote at this point to a note on p. 23 of Russo's edition of *The Prince* (Florence, 1931). Most of the paragraph which follows is in fact a close paraphrase or quotation from this note of Russo's. Russo's other writings on Machiavelli, including the introduction to his edition (but not the commentary, from which this quotation is taken), have been published in volume form (Florence, 1945).

[59] Literally "virtue", but in connection with Machiavelli better rendered by a word without moral overtones, such as "prowess". In *The Prince* Machiavelli sets up an opposition between *fortuna* (roughly—"circumstance") and *virtù*—the ability of the individual to act on and overcome the given world of circumstance. In Latin *virtus* meant an inherent quality such as (for example and in particular) military valour: Machiavelli tends to make it rather a quality of the will. The moral sense of the English word "virtue" evolved through an intermediary phase in Stoic and Early Christian thought where it meant "inner strength" and hence the ability to act well.

man's will. Machiavelli's "*virtù*", as Russo puts it, is no longer the *virtus* of the scholastics, which has an ethical character and takes its power from heaven, nor that of Livy, which generally means military valour, but it is the *virtù* of Renaissance man, which is capacity, ability, industriousness, individual strength, sensibility, intuition of opportunity and a measure of one's own possibilities.

After this Russo vacillates in his analysis. For him the concept of *fortune*, as force of circumstances, which in Machiavelli as in the Renaissance humanists still retains a *naturalistic and mechanical character*, will beome *truth* and deepened historical perception only in the *rational providence* of Vico and Hegel. But it is important to point out that such concepts in Machiavelli never have a metaphysical character, as they do in the philosophers proper of humanism, but are simple and profound intuitions (and therefore philosophy!) of life, and are to be understood and explained as symbols of sentiments.*

A repertory of the Philosophy of Praxis

An extremely useful thing would be a critical inventory of all the questions that have been raised and discussed in connection with the philosophy of praxis, together with full critical bibliographies. The material for such a specialised, encyclopaedic work is so extensive, so disparate, so varied in quality and in so many languages that only an editorial committee would be able to prepare it within a reasonable length of time. But the usefulness that a compilation of this type would have would be of tremendous importance both in the scientific field, in that of education and among independent scholars. It would become an instrument of prime importance for the dissemination of the study of the philosophy of praxis and for its consolidation into a scientific discipline. It would mark a definite split between two epochs, a modern age and the previous period of elementary fumblings, parrot-like repetitions and journalistic amateurism.

In order to set up the project one would have to study all the material of the same type published by the Catholics, in various countries, in relation to the Bible, the Gospels, the Early Fathers, the Liturgy and Apologetics, great specialised encyclopaedias of

---

* On the gradual metaphysical formation of these concepts, for the pre-Machiavellian period, Russo refers to Gentile, *Giordano Bruno e il pensiero del Rinascimento* (Chapter on "*Il concetto dell'uomo nel Rinascimento*" and appendix), Florence, Vallecchi. For these concepts in Machiavelli, see F. Ercole, *La Politica di Machiavelli* [Rome 1920].

uneven value which are continually being published and which maintain the ideological unity of the hundreds of thousands of priests and other cadres [*dirigenti*] who provide the framework and the strength of the Catholic Church. (For the bibliography of the philosophy of praxis in Germany one should look at the compilations of Ernest Drahn, mentioned by Drahn himself in his introduction to numbers 6068–6069 of the *Reklam Universal Bibliothek*.)

One would have to do for the philosophy of praxis something similar to the work Bernheim did for the historical method.* Bernheim's book is not a treatise on the philosophy of historicism, bnt it is implicitly linked to that. A so-called "sociology of the philosophy of praxis" should stand in the same relation to the philosophy itself as Bernheim's book does to historicism in general. In other words it should be a systematic exposition of practical canons of research and interpretation of history—and politics; a collection of immediate criteria, of critical precautions, etc., a philology of history and politics as they are conceived by the philosophy of praxis. It would also, in certain ways, be useful to prepare a critique of a number of tendencies within the philosophy of praxis, tendencies which because of their sheer crudeness would probably prove among the most widespread. This would take the same form as the critique that modern historicism has made of the old historical method and old-fashioned philology, which have led to the growth of naive forms of dogmatism and replaced interpretations and historical construction with external description and the cataloguing of unevaluated sources put together often in a disordered and incoherent way. The strength of these publications consisted for the most part of a kind of dogmatic mysticism which had grown up and become popularised and which expressed itself in the unjustified claim to be followers of the historical method and of science.*

The Founders of the Philosophy of Praxis and Italy

A systematic collection of all the writings (including letters) [of Marx and Engels] that concern Italy or treat of Italian problems. But a collection that limited itself to a choice of this kind would

---

* E. Bernheim. *Lehrbuch der Historischen Methode*, 6th Edition, 1908. Leipzig, Dunker and Humblot. Translated into Italian and published by Sandron, Palermo [Partial translation only].

* On this question see some of the observations made elsewhere in the series *Riviste Tipo* and those concerning the "Dizionario Critico".[60]

[60] See Int., pp. 137–43.

not be organic and properly complete. There are writings of these authors which, although they do not concern themselves specifically with Italy, nonetheless have a significance for Italy (and not just a generic significance, needless to add, for in that case one could claim that all their works were relevant to Italy). The plan of the collection could be designed according to the following criteria:

1. writings with specific reference to Italy;

2. writings on "specific" arguments of historical and political criticism which, although not referring to Italy have a relevance to Italian problems. Examples: the article on the Spanish Constitution of 1812 has a relevance to Italy because of the political function that this constitution had in Italian political movements up to 1848. Similarly the critique in *The Poverty of Philosophy* against the falsification of Hegelian dialectics made by Proudhon is also relevant to Italy in that this falsification finds its reflection in corresponding Italian intellectual movements (Gioberti, the Hegelianism of the Moderates, concept of passive revolution, dialectic revolution/restoration). The same could be said of Engels' writings on the Spanish libertarian movements of 1873 (after the abdication of Amadeus of Savoy), again relevant to Italy, etc. For this second series of writings there is no need perhaps to produce a collection, but just to offer a critico-analytical exposition. Perhaps the most organic plan might be one in three parts:

1. historico-critical introduction;

2. writings on Italy;

3. analysis of writings indirectly relevant to Italy—i.e. those which set out to resolve questions which are essential and specific for Italy as well.

Hegemony of Western Culture over the whole World Culture

1. Even if one admits that other cultures have had an importance and a significance in the process of "hierarchical" unification of world civilisation (and this should certainly be admitted without question), they have had a universal value only in so far as they have become constituent elements of European culture, which is the only historically and concretely universal culture—in so far, that is, as they have contributed to the process of European thought and been assimilated by it.

2. However, even European culture has undergone a process of unification and, in the historical moment that interests us, this has culminated in Hegel and the critique of Hegelianism.

3. It emerges from these two points that we are dealing with the cultural process that is personified in the intellectuals; one should not talk about popular cultures in this connection, since with regard to these one cannot speak of critical elaboration and process of development.

4. Nor is one speaking here of those cultural processes which culminate in real activity, such as that which took place in France in the eighteenth century: or rather one should speak of them only in connection with the process that culminated in Hegel and in classical German philosophy, using them as a "practical" confirmation (in the sense referred to frequently elsewhere)[61] of the reciprocal translatability of the two processes; one, the French, political and juridical, the other, German, theoretical and speculative.

5. From the disintegration of Hegelianism derives the beginning of a new cultural process, different in character from its predecessors, a process in which practical movement and theoretical thought are united (or are trying to unite through a struggle that is both theoretical and practical).

6. It is not important that this movement had its origins in mediocre philosophical works, or at best, in works that were not philosophical masterpieces. What matters is that a new way of conceiving the world and man is born and that this conception is no longer reserved to the great intellectuals, to professional philosophers, but tends rather to become a popular, mass phenomenon, with a concretely world-wide character, capable of modifying (even if the result includes hybrid combinations) popular thought and mummified popular culture.

7. One should not be surprised if this beginning arises from the convergence of various elements, apparently heterogenous—Feuerbach, in his role as a critic of Hegel, the Tübingen school as an affirmation of the historical and philosophical critique of religion, etc. Indeed it is worth nothing that such an overthrow could not but have connections with religion.

8. The philosophy of praxis as the result and the crowning point of all previous history. Out of the critique of Hegelianism arose modern idealism and the philosophy of praxis. Hegelian immanentism becomes historicism, but it is absolute historicism only with the philosophy of praxis—absolute historicism or absolute humanism. (Ambiguity of atheism and of deism in many modern idealist

---

[61] See MS. pp. 63–71, etc. See also p. 400 above.

philosophers: it is clear that atheism is a purely negative and sterile form, unless it is to be conceived as a period of pure popular literary polemic.)

Passage from Knowing to Understanding and to Feeling and vice versa from Feeling to Understanding and to Knowing

The popular element "feels" but does not always know or understand; the intellectual element "knows" but does not always understand and in particular does not always feel. The two extremes are therefore pedantry and philistinism on the one hand and blind passion and sectarianism on the other. Not that the pedant cannot be impassioned; far from it. Impassioned pedantry is every bit as ridiculous and dangerous as the wildest sectarianism and demagogy. The intellectual's error consists in believing that one can know without understanding and even more without feeling and being impassioned (not only for knowledge in itself but also for the object of knowledge): in other words that the intellectual can be an intellectual (and not a pure pedant) if distinct and separate from the people-nation, that is, without feeling the elementary passions of the people, understanding them and therefore explaining and justifying them in the particular historical situation and connecting them dialectically to the laws of history and to a superior conception of the world, scientifically and coherently elaborated—i.e. knowledge. One cannot make politics-history without this passion, without this sentimental connection between intellectuals and people-nation. In the absence of such a nexus the relations between the intellectual and the people-nation are, or are reduced to, relationships of a purely bureaucratic and formal order; the intellectuals become a caste, or a priesthood (so-called organic centralism).[62]

If the relationship between intellectuals and people-nation, between the leaders and the led, the rulers and the ruled, is provided by an organic cohesion in which feeling-passion becomes understanding and thence knowledge (not mechanically but in a way that is alive), then and only then is the relationship one of representation. Only then can there take place an exchange of individual elements between the rulers and ruled, leaders [*dirigenti*] and led, and can the shared life be realised which alone is a social force—with the creation of the "historical bloc".

De Man "studies" popular feelings: he does not feel with them

---

[62] See note 83 on p. 187.

to guide them, and lead them into a catharsis of modern civilisation. His position is that of the scholarly student of folklore who is permanently afraid that modernity is going to destroy the object of his study. What one finds in his book is the pedantic reflection of what is, however, a real need: for popular feelings to be known and studied in the way in which they present themselves objectively and for them not to be considered something negligible and inert within the movement of history.

CRITICAL NOTES ON AN ATTEMPT AT POPULAR SOCIOLOGY

A work like the *Popular Manual*,[63] which is essentially destined for a community of readers who are not professional intellectuals, should have taken as its starting point a critical analysis of the philosophy of common sense, which is the "philosophy of non-philosophers", or in other words the conception of the world which is uncritically absorbed by the various social and cultural environments in which the moral individuality of the average man is developed. Common sense is not a single unique conception, identical in time and space. It is the "folklore" of philosophy, and, like folklore, it takes countless different forms. Its most fundamental characteristic is that it is a conception which, even in the brain of one individual, is fragmentary, incoherent and inconseqential, in conformity with the social and cultural position of those masses whose philosophy it is. At those times in history when a homogeneous social group is brought into being, there comes into being also, in opposition to common sense, a homogeneous—in other words coherent and systematic—philosophy.[64]

The first mistake of the *Popular Manual* is that it starts, at least implicitly, from the assumption that the elaboration of an original philosophy of the popular masses is to be opposed to the great systems of traditional philosophy and the religion of the leaders of the clergy—i.e. the conception of the world of the intellectuals and of high culture. In reality these systems are unknown to the

---

[63] i.e. Bukharin's *Theory of Historical Materialism: A Popular Manual of Marxist Sociology* (see introduction to this section). For reasons of censorship Gramsci refers to Bukharin throughout this section simply as "the author" and to his book as the "Popular Manual" (*Saggio popolare*) or just "the Manual".

[64] For a more systematic exposition of Gramsci's own ideas on common sense, and therefore on the correct starting point for a popular work on Marxism, see the opening pages of "Some Preliminary Points of Reference", p. 323 ff.

multitude and have no direct influence on its way of thinking and acting. This does not mean of course that they are altogether without influence but it is influence of a different kind. These systems influence the popular masses as an external political force, an element of cohesive force exercised by the ruling classes and therefore an element of subordination to an external hegemony. This limits the original thought of the popular masses in a negative direction, without having the positive effect of a vital ferment of interior transformation of what the masses think in an embryonic and chaotic form about the world and life. The principal elements of common sense are provided by religion, and consequently the relationship between common sense and religion is much more intimate than that between common sense and the philosophical systems of the intellectuals. But even within religion some critical distinctions should be made. Every religion, even Catholicism (indeed Catholicism more than any, precisely because of its efforts to retain a "surface" unity and avoid splintering into national churches and social stratifications), is in reality a multiplicity of distinct and often contradictory religions: there is one Catholicism for the peasants, one for the *petits-bourgeois* and town workers, one for women, and one for intellectuals which is itself variegated and disconnected. But common sense is influenced not only by the crudest and least elaborated forms of these sundry Catholicisms as they exist today. Previous religions have also had an influence and remain components of common sense to this day, and the same is true of previous forms of present Catholicism—popular heretical movements, scientific superstitions connected with past cults, etc. In common sense it is the "realistic", materialistic elements which are predominant, the immediate product of crude sensation. This is by no means in contradiction with the religious element, far from it. But here these elements are "superstitious" and acritical. This, then, is a danger of the *Popular Manual*, which often reinforces, instead of scientifically criticising, these acritical elements which have caused common sense to remain Ptolemaic, anthropomorphic and anthropocentric.

The above remarks about the way in which the *Popular Manual* criticises systematic philosophies instead of starting from a critique of common sense, should be understood as a methodological point and within certain limits. Certainly they do not mean that the critique of the systematic philosophies of the intellectuals is to be neglected. When an individual from the masses succeeds in criticising and going beyond common sense, he by this very fact accepts a new philosophy. Hence the necessity, in an exposition of the philosophy of praxis, of a polemic with traditional philosophies. Indeed, because by its nature it tends towards being a mass philosophy, the philosophy of praxis can only be conceived in a polemical form and in the form of a perpetual struggle. None the less the starting point must always be that common sense which is the spontaneous philosophy of the multitude and which has to be made ideologically coherent.

More than in any other national literature there exist in French philosophical literature treatments of "common sense": this is due to the more strictly "popular-national"[65] character of French culture, in other words to the fact that the intellectuals, because of certain specific traditional conditions, tend more than elsewhere to approach the people in order to guide it ideologically and keep it linked with the leading group. One will be able to find in French literature a lot of material on common sense that can be used and elaborated. The attitude of French philosophical culture towards common sense can indeed offer a model of hegemonic ideological construction. American and English culture can also offer some suggestions, but not in such an organic and complete way as the French. "Common sense" has been treated in various ways. Sometimes it has even been taken as the base of philosophy itself. Alternatively it has been criticised from the point of view of another philosophy. In reality, in either case, the result was to transcend a particular form of common sense and to create another which was closer to the conception of the world of the leading group. In an article on Léon Brunschvicg[66] in *Les Nouvelles Littéraires* of the 17 October 1931, Henri Gouhier writes, on the subject of Brunschvicg's philosophy: "There is but one sole movement of spiritualisation, be it in mathematics, physics, biology, philosophy or morals: it is the effort through which the spirit frees itself from common sense and from its spontaneous metaphysics which envisages

---

[65] The notion of the "popular-national" (or, more frequently "national-popular") is one of the most interesting and also most widely criticised ideas in Gramsci's thought. Supposedly at the origin of the cultural policy of the PCI since the war, it is perhaps best taken as describing a sort of "historic bloc" between national and popular aspirations in the formation of which the intellectuals, in the wide, Gramscian use of the term play an essential mediating role. It is important to stress, however, that it is a cultural concept, relating to the position of the masses within the culture of the nation, and radically alien to any form of populism or "national socialism".

[66] Léon Brunschvicg (1869–1944): French philosopher, most famous, apart from his work on Pascal, for his application of a neo-Kantian problematic to the philosophy of mathematics and science.

a world of real sensible things and man in the middle of this world".*

Croce's attitude towards "common sense" seems unclear. In Croce, the proposition that all men are philosophers has an excessive influence on his judgment about common sense. It seems that Croce often likes to feel that certain philosophical propositions are shared by common sense. But what can this mean concretely? Common sense is a chaotic aggregate of disparate conceptions, and one can find there anything that one likes. Furthermore, this attitude of Croce's towards common sense has not led to a conception of culture which is productive from the national-popular point of view, that is to a more concretely historicist conception of philosophy—but that in any case could happen only with the philosophy of praxis.

As far as Gentile is concerned one must look at his article *La concezione umanistica del mondo* [The humanistic conception of the world] (in *La Nuova Antologia*, 1 June 1931). Gentile writes: "Philosophy could be defined as a great effort accomplished by reflective thought to gain critical certainty of the truths of common sense and of the naïve consciousness, of those truths of which it can be said that every man feels them naturally and which constitute the solid structure of the mentality he requires for everyday life." This seems yet another example of the disordered crudity of Gentile's thought. Gentile's affirmation seems to be "naively" derived from Croce's affirmations on popular modes of thought as the confirmation of the truth of certain philosophical propositions. Further on Gentile writes: "The healthy man believes in God and in the freedom of his spirit". Thus just in these two propositions of Gentile's we find: 1. an extra-historical "human nature" which one can't see quite what it is; 2. the human nature of the healthy man; 3. the common sense of the healthy man and therefore also a common sense of the non-healthy. But what is meant by healthy man? Physically healthy? Or not mad?[67] Or someone who thinks in a healthy way, right-thinking, philistine, etc.? And what does a "truth of common sense" mean? Gentile's philosophy, for example, is utterly contrary to common sense, whether one understands thereby the naïve philosophy of the people, which revolts against any form of subjectivist idealism, or whether one understands it

---

* Brunschvicg's works—*Les Etapes de la Philosophie Mathématique*, *L'Expérience Humaine et la Causalité Physique*, *Le Progrès de la Conscience dans la Philosophie Occidentale*, *La Connaissance de Soi*.

[67] The sense of this passage is dependent on an ambiguity in the Italian word *sano*, which means both "healthy" in the physical sense and mentally "sane".

to be good sense and a contemptuous attitude to the abstruseness, ingenuities and obscurity of certain forms of scientific and philosophical exposition. This flirtation of Gentile with common sense is quite comical.

What was said above does not mean that there are no truths in common sense. It means rather that common sense is an ambiguous, contradictory and multiform concept, and that to refer to common sense as a confirmation of truth is a nonsense. It is possible to state correctly that a certain truth has become part of common sense in order to indicate that it has spread beyond the confines of intellectual groups, but all one is doing in that case is making a historical observation and an assertion of the rationality of history. In this sense, and used with restraint, the argument has a certain validity, precisely because common sense is crudely neophobe and conservative so that to have succeeded in forcing the introduction of a new truth is a proof that the truth in question has exceptional evidence and capacity for expansion.

Recall Giusti's epigram:

"Good sense, which once ruled far and wide,
Now in our schools to rest is laid.
Science, its once beloved child,
Killed it to see how it was made."[68]

This quotation can serve to indicate how the terms good sense and common sense are used ambiguously: as "philosophy", as a specific mode of thought with a certain content of beliefs and opinions, and as an attitude of amiable indulgence, though at the same time contemptuous, towards anything abstruse and ingenious. It was therefore necessary for science to kill a particular form of traditional good sense, in order to create a "new" good sense.

References to common sense and to the solidity of its beliefs are frequent in Marx.[69] But Marx is referring not to the validity of the content of these beliefs but rather to their formal solidity and

---

[68] "*Il buon senso che un dí fu caposcuola*
Or nelle nostre scuole è morto affatto.
La scienza, sua figliola,
L'uccise per veder com' era fatto." (Giusti, *Epigrammi.*)

Giuseppe Giusti (1808–50) was a radical poet and satirist, who combined a fierce hatred of reaction and restoration with an old-fashioned Enlightenment rationalism. This epigram dates from 1849, and in its correct version differs slightly from the text quoted, probably from memory, by Gramsci.

[69] See note 44 on p. 404.

to the consequent imperative character they have when they produce norms of conduct. There is, further, implicit in these references an assertion of the necessity for new popular beliefs, that is to say a new common sense and with it a new culture and a new philosophy which will be rooted in the popular consciousness with the same solidity and imperative quality as traditional beliefs.

Note I. One should add on the subject of Gentile's propositions about common sense, that his language is deliberately equivocal for disreputable opportunistic ideological reasons. When he writes, as an example of one of those truths of common sense whose critical certainty is elaborated by reflective thought, that "the healthy man believes in God and in the freedom of his spirit", he wants it to be believed that his philosophy is the conquest of the critical certainty of the truths of Catholicism, but the Catholics do not take the bait and continue to maintain that Gentile's idealism is the purest paganism, etc. None the less Gentile insists and perpetuates an ambiguity which is not without consequence in creating a climate of demi-mondaine culture, in which all cats are grey, religion embraces atheism, immanence flirts with transcendence and Antonio Bruers has a field day, because the more the threads get tangled and thought becomes obscure the more he feels himself justified in his macaronic "syncretism". If Gentile's words meant what they literally say, actual idealism[70] would have become indeed the "manservant of theology".

Note II. In the teaching of philosophy which is aimed not at giving the student historical information about the development of past philosophy, but at giving him a cultural formation and helping him to elaborate his own thought critically so as to be able to participate in an ideological and cultural community, it is necessary to take as one's starting point what the student already knows and his philosophical experience (having first demonstrated to him precisely that he has such an experience, that he is a "philosopher" without knowing it). And since one presupposes a certain average cultural and intellectual level among the students, who in all probability have hitherto only

[70] "Actual idealism": i.e. the philosophy of Gentile, Spirito and others, so called because it saw the spirit as existing concretely in the "act" rather than in self-reflecting consciousness. (See G. Gentile, *Teoria dello spirito come atto puro*, 1916.) For Antonio Bruers, described by Gramsci as "a notorious muddle-headed prattler", see LVN. p. 190.

acquired scattered and fragmentary bits of information and have no methodological and critical preparation, one cannot but start in the first place from common sense, then secondly from religion, and only at a third stage move on to the philosophical systems elaborated by traditional intellectual groups.

GENERAL QUESTIONS

Historical Materialism and Sociology

One preliminary observation to be made is this: that the title does not correspond to the content of the book.[71] "Theory of the philosophy of praxis" ought to mean a logical and coherent systematic treatment of the philosophical concepts generically known under the title of historical materialism (many of which are spurious and come from other sources and as such require to be criticised and eliminated). The first chapters should treat the following questions: What is philosophy? In what sense can a conception of the world be called a philosophy? How has philosophy been conceived hitherto? Does the philosophy of praxis renew this conception? What is meant by a "speculative" philosophy? Would the philosophy of praxis ever be able to have a speculative form? What are the relationships between ideologies, conceptions of the world and philosophies? What is or should be the relationship between theory and practice? How do traditional philosophies conceive of this relationship? etc. The answer to these and other questions constitutes the "theory" of the philosophy of praxis.[72]

In the *Popular Manual* there is not even a coherent justification offered of the premiss implicit in the exposition and explicitly referred to elsewhere, quite casually, that the *true* philosophy is philosophical materialism and that the philosophy of praxis is purely a "sociology". What does this assertion really mean? If it were true, then the theory of the philosophy of praxis would be

---

[71] The title is "Theory of Historical Materialism", and the sub-title "A Popular Manual of Marxist Sociology". Gramsci goes on to argue below that only the sub-title is in any way an exact description of the content of Bukharin's work, and even then only "on condition that one gives an extremely restricted meaning to the term 'sociology' ". It should be noted that Gramsci himself vacillates slightly in his notion of what sociology is. His main targets would appear to be empiricism and positivism applied to the science of society, and the reflection of these doctrines, in the guise of "materialism", in Bukharin's *Manual*.

[72] These questions are effectively those to which Gramsci himself attempts to give an answer in his own philosophical writings. See in particular pp. 343–377.

philosophical materialism. But in that case what does it mean to say that the philosophy of praxis is a sociology? What sort of thing would this sociology be? A science of politics and historiography? Or a systematic collection, classified in a particular ordered form, of purely empirical observations on the art of politics and of external canons of historical research? Answers to these questions are not to be found in the book. But only they could be a theory. Thus the connection between the general title "Theory [of historical materialism]" and the sub-title "Popular Manual [of Marxist sociology]" is unjustified. The sub-title would be a more exact title, on condition that one gave an extremely restricted meaning to the term "sociology". In fact the question arises of what is "sociology". Is not sociology an attempt to produce a so-called exact (i.e. positivist) science of social facts, that is of politics and history—in other words a philosophy in embryo? Has not sociology tried to do something similar to the philosophy of praxis?[73] One must however be clear about this: the philosophy of praxis was born in the form of aphorisms and practical criteria for the purely accidental reason that its founder dedicated his intellectual forces to other problems, particularly economic (which he treated in systematic form); but in these practical criteria and these aphorisms is implicit an entire conception of the world, a philosophy.

Sociology has been an attempt to create a method of historical and political science in a form dependent on a pre-elaborated philosophical system, that of evolutionist positivism, against which sociology reacted, but only partially. It therefore became a tendency on its own; it became the philosophy of non-philosophers, an attempt to provide a schematic description and classification of historical and political facts, according to criteria built up on the model of natural science. It is therefore an attempt to derive "experimentally" the laws of evolution of human society in such a way as to "predict" that the oak tree will develop out of the acorn. Vulgar evolutionism is at the root of sociology, and sociology cannot know the dialectical principle with its passage from quantity to quality. But this passage disturbs any form of evolution and any law of uniformity understood in a vulgar evolutionist sense. In any case, any sociology presupposes a philosophy, a conception of the

[73] What Gramsci has in mind at this point is less the empiricism which is his most usual target than the attempts, notably by Max Weber but also by Pareto and Michels, to construct a general and comprehensive theory of man and society, under the general title (first coined by Auguste Comte) of "sociology".

world, of which it is but a subordinate part. Nor should the particular internal "logic" of the varying forms of sociology, which is what gives them a mechanical coherence, be confused with general theory, that is to say philosophy. Naturally this does not mean that the search for "laws" of uniformity is not a useful and interesting pursuit or that a treatise of immediate observations on the art of politics does not have its purpose. But one should call a spade a spade, and present treatises of this kind for what they really are.

All these are "theoretical" problems, while those that the author of the *Manua* considers as such are not. The questions which he poses are all of an immediate political and ideological order (understanding ideology as an intermediate phase between philosophy and day-to-day practice); they are reflections on disconnected and casual individual historical and political facts. One theoretical question arises for the author right at the beginning, when he refers to a tendency which denies that it is possible to construct a sociology of the philosophy of praxis and which maintains that this philosophy can be expressed only through concrete historical works. This objection, which is extremely important, is not resolved by the author except on the level of phrasemongering. Certainly the philosophy of praxis is realised through the concrete study of past history and through present activity to construct new history. But a theory of history and politics can be made, for even if the facts are always unique and changeable in the flux of movement of history, the concepts can be theorised. Otherwise one would not even be able to tell what movement is, or the dialectic, and one would fall back into a new form of nominalism.*

The reduction of the philosophy of praxis to a form of sociology has represented the crystallisation of the degenerate tendency, already criticised by Engels (in the letters to two students published in the *Sozial. Akademiker*),[74] and which consists in reducing a con-

* It is because he has not posed with any exactitude the question of what "theory" is that the author has been prevented from posing the further question of what is religion and from offering a realistic historical judgment of past philosophies, all of which he presents as pure delirium and folly.

[74] F. Engels. Letters to Josef Bloch and to Heinz Starkenburg, 21 September 1890 and 25 January 1894, published in *Der Sozialistischer Akademiker*, 1 and 15 October 1895. In the letter to Bloch, Engels writes: "According to the materialist conception of history the determining moment in history is *ultimately* the production and reproduction of real life. More than this neither Marx nor I have ever asserted. If therefore somebody twists this into the statement that the economic moment is the only determining one, he transforms it into a meaningless, abstract and absurd phrase." Both letters are in fact intended as correctives to the pseudo-Marxist reductionism which Gramsci is also concerned to attack. (See also note 123 below.)

ception of the world to a mechanical formula which gives the impression of holding the whole of history in the palm of its hand. This has provided the strongest incentive to the "pocket-geniuses", with their facile journalistic improvisations. The experience on which the philosophy of praxis is based cannot be schematised; it is history in all its infinite variety and multiplicity, whose study can give rise to "philology"[75] as a method of scholarship for ascertaining particular facts and to philosophy understood as a general methodology of history. This perhaps is what was meant by those writers who, as is mentioned in rather summary fashion in the first chapter of the *Manual*, deny that one can make a sociology of the philosophy of praxis and maintain rather that this philosophy lives only in particular historical essays (this assertion, in such a bald and crude form, is certainly erroneous and seems like a new and curious form of nominalism and philosophical scepticism).

To deny that one can construct a sociology, understood in the sense of a science of society, that is a science of history and politics, which is not co-terminous with the philosophy of praxis itself, does not mean that one cannot build up an empirical compilation of practical observations which extend the sphere of philology as traditionally understood. If philology is the methodological express sion of the importance of ascertaining and precising particular fact- in their unique and unrepeatable individuality, one cannot however exclude the practical utility of isolating certain more general "laws of tendency" corresponding in the political field to the laws of statistics or to the law of large numbers which have helped to advance various of the natural sciences.[76] But the fact has not been properly emphasised that statistical laws can be employed in the science and art of politics only so long as the great masses of the population remain (or at least are reputed to remain) essentially passive, in relation to the questions which interest historians and politicians. Furthermore the extension of statistics to the science and art of politics can have very serious consequences to the extent that it is adopted for working out future perspectives and programmes of action. In the natural sciences the worst that statistics

---

[75] "Philology": Gramsci uses the word here partly in its conventional sense of the study of linguistic and historical documents (i.e. the primary sources of historiography and literary history) but partly in the sense resuscitated by Croce from the writings of Vico, which divides knowledge into philosophy as the science of the True and philology as the pursuit of the Certain. (See also note 11 on p. 35.)

[76] For the law of large numbers and for Gramsci's use of the notion of a law of tendency see notes 55 and 40 on pp. 412 and 401.

can do is produce blunders and irrelevances which can easily be corrected by further research and which in any case simply make the individual scientist who used the technique look a bit ridiculous. But in the science and art of politics it can have literally catastrophic results which do irreparable harm. Indeed in politics the assumption of the law of statistics as an essential law operating of necessity is not only a scientific error, but becomes a practical error in action. What is more it favours mental laziness and a superficiality in political programmes. It should be observed that political action tends precisely to rouse the masses from passivity, in other words to destroy the law of large numbers. So how can that law be considered a law of sociology? If one thinks about it even the demand for a planned, i.e. guided, economy is destined to break down the statistical law understood in a mechanical sense, that is statistics produced by the fortuitous putting together of an infinity of arbitrary individual acts. Planning of this kind must be based on statistics, but that is not the same thing. Human awareness replaces naturalistic "spontaneity". A further element which, in the art of politics, leads to the overthrow of the old naturalistic schema is the replacement by political organisms (parties) of single individuals and individual (or charismatic,[77] as Michels calls them) leaders. With the extension of mass parties and their organic coalescence with the intimate (economic-productive) life of the masses themselves, the process whereby popular feeling is standardised ceases to be mechanical and casual (that is produced by the conditioning of environmental factors and the like) and becomes conscious and critical. Knowledge and a judgment of the importance of this feeling on the part of the leaders is no longer the product of hunches backed up by the identification of statistical laws, which leaders then translate into ideas and words-as-force. (This is the rational and intellectual way and is all too often fallacious.) Rather it is acquired by the collective organism through "active and conscious co-participation", through "compassionality", through experience of immediate particulars, through a system which one could call "living philology". In this way a close link is formed between great mass, party and leading group; and the whole complex, thus articulated, can move together as "collective-man".

---

[77] The notion of "charisma" as a quality which causes leaders to be followed in spite of their lack of legitimate or institutional authority derives in fact not from Michels but from Max Weber, who in turn took it from the jurist and church historian Rudolf Sohm. For Michels see note 79 below.

Henri De Man's book,[78] if it has any value, has it precisely in this sense, in that he invites us to "inform" ourselves in more detail about the real feelings of groups and individuals and not those that are assumed on the basis of sociological laws. But De Man has made no original discoveries, nor has he found any original principle which goes beyond the philosophy of praxis or scientifically proves it to be sterile or mistaken. He has elevated to the status of a scientific principle an empirical criterion of the art of politics which was already well known and had been applied, although it had perhaps been insufficiently defined and developed. But De Man has not even been able to establish the exact limits of his criterion, for he has finished up by just producing a new statistical law and, unconsciously and under another name, a new method of social mathematics and of external classification, a new abstract sociology.

Note I. The so-called laws of sociology which are assumed as laws of causation (such-and-such a fact occurs because of such-and-such a law, etc.) have no causal value: they are almost always tautologies and paralogisms. Usually they are no more than a duplicate of the observed fact itself. A fact or a series of facts is described according to a mechanical process of abstract generalisation, a relationship of similarity is derived from this and given the title of law and the law is then assumed to have causal value. But what novelty is there in that? The only novelty is the collective name given to a series of petty facts, but names are not an innovation. (In Michels' treatises[79] one can find a whole catalogue of similar tautological generalisations, the last and most famous being that about the "charismatic leader".) What is not realised is that in this way one falls into a baroque form of Platonic idealism, since these abstract laws have a strange resemblance to Plato's pure ideas which are the essence of real earthly facts.

---

[78] *Au delà du Marxisme*. See note 74 on p. 376.

[79] See in particular "Political Parties" (*Zur Soziologie des Parteiwesens*, 1911. English translation, from the Italian, 1915). Robert Michels (1876–1936) was a German sociologist of (originally) Social-Democratic leanings who emigrated first to Switzerland and then to Italy, where he became a naturalised citizen under the Mussolini régime. Michels is most famous for his "iron law of oligarchy" and together with Mosca and Pareto is an originator of the theory of political *élites*. Despite Gramsci's evident contempt for Michels' method and distaste for his politics, it has been argued that there was a certain indirect influence of Michels and élite theory on his own theory of social and political structures in non-revolutionary periods. (See G. Galli, "Gramsci e le teorie delle élites", in *Gramsci e la cultura contemporanea*, vol. II, pp. 201–217.)

The Constituent Parts of the Philosophy of Praxis

A systematic treatment of the philosophy of praxis cannot afford to neglect any of the constituent parts of the doctrines of its founder [Marx]. But how should this be understood? It should deal with all the general philosophical part, and then should develop in a coherent fashion all the general concepts of a methodology of history and politics and, in addition, of art, economics and ethics, finding place in the overall construction for a theory of the natural sciences. One widespread conception is that the philosophy of praxis is a pure philosophy, the science of dialectics, the other parts of it being economics and politics, and it is therefore maintained that the doctrine is formed of three constituent parts, which are at the same time the consummation and the transcending of the highest level reached around 1848 by science in the most advanced countries of Europe: classical German philosophy, English classical economics and French political activity and science. This conception, which reflects rather a generic search for historical sources than a classification drawn from the heart of the doctrine itself, cannot be set up in opposition, as a definitive scheme, to some other definition of the doctrine which is closer to reality. It will be asked whether the philosophy of praxis is not precisely and specifically a theory of history, and the answer must be that this is indeed true but that one cannot separate politics and economics from history, even the specialised aspects of political science and art and of economic science and policy. This means that, after having accomplished the principal task in the general philosophical part, which deals with the philosophy of praxis proper—the science of dialectics or the theory of knowledge, within which the general concepts of history, politics and economics are interwoven in an organic unity—it would be useful, in a popular manual, to give a general outline of each moment or constituent part, even to the extent of treating them as independent and distinct sciences. On close examination it is clear that in the *Popular Manual* all these points are at least referred to, but casually and incoherently, in a quite chaotic and indistinct way, because there is no clear and precise concept of what the philosophy of praxis itself actually is.

Structure and Historical Movement

This fundamental point is not dealt with: how does the historical movement arise on the structural base? The problem is however referred to in Plekhanov's *Fundamentals*[80] and could be developed. This is furthermore the crux of all the questions that have arisen around the philosophy of praxis and without resolving this one cannot resolve the corresponding problem about the relationship between society and "nature", to which the *Manual* devotes a special chapter. It would have been necessary to analyse the full import and consequences of the two propositions in the Preface to *A Contribution to the Critique of Political Economy* to the following effect: 1. Mankind only poses for itself such tasks as it can resolve; . . . the task itself only arises when the material conditions for its resolution already exist or at least are in the process of formation. 2. A social order does not perish until all the productive forces for which it still has room have been developed and new and higher relations of production have taken their place, and until the material conditions of the new relations have grown up within the womb of the old society. Only on this basis can all mechanicism and every trace of the superstitiously "miraculous" be eliminated, and it is on this basis that the problem of the formation of active political groups, and, in the last analysis, even the problem of the historical function of great personalities must be posed.

The Intellectuals

It would be worth compiling a "reasoned" catalogue of the men of learning whose opinions are widely quoted or contested in the book, each name to be accompanied by notes on their significance and scientific importance (this to be done also for the supporters of the philosophy of praxis who are certainly not quoted in the light of their originality and significance). In fact there are only the most passing references to the great intellectuals. The question is raised: would it not have been better to have referred only to the major intellectuals on the enemy side, leaving aside the men in the second rank, the regurgitators of second-hand phrases? One gets the impression that the author wants to combat only the weakest of his adversaries and the weakest of their positions (or the ones which the weakest adversaries have maintained least adequately), in order to obtain facile verbal victories—for one can hardly speak of real victories. The illusion is created that there exists some kind of more than formal and metaphorical resemblance between an ideological and a politico-military front. In the political and military

---

[80] G. Plekhanov, *Fundamental Problems of Marxism*, 1908.

struggle it can be correct tactics to break through at the points of least resistance in order to be able to assault the strongest point with maximum forces that have been precisely made available by the elimination of the weaker auxiliaries. Political and military victories, within certain limits, have a permanent and universal value and the strategic end can be attained decisively with a general effect for everyone. On the ideological front, however, the defeat of the auxiliaries and the minor hangers-on is of all but negligible importance. Here it is necessary to engage battle with the most eminent of one's adversaries. Otherwise one confuses newspapers with books, and petty daily polemic with scientific work. The lesser figures must be abandoned to the infinite casebook of newspaper polemic.

A new science proves its efficacy and vitality when it demonstrates that it is capable of confronting the great champions of the tendencies opposed to it and when it either resolves by its own means the vital questions which they have posed or demonstrates, in peremptory fashion, that these questions are false problems.

It is true that an historical epoch and a given society are characterised rather by the average run of intellectuals, and therefore by the more mediocre. But widespread, mass ideology must be distinguished from the scientific works and the great philosophical syntheses which are its real cornerstones. It is the latter which must be overcome, either negatively, by demonstrating that they are without foundation, or positively, by opposing to them philosophical syntheses of greater importance and significance. Reading the *Manual* one has the impression of someone who cannot sleep for the moonlight and who struggles to massacre the fireflies in the belief that by so doing he will make the brightness lessen or disappear.

Science and System

Is it possible to write an elementary book, a handbook, a "Popular Manual", on a doctrine that is still at the stage of discussion, polemic and elaboration? A popular manual cannot be conceived other than as a formally dogmatic, stylistically poised and scientifically balanced exposition of a particular subject. It can only be an introduction to scientific study, and not an exposition of original scientific researches, since it is written for young people or for a public which, from the point of view of scientific discipline, is in a condition like that of youth and therefore has an immediate need for "certainties", for opinions which, at least on a formal level, appear as reliably true and indisputable. If the doctrine in question has not yet reached this "classical" phase of its development, any attempt to "manualise" it is bound to fail, its logical ordering will be purely apparent and illusory, and one will get, as with the "Popular Manual", just a mechanical juxtaposition of disparate elements which remain inexorably disconnected and disjointed in spite of the unitary varnish provided by the literary presentation. Why not therefore pose the question in its correct theoretical and historical terms and rest content with a book in which each of the essential problems of the doctrine receives separate monographic treatment? This would be more serious and more "scientific". But the vulgar contention is that science must absolutely mean "system", and consequently systems of all sorts are built up which have only the mechanical exteriority of a system and not its necessary inherent coherence.

The Dialectic

The *Manual* contains no treatment of any kind of the dialectic. The dialectic is presupposed, in a very superficial manner, but is not expounded, and this is absurd in a manual which ought to contain the essential elements of the doctrine under discussion and whose bibliographical references should be aimed at stimulating study in order to widen and deepen understanding of the subject and not at replacing the manual itself. The absence of any treatment of the dialectic could have two origins. The first of these would be the fact that philosophy of praxis is envisaged as split into two elements: on the one hand a theory of history and politics conceived as sociology—i.e. one that can be constructed according to the methods of natural science (experimental in the crudest positivist sense); and on the other hand a philosophy proper, this being philosophical alias metaphysical or mechanical (vulgar) materialism.

Even after the great debate which has taken place against mechanicism, the author of the *Manual* does not appear to have changed very much his way of posing the philosophical problem. It would appear from the contribution presented at the London Congress on the History of Science[81] that he continues to maintain that the philosophy of praxis has always been split into two: a

[81] See Introduction to this Section.

doctrine of history and politics, and a philosophy, although he now calls the latter dialectical materialism. But if the question is framed in this way, one can no longer understand the importance and significance of the dialectic, which is relegated from its position as a doctrine of knowledge and the very marrow of historiography and the science of politics, to the level of a sub-species of formal logic and elementary scholastics. The true fundamental function and significance of the dialectic can only be grasped if the philosophy of praxis is conceived as an integral and original philosophy which opens up a new phase of history and a new phase in the development of world thought. It does this to the extent that it goes beyond both traditional idealism and traditional materialism, philosophies which are expressions of past societies, while retaining their vital elements. If the philosophy of praxis is not considered except in subordination to another philosophy, then it is not possible to grasp the new dialectic, through which the transcending of old philosophies is effected and expressed.

The second origin would appear to be psychological. It is felt that the dialectic is something arduous and difficult, in so far as thinking dialectically goes against vulgar common sense, which is dogmatic and eager for peremptory certainties and has as its expression formal logic. To understand this better one can think of what would happen if in primary and secondary schools natural and physical sciences were taught on the basis of Einsteinian relativity and the traditional notion of a "law of nature" was accompanied by that of a statistical law or of the law of large numbers. The children would not understand anything at all and the clash between school teaching and family and popular life would be such that the school would become an object of ridicule and caricature.

This motivation seems to me to act as a psychological brake on the author of the *Manual*; he really does capitulate before common sense and vulgar thought, since he has not put the problem in exact theoretical terms and is therefore in practice disarmed and impotent. The uneducated and crude environment has dominated the educator and vulgar common sense has imposed itself on science rather than the other way round. If the environment is the educator, it too must in turn be educated,[82] but the *Manual* does not understand this revolutionary dialectic. The source of all the errors of the *Manual*, and of its author (who does not seem to have changed

---

[82] Cf. the third of Marx's *Theses on Feuerbach*.

his position, even after the great debate which apparently, or so it would appear from the text presented at the London Congress, resulted in his repudiating the book), consists precisely in this pretension to divide the philosophy of praxis into two parts: a "sociology" and a systematic philosophy. Separated from the theory of history and politics philosophy cannot be other than metaphysics, whereas the great conquest in the history of modern thought, represented by the philosophy of praxis, is precisely the concrete historicisation of philosophy and its identification with history.

On Metaphysics

Can one extract from the Popular Manual a critique of metaphysics and of speculative philosophy? It has to be said that the author fails to grasp the very concept of metaphysics, just as he fails to grasp the concepts of historical movement, of becoming and, therefore, of the dialectic itself. To think of a philosophical affirmation as true in a particular historical period (that is, as the necessary and inseparable expression of a particular historical action, of a particular praxis) but as superseded and rendered "vain" in a succeeding period, without however falling into scepticism and moral and ideological relativism, in other words to see philosophy as historicity, is quite an arduous and difficult mental operation. The author, however, falls headlong into dogmatism and therefore into a form, though a naïve one, of metaphysics. This is clear from the beginning in the way in which the problem is situated and from the desire to construct a systematic "sociology" of the philosophy of praxis—sociology, in this case, meaning precisely naïve metaphysics. In the final section of the introduction the author is incapable of replying to those critics who maintain that the philosophy of praxis can live only in concrete works of history. He does not succeed in elaborating the concept of philosophy of praxis as "historical methodology", and of that in turn as "philosophy", as the only concrete philosophy. That is to say he does not succeed in posing and resolving, from the point of view of the real dialectic, the problem which Croce has posed and has attempted to resolve from the speculative point of view. Instead of a historical methodology, of a philosophy, he constructs a casebook of particular questions which he envisages and resolves in a dogmatic fashion, and sometimes purely verbally, with paralogisms that are as pretentious as they are naïve. This casebook could be useful and interesting if it was presented as such, with no pretension beyond that of giving approximate schemas of an empirical character, useful for immediate practice. But one can see why this is bound to happen since in the *Popular Manual* the philosophy of praxis is not an autonomous and original philosophy but the "sociology" of metaphysical materialism. As far as the book is concerned, metaphysics means only a specific philosophical formulation, that of speculative idealism, rather than any systematic formulation that is put forward as an extra-historical truth, as an abstract universal outside of time and space.

The philosophy implicit in the *Popular Manual* could be called a positivistic Aristotelianism, an adaptation of formal logic to the methods of physical and natural science. The historical dialectic is replaced by the law of causality and the search for regularity, normality and uniformity. But how can one derive from this way of seeing things the overcoming, the "overthrow" of praxis?[83] In mechanical terms, the effect can never transcend the cause or the system of causes, and therefore can have no development other than the flat vulgar development of evolutionism.

If "speculative idealism" is the science of categories and of the *a priori* synthesis of the spirit, i.e. a form of anti-historicist abstraction, the philosophy implicit in the Popular Manual is idealism upside down, in the sense that the speculative categories are replaced by empirical concepts and classifications which are no less abstract and anti-historical.

One of the most blatant traces of old-fashioned metaphysics in the *Popular Manual* is the attempt to reduce everything to a single ultimate or final cause. One could reconstruct the history of the problem of the single ultimate cause and demonstrate that it is one manifestation of the "search for God". In opposition to this dogmatism recall once again the two letters of Engels published in the *Sozial. Akademiker*.[84]

The Concept of "Science"

The situating of the problem as a search for laws and for constant, regular and uniform lines is connected to a need, conceived in a somewhat puerile and ingenuous way, to resolve in peremptory fashion the practical problem of the predictability of historical events. Since it "appears", by a strange inversion of the perspectives,

---

[83] *il "rovesciamento" della prassi.* See note 56 on p. 366.

[84] See note 74 on p. 427.

that the natural sciences provide us with the ability to foresee the evolution of natural processes, historical methodology is "scientifically" conceived only if, and in so far as, it permits one "abstractly" to foresee the future of society. Hence the search for essential causes, indeed for the "first cause", for the "cause of causes". But the *Theses on Feuerbach* had already criticised in advance this simplistic conception. In reality one can "scientifically" foresee only the struggle, but not the concrete moments of the struggle, which cannot but be the results of opposing forces in continuous movement, which are never reducible to fixed quantities since within them quantity is continually becoming quality. In reality one can "foresee" to the extent that one acts, to the extent that one applies a voluntary effort and therefore contributes concretely to creating the result "foreseen". Prediction reveals itself thus not as a scientific act of knowledge, but as the abstract expression of the effort made, the practical way of creating a collective will.

And how could prediction be an act of knowledge? One knows what has been and what is, not what will be, which is something "non-existent" and therefore unknowable by definition. Prediction is therefore only a practical act which cannot, at the risk of being an utterly futile waste of time, have any other explanation than that given above. It is necessary to pose in exact terms the problem of the predictability of historical events in order to be able to criticise exhaustively the conception of mechanical causalism, to rid it of any scientific prestige and reduce it to a pure myth which perhaps was useful in the past in a backward period of development of certain subaltern social groups.

But it is the concept itself of "science", as it merges from the *Popular Manual*, which requires to be critically destroyed. It is taken root and branch from the natural sciences, as if these were the only sciences or science *par excellence*, as decreed by positivism. But in the *Popular Manual* the term science is used in several meanings, some explicit, some only by implication or barely mentioned. The explicit sense is the one that "science" has in physical research. At other times however it seems to indicate the method. But does there exist a method in general, and if it does exist surely then it can only mean philosophy? At other times it could mean nothing more than formal logic: but can one call that a method and a science? It has to be established that every research has its own specific method and constructs its own specific science, and that the method has developed and been elaborated together with the development and elaboration of this specific research and science and forms with them a single whole. To think that one can advance the progress of a work of scientific research by applying to it a standard method, chosen because it has given good results in another field of research to which it was naturally suited, is a strange delusion which has little to do with science. There do however exist certain general criteria which could be held to constitute the critical consciousness of every man of science whatever his "specialisation", criteria which should always be spontaneously vigilant in his work. Thus one can say someone is not a scientist if he displays a lack of sureness in his particular criteria, if he does not have a full understanding of the concepts he is using, if he has scant information on and understanding of the previous state of the problems he is dealing with, if he is not very cautious in his assertions, if he does not proceed in a necessary but in an arbitrary and disconnected fashion, if he cannot take account of the gaps that exist in knowledge acquired but covers them over and contents himself with purely verbal solutions and connections instead of stating that one is dealing with provisional positions which may have to be gone over again and developed, etc.

One observation which could be made on many polemical references in the *Manual* is its systematic failure to recognise the possibility of error on the part of individual authors quoted, with the result that a social group—of which the men of science are always assumed to be the representatives—finds attributed to it the most disparate opinions and the most contradictory intentions. This is connected precisely to a more general criterion of method which is this: it is not very "scientific", or more simply it is not very "serious", to choose to combat the stupidest and most mediocre of one's opponents or even to choose the least essential and the most occasional of their opinions and then to presume thereby to have "destroyed" "all" the enemy because one has destroyed a secondary and incidental opinion of his or to have destroyed an ideology or a doctrine because one has demonstrated the theoretical inadequacy of its third- or fourth-rate champions. Further: "one must be fair to one's enemies", in the sense that one must make an effort to understand what they really meant to say and not maliciously stop short at the superficial immediate meaning of their expressions. That is to say, if the end proposed is that of raising the tone and intellectual level of one's followers and not just the immediate aim of creating a desert around oneself by all means possible. The point of view to be adopted is this: one's supporter must discuss and uphold his own point of view in debate with capable and intelligent opponents and not just with clumsy untrained people who are convinced "by authority" or "by emotion". The possibility of error must be asserted and justified, but without being untrue to one's own conception, because what counts is not the opinion of Tom, Dick and Harry, but that ensemble of opinions which have become collective, a social element and a social force. These are the opinions that must be refuted, in the person of those of their theoretical exponents who are most representative and indeed worthy of respect for the high quality of their thought and for their "disinterestedness" in the immediate term. Nor should this be done with the idea that one has thereby destroyed the corresponding social element and social force (which would be pure enlightenment rationalism) but only with the idea of having contributed 1. to maintaining and strengthening among one's own side the spirit of distinction and division; and 2. to preparing the ground for one's own side to absorb and give life to an original doctrine of its own, corresponding to its own conditions of life.

It is worth observing that many of the deficiencies of the *Popular Manual* are connected with its "oratory". The author refers in the preface, as if with pride, to the "spoken" origin of his work. But as Macaulay observed long ago in connection with oral discussions in Greece, it is precisely "oral demonstrations" and the mentality of orators which tend to be connected with the most incredible superficialities of logic and argumentation. In any case this does not lessen the responsibility of authors who do not revise before printing the text of lectures delivered orally often with improvisation in which a mechanical and casual association of ideas often replaces the sinew of the argument. The worst thing is when, as a result of this oratorical practice, the facile attitude of mind is consolidated and critical restraints cease to function. One could make a list of the "*ignorantiae*", "*mutationes*", "*elenchi*"[85] of the *Popular Manual*, due in all probability to its oratorical "ardour". A typical example, in my opinion, would be the section devoted to Professor Stammler, which is quite exceptionally superficial and sophistic.

The So-Called "Reality of the External World"

The entire polemic against the subjectivist conception of reality, with the "fearsome" question of the "objective reality of the external world", is badly framed and conducted worse and is to a great degree

---

[85] Types of error of reasoning as categorised in scholastic logic.

futile and superfluous. (I refer here also to the paper presented at the Congress of History of Science, held in London in June–July 1931.) From the point of view of a popular manual the whole treatment is more a response to an intellectual pedantic itch than to any logical necessity. The popular public does not think that a problem such as whether the external world exists objectively can even be asked. One just has to enunciate the problem in these terms to provoke an irresistible and gargantuan outburst of laughter. The public "believes" that the external world is objectively real, but it is precisely here that the question arises: what is the origin of this "belief" and what critical value does it "objectively" have? In fact the belief is of religious origin, even if the man who shares it is indifferent to religion. Since all religions have taught and do teach that the world, nature, the universe were created by God before the creation of man, and therefore man found the world all ready made, catalogued and defined once and for all, this belief has become an iron fact of "common sense" and survives with the same solidity even if religious feeling is dead or asleep. It follows therefore that to base oneself on this experience of common sense in order to destroy the subjectivist conception by "poking fun" at it has a rather "reactionary" significance, an implicit return to religious feeling. Indeed Catholic writers and orators have recourse to the same means in order to obtain the same effect of corrosive ridicule.*

In the paper presented at the London Congress the author of the *Popular Manual* replies implicitly to this observation (which, though it has its importance, is of an external character), noting that Berkeley, to whom we owe the first worked out enunciation of the subjectivist conception, was an archbishop[86] (from which, it seems, one could deduce the religious origin of the theory) and then saying that only "Adam", finding himself on the world for the first time, could think that the world exists only because he thinks (and here again the religious origin of the theory is insinuated, though without much, or any, force of conviction).

---

* The Church (through the Jesuits and in particular the neo-scholastics: Universities of Louvain and of the Sacred Heart in Milan) has attempted to absorb positivism and indeed takes advantage of this reasoning to ridicule the idealists in the eyes of the crowd: "The idealists are the people who think that this or that tower only exists because you think it; if you didn't think it the tower would no longer exist."

[86] George Berkeley subsequently became Bishop of Cloyne, in Ireland, but he was only a minor cleric at the time when, in his youth, he published his subjectivist philosophy.

The problem on the other hand, it seems to me, is this: how can one explain how such a conception, which is certainly not pure futility, even for a philosophy of praxis, should today, when exposed to the public, provoke only laughter and mockery? This seems to me the most typical cause of the distance that has grown up between science and life, between certain groups of intellectuals—who are however in "central" positions of command in high culture—on the one hand, and the great popular masses on the other; and a cause also of the way in which the language of philosophy has become a jargon which produces the same effect as that of Harlequin. But if common sense finds it funny, the philosopher of praxis should all the same look for an explanation both of the real meaning which the conception has and of the reason why it was born and became diffused among the intellectuals, and also of the reason why it is found laughable by common sense. Without doubt the subjectivist conception is proper to modern philosophy in its most achieved and advanced form, in that it gave birth to, and was superseded by, historical materialism, a philosophy which, in its theory of superstructures, poses in realistic and historicist terms what traditional philosophy expressed in a speculative form. A demonstration of this point, which is hardly referred to in the book, would have the greatest cultural significance because it would put an end to a whole series of futile and irrelevant discussions and permit an organic development of the philosophy of praxis even to the point of it becoming the hegemonic exponent of high culture. It is surprising that there has been no proper affirmation and development of the connection between the idealist assertion of the reality of the world as a creation of the human spirit and the affirmation made by the philosophy of praxis of the historicity and transience of ideologies on the grounds that ideologies are expressions of the structure and are modified by modifications of the structure.

The question is closely connected, for obvious reasons, with the question of the value of the so-called exact or physical sciences and the position they have come to acquire within the philosophy of praxis, a position of near-fetishism, in which indeed they are regarded as the only true philosophy or knowledge of the world.

But what are we to understand by the subjectivist conception of reality? Can we take up any one of the countless subjectivist theories thought up by a whole series of philosophers and professors stretching right through into solipsism? It is clear that here again the philosophy of praxis can be compared only with Hegelianism, which represents the most brilliant and achieved form of this conception, and that from subsequent theories one need take into consideration only certain partial aspects and instrumental values. It is also worth looking into the more bizarre forms taken by the conception, whether amongst its adherents or amongst its critics of greater or lesser intelligence. Thus it is worth recalling what Tolstoy writes in his Memoirs of Childhood, Boyhood and Youth. He writes there that he became so enthused with the subjectivist conception of reality that he often used to make himself dizzy with suddenly turning faceabout, convinced that he could thus capture the moment in which he would see nothing because his spirit would not have had time to "create" reality (or something of the kind: the passage of Tolstoy is characteristic and of great literary interest).*

Thus too in his *Linee di filosofia critica*[87] (p. 159) Bernardino Varisco writes: "I open the newspaper for information on the news; how can you maintain that I myself created the news by opening the paper?" That Tolstoy should have given such an immediate and mechanical significance to the subjectivist proposition is understandable. But is it not incredible that Varisco should write in this way, for, although nowadays he is oriented towards religion and transcendental dualism, he is nevertheless a serious scholar and should know his own subject? Varisco's is a common-sense critique, and it is worth noting that such a critique is disregarded by the idealist philosophers despite its extreme importance in hindering the diffusion of a mode of thought and of a culture. One can recall an article by Mario Missiroli in *L'Italia Letteraria*, where he writes

---

* L. Tolstoy. *Childhood, Boyhood and Youth*. Ch. XIX of the "Boyhood" section. "But by none of my philosophical tendencies was I so carried away as by scepticism, which at one time led me to the verge of insanity. I imagined that besides myself nobody existed in the universe, that objects were not objects at all, but images which appeared only when I paid attention to them, and that as soon as I left off thinking of them these images immediately disappeared. In a word, I coincided with Schelling in the conviction that not objects exist but my relation to them. There were moments when, under the influence of this *idée fixe*, I reached such a state of insanity that I sometimes looked rapidly round to one side, hoping to catch emptiness (*le néant*) unawares where I was not."

Apart from the Tolstoy example, recall the facetious way in which a journalist described the "professional or traditional" philosopher (represented by Croce in the chapter "The Philosopher") who had sat for years at his desk staring at the ink-well and asking himself "Is this ink-well inside me or outside?".

[87] B. Varisco, *Linee di filosofia critica*, 1925. Bernardino Varisco (1850–1933) was trained as a scientist and became a noted positivist philosopher, but gradually moved towards idealism and then to a form of religious philosophy which saw in God the "absolute subject" validating the reality of the world.

that he would feel very embarrassed if he found himself obliged, in front of an ordinary public and in debate with a neo-scholastic, to defend, for example, the subjectivist point of view. He also observes how Catholicism tends, in its competition with idealist philosophy, to appropriate to its side natural and physical science. Elsewhere Missiroli has written that he foresees a period of decline of speculative philosophy and an ever-increasing diffusion of the experimental and "realistic" sciences. (In this other text, however, published by *Il Saggiatore*, he also foresees a wave of anti-clericalism. In other words he apparently no longer believes in the appropriation of science by Catholicism.) Also worth recalling is the "pumpkin polemic"[88] to be found in the volume of writings of Roberto Ardigò (*Scritti vari*, collected and arranged by G. Marchesini, Lemonnier, 1922). In a minor provincial clerical paper, some writer (a priest of the Episcopal Curia), in order to disqualify Ardigò in the eyes of a popular public, called him more or less "one of those philosophers who maintain that the cathedral (of Mantua or wherever it may be) only exists because they think it, and when they cease to think it the cathedral disappears" (etc.), a charge which was sharply resented by Ardigò who was a positivist and agreed with the Catholics as to the way of conceiving external reality.

It must be demonstrated that while the "subjectivist" conception has had its usefulness as a criticism of the philosophy of transcendence on the one hand and the naïve metaphysics of common sense and of philosophical materialism on the other, it can find its truth and its historicist interpretation only in the concept of superstructures. As for its speculative form, it is no more than a mere philosophical romance.*

The point that must be made against the *Popular Manual* is that it has presented the subjectivist conception just as it appears from the point of view of common-sense criticism and that it has adopted the conception of the objective reality of the external world in its most trivial and uncritical sense without so much as a suspicion that

---

[88] The so-called *polemica della zucca*.

* A reference to a somewhat more realistic interpretation of subjectivism in classical German philosophy can be found in a review by G. De Ruggiero of some posthumous writings (letters, I think) of B. Constant published in *Critica* some years ago.[89]

[89] The book referred to is the *Journal intime et lettres à sa famille* of Benjamin Constant (1767–1830), reviewed in *Critica*, January 1929.

it can run into objections on the grounds of mysticism, as indeed it has.*

However, if one analyses this idea it is not all that easy to justify a view of external objectivity understood in such a mechanical way. It might seem that there can exist an extra-historical and extra-human objectivity. But who is the judge of such objectivity? Who is able to put himself in this kind of "standpoint of the cosmos in itself" and what could such a standpoint mean? It can indeed be maintained that here we are dealing with a hangover of the concept of God, precisely in its mystic form of a conception of an unknown God. Engels' formulation that "the unity of the world consists in its materiality demonstrated by the long and laborious development of philosophy and natural science"[91] contains the germ of the correct conception in that it has recourse to history and to man in order to demonstrate objective reality. Objective always means "humanly objective" which can be held to correspond exactly to "historically subjective": in other words, objective would mean "universal subjective".[92] Man knows objectively in so far as knowledge is real for the whole human race *historically* unified in a single unitary cultural system. But this process of historical unification takes place through the disappearance of the internal contradictions which tear apart human society, while these contradictions themselves are the condition for the formation of groups and for the birth of ideologies which are not concretely universal but are immediately rendered transient by the practical origin of their substance. There exists therefore a struggle for objectivity (to free oneself from partial and fallacious ideologies) and this struggle is the same as the struggle for the cultural unification of the human race. What the idealists call "spirit" is not a point of departure but

---

* In the text presented to the London Congress the author of the *Popular Manual* refers to an accusation of mysticism, attributing it to Sombart and dismissing it contemptuously. Sombart certainly took it from Croce.[90]

[90] Werner Sombart (1863–1941): German economist and sociologist who became an ideologue of the conservative Right in the Weimar period.

[91] F. Engels, *Anti-Dühring* (*Herr Eugen Dühring's Revolution in Science*, translated by Emil Burns, London [n.d.], p. 54). "The real unity of the world consists in its materiality, and this is proved not by a few juggling phrases but by a long and tedious development of philosophy and natural science."

[92] The original phrase is *universale soggettivo* which is slightly ambiguous, as it could also be translated "subjective universal". The basic sense however would be the same: viz. that the unity of knowledge and being demanded by the subjectivists can only avoid the pitfalls of arbitrary relativism when there is a single knowing subject and an undivided human race so that knowledge becomes the same for all.

a point of arrival, it is the *ensemble* of the superstructures moving towards concrete and objectively universal unification and it is not a unitary presupposition.

Up to now experimental science has provided the terrain on which a cultural unity of this kind has reached its furthest extension. This has been the element of knowledge that has contributed most to unifying the "spirit" and making it more universal. It is the most objectivised and concretely universalised subjectivity.

The idea of "objective" in metaphysical materialism would appear to mean an objectivity that exists even apart from man; but when one affirms that a reality would exist even if man did not, one is either speaking metaphorically or one is falling into a form of mysticism. We know reality only in relation to man, and since man is historical becoming, knowledge and reality are also a becoming and so is objectivity, etc.

Engels' phrase that "the materiality of the world is demonstrated by the long and laborious development of philosophy and natural science" should be analysed and made more precise. Does science mean theoretical activity or the practical-experimental activity of scientists, or a synthesis of the two? One might say that the typical unitary process of reality is found here in the experimental activity of the scientist, which is the first model of dialectical mediation between man and nature, and the elementary historical cell through which man puts himself into relation with nature by means of technology, knows her and dominates her. There can be no doubt that the rise of the experimental method separates two historical worlds, two epochs, and initiates the process of dissolution of theology and metaphysics and the process of development of modern thought whose consummation is in the philosophy of praxis. Scientific experiment is the first cell of the new method of production, of the new form of active union of man and nature. The scientist-experimenter is also a worker, not a pure thinker, and his thought is continually controlled by practice and vice versa, until there is formed the perfect unity of theory and practice.

The neo-scholastic Casotti writes:*

"The researches of naturalists and biologists presuppose life and real organisms already in existence", an expression which relates to that of Engels in *Anti-Dühring*.

Agreement of Catholicism and Aristotelianism on the question of the objectivity of the real.

---

* Mario Casotti, *Maestro e scolaro* [Milan, 1930], p. 49.

To understand exactly what might be meant by the problem of the reality of the external world it might be worth taking up the example of the notions of "East" and "West" which do not cease to be "objectively real" even though analysis shows them to be no more than a conventional, that is "historico-cultural" construction. (The terms "artificial" and "conventional" often indicate "historical" facts which are products of the development of civilisation and not just rationalistically arbitrary or individually contrived constructions.) One can also recall the example contained in a little book by Bertrand Russell.[93] Russell says approximately this: "We cannot, without the existence of man on the earth, think of the existence of London or Edinburgh, but we can think of the existence of two points in space, one to the North and one to the South, where London and Edinburgh now are." It could be objected that without the existence of man one cannot think of "thinking", one canot think at all of any fact or relationship which exists only in so far as man exists. What would North–South or East–West mean without man? They are real relationships and yet they would not exist without man and without the development of civilisation. Obviously East and West are arbitrary and conventional, that is historical, constructions, since outside of real history every point on the earth is East and West at the same time. This can be seen more clearly from the fact that these terms have crystallised not from the point of view of a hypothetical melancholic man in general but from the point of view of the European cultured classes who, as a result of their world-wide hegemony, have caused them to be accepted everywhere. Japan is the Far East not only for Europe but also perhaps for the American from California and even for the Japanese himself, who, through English political culture, may then call Egypt the Near East. So because of the historical content that has become attached to the geographical terms, the expressions East and West have finished up indicating specific relations between different cultural complexes. Thus Italians often, when speaking of Morocco, call it an "Eastern" country, to refer to its Moslem and Arab civilisation. And yet these references are real; they correspond to real facts, they allow one to travel by land and by sea, to arrive where one has decided to arrive, to "foresee"

---

[93] Bertrand Russell, *The Problems of Philosophy*, 1912. "The part of the earth's surface where Edinburgh stands would be North of the part where London stands even if there were no human beings to know about North and South and even if there were no minds at all in the universe." (1967 edition, p. 56.)

the future, to objectivise reality, to understand the objectivity of the external world. Rational and real become one.

Without having understood this relationship it seems that one cannot understand the philosophy of praxis, its position in comparison with idealism and with mechanical materialism, the importance and significance of the doctrine of superstructures. It is not exact, as Croce maintains, to say that in the philosophy of praxis the Hegelian "idea" has been replaced by the "concept" of structure. The Hegelian "idea" has been resolved both in the structure and in the superstructures and the whole way of conceiving philosophy has been "historicised", that is to say a new way of philosophising which is more concrete and historical than what went before it has begun to come into existence.

Note. One must study the position of Professor Lukács towards the philosophy of praxis. It would appear that Lukács maintains that one can speak of the dialectic only for the history of men and not for nature. He might be right and he might be wrong. If his assertion presupposes a dualism between nature and man he is wrong because he is falling into a conception of nature proper to religion and to Graeco-Christian philosophy and also to idealism which does not in reality succeed in unifying and relating man and nature to each other except verbally. But if human history should be conceived also as the history of nature (also by means of the history of science) how can the dialectic be separated from nature? Perhaps Lukács, in reaction to the baroque theories of the *Popular Manual*, has fallen into the opposite error, into a form of idealism.[94]

Judgment on Past Philosophies

The superficial critique of subjectivism in the *Popular Manual* is part of a more general question, which is that of the attitude taken up

[94] It is not entirely clear on the basis of what evidence Gramsci makes this admittedly very tentative criticism. In his own essay on Bukharin's *Manual* (see introduction to this section) Lukács observes ". . . [the realm of the dialectic] is that of the historical process as a whole, whose individual, concrete, unrepeatable moments reveal its dialectical essence precisely in the qualitative differences between them and in the continuous transformation of their objective structure". Even in his supposedly most "idealist" work, *History and Class Consciousness*, Lukács does not appear to maintain a dualism between natural and human history. Nor does the reference in OC (p. 153n) to the essay *Mein Weg zu Marx* (1933) bear out Gramsci's observation, which is probably based on reports of the criticisms of Lukács made by Deborin and others about that time.

towards past philosophies and philosophers. To judge the whole of past philosophy as delirium and folly is not only an anti-historical error in that it makes the anachronistic claim that people in the past should have thought as we do today; it is also a real hang-over from metaphysics in that it presumes a dogmatic form of thought, valid at all times and in all countries, in the light of which the past can be judged. Methodical anti-historicism is sheer metaphysics. The fact that philosophical systems have been superseded does not exclude their once having been historically valid and having performed a necessary function. The fact that they fall by the wayside is to be considered from the point of view of the entire development of history and of the real dialectic. That they were *worthy* of falling is not a moral judgment nor one of mental hygiene, made from an objective point of view, but a dialectical-historical judgment. One should compare Engels' presentation of Hegel's proposition that "all that is rational is real and the real is rational",[95] a proposition which should be equally valid for the past.

In the *Manual* the past is judged as "irrational" and "monstrous" and the history of philosophy becomes a historical treatise on teratology; because the starting-point is metaphysical. (*The* [*Communist*] *Manifesto*, by contrast, contains the highest praises for the world that is a-dying.) If this way of judging the past is a theoretical error, a deviation from the philosophy of praxis, can it have any educative value or inspire energetic activity? It would seem not, because the matter becomes reduced to the presumption of being someone by virtue of the simple fact of being born at the present time instead of in some past century. But in every age there has been a past and a present, and the title "contemporary" belongs strictly to the world of comic anecdote.*

Immanence and the Philosophy of Praxis

The point is made in the *Manual* that the words "immanence" and "immanent" are indeed used in the philosophy of praxis but that "evidently" this use is purely metaphorical. Fine. But is it explained what immanence and immanent "metaphorically" mean?

---

[95] In *Ludwig Feuerbach and the End of Classical German Philosophy*. The maxim of Hegel comes from his *Philosophy of Right*. See note 57 on p. 366.

* The story is told of the little French bourgeois who had the word "Contemporary" printed on his visiting-card. He had thought he was a nobody and then one day he discovered he was somebody after all—he was a contemporary.

Why have these terms continued to be used and not been replaced? Is it just through a revulsion against creating new words? Usually, when a new conception replaces the previous one, the previous language continues to be used but is, precisely, used metaphorically. The whole of language is a continuous process of metaphor, and the history of semantics is an aspect of the history of culture; language is at the same time a living thing and a museum of fossils of life and civilisations. When I use the word "disaster" no one can accuse me of believing in astrology, and when I say "by Jove!" no one can assume that I am a worshipper of pagan divinities. These expressions are however a proof that modern civilisation is also a development of paganism and astrology. The term "immanence" has in the philosophy of praxis a quite precise meaning which is concealed beneath the metaphor and this meaning had to be defined and made precise. Such a definition would in reality have been genuinely "theory". The philosophy of praxis continues the philosophy of immanence but purifies it of all its metaphysical apparatus and brings it onto the concrete terrain of history. The use is metaphorical only in the sense that the old immanence has been superseded—that it has been superseded but is still assumed as a link in the process of thought out of which the new usage has come. And besides, is the new concept of immanence completely new? It would seem that in Giordano Bruno,[96] for example, there are many traces of a new conception of this type. The founders of the philosophy of praxis were acquainted with Bruno. They knew his writings and their marginal notes on copies of his works still survive. Furthermore, Bruno was not without influence on classical German philosophy (etc.). Here are a number of problems in the history of philosophy which could be usefully pursued.

The question of the relationship between language and metaphor is far from simple. Language, moreover, is always metaphorical. If perhaps it cannot quite be said that all discourse is metaphorical in respect of the thing or material and sensible object referred to (or the abstract concept) so as not to widen the concept of metaphor excessively, it can however be said that present language is metaphorical with respect to the meanings and the ideological content which the words used had in preceding periods of civilisation. A

---

[96] The notion that the thought of Bruno, together with that of other unorthodox sixteenth-century philosophers such as Telesius and Campanella, contained the germs of a "modern" anti-transcendentalist form of thought is one that has been repeatedly put forward by idealist commentators since Croce and has received reserved support even from Marxists.

treatise of semantics (that of Michel Bréal[97] for example) can provide an historically and critically reconstructed catalogue of the semantic mutations of given groups of words. A failure to take account of this fact, that is to say the absence of a critical and historicist conception of the phenomenon of language, can lead to many errors in both the scientific and the practical field:

1. An error of an aesthetic nature, which today is increasingly being corrected but which in the past used to be a dominant doctrine, is the notion that certain expressions as opposed to others are "beautiful" in themselves in that they are crystallised metaphors: rhetoricians and grammarians drool on about certain little phrases in which they discern God knows what abstract artistic virtues and essentiality. The purely bookish "joy" of the philologist ecstatic over the result of some of his etymological or semantic researches is confused with artistic enjoyment proper. A recent pathological example of this is the case of Giulio Bertoni's *Linguaggio e Poesia*.

2. A practical error which has many adherents is the utopia of fixed and universal languages.

3. An arbitrary trend towards neologism, which arises from the question posed by Pareto and the pragmatists about "language as a source of error".[98] Both Pareto and the pragmatists claim to have originated a new conception of the world or at least to have renewed a particular science and therefore to have given a new meaning or at least a new nuance to words or to have created new concepts. They then find themselves faced with the fact that traditional words, particularly as commonly used but also in the usage of the educated classes and even in the usage of specialists in the same science, continue to retain their old meaning despite the change of content, and they react against it. Pareto creates his own "dictionary", demonstrating his tendency to create his own "pure" or "mathematical" language. The pragmatists theorise abstractly about language as a source of error (see Prezzolini's little book). But is it possible to remove from language its metaphorical and extensive meanings? It is not possible. Language is transformed with the transformation of the whole of civilisation, through the acquisition of culture by new classes and through the hegemony exercised by one national language over others, etc., and what it

[97] M. Bréal, *Essai de sémantique*, Paris, 1897: English translation, *Semantics, Studies in the Science of Meaning*, London, 1900.

[98] See p. 348.

does is precisely to absorb in metaphorical form the words of previous civilisations and cultures. Nobody today thinks that the word "dis-aster" is connected with astrology or can claim to be misled about the opinions of someone who uses the word. Similarly even an atheist can speak of "dis-grace" without being thought to be a believer in predestination (etc.).[99] The new "metaphorical" meaning spreads with the spread of the new culture, which furthermore also coins brand-new words or absorbs them from other languages as loan-words giving them a precise meaning and therefore depriving them of the extensive halo they possessed in the original language. Thus it is probable that for many people the term "immanence" is known, understood and used for the first time only in the new "metaphorical" sense given to it by the philosophy of praxis.

Questions of Nomenclature and Content

One of the characteristics of the intellectuals as a crystallised social group (one, that is, which sees itself as continuing uninterruptedly through history and thus independent of the struggle of groups[100] rather than as the expression of a dialectical process through which every dominant social group elaborates its own category of intellectuals) is precisely that of connecting itself, in the ideological sphere, with a preceding intellectual category by means of a common conceptual nomenclature. Every new social organism (type of society) creates a new superstructure whose specialised representatives and standard-bearers (the intellectuals) can only be conceived as themselves being "new" intellectuals who have come

---

[99] Literally "dis-grace" means the withdrawal of Divine Grace, and therefore logically implies a notion of predestination. Similarly "dis-aster" refers to an unfavourable conjunction of the stars. Both words have, however, lost their original connotations in the modern language. On the other hand, as Gramsci points out in another note (MS. 159), the case for systematic neologism as a means of avoiding any possible confusion in the application of terms has a long and interesting history. In this note Gramsci refers to a conversation with Napoleon in 1805, recalled by Pietro Giordani some years later, in which Napoleon is reported to have said ". . . I think that in science when something really new is discovered a completely new word must be given to it, so that the idea remains precise and distinct. If you give a new meaning to an old word, then however strongly you assert that the new idea attached to that word has nothing in common with the idea newly attributed to it the human mind cannot ever refrain from imagining some resemblance and connection between the old and the new idea."

[100] Euphemism (for reasons of censorship) for the class struggle. For the notion below of the dominant social group elaborating its own category of intellectuals see the essay "The Formation of the Intellectuals", pp. 5–14.

out of the new situation and are not a continuation of the preceding intellectual milieu. If the "new" intellectuals put themselves forward as the direct continuation of the previous "intelligentsia", they are not new at all (that is, not tied to the new social group which organically represents the new historical situation) but are a conservative and fossilised left-over of the social group which has been historically superseded. (This is another way of saying that the new historical situation has not reached the level of development necessary for it to have the capacity to create new superstructures but continues to live in the worm-eaten integument of old history.)

It must however be borne in mind that no new historical situation, however radical the change that has brought it about, completely transforms language, at least in its external formal aspect. But the content of language must be changed, even if it is difficult to have an exact consciousness of the change in immediate terms. The phenomenon is, moreover, historically complex and complicated by the existence of characteristic cultures among the various strata of the new social group, some of whom, in the ideological field, are still immersed in the culture of preceding historical situations, including sometimes the one that has most recently been superseded. A class some of whose strata still have a Ptolemaic conception of the world can none the less be the representative of a very advanced historical situation. Ideologically backward (or at least in certain aspects of their conception of the world, which remains disconnected and ingenuous), these strata are nevertheless very advanced on a practical level, in terms, that is, of economic and political function. If the task of the intellectuals is to determine and to organise the reform of moral and intellectual life, in words to fit culture to the sphere of practice, it is clear that "crystallised" intellectuals are conservative and reactionary. For while the new social group at least feels itself split off and distinct from its predecessor, these intellectuals are not even conscious of this distinction, but think that they can reconnect themselves with the past.

This is not to say, however, that the whole heritage of the past must be rejected. There are "instrumental values" which cannot but be absorbed in their entirety in order to continue to be elaborated and refined. But how is one to distinguish the instrumental value from the transient philosophical value that has to be rejected outright? It often happens that, because one has accepted a transient philosophical value belonging to a particular past tendency, one then rejects an instrumental value from another tendency because it conflicts with the first, even though this instrumental value could have been useful to express the new historical cultural content.

Thus we have seen the term "materialism" accepted with its past content, while the term "immanence" was rejected because in the past it had a particular historical cultural content. The difficulty of fitting literary expression to conceptual content and the confusion of questions of terminology with questions of substance and vice versa is typical of philosophical dilettantism and of the lack of an historical sense in grasping the different moments of a process of cultural development, typical, in other words, of an anti-dialectical and dogmatic conception, imprisoned within the abstract schemas of formal logic.

The term "materialism" in the first fifty years of the nineteenth century should be understood not only in its restricted technical philosophical sense but with the more extended meaning that it acquired polemically in the debates that grew up in Europe with the rise and victorious development of modern culture. The name materialism was given to any philosophical doctrine which excluded transcendence from the realm of thought. It was given therefore, not only to pantheism and immanentism, but to any practical attitude inspired by political realism—i.e. to any that was opposed to certain of the worst currents of political romanticism such as the popularisations of the doctrines of Mazzini[101] which carried on all the time about "missions" and "ideals" and suchlike vague, nebulous and sentimental abstractions. Even today in Catholic polemics the term materialism is often used in this sense; materialism is the opposite of spiritualism in the strict sense, i.e. religious spiritualism, and therefore one can include under the heading materialism the whole of Hegelianism and classical German philosophy in general, as well as sensationalism and the philosophy of the French Enlightenment. Similarly, in the terminology of common sense, materialism includes everything that tends to locate the purpose of life on this earth and not in paradise. Any form of

---

[101] Not only the popularisations but Mazzini's original doctrines themselves were in point of fact extremely vague and devoid of content. Despite his active participation in the Roman Republic of 1849, Mazzini never succeeded, particularly in the crucial years 1860–70, in formulating a clear policy towards the position of the Church and the Papacy, and his slogan "*Dio e popolo*" (God and People) provided a political and ideological cover for all sorts of liberal and neo-Catholic sentimentalisms. On an ideological level (and Mazzini's influence after 1850 was mainly ideological rather than directly political) Mazzinianism represented the degeneration of the romantic patriotic impulse of the Risorgimento, co-incidental with the rise of "materialistic" positivism.

economic activity which went beyond the bounds of mediaeval production was "materialism" because it seemed an "end in itself", economics for the sake of economics, activity for the sake of activity, just as today for the average European America is "materialist" because the use of machinery and the scale of firms and businesses goes beyond the limit which the average European considers "just"—that within which "spiritual" demands are not mortified. Thus a polemical riposte made by feudal culture against the developing bourgeoisie has now been appropriated by European bourgeois culture, on the one hand against a more developed form of capitalism than the European, and on the other hand against the practical activity of subaltern social groups. (For these groups at the outset and for a whole historical epoch, until they have been able to construct an economy and a social structure of their own, activity cannot but be prevalently economic or at least expressed in economic and structural terms.) Traces of this conception of materialism remain in language. The German *geistlich* [spiritual] also means "clerical", proper to the clergy, and so does the Russian *dukhoviez*. How prevalent it is can be seen from many writers of the philosophy of praxis, for whom, precisely, religion, theism, etc., are the points of reference for recognising "thorough-going materialists".

One of the reasons, and perhaps the most important, for the reduction of historical materialism to traditional metaphysical materialism is to be looked for in the fact that historical materialism could not but be a mainly critical and polemical phase of philosophy, while there was a need for an achieved and perfected system. But achieved and perfected systems are always the work of single philosophers, and in them, side by side with the historically relevant part, the part, that is, which corresponds to contemporary conditions of life, there always exists an abstract part, which is "ahistorical" in the sense that it is tied to preceding philosophies and corresponds to external pedantic necessities of the architecture of the system or is due to personal idiosyncracies. Therefore the philosophy of an epoch cannot be any systematic tendency or individual system. It is the *ensemble* of all individual philosophies and philosophical tendencies, plus scientific opinions, religion and common sense. Can a system of this type be created artificially? And if so, by individuals or by groups? Critical activity is the only kind possible, particularly in the sense of posing and resolving critically the problems that present themselves as an expression of historical development. But the first problem which has to be formulated and understood is this: that the new philosophy cannot coincide with any past system, under whatever name. Identity of terms does not mean identity of concepts.

A book worth looking at in connection with this question is Lange's *History of Materialism.*[102] This work may have been more or less superseded by subsequent studies of individual materialist philosophers, but from our point of view its cultural importance remains intact. A whole series of adherents of historical materialism have referred to it, for information on their forerunners and for the fundamental concepts of materialism. It could be said, schematically, that what has happened is this. One starts from the dogmatic presupposition that historical materialism is straightforward traditional materialism slightly revised and corrected (corrected by the "dialectic", which therefore becomes absorbed as a chapter of formal logic and not as a logic of its own, that is a theory of knowledge); and one then studies in Lange what traditional materialism was, and concepts of this materialism are represented as the concepts of historical materialism. So that it could be said that the major part of the corpus of concepts that goes under the label of historical materialism have as their founder and fountainhead none other than Lange. For this reason the study of this work is of great cultural and critical interest, all the more so because Lange is a conscientious and acute historian who has a quite precise, definite and limited conception of materialism and therefore, to the great surprise and even indignation of certain people (such as Plekhanov) does not regard as materialist either historical materialism or even the philosophy of Feuerbach.[103] Here again one can see how the terminology is conventional but not without importance in making for errors and deviations as soon as one forgets that it is always necessary to return to the cultural sources in order to identify the exact value of concepts, since there may be different heads under the same hat. It is well known, moreover, that the originator of the philosophy of praxis [Marx] never called his own conception materialist and that when writing about French materialism he criticises it and affirms that the critique ought to be more exhaustive.[104] Thus he never uses the formula "materialist dialectic", but

---

[102] Friedrich Albert Lange, *Geschichte des Materialismus und Kritik seiner Bedeutung in der Gegenwart*, 2nd revised edition 1873–75.

[103] Feuerbachian materialism, as defined and attacked in *The German Ideology* and in the *Theses on Feuerbach*, is not strictly materialist in that it is founded on a basic dualism between an objective reality and a separate realm of human subjectivity.

[104] The reference would appear to be to the section on French Materialism in *The Holy Family* (VI, 3(d)), except that in this section Marx is far less critical of French Materialism in its classic form than Gramsci suggests.

calls it "rational" as opposed to "mystical", which gives the term "rational" a quite precise meaning.*[105]

Science and the Instruments of Science

It is affirmed, in the *Popular Manual*, that the progress of science is dependent, as an effect from a cause, on the development of the instruments of science. This is a corollary of the general principle adopted by the *Manual*, originating with Loria,[106] about the historical function of the "instrument of production and work" (which is substituted for the *ensemble* of social relations of production). But in the science of geology no instruments except a hammer are used and the technical progress in hammers is in no way comparable with progress in geology. If the history of sciences can be reduced, as the *Manual* claims, to the history of their particular instruments, how can one produce a history of geology? It is no good saying that geology is based also on the progress of a complex of other sciences so that the history of the instruments of these sciences helps to describe the history of geology, because with this let-out one ends up with an empty generalisation and a recourse to ever-wider movements right up to the relations of production. It is very apt that the motto of geology should be "mente et malleo" [with the mind and with the hammer].

It can be said in general that the advance of science cannot be *materially* documented. The history of the sciences can at most be brought alive in the memory, and that not in all cases, through the description of the successive perfecting of the instruments which have been one means of advance and through the description of the machines which have been applications of the science itself. The principal "instruments" of scientific progress are of an intellectual (and even political) and methodological order, and Engels has written[107] that "intellectual instruments" are not born from

* On this question it is worth looking again at the essays of Antonio Labriola.

[105] See Marx's Afterword to the Second German Edition of *Capital*, where he argues that in Hegel the dialectic stood on its head and that in order to make it stand properly on its feet it is necessary to extract the rational kernel from the mystic shell. The rational dialectic, therefore, is defined in specific opposition to the way it was developed by Hegel, but this is not tantamount to saying that from "idealist" it should become "materialist", which is a Feuerbachian rather than a Marxist conception.

[106] For Loria see note 108 on p. 458.

[107] See Engels, *Anti-Dühring* (cit.), Introduction, ". . . The art of working with concepts is not inborn and also is not given with ordinary everyday consciousness, but requires real thought, and . . . this thought similarly has a long empirical history, not more and not less than empirical natural science."

See also the Letter to Starkenburg (cit. above, note 74).

nothing and are not innate in man, but are acquired, have developed and are developing historically. How great a contribution to the progress of science was made by the expulsion from the scientific fields of the authority of Aristotle and the Bible? And was not this expulsion due to the general progress of modern society? Recall the example of theories on the origin of springs. The first exact formulation of the way that springs are produced is to be found in the *Encyclopaedia* of Diderot, etc. While the ordinary people can be shown to have had correct opinions on the question before then, in the scientific world there were a succession of the most arbitrary and bizarre theories which aimed to reconcile the Bible and Aristotle with the experimental observations of good sense.

Another question is this. If the affirmation in the *Manual* were true, what would distinguish the history of the sciences from the history of technology? With the development of the "material" instruments of science, which begins historically with the coming of the experimental method, a particular science has developed, the science of instruments, which is closely connected with the general development of production and technology.*

How superficial the affirmation in the *Manual* is can be seen from the example of the mathematical sciences which have no need of any material instruments (the development of the abacus, is not, I think, a valid counter-example) and which are themselves an "instrument" of all the natural sciences.

The "Technical Instrument"

The notion of the "technical instrument" in the *Popular Manual* is completely mistaken. From Croce's essay on Achille Loria[108] in *Materialismo storico ed economia marxistica* it seems that Loria was the first person who arbitrarily (or else through the puerile desire

* On this question see G. Boffito, *Gli strumenti della scienza e la scienza degli strumenti*, Libreria Internazionale Seeber, Firenze, 1929.

[108] Croce's essay on Loria dates from 1896, when Croce was a Marxist, albeit of an unorthodox kind, and was reprinted in the volume *Materialismo storico ed economia marxistica* (1900. Collected Works, Vol. II, 4, pp. 23–56). Basically it is an amplification of the attack on Loria's vulgarisation and plagiarism of Marx made by Engels in the Preface to *Capital*, Vol. II. Achille Loria (1857–1943) was an academic economist who put himself forward as an original thinker and enjoyed a certain vogue, not only in Italy, in the 1880s and 1890s. Loria's theory, to which he gave the name "historical economism", was a mish-mash of vulgar economy and vulgar Marxism, of no intrinsic distinction but interesting, in Gramsci's eyes, as an example of "certain degenerate and bizarre aspects of the mentality of a group of Italian intellectuals and therefore of the national culture. . . .". (Int. p. 169) to which he gave the name "*lorianismo*".

for original discovery) put the expression "technical instrument" in the place of "material forces of production" or "complex of social relations".

The Preface to *A Contribution to the Critique of Political Economy* states:

"In the social production of their life men enter into relations with each other which are determined, necessary and independent of their will, that is into relations of production, which correspond to a given level of development of the material forces of production. The ensemble of these relations constitutes the economic structure of society, in other words the real base on top of which is raised a political and juridical superstructure and to which correspond given social forms of consciousness. . . . At a given point in their development, the material productive forces of society enter into contradiction with the pre-existing relations of production (that is the property relations, which is the juridical equivalent of that expression) within which these forces had previously moved. These relations of production, from a form of development of the productive forces, are converted into an obstacle to them. And then there arrives an age of social revolution. With the change in the economic base the colossal overhanging superstructure is revolutionised and collapses more or less rapidly . . . A social formation does not perish until all the productive forces for which there is room in it have been developed and new relations of production do not take their place until the material conditions of their existence have matured in the womb of the existing society."

(Translation by Antonio Labriola in his essay, *In Memoria* [In Memory of the Communist Manifesto].)[109]

And here is a rehash by Loria (taken from *La terra e il sistema sociale*, p. 19, Verona, Drucker, 1892; Croce maintains that similar statements are to be found in other writings of Loria):

"To a certain stage of the productive instrument there corresponds, and is built upon it, a given system of production, and

[109] Quoted in Croce, *Materialismo* (cit.), pp. 41–2, which is also the source for the Loria quotation and certain further remarks below. Since Gramsci had access to few Marxist texts while in prison, this quotation from Marx, here retranslated from the Italian version, came to assume exceptional importance for him.

thus of economic relations, which then shape the whole mode of being of society. But the incessant evolution of productive methods generates sooner or later a radical metamorphosis of the technical instrument which renders intolerable the system of production and economy on which the previous stage of technique was founded. Then the outdated economic form is destroyed through a social revolution and replaced by a superior economic form, which corresponds to the new phase of the productive instrument."

Croce adds that in *Capital* (volume I, Ch. III, sec. 3, and Ch. XIV) and elsewhere the importance of technical inventions is stressed and a history of techniques is invoked, but that there is no text in which the "technical instrument" is turned into the unique and supereme cause of economic development. The passage from *Zur Kritik* contains the phrases "level of development of the material forces of production", "mode of production of material life", "economic conditions of production" and the like, which certainly affirm that economic development is determined by material conditions, but it never reduces these to the mere "metamorphosis of the technical instrument". Croce then adds that the founder of the philosophy of praxis never framed his enquiry around the ultimate cause of economic life. "His philosophy was not that cheap. He had not 'flirted' in vain with the Hegelian dialectic to go then in search of ultimate causes."[110]

It is worth noting that the *Popular Manual* does not quote the passage from the Preface to the *Zur Kritik* nor even refer to it. This is pretty strange, given that this is the most important authentic source for a reconstruction of the philosophy of praxis.[111] Furthermore, in this respect the mode of thinking expounded in the *Manual* is no different from that of Loria, if not indeed even more superficial and open to criticism. It is hard to tell what the *Manual* means by structure, superstructure or technical instrument. All its general concepts are nebulous and vague. The technical instrument is

---

[110] Croce, *op. cit.*, p. 43. For Marx's "flirting" or "coquetting" (*kokettieren*) with Hegel see the Afterword to *Capital*, I.

[111] See "Questions of Method", pp. 382–386 above. Gramsci's position was that Marx, engaged for the last years of his life on the concrete study of economics, left behind little writing of a philosophical nature, with the result that the gaps in Marx's philosophy tended to be filled by Engels. With these restrictions, reinforced by the fact that Gramsci either could not or did not know certain works of Marx whose importance has emerged subsequently, his emphasis on the unique importance of the Preface is of extreme importance, both as a source for Gramsci's own Marxism and as a guideline for other Marxists.

conceived in such a generic way that it can mean any form of equipment or utensil, including the instruments used by scientists in their experiments and . . . musical instruments. This way of treating the question just makes matters uselessly complicated.

If one starts from this baroque way of thinking a whole series of baroque questions are thrown up. For example, are libraries structure or superstructure? Or the specialised laboratories of scientists? If it can be maintained that an art or a science is developed through the developments of its technical instruments, why could one not maintain quite the contrary or argue that certain instrumental forms are structure and superstructure at the same time? Thus it could be said that certain superstructures have a particular structure of their own while remaining superstructures. The art of typography would be the material structure of a whole series of ideologies, indeed of all ideologies, and the existence of the printing industry would be sufficient to provide a materialistic justification of the whole of history. There would then remain the case of pure mathematics and algebra which, having no instruments of their own, could not develop. It is clear that the whole theory of the technical instrument in the *Manual* is pure *abracadabra* and comparable to the theory of memory concocted by Croce to explain why artists are not content to conceive their works purely in an ideal form but write them or sculpt them, etc. (with Tilgher's phenomenal objection that in the case of architecture it would be a bit much to think of an engineer constructing a building just to preserve the memory of his idea). There is no doubt that all this is just an infantile deviation of the philosophy of praxis generated by the baroque conviction that the more one goes back to "material" objects the more orthodox one must be.

Objection to empiricism

An enquiry into a series of facts to discover the relations between them presupposes a "concept" that permits one to distinguish that series from other possible series of facts. How can there take place a choice of facts to be adduced as proof of the truth of one's own assumption if one does not have a pre-existing criterion of choice? But what is this criterion of choice to be, if not something superior to each single fact under enquiry? An intuition, a conception, which must be regarded as having a complex history, a process that is to be connected with the whole process of the development of culture (etc.). This observation may be connected with the other one on the "sociological law", in which one simply repeats the same fact twice, the first time as a fact and the second time as a law, and which is a sophism of the double fact and not a law at all.

Concept of "orthodoxy"

From a few of the points developed above it emerges that the concept of "orthodoxy" requires to be renewed and brought back to its authentic origins. Orthodoxy is not to be looked for in this or that adherent of the philosophy of praxis, or in this or that tendency connected with currents extraneous to the original doctrine, but in the fundamental concept that the philosophy of praxis is "sufficient unto itself", that it contains in itself all the fundamental elements needed to construct a total and integral conception of the world, a total philosophy and theory of natural science, and not only that but everything that is needed to give life to an integral practical organisation of society, that is, to become a total integral civilisation.

This concept of orthodoxy, thus renewed, helps to give a better definition of the attribute "revolutionary" which is applied with such facility to various conceptions of the world, theories or philosophies. Christianity was revolutionary in relation to paganism because it was an element of complete split between the supporters of the old and new worlds. A theory is "revolutionary" precisely to the extent that it is an element of conscious separation and distinction into two camps and is a peak inaccessible to the enemy camp. To maintain that the philosophy of praxis is not a completely autonomous and independent structure of thought in antagonism to all traditional philosophies and religions, means in reality that one has not severed one's links with the old world, if indeed one has not actually capitulated. The philosophy of praxis has no need of support from alien sources. It is sufficiently robust and rich in new truths for the old world to come to it to supply itself with a more modern and efficacious arsenal of weapons. This means that the philosophy of praxis is beginning to exercise its own hegemony over traditional culture. But traditional culture, which is still strong and above all is more polished and refined, is trying to react like Greece in defeat which finished by vanquishing its uncouth Roman conqueror.

It could be said that a large part of the philosophy of Croce represents this attempt to reabsorb the philosophy of praxis and incorporate it as the handmaid of traditional culture. But, as the

Manual demonstrates, even some self-styled "orthodox" adherents of the philosophy of praxis fall into the trap and themselves conceive their philosophy as surbordinated to a general (vulgar) materialist philosophy just as others are to idealism. (This does not mean that there are no points of relationship between the philosophy of praxis and the old philosophies, but they are less than those that exist between Christianity and Greek philosophy.) In Otto Bauer's little book on religion[112] one can find a number of references to the combinations that have been given rise to by this erroneous notion that the philosopy of praxis is not autonomous and independent but needs the support, as need arises, of some other materialist or idealist philosophy. Bauer maintains as a political thesis the agnosticism of parties and the granting of permission to party members to group themselves into idealists, materialists, atheists, catholics, etc.

Note. People tend to look for a general philosophy underlying the philosophy of praxis and implicitly to deny to it any originality of content and method. One case of this error would appear to be this: that a confusion is made between on the one hand the personal culture of the founder of the philosophy of praxis, i.e. the philosophical currents and the great philosophers in which he was very interested in his youth and whose language he often reproduces (always however with detachment and often with the observation that he uses it in order to make his own concept easier to understand) and on the other the origins or constituent parts of the philosophy of praxis. This error has a long history, particularly in the field of literary criticism. It is well known that the business of reducing great poetic works to their sources became at one period the major task of many distinguished scholars. This problem comes up in its external form in so-called plagiaries, but it is also true that even in the case of a number of "plagiaries" and indeed literal reproductions it is not impossible to claim originality for the plagiarism or reproduction.[113] Two notable examples can be cited: 1. the sonnet of Tansillo reproduced by Giordano Bruno in *Degli eroici furori* (or in *La Cena delle Ceneri*) "Poiché spiegate ho l'ali al bel desio", which in Tansillo was a love poem to the Marchesa del

---

[112] Otto Bauer, *Sozialdemokratie, Religion und Kirche*. See note 13 on p. 387.

[113] Gramsci says "*per l'opera plagiata o riprodotta*", which is presumably a slip of the pen.

Vasto;[114] 2. the verses for the dead of Dogali which D'Annunzio put forward as his own, having in fact copied them word for word from a collection by Tommaseo of Serbian songs.[115] In both Bruno and D'Annunzio these reproductions acquire a new and original flavour which makes one forget their origins.

The study of the philosophical culture of a man like Marx is not only interesting but necessary. But one must not forget that it belongs exclusively to the field of the reconstruction of his intellectual biography. The elements of Spinoza, Feuerbach, Hegel, French materialism, etc., are in no way essential parts of the philosophy of praxis, nor can that philosophy be reduced to those elements. What is interesting is precisely the transcending of the old philosophies, the new synthesis or the elements of a new synthesis and the way of conceiving philosophy. One should further bear in mind that the elements of this new mode of conceiving philosophy are contained in aphorisms or in some way dispersed throughout the writings of the founder of the philosophy of praxis, and that it is necessary precisely to distinguish these elements and develop them coherently. At the level of theory the philosophy of praxis cannot be confounded with or reduced to any other philosophy. Its originality lies not only in its transcending of previous philosophies but also and above all in that it opens up a completely new road, renewing from head to toe the whole way of conceiving philosophy itself. At the level of historical biographical research, however, one can study those interests which provided the occasion for the philosophical activity of the founder of the philosophy of praxis. Here one should bear in mind the psychology of the young scholar who every so often allows himself to be intellectually attracted by whatever new current he is studying and examining and who forms his own individuality as a result of this very process—a critical spirit and a power of original thought being generated as a result of having tried out and compared with each other so many contrasting ideas. For this one must therefore locate which

---

[114] Luigi Tansillo (1510–1568) was a minor Renaissance poet, who appears as one of the imaginary interlocutors of Giordano Bruno's dialogue *Degli eroici furori*. In the dialogue Tansillo acts as the mouthpiece for Bruno's philosophy and, as in this example from Dialogue III, is made to quote some of his own love poetry as if its content were a desire not for a woman but for knowledge. The aesthetic significance of this is discussed by Croce in an essay in *Problemi di estetica* (1910) which is also Gramsci's source.

[115] The battle of Dogali (1887) involved the annihilation of an entire Italian advance guard during the imperialist campaign in Eritrea.

elements he has incorporated and made homogeneous with his own thought and especially what is new creation. There is no doubt that Hegelianism is (relatively speaking) the most important of the philosophical motivations of our author, particularly because it attempted to go beyond the traditional conceptions of idealism and materialism in a new synthesis which undoubtedly had a quite exceptional importance and which represents a world-historical moment of philosophical inquiry. So when the *Manual* says that the term "immanence" in the philosophy of praxis is used in a metaphorical sense, it is saying nothing. In reality the term immanence has here acquired a special meaning which is not that of the "pantheists" nor any other metaphysical meaning but one which is new and needs to be specified. It has been forgotten that in the case of a very common expression [historical materialism] one should put the accent on the first term—"historical"—and not on the second, which is of metaphysical origin. The philosophy of praxis is absolute "historicism", the absolute secularisation and earthliness of thought, an absolute humanism of history. It is along this line that one must trace the thread of the new conception of the world.

"*Matter*"

What does the *Popular Manual* mean by matter? A popular handbook, even more than a book for specialists, particularly a book like this which claims to be the first of its kind, must define exactly not only its fundamental concepts, but its entire terminology, in order to avoid the sources of error deriving from the popular and vulgar usages of scientific words. Clearly, for the philosophy of praxis, "matter" should be understood neither in the meaning that it has acquired in natural science (physics, chemistry, mechanics, etc.—meanings to be noted and studied in the terms of their historical development), nor in any of the meanings that one finds in the various materialistic metaphysics. The various physical (chemical, mechanical, etc.) properties of matter which together constitute matter itself (unless one is to fall back on a conception of the Kantian noumenon)[116] should be considered, but only to the extent that they become a productive "economic element". Matter as such therefore is not our subject but how it is socially and historically organised for production, and natural science should be

---

[116] See note 61 on p. 367.

seen correspondingly as essentially an historical category, a human relation. Has the *ensemble* of the properties of all forms of matter always been the same? The history of the technical sciences shows that it has not. For how long was the mechanical power of steam neglected? Can it be claimed that this mechanical power existed before it was harnessed by man-made machines? Might it not be said in a sense, and up to a certain point, that what nature provides the opportunity for are not discoveries and inventions of pre-existing forces—of pre-existing qualities of matter—but "creations", which are closely linked to the interests of society and to the development and further necessities of development of the forces of production? And might not the idealistic conception[117] according to which nature is none other than the economic category be reduced, once cleansed of its speculative superstructures, into the terms of the philosophy of praxis and demonstrated to be historically linked to and a development of that philosophy? In reality the philosophy of praxis does not study a machine in order to know about and to establish the atomic structure of its materials or the physical, chemical and mechanical properties of its natural components (which is the business of the exact sciences and of technology) but only in so far as it is a moment of the material forces of production, is an object of property of particular social forces, and expresses a social relation which in turn corresponds to a particular historical period. The ensemble of the material forces of production is the least variable element in historical development: it is the one which at any given time can be ascertained and measured with mathematical exactitude and can therefore give rise to observations and criteria of an experimental character and thus to the reconstruction of a solid skeleton of the historical process. The variability of the ensemble of the material forces of production can also be measured, and one can establish with a fair degree of precision the point at which its development ceases to be merely quantitative and becomes qualitative. The ensemble of the material forces of production is at the same time a crystallisation of all past history and the basis of present and future history: it is both a document and an active and actual propulsive force. But the concept of activity applied to forces of this kind must not be confused or even compared with activity in either the physical or the metaphysical sense. Electricity is historically active, not merely however

---

[117] In Crocean metaphysics "Economics" is a distinct "category", along with Logic, Aesthetics and Ethics. See General Introduction and also note 58 on p. 366.

as a natural force (e.g. an electrical discharge which causes a fire) but as a productive element dominated by man and incorporated into the ensemble of the material forces of production, an object of private property. As an abstract natural force electricity existed even before its reduction to a productive force, but it was not historically operative and was just a subject of hypothetical discourse in natural history (earlier still it was historical "nothingness", since no one was interested in it or indeed knew anything about it).

These observations help to explain how the element of causality used by the natural sciences to explain human history is in fact quite an arbitrary assumption, if not actually a return to old ideological interpretations. For example the *Manual* affirms that modern atomic theory destroys individualism (Robinsonades).[118] But what does this mean? What is implied in this juxtaposition of politics and scientific theories, if not that history is moved by these scientific theories, in other words by ideologies? So that by trying to be ultra-materialist one falls into a baroque form of abstract idealism. And it cannot be maintained that it is not atomic theory but the natural reality that the theory observes and describes that has destroyed individualism, but without falling into further complicated contradictions in that this natural reality is supposed to be prior to the theory and therefore already operative even when individualism was at its height. How could "atomistic" reality, if it is and was a natural law, not have been always in operation but have needed the construction of a theory on the part of mankind for it to come into operation? Do men only obey the laws they know, as if these laws were Acts of Parliament? And who could have imposed on mankind observation of laws of which they were unaware, on the principle of modern legislation according to which ignorance of the law is no excuse? Nor, again, can it be held that the laws of a given natural science are identical with the laws of history, or that, because the whole complex of scientific ideas is a homogeneous unity, one can reduce one science to another or one law to another. For in this case by what right does this particular element of physics rather than any other become the one that can be reduced to the unity of the conception of the world?

This is indeed just one of many elements in the *Popular Manual* which demonstrate the superficial way in which it has posed the

---

[118] "Robinsonades" is the name given (e.g. by Marx) to the speculative reasoning that derives forms of social life from the needs of an imaginary isolated individual, after the pattern of Defoe's *Robinson Crusoe*.

problem of the philosophy of praxis and its failure to give to this conception of the world its proper scientific autonomy and the position due to it in relation to natural science—or even, what is worse, in relation to that vague concept of science in general which is typical of the vulgar popular conception which regards even conjuring tricks as science. Is modern atomic theory a "definitive" theory, established once and for all? What scientist would dare make such an assertion? Might it not rather be simply a scientific hypothesis which may be superseded, that is to say, absorbed into a vaster and more comprehensive theory? Why then should reference to this theory be so decisive and have put an end to the question of individualism and of Robinsonades? (Quite apart from the fact that Robinsonades can sometimes be practical models constructed to indicate a tendency or for the purposes of a demonstration *ad absurdum*: even the author of the critical economy [Marx] had recourse to Robinsonades.) But there are further questions. If atomic theory is what the *Manual* makes it out to be, given that the history of society is a series of upheavals and there have been many forms of society whereas atomic theory would appear to be the reflection of an ever-constant natural reality, how then has society not always obeyed this law? Or is it being claimed that the change from the mediaeval corporate regime to economic individualism was anti-scientific, a mistake of history and of nature? According to the theory of praxis it is evident that it is not atomic theory that explains human history but the other way about: in other words that atomic theory and all scientific hypotheses and opinions are superstructures.*

Quantity and Quality

In the *Popular Manual* it is said (but only in passing, for the assertion is not justified or evaluated and does not express a fertile concept, but is casual, with no links with what goes before or comes after) that every society is more than the mere sum of its individual components. This is true in the abstract, but what does it mean concretely? The explanation given—empirically—is often baroque. It is said that a hundred cows taken one at a time are quite different from a hundred cows together which are then a herd—thus reducing the question to one of terminology. Similarly it is said that in

* Atomistic theory can be used to explain biological man as an aggregate of various bodies and so explain the society of man. Talk about a comprehensive theory!

numbers when we get to twelve we have a dozen, as if there didn't also exist couples, triplets and quartets, etc., i.e. simply different ways of counting. The most concrete theoretico-practical explanation, however, is that to be found in the first volume of *Capital*, where it is demonstrated that in the factory system there exists a quota of production which cannot be attributed to any individual worker but to the ensemble of the labour force, to collective man. A similar process takes place for the whole of society, which is based on the division of labour and of functions and for this reason is worth more than the sum of its parts. How the philosophy of praxis has "concretised" the Hegelian law about quantity becoming quality is another of those knotty theoretical problems which the *Popular Manual* does not go into but regards as already known, contenting itself with wordplay about water changing its state (ice, liquid, gas) with changes in temperature, a purely mechanical fact determined by external agents (fire, sun, evaporation of carbonic acid, etc.).

In the case of man, who is this external agent? In the factory it is the division of labour, etc., conditions created by man himself. In society it is the ensemble of productive forces. But the author of the *Manual* has not considered that, if every social aggregate is something more (and different) than the sum of its components, this must mean that the law or principle which explains the development of society cannot be a physical law, since in physics one does not get out of the quantitative sphere except metaphorically. However, in the philosophy of praxis quality is also connected to quantity and this connection is perhaps its most fertile contribution. Idealism, on the other hand, hypostasises this mysterious something else known as quality, it makes it into an entity of its own, "spirit", just as religion had done with the idea of divinity. But if the notion of quality is a hypostasis in religious thought and in idealism, that is to say an arbitrary abstraction rather than a process of analytical distinction necessary for explanatory purposes, then the same is true in the case of vulgar materialism, which "divinises" a hypostasis of matter.

This way of looking at the conception of society should be compared with the conception of the State typical of the actual idealists.[119] For the actualists the State has ended up being precisely this sort of entity superior to individuals (though in the light of the consequences derived by Spirito from the idealist identification of

[119] See succeeding note and also note 70 on p. 424.

State and individual in relation to property, Gentile in *L'Educazione Fascista* of August 1932 has been careful to make some qualifications.[120] The ideas of the vulgar actualists had degenerated into such parrot talk that the only possible critique was humorous caricature. Thus one could imagine a recruit explaining to the recruiting officers the theory of the State as superior to individuals and demanding that they should leave in liberty his physical and material person and just enrol that mysterious something that contributes to building that national something known as the State. Or recall the story in the *Novellino*[121] in which the wise Saladin decides the issue between the innkeeper who wants to be paid for the consumption of the aroma emanating from his meat and the beggar who does not want to pay: Saladin pays him with the chinking of coin and tells the innkeeper to pocket the sound in the same way as the beggar ate the aromatic exhalations.

Teleology

The treatment of the question of teleology brings out even more blatantly the *Manual's* weakness for presenting the philosophical doctrines of the past as all equally trival and banal, so that the reader gets the impression that all past culture was a phantasmagoric sequence of Bacchantae in delirium. The method is reprehensible from various points of view. The serious reader, aiming to broaden his knowledge and deepen his understanding, believes that he is being fooled and extends his suspicions to the whole of the system. It is easy to think one has got beyond a position by denigrating it, but this is a pure verbal illusion. To give a burlesque treatment to questions can be valid for Voltaire, but not everyone can be a Voltaire, i.e. a great artist.

Thus the *Manual* presents the question of teleology in its most infantile manifestations, while ignoring the solution to the problem

---

[120] Spirito was an ideologue of the corporate State and an idealist philosopher. Originally a student and follower of Gentile, he departed from Gentile's actualism in the 1930s. Around 1930 he was aligned with Gentile against Croce and Einaudi over the role of the State, but his position over the subordination of the citizen to the State through the mediation of the "corporation" was more extreme than that of Gentile and contained anti-capitalist implications (the "corporation as property": see p. 291 of this volume) which were no doubt a reason for Gentile's qualifications. For Gramsci's assessment of the overall debate see pp. 271–272 and also PP. pp. 31–2, and MS. 275–277.

[121] The *Novellino*, otherwise known as the *Cento Novelle Antiche*, is the earliest extant collection of Italian short stories, dating from the thirteenth century. The story in question, rather inaccurately recalled by Gramsci, is No. IX.

offered by Kant. It could perhaps be demonstrated that in the *Manual* there survives a lot of unconscious teleology which without knowing it reproduces the Kantian point of view. See for example the chapter on the "Equilibrium of Nature and Society".*

On Art

In the chapter devoted to Art it is affirmed that the most recent works on aesthetics maintain the unity of form and content. This can be seen as one of the most glaring examples of the author's critical inability to establish the history of concepts and to identify the real significance of the concepts themselves within various theories. In point of fact the identification of content and form is affirmed by idealist aesthetics (Croce), but on idealistic premisses and with idealistic terminology. "Content" and "form" do not therefore have the meaning the *Manual* supposes. That form and content are identified means that in art the content is not the "abstract subject", that is the novelistic plot and a particular mass of generic sentiments, but is art itself, a philosophical category, a "distinct" moment of the spirit, etc. Nor does form mean "technique" as the *Manual* maintains.

All the points and references to aesthetics and to artistic criticism in the *Manual* should be collected and analysed. Meanwhile one can take as an example the section devoted to Goethe's *Prometheus*. The judgment given is superficial and extremely generic. The author, as far as one can gather, knows neither the exact history of

---

* From Goethe's *Xenien*: "*The Teleologist*"—"We most humbly adore the world's good Creator who when/The cork-tree first he made, also invented the cork".[122] Croce in his volume on Goethe (*Opere* III, 12(i), p. 279) adds this note: "In opposition to extrinsic finalism, generally accepted in the eighteenth century and recently criticised by Kant, who had replaced it with a more profound conception of finality." Elsewhere and in another form Goethe repeats the same motif and claims to have derived it from Kant: "Kant is the most eminent of modern philosophers, the man whose doctrines have most influenced my formation. The distinction of subject and object and the scientific principle that everything exists and develops for its own proper intrinsic reasons (that the cork tree, to use a proverbial example, does not come into being to provide stoppers for our bottles) was something I held in common with Kant, and later I devoted much study to his philosophy." Might one not trace to a teleological root the expression "historic mission"? In many cases indeed this expression has acquired an equivocal and mystical meaning. But in other cases it does have a meaning, which, in the light of the Kantian conception of teleology, could be maintained and justified by the philosophy of praxis.

122 The *Xenien* are a collection of epigrams written by Goethe and Schiller in elegiac couplets. The translation here is from the Italian version given by Croce as we have been unable to trace the original.

this ode of Goethe's nor the history of the Prometheus myth in world literature prior to Goethe and particularly in the period before and during Goethe's literary activity. But is it possible to give a judgment, of the type given in the *Manual*, without knowing precisely these elements? How, in their absence, can one distinguish what is strictly personal to Goethe from what is representative of an age and of a social group? Judgments of this type are justified only to the extent that they are not empty generalities containing in themselves the most disparate things but are precise, proven and decisive. Failing this they can only serve to disparage a theory and to encourage a superficial way of looking at questions. (It is again worth recalling Engels' phrase contained in the letter to a student published in the *Sozial. Akademiker*.)[123]

---

[123] See Engels, Letter to Bloch, 21 September 1890 (cit. above, note 74): "Unfortunately, however, it happens only too often that people think they have understood a theory and can apply it without more ado from the moment they have mastered its main principles, and those even not always correctly. And I cannot exempt many of the more recent "Marxists" from this reproach, for the most wonderful rubbish has been produced from this quarter too."

NAME INDEX

Pseudonymous references, e.g. "the founder of the philosophy of praxis" for Marx or "Ilich" for Lenin, are given under the normal name of the person. The letter *n* after a page number refers to Gramsci's own (asterisked) footnotes and the letter *f* to editorial (numbered) footnotes.

SUBJECT INDEX

This index is intended as a guide to the occurrence of subjects and concepts in Gramsci's text. In the majority of cases references are to the words used by Gramsci, but a number of phrases have been "decoded" and some general subject references inserted. The letter *n* after a page number refers to Gramsci's own (asterisked) footnotes and the letter *f* to editorial (numbered) footnotes.